Related Books of Interest

The IBM Style Guide

Conventions for Writers and Editors

by Francis DeRespinis, Peter Hayward, Jana Jenkins, Amy Laird, Leslie McDonald, Eric Radzinski

ISBN: 0-13-210130-0

The IBM Style Guide distills IBM wisdom for developing superior content: information that is consistent, clear, concise, and easy to translate. This expert guide contains practical guidance on topic-based writing, writing content for different media types, and writing for global audiences and can help any organization improve and standardize content across authors, delivery mechanisms, and geographic locations.

The IBM Style Guide can help any organization or individual create and manage content more effectively. The guidelines are especially valuable for businesses that have not previously adopted a corporate style guide, for anyone who writes or edits for IBM as an employee or outside contractor, and for anyone who uses modern approaches to information architecture.

DITA Best Practices

By Laura Bellamy, Michelle Carey, and Jenifer Schlotfeldt

ISBN: 0-13-248052-2

Darwin Information Typing Architecture (DITA) is today's most powerful toolbox for constructing information. By implementing DITA, organizations can gain more value from their technical documentation than ever before. In *DITA Best Practices*, three DITA pioneers offer the first complete roadmap for successful DITA adoption, implementation, and usage. Drawing on years of experience helping large organizations adopt DITA, the authors answer crucial questions the "official" DITA documents ignore. An indispensable resource for every writer, editor, information architect, manager, or consultant involved with evaluating, deploying, or using DITA.

Sign up for the monthly IBM Press newsletter at ibmpressbooks/newsletters

Related Books of Interest

Search Engine Marketing, Inc.

By Mike Moran and Bill Hunt

ISBN: 0-13-606868-5

The #1 Step-by-Step Guide to Search Marketing Success...Now Completely Updated with New Techniques, Tools, Best Practices, and Value-Packed Bonus DVD!

In this book, two world-class experts present today's best practices, step-by-step techniques, and hard-won tips for using search engine marketing to achieve your sales and marketing goals, whatever they are. Mike Moran and Bill Hunt thoroughly cover both the business and technical aspects of contemporary search engine marketing, walking beginners through all the basics while providing reliable, up-to-the-minute insights for experienced professionals.

Thoroughly updated to fully reflect today's latest search engine marketing opportunities, this book guides you through profiting from social media marketing, site search, advanced keyword tools, hybrid paid search auctions, and much more.

Listen to the author's podcast at:
ibmpressbooks.com/podcasts

Do It Wrong Quickly

How the Web Changes the Old Marketing Rules

Moran

ISBN: 0-13-225596-0

Get Bold

Using Social Media to Create a New Type of Social Business

Carter

ISBN: 0-13-261831-1

The Social Factor

Innovate, Ignite, and Win through Mass Collaboration and Social Networking

Azua

ISBN: 0-13-701890-8

Audience, Relevance, and Search

Targeting Web Audiences with Relevant Content

Mathewson, Donatone, Fishel

ISBN: 0-13-700420-6

Making the World Work Better

The Ideas That Shaped a Century and a Company

Maney, Hamm, O'Brien

ISBN: 0-13-275510-6

Sign up for the monthly IBM Press newsletter at
ibmpressbooks/newsletters

Multilingual Natural Language Processing Applications

Multilingual Natural Language Processing Applications

From Theory to Practice

Edited by Daniel M. Bikel Imed Zitouni

IBM Press
Pearson plc
Upper Saddle River, NJ • Boston • Indianapolis • San Francisco
New York • Toronto • Montreal • London • Munich • Paris • Madrid
Capetown • Sydney • Tokyo • Singapore • Mexico City

ibmpressbooks.com

IBM Press Program Managers: Steven M. Stansel, Ellice Uffer
Cover design: IBM Corporation

Executive Editor: Bernard Goodwin
Marketing Manager: Stephane Nakib
Publicist: Heather Fox
Managing Editor: John Fuller
Designer: Alan Clements
Project Editor: Elizabeth Ryan
Copy Editor: Carol Lallier
Indexer: Jack Lewis
Compositor: LaurelTech
Proofreader: Kelli M. Brooks
Manufacturing Buyer: Dan Uhrig

Published by Pearson plc
Publishing as IBM Press

IBM Press offers excellent discounts on this book when ordered in quantity for bulk purchases or special sales, which may include electronic versions and/or custom covers and content particular to your business, training goals, marketing focus, and branding interests. For more information, please contact

U.S. Corporate and Government Sales
1-800-382-3419
corpsales@pearsontechgroup.com

For sales outside the United States, please contact
International Sales
international@pearson.com

Library of Congress Cataloging-in-Publication Data is on file with the Library of Congress.

ISBN-13: 978-0-13-715144-8
ISBN-10: 0-13-715144-6

Text printed in the United States on recycled paper at Courier in Westford, Massachusetts.
First printing, May 2012

I dedicate this book to
my mother Rita, my brother Robert, my sister-in-law Judi,
my nephew Wolfie, and my niece Freya—Bikels all.
I also dedicate it to Science.

DMB

I dedicate this book to
my parents Ali and Radhia, who taught me the love of science,
my wife Barbara, for her support and encouragement,
my kids Nassim and Ines, for the joy they give me.
I also dedicate it to my grandmother Zohra,
my brother Issam, my sister-in-law Chahnez,
as well as my parents-in-law Alain and Pilar.

IZ

Contents

Preface

Almost everyone on the planet, it seems, has been touched in some way by advances in information technology and the proliferation of the Internet. Recently, multimedia information sources have become increasingly popular. Nevertheless, the sheer volume of raw natural language text keeps increasing, and this text is being generated in all the major languages on Earth. For example, the English Wikipedia reports that 101 language-specific Wikipedias exist with at least 10,000 articles each. There is therefore a pressing need for countries, companies, and individuals to analyze this massive amount of text, translate it, and synthesize and distill it.

Previously, to build robust and accurate multilingual natural language processing (NLP) applications, a researcher or developer had to consult several reference books and dozens, if not hundreds, of journal and conference papers. Our aim for this book is to provide a "one-stop shop" that offers all the requisite background and practical advice for building such applications. Although it is quite a tall order, we hope that, at a minimum, you find this book a useful resource.

In the last two decades, NLP researchers have developed exciting algorithms for processing large amounts of text in many different languages. By far, the dominant approach has been to build a statistical model that can learn from examples. In this way, a model can be robust to changes in the type of text and even the language of text on which it operates. With the right design choices, the same model can be trained to work in a new domain or new language simply by providing new examples in that domain. This approach also obviates the need for researchers to lay out, in a painstaking fashion, all the rules that govern the problem at hand and the manner in which those rules must be combined. Rather, a statistical system typically allows for researchers to provide an abstract expression of possible *features* of the input, where the relative importance of those features can be learned during the *training* phase and can be applied to new text during the *decoding*, or *inference*, phase.

The field of statistical NLP is rapidly changing. Part of the change is due to the field's growth. For example, one of the main conferences in the field is that of the Association of Computational Linguistics, where conference attendance has doubled in the last five years. Also, the share of NLP papers in the IEEE speech and language processing conferences and journals more than doubled in the last decade; IEEE constitutes one of the world's largest professional associations for the advancement of technology. Not only are NLP researchers making inherent progress on the various subproblems of the field, but NLP continues to benefit (and borrow) heavily from progress in the machine learning community and linguistics alike. This book devotes some attention to cutting-edge algorithms and techniques, but its primary purpose is to be a thorough explication of best practices in the field. Furthermore, every chapter describes how the techniques discussed apply in a *multilingual* setting.

This book is divided into two parts. Part I, In Theory, includes the first seven chapters and lays out the various core NLP problems and algorithms to attack those problems. The first three chapters focus on finding structure in language at various levels of granularity. Chapter 1 introduces the important concept of *morphology*, the study of the structure of words, and ways to process the diverse array of morphologies present in the world's languages. Chapter 2 discusses the methods by which documents may be decomposed into more manageable parts, such as sentences and larger units related by topic. Finally, in this initial trio of chapters, Chapter 3 investigates the various methods of uncovering a sentence's internal structure, or *syntax*. Syntax has long been a dominant area of research in linguistics, and that dominance has been mirrored in the field of NLP as well. The dominance, in part, stems from the fact that the structure of a sentence bears relation to the sentence's meaning, so uncovering syntactic structure can serve as a first step toward a full "understanding" of a sentence.

Finding a structured meaning representation for a sentence, or for some other unit of text, is often called *semantic parsing*, which is the concern of Chapter 4. That chapter covers, inter alia, a related subproblem that has garnered much attention in recent years known as *semantic role labeling*, which attempts to find the syntactic phrases that constitute the *arguments* to some verb or predicate. By identifying and classifying a verb's arguments, we come one step closer to producing a *logical form* for a sentence, which is one way to represent a sentence's meaning in such a way as to be readily processed by machine, using the rich array of tools available from logic that mankind has been developing since ancient times.

But what if we do not want or need the deep syntactico-semantic structure that semantic parsing would provide? What if our problem is simply to decide which among many candidate sentences is the most likely sentence a human would write or speak? One way to do so would be to develop a model that could score each sentence according to its grammaticality and pick the sentence with the highest score. The problem of producing a score or probability estimate for a sequence of word tokens is known as *language modeling* and is the subject of Chapter 5.

Representing meaning and judging a sentence's grammaticality are only two of many possible first steps toward processing language. Moving further toward some sense of understanding, we might wish to have an algorithm make *inferences* about facts expressed in a piece of text. For example, we might want to know if a fact mentioned in one sentence is *entailed* by some previous sentence in a document. This sort of inference is known as *recognizing textual entailment* and is the subject of Chapter 6.

Finding which facts or statements are entailed by others is clearly important to the automatic understanding of text, but there is also the *nature* of those statements. Understanding which statements are subjective and the polarity of the opinion expressed is the subject matter of Chapter 7. Given how often people express opinions, this is clearly an important problem area, all the more so in an age when social networks are fast becoming the dominant form of person-to-person communication on the Internet. This chapter rounds out Part I of our book.

Part II, In Practice, takes the various core areas of NLP described in Part I and explains how to apply them to the diverse array of real-world NLP applications. Engineering is often about trade-offs, say, between time and space, and so the chapters in this applied part of our book explore the trade-offs in making various algorithmic and design choices when building a robust, multilingual NLP application.

Chapter 8 describes ways to identify and classify *named entities* and other mentions of those entities in text, as well as methods to identify when two or more entity mentions *corefer*. These two problems are typically known as *mention detection* and *coreference resolution*; they are two of the core parts of a larger application area known as *information extraction*.

Chapter 9 continues the information extraction discussion, exploring techniques for finding out how two entities are related to each other, known as *relation extraction*, and identifying and classifying events, or *event extraction*. An event, in this case, is when something happens involving multiple entities, and we would like a machine to uncover who the participants are and what their roles are. In this way, event extraction is closely related to the core NLP problem of semantic role labeling.

Chapter 10 describes one of the oldest problems in the field, and one of the few that is an inherently multilingual NLP problem: *machine translation*, or *MT*. Automatically translating from one language to another has long been a holy grail of NLP research, and in recent years the community has developed techniques and can obtain hardware that make MT a practical reality, reaping rewards after decades of effort.

It is one thing to translate text, but how do we make sense of all the text out there in seemingly limitless quantity? Chapters 8 and 9 make some headway in this regard by helping us automatically produce structured records of information in text. Another way to tackle the quantity problem is to narrow down the scope by finding the few documents, or subparts of documents, that are relevant based on a search query. This problem is known as *information retrieval* and is the subject of Chapter 11. In many ways, commercial search engines such as Google are large-scale information retrieval systems. Given the popularity of search engines, this is clearly an important NLP problem—all the more so given the number of corpora that are *not* public and therefore searchable by commercial engines.

Another way we might tackle the sheer quantity of text is by automatically summarizing it, which is the topic of Chapter 12. This very difficult problem involves either finding the sentences, or bits of sentences, that contribute to providing a relevant summary of a larger quantity of text or else ingesting the text summarizing its meaning in some internal representation, and then *generating* the text that constitutes a summary, much as a human might do.

Often, humans would like machines to process text automatically because they have questions they seek to answer. These questions can range from simple, factoid-like questions, such as "When was John F. Kennedy born?" to more complex questions such as "What is the largest city in Bavaria, Germany?" Chapter 13 discusses ways to build systems to answer these types of questions automatically.

What if the types of questions we might like to answer are even *more* complex? Our queries might have multiple answers, such as "Name all the foreign heads of state President Barack Obama met with in 2010." These types of queries are handled by a relatively new subdiscipline within NLP known as *distillation*. In a very real way, distillation combines the techniques of information retrieval with information extraction and adds a few of its own.

In many cases, we might like to have machines process language in an interactive way, making use of speech technology that both recognizes and synthesizes speech. Such systems are known as *dialog systems* and are covered in Chapter 15. Due to advances in speech recognition, dialog management, and speech synthesis, such systems are becoming increasingly practical and are seeing widespread, real-world deployment.

Finally, we, as NLP researchers and engineers, might like to build systems using diverse arrays of components developed across the world. This aggregation of processing engines is described in Chapter 16. Although it is the final chapter of our book, in some ways it represents a beginning, not an end, to processing text, for it describes how a common infrastructure can be used to produce a combinatorically diverse array of processing pipelines.

As much as we hope this book is self-contained, we also hope that for you it serves as the beginning and not an end. Each chapter has a long list of relevant work upon which it is based, allowing you to explore any subtopic in great detail. The large community of NLP researchers is growing throughout the world, and we hope you join us in our exciting efforts to process text automatically and that you interact with us at universities, at industrial research labs, at conferences, in blogs, on social networks, and elsewhere. The multilingual NLP systems of the future are going to be even more exciting than the ones we have now, and we look forward to all your contributions!

Acknowledgments

This book was, from its inception, designed as a highly collaborative effort. We are immensely grateful for the encouraging support obtained from the beginning from IBM Press/Prentice Hall, especially from Bernard Goodwin and all the others at IBM Press who helped us get this project off the ground and see it to completion. A book of this kind would also not have been possible without the generous time, effort, and technical acumen of our fellow chapter authors, so we owe huge thanks to Otakar Smrž, Hyun-Jo You, Dilek Hakkani-Tür, Gokhan Tur, Benoit Favre, Elizabeth Shriberg, Anoop Sarkar, Sameer Pradhan, Katrin Kirchhoff, Mark Sammons, V.G.Vinod Vydiswaran, Dan Roth, Carmen Banea, Rada Mihalcea, Janyce Wiebe, Xiaqiang Luo, Philipp Koehn, Philipp Sorg, Philipp Cimiano, Frank Schilder, Liang Zhou, Nico Schlaefer, Jennifer Chu-Carroll, Vittorio Castelli, Radu Florian, Roberto Pieraccini, David Suendermann, John F. Pitrelli, and Burn Lewis. Daniel M. Bikel is also grateful to Google Research, especially to Corinna Cortes, for her support during the final stages of this project. Finally, we—Daniel M. Bikel and Imed Zitouni—would like to express our great appreciation for the backing of IBM Research, with special thanks to Ellen Yoffa, without whom this project would not have been possible.

About the Authors

Daniel M. Bikel (dbikel@google.com) is a senior research scientist at Google. He graduated with honors from Harvard in 1993 with a degree in Classics–Ancient Greek and Latin. From 1994 to 1997, he worked at BBN on several natural language processing problems, including development of the first high-accuracy stochastic name-finder, for which he holds a patent. He received M.S. and Ph.D. degrees in computer science from the University of Pennsylvania, in 2000 and 2004 respectively, discovering new properties of statistical parsing algorithms. From 2004 through 2010, he was a research staff member at IBM Research, working on a wide variety of natural language processing problems, including parsing, semantic role labeling, information extraction, machine translation, and question answering. Dr. Bikel has been a reviewer for the *Computational Linguistics* journal, and has been on the program committees of the ACL, NAACL, EACL, and EMNLP conferences. He has published numerous peer-reviewed papers in the leading conferences and journals and has built software tools that have seen widespread use in the natural language processing community. In 2008, he won a Best Paper Award (Outstanding Short Paper) at the ACL-08: HLT conference. Since 2010, Dr. Bikel has been doing natural language processing and speech processing research at Google.

Imed Zitouni (izitouni@us.ibm.com) is a senior researcher working for IBM since 2004. He received his M.Sc. and Ph.D. in computer science with honors from University of Nancy, France in 1996 and 2000 respectively. In 1995, he obtained an MEng degree in computer science from Ecole Nationale des Sciences de l'Informatique, a prestigious national computer institute in Tunisia. Before joining IBM, he was a principal scientist at a startup company, DIALOCA, in 1999 and 2000. He then joined Bell Laboratories Lucent-Alcatel between 2000 and 2004 as a research staff member. His research interests include natural language processing, language modeling, spoken dialog systems, speech recognition, and machine learning. Dr. Zitouni is a member of the IEEE Speech and Language Technical Committee in 2009–2011. He is the associate editor of the *ACM Transactions on Asian Language Information Processing* and the information officer of the Association for Computational Linguistics (ACL) Special Interest Group on Computational Approaches to Semitic Languages. He is a senior member of IEEE and member of ISCA and ACL. He served on the program committee and as a chair for several peer-review conferences and journals. He holds several patents in the field and authored more than seventy-five papers in peer-review conferences and journals.

Carmen Banea (carmen.banea@gmail.com) is a doctoral student in the Department of Computer Science and Engineering, University of North Texas. She is working in the field of natural language processing. Her research work focuses primarily on multilingual approaches to subjectivity and sentiment analysis, where she developed both dictionary- and corpus-based methods that leverage languages with rich resources to create tools and data in other languages. Carmen has authored papers in major natural language processing conferences, including the Association for Computational Linguistics, Empirical Methods in Natural Language Processing, and the International Conference on Computational Linguistics. She served as a program committee member in numerous large conferences and was also a reviewer for the *Computational Linguistics Journal* and the *Journal of Natural Language Engineering*. She cochaired the TextGraphs 2010 Workshop collocated with ACL 2010 and was one of the organizers of the University of North Texas site of the North American Computational Linguistics Olympiad in 2009 to 2011.

Vittorio Castelli (vittorio@us.ibm.com) received a Laurea degree in electrical engineering from Politecnico di Milano in 1988, an M.S. in electrical engineering in 1990, an M.S. in statistics in 1994, and a Ph.D. in electrical engineering in 1995, with a dissertation on information theory and statistical classification. In 1995 he joined the IBM T. J. Watson Research Center. His recent work is in natural language processing, specifically in information extraction; he has worked on the DARPA GALE and machine reading projects. Vittorio previously started the Personal Wizards project, aimed at capturing procedural knowledge from observation of experts performing a task. He has also done work on foundations of information theory, memory compression, time series prediction and indexing, performance analysis, methods for improving the reliability and serviceability of computer systems, and digital libraries for scientific imagery. From 1996 to 1998 he was coinvestigator of the NASA/CAN project no. NCC5-101. His main research interests include information theory, probability theory, statistics, and statistical pattern recognition. From 1998 to 2005 he was an adjunct assistant professor at Columbia University, teaching information theory and statistical pattern recognition. He is a member of Sigma Xi, of the IEEE IT Society, and of the American Statistical Association. Vittorio has published papers on natural language processing computer-assisted instruction, statistical classification, data compression, image processing, multimedia databases, database mining and multidimensional indexing structures, intelligent user interfactes, and foundational problems in information theory, and he coedited *Image Databases: Search and Retrieval of Digital Imagery* (Wiley, 2002).

Jennifer Chu-Carroll (jencc@us.ibm.com) is a research staff member in the Semantic Analysis and Integration Department at the IBM T. J. Watson Research Center. Before joining IBM in 2001, she spent five years as a member of technical staff at Lucent Technologies Bell Labratories. Her research interests include question answering, semantic search, discourse processing, and spoken dialog management.

Philipp Cimiano (cimiano@cit-ec.uni-bielefeld.de) is professor in computer science at the University of Bielefeld, Germany. He leads the Semantic Computing Group that is affiliated with the Cognitive Interaction Technology Excellence Center, funded by the Deutsche Forschungsgemeinschaft in the framework of the excellence initiative. Philipp Cimiano graduated in computer science (major) and computational linguistics (minor) from the University of Stuttgart. He obtained his doctoral degree (summa cum laude) from the University of Karlsruhe. His main research interest lies in the combination of natural language with semantic technologies. In the last several years, he has focused on multilingual information access. He has been involved as main investigator in a number of European (Dot.Kom, X-Media, Monnet) as well as national research projects such as SmartWeb (BMBF) and Multipla (DFG).

Benoit Favre (benoit.favre@lif.univ-mrs.fr) is an associate professor at Aix-Marseille Université, Marseille, France. He is a researcher in the field of natural language understanding. His research interests are in speech and text understanding with a focus on machine learning approaches. He received his Ph.D. from the University of Avignon, France, in 2007 on the topic of automatic speech summarization. Benoit was a teaching assistant at University of Avignon between 2003 and 2007 and a research engineer at Thales Land & Joint Systems, Paris, during the same period. Between 2007 and 2009, Benoit held a postdoctoral position at the International Computer Institute (Berkeley, CA) working with the speech group. From 2009 to 2010, he held a postdoctoral position at University of Le Mans, France. Since 2010, he is a tenured associate professor at Aix-Marseille Université, member of Laboratoire d'Informatique Fondamentale. Benoit is the coauthor of more than thirty refereed papers in international conferences and journals. He was a reviewer for major conferences in the field (ICASSP, Interspeech, ACL, EMNLP, Coling, NAACL) and for the *IEEE Transactions on Speech and Language Processing*. He is a member of the International Speech Communication Association and IEEE.

Radu Florian (raduf@us.ibm.com) is the manager of the Statistical Content Analytics (Information Extraction) group at IBM. He received his Ph.D. in 2002 from Johns Hopkins University, when he joined the Multilingual NLP group at IBM. At IBM, he has worked on a variety of research projects in the area of information extraction: mention detection, coreference resolution, relation extraction, cross-document coreference, and targeted information retrieval. Radu led research groups participating in several DARPA programs (GALE Distillation, MRP) and NIST-organized evaluations (ACE, TAC-KBP) and joint development programs with IBM partners for text mining in the medical domain (with Nuance), and contributed to the Watson *Jeopardy!* project.

Dilek Hakkani-Tür (Dilek.Hakkani-Tur@microsoft.com) is a principal scientist at Microsoft. Before joining Microsoft, she was with the International Computer Science Institute (ICSI) speech group (2006–2010) and AT&T Labs–Research (2001–2005). She received her B.Sc. degree from Middle East Technical University in 1994, and M.Sc. and Ph.D. degrees from Bilkent University, department of computer engineering, in 1996 and 2000 respectively. Her Ph.D. thesis is on statistical language modeling for agglutinative languages. She worked on machine translation at Carnegie Mellon University, Language Technologies Institute, in 1997 and at Johns Hopkins University in 1998. Between 1998 and 1999, Dilek worked on using lexical and prosodic information for information extraction from speech at SRI International. Her research interests include natural language and speech processing, spoken dialog systems, and active and unsupervised learning for language processing. She holds 13 patents and has coauthored over one hundred papers in natural language and speech processing. She was an associate editor of *IEEE Transactions on Audio, Speech and Language Processing* between 2005 and 2008 and currently serves as an elected member of the IEEE Speech and Language Technical Committee (2009–2012).

Katrin Kirchhoff (kk2@u.washington.edu) is a research associate professor in electrical engineering at the University of Washington. Her main research interests are automatic speech recognition, natural language processing, and human–computer interfaces, with particular emphasis on multilingual applications. She has authored over seventy peer-reviewed publications and is coeditor of *Multilingual Speech Processing*. Katrin currently serves as a member of the IEEE Speech Technical Committee and on the editorial boards of *Computer, Speech and Language* and *Speech Communication*.

Philipp Koehn (pkoehn@inf.ed.ac.uk) is a reader at the University of Edinburgh. He received his Ph.D. from the University of Southern California, where he was a research assistant at the Information Sciences Institute from 1997 to 2003. He was a postdoctoral research associate at the Massachusetts Institute of Technology in 2004 and joined the University of Edinburgh as a lecturer in 2005. His research centers on statistical machine translation, but he has also worked on speech, text classification, and information extraction. His major contribution to the machine translation community are the preparation and release of the Europarl corpus as well as the Pharaoh and Moses decoder. He is president of the ACL Special Interest Group on Machine Translation and author of *Statistical Machine Translation* (Cambridge University Press, 2010).

Burn L. Lewis (burn@us.ibm.com) is a member of the computer science department at the IBM Thomas J. Watson Research Center. He received B.E. and M.E. degrees in electrical engineering from the University of Auckland in 1967 and 1968, respectively, and a Ph.D. in electrical engineering and computer science from the University of California–Berkeley in 1974. He subsequently joined IBM at the T. J. Watson Research Center, where he has worked on speech recognition and unstructured information management.

Xiaqiang Luo (xiaoluo@us.ibm.com) is a research staff member at IBM T. J. Watson Research Center. He has extensive experiences in human language technology, including speech recognition, spoken dialog systems, and natural language processing. He is a major contributor to IBM's success in many government-sponsored projects in the area of speech and language technology. He received the prestigious IBM Outstanding Technical Achievement Award in 2007, IBM ThinkPlace Bravo Award in 2006, and numerous invention achievement awards. Dr. Luo received his Ph.D. and M.S. in electrical engineering from Johns Hopkins University in 1999 and 1995, respectively, and B.A. in electrical engineering from University of Science and Technology of China in 1990. Dr. Luo is a member of the Association of Computational Linguistics and has served as program committee member for major technical conferences in the area of human language and artificial intelligence. He is a board member of the Chinese Association for Science and Technology (Greater New York Chapter). He served as an associate editor for *ACM Transactions on Asian Language Information Processing (TALIP)* from 2007 to 2010.

Rada Mihalcea (rada@cs.unt.edu) is associate professor in the Department of Computer Science and Engineering, University of North Texas. Her research interests are in computational linguistics, with a focus on lexical semantics, graph-based algorithms for natural language processing, and multilingual natural language processing. She is currently involved in a number of research projects, including word sense disambiguation, monolingual and crosslingual semantic similarity, automatic keyword extraction and text summarization, emotion and sentiment analysis, and computational humor. Rada serves or has served on the editorial boards of the *Journals of Computational Linguistics, Language Resources and Evaluations, Natural Language Engineering*, and *Research in Language in Computation.* Her research has been funded by the National Science Foundation, Google, the National Endowment for the Humanities, and the State of Texas. She is the recipient of a National Science Foundation CAREER award (2008) and a Presidential Early Career Award for Scientists and Engineers (PECASE, 2009).

Roberto Pieraccini (www.robertopieraccini.com) is chief technology officer of SpeechCycle Inc. Roberto graduated in electrical engineering at the University of Pisa, Italy, in 1980. In 1981 he started working as a speech recognition researcher at CSELT, the research institution of the Italian telephone operating company. In 1990 he joined Bell Laboratories (Murray Hill, NJ) as a member of technical staff where he was involved in speech recognition and spoken language understanding research. He then joined AT&T Labs in 1996, where he started working on spoken dialog research. In 1999 he was director of R&D for SpeechWorks International. In 2003 he joined IBM T. J. Watson Research where he managed the Advanced Conversational Interaction Technology department, and then joined SpeechCycle in 2005 as their CTO. Roberto Pieraccini is the author of more than one hundred twenty papers and articles on speech recognition, language modeling, character recognition, language understanding, and automatic spoken dialog management. He is an ISCA and IEEE Fellow, a member of the editorial board of the *IEEE Signal Processing Magazine* and of the *International Journal of Speech Technology.* He is also a member of the Applied Voice Input Output Society and Speech Technology Consortium boards.

John F. Pitrelli (pitrelli@us.ibm.com) is a member of the Multilingual Natural Language Processing department at the IBM T. J. Watson Research Center in Yorktown Heights, New York. He received S.B., S.M., and Ph.D. degrees in electrical engineering and computer science from the Massachusetts Institute of Technology in 1983, 1985, and 1990 respectively, with graduate work in speech recognition and synthesis. Before his current position, he worked in the Speech Technology Group at NYNEX Science & Technology, Inc., in White Plains, New York; was a member of the IBM Pen Technologies Group; and worked on speech synthesis and prosody in the Human Language Technologies group at Watson. John's research interests include natural language processing, speech synthesis, speech recognition, handwriting recognition, statistical language modeling, prosody, unstructured information management, and confidence modeling for recognition. He has published forty papers and holds four patents.

Sameer Pradhan (sameer.pradhan@Colorado.edu) is a scientist at BBN Technologies in Cambridge, Massachusetts. He is the author of a number of widely cited articles and chapters in the field of computational semantics. He is currently creating the next generation of semantic analysis engines and their applications, through algorithmic innovation, wide distribution of research tools such as Automatic Statistical SEmantic Role Tagger (ASSERT), and through the generation of rich, multilayer, multilingual, integrated resources, such as OntoNotes, that serve as a platform. Eventually these models of semantics should replace the currently impoverished, mostly word-based models, prevalent in most application domains, and help take the area of language understanding to a new level of richness. Sameer received his Ph.D. from the University of Colorado in 2005, and since then has been working at BBN Technologies developing the OntoNotes corpora as part of the DARPA Global Autonomus Language Exploitation program. He is a member of ACL, and is a founding member of ACL's Special Interest Group for Annotation, promoting innovation in the area of annotation. He has regularly been on the program committees of various natural language processing conferences and workshops such as ACL, HLT, EMNLP, CoNLL, COLING, LREC, and LAW. He is also an accomplished chef.

Dan Roth (danr@illinois.edu) is a professor in the department of computer science and the Beckman Institute at the University of Illinois at Urbana-Champaign. He is a Fellow of AAAI, a University of Illinois Scholar, and holds faculty positions at the statistics and linguistics departments and at the Graduate School of Library and Information Science. Professor Roth's research spans theoretical work in machine learning and intelligent reasoning with a specific focus on learning and inference in natural language processing and intelligent access to textual information. He has published over two hundred papers in these areas and his papers have received multiple awards. He has developed advanced machine learning-based tools for natural language applications that are being used widely by the research community, including an award-winning semantic parser. He was the program chair of AAAI'11, CoNLL'02, and ACL'03, and is or has been on the editorial board of several journals in his research areas. He is currently an associate editor for the *Journal of Artificial Intelligence Research* and the *Machine Learning Journal.* Professor Roth got his B.A. summa cum laude in mathematics from the Technion, Israel, and his Ph.D. in computer science from Harvard University.

Mark Sammons (mssammon@illinois.edu) is a principal research scientist working with the Cognitive Computation Group at the University of Illinois at Urbana-Champaign. His primary interests are in natural language processing and machine learning, with a focus on integrating diverse information sources in the context of textual entailment. His work has focused on developing a textual entailment framework that can easily incorporate new resources, designing appropriate inference procedures for recognizing entailment, and identifying and developing automated approaches to recognize and represent implicit content in natural language text. Mark received his M.Sc. in computer science from the University of Illinois in 2004 and his Ph.D. in mechanical engineering from the University of Leeds, England, in 2000.

Anoop Sarkar (www.cs.sfu.ca/~anoop) is an associate professor of computing science at Simon Fraser University in British Columbia, Canada, where he codirects the Natural Language Laboratory (http://natlang.cs.sfu.ca). He received his Ph.D. from the Department of Computer and Information Sciences at the University of Pennsylvania under Professor Aravind Joshi for his work on semi-supervised statistical parsing and parsing for tree-adjoining grammars. Anoop's current research is focused on statistical parsing and machine translation (exploiting syntax or morphology, or both). His interests also include formal language theory and stochastic grammars, in particular tree automata and tree-adjoining grammars.

Frank Schilder (frank.schilder@thomsonreuters.com) is a lead research scientist at the Research & Development department of Thomson Reuters. He joined Thomson Reuters in 2004, where he has been doing applied research on summarization technologies and information extraction systems. His summarization work has been implemented as the snippet generator for search results of WestLawNext, the new legal research system produced by Thomson Reuters. His current research activities involve the participation in different research competitions such as the Text Analysis Conference carried out by the National Institute of Standards and Technology. He obtained a Ph.D. in cognitive science from the University of Edinburgh, Scotland, in 1997. From 1997 to 2003, he was employed by the Department for Informatics at the University of Hamburg, Germany, first as a postdoctoral researcher and later as an assistant professor. Frank has authored several journal articles and book chapters, including "Natural Language Processing: Overview" from the *Encyclopedia of Language and Linguistics* (Elsevier, 2006), coauthored with Peter Jackson, the chief scientist of Thomson Reuters. In 2011, he jointly won the Thomson Reuters Innovation challenge. He serves as reviewer for journals in computational linguistics and as program committee member of various conferences organized by the Association of Computational Linguistics.

Nico Schlaefer (nico@cs.cmu.edu) is a Ph.D. candidate in the School of Computer Science at Carnegie Mellon University and an IBM Ph.D. Fellow. His research focus is the application of machine learning techniques to natural language processing tasks. Schlaefer developed algorithms that enable question-answering systems to find correct answers, even if the original information sources contain little relevant content, and a flexible architecture that supports the integration of such algorithms. Schlaefer is the primary author of OpenEphyra, one of the most widely used open-source question-answering systems. Nico also contributed a statistical source expansion approach to Watson, the computer that won against human champions in the *Jeopardy!* quiz show. His approach automatically extends knowledge sources with related content from the Web and other large text corpora, making it easier for Watson to find answers and supporting evidence.

Elizabeth Shriberg (elshribe@microsoft.com) is currently a principal scientist at Microsoft; previously she was at SRI International (Menlo Park, CA). She is also affiliated with the International Computer Science Institute (Berkeley, CA) and CASL (University of Maryland). She received a B.A. from Harvard (1987) and a Ph.D. from the University of California–Berkeley (1994). Elizabeth's main interest is in modeling spontaneous speech using both lexical and prosodic information. Her work aims to combine linguistic knowledge with corpora and techniques from automatic speech and speaker recognition to advance both scientific understanding and technology. She has published roughly two hundred papers in speech science and technology and has served as associate editor of language and speech, on the boards of Speech Communication and Computational Linguistics, on a range of conference and workshop boards, on the ISCA Advisory Council, and on the ICSLP Permanent Council. She has organized workshops and served on boards for the National Science Foundation, the European Commission, NWO (Netherlands), and has reviewed for an interdisciplinary range of conferences, workshops, and journals (e.g., *IEEE Transactions on Speech and Audio Processing, Journal of the Acoustical Society of America, Nature, Journal of Phonetics, Computer Speech and Language, Journal of Memory and Language, Memory and Cognition, Discourse Processes*). In 2009 she received the ISCA Fellow Award. In 2010 she became a Fellow of SRI.

Otakar Smrž (otakar.smrz@cmu.edu) is a postdoctoral research associate at Carnegie Mellon University in Qatar. He focuses on methods of learning from comparable corpora to improve statistical machine translation from and into Arabic. Otakar completed his doctoral studies in mathematical linguistics at Charles University in Prague. He designed and implemented the ElixirFM computational model of Arabic morphology using functional programming and has developed other open source software for natural language processing. He has been the principal investigator of the Prague Arabic Dependency Treebank. Otakar used to work as a research scientist at IBM Czech Republic, where he explored unsupervised semantic parsing as well as acoustic modeling for multiple languages. Otakar is a cofounder of the Džám-e Džam Language Institute in Prague.

Philipp Sorg (philipp.sorg@kit.edu) is a Ph.D. student at the Karlsruhe Institute of Technology, Germany. He has a researcher position at the Institute of Applied Informatics and Formal Description Methods. Philipp graduated in computer science at the University of Karlsruhe. His main research interest lies in multilingual information retrieval. His special focus is the exploitation of social semantics in the context of the Web 2.0. He has been involved in the European research project Active, as well as in the national research project Multipla (DFG).

David Suendermann (david@speechcycle.com) is the principal speech scientist at SpeechCycle Labs (New York). Dr. Suendermann has been working on various fields of speech technology research for the last ten years. He worked at multiple industrial and academic institutions including Siemens (Munich), Columbia University (New York), University of Southern California (Los Angeles), Universitat Politècnica de Catalunya (Barcelona), and Rheinisch Westfälische Technische Hochschule (Aachen, Germany). He has authored more than sixty publications and patents, including a book and five book chapters, and holds a Ph.D. from the Bundeswehr University in Munich.

Gokhan Tur (gokhan.tur@ieee.org) is currently with Microsoft working as a principal scientist. He received his B.S., M.S., and Ph.D. from the Department of Computer Science, Bilkent University, Turkey in 1994, 1996, and 2000 respectively. Between 1997 and 1999, Tur visited the Center for Machine Translation of Carnegie Mellon University, then the Department of Computer Science of Johns Hopkins University, and then the Speech Technology and Research Lab of SRI International. He worked at AT&T Labs–Research from 2001 to 2006 and at the Speech Technology and Research Lab of SRI International from 2006 to 2010. His research interests include spoken language understanding, speech and language processing, machine learning, and information retrieval and extraction. Tur has coauthored more than one hundred papers published in refereed journals or books and presented at international conferences. He is the editor of *Spoken Language Understanding: Systems for Extracting Semantic Information from Speech* (Wiley, 2011). Dr. Tur is a senior member of IEEE, ACL, and ISCA, was a member of IEEE Signal Processing Society (SPS), Speech and Language Technical Committee (SLTC) for 2006–2008, and is currently an associate editor for *IEEE Transactions on Audio, Speech, and Language Processing.*

V. G. Vinod Vydiswaran (vgvinodv@illinois.edu) is currently a Ph.D. student in the Department of Computer Science at the University of Illinois, Urbana-Champaign. His thesis is on modeling information trustworthiness on the Web and is advised by professors ChengXiang Zhai and Dan Roth. His research interests include text informatics, natural language processing, machine learning, and information extraction. V. G. Vinod's work has included developing a textual entailment system and applying textual entailment to relation extraction and information retrieval. He received his M.S. from Indian Institute of Technology-Bombay in 2004, where he worked on conditional models for information extraction with Professor Sunita Sarawagi. Later, he worked at Yahoo! Research & Development Center at Bangalore, India, on scaling information extraction technologies over the Web.

Janyce Wiebe (wiebe@cs.pitt.edu) is a professor of computer science and codirector of the Intelligent Systems Program at the University of Pittsburgh. Her research with students and colleagues has been in discourse processing, pragmatics, word-sense disambiguation, and probabilistic classification in natural language processing. A major concentration of her research is subjectivity analysis, recognizing and interpretating expressions of opinions and sentiments in text, to support natural language processing applications such as question answering, information extraction, text categorization, and summarization. Janyce's current and past professional roles include ACL program cochair, NAACL program chair, NAACL executive board member, computational linguistics, and language resources and evaluation, editorial board member, AAAI workshop cochair, ACM special interest group on artificial intelligence (SIGART) vice-chair, and ACM-SIGART/AAAI doctoral consortium chair.

Hyun-Jo You (youhyunjo@gmail.com) is currently a lecturer in the Department of Linguistics, Seoul National University. He received his Ph.D. from Seoul National University. His research interests include quantitative linguistics, statistical language modeling, and computerized corpus analysis. He is especially interested in studying the morpho-syntactic and discourse structure in morphologically rich, free word order languages such as Korean, Czech, and Russian.

Liang Zhou (liangz@isi.edu) is a research scientist at Thomson Reuters Corporation. She has extensive knowledge in natural language processing, including sentiment analysis, automated text summarization, text understanding, information extraction, question answering, and information distillation. During her graduate studies at the Information Sciences Institute, she was actively involved in various government-sponsored projects, such as NIST Document Understanding conferences and DARPA Global Autonomous Language Exploitation. Dr. Zhou received her Ph.D. from the University of Southern California in 2006, M.S. from Stanford University in 2001, and B.S. from the University of Tennessee in 1999, all in computer science.

Part I

In Theory

Chapter 1, "Finding the Structure of Words," describes how to identify distinct types of words in human languages and how the internal structure of words can be modeled in connection with grammatical properties and lexical concepts.

Chapter 2, "Finding the Structure of Documents," discusses how to find the structure of documents, breaking them down into more manageable units, such as sentences and pieces of text grouped by topic.

Chapter 3, "Syntax," describes how to find the structure of sentences.

Chapter 4, "Semantic Parsing," explores automatic methods for finding meaning representations for sentences.

Chapter 5, "Language Modeling," discusses the problem of building a model that assigns a probability estimate or score for every possible finite-length sequence of words.

Chapter 6, "Recognizing Textual Entailment," discusses methods for determining whether a fact predicated in one piece of text is entailed by a fact in another piece of text.

Chapter 7, "Multilingual Sentiment and Subjectivity Analysis," explores ways of determining whether sentences are subjective and determining the polarity and nature of the opinion expressed.

Chapter 1

Finding the Structure of Words

Otakar Smrž and Hyun-Jo You

Human language is a complicated thing. We use it to express our thoughts, and through language, we receive information and infer its meaning. Linguistic expressions are not unorganized, though. They show structure of different kinds and complexity and consist of more elementary components whose co-occurrence in context refines the notions they refer to in isolation and implies further meaningful relations between them.

Trying to understand language en bloc is not a viable approach. Linguists have developed whole disciplines that look at language from different perspectives and at different levels of detail. The point of morphology, for instance, is to study the variable forms and functions of words, while syntax is concerned with the arrangement of words into phrases, clauses, and sentences. Word structure constraints due to pronunciation are described by phonology, whereas conventions for writing constitute the orthography of a language. The meaning of a linguistic expression is its semantics, and etymology and lexicology cover especially the evolution of words and explain the semantic, morphological, and other links among them.

Words are perhaps the most intuitive units of language, yet they are in general tricky to define. Knowing how to work with them allows, in particular, the development of syntactic and semantic abstractions and simplifies other advanced views on language. Morphology is an essential part of language processing, and in multilingual settings, it becomes even more important.

In this chapter, we explore how to identify words of distinct types in human languages, and how the internal structure of words can be modeled in connection with the grammatical properties and lexical concepts the words should represent. The discovery of word structure is **morphological parsing**.

How difficult can such tasks be? It depends. In many languages, words are delimited in the orthography by whitespace and punctuation. But in many other languages, the writing system leaves it up to the reader to tell words apart or determine their exact phonological forms. Some languages use words whose form need not change much with the varying context; others are highly sensitive about the choice of word forms according to particular syntactic and semantic constraints and restrictions.

1.1 Words and Their Components

Words are defined in most languages as the smallest linguistic units that can form a complete utterance by themselves. The minimal parts of words that deliver aspects of meaning to them are called morphemes. Depending on the means of communication, morphemes are spelled out via graphemes—symbols of writing such as letters or characters—or are realized through phonemes, the distinctive units of sound in spoken language.[1] It is not always easy to decide and agree on the precise boundaries discriminating words from morphemes and from phrases [1, 2].

1.1.1 Tokens

Suppose, for a moment, that words in English are delimited only by whitespace and punctuation [3], and consider Example 1–1:

Example 1–1: Will you read the newspaper? Will you read it? I won't read it.

If we confront our assumption with insights from etymology and syntax, we notice two words here: *newspaper* and *won't*. Being a compound word, *newspaper* has an interesting derivational structure. We might wish to describe it in more detail, once there is a lexicon or some other linguistic evidence on which to build the possible hypotheses about the origins of the word. In writing, *newspaper* and the associated concept is distinguished from the isolated *news* and *paper*. In speech, however, the distinction is far from clear, and identification of words becomes an issue of its own.

For reasons of generality, linguists prefer to analyze *won't* as two syntactic words, or tokens, each of which has its independent role and can be reverted to its normalized form. The structure of *won't* could be parsed as *will* followed by *not*. In English, this kind of **tokenization** and **normalization** may apply to just a limited set of cases, but in other languages, these phenomena have to be treated in a less trivial manner.

In Arabic or Hebrew [4], certain tokens are concatenated in writing with the preceding or the following ones, possibly changing their forms as well. The underlying lexical or syntactic units are thereby blurred into one compact string of letters and no longer appear as distinct words. Tokens behaving in this way can be found in various languages and are often called clitics.

In the writing systems of Chinese, Japanese [5], and Thai, whitespace is not used to separate words. The units that are delimited graphically in some way are sentences or clauses. In Korean, character strings are called *eojeol* 'word segment' and roughly correspond to speech or cognitive units, which are usually larger than words and smaller than clauses [6], as shown in Example 1–2:

Example 1–2: 학생들에게만 주셨는데
hak.sayng.tul.ey.key.man cwu.syess.nun.te[2]
haksayng-tul-eykey-man cwu-si-ess-nunte
student+*plural*+*dative*+only give+*honorific*+*past*+while
while (he/she) gave (it) only to the students

1. Signs used in sign languages are composed of elements denoted as phonemes, too.
2. We use the Yale romanization of the Korean script and indicate its original characters by dots. Hyphens mark morphological boundaries, and tokens are separated by plus symbols.

Nonetheless, the elementary morphological units are viewed as having their own syntactic status [7]. In such languages, tokenization, also known as **word segmentation**, is the fundamental step of morphological analysis and a prerequisite for most language processing applications.

1.1.2 Lexemes

By the term word, we often denote not just the one linguistic form in the given context but also the concept behind the form and the set of alternative forms that can express it. Such sets are called lexemes or lexical items, and they constitute the lexicon of a language. Lexemes can be divided by their behavior into the lexical categories of verbs, nouns, adjectives, conjunctions, particles, or other parts of speech. The citation form of a lexeme, by which it is commonly identified, is also called its lemma.

When we convert a word into its other forms, such as turning the singular *mouse* into the plural *mice* or *mouses*, we say we inflect the lexeme. When we transform a lexeme into another one that is morphologically related, regardless of its lexical category, we say we derive the lexeme: for instance, the nouns *receiver* and *reception* are derived from the verb *to receive*.

EXAMPLE 1–3: Did you see him? I didn't see him. I didn't see anyone.

Example 1–3 presents the problem of tokenization of *didn't* and the investigation of the internal structure of *anyone*. In the paraphrase *I saw no one*, the lexeme *to see* would be inflected into the form *saw* to reflect its grammatical function of expressing positive past tense. Likewise, *him* is the oblique case form of *he* or even of a more abstract lexeme representing all personal pronouns. In the paraphrase, *no one* can be perceived as the minimal word synonymous with *nobody*. The difficulty with the definition of what counts as a word need not pose a problem for the syntactic description if we understand *no one* as two closely connected tokens treated as one fixed element.

In the Czech translation of Example 1–3, the lexeme *vidět* 'to see' is inflected for past tense, in which forms comprising two tokens are produced in the second and first person (i.e., *viděla jsi* 'you-FEM-SG saw' and *neviděla jsem* 'I-FEM-SG did not see'). Negation in Czech is an inflectional parameter rather than just syntactic and is marked both in the verb and in the pronoun of the latter response, as in Example 1–4:

EXAMPLE 1–4: Vidělas ho? Neviděla jsem ho. Neviděla jsem nikoho.
saw+you-are him? not-saw I-am him. not-saw I-am no-one.

Here, *vidělas* is the contracted form of *viděla jsi* 'you-FEM-SG saw'. The *s* of *jsi* 'you are' is a clitic, and due to free word order in Czech, it can be attached to virtually any part of speech. We could thus ask a question like *Nikohos neviděla?* 'Did you see no one?' in which the pronoun *nikoho* 'no one' is followed by this clitic.

1.1.3 Morphemes

Morphological theories differ on whether and how to associate the properties of word forms with their structural components [8, 9, 10, 11]. These components are usually called **segments** or **morphs**. The morphs that by themselves represent some aspect of the meaning of a word are called **morphemes** of some function.

Human languages employ a variety of devices by which morphs and morphemes are combined into word forms. The simplest morphological process concatenates morphs one by one, as in *dis-agree-ment-s*, where *agree* is a free lexical morpheme and the other elements are bound grammatical morphemes contributing some partial meaning to the whole word.

In a more complex scheme, morphs can interact with each other, and their forms may become subject to additional phonological and orthographic changes denoted as morphophonemic. The alternative forms of a morpheme are termed **allomorphs**.

Examples of morphological alternation and phonologically dependent choice of the form of a morpheme are abundant in the Korean language. In Korean, many morphemes change their forms systematically with the phonological context. Example 1–5 lists the allomorphs *-ess-*, *-ass-*, *-yess-* of the temporal marker indicating past tense. The first two alter according to the phonological condition of the preceding verb stem; the last one is used especially for the verb *ha-* 'do'. The appropriate allomorph is merely concatenated after the stem, or it can be further contracted with it, as was *-si-ess-* into *-syess-* in Example 1–2. During morphological parsing, normalization of allomorphs into some canonical form of the morpheme is desirable, especially because the contraction of morphs interferes with simple segmentation:

EXAMPLE 1–5:

	concatenated		contracted		
(a)	보았-	*po-ass-*	봤-	*pwass-*	'have seen'
(b)	가지었-	*ka.ci-ess-*	가졌-	*ka.cyess-*	'have taken'
(c)	하였-	*ha-yess-*	했-	*hayss-*	'have done'
(d)	되었-	*toy-ess-*	됐-	*twayss-*	'have become'
(e)	놓았-	*noh-ass-*	놨-	*nwass-*	'have put'

Contractions (a, b) are ordinary but require attention because two characters are reduced into one. Other types (c, d, e) are phonologically unpredictable, or lexically dependent. For example, *coh-ass-* 'have been good' may never be contracted, whereas *noh-* and *-ass-* are merged into *nwass-* in (e).

There are yet other linguistic devices of word formation to account for, as the morphological process itself can get less trivial. The concatenation operation can be complemented with infixation or intertwining of the morphs, which is common, for instance, in Arabic. Nonconcatenative inflection by modification of the internal vowel of a word occurs even in English: compare the sounds of *mouse* and *mice*, *see* and *saw*, *read* and *read*.

Notably in Arabic, internal inflection takes place routinely and has a yet different quality. The internal parts of words, called stems, are modeled with root and pattern morphemes. Word structure is then described by templates abstracting away from the root but showing the pattern and all the other morphs attached to either side of it.

EXAMPLE 1–6: `hl stqrO h*h AljrA}d?`[3] هل ستقرأ هذه الجرائد؟
hal sa-taqraʾu hāḏihi ʾl-ǧarāʾida?
whether will+you-read this the-newspapers?

`hl stqrWhA? ln OqrOhA.` هل ستقرؤها؟ لن أقرأها.
hal sa-taqraʾuhā? lan ʾaqraʾahā.
whether will+you-read+it? not-will I-read+it.

3. The original Arabic script is transliterated using Buckwalter notation. For readability, we also provide the standard phonological transcription, which reduces ambiguity.

The meaning of Example 1–6 is similar to that of Example 1–1, only the phrase *hāḏihi 'l-ǧarāʾida* refers to 'these newspapers'. While *sa-taqraʾu* 'you will read' combines the future marker *sa-* with the imperfective second-person masculine singular verb *taqraʾu* in the indicative mood and active voice, *sa-taqraʾuhā* 'you will read it' also adds the cliticized feminine singular personal pronoun in the accusative case.[4]

The citation form of the lexeme to which *taqraʾu* 'you-MASC-SG read' belongs is *qaraʾ*, roughly 'to read'. This form is classified by linguists as the basic verbal form represented by the template *faʿal* merged with the consonantal root *q r ʾ*, where the *f ʿ l* symbols of the template are substituted by the respective root consonants. Inflections of this lexeme can modify the pattern *faʿal* of the stem of the lemma into *fʿal* and concatenate it, under rules of morphophonemic changes, with further prefixes and suffixes. The structure of *taqraʾu* is thus parsed into the template *ta-fʿal-u* and the invariant root.

The word *al-ǧarāʾida* 'the newspapers' in the accusative case and definite state is another example of internal inflection. Its structure follows the template *al-faʿāʾil-a* with the root *ǧ r d*. This word is the plural of *ǧarīdah* 'newspaper' with the template *faʿīl-ah*. The links between singular and plural templates are subject to convention and have to be declared in the lexicon.

Irrespective of the morphological processes involved, some properties or features of a word need not be apparent explicitly in its morphological structure. Its existing structural components may be paired with and depend on several functions simultaneously but may have no particular grammatical interpretation or lexical meaning.

The *-ah* suffix of *ǧarīdah* 'newspaper' corresponds with the inherent feminine gender of the lexeme. In fact, the *-ah* morpheme is commonly, though not exclusively, used to mark the feminine singular forms of adjectives: for example, *ǧadīd* becomes *ǧadīdah* 'new'. However, the *-ah* suffix can be part of words that are not feminine, and there its function can be seen as either emptied or overridden [12]. In general, linguistic forms should be distinguished from functions, and not every morph can be assumed to be a morpheme.

1.1.4 Typology

Morphological typology divides languages into groups by characterizing the prevalent morphological phenomena in those languages. It can consider various criteria, and during the history of linguistics, different classifications have been proposed [13, 14]. Let us outline the typology that is based on quantitative relations between words, their morphemes, and their features:

Isolating, or **analytic**, languages include no or relatively few words that would comprise more than one morpheme (typical members are Chinese, Vietnamese, and Thai; analytic tendencies are also found in English).

Synthetic languages can combine more morphemes in one word and are further divided into agglutinative and fusional languages.

Agglutinative languages have morphemes associated with only a single function at a time (as in Korean, Japanese, Finnish, and Tamil, etc.).

4. The logical plural of things is formally treated as feminine singular in Arabic.

Fusional languages are defined by their feature-per-morpheme ratio higher than one (as in Arabic, Czech, Latin, Sanskrit, German, etc.).

In accordance with the notions about word formation processes mentioned earlier, we can also discern:

Concatenative languages linking morphs and morphemes one after another.

Nonlinear languages allowing structural components to merge nonsequentially to apply tonal morphemes or change the consonantal or vocalic templates of words.

While some morphological phenomena, such as orthographic collapsing, phonological contraction, or complex inflection and derivation, are more dominant in some languages than in others, in principle, we can find, and should be able to deal with, instances of these phenomena across different language families and typological classes.

1.2 Issues and Challenges

Morphological parsing tries to eliminate or alleviate the variability of word forms to provide higher-level linguistic units whose lexical and morphological properties are explicit and well defined. It attempts to remove unnecessary irregularity and give limits to ambiguity, both of which are present inherently in human language.

By irregularity, we mean existence of such forms and structures that are not described appropriately by a prototypical linguistic model. Some irregularities can be understood by redesigning the model and improving its rules, but other lexically dependent irregularities often cannot be generalized.

Ambiguity is indeterminacy in interpretation of expressions of language. Next to accidental ambiguity and ambiguity due to lexemes having multiple senses, we note the issue of **syncretism**, or systematic ambiguity.

Morphological modeling also faces the problem of productivity and creativity in language, by which unconventional but perfectly meaningful new words or new senses are coined. Usually, though, words that are not licensed in some way by the lexicon of a morphological system will remain completely unparsed. This **unknown word** problem is particularly severe in speech or writing that gets out of the expected domain of the linguistic model, such as when special terms or foreign names are involved in the discourse or when multiple languages or dialects are mixed together.

1.2.1 Irregularity

Morphological parsing is motivated by the quest for generalization and abstraction in the world of words. Immediate descriptions of given linguistic data may not be the ultimate ones, due to either their inadequate accuracy or inappropriate complexity, and better formulations may be needed. The design principles of the morphological model are therefore very important.

In Arabic, the deeper study of the morphological processes that are in effect during inflection and derivation, even for the so-called irregular words, is essential for mastering the whole morphological and phonological system. With the proper abstractions made, irregular morphology can be seen as merely enforcing some extended rules, the nature of which is phonological, over the underlying or prototypical regular word forms [15, 16].

EXAMPLE 1–7: `hl rOyth? lm Orh. lm Or OHdA.` هل رأيته؟ لم أره. لم أر أحدا.
hal raʾaytihi? lam ʾarahu. lam ʾara ʾaḥadan.
whether you-saw+him? not-did I-see+him. not-did I-see anyone.

In Example 1–7, *raʾayti* is the second-person feminine singular perfective verb in active voice, member of the *raʾā* 'to see' lexeme of the *r ʾ y* root. The prototypical, regularized pattern for this citation form is *faʿal*, as we saw with *qaraʾ* in Example 1–6. Alternatively, we could assume the pattern of *raʾā* to be *faʿā*, thereby asserting in a compact way that the final root consonant and its vocalic context are subject to the particular phonological change, resulting in *raʾā* like *faʿā* instead of *raʾay* like *faʿal*. The occurrence of this change in the citation form may have possible implications for the morphological behavior of the whole lexeme.

Table 1–1 illustrates differences between a naive model of word structure in Arabic and the model proposed in Smrž [12] and Smrž and Bielický [17] where morphophonemic merge rules and templates are involved. Morphophonemic templates capture morphological processes by just organizing stem patterns and generic affixes without any context-dependent variation of the affixes or ad hoc modification of the stems. The merge rules, indeed very terse, then ensure that such structured representations can be converted into exactly the surface forms, both orthographic and phonological, used in the natural language. Applying the merge rules is independent of and irrespective of any grammatical parameters or information other than that contained in a template. Most morphological irregularities are thus successfully removed.

Table 1–1: Discovering the regularity of Arabic morphology using morphophonemic templates, where uniform structural operations apply to different kinds of stems. In rows, surface forms S of *qaraʾ* 'to read' and *raʾā* 'to see' and their inflections are analyzed into immediate I and morphophonemic M templates, in which dashes mark the structural boundaries where merge rules are enforced. The outer columns of the table correspond to P perfective and I imperfective stems declared in the lexicon; the inner columns treat active verb forms of the following morphosyntactic properties: I indicative, S subjunctive, J jussive mood; 1 first, 2 second, 3 third person; M masculine, F feminine gender; S singular, P plural number

P-STEM	P–3MS	P–2FS	P–3MP	II2MS	IS1–S	IJ1–S	I-STEM	
qaraʾ	*qaraʾa*	*qaraʾti*	*qaraʾū*	*taqraʾu*	*ʾaqraʾa*	*ʾaqraʾ*	*qraʾ*	S
faʿal	*faʿal-a*	*faʿal-ti*	*faʿal-ū*	*ta-fʿal-u*	*ʾa-fʿal-a*	*ʾa-fʿal*	*fʿal*	I
faʿal	*faʿal-a*	*faʿal-ti*	*faʿal-ū*	*ta-fʿal-u*	*ʾa-fʿal-a*	*ʾa-fʿal-*	*fʿal*	M
...	**...-a**	**...-ti**	**...-ū**	**ta-...-u**	**ʾa-...-a**	**ʾa-...-**	**...**	
faʿā	*faʿā-a*	*faʿā-ti*	*faʿā-ū*	*ta-fā-u*	*ʾa-fā-a*	*ʾa-fā-*	*fā*	M
faʿā	*faʿā*	*faʿal-ti*	*faʿ-aw*	*ta-fā*	*ʾa-fā*	*ʾa-fa*	*fā*	I
raʾā	*raʾā*	*raʾayti*	*raʾaw*	*tarā*	*ʾarā*	*ʾara*	***rā***	S

Table 1–2: Examples of major Korean irregular verb classes compared with regular verbs

Base Form		(-*e*)		Meaning	Comment
집-	*cip-*	집어	*cip.e*	'pick'	regular
깁-	*kip-*	기워	*ki.we*	'sew'	*p*-irregular
믿-	*mit-*	믿어	*mit.e*	'believe'	regular
싣-	*sit-*	실어	*sil.e*	'load'	*t*-irregular
씻-	*ssis-*	씻어	*ssis.e*	'wash'	regular
잇-	*is-*	이어	*i.e*	'link'	*s*-irregular
낳-	*nah-*	낳아	*nah.a*	'bear'	regular
까맣-	*kka.mah-*	까매	*kka.may*	'be black'	*h*-irregular
치르-	*chi.lu-*	치러	*chi.le*	'pay'	regular *u*-ellipsis
이르-	*i.lu-*	이르러	*i.lu.le*	'reach'	*le*-irregular
흐르-	*hu.lu-*	흘러	*hul.le*	'flow'	*lu*-irregular

In contrast, some irregularities are bound to particular lexemes or contexts, and cannot be accounted for by general rules. Korean irregular verbs provide examples of such irregularities.

Korean shows exceptional constraints on the selection of grammatical morphemes. It is hard to find irregular inflection in other agglutinative languages: two irregular verbs in Japanese [18], one in Finnish [19]. These languages are abundant with morphological alternations that are formalized by precise phonological rules. Korean additionally features lexically dependent stem alternation. As in many other languages, *i-* 'be' and *ha-* 'do' have unique irregular endings. Other irregular verbs are classified by the stem final phoneme. Table 1–2 compares major irregular verb classes with regular verbs in the same phonological condition.

1.2.2 Ambiguity

Morphological ambiguity is the possibility that word forms be understood in multiple ways out of the context of their discourse. Words forms that look the same but have distinct functions or meaning are called homonyms.

Ambiguity is present in all aspects of morphological processing and language processing at large. Morphological parsing is not concerned with complete disambiguation of words in their context, however; it can effectively restrict the set of valid interpretations of a given word form [20, 21].

In Korean, homonyms are one of the most problematic objects in morphological analysis because they prevail all around frequent lexical items. Table 1–3 arranges homonyms on the basis of their behavior with different endings. Example 1–8 is an example of homonyms through nouns and verbs.

Table 1–3: Systematic homonyms arise as verbs combined with endings in Korean

(-*ko*)		(-*e*)		(-*un*)		Meaning
묻고	***mwut.ko***	묻어	*mwut.e*	묻은	*mwut.un*	'bury'
묻고	***mwut.ko***	물어	***mwul.e***	물은	*mwul.un*	'ask'
물고	*mwul.ko*	물어	***mwul.e***	문	*mwun*	'bite'
걷고	***ket.ko***	걷어	*ket.e*	걷은	*ket.un*	'roll up'
걷고	***ket.ko***	걸어	***kel.e***	걸은	*kel.un*	'walk'
걸고	*kel.ko*	걸어	***kel.e***	건	*ken*	'hang'
굽고	***kwup.ko***	굽어	*kwup.e*	굽은	*kwup.un*	'be bent'
굽고	***kwup.ko***	구워	*kwu.we*	구운	*kwu.wun*	'bake'
이르고	***i.lu.ko***	이르러	*i.lu.le*	이른	***i.lun***	'reach'
이르고	***i.lu.ko***	일러	*il.le*	이른	***i.lun***	'say'

EXAMPLE 1–8: 난 'orchid' ← 난 *nan* 'orchid'
난 'I' ← 나 *na* 'I' + -*n* (topic)
난 'which flew' ← 날- *nal*- 'fly' + -*n* (relative, past)
난 'which got out' ← 나- *na*- 'get out' + -*n* (relative, past)

We could also consider ambiguity in the senses of the noun *nan*, according to the Standard Korean Language Dictionary: nan^1 'egg', nan^2 'revolt', nan^5 'section (in newspaper)', nan^6 'orchid', plus several infrequent readings.

Arabic is a language of rich morphology, both derivational and inflectional. Because Arabic script usually does not encode short vowels and omits yet some other diacritical marks that would record the phonological form exactly, the degree of its morphological ambiguity is considerably increased. In addition, Arabic orthography collapses certain word forms together. The problem of morphological disambiguation of Arabic encompasses not only the resolution of the structural components of words and their actual morphosyntactic properties (i.e., morphological tagging [22, 23, 24]) but also tokenization and normalization [25], lemmatization, stemming, and diacritization [26, 27, 28].

When inflected syntactic words are combined in an utterance, additional phonological and orthographic changes can take place, as shown in Figure 1–1. In Sanskrit, one such euphony rule is known as external *sandhi* [29, 30]. Inverting *sandhi* during tokenization is usually nondeterministic in the sense that it can provide multiple solutions. In any language, tokenization decisions may impose constraints on the morphosyntactic properties of the tokens being reconstructed, which then have to be respected in further processing. The tight coupling between morphology and syntax has inspired proposals for disambiguating them jointly rather than sequentially [4].

Czech is a highly inflected fusional language. Unlike agglutinative languages, inflectional morphemes often represent several functions simultaneously, and there is no particular one-to-one correspondence between their forms and functions. Inflectional **paradigms**

dirāsatī	دراستي	`drAsty`	→	*dirāsatu ī*	دراسة ي	`drAsp y`
			→	*dirāsati ī*	دراسة ي	`drAsp y`
			→	*dirāsata ī*	دراسة ي	`drAsp y`
muʿallimīya	معلمي	`mElmy`	→	*muʿallimū ī*	معلمو ي	`mElmw y`
			→	*muʿallimī ī*	معلمي ي	`mElmy y`
katabtumūhā	كتبتموها	`ktbtmwhA`	→	*katabtum hā*	كتبتم ها	`ktbtm hA`
ʾiǧrāʾuhu	إجراؤه	`IjrAWh`	→	*ʾiǧrāʾu hu*	إجراء ه	`IjrA' h`
ʾiǧrāʾihi	إجرائه	`IjrA}h`	→	*ʾiǧrāʾi hu*	إجراء ه	`IjrA' h`
ʾiǧrāʾahu	إجراءه	`IjrA'h`	→	*ʾiǧrāʾa hu*	إجراء ه	`IjrA' h`
li-'l-ʾasafi	للأسف	`llOsf`	→	*li 'l-ʾasafi li*	ل الأسف	`l AlOsf`

Figure 1–1: Complex tokenization and normalization of euphony in Arabic. Three nominal cases are expressed by the same word form with *dirāsatī* 'my study' and *muʿallimīya* 'my teachers', but the original case endings are distinct. In *katabtumūhā* 'you-MASC-PL wrote them', the liaison vowel *ū* is dropped when tokenized. Special attention is needed to normalize some orthographic conventions, such as the interaction of *ʾiǧrāʾ* 'carrying out' and the cliticized *hu* 'his' respecting the case ending or the merge of the definite article of *ʾasaf* 'regret' with the preposition *li* 'for'

(i.e., schemes for finding the form of a lexeme associated with the required properties) in Czech are of numerous kinds, yet they tend to include nonunique forms in them.

Table 1–4 lists the paradigms of several common Czech words. Inflectional paradigms for nouns depend on the grammatical gender and the phonological structure of a lexeme. The individual forms in a paradigm vary with grammatical number and case, which are the free parameters imposed only by the context in which a word is used.

Looking at the morphological variation of the word *stavení* 'building', we might wonder why we should distinguish all the cases for it when this lexeme can take only four different forms. Is the detail of the case system appropriate? The answer is yes, because we can find linguistic evidence that leads to this case category abstraction. Just consider other words of the same meaning in place of *stavení* in various contexts. We conclude that there is indeed a case distinction made by the underlying system, but it need not necessarily be expressed clearly and uniquely in the form of words.

The morphological phenomenon that some words or word classes show instances of systematic homonymy is called syncretism. In particular, homonymy can occur due to **neutralization** and **uninflectedness** with respect to some morphosyntactic parameters. These cases of morphological syncretism are distinguished by the ability of the context to demand the morphosyntactic properties in question, as stated by Baerman, Brown, and Corbett [10, p. 32]:

> Whereas *neutralization* is about syntactic irrelevance as reflected in morphology, *uninflectedness* is about morphology being unresponsive to a feature that is syntactically relevant.

For example, it seems fine for syntax in Czech or Arabic to request the personal pronoun of the first-person feminine singular, equivalent to 'I', despite it being homonymous with

Table 1–4: Morphological paradigms of the Czech words dům 'house', budova 'building', stavba 'building', stavení 'building'. Despite systematic ambiguities in them, the space of inflectional parameters could not be reduced without losing the ability to capture all distinct forms elsewhere: S singular, P plural number; 1 nominative, 2 genitive, 3 dative, 4 accusative, 5 vocative, 6 locative, 7 instrumental case

	Masculine inanimate	Feminine	Feminine	Neuter
S1	dům	budova	stavba	stavení
S2	domu	budovy	stavby	stavení
S3	domu	budově	stavbě	stavení
S4	dům	budovu	stavbu	stavení
S5	dome	budovo	stavbo	stavení
S6	domu / domě	budově	stavbě	stavení
S7	domem	budovou	stavbou	stavením
P1	domy	budovy	stavby	stavení
P2	domů	budov	staveb	stavení
P3	domům	budovám	stavbám	stavením
P4	domy	budovy	stavby	stavení
P5	domy	budovy	stavby	stavení
P6	domech	budovách	stavbách	staveních
P7	domy	budovami	stavbami	staveními

the first-person masculine singular. The reason is that for some other values of the person category, the forms of masculine and feminine gender are different, and there exist syntactic dependencies that do take gender into account. It is not the case that the first-person singular pronoun would have no gender nor that it would have both. We just observe uninflectedness here. On the other hand, we might claim that in English or Korean, the gender category is syntactically neutralized if it ever was present, and the nuances between *he* and *she*, *him* and *her*, *his* and *hers* are only semantic.

With the notion of paradigms and syncretism in mind, we should ask what is the minimal set of combinations of morphosyntactic inflectional parameters that covers the inflectional variability in a language. Morphological models that would like to define a joint system of underlying morphosyntactic properties for multiple languages would have to generalize the parameter space accordingly and neutralize any systematically void configurations.

1.2.3 Productivity

Is the inventory of words in a language finite, or is it unlimited? This question leads directly to discerning two fundamental approaches to language, summarized in the distinction between *langue* and *parole* by Ferdinand de Saussure, or in the competence versus performance duality by Noam Chomsky.

In one view, language can be seen as simply a collection of utterances (parole) actually pronounced or written (performance). This ideal data set can in practice be approximated by linguistic corpora, which are finite collections of linguistic data that are studied with empirical methods and can be used for comparison when linguistic models are developed.

Yet, if we consider language as a system (langue), we discover in it structural devices like recursion, iteration, or compounding that allow to produce (competence) an infinite set of concrete linguistic utterances. This general potential holds for morphological processes as well and is called morphological productivity [31, 32].

We denote the set of word forms found in a corpus of a language as its vocabulary. The members of this set are word types, whereas every original instance of a word form is a word token.

The distribution of words [33] or other elements of language follows the "80/20 rule," also known as the law of the vital few. It says that most of the word tokens in a given corpus can be identified with just a couple of word types in its vocabulary, and words from the rest of the vocabulary occur much less commonly if not rarely in the corpus. Furthermore, new, unexpected words will always appear as the collection of linguistic data is enlarged.

In Czech, negation is a productive morphological operation. Verbs, nouns, adjectives, and adverbs can be prefixed with *ne-* to define the complementary lexical concept. In Example 1–9, *budeš* 'you will be' is the second-person singular of *být* 'to be', and *nebudu* 'I will not be' is the first-person singular of *nebýt*, the negated *být*. We could easily have *číst* 'to read' and *nečíst* 'not to read', or we could create an adverbial phrase like *noviny nenoviny* that would express 'indifference to newspapers' in general:

Example 1–9: Budeš číst ty noviny? Budeš je číst? Nebudu je číst.
you-will read the newspaper? you-will it read? not-I-will it read.

Example 1–9 has the meaning of Example 1–1 and Example 1–6. The word *noviny* 'newspaper' exists only in plural whether it signifies one piece of newspaper or many of them. We can literally translate *noviny* as the plural of *novina* 'news' to see the origins of the word as well as the fortunate analogy with English.

It is conceivable to include all negated lexemes into the lexicon and thereby again achieve a finite number of word forms in the vocabulary. Generally, though, the richness of a morphological system of a language can make this approach highly impractical.

Most languages contain words that allow some of their structural components to repeat freely. Consider the prefix *pra-* related to a notion of 'generation' in Czech and how it can or cannot be iterated, as shown in Example 1–10:

Example 1–10:		
	vnuk 'grandson'	*pravnuk* 'great-grandson'
		prapra...vnuk 'great-great-...grandson'
	les 'forest'	*prales* 'jungle', 'virgin forest'
	zdroj 'source'	*prazdroj* 'urquell', 'original source'
	starý 'old'	*prastarý* 'time-honored', 'dateless'

In creative language, such as in blogs, chats, and emotive informal communication, iteration is often used to accent intensity of expression. Creativity may, of course, go beyond the rules of productivity itself [32].

Let us give an example where creativity, productivity, and the issue of unknown words meet nicely. According to Wikipedia, the word *googol* is a made-up word denoting the number "one followed by one hundred zeros," and the name of the company Google is an inadvertent misspelling thereof. Nonetheless, both of these words successfully entered the lexicon of English where morphological productivity started working, and we now know the verb *to google* and nouns like *googling* or even *googlish* or *googleology* [34].

The original names have been adopted by other languages, too, and their own morphological processes have been triggered. In Czech, one says *googlovat*, *googlit* 'to google' or *vygooglovat*, *vygooglit* 'to google out', *googlování* 'googling', and so on. In Arabic, the names are transcribed as *ǧūǧūl* 'googol' and *ǧūǧil* 'Google'. The latter one got transformed to the verb *ǧawǧal* 'to google' through internal inflection, as if there were a genuine root *ǧ w ǧ l*, and the corresponding noun *ǧawǧalah* 'googling' exists as well.

1.3 Morphological Models

There are many possible approaches to designing and implementing morphological models. Over time, computational linguistics has witnessed the development of a number of formalisms and frameworks, in particular grammars of different kinds and expressive power, with which to address whole classes of problems in processing natural as well as formal languages.

Various domain-specific programming languages have been created that allow us to implement the theoretical problem using hopefully intuitive and minimal programming effort. These special-purpose languages usually introduce idiosyncratic notations of programs and are interpreted using some restricted model of computation. The motivation for such approaches may partly lie in the fact that, historically, computational resources were too limited compared to the requirements and complexity of the tasks being solved. Other motivations are theoretical given that finding a simple but accurate and yet generalizing model is the point of scientific abstraction.

There are also many approaches that do not resort to domain-specific programming. They, however, have to take care of the runtime performance and efficiency of the computational model themselves. It is up to the choice of the programming methods and the design style whether such models turn out to be pure, intuitive, adequate, complete, reusable, elegant, or not.

Let us now look at the most prominent types of computational approaches to morphology. Needless to say, this typology is not strictly exclusive in the sense that comprehensive morphological models and their applications can combine various distinct implementational aspects, discussed next.

1.3.1 Dictionary Lookup

Morphological parsing is a process by which word forms of a language are associated with corresponding linguistic descriptions. Morphological systems that specify these associations by merely enumerating them case by case do not offer any generalization means. Likewise for systems in which analyzing a word form is reduced to looking it up verbatim in word lists, dictionaries, or databases, unless they are constructed by and kept in sync with more sophisticated models of the language.

In this context, a dictionary is understood as a data structure that directly enables obtaining some precomputed results, in our case word analyses. The data structure can be optimized for efficient lookup, and the results can be shared. Lookup operations are relatively simple and usually quick. Dictionaries can be implemented, for instance, as lists, binary search trees, tries, hash tables, and so on.

Because the set of associations between word forms and their desired descriptions is declared by plain enumeration, the coverage of the model is finite and the generative potential of the language is not exploited. Developing as well as verifying the association list is tedious, liable to errors, and likely inefficient and inaccurate unless the data are retrieved automatically from large and reliable linguistic resources.

Despite all that, an enumerative model is often sufficient for the given purpose, deals easily with exceptions, and can implement even complex morphology. For instance, dictionary-based approaches to Korean [35] depend on a large dictionary of all possible combinations of allomorphs and morphological alternations. These approaches do not allow development of reusable morphological rules, though [36].

The word list or dictionary-based approach has been used frequently in various ad hoc implementations for many languages. We could assume that with the availability of immense online data, extracting a high-coverage vocabulary of word forms is feasible these days [37]. The question remains how the associated annotations are constructed and how informative and accurate they are. References to the literature on the unsupervised learning and induction of morphology, which are methods resulting in structured and therefore nonenumerative models, are provided later in this chapter.

1.3.2 Finite-State Morphology

By finite-state morphological models, we mean those in which the specifications written by human programmers are directly compiled into finite-state transducers. The two most popular tools supporting this approach, which have been cited in literature and for which example implementations for multiple languages are available online, include XFST (Xerox Finite-State Tool) [9] and LexTools [11].[5]

Finite-state transducers are computational devices extending the power of finite-state automata. They consist of a finite set of nodes connected by directed edges labeled with pairs of input and output symbols. In such a network or graph, nodes are also called states, while edges are called arcs. Traversing the network from the set of initial states to the set of final states along the arcs is equivalent to reading the sequences of encountered input symbols and writing the sequences of corresponding output symbols.

The set of possible sequences accepted by the transducer defines the input language; the set of possible sequences emitted by the transducer defines the output language. For example, a finite-state transducer could translate the infinite regular language consisting of the words *vnuk*, *pravnuk*, *prapravnuk*, ... to the matching words in the infinite regular language defined by *grandson*, *great-grandson*, *great-great-grandson*, ...

5. See http://www.fsmbook.com/ and http://compling.ai.uiuc.edu/catms/ respectively.

The role of finite-state transducers is to capture and compute **regular relations** on sets [38, 9, 11].[6] That is, transducers specify relations between the input and output languages. In fact, it is possible to invert the domain and the range of a relation, that is, exchange the input and the output. In finite-state computational morphology, it is common to refer to the input word forms as **surface strings** and to the output descriptions as **lexical strings**, if the transducer is used for morphological analysis, or vice versa, if it is used for morphological generation.

The linguistic descriptions we would like to give to the word forms and their components can be rather arbitrary and are obviously dependent on the language processed as well as on the morphological theory followed. In English, a finite-state transducer could analyze the surface string `children` into the lexical string `child [+plural]`, for instance, or generate `women` from `woman [+plural]`. For other examples of possible input and output strings, consider Example 1–8 or Figure 1–1.

Relations on languages can also be viewed as functions. Let us have a relation $\mathcal{R}$, and let us denote by $[\Sigma]$ the set of all sequences over some set of symbols Σ, so that the domain and the range of $\mathcal{R}$ are subsets of $[\Sigma]$. We can then consider $\mathcal{R}$ as a function mapping an input string into a set of output strings, formally denoted by this type signature, where $[\Sigma]$ equals *String*:

$$\mathcal{R} :: [\Sigma] \rightarrow \{[\Sigma]\} \qquad\qquad \mathcal{R} :: String \rightarrow \{String\} \tag{1.1}$$

Finite-state transducers have been studied extensively for their formal algebraic properties and have proven to be suitable models for miscellaneous problems [9]. Their applications encoding the surface rather than lexical string associations as **rewrite rules** of phonology and morphology have been around since the two-level morphology model [39], further presented in *Computational Approaches to Morphology and Syntax* [11] *and Morphology and Computation* [40].

Morphological operations and processes in human languages can, in the overwhelming number of cases and to a sufficient degree, be expressed in finite-state terms. Beesley and Karttunen [9] stress concatenation of transducers as the method for factoring surface and lexical languages into simpler models and propose a somewhat unsystematic **compile-replace** transducer operation for handling nonconcatenative phenomena in morphology. Roark and Sproat [11], however, argue that building morphological models in general using transducer composition, which is pure, is a more universal approach.

A theoretical limitation of finite-state models of morphology is the problem of capturing **reduplication** of words or their elements (e.g., to express plurality) found in several human languages. A formal language that contains only words of the form λ^{1+k}, where λ is some arbitrary sequence of symbols from an alphabet and $k \in \{1, 2, \dots\}$ is an arbitrary natural number indicating how many times λ is repeated after itself, is not a regular language, not even a context-free language. General reduplication of strings of unbounded length is thus not a regular-language operation. Coping with this problem in the framework of finite-state transducers is discussed by Roark and Sproat [11].

6. Regular relations and regular languages are restricted in their structure by the limited memory of the device (i.e., the finite set of configurations in which it can occur). Unlike with regular languages, intersection of regular relations can in general yield nonregular results [38].

Finite-state technology can be applied to the morphological modeling of isolating and agglutinative languages in a quite straightforward manner. Korean finite-state models are discussed by Kim et al. [41], Lee and Rim [42], and Han [43], to mention a few. For treatments of nonconcatenative morphology using finite-state frameworks, see especially Kay [44], Beesley [45], Kiraz [46], and Habash, Rambow, and Kiraz [47]. For comparison with finite-state models of the rich morphology of Czech, compare Skoumalová [48] and Sedláĉek and Smrž [49].

Implementing a refined finite-state morphological model requires careful fine-tuning of its lexicons, rewrite rules, and other components, while extending the code can lead to unexpected interactions in it, as noted by Oazer [50]. Convenient specification languages like those mentioned previously are needed because encoding the finite-state transducers directly would be extremely arduous, error prone, and unintelligible.

Finite-state tools are available in most general-purpose programming languages in the form of support for regular expression matching and substitution. While these may not be the ultimate choice for building full-fledged morphological analyzers or generators of a natural language, they are very suitable for developing tokenizers and morphological guessers capable of suggesting at least some structure for words that are formed correctly but cannot be identified with concrete lexemes during full morphological parsing [9].

1.3.3 Unification-Based Morphology

Unification-based approaches to morphology have been inspired by advances in various formal linguistic frameworks aiming at enabling complete grammatical descriptions of human languages, especially head-driven phrase structure grammar (HPSG) [51], and by development of languages for lexical knowledge representation, especially DATR [52]. The concepts and methods of these formalisms are often closely connected to those of logic programming. In the excellent thesis by Erjavec [53], the scientific context is discussed extensively and profoundly; refer also to the monographs by Carpenter [54] and Shieber [55].

In finite-state morphological models, both surface and lexical forms are by themselves unstructured strings of atomic symbols. In higher-level approaches, linguistic information is expressed by more appropriate data structures that can include complex values or can be recursively nested if needed. Morphological parsing $\mathcal{P}$ thus associates linear forms ϕ with alternatives of structured content ψ, cf. (1.1):

$$\mathcal{P} :: \phi \rightarrow \{\psi\} \qquad\qquad \mathcal{P} :: form \rightarrow \{content\} \tag{1.2}$$

Erjavec [53] argues that for morphological modeling, word forms are best captured by regular expressions, while the linguistic content is best described through **typed feature structures**. Feature structures can be viewed as directed acyclic graphs. A node in a feature structure comprises a set of attributes whose values can be feature structures again. Nodes are associated with types, and atomic values are attributeless nodes distinguished by their type. Instead of unique instances of values everywhere, references can be used to establish value instance identity. Feature structures are usually displayed as attribute-value matrices or as nested symbolic expressions.

Unification is the key operation by which feature structures can be merged into a more informative feature structure. Unification of feature structures can also fail, which means that the information in them is mutually incompatible. Depending on the flavor of the processing logic, unification can be monotonic (i.e., information-preserving), or it can allow inheritance of default values and their overriding. In either case, information in a model can be efficiently shared and reused by means of inheritance hierarchies defined on the feature structure types.

Morphological models of this kind are typically formulated as logic programs, and unification is used to solve the system of constraints imposed by the model. Advantages of this approach include better abstraction possibilities for developing a morphological grammar as well as elimination of redundant information from it.

However, morphological models implemented in DATR can, under certain assumptions, be converted to finite-state machines and are thus formally equivalent to them in the range of morphological phenomena they can describe [11]. Interestingly, one-level phonology [56] formulating phonological constraints as logic expressions can be compiled into finite-state automata, which can then be intersected with morphological transducers to exclude any disturbing phonologically invalid surface strings [cf. 57, 53]

Unification-based models have been implemented for Russian [58], Czech [59], Slovene [53], Persian [60], Hebrew [61], Arabic [62, 63], and other languages. Some rely on DATR; some adopt, adapt, or develop other unification engines.

1.3.4 Functional Morphology

This group of morphological models includes not only the ones following the methodology of functional morphology [64], but even those related to it, such as morphological resource grammars of Grammatical Framework [65]. Functional morphology defines its models using principles of functional programming and type theory. It treats morphological operations and processes as pure mathematical functions and organizes the linguistic as well as abstract elements of a model into distinct types of values and type classes.

Though functional morphology is not limited to modeling particular types of morphologies in human languages, it is especially useful for fusional morphologies. Linguistic notions like paradigms, rules and exceptions, grammatical categories and parameters, lexemes, morphemes, and morphs can be represented intuitively and succinctly in this approach. Designing a morphological system in an accurate and elegant way is encouraged by the computational setting, which supports logical decoupling of subproblems and reinforces the semantic structure of a program by strong type checking.

Functional morphology implementations are intended to be reused as programming libraries capable of handling the complete morphology of a language and to be incorporated into various kinds of applications. Morphological parsing is just one usage of the system, the others being morphological generation, lexicon browsing, and so on. Next to parsing (1.2), we can describe inflection $\mathcal{I}$, derivation $\mathcal{D}$, and lookup $\mathcal{L}$ as functions of these generic types:

$$\mathcal{I} :: \textit{lexeme} \to \{\textit{parameter}\} \to \{\textit{form}\} \tag{1.3}$$

$$\mathcal{D} :: \textit{lexeme} \to \{\textit{parameter}\} \to \{\textit{lexeme}\} \tag{1.4}$$

$$\mathcal{L} :: \textit{content} \to \{\textit{lexeme}\} \tag{1.5}$$

A functional morphology model can be compiled into finite-state transducers if needed, but can also be used interactively in an interpreted mode, for instance. Computation within a model may exploit lazy evaluation and employ alternative methods of efficient parsing, lookup, and so on [see 66, 12].

Many functional morphology implementations are embedded in a general-purpose programming language, which gives programmers more freedom with advanced programming techniques and allows them to develop full-featured, real-world applications for their models. The Zen toolkit for Sanskrit morphology [67, 68] is written in OCaml. It influenced the functional morphology framework [64] in Haskell, with which morphologies of Latin, Swedish, Spanish, Urdu [69], and other languages have been implemented.

In Haskell, in particular, developers can take advantage of its syntactic flexibility and design their own notation for the functional constructs that model the given problem. The notation then constitutes a so-called domain-specific embedded language, which makes programming even more fun. Figure 1–2 illustrates how the ElixirFM implementation of Arabic morphology [12, 17] captures the structure of words and defines the lexicon. Despite the entries being most informative, their format is simply similar to that found in printed dictionaries. Operators like >|, |<, |<< and labels like verb are just infix functions; patterns and affixes like FaCY, FCI, At are data constructors.

```
|> "d r y" <| [
FaCY                          `verb`   [ "know", "notice" ]
        `imperf`   FCI,
FACY                          `verb`   [ "flatter", "deceive" ],
HaFCY                         `verb`   [ "inform", "let know" ],
IA >| "'a" >>| FCI |<< "ly"        `adj`   [ "agnostic" ],
FiCAL |< aT                   `noun`   [ "knowledge", "knowing" ],
MuFACY |< aT                  `noun`   [ "flattery" ]
        `plural`   MuFACY |< At,
FACI                          `adj`    [ "aware", "knowing" ] ]
```

d r y دري
faʿā
fʿī
fāʿā
ʾafʿā
lā-ʾa-fʿī-īy
fiʿāl-ah
mufāʿā-ah
mufāʿā-āt
fāʿī

know, notice	I (*i*) *darā* درى	knowledge, knowing	*dirāyah* دراية
flatter, deceive	III *dārā* دارى	flattery	*mudārāh* مداراة
inform, let know	IV *ʾadrā* أدرى		(*mudārayāt* مداريات)
agnostic	*lā-ʾadrīy* لاأدري	aware, knowing	*dārin* دار

Figure 1–2: Excerpt from the ElixirFM lexicon and a layout generated from it. The source code of entries nested under the *d r y* root is shown in monospace font. Note the custom notation and the economy yet informativeness of the declaration

Even without the options provided by general-purpose programming languages, functional morphology models achieve high levels of abstraction. Morphological grammars in Grammatical Framework [65] can be extended with descriptions of the syntax and semantics of a language. Grammatical Framework itself supports multilinguality, and models of more than a dozen languages are available in it as open-source software [70, 71].

Grammars in the OpenCCG project [72] can be viewed as functional models, too. Their formalism discerns declarations of features, categories, and families that provide type-system-like means for representing structured values and inheritance hierarchies on them. The grammars leverage heavily the functionality to define parametrized macros to minimize redundancy in the model and make required generalizations. Expansion of macros in the source code has effects similar to inlining of functions. The original text of the grammar is reduced to associations between word forms and their morphosyntactic and lexical properties.

1.3.5 Morphology Induction

We have focused on finding the structure of words in diverse languages supposing we know what we are looking for. We have not considered the problem of discovering and inducing word structure without the human insight (i.e., in an unsupervised or semi-supervised manner). The motivation for such approaches lies in the fact that for many languages, linguistic expertise might be unavailable or limited, and implementations adequate to a purpose may not exist at all. Automated acquisition of morphological and lexical information, even if not perfect, can be reused for bootstrapping and improving the classical morphological models, too.

Let us skim over the directions of research in this domain. In the studies by Hammarström [73] and Goldsmith [74], the literature on unsupervised learning of morphology is reviewed in detail. Hammarström divides the numerous approaches into three main groups. Some works compare and cluster words based on their similarity according to miscellaneous metrics [75, 76, 77, 78]; others try to identify the prominent features of word forms distinguishing them from the unrelated ones. Most of the published approaches cast morphology induction as the problem of word boundary and morpheme boundary detection, sometimes acquiring also lexicons and paradigms [79, 80, 81, 82, 83].[7]

There are several challenging issues about deducing word structure just from the forms and their context. They are caused by ambiguity [76] and irregularity [75] in morphology, as well as by orthographic and phonological alternations [85] and nonlinear morphological processes [86, 87].

In order to improve the chances of statistical inference, parallel learning of morphologies for multiple languages is proposed by Snyder and Barzilay [88], resulting in discovery of abstract morphemes. The discriminative log-linear model of Poon, Cherry, and Toutanova [89] enhances its generalization options by employing overlapping contextual features when making segmentation decisions [cf. 90].

7. Compare these with a semisupervised approach to word hyphenation [84].

1.4 Summary

In this chapter, we learned that morphology can be looked at from opposing viewpoints: one that tries to find the structural components from which words are built versus a more syntax-driven perspective wherein the functions of words are the focus of the study. Another distinction can be made between analytic and generative aspects of morphology or can consider man-made morphological frameworks versus systems for unsupervised induction of morphology. Yet other kinds of issues are raised about how well and how easily the morphological models can be implemented.

We described morphological parsing as the formal process recovering structured information from a linear sequence of symbols, where ambiguity is present and where multiple interpretations should be expected.

We explored interesting morphological phenomena in different types of languages and mentioned several hints in respect to multilingual processing and model development.

With Korean as a language where agglutination moderated by phonological rules is the dominant morphological process, we saw that a viable model of word decomposition can work at the morphemes level, regardless of whether they are lexical or grammatical.

In Czech and Arabic as fusional languages with intricate systems of inflectional and derivational parameters and lexically dependent word stem variation, such factorization is not useful. Morphology is better described via paradigms associating the possible forms of lexemes with their corresponding properties.

We discussed various options for implementing either of these models using modern programming techniques.

Acknowledgment

We would like to thank Petr Novák for his valuable comments on an earlier draft of this chapter.

Bibliography

[1] M. Liberman, "Morphology." Linguistics 001, Lecture 7, University of Pennsylvania, 2009. http://www.ling.upenn.edu/courses/Fall_2009/ling001/morphology.html.

[2] M. Haspelmath, "The indeterminacy of word segmentation and the nature of morphology and syntax," *Folia Linguistica*, vol. 45, 2011.

[3] H. Kučera and W. N. Francis, *Computational Analysis of Present-Day American English.* Providence, RI: Brown University Press, 1967.

[4] S. B. Cohen and N. A. Smith, "Joint morphological and syntactic disambiguation," in *Proceedings of the 2007 Joint Conference on Empirical Methods in Natural Language Processing and Computational Natural Language Learning (EMNLP-CoNLL)*, pp. 208–217, 2007.

[5] T. Nakagawa, "Chinese and Japanese word segmentation using word-level and character-level information," in *Proceedings of 20th International Conference on Computational Linguistics*, pp. 466–472, 2004.

[6] H. Shin and H. You, "Hybrid *n*-gram probability estimation in morphologically rich languages," in *Proceedings of the 23rd Pacific Asia Conference on Language, Information and Computation*, 2009.

[7] D. Z. Hakkani-Tür, K. Oflazer, and G. Tür, "Statistical morphological disambiguation for agglutinative languages," in *Proceedings of the 18th Conference on Computational Linguistics*, pp. 285–291, 2000.

[8] G. T. Stump, *Inflectional Morphology: A Theory of Paradigm Structure.* Cambridge Studies in Linguistics, New York: Cambridge University Press, 2001.

[9] K. R. Beesley and L. Karttunen, *Finite State Morphology.* CSLI Studies in Computational Linguistics, Stanford, CA: CSLI Publications, 2003.

[10] M. Baerman, D. Brown, and G. G. Corbett, *The Syntax-Morphology Interface. A Study of Syncretism.* Cambridge Studies in Linguistics, New York: Cambridge University Press, 2006.

[11] B. Roark and R. Sproat, *Computational Approaches to Morphology and Syntax.* Oxford Surveys in Syntax and Morphology, New York: Oxford University Press, 2007.

[12] O. Smrž, "Functional Arabic morphology. Formal system and implementation," PhD thesis, Charles University in Prague, 2007.

[13] H. Eifring and R. Theil, *Linguistics for Students of Asian and African Languages.* Universitetet i Oslo, 2005.

[14] B. Bickel and J. Nichols, "Fusion of selected inflectional formatives & exponence of selected inflectional formatives," in *The World Atlas of Language Structures Online* (M. Haspelmath, M. S. Dryer, D. Gil, and B. Comrie, eds.), ch. 20 & 21, Munich: Max Planck Digital Library, 2008.

[15] W. Fischer, *A Grammar of Classical Arabic.* Trans. Jonathan Rodgers. Yale Language Series, New Haven, CT: Yale University Press, 2002.

[16] K. C. Ryding, *A Reference Grammar of Modern Standard Arabic.* New York: Cambridge University Press, 2005.

[17] O. Smrž and V. Bielický, "ElixirFM." Functional Arabic Morphology, SourceForge.net, 2010. http://sourceforge.net/projects/elixer-fm/.

[18] T. Kamei, R. Kōno, and E. Chino, eds., *The Sanseido Encyclopedia of Linguistics, Volume 6 Terms* (in Japanese). Sanseido, 1996.

[19] F. Karlsson, *Finnish Grammar.* Helsinki: Werner Söderström Osakenyhtiö, 1987.

[20] J. Hajič and B. Hladká, "Tagging inflective languages: Prediction of morphological categories for a rich, structured tagset," in *Proceedings of COLING-ACL 1998*, pp. 483–490, 1998.

[21] J. Hajič, "Morphological tagging: Data vs. dictionaries," in *Proceedings of NAACL-ANLP 2000*, pp. 94–101, 2000.

[22] N. Habash and O. Rambow, "Arabic tokenization, part-of-speech tagging and morphological disambiguation in one fell swoop," in *Proceedings of the 43rd Annual Meeting of the Association for Computational Linguistics (ACL'05)*, pp. 573–580, 2005.

[23] N. A. Smith, D. A. Smith, and R. W. Tromble, "Context-based morphological disambiguation with random fields," in *Proceedings of HLT/EMNLP 2005*, pp. 475–482, 2005.

[24] J. Hajič, O. Smrž, T. Buckwalter, and H. Jin, "Feature-based tagger of approximations of functional Arabic morphology," in *Proceedings of the 4th Workshop on Treebanks and Linguistic Theories (TLT 2005)*, pp. 53–64, 2005.

[25] T. Buckwalter, "Issues in Arabic orthography and morphology analysis," in *COLING 2004 Computational Approaches to Arabic Script-based Languages*, pp. 31–34, 2004.

[26] R. Nelken and S. M. Shieber, "Arabic diacritization using finite-state transducers," in *Proceedings of the ACL Workshop on Computational Approaches to Semitic Languages*, pp. 79–86, 2005.

[27] I. Zitouni, J. S. Sorensen, and R. Sarikaya, "Maximum entropy based restoration of Arabic diacritics," in *Proceedings of the 21st International Conference on Computational Linguistics and 44th Annual Meeting of the Association for Computational Linguistics*, pp. 577–584, 2006.

[28] N. Habash and O. Rambow, "Arabic diacritization through full morphological tagging," in *Human Language Technologies 2007: The Conference of the North American Chapter of the Association for Computational Linguistics; Companion Volume, Short Papers*, pp. 53–56, 2007.

[29] G. Huet, "Lexicon-directed segmentation and tagging of Sanskrit," in *Proceedings of the XIIth World Sanskrit Conference*, pp. 307–325, 2003.

[30] G. Huet, "Formal structure of Sanskrit text: Requirements analysis for a mechanical Sanskrit processor," in *Sanskrit Computational Linguistics: First and Second International Symposia* (G. Huet, A. Kulkarni, and P. Scharf, eds.), vol. 5402 of *LNAI*, pp. 162–199, Berlin: Springer, 2009.

[31] F. Katamba and J. Stonham, *Morphology*. Basingstoke: Palgrave Macmillan, 2006.

[32] L. Bauer, *Morphological Productivity*, Cambridge Studies in Linguistics. New York: Cambridge University Press, 2001.

[33] R. H. Baayen, *Word Frequency Distributions*, Text, Speech and Language Technology. Boston: Kluwer Academic Publishers, 2001.

[34] A. Kilgarriff, "Googleology is bad science," *Computational Linguistics*, vol. 33, no. 1, pp. 147–151, 2007.

[35] H.-C. Kwon and Y.-S. Chae, "A dictionary-based morphological analysis," in *Proceedings of Natural Language Processing Pacific Rim Symposium*, pp. 178–185, 1991.

[36] D.-B. Kim, K.-S. Choi, and K.-H. Lee, "A computational model of Korean morphological analysis: A prediction-based approach," *Journal of East Asian Linguistics*, vol. 5, no. 2, pp. 183–215, 1996.

[37] A. Halevy, P. Norvig, and F. Pereira, "The unreasonable effectiveness of data," *IEEE Intelligent Systems*, vol. 24, no. 2, pp. 8–12, 2009.

[38] R. M. Kaplan and M. Kay, "Regular models of phonological rule systems," *Computational Linguistics*, vol. 20, no. 3, pp. 331–378, 1994.

[39] K. Koskenniemi, "Two-level morphology: A general computational model for word form recognition and production," PhD thesis, University of Helsinki, 1983.

[40] R. Sproat, *Morphology and Computation.* ACL–MIT Press Series in Natural Language Processing. Cambridge, MA: MIT Press, 1992.

[41] D.-B. Kim, S.-J. Lee, K.-S. Choi, and G.-C. Kim, "A two-level morphological analysis of Korean," in *Proceedings of the 15th International Conference on Computational Linguistics*, pp. 535–539, 1994.

[42] S.-Z. Lee and H.-C. Rim, "Korean morphology with elementary two-level rules and rule features," in *Proceedings of the Pacific Association for Computational Linguistics*, pp. 182–187, 1997.

[43] N.-R. Han, "Klex: A finite-state trancducer lexicon of Korean," in *Finite-state Methods and Natural Language Processing: 5th International Workshop, FSMNLP 2005*, pp. 67–77, Springer, 2006.

[44] M. Kay, "Nonconcatenative finite-state morphology," in *Proceedings of the Third Conference of the European Chapter of the ACL (EACL-87)*, pp. 2–10, ACL, 1987.

[45] K. R. Beesley, "Arabic morphology using only finite-state operations," in *COLING-ACL'98 Proceedings of the Workshop on Computational Approaches to Semitic languages*, pp. 50–57, 1998.

[46] G. A. Kiraz, *Computational Nonlinear Morphology with Emphasis on Semitic Languages.* Studies in Natural Language Processing, Cambridge: Cambridge University Press, 2001.

[47] N. Habash, O. Rambow, and G. Kiraz, "Morphological analysis and generation for Arabic dialects," in *Proceedings of the ACL Workshop on Computational Approaches to Semitic Languages*, pp. 17–24, 2005.

[48] H. Skoumalová, "A Czech morphological lexicon," in *Proceedings of the Third Meeting of the ACL Special Interest Group in Computational Phonology*, pp. 41–47, 1997.

[49] R. Sedláček and P. Smrž, "A new Czech morphological analyser `ajka`," in *Text, Speech and Dialogue*, vol. 2166, pp. 100–107, Berlin: Springer, 2001.

[50] K. Oflazer, "Computational morphology." ESSLLI 2006 European Summer School in Logic, Language, and Information, 2006.

[51] C. Pollard and I. A. Sag, *Head-Driven Phrase Structure Grammar.* Chicago: University of Chicago Press, 1994.

[52] R. Evans and G. Gazdar, "DATR: A language for lexical knowledge representation," *Computational Linguistics*, vol. 22, no. 2, pp. 167–216, 1996.

[53] T. Erjavec, "Unification, inheritance, and paradigms in the morphology of natural languages," PhD thesis, University of Ljubljana, 1996.

[54] B. Carpenter, *The Logic of Typed Feature Structures.* Cambridge Tracts in Theoretical Computer Science 32, New York: Cambridge University Press, 1992.

[55] S. M. Shieber, *Constraint-Based Grammar Formalisms: Parsing and Type Inference for Natural and Computer Languages.* Cambridge, MA: MIT Press, 1992.

[56] S. Bird and T. M. Ellison, "One-level phonology: Autosegmental representations and rules as finite automata," *Computational Linguistics*, vol. 20, no. 1, pp. 55–90, 1994.

[57] S. Bird and P. Blackburn, "A logical approach to Arabic phonology," in *Proceedings of the 5th Conference of the European Chapter of the Association for Computational Linguistics*, pp. 89–94, 1991.

[58] G. G. Corbett and N. M. Fraser, "Network morphology: A DATR account of Russian nominal inflection," *Journal of Linguistics*, vol. 29, pp. 113–142, 1993.

[59] J. Hajič, "Unification morphology grammar. Software system for multilanguage morphological analysis," PhD thesis, Charles University in Prague, 1994.

[60] K. Megerdoomian, "Unification-based Persian morphology," in *Proceedings of CICLing 2000*, 2000.

[61] R. Finkel and G. Stump, "Generating Hebrew verb morphology by default inheritance hierarchies," in *Proceedings of the Workshop on Computational Approaches to Semitic Languages*, pp. 9–18, 2002.

[62] S. R. Al-Najem, "Inheritance-based approach to Arabic verbal root-and-pattern morphology," in *Arabic Computational Morphology. Knowledge-based and Empirical Methods* (A. Soudi, A. van den Bosch, and G. Neumann, eds.), vol. 38, pp. 67–88, Berlin: Springer, 2007.

[63] S. Köprü and J. Miller, "A unification based approach to the morphological analysis and generation of Arabic," in *CAASL-3: Third Workshop on Computational Approaches to Arabic Script-based Languages*, 2009.

[64] M. Forsberg and A. Ranta, "Functional morphology," in *Proceedings of the 9th ACM SIGPLAN International Conference on Functional Programming, ICFP 2004*, pp. 213–223, 2004.

[65] A. Ranta, "Grammatical Framework: A type-theoretical grammar formalism," *Journal of Functional Programming*, vol. 14, no. 2, pp. 145–189, 2004.

[66] P. Ljunglöf, "Pure functional parsing. An advanced tutorial," Licenciate thesis, Göteborg University & Chalmers University of Technology, 2002.

[67] G. Huet, "The Zen computational linguistics toolkit," ESSLLI 2002 European Summer School in Logic, Language, and Information, 2002.

[68] G. Huet, "A functional toolkit for morphological and phonological processing, application to a Sanskrit tagger," *Journal of Functional Programming*, vol. 15, no. 4, pp. 573–614, 2005.

[69] M. Humayoun, H. Hammarström, and A. Ranta, "Urdu morphology, orthography and lexicon extraction," in *CAASL-2: Second Workshop on Computational Approaches to Arabic Script-based Languages*, pp. 59–66, 2007.

[70] A. Dada and A. Ranta, "Implementing an open source Arabic resource grammar in GF," in *Perspectives on Arabic Linguistics* (M. A. Mughazy, ed.), vol. XX, pp. 209–231, John Benjamins, 2007.

[71] A. Ranta, "Grammatical Framework." Programming Language for Multilingual Grammar Applications, http://www.grammaticalframework.org/, 2010.

[72] J. Baldridge, S. Chatterjee, A. Palmer, and B. Wing, "DotCCG and VisCCG: Wiki and programming paradigms for improved grammar engineering with OpenCCG," in *Proceedings of the Workshop on Grammar Engineering Across Frameworks*, 2007.

[73] H. Hammarström, "Unsupervised learning of morphology and the languages of the world," PhD thesis, Chalmers University of Technology and University of Gothenburg, 2009.

[74] J. A. Goldsmith, "Segmentation and morphology," in *Computational Linguistics and Natural Language Processing Handbook* (A. Clark, C. Fox, and S. Lappin, eds.), pp. 364–393, Chichester: Wiley-Blackwell, 2010.

[75] D. Yarowsky and R. Wicentowski, "Minimally supervised morphological analysis by multimodal alignment," in *Proceedings of the 38th Meeting of the Association for Computational Linguistics*, pp. 207–216, 2000.

[76] P. Schone and D. Jurafsky, "Knowledge-free induction of inflectional morphologies," in *Proceedings of the North American Chapter of the Association for Computational Linguistics*, pp. 183–191, 2001.

[77] S. Neuvel and S. A. Fulop, "Unsupervised learning of morphology without morphemes," in *Proceedings of the ACL-02 Workshop on Morphological and Phonological Learning*, pp. 31–40, 2002.

[78] N. Hathout, "Acquistion of the morphological structure of the lexicon based on lexical similarity and formal analogy," in *Coling 2008: Proceedings of the 3rd Textgraphs Workshop on Graph-based Algorithms for Natural Language Processing*, pp. 1–8, 2008.

[79] J. Goldsmith, "Unsupervised learning of the morphology of a natural language," *Computational Linguistics*, vol. 27, no. 2, pp. 153–198, 2001.

[80] H. Johnson and J. Martin, "Unsupervised learning of morphology for English and Inuktikut," in *Companion Volume of the Proceedings of the Human Language Technologies: The Annual Conference of the North American Chapter of the Association for Computational Linguistics 2003: Short Papers*, pp. 43–45, 2003.

[81] M. Creutz and K. Lagus, "Induction of a simple morphology for highly-inflecting languages," in *Proceedings of the 7th Meeting of the ACL Special Interest Group in Computational Phonology*, pp. 43–51, 2004.

[82] M. Creutz and K. Lagus, "Unsupervised models for morpheme segmentation and morphology learning," *ACM Transactions on Speech and Language Processing*, vol. 4, no. 1, pp. 1–34, 2007.

[83] C. Monson, J. Carbonell, A. Lavie, and L. Levin, "ParaMor: Minimally supervised induction of paradigm structure and morphological analysis," in *Proceedings of Ninth Meeting of the ACL Special Interest Group in Computational Morphology and Phonology*, pp. 117–125, 2007.

[84] F. M. Liang, "Word Hy-phen-a-tion by Com-put-er," PhD thesis, Stanford University, 1983.

[85] V. Demberg, "A language-independent unsupervised model for morphological segmentation," in *Proceedings of the 45th Annual Meeting of the Association of Computational Linguistics*, pp. 920–927, 2007.

[86] A. Clark, "Supervised and unsupervised learning of Arabic morphology," in *Arabic Computational Morphology. Knowledge-based and Empirical Methods* (A. Soudi, A. van den Bosch, and G. Neumann, eds.), vol. 38, pp. 181–200, Berlin: Springer, 2007.

[87] A. Xanthos, *Apprentissage automatique de la morphologie: le cas des structures racine-schème.* Sciences pour la communication, Bern: Peter Lang, 2008.

[88] B. Snyder and R. Barzilay, "Unsupervised multilingual learning for morphological segmentation," in *Proceedings of ACL-08: HLT*, pp. 737–745, 2008.

[89] H. Poon, C. Cherry, and K. Toutanova, "Unsupervised morphological segmentation with log-linear models," in *Proceedings of Human Language Technologies: Annual Conference of the North American Chapter of the Association for Computational Linguistics*, pp. 209–217, 2009.

[90] S. Della Pietra, V. Della Pietra, and J. Lafferty, "Inducing features of random fields," *IEEE Transactions on Pattern Analysis and Machine Intelligence*, vol. 19, no. 4, pp. 380–393, 1997.

Chapter 2

Finding the Structure of Documents

Dilek Hakkani-Tür, Gokhan Tur, Benoit Favre, and Elizabeth Shriberg

2.1 Introduction

In human language, words and sentences do not appear randomly but usually have a structure. For example, combinations of words form sentences—meaningful grammatical units, such as statements, requests, and commands. Likewise, in written text, sentences form paragraphs—self-contained units of discourse about a particular point or idea. Sentences may also be related to each other by explicit discourse connectives such as *therefore*.

Automatic extraction of structure of documents helps subsequent natural language processing (NLP) tasks; for example, parsing, machine translation, and semantic role labeling use sentences as the basic processing unit [1, 2]. Sentence boundary annotation is also important for aiding human readability of the output of automatic speech recognition (ASR) systems [3]. Furthermore, chunking the input text or speech into topically coherent blocks provides better organization and indexing of the data. For example, portions related to specific topics can be extracted from a long speech. Similarly, articles belonging to the same topic may be categorized and processed further. Given the ever-growing problem of written and spoken information overload, extracting the structure of textual and audio documents is a meaningful and sometimes necessary first step in most speech and language processing applications.

Here, we discuss methods for finding the structure of documents; for simplicity, only the sentence and group of sentences related to a topic are considered as the structure elements.

In this chapter, we call the task of deciding where sentences start and end given a sequence of characters (made of words and typographical cues) **sentence boundary detection**. Similarly, we refer to **topic segmentation** as the task of determining when a topic starts and ends in a sequence of sentences. We present statistical classification approaches that try to infer the presence of sentence and topic boundaries given human-annotated training data, for segmentation.[1] These methods base their predictions on **features** of the input: local characteristics that give evidence toward the presence or absence of a sentence or topic boundary, such as a punctuation sign, a pause in speech, and a new word in a document. Features are the core of classification approaches and require careful design and selection in order to be successful and prevent overfitting and noise problems.

1. *Segmentation* refers to both tasks.

Note that while most statistical approaches described in this chapter are language independent, every language is a challenge in itself. For example, for processing of Chinese documents, the processor may need to first segment character sequences into words, as the words usually are not separated by a space. Similarly, for morphologically rich languages, the word structure may need to be analyzed to extract additional features. Such processing is usually done in a preprocessing step, where a sequence of tokens is determined. Tokens can be words or subword units, depending on the task and language. These algorithms are then applied on tokens. Segmentation aims to decide whether or not a boundary between two tokens should be marked as a sentence (or a topic) boundary.

Instead of focusing on techniques used for sentence and topic segmentation individually, we first formally define these tasks and present techniques for sentence and topic segmentation in a unified framework. Then, we present the features used for segmenting text or speech.

2.1.1 Sentence Boundary Detection

Sentence boundary detection (also called sentence segmentation) deals with automatically segmenting a sequence of word tokens into sentence units. In written text in English and some other languages, the beginning of a sentence is usually marked with an uppercase letter, and the end of a sentence is explicitly marked with a period (.), a question mark (?), an exclamation mark (!), or another type of punctuation. However, in addition to their role as sentence boundary markers, capitalized initial letters are used to distinguish proper nouns, periods are used in abbreviations, and numbers and other punctuation marks are used inside proper names. For instance, 10% of the periods in the Brown corpus are abbreviations [4] such as "Dr." that can be an abbreviation for the words *doctor* and *drive*. And the period at the end of an abbreviation can mark a sentence boundary at the same time. For example, consider the following two sentences: *I spoke with Dr. Smith.* and *My house is on Mountain Dr.* In the first sentence, the abbreviation *Dr.* does not end a sentence, and in the second it does. This percentage of periods that are used to mark an abbreviation rises to 47% in the Wall Street Journal Corpus [5]. For example, in the following sentence, partly taken from the Wall Street Journal part of the OntoNotes [6] corpus, only the last period ends the sentence:

> *"This year has been difficult for both Hertz and Avis," said Charles Finnie, car-rental industry analyst—yes, there is such a profession—at Alex. Brown & Sons.*

Such sentences containing other sentences are not infrequent. Especially quoted sentences are always problematic, as the speaker may have uttered multiple sentences, and sentence boundaries inside the quotes are also marked with punctuation marks. An automatic method that outputs word boundaries as ending sentences according to the presence of such punctuation marks would result in cutting some sentences incorrectly. Furthermore, if the preceeding sentence is spoken instead of written, prosodic cues usually mark structure.

Ambiguous abbreviations and capitalizations are not the only problem of sentence segmentation in written text. "Spontaneously" written texts, such as short message service (SMS) texts or instant messaging (IM) texts, tend to be nongrammatical and have poorly used or missing punctuation, which makes sentence segmentation even more challenging [7, 8].

Similarly, if the text input to be segmented into sentences comes from an automatic system, such as optical character recognition (OCR) or ASR, that aims to translate images of handwritten, typewritten, or printed text or spoken utterances into machine-editable text, the finding of sentence boundaries must deal with the errors of those systems as well. For example, Taghva et al. [9] observed that an OCR system easily confuses periods and commas and can result in meaningless sentences. ASR transcripts typically lack punctuation marks and are usually monocase; hence, all ASR output word boundaries can be ending or beginning a sentence. Stevenson and Gaizauskas [10] asked human participants to repunctuate monocase texts, and they performed at an F_1-measure of about 80%, which illustrates the difficulty of the task. In such input, sentence segmentation methods usually hypothesize a sentence boundary between every two tokens.

On the other hand, for conversational speech or text or multiparty meetings with ungrammatical sentences and disfluencies, in most cases it is not clear where the boundaries are. The interannotator agreement was quite low [11] during the segmentation of the Linguistic Data Consortium (LDC) distributed ICSI Meeting Corpus [12]. In an example utterance of *okay no problem*, it is not clear whether there is a single sentence or two. The problem may be redefined for the conversational domain as the task of dialog act segmentation, because dialog acts are better defined for conversational speech using a number of markup standards such as Dialog Act Markup in Several Layers (DAMSL) [13] or Meeting Recorder Dialog Act (MRDA) [14]. According to these standards, the example sentence *okay no problem* consists of two sentential units (or dialog act units): *okay* and *no problem*.

In most practical applications relying on automatic sentence segmentation, the task can be redefined according to the need of the following task. For example, the sentence *I think so but you should also ask him* may be a grammatical sentence as a whole, but for DAMSL and MRDA standards, there are two dialog act tags, one affirmation and one suggestion. Such a modification may be needed for conversation analysis, such as speaker role detection or sentiment analysis. This task can be seen as a semantic boundary detection task instead of syntactic.

Code switching—that is, the use of words, phrases, or sentences from multiple languages by multilingual speakers—is another problem that can affect the characteristics of sentences. For example, when switching to a different language, the writer can either keep the punctuation rules from the first language or resort to the code of the second language (e.g., Spanish uses the inverted question mark to precede questions). Code switching also affects technical texts for which the meanings of punctuation signs can be redefined, as in uniform resource locators (URLs), programming languages, and mathematics. We must detect and parse those specific constructs in order to process technical texts adequately.

Conventional rule-based sentence segmentation systems in well-formed texts rely on patterns to identify potential ends of sentences and lists of abbreviations for disambiguating them [5, 15, 16, 17]. For example if the word before the boundary is a known abbreviation, such as "Mr." or "Gov.," the text is not segmented at that position even though some periods are exceptions. Although rules cover most of these cases, they do not address unknown abbreviations, abbreviations at the ends of sentences, or typos in the input text. Furthermore, such rules are not robust to text that is not well formed, such as forums, chats, and blogs, or to spoken input that completely lacks typographic cues. Moreover, each language requires a specific set of rules.

To improve on such a rule-based approach, sentence segmentation is stated as a classification problem. Given training data where all sentence boundaries are marked, we can train a classifier to recognize them, as described in Section 2.2. Sentence segmentation in text usually uses the punctuation marks as delimiters and aims to categorize them as sentence-ending/beginning or not. On the other hand, for speech input, all word boundaries are usually considered as candidate sentence boundaries.

2.1.2 Topic Boundary Detection

Topic segmentation (sometimes called discourse or text segmentation) is the task of automatically dividing a stream of text or speech into topically homogeneous blocks. That is, given a sequence of (written or spoken) words, the aim of topic segmentation is to find the boundaries where topics change. Figure 2–1 gives an example of a topic change boundary from a broadcast news program.

Topic segmentation is an important task for various language-understanding applications, such as information extraction and retrieval and text summarization. For example, in information retrieval, if long documents can be segmented into shorter, topically coherent segments, then only the segment that is about the user's query could be retrieved.

During the late 1990s, the U.S. Defense Advanced Research Projects Agency (DARPA) initiated the Topic Detection and Tracking (TDT) program to further the state of the art in finding and following new topics in a stream of broadcast news stories [18]. One of the tasks in the TDT effort was segmenting a news stream into individual stories. TDT established a common test bed, but most researchers also use simulated environments such as by concatenating news stories from Reuters.

For multiparty meetings, the task of topic segmentation is inspired by discourse analysis. For official and well-structured meetings, the topics are segmented according to the agenda items, whereas for more casual conversational-style meetings, the boundaries are less clear.

Topic segmentation is a nontrivial problem without a very high human agreement because of many natural-language-related issues and hence requires a good definition of topic categories and their granularities. For example, topics are not typically flat but occur in a semantic hierarchy. When a sentence about soccer is followed by a sentence about baseball, one annotator may mark a topic change and the other may not, considering that soccer and baseball both belong to the topic sports. This is also the case for finer-grained distinctions. Even though the annotators are told to segment the text into a predefined number

> Tens of thousands of people are homeless in northern China tonight after a powerful earthquake hit an earthquake registering 6.2 on the Richter scale at least 47 people are dead. Few pictures available from the region but we do know temperatures there will be very cold tonight -7 degrees. <TOPIC_CHANGE> Peace talks expected to resume on Monday in Belfast, Northern Ireland. . . .

Figure 2–1: Example of a topic boundary in a news article

of topics, it is hard to define the concept of topic because it varies greatly depending on the semantic content. While high interannotator agreement (with Cohen's kappa values of 0.7–0.9) has been achieved for the TDT corpus [19], which includes broadcast news, documents and hence stories, news, or topics usually had the same boundary. For topic segmentation of multiparty meetings, the agreement is lower [20] (with kappa values of 0.6–0.7). Note that for conversational speech, the topic boundaries may not be absolute. For example, in a multiparty meeting, a few turns after switching the topic, a participant may utter a sentence about the previous topic.

In text, topic boundaries are usually marked with distinct segmentation cues, such as headlines and paragraph breaks. These cues are absent in speech. However, speech provides other cues, such as pause duration and speaker changes. This is analogous to differences between sentence segmentation of text and speech. In Section 2.5 these feature types are analyzed in more detail.

2.2 Methods

Sentence segmentation and topic segmentation have mainly been considered as a boundary classification problem. Given a boundary candidate (between two word tokens for sentence segmentation and between two sentences for topic segmentation), the goal is to predict whether or not the candidate is an actual boundary (sentence or topic boundary). Formally, let $\mathbf{x} \in \mathcal{X}$ be the vector of features (the observation) associated with a candidate and $y \in \mathcal{Y}$ be the label predicted for that candidate. The label y can be b for boundary and $\bar{b}$ for nonboundary. This results in a classification problem: given a set of training examples $\{\mathbf{x}, y\}_{train}$, find a function that will assign the most accurate possible label y of unseen examples $\mathbf{x}_{unseen}$. Alternatively to the binary classification problem, it is possible to model boundary types using finer-grained categories. For example, Gillick [21] suggests that sentence segmentation in text be framed as a three-class problem: sentence boundary with an abbreviation b^a, without an abbreviation $b^{\bar{a}}$, and abbreviation not at a boundary $\bar{b}^a$. Similarly, in spoken language, a three-way classification can be made between nonboundaries $\bar{b}$, statement b^s, and question boundaries b^q.

Features can be the presence of specific word n-grams around the candidate boundary; an indicator of being inside a quotation in text; an indicator of presence of the preceding word tokens in an abbreviation list; or duration of pause, pitch, energy, and other duration-related features in speech. A more detailed discussion of features is presented in Section 2.5.

For sentence or topic segmentation, the problem is defined as finding the most probable sentence or topic boundaries. The natural unit of sentence segmentation is words and of topic segmentation is sentences, as we can assume that topics typically do not change in the middle of a sentence.[2] The words or sentences are then grouped into contiguous stretches belonging to one sentence or topic—that is, the word or sentence boundaries are classified

2. Similarly, it is sometimes assumed for topic-segmentation purposes that topics change only at paragraph boundaries [22].

into sentence or topic boundaries and nonboundaries. The classification can be done at each potential boundary i (local modeling); then, the aim is to estimate the most probable boundary type, $\widehat{y_i}$, for each candidate example, $\mathbf{x}_i$:

$$\widehat{y_i} = \underset{y_i in \mathcal{Y}}{\operatorname{argmax}} P(y_i|\mathbf{x}_i) \tag{2.1}$$

Here, the $\widehat{\ }$ is used to denote estimated categories, and a variable without a $\widehat{\ }$ is used to show possible categories. In this formulation, a category is assigned to each example in isolation; hence, the decision is made locally. However, the consecutive boundary types can be related to each other. For example, in broadcast news speech, two consecutive sentence boundaries that form a single word sentence are very infrequent. In local modeling, features can be extracted from the surrounding example context of the candidate boundary to model such dependencies. It is also possible to see the candidate boundaries as a sequence and search for the sequence of boundary types, $\widehat{Y} = \widehat{y_1}, \ldots, \widehat{y_n}$, that have the maximum probability given the candidate examples, $X = \mathbf{x}_1, \ldots, \mathbf{x}_n$:

$$\widehat{Y} = \underset{Y}{\operatorname{argmax}} P(Y|X) \tag{2.2}$$

In the following discussion, we categorize the methods into local and sequence classification. Another categorization of methods is done according to the type of the machine learning algorithm: generative versus discriminative. Generative sequence models estimate the joint distribution of the observations, $P(X, Y)$ (e.g., words, punctuation) and the labels (sentence boundary, topic boundary), which requires specific assumptions (such as backoff to account for unseen events) and have good generalization properties. Discriminative sequence models, however, focus on features that characterize the differences between the labeling of the examples.

Such methods (as described in the following sections) can be used for sentence and topic segmentation in both written and spoken language, with one difference: in text, the category of all boundaries that do not include a potential end-of-sentence delimiter (period, question mark, exclamation mark) is preset to nonsentence or nontopic, and a category is estimated for only those word boundaries that include a delimiter, whereas in speech, all boundaries between consecutive tokens are usually considered.

2.2.1 Generative Sequence Classification Methods

The most commonly used generative sequence classification method for topic and sentence segmentation is the hidden Markov model (HMM). The probability in Equation 2.2 is rewritten as the following, using the Bayes rule:

$$\widehat{Y} = \underset{Y}{\operatorname{argmax}} P(Y|X) = \underset{Y}{\operatorname{argmax}} \frac{P(X|Y)P(Y)}{P(X)} = \underset{Y}{\operatorname{argmax}} P(X|Y)P(Y) \tag{2.3}$$

$P(X)$ in the denominator is dropped because it is fixed for different Y and hence does not change the argument of *max*. $P(X|Y)$, and $P(Y)$ can be estimated as

$$P(X|Y) = \prod_{i=1}^{n} P(\mathbf{x}_i|y_1, \ldots, y_i) \tag{2.4}$$

and

$$P(Y) = \prod_{i=1}^{n} P(y_i|y_1, \dots y_{i-1}) \tag{2.5}$$

Simplifying assumptions can be made to make the computation of these probabilities tractable:

$$P(\mathbf{x}_i|y_1, \dots, y_i) \approx P(\mathbf{x}_i|y_i) \tag{2.6}$$

and a bigram model can be assumed for modeling output categories:

$$P(y_i|y_1, \dots, y_{i-1}) \approx P(y_i|y_{i-1}) \tag{2.7}$$

The bigram case is modeled by a fully connected m-state Markov model, where m is the number of boundary categories. The states emit words (sentences or paragraphs) for sentence (topic) segmentation, and the state sequence that most likely generated the word (sentence) sequence is estimated. State transition probabilities, $P(y_i|y_{i-1})$, and state observation likelihoods, $P(\mathbf{x}_i|y_i)$, are estimated using the training data. The most probable boundary sequence is obtained by dynamic programming, thanks to the Viterbi algorithm that is used for decoding Markov models [23]. The bigram case can be extended to higher-order n-grams at the cost of an increased complexity.

For example, Figure 2–2 shows the model for the two-class problem, for example *nonboundary* (NB) and *sentence boundary* (SB) for sentence segmentation. Table 2–1 shows an example sequence of words emitted.

For topic segmentation, typically instead of using two states, n states are used, where n is the number of topics. However, obtaining state observation likelihoods without knowing the topic categories is the main challenge. Yamron et al. [24] model topics with unigram language models, and the state observation likelihoods are trained using the k-means clustering algorithm.

Note that this is not different from using an HMM, as is typically done in similar tagging tasks, such as part-of-speech (POS) tagging [25] or named entity extraction [26]. However, it

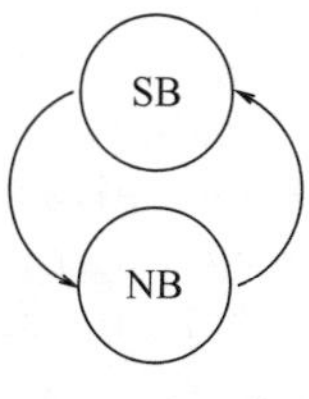

Figure 2–2: Conceptual hidden Markov model for segmentation with two states: one for segment boundaries, one for others

Table 2–1: Sentence segmentation with simple two-state Markov model

Emitted Words	...	people	are	dead	few	pictures	...
State Sequence	...	NB	NB	SB	NB	NB	...

has been shown that the conventional HMM approach has certain weaknesses. For example, it is not possible to use any information beyond words, such as POS tags of the words or prosodic cues, for speech segmentation.

To this end, two simple extensions have been proposed: Shriberg et al. [27] suggested using explicit states to emit the boundary tokens, hence incorporating nonlexical information via combination with other models. This approach is used for sentence segmentation and is inspired by the hidden event language model (HELM), as introduced by Stolcke and Shriberg [28], which was originally designed for speech disfluencies. The approach was to treat such events as extra meta tokens. In this model, one state is reserved for each boundary token, SB and NB, and the rest of the states are for generating words. To ease the computation, an imaginary token is inserted between all consecutive words in case the word preceding the boundary is not part of a disfluency. Example 2–1 is a conceptual representation of a sequence with boundary tokens:

EXAMPLE 2–1: ... *people NB are NB dead YB few NB pictures* ...

The most probable boundary token sequence is again obtained simply by Viterbi decoding. The conceptual HELM for segmentation is depicted in Figure 2–3.

These extra boundary tokens are then used to capture other meta-information. The most commonly used meta-information is the feedback obtained from other classifiers. Typically, the posterior probability of being in that boundary state is used as a state observation likelihood after being divided by prior probabilities [27]. These other classifiers also may be trained with other feature sets, such as prosodic or syntactic. This hybrid approach is presented in Section 2.2.4.

For topic segmentation, Tur et al. [29] used the same idea and modeled topic-start and topic-final sections explicitly, which helped greatly for broadcast news topic segmentation.

The second extension is inspired from factored language models [30], which capture not only words but also morphological, syntactic, and other information. Guz et al. [31] proposed using factored HELM (fHELM) for sentence segmentation using POS tags in addition to words.

2.2.2 Discriminative Local Classification Methods

Discriminative classifiers aim to model $P(y_i|\mathbf{x}_i)$ of Equation 2.1 directly. The most important distinction is that whereas class densities, $p(\mathbf{x}|y)$, are model assumptions in generative approaches, such as saive Bayes, in discriminative methods, discriminant functions of the feature space define the model. A number of discriminative classification approaches, such as support vector machines, boosting, maximum entropy, and regression, are based on very

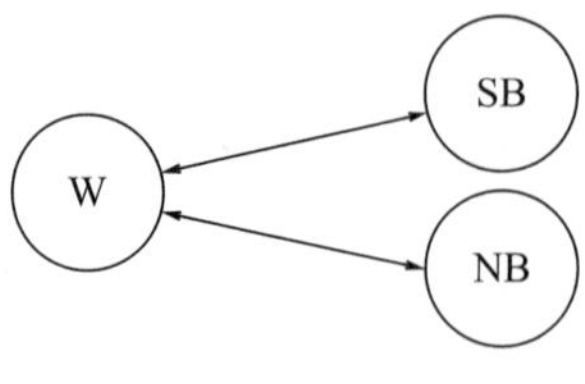

Figure 2–3: Conceptual hidden event language model for segmentation

different machine learning algorithms. While discriminative approaches have been shown to outperform generative methods in many speech and language processing tasks, training typically requires iterative optimization.

In discriminative local classification, each boundary is processed separately with local and contextual features. No global (i.e., sentence or document wide) optimization is performed, unlike in sequence classification models. Instead, features related to a wider context may be incorporated into the feature set. For example, the predicted class of the previous or next boundary can be used in an iterative fashion.

For sentence segmentation, supervised learning methods have primarily been applied to newspaper articles. Stamatatos, Fakotakis, and Kokkinakis [32] used transformation-based learning (TBL) to infer rules for finding sentence boundaries. Many classifiers have been tried for the task: regression trees [33], neural networks [34, 35], a C4.5 classification tree [36], maximum entropy classifiers [37, 38], support vector machines (SVMs), and naive Bayes classifiers [21]. Mikheev treated the sentence segmentation problem as a subtask for POS tagging by assigning a tag to punctuation similar to other tokens [39]. For tagging he employed a combination of HMM and maximum entropy approaches.

The popular TextTiling method of Hearst for topic segmentation [40, 22] uses a lexical cohesion metric in a word vector space as an indicator of topic similarity. TextTiling can be seen as a local classification method with a single feature of similarity. Figure 2–4 depicts a typical graph of similarity with respect to consecutive segmentation units. The document is chopped when the similarity is below some threshold.

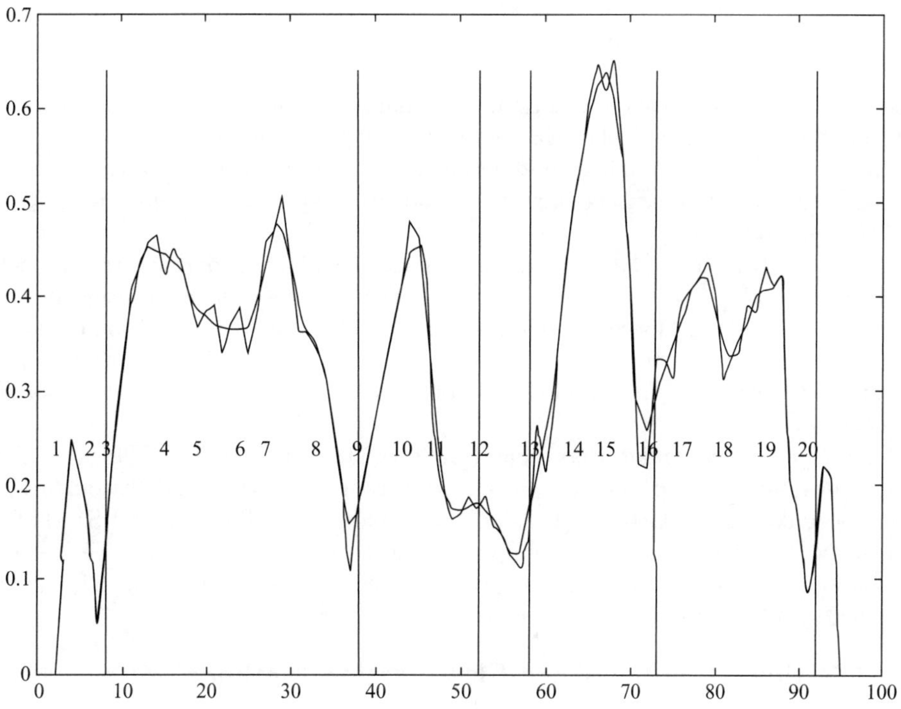

Figure 2–4: Text Tiling example (from [22])

Originally, two methods for computing the similarity scores were proposed: block comparison and vocabulary introduction. The first, block comparison, compares adjacent blocks of text to see how similar they are according to how many words the adjacent blocks have in common. The block size can be variable, not necessarily looking only at the consecutive blocks but instead at a window. Given two blocks, b_1 and b_2, each having k tokens (sentences or paragraphs), the similarity (or topical cohesion) score is computed by the formula:

$$\frac{\sum_t w_{t,b_1}.w_{t,b_2}}{\sqrt{\sum_t w_{t,b_1}^2 \sum_t w_{t,b_2}^2}}$$

where $w_{t,b}$ is the weight assigned to term t in block b. The weights can be binary or may be computed using other information retrieval–based metrics such as term frequency.

The second, the vocabulary introduction method, assigns a score to a token-sequence gap on the basis of how many new words are seen in the interval in which it is the midpoint. Similar to the block comparison formulation, given two consecutive blocks, b_1 and b_2, of equal number of words, w, the topical cohesion score is computed with the following formula:

$$\frac{NumNewTerms(b_1) + NumNewTerms(b_2)}{2 \times w}$$

where $NumNewTerms(b)$ returns the number of terms in block b, seen for the first time in text.

Brants, Chen, and Tsochantaridis [41] extended this method to exploit latent semantic analysis. Instead of simply looking at all words, they worked on the transformed lexical space, which has led to improved results because this approach also captures semantic similarities implicitly.

Morris and Hirst [42] proposed using lexical chains instead of lexical similarity for estimating cohesion. Later, Kan, Klavans, and McKeown [43] proposed using a simpler interpretation of lexical chains, linking nonfunction words and syntactic phrases to each other only if they occur within n sentences, where n and the weights of the links are tuned on the basis of the syntactic category.

Banerjee and Rudnicky [44] applied the original TextTiling approach to the meetings domain. Galley et al. [45] used a similar approach with chains of repeated terms for meeting segmentation. Hsueh and Moore [20] extended this approach by using decision trees. Purver et al. [46] used a generative topic model with a variant of Latent Dirichlet allocation to learn models of the topics in an unsupervised fashion, simultaneously producing a segmentation of the meetings.

Reynar [47] and Beeferman, Berger, and Lafferty [48] extended TextTiling-based methods using maximum entropy models with a wide range of lexical and discourse features tracking vocabulary shift. Georgescul, Clark, and Armstrong [49] employed SVMs for this task. Rosenberg and Hirschberg [50] employed the Ripper algorithm with lexical chains, cue words, and prosodic features. Levow [51] used decision trees with cosine similarity and prosodic features for broadcast news segmentation.

2.2.3 Discriminative Sequence Classification Methods

In segmentation tasks, the sentence or topic decision for a given example (word, sentence, paragraph) highly depends on the decision for the examples in its vicinity. Discriminative sequence classification methods are in general extensions of local discriminative models with additional decoding stages that find the best assignment of labels by looking at neighboring decisions to label an example. Conditional random fields (CRFs) [52] are an extension of maximum entropy, SVM struct [53] is an extension of SVM to handle structured outputs, and maximum margin Markov networks (M^3N) are extensions of HMMs [54]. The margin infused relaxed algorithm (MIRA) is an online learning approach that requires loading of one sequence at a time during training [55]. For conciseness, we present only CRFs, which have been successful for many sequence labeling tasks, including sentence segmentation in speech.

CRFs are a class of log-linear models for labeling structures [52]. Contrary to local classifiers that predict sentence or topic boundaries independently, CRFs can oversee the whole sequence of boundary hypotheses to make their decisions. Formally, they model the conditional probability of a sequence of boundary labels ($Y = y_1, \ldots, y_n$) given the sequence of feature sets extracted from the context in which they occur ($X = \mathbf{x}_1, \ldots, \mathbf{x}_n$).

$$P(Y|X) \sim \frac{1}{Z(X)} \exp\left(\sum_{t=1}^{n}\sum_{i=1}^{m} \lambda_i f_i(y_{t-1}, y_t, y_t)\right) \tag{2.8}$$

$$Z(X) = \sum_{Y} \exp\left(\sum_{t=1}^{n}\sum_{i=1}^{m} \lambda_i f_i(y_{t-1}, y_t, y_t)\right)$$

where $f_i(\cdot)$ are feature functions of the observations and a clique of labels, and λ_i are the corresponding weights. $Z(\cdot)$ is a normalization function dependent only on the observations. CRFs are trained by finding the λ parameters that maximize the likelihood of the training data, usually with a regularization term to avoid overfitting. Gradient, conjugate gradient, or online methods are used for training [56, 57, 58]. Dynamic programming (Viterbi decoding) is used to find the most probable assignment of labels at test time or to compute the $Z(\cdot)$ function.

2.2.4 Hybrid Approaches

Nonsequential discriminative classification algorithms typically ignore the context, which is critical for the segmentation task. While we may add context as a feature or simply use CRFs, which inherently consider context, these approaches are suboptimal when dealing with real-valued features, such as pause duration or pitch range. Most earlier studies simply tackled this problem by binning the feature space either manually or automatically [59].

An alternative is to use a hybrid classification approach, as suggested by Shriberg et al. [27]. The main idea is to use the posterior probabilities, $P_c(y_i|\mathbf{x}_i)$, for each boundary candidate, obtained from the other classifiers, such as boosting or CRF, by simply converting them to state observation likelihoods by dividing to their priors following the well-known Bayes rule:

$$\underset{y_i}{\operatorname{argmax}} \frac{P_c(y_i|\mathbf{x}_i)}{P(y_i)} = \underset{y_i}{\operatorname{argmax}} P(\mathbf{x}_i|y_i) \tag{2.9}$$

Applying the Viterbi algorithm to the HMM then returns the most likely segmentation. To handle dynamic ranges of state transition probabilities and observation likelihoods, a weighting scheme as is usually described in the literature can be applied:

$$\underset{y_i}{\operatorname{argmax}}\, P_c(\mathbf{x}_i|y_i)^{\alpha} \times P(y_i)^{\beta} \tag{2.10}$$

where $P(y_i)$ is estimated by the HELM, and α and β are optimized using a held-out set.

Zimmerman et al. compared various discriminative local classification methods, namely boosting, maximum entropy, and decision trees, along with their hybrid versions for sentence segmentation of multilingual speech [60]. They concluded that hybrid approaches are always superior, and Guz et al. [31] concluded that this is also true with CRF, although to a lesser degree.

2.2.5 Extensions for Global Modeling for Sentence Segmentation

So far, most approaches to sentence segmentation have focused on recognizing boundaries rather than sentences in themselves. This has occurred because of the quadratic number of sentence hypotheses that must be assessed in comparison to the number of boundaries. To tackle that problem, Roark et al. [61] segment the input according to likely sentence boundaries established by a local model, and then train a reranker on the n-best lists of segmentations. This approach allows leveraging of sentence-level features such as scores from a syntactic parser or global prosodic features. Favre et al. [62] proposed to extend this concept to a pruned sentence lattice, which allows combining local scores with sentence-level scores in a more efficient manner.

2.3 Complexity of the Approaches

The approaches described here have advantages and disadvantages. In a given context and under a set of observation features, one approach may be better than another. These approaches can be rated in terms of complexity (time and memory) of their training and prediction algorithms and in terms of their performance on real-world datasets. Some may also require specific preprocessing, such as converting or normalizing continuous features to discrete features.

In terms of complexity, training of discriminative approaches is more complex than training of generative ones because they require multiple passes over the training data to adjust for their feature weights. However, generative models such as HELMs can handle multiple orders of magnitude larger training sets and benefit, for instance, from decades of news wire transcripts. On the other hand, they work with only a few features (only words for HELM) and do not cope well with unseen events. Discriminative classifiers allow for a wider variety of features and perform better on smaller training sets. Predicting with discriminative classifiers is also slower, even though the models are relatively simple (linear or log-linear), because it is dominated by the cost of extracting more features.

Compared to local approaches, sequence approaches bring the additional complexity of decoding: finding the best sequence of decisions requires evaluating all possible sequences of decisions. Fortunately, conditional independence assumptions allow the use of dynamic programming to trade time for memory and decode in polynomial time. This complexity is then exponential in the order of the model (number of boundary candidates processed together) and the number of classes (number of boundary states). Discriminative sequence classifiers, such as CRFs, also need to repeatedly perform inference on the training data, which might become expensive.

2.4 Performances of the Approaches

For sentence segmentation in speech, performance is usually evaluated using the error rate (ratio of number of errors to the number of examples), F_1-measure (the harmonic mean of recall and precision, where recall is defined as the ratio of the number of correctly returned sentence boundaries to the number of sentence boundaries in the reference annotations and precision is the ratio of the number of correctly returned sentence boundaries to the number of all automatically estimated sentence boundaries), and the National Institute of Standards and Technology (NIST) error rate (number of candidates wrongly labeled divided by the number of actual boundaries).

For sentence segmentation in text, researchers have reported error rate results on a subset of the Wall Street Journal Corpus of about 27,000 sentences. For instance, Mikheev [39] reports that his rule-based system performs at an error rate of 1.41%. The addition of an abbreviation list to this system lowers its error rate to 0.45%, and combining it with a supervised classifier using POS tag features leads to an error rate of 0.31%. Without requiring handcrafted rules or an abbreviation list, Gillick's SVM-based system [21] obtains even fewer errors, at 0.25%. Even though the error rates presented seem low, sentence segmentation is one of the first processing steps for any NLP task, and each error impacts subsequent steps, especially if the resulting sentences are presented to the user as for example, in extractive summarization.

For sentence segmentation in speech, Doss et al. [63] report on the Mandarin TDT4 Multilingual Broadcast News Speech Corpus an F_1-measure of 69.1% for a MaxEnt classifier, 72.6% with Adaboost, and 72.7% with SVMs, using the same set of features. A combination of the three classifiers using logistic regression is also proposed. On a Turkish broadcast news corpus, Guz et al. [31] report an F_1-measure of 78.2% with HELM, 86.2% with fHELM with morphology features, 86.9% with Adaboost, and 89.1% with CRFs. In these results, HELMs (and fHELMs) were trained on the same corpus as the other classifiers. They can, however, be trained on a much larger corpus and improve performance when combined with discriminative classifiers. For instance, Zimmerman et al. [64] report that on the English TDT4 broadcast news corpus, Adaboost combined with HELM performs at an F_1-measure of 67.3% compared to 65.5% for Adaboost alone.

2.5 Features

Although most approaches are tightly related to the kinds of features employed, it is beneficial for demonstrative purposes to decouple these. Similarly, although most feature categories, such as lexical or prosodic features, are common in sentence and topic segmentation, their usage is very different. We refer to "segmentation" when features apply to both sentence and topic segmentation and explicitly state the kind of segmentation otherwise.

In this section, we describe the features of a potential boundary observation as the dimensions of the vector **x**. A feature f can be either binary (presence of a trigger word denoted by $x_f = 1$ or absence thereof denoted by $x_f = 0$) or can take values with $x_f \in \mathbb{R}$ (e.g., the length of a sentence, the duration of a pause). For binary features, in the following, we replace $x_f = 1$ by x_f and omit $x_f = 0$.

Certain classifiers assume properties for the input features and may require that they are all binary or may prefer that their distribution be standardized. Real-valued features can be converted to binary features by quantification and projection in a space of larger dimension so that the value of the feature being in an interval results in its corresponding dimension in the projected space having a value of 1 while the others yield 0.

2.5.1 Features for Both Text and Speech

Lexical Features

For both text and speech and for both sentence and topic segmentation, lexical features are the key features. Sentence and topic initial and final tokens and phrases can be captured via statistical machine learning methods, as described earlier. Typically, windows of n tokens (or sentences) are analyzed for sentence (or topic) segmentation. Whereas sequence classification methods perform this analysis implicitly, local classification methods can be fed corresponding features, such as the overlap of content words compared to the previous sentence.

For sentence segmentation of text, the lexical cues are tokens in text, and the task is mainly disambiguating sentence final punctuation. For speech, the lexical cues are raw tokens because speech lacks typographic cues.

Note that lexical features have two kinds of usage. The first one is based on the occurrence of lexical features around boundaries, such as cue phrases. For example, in the Broadcast News corpus of TDT, the news elements (i.e., topics) typically end with similar phrases. This first usage is described as "discourse features." The second is similar to TextTiling-based approaches, which typically employ stems of content words that are used while computing the cosine distance. The former usage is dependent on the genre and language, and the second usage is domain independent. These two usages are not alternatives to each other and can be combined in a single classification framework. Reynar's work [47] can be seen as a pioneering study for achieving this framework. In a maximum entropy framework, Reynar used the count of content words and names repeated in the window before and after the boundary.

More formally, let $w_1, w_2, \ldots, w_n$ be the tokens of the input, and let us extract lexical features for the boundary candidate between w_i and w_{i+1}. For sentence segmentation, the most relevant features are generally token n-grams before, after, and across the boundary. For the case of bigrams, this results in extracting the following features: x_{w_{i-1},w_i}, $x_{w_{i+1},w_{i+2}}$ and $x_{w_i,w_{i+1}}$. The cross-boundary features, for example, capture the fact that a sentence boundary is unlikely after *Gov. Smith*, but is likely in *government. The.*

For topic segmentation, boundary candidates occur between sentences. If the sentence before the boundary is denoted s_i, and the sentence after the boundary is denoted s_{i+1}, the presence of cue phrase c in those sentences will be represented as $x_{c \in s_i}$ and $x_{c \in s_{i+1}}$.

A second type of feature is the similarity of the content before and after the boundary, typically expressed as the cosine similarity between the previous and next sentences.

$$x_{\text{cosine}(s_i, s_{i+1})} = \frac{\sum_w \text{tf}(w, s_i)\text{tf}(w, s_{i+1})\text{idf}(w)}{\sqrt{\sum_w (\text{tf}(w, s_i)\text{idf}(w))^2}\sqrt{\sum_w (\text{tf}(w, s_{i+1})\text{idf}(w))^2}}$$

where $\text{tf}(w, s) = \frac{n_{w,s}}{\sum_u n_{u,s}}$ represents the term frequency of token w in sentence s and $\text{idf}(w) = \log \frac{D}{\text{df}(w)}$ is the inverse document frequency of that token, which show how common it is, generally computed on a separate corpus (D is the total number of documents, $\text{df}(w)$ is the number of documents containing w). The content can be compared at different levels: for instance, n sentences before the boundary and n sentences after the boundary.

Lexical chains are another relevant feature for topic segmentation. We usually compute the number of chains that start and stop at a candidate boundary. Let $c \in \mathcal{C}$ be a set of words referring to a lexical chain (for example, *leaf, rose, flower*). For practical reasons, a lexical chain is often reduced to a single token (all occurrences of *leaf*). Then, for a candidate boundary between w_i and w_{i+1}, the broken-lexical-chain feature can be computed as

$$x_{\text{chain}} = \left| \left\{ c \in \mathcal{C} : \min_{\substack{w_k, w_l \in c \times c \\ k \leq i, l > i}} l - k > d_{\text{min}} \right\} \right|$$

Most automatic topic segmentation work based on text sources has explored topical word usage cues in one form or other. Kozima [65] used mutual similarity of words in a sequence of text as an indicator of text structure. Reynar [66] presented a method that finds topically similar regions in the text by graphically modeling the distribution of word repetitions. Ponte and Croft [67] extracted related word sets for topic segments with the information retrieval technique of local context analysis and then compared the expanded word sets.

Beeferman et al. [48] combined a large set of automatically selected lexical discourse cues in a maximum entropy model. They also incorporated topical word usage into the model by building two statistical language models: one static (topic independent) and one that adapts its word predictions on the basis of past words. They showed that the log likelihood ratio of the two predictors behaves as an indicator of topic boundaries and can thus be used as an additional feature in the exponential model classifier.

Syntactic Features

Syntactic information has been successfully captured by a number of studies. Mikheev [39] implicitly used POS tags for sentence segmentation. Similarly, for global reranking approaches as described in Section 2.2.5, syntactic features in the form of constituency trees or dependency parse trees are also used.

For morphologically rich languages, such as Czech and Turkish, morphological analyses of words are used as additional cues [31, 68].

Formally, let $t_1, \ldots, t_n$ be the sequence of POS or morphologic tags extracted for words $w_1, \ldots, w_n$. The same features can be extracted as for words (n-grams before, after, and across the candidate boundary), for example, x_{t_{i-1},t_i}, $x_{t_i,t_{i+1}}$ and $x_{t_{i+1},t_{i+2}}$. Syntactic features are typically less useful for topic segmentation because topic changes are usually characterized by content shifts.

To assess the grammaticality of a sentence candidate in the global model under a probabilistic context-free grammar (PCFG), we can compute the sum of the probability of all valid parse trees for that sentence:

$$x_{\text{pcfg}} = \sum_{t:s_i} P(t) = \sum_{t:s_i} \prod_{r \in t} P(r)$$

where t is a parse tree and r is a production rule used in that tree [69].

Discourse Features

Speech or text, discourse features are always important for segmentation. For example, in a broadcast news show, the anchor first gives the headlines, then a commercial follows, and then the stories are presented one by one with optional anchor/reporter interaction and typical topic start and end phrases.

Previous work on both text and speech segmentation has shown that cue phrases or discourse particles (items such as *now* or *by the way*), as well as other lexical cues, can provide valuable indicators of structural units in discourse [e.g., 70,71]. Similarly, for speech, change of speaker may indicate a sentence boundary, and commercials may indicate a topic boundary in broadcast news or conversations. Formally, for all events $e \in \mathcal{E}$ that appear in the vicinity of a boundary, a feature x_e can be generated to represent the occurrence of that event, and if relevant, $x_{\overline{e}}$ will be used to represent the nonoccurrence of that event. Events have to be detected using additional systems not detailed in this book (such as a commercial detector) that may output confidence scores. In this case, the feature will be $x_e = cs$ where cs is the confidence score for that event to be recognized.

Whereas earlier approaches try to capture such predetermined discourse cues, more corpus-based studies rely on the machine learning approaches to automatically learn such patterns using informative feature sets. For example, Tur et al. [29] used explicit HMM states for topic initial and final sentences, which improved performance greatly. Rosenberg and Hirschberg [50] used statistical hypothesis testing for predetermining such phrases.

For meeting or conversation segmentation, discourse features are more complex and rely on argumentation structure. Most studies simply use previous and next turns as discourse features, but higher-level semantic information such as dialog act tags or meeting agenda items can also be used for exploiting discourse information [72].

2.5.2 Features Only for Text

Typographical and Structural Features

For sentence and topic segmentation, typographical and structural cues, such as punctuation and headlines, are very informative. Sentence segmentation systems use words and punctuation before and after the boundary, capitalization and POS tags of those words, their length, and how frequently they are used in nonsentence boundary contexts (e.g., before a lowercase word) compared to at the end/beginning of a sentence. Similarly, gazetteer information containing abbreviations and preprocessing and postprocessing patterns is employed to process text.

Formally, let g be a set of words that appear in a gazetteer. A feature is generated so that $x_{g(w)} = 1$ if $w \in g$. Similarly, the feature that denotes the frequency of the lowercase form (flc) of a word can be computed as $x_{flc(w)} = \frac{|lc(w)|}{|w|}$ where $lc(w)$ denotes the lowercase version of w.

In his work on sentence segmentation, Gillick [21] observed that on a given set of features, the choice of a classifier had a much smaller impact than a mismatch between the training and the test data or a mismatch on the tokenization of the input words. Kiss and Strunk [73] proposed an unsupervised approach for finding sentence boundaries that learns abbreviations using global statistics on an unlabeled corpus. Even though the approach is independent of the language, it is unable to identify abbreviations if they are not used multiple times in the test corpus.

Other structural cues include paragraph boundaries, headlines, and section numbering. Such cues appear only in structured textual sources and may not exist in certain text such as blogs and chatrooms.

2.5.3 Features for Speech

When working with speech recognition output, some words may be incorrect due to recognition errors, degrading the quality of lexical features. Similarly, token start times and their durations may also be wrongly estimated, causing errors in prosodic feature computation. Typically, a large set of prosodic features are extracted for robustness to these errors.

Prosodic Features

When applying segmentation to speech rather than written text, many of the same approaches can be used, but with some important considerations. First, in the case of automatic processing of speech, lexical information comes from the output of a speech recognition, which typically contains errors. Second, spoken language lacks explicit punctuation, capitalization, and formatting information. Rather, this information is conveyed through the language and also through prosody, as explained shortly. Third, although some spoken language, such as news broadcasts, is read from a text, most natural speech is conversational. In natural, spontaneous speech, sentences can be "ungrammatical" (from the perspective of formal syntax) and typically contain significant numbers of normal speech disfluencies, such as filled pauses, repetitions, and repairs.

Spoken language input, on the other hand, provides additional, "beyond words" information through its intonational and rhythmic information, that is, through its **prosody**. Prosody refers to patterns in pitch (fundamental frequency), loudness (energy), and timing (as conveyed through pausing and phonetic durations). Prosodic cues are known to be relevant to discourse structure in spontaneous speech and can therefore be expected to play a role in indicating sentence boundaries and topic transitions. Furthermore, prosodic cues by their nature are in principle independent of word identity. Thus they tend to suffer less than do lexical features from errors in automatic speech recognition.

Figure 2–5 depicts some general prosodic features used for segmenting speech into sentences along with lexical features. Broadly speaking, the prosodic features associated with sentence boundaries are similar to those for topic boundaries because both involve conveying a break that serves to chunk information. Pause length, and pitch and energy resets are generally greater in magnitude for the larger (i.e., topic) breaks, but similar types of prosodic features can be used for both tasks, trained of course for the task at hand.

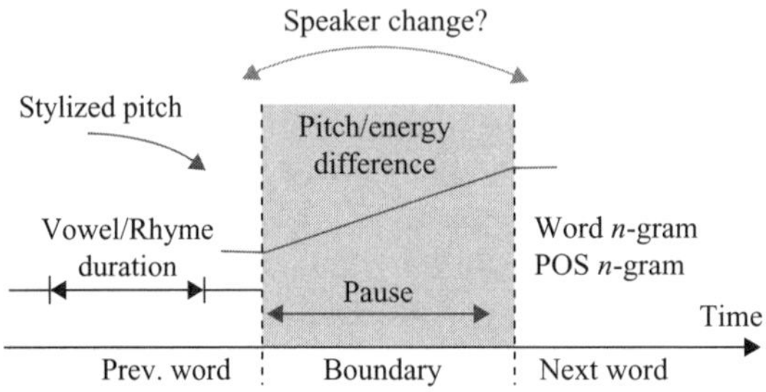

Figure 2–5: Some basic prosodic and lexical features for speech segmentation

Prosodic features for sentence segmentation have been used in a number of studies [74, 75, 27, 76, 77, 78, 51, 11, 79, 60, 80]. The simplest and most often used feature is a pause at the boundary of interest. For automatic processing, pauses are more easily obtained than other prosodic features because, unlike pitch and energy features, pause information can be extracted from automatic speech recognition output. Of course, not all sentence boundaries contain pauses, particularly in spontaneous speech. And conversely, not all pauses correspond to sentence boundaries. For example, many sentence-internal disfluencies also contain pauses. Some methods use simply the presence of a pause; others model the duration of the pause. Pause durations can be quite large in the case of turn-final sentence boundaries in conversation because such regions correspond to time during which another participant is talking. Sentence segmentation for certain dialog acts, such as backchannels (e.g., "uh-huh"), which tend to occur in isolated turns, can thus be achieved fairly successfully using only pause information.

The pause feature is computed as $x_{pause} = start(w_{i+1}) - end(w_i)$ where $start()$ and $end()$ represent the timing in seconds of the beginning and the end of a word in the speech recognition output. Relevant side features are the pause before the word (to know if it is isolated) and the quantized pause $x_{qpause}(w_i) = 1 \quad \text{iff} \quad x_{pause} > thr_{pause}$, where thr_{pause} is set to, for example, 0.2 second. Pause duration does not follow a normal distribution, by nature, and tends to confuse classifiers that expect such a distribution. However, this single feature is often the most relevant one for segmenting speech.

More detailed prosodic modeling has included pitch, phone duration, and energy information. Pitch is captured by modeling fundamental frequency during voiced regions of speech. Pitch conveys a wide range of types of information, including information about the prominence of a syllable, but for sentence segmentation the goal is usually to capture a reset in pitch. Thus, methods have looked at pitch differences across a word boundary, with a larger negative difference indicating higher probability of a sentence boundary. In addition to modeling the break in pitch across a word boundary, some approaches [27] have also modeled a speaker-specific value to which pitch falls at the ends of utterances, which not only improves performance but also allows for causal modeling because it does not rely on speech after the pause [81].

Pitch is not a continuous function and cannot be computed outside of voiced regions. Therefore, pitch features can be undefined for a given boundary candidate, which might be a problem with certain classifiers. Computing pitch, smoothing and interpolating it properly, is not the matter of this book and should be handled by appropriate software, such as the widely used Praat toolkit [82]. Typically, features are computed from statistics of pitch values in a window before the end of the word before the candidate boundary and after the beginning of the word after the boundary. For example, the pitch difference feature described in the previous paragraph results in

$$x_{\text{pitch}} = \left(\max_{t \in W_e(w_i)} \text{pitch}(t) \right) - \left(\min_{t \in W_s(w_{i+1})} \text{pitch}(t) \right)$$

where *pitch*(t) is the pitch value at time t, $W_e(w_i)$ is a temporal window anchored at the end of word w_i, and $W_s(w_{i+1})$ is a similar window at the start of word w_{i+1}. Variants of this feature can be created by changing the window size (i.e., 200 ms, 500 ms), changing the statistics computed on both sides of the boundary (i.e., min, max, mean), and normalizing pitch values according to different factors (i.e., log space projection, standardization of the distribution of pitch values of the current speaker).

Duration features for sentence segmentation aim to capture a phenomenon known as **preboundary lengthening** in which the last region of speech before the end of a unit is stretched out in duration. (Interestingly, this phenomenon is also observed in music and even in bird song [83].) Automatic modeling methods best capture preboundary lengthening when phone durations are normalized by the average duration of those phones in a corpus of similar speaking style. The duration of the rhyme (the vowel and any following consonants) of a prefinal syllable typically shows more lengthening than does the onset of that syllable.

For example, let v be the last vowel in w_i, the word before the boundary candidate. A feature can be computed as the relative duration of that vowel compared to its average duration in a corpus $\mathcal{C}$.

$$x_{\text{vowel}} = \frac{\text{end}(v_{w_i}) - \text{start}(v_{w_i})}{\sum_{w \in \mathcal{C}} \text{end}(v_w) - \text{start}(v_w)}$$

Energy features have also been employed in sentence boundary modeling, but with less success. From a descriptive point of view, energy behaves somewhat like pitch, falling toward the end of a sentence and often showing a reset for the next sentence. However, energy is affected by a myriad of factors, including the recording itself, and can be difficult to normalize both within and across talkers. Thus it has in general been less successful than pause, pitch, and duration features for automatic segmentation.

A final feature that is sometimes considered in prosodic modeling is voice quality. Descriptive work has shown an association between sentence boundaries and voice quality changes, but because such phenomena are highly speaker dependent and difficult to capture automatically, most automatic segmentation work has relied on the previously mentioned prosodic features.

Descriptive work on topic boundaries has found that major shifts in topic typically show longer pauses, an extra-high F0 onset or reset, a higher maximum accent peak, shifts in speaking rate, and greater range in F0 and intensity [e.g., 84, 85, 86, 87, 27]. Such cues are known to be salient for human listeners; in fact, subjects can perceive major discourse boundaries even if the speech itself is made unintelligible via spectral filtering [88]. In automatic studies of topic shifts, Galley et al. [45] found that features such as changes in speaker activity, amounts of silence and overlapping speech, and the presence of certain cue phrases were all indicative of changes in topic, and adding them to their approach improved their segmentation accuracy significantly. Georgescul, Clark, and Armstrong [89] found that similar features also gave some improvement with their approach. However, Hsueh, Moore, and Renals [90] found this to be true only for coarse-grained topic shifts (corresponding in many cases to changes in the activity or state of the meeting, such as introductions or closing review) and that detection of finer-grained shifts in subject matter showed no improvement.

2.6 Processing Stages

Usually, the first step in the segmentation tasks is preprocessing to determine tokens and candidate boundaries. In language like English, words are candidate tokens, but special cases like abbreviations and acronyms exist. In languages like Mandarin, with textual sources, a preceding word segmentation step can be employed.

Then a set of features, as described in the previous section, is extracted for each candidate. For speech data, token start times and durations are usually not available in the reference annotations of the spoken utterances, but these are necessary for computing prosodic features. Usually, a forced alignment of decoding step is performed to obtain these features.

Once the features are extracted, each candidate boundary is classified using one of the methods described in the previous sections.

For testing, the automatically estimated token boundaries are compared to the boundaries in reference transcriptions. When speech recognition output is used for training or testing, reference tokens are aligned with speech recognition output words using dynamic programming to minimize alignment error (such as using NIST `sclite` alignment tools), and boundary annotations are transferred to the speech recognition output. Unfortunately, sometimes perfect alignment is not possible. For example, two tokens in reference annotations with a sentence boundary between them may be recognized by the speech recognizer as a single token. In such cases, it is not clear if the sentence boundary should be omitted from the speech recognition annotations or should be included so a heuristic rule is used.

2.7 Discussion

Although sentence segmentation is a useful step for many language processing tasks, careful optimization of the segmentation parameters directly for the following task in comparison to independent optimization for segmentation quality of the predicted sentence boundaries has been empirically shown to be useful. For example, Walker et al. [91] observed that the hardcoded rules for sentence segmentation in a machine translation system resulted in very poor sentence segmentation generalization performance compared to the use of a machine learning approach. Matusov et al. [92] show that optimizing parameters of sentence segmentation in the source language is useful for machine translation of spoken documents. Similarly, Favre et al. [93] and Liu and Xie [94] study the effect of parameter optimization on information extraction and speech summarization, respectively, instead of optimization on the sentence segmentation task itself.

Regarding topic segmentation, automatic transcription of speech uses language models to predict topical information in the language model, and this has been shown to improve ASR, either by selecting a language model trained on a matching topic or by building a general language model wherein the topic is a latent variable estimated during decoding. More generally, topic-driven domain adaptation is used in a wide range of natural language processing tasks. In information retrieval, topic is modeled explicitly [95] by allowing words to contribute differently in function of the topic in which they occur or implicitly [96] using co-occurrence space reduction techniques. In automatic summarization, Tang, Yao, and Chen [97] propose to reconsider the common assumption that a document is made of a single topic and include topic-specific information in their model. Word-sense disambiguation also benefits from topic information, as many words have probably a dominant sense in a given topic [98].

2.8 Summary

We described the tasks of sentence and topic segmentation for text and speech input. We described learning algorithms for these tasks in several categories. Depending on the type of input (i.e., text versus speech), several different types of features may be used for these tasks. For example, in text, typographical cues such as capitalization and punctuation can be benefical, whereas in speech, prosodic features may be useful.

In parallel with the recent advances in speech processing and discriminative machine learning methods, performance of sentence and topic segmentation systems have improved by exploiting very high-dimensional feature sets. However, these systems still make errors, requiring the follow-on processing stages, such as machine translation, to be robust to such noise. Further research is required for jointly optimizing the segmentation stage with the follow-on processing systems.

Bibliography

[1] J. Mrozinski, E. W. D. Whittaker, P. Chatain, and S. Furui, "Automatic sentence segmentation of speech for automatic summarization," in *Proceedings of the International Conference on Acoustics, Speech and Signal Processing (ICASSP)*, 2005.

[2] J. Makhoul, A. Baron, I. Bulyko, L. Nguyen, L. Ramshaw, D. Stallard, R. Schwartz, and B. Xiang, "The effects of speech recognition and punctuation on information extraction performance," in *Proceedings of International Conference on Spoken Language Processing (Interspeech)*, 2005.

[3] D. Jones, W. Shen, E. Shriberg, A. Stolcke, T. Kamm, and D. Reynolds, "Two experiments comparing reading with listening for human processing of conversational telephone speech," in *Proceedings of EUROSPEECH*, pp. 1145–1148, 2005.

[4] W. Francis, H. Kučera, and A. Mackie, *Frequency Analysis of English Usage: Lexicon and Grammar*. Boston: Houghton Mifflin, 1982.

[5] M. Liberman and K. Church, "Text analysis and word pronunciation in text-to-speech synthesis," in *Advances in Speech Signal Processing* (S. Furui and M. M. Sondi, eds.), pp. 791–831, New York: Marcel Dekker, 1992.

[6] E. Hovy, M. Marcus, M. Palmer, L. Ramshaw, and R. Weischedel, "OntoNotes: The 90% Solution," in *Proceedings of the Human Language Technologies: The Annual Conference of the North American Chapter of the Association for Computational Linguistics*, p. 57, 2007.

[7] L. Zhou and D. Zhang, "A heuristic approach to establishing punctuation convention in instant messaging," *IEEE Transactions on Professional Communication*, vol. 48, no. 4, pp. 391–400, 2005.

[8] A. Aw, M. Zhang, J. Xiao, and J. Su, "A phrase-based statistical model for SMS text normalization," in *Proceedings of the COLING/ACL*, 2006.

[9] K. Taghva, A. Condit, J. Borsack, and S. Erva, "Structural markup of OCR generated text," *Information Science Research Institute 1994 Annual Research Report*, p. 61, 1994.

[10] M. Stevenson and R. Gaizauskas, "Experiments on sentence boundary detection," in *Proceedings of the Conference on Applied Natural Language Processing (ANLP)*, 2000.

[11] J. Kolar, E. Shriberg, and Y. Liu, "Using prosody for automatic sentence segmentation of multi-party meetings," in *Proceedings of the International Conference on Text, Speech, and Dialogue (TSD)*, 2006.

[12] A. Janin, J. Ang, S. Bhagat, R. Dhillon, J. Edwards, J. Macias-Guarasa, N. Morgan, B. Peskin, E. Shriberg, A. Stolcke, C. Wooters, and B. Wrede, "The ICSI meeting project: Resources and research," in *Proceedings of the International Conference on Acoustics, Speech and Signal Processing (ICASSP)*, 2004.

[13] M. Core and J. Allen, "Coding dialogs with the DAMSL annotation scheme," in *Proceedings of the Working Notes of the Conference of the American Association for Artificial Intelligence (AAAI) Fall Symposium on Communicative Action in Humans and Machines*, 1997.

[14] E. Shriberg, R. Dhillon, S. Bhagat, J. Ang, and H. Carvey, "The ICSI Meeting Recorder Dialog Act (MRDA) Corpus," in *Proceedings of the SigDial Workshop*, 2004.

[15] C. Hoffmann, "Automatische Disambiguierung von Satzgrenzen in einem maschinenlesbaren deutschen Korpus," Manuscript, University of Trier, Germany, 1994.

[16] G. Grefenstette and P. Tapanainen, "What is a word, what is a sentence? Problems of tokenization," Rank Xerox Research Centre, 1994.

[17] T. Briscoe, J. Carroll, and R. Watson, "The second release of the RASP system," in *Proceedings of the Interactive Demo Session of COLING/ACL*, vol. 6, 2006.

[18] C. L. Wayne, "Topic Detection and Tracking (TDT) overview and perspective," in *Proceedings of the DARPA Broadcast News Transcription and Understanding Workshop*, 1998.

[19] G. Doddington, "The Topic Detection and Tracking Phase 2 (TDT2) evaluation plan," in *Proceedings of the DARPA Broadcast News Transcription and Understanding Workshop*, 1998.

[20] P.-Y. Hsueh and J. Moore, "Automatic topic segmentation and labeling in multiparty dialogue," in *Proceedings of the 1st IEEE/ACM Workshop on Spoken Language Technology (SLT)*, 2006.

[21] D. Gillick, "Sentence boundary detection and the problem with the U.S.," in *Proceedings of NAACL: Short Papers*, 2009.

[22] M. A. Hearst, "TexTiling: Segmenting text info multi-paragraph subtopic passages," *Computational Linguistics*, vol. 23, no. 1, pp. 33–64, 1997.

[23] A. Viterbi, "Error bounds for convolutional codes and an asymptotically optimum decoding algorithm," *IEEE Transactions on Information Theory*, pp. 1260–1269, 1967.

[24] J. Yamron, I. Carp, L. Gillick, S. Lowe, and P. van Mulbregt, "A hidden Markov model approach to text segmentation and event tracking," in *Proceedings of the IEEE Conference on Acoustics, Speech, and Signal Processing*, vol. 1, pp. 333–336, May 1998.

[25] K. W. Church, "A stochastic parts program and noun phrase parser for unrestricted text," in *Proceedings of the Conference on Applied Natural Language Processing (ANLP)*, pp. 136–143, 1988.

[26] D. M. Bikel, R. Schwartz, and R. M. Weischedel, "An algorithm that learns what's in a name," *Machine Learning Journal Special Issue on Natural Language Learning*, vol. 34, no. 1-3, pp. 211–231, 1999.

[27] E. Shriberg, A. Stolcke, D. Hakkani-Tür, and G. Tur, "Prosody-based automatic segmentation of speech into sentences and topics," *Speech Communication*, vol. 32, no. 1-2, pp. 127–154, 2000.

[28] A. Stolcke and E. Shriberg, "Statistical language modeling for speech disfluencies," in *Proceedings of the International Conference on Acoustics, Speech and Signal Processing (ICASSP)*, 1996.

[29] G. Tur, D. Hakkani-Tür, A. Stolcke, and E. Shriberg, "Integrating prosodic and lexical cues for automatic topic segmentation," *Computational Linguistics*, vol. 27, no. 1, pp. 31–57, 2001.

[30] J. A. Bilmes and K. Kirchhoff, "Factored language models and generalized parallel backoff," in *Proceedings of the Human Language Technology Conference (HLT)-Conference of the North American Chapter of the Association for Computational Linguistics (NAACL)*, 2003.

[31] U. Guz, B. Favre, G. Tur, and D. Hakkani-Tür, "Generative and discriminative methods using morphological information for sentence segmentation of Turkish," *IEEE Transactions on Audio, Speech, and Language Processing*, vol. 17, no. 5, pp. 895–903, 2009.

[32] E. Stamatatos, N. Fakotakis, and G. Kokkinakis, "Automatic extraction of rules for sentence boundary disambiguation," in *Proceedings of the Workshop on Machine Learning in Human Language Technology*, pp. 88–92, 1999.

[33] M. D. Riley, "Some applications of tree-based modelling to speech and language indexing," in *Proceedings of the DARPA Speech and Natural Language Workshop*, pp. 339–352, 1989.

[34] D. Palmer and M. Hearst, "Adaptive sentence boundary disambiguation," in *Proceedings of the Fourth ACL Conference on Applied Natural Language Processing*, 1994.

[35] T. Humphrey and F. Zhou, "Period disambiguation using a neural network," in *Proceedings of the International Joint Conference on Neural Networks (IJCNN)*, p. 606, 1989.

[36] J. Shim, D. Kim, J. Cha, G. Lee, and J. Seo, "Multistrategic integrated web document pre-processing for sentence and word boundary detection," *Information Processing and Management*, vol. 38, no. 4, pp. 509–527, 2002.

[37] J. Reynar and A. Ratnaparkhi, "A maximum entropy approach to identifying sentence boundaries," in *Proceedings of the Conference on Applied Natural Language Processing (ANLP)*, 1997.

[38] H. Le and T. Ho, "A maximum entropy approach to sentence boundary detection of Vietnamesetexts," in *IEEE International Conference on Research, Innovation and Vision for the Future*, 2008.

[39] A. Mikheev, "Tagging sentence boundaries," in *Proceedings of the Annual International ACM SIGIR Conference on Research and Development in Information Retrieval*, 2000.

[40] M. A. Hearst, "Multi-paragraph segmentation of expository text," in ACL [99], pp. 9–16.

[41] T. Brants, F. Chen, and I. Tsochantaridis, "Topic-based document segmentation with probabilistic latent semantic analysis," in *Proceedings of the ACM International Conference on Information and Knowledge Management (CIKM)*, 2002.

[42] J. Morris and G. Hirst, "Lexical cohesion computed by thesaural relations as an indicator of the structure of text," *Computational Linguistics*, vol. 17, no. 1, pp. 21–48, 1991.

[43] M.-Y. Kan, J. L. Klavans, and K. R. McKeown, "Linear segmentation and segment significance," in *Proceedings ACL/COLING Workshop on Very Large Corpora*, Canada 1998.

[44] S. Banerjee and A. Rudnicky, "A TextTiling based approach to topic boundary detection in meetings," in *Proceedings of the International Conference on Spoken Language Processing (ICSLP)*, 2006.

[45] M. Galley, K. McKeown, E. Fosler-Lussier, and H. Jing, "Discourse segmentation of multi-party conversation," in *Proceedings of the Annual Meeting of the Association for Computational Linguistics (ACL)*, 2003.

[46] M. Purver, K. Körding, T. Griffiths, and J. Tenenbaum, "Unsupervised topic modelling for multi-party spoken discourse," in *Proceedings of the International Conference on Computational Linguistics (COLING)—Annual Meeting of the Association for Computational Linguistics (ACL)*, pp. 17–24, 2006.

[47] J. Reynar, "Statistical models for topic segmentation," in *Proceedings of the Annual Meeting of the Association for Computational Linguistics (ACL)*, pp. 357–364, 1999.

[48] D. Beeferman, A. Berger, and J. Lafferty, "Statistical models for text segmentation," *Machine Learning*, vol. 34, no. 1-3, pp. 177–210, 1999.

[49] M. Georgescul, A. Clark, and S. Armstrong, "Word distributions for thematic segmentation in a support vector machine approach," in *Proceedings of the Conference on Computational Natural Language Learning (CoNLL)*, pp. 101–108, 2006.

[50] A. Rosenberg and J. Hirschberg, "Story segmentation of broadcast news in English, Mandarin, and Arabic," in *Proceedings of the Human Language Technology Conference (HLT) and Conference of the North American Chapter of the Association for Computational Linguistics (NAACL)*, 2006.

[51] G. A. Levow, "Assessing prosodic and text features for segmentation of Mandarinbroadcast news," in *Proceedings of the Human Language Technology Conference (HLT)-Conference of the North American Chapter of the Association for Computational Linguistics (NAACL) 2004*, 2004.

[52] J. D. Lafferty, A. McCallum, and F. C. N. Pereira, "Conditional random fields: Probabilistic models for segmenting and labeling sequence data," in *Proceedings of the 18th International Conference on Machine Learning (ICML)*, pp. 282–289, 2001.

[53] I. Tsochantaridis, T. Hofmann, T. Joachims, and Y. Altun, "Support vector machine learning for interdependent and structured output spaces," in *Proceedings of the International Conference on Machine Learning (ICML)*, 2004.

[54] B. Taskar, "Learning structured prediction models: A large margin approach," PhD thesis, Stanford University, 2004.

[55] K. Crammer, R. Mcdonald, and F. Pereira, "Scalable large-margin online learning for structured classification," in *Annual Conference on Neural Information Processing Systems (NIPS)*, 2005.

[56] H. Wallach, "Efficient training of conditional random fields," in *Proceedings of the Annual CLUK Research Colloquium*, vol. 112, 2002.

[57] S. Vishwanathan, N. Schraudolph, M. Schmidt, and K. Murphy, "Accelerated training of conditional random fields with stochastic gradient methods," in *Proceedings of the International Conference on Machine Learning (ICML)*, 2006.

[58] S. Sarawagi and W. Cohen, "Semi-Markov conditional random fields for information extraction," *Advances in Neural Information Processing Systems*, vol. 17, pp. 1185–1192, 2005.

[59] H.-K. J. Kuo and Y. Gao, "Maximum entropy direct models for speech recognition," *IEEE Transactions on Speech and Audio Processing*, vol. 14, no. 3, pp. 873–881, 2006.

[60] M. Zimmerman, D. Hakkani-Tür, J. Fung, N. Mirghafori, L. Gottlieb, E. Shriberg, and Y. Liu, "The ICSI+ multilingual sentence segmentation system," in *Proceedings of the International Conference on Spoken Language Processing (ICSLP)*, 2006.

[61] B. Roark, Y. Liu, M. Harper, R. Stewart, M. Lease, M. Snover, I. Shafran, B. Dorr, J. Hale, A. Krasnyanskaya, and L. Yung, "Reranking for sentence boundary detection in conversational speech," in *Proceedings of the International Conference on Acoustics, Speech and Signal Processing (ICASSP)*, 2006.

[62] B. Favre, D. Hakkani-Tür, S. Petrov, and D. Klein, "Efficient sentence segmentation using syntactic features," in *Proceedings of the IEEE/ACL Spoken Language Technologies (SLT) Workshop*, 2008.

[63] M. Doss, D. Hakkani-Tür, O. Cetin, E. Shriberg, J. Fung, and N. Mirghafori, "Entropy based classifier combination for sentence segmentation," in *Proceedings of the IEEE ICASSP Conference*, pp. 189–192, 2007.

[64] M. Zimmerman, D. Hakkani-Tür, J. Fung, N. Mirghafori, L. Gottlieb, E. Shriberg, and Y. Liu, "The ICSI+ multilingual sentence segmentation system," in *Proceedings of the 9th International Conference on Spoken Language Processing*, ISCA, 2006.

[65] H. Kozima, "Text segmentation based on similarity between words," in *Proceedings of the 31st Annual Meeting of the Association for Computational Linguistics*, pp. 286–288, 1993.

[66] J. C. Reynar, "An automatic method of finding topic boundaries," in ACL [99], pp. 331–333.

[67] J. M. Ponte and W. B. Croft, "Text segmentation by topic," in *Proceedings of the First European Conference on Research and Advanced Technology for Digital Libraries*, pp. 120–129, 1997.

[68] J. Kolar, Y. Liu, and E. Shriberg, "Genre effects on automatic sentence segmentation of speech: A comparison of broadcast news and broadcast conversations," in *Proceedings of the International Conference on Acoustics, Speech and Signal Processing (ICASSP)*, 2009.

[69] M. Johnson, "PCFG models of linguistic tree representations," *Computational Linguistics*, vol. 24, no. 4, pp. 613–632, 1998.

[70] B. Grosz and C. Sidner, "Attention, intention, and the structure of discourse," *Computational Linguistics*, vol. 12, no. 3, pp. 175–204, 1986.

[71] R. J. Passonneau and D. J. Litman, "Discourse segmentation by human and automated means," *Computational Linguistics*, vol. 23, no. 1, pp. 103–139, 1997.

[72] S. Banerjee and A. Rudnicky, "Segmenting meetings into agenda items by extracting implicit supervision from human note-taking," in *Proceedings of the International Conference on Intelligent User Interfaces (IUI'07)*, 2007.

[73] T. Kiss and J. Strunk, "Unsupervised multilingual sentence boundary detection," *Computational Linguistics*, vol. 32, no. 4, pp. 485–525, 2006.

[74] V. Warnke, R. Kompe, H. Niemann, and E. Nöth, "Integrated dialog act segmentation and classification using prosodic features and language models," in *Proceedings of the 5th European Conference on Speech Communication and Technology*, pp. 207–210, 1997.

[75] C. Chen, "Speech recognition with automatic punctuation," in *Proceedings of EUROSPEECH*, pp. 447–450, 1999.

[76] H. Christensen, Y. Gotoh, and S. Renals, "Punctuation annotation using statistical prosody models," in *Proceedings of the ISCA Workshop on Prosody in Speech Recognition and Understanding*, 2001.

[77] A. Srivastava and F. Kubala, "Sentence boundary detection in Arabicspeech," in *Proceedings of EUROSPEECH*, 2003.

[78] J.-H. Kim and P. C. Woodland, "A combined punctuation generation and speech recognition system and its performance enhancement using prosody," *Computer Speech and Language*, vol. 41, no. 4, pp. 563–577, Nov. 2003.

[79] M. Tomalin and P. C.Woodland, "Discriminatively trained Gaussianmixture models for sentence boundary detection," in *Proceedings of ICASSP*, pp. 549–552, 2006.

[80] Y. Liu, E. Shriberg, A. Stolcke, D. Hillard, M. Ostendorf, and M. Harper, "Enriching speech recognition with automatic detection of sentence boundaries and disfluencies," *IEEE Transactions on Audio, Speech, and Language Processing*, vol. 14, no. 5, pp. 1526–1540, 2006.

[81] L. Ferrer, E. Shriberg, and A. Stolcke, "Is the speaker done yet? Faster and more accurate end-of-utterance detection using prosody in human-computer dialog," in *Proceedings of the International Conference on Spoken Language Processing*, pp. 2061–2064, 2002.

[82] P. Boersma and D. Weenink, "Praat, a system for doing phonetics by computer, version 3.4," Tech. Rep. 132, Institute of Phonetic Sciences of the University of Amsterdam, 1996.

[83] J. Vaissière, "Language-independent prosodic features," in *Prosody: Models and Measurements* (A. Cutler and D. R. Ladd, eds.), ch. 5, pp. 53–66, Berlin: Springer, 1983.

[84] B. Grosz and J. Hirschberg, "Some intonational characteristics of discourse structure," in Ohala et al. [100], pp. 429–432.

[85] S. Nakajima and J. F. Allen, "A study on prosody and discourse structure in cooperative dialogues," *Phonetica*, vol. 50, pp. 197–210, 1993.

[86] J. Hirschberg and C. Nakatani, "A prosodic analysis of discourse segments in direction-giving monologues," in *Proceedings of the 34th Annual Meeting of the Association for Computational Linguistics*, pp. 286–293, 1996.

[87] M. Swerts, "Prosodic features at discourse boundaries of different strength," *Journal of the Acoustical Society of America*, vol. 101, pp. 514–521, 1997.

[88] M. Swerts, R. Geluykens, and J. Terken, "Prosodic correlates of discourse units in spontaneous speech," in Ohala et al. [100] pp. 421–424.

[89] M. Georgescul, A. Clark, and S. Armstrong, "Exploiting structural meeting-specific features for topic segmentation," in *Actes de la 14è me Conférence sur le Traitement Automatique des Langues Naturelles*, Association pour le Traitement Automatique des Langues, June 2007.

[90] P.-Y. Hsueh, J. Moore, and S. Renals, "Automatic segmentation of multiparty dialogue," in *Proceedings of the Conference of the European Chapter of the Association for Computational Linguistics (EACL)*, 2006.

[91] D. Walker, D. Clements, M. Darwin, and J. Amtrup, "Sentence boundary detection: A comparison of paradigms for improving MT quality," in *Proceedings of the MT Summit VIII*, 2001.

[92] E. Matusov, D. Hillard, M. Magimai-Doss, D. Hakkani-Tür, M. Ostendorf, and H. Ney, "Improving speech translation with automatic boundary prediction," in *Proceedings of International Conference on Spoken Language Processing (Interspeech)*, 2007.

[93] B. Favre, R. Grishman, D. Hillard, H. Ji, D. Hakkani-Tür, and M. Ostendorf, "Punctuating speech for information extraction," in *Proceedings of IEEE International Conference on Acoustics, Speech, and Signal Processing (ICASSP)*, 2008.

[94] Y. Liu and S. Xie, "Impact of automatic sentence segmentation on meeting summarization," in *Proceedings of IEEE International Conference on Acoustics, Speech, and Signal Processing (ICASSP)*, 2008.

[95] J. Becker and D. Kuropka, "Topic-based vector space model," in *Proceedings of the 6th International Conference on Business Information Systems*, pp. 7–12, 2003.

[96] S. Deerwester, S. Dumais, G. Furnas, T. Landauer, and R. Harshman, "Indexing by latent semantic analysis," *Journal of the American Society for Information Science*, vol. 41, no. 6, pp. 391–407, 1990.

[97] J. Tang, L. Yao, and D. Chen, "Multi-topic based query-oriented summarization," in *Proceedings of SDM*, 2009.

[98] J. Boyd-Graber, D. Blei, and X. Zhu, "A topic model for word sense disambiguation," in *Proceedings of the the Joint Conference on Empirical Methods in Natural Language Processing and Computational Natural Language Learning*, pp. 1024–1033, 2007.

[99] *Proceedings of the 32nd Annual Meeting of the Association for Computational Linguistics, New Mexico State University, Las Cruces, New Mexico.* Morriston, NJ: ACL, 1994.

[100] J. J. Ohala, T. M. Nearey, B. L. Derwing, M. M. Hodge, and G. E. Wiebe, eds., *Proceedings of the International Conference on Spoken Language Processing*, Edmonton: University of Alberta, 1992.

Chapter 3

Syntax

Anoop Sarkar

Parsing uncovers the hidden structure of linguistic input. In many applications involving natural language, the underlying predicate-argument structure of sentences can be useful. The syntactic analysis of language provides a means to explicitly discover the various predicate-argument dependencies that may exist in a sentence. In natural language processing (NLP), the syntactic analysis of natural language input can vary from being very low-level, such as simply tagging each word in the sentence with a part of speech (POS), or very high level, such as recovering a structural analysis that identifies the dependency between each predicate in the sentence and its explicit and implicit arguments. The major bottleneck in parsing natural language is the fact that ambiguity is so pervasive. In syntactic parsing, ambiguity is a particularly difficult problem because the most plausible analysis has to be chosen from an exponentially large number of alternative analyses. From tagging to full parsing, algorithms that can handle such ambiguity have to be carefully chosen. This chapter explores syntactic analysis methods from tagging to full parsing and the use of supervised machine learning to deal with ambiguity.

3.1 Parsing Natural Language

In a text-to-speech application, input sentences are to be converted to a spoken output that should sound like it was spoken by a native speaker of the language. Consider the following pair of sentences (imagine them spoken rather than written):[1]

1. He wanted to go for a drive in movie.
2. He wanted to go for a drive in the country.

There is a natural pause between the words *drive* and *in* in sentence 2 that reflects an underlying hidden structure to the sentence. Parsing can provide a structural description that identifies such a break in the intonation. A simpler case occurs in the following sentence:

3. The cat who lives dangerously had nine lives.

1. When written, *drive in* would probably be hyphenated in the second utterance.

In this case, a text-to-speech system needs to know that the first instance of the word *lives* is a verb and the second instance is a noun before it can begin to produce the natural intonation for this sentence. This is an instance of the part-of-speech (POS) tagging problem where each word in the sentence is assigned a most likely part of speech. These examples come from the open-source Festival text-to-speech system (www.festvox.org), which uses parsing to disambiguate these cases.

Another motivation for parsing comes from the natural language task of summarization, in which several documents about the same topic should be condensed down to a small digest of information typically limited in size to 100 or 250 words. Such a summary may be in response to a question that is answered (perhaps in different ways) in the set of documents. In this case, a useful subtask is to compress an individual sentence so that only the relevant portions of a sentence is included in the summary [1]. This allows the summary to be concise, informative, and fluent. For example, we may want to compress sentence 4 to a shorter sentence 5.

4. Beyond the basic level, the operations of the three products vary widely.
5. The operations of the products vary.

An elegant way to approach this task is to first parse the sentence to find the various constituents: where we recursively partition the words in the sentence into individual phrases such as a verb phrase or a noun phrase. The output of the parser for the input sentence 4 is shown in Figure 3–1. The parse tree produced by the parser can now be edited using a compression model that is aware of constituents, and a few choice constituent deletions can produce a fluent compressed version of the original sentence.

Another example is the paraphrasing of text [2]. In the sentence fragment 6, the capitalized phrase EUROPEAN COUNTRIES can be replaced with other phrases without changing the essential meaning of the sentence. A few examples of replacement phrases are shown in italics in sentence fragments 7 to 11. This kind of replacement cannot simply rely on substitution of arbitrary words in the sentence because such an approach can lead to

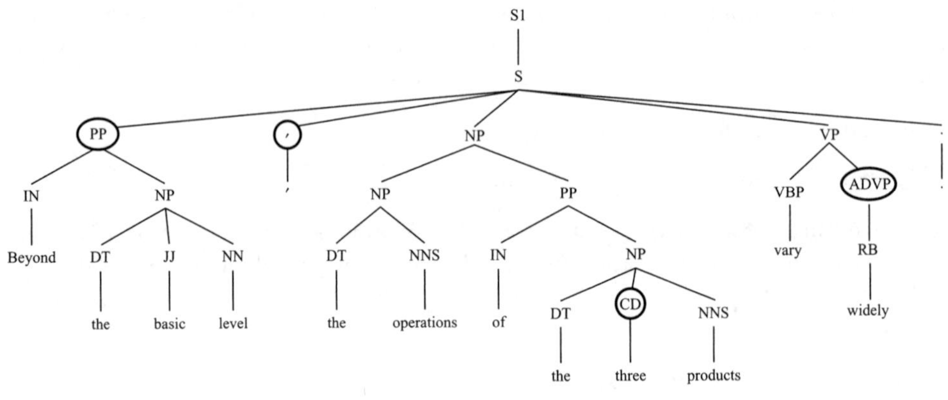

Figure 3–1: Parser output for sentence 4. Deleting the circled constituents PP, ,, CD, and ADVP results in the shorter fluent sentence *The operations of the products vary.* (example from Knight and Marcu [1])

incoherent and disfluent paraphrases. Paraphrasing models build on top of parsers to identify target constituents to replace and also to find appropriate replacement phrases that can substitute for the original phrase. Paraphrases of this type have been shown to be useful in applications such as statistical machine translation.

6. open borders imply increasing racial fragmentation in EUROPEAN COUNTRIES.
7. open borders imply increasing racial fragmentation in *the countries of europe.*
8. open borders imply increasing racial fragmentation in *european states.*
9. open borders imply increasing racial fragmentation in *europe.*
10. open borders imply increasing racial fragmentation in *european nations.*
11. open borders imply increasing racial fragmentation in *the european countries.*

In contemporary NLP, syntactic parsers are routinely used in many applications, including but not limited to statistical machine translation [3], information extraction from text collections [4], language summarization [5], producing entity grids for language generation [6], error correction in text [7], knowledge acquisition from language (e.g., discovering semantic classes or x IS-A y relationships) [8], in speech recognition systems as language models (a language model assigns a probability to a candidate output sentence—syntax is useful in particular for disfluent or error-prone speech input) [7], dialog systems [9], and text-to-speech systems (www.festvox.org). Parsers have been written for a large number of languages around the world and are an essential component in many kinds of multilingual processing tasks.

3.2 Treebanks: A Data-Driven Approach to Syntax

Parsing recovers information that is not explicit in the input sentence. This implies that a parser requires some knowledge in addition to the input sentence about the kind of syntactic analysis that should be produced as output. One method to provide such knowledge to the parser is to write down a grammar of the language—a set of rules of syntactic analysis. For instance, we might write down the rules of syntax as a context-free grammar (CFG). In the rest of this chapter we assume some familiarity with CFGs (please refer to Sipser [10] for a good introduction to the notion of a formal grammar and the formal languages they generate and CFGs in particular).

The following CFG (written in a simple Backus-Naur form) represents a simple grammar of transitive verbs in English, verbs (V) that have a subject and object noun phrase (NP), plus modifiers of verb phrases (VP) in the form of prepositional phrases (PP).

```
S -> NP VP
NP -> 'John' | 'pockets' | D N | NP PP
VP -> V NP | VP PP
V -> 'bought'
D -> 'a'
```

```
N -> 'shirt'
PP -> P NP
P -> 'with'
```

Natural language grammars typically have the words w as terminal symbols in the CFG, and they are generated by rules of type $X \rightarrow w$, where X is the part of speech for the word w. For example, in the preceding CFG, the rule `V -> 'saw'` has the POS symbol V generating the verb *saw*. Such nonterminals are called **part-of-speech tags** or **preterminals**. The preceding CFG can produce a syntax analysis of a sentence like *John bought a shirt with pockets* with S as the start symbol of the grammar. Parsing the sentence with the CFG rules gives us two possible derivations for this sentence. In one parse, pockets are a kind of currency that can be used to buy a shirt, and the other parse, which is the more plausible one, John is purchasing a kind of shirt that has pockets.

```
(S (NP John)
   (VP (VP (V bought)
           (NP (D a)
               (N shirt)))
       (PP (P with)
           (NP pockets))))
```

```
(S (NP John)
   (VP (V bought)
       (NP (NP (D a)
               (N shirt))
           (PP (P with)
               (NP pockets)))))
```

However, writing down a CFG for the syntactic analysis of natural language is problematic. Unlike a programming language, natural language is far too complex to simply list all the syntactic rules in terms of a CFG. A simple list of rules does not consider interactions between different components in the grammar. We could extend this grammar to include other types of verbs and other syntactic constructions, but listing all possible syntactic constructions in a language is a difficult task. In addition, it is difficult to exhaustively list lexical properties of words, for instance, to list all the grammar rules in which a particular word can be a participant. This is a typical knowledge acquisition problem.

Apart from this knowledge acquisition problem, there is a less apparent problem: it turns out that the rules interact with each other in combinatorially explosive ways. Consider a simple CFG that provides a syntactic analysis of noun phrases as a binary branching tree:

```
N -> N N
N -> 'natural' | 'language' | 'processing' | 'book'
```

Recursive rules produce ambiguity: with N as the start symbol, for the input *natural* there is one parse tree `(N natural)`; for the input *natural language* we use the recursive rule once and obtain one parse tree `(N (N natural) (N language))`; for the input *natural language processing* we use the recursive rule twice in each parse, and there are two ambiguous parses:

```
(N (N (N natural)
      (N language))
   (N processing))
```

```
(N (N natural)
   (N (N language)
      (N processing)))
```

Note that the ambiguity in the syntactic analysis reflects a real ambiguity: is it a processing of natural language, or is it a natural way to do language processing? So this issue cannot be resolved by changing the formalism in which the rules are written (e.g., by using finite-state automata, which can be deterministic but cannot simultaneously model both meanings in a single grammar). Any system of writing down syntactic rules should represent this ambiguity. However, by using the recursive rule three times, we get five parses for *natural language processing book* and for longer and longer input noun phrases, using the recursive rule four times, we get 14 parses; using it five times, we get 42 parses; using it six times, we get 132 parses. In fact, for CFGs it can be proved that the number of parses obtained by using the recursive rule n times is the Catalan number of n:

$$\text{Cat}(n) = \frac{1}{n+1}\binom{2n}{n}$$

This occurs not only for coordinate structures such as the noun phrase grammar but also when you have recursive rules to deal with modifiers such as the recursive rule for prepositional phrase modification `VP -> VP PP` in the first CFG in this section. In fact, the ambiguity of PP modification is not independent of the ambiguity of coordination: in a sentence with both types of ambiguity, the total number of parses is the cross product of the parses from each subgrammar. This poses a serious computational problem for parsers. For an input with n words, the number of possible parses is exponential in n.

For most natural language tasks, we do not wish to explore this entire space of ambiguity, even if, as we show later, it is possible to produce a compact representation of the entire exponential number of parses in polynomial time (for CFGs, $\mathcal{O}(n^3)$ is the worst-case time complexity) and store it in polynomial space (for CFGs, the space needed is proportional to n^2).

For example, for the input *natural language processing book*, only one out of the five parses obtained using the CFG above is intuitively correct (corresponding to a book about the processing of natural language):

```
(N (N (N (N natural)
         (N language))
      (N processing))
   (N book))
```

This is a second knowledge acquisition problem—not only do we need to know the syntactic rules for a particular language, but we also need to know which analysis is the most plausible for a given input sentence. The construction of a **treebank** is a data-driven approach to syntax analysis that allows us to address both of these knowledge acquisition bottlenecks in one stroke.

A treebank is simply a collection of sentences (also called a corpus of text), where each sentence is provided a complete syntax analysis. The syntactic analysis for each sentence has been judged by a human expert as the most plausible analysis for that sentence. A lot of care is taken during the human annotation process to ensure that a consistent treatment is provided across the treebank for related grammatical phenomena. A style book or set of **annotation guidelines** is typically written before the annotation process to ensure a consistent scheme of annotation throughout the treebank.

There is no set of syntactic rules or linguistic grammar explicitly provided by a treebank, and typically there is no list of syntactic constructions provided explicitly in a treebank. In fact, no exhaustive set of rules is even assumed to exist, even though assumptions about syntax are implicit in a treebank. A detailed set of assumptions about syntax is typically used as an annotation guideline to help the human experts produce the single-most plausible syntactic analysis for each sentence in the corpus. The consistency of syntax analysis in a treebank is measured using interannotator agreement by having approximately 10% overlapped material annotated by more than one annotator.

Treebanks provide a solution to the two kinds of knowledge acquisition bottlenecks we discussed. Treebanks provide annotations of syntactic structure for a large sample of sentences. We can use supervised machine learning methods to train a parser to produce a syntactic analysis for input sentences by generalizing appropriately from the training data extracted from the treebank.

Treebanks solve the first knowledge acquisition problem of finding the grammar underlying the syntax analysis because the syntactic analysis is directly given instead of a grammar. In fact, the parser does not necessarily need any explicit grammar rules as long as it can faithfully produce a syntax analysis for an input sentence, although the information used by the trained parser can be said to represent a set of implicit grammar rules. Nivre [11] discusses in further detail this subtle difference between parsing using a grammar and parsing a text using data-driven methods that may or may not be grammar-based.

Treebanks solve the second knowledge acquisition problem as well. Because each sentence in a treebank has been given its most plausible syntactic analysis, supervised machine learning methods can be used to learn a scoring function over all possible syntax analyses. A statistical parser trained on the treebank tries to mimic the human annotation decisions by using indicators from the input and previous decisions made in the parser itself to learn such a scoring function. For a given sentence not seen in the training data, a statistical parser can use this scoring function to return the syntax analysis that has the highest score, which is taken to be the most plausible analysis for that sentence. The scoring function can also be used to produce the k-best syntax analyses for a sentence.

Two main approaches to syntax analysis are used to construct treebanks: dependency graphs and phrase structure trees. These two representations are very closely related to each other, and under some assumptions, one representation can be converted to another. Dependency analysis is typically favored for languages such as Czech and Turkish, that have free(er) word order, where the arguments of a predicate are often seen in different ordering in the sentence, while phrase structure analysis is often used to provide additional information about long-distance dependencies and mostly in languages like English and French, where the word order is less flexible.

In the rest of this chapter, we examine three main components for building a parser: the representation of the syntactic structure, which involves the use of a varying amount of linguistic knowledge to build a treebank (§3.3); the training and decoding algorithms for the model that deal with the potentially exponential search space (§3.4); methods to model ambiguity and provide a way to rank parses so that we can recover the most likely parse (§3.5).

3.3 Representation of Syntactic Structure

3.3.1 Syntax Analysis Using Dependency Graphs

The main philosophy behind dependency graphs is to connect a word—the **head** of a phrase—with the dependents in that phrase. The notation connects a head with its dependent using a directed (hence asymmetric) connection [12]. Dependency graphs, just like phrase structure trees, is a representation that is consistent with many different linguistic frameworks. The head-dependent relationship could be either semantic (head-modifier) or syntactic (head-specifier). The main difference between dependency graphs and phrase structure trees is that dependency analyses typically make minimal assumptions about syntactic structure and to avoid any annotation of hidden structure such as, for example, using empty elements as placeholders to represent missing or displaced arguments of predicates, or any unnecessary hierarchical structure. The words in the input sentence are treated as the only vertices in the graph, which are linked together by directed arcs representing syntactic dependencies. The CoNLL 2007 shared task on dependency parsing [13] provides the following definition of a **dependency graph**:

> In dependency-based syntactic parsing, the task is to derive a syntactic structure for an input sentence by identifying the syntactic *head* of each word in the sentence. This defines a *dependency graph*, where the nodes are the words of the input sentence and the arcs are the binary relations from head to dependent. Often, but not always, it is assumed that all words except one have a syntactic head, which means that the graph will be a tree with the single independent node as the root. In *labeled* dependency parsing, we additionally require the parser to assign a specific type (or label) to each dependency relation holding between head word and dependent word.

As in this definition, we will restrict ourselves to dependency tree analyses, where each word depends on exactly one parent, either another word or a dummy root symbol. By convention, in dependency trees the 0 index is used to indicate the root symbol, and the directed arcs are drawn from the head word to the dependent word. For example, Figure 3–2 shows an example of a dependency tree for a Czech sentence taken from the Prague Dependency Treebank, which is a large corpus of Czech text annotated with dependency trees. Each treebank has its own annotation flavor, and the Prague treebank annotates other levels of information as well, such as topic and focus structure of the sentence, but we only show the dependency tree information here.

There are many variants of dependency syntactic analysis, but the basic textual format for a dependency tree can be written in the following form, where each dependent word specifies the head word in the sentence, and exactly one word is dependent to the root of the sentence. The following shows a typical textual representation of a labeled dependency tree:

Index	Word	Part of Speech	Head	Label
1	They	PRP	2	SBJ
2	persuaded	VBD	0	ROOT
3	Mr.	NNP	4	NMOD
4	Trotter	NNP	2	IOBJ
5	to	TO	6	VMOD
6	take	VB	2	OBJ
7	it	PRP	6	OBJ
8	back	RB	6	PRT
9	.	.	2	P

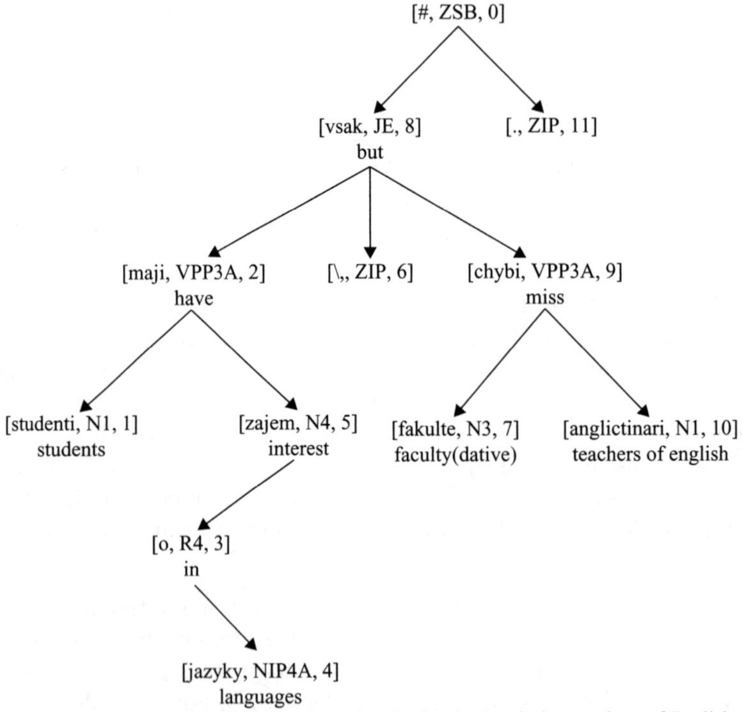

The students are interested in languages, but the faculty is missing teachers of English.

Figure 3–2: An example of a dependency graph syntax analysis for a Czech sentence taken from the Prague Dependency Treebank. Each node in the graph is a word, its part of speech, and the position of the word in the sentence; for example, [fakulte, N3, 7] is the seventh word in the sentence with POS tag N3, which also tells us that the word has dative case. The node [#,ZSB,0] is the root node of the dependency tree. The English equivalent is provided for each node

An important notion in dependency analysis is the notion of **projectivity**, which is a constraint imposed by the linear order of words on the dependencies between words [14]. A **projective dependency tree** is one where if we put the words in a linear order based

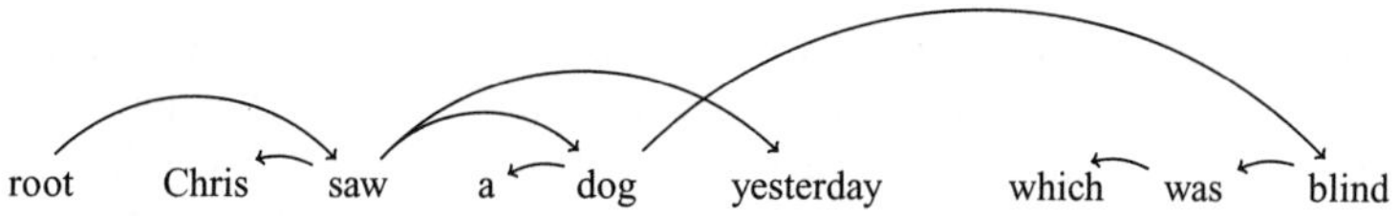

Figure 3–3: An unlabeled nonprojective dependency tree with a crossing dependency

Table 3–1: A multilingual comparison of percentage of crossing dependencies and percentage of sentences with nonprojectivity taken from the CoNLL 2007 shared task data set. Ar = Arabic, Ba = Basque, Ca = Catalan, Ch = Chinese, Cz = Czech, En = English, Gr = Greek, Hu = Hungarian, It = Italian, Tu = Turkish. Note that in some cases the dependency trees were created by conversion via heuristic rules from an original phrase structure tree. From Nivre et al. [13]

	Ar	Ba	Ca	Ch	Cz	En	Gr	Hu	It	Tu
% deps	0.4	2.9	0.1	0.0	1.9	0.3	1.1	2.9	0.5	5.5
% sents	10.1	26.2	2.9	0.0	23.2	6.7	20.3	26.4	7.4	33.3

on the sentence with the root symbol in the first position, the dependency arcs can be drawn above the words without any crossing dependencies. Another way to state projectivity is to say that for each word in the sentence, its descendants form a contiguous substring of the sentence. For example, Figure 3–3 shows a natural analysis of an English sentence that contains an extraposition to the right of a noun phrase modifier phrase, which as a result requires a crossing dependency. However, English has very few cases in a treebank that will need such a nonprojective analysis. In other languages, such Czech and Turkish, the number of nonprojective dependencies can be much higher. As a percentage of the total number of dependencies, crossing dependencies even in those languages are a small percentage. However, a substantial percentage of sentences contain at least one crossing dependency, making it an important issue in some languages. Table 3–1 contains a multilingual comparison of crossing dependencies across the languages that were part of the CoNLL 2007 shared task on dependency parsing.

Dependency graphs in treebanks do not explicitly distinguish between projective and **nonprojective dependency tree** analyses. However, parsing algorithms are sometimes forced to distinguish between projective and nonprojective dependencies. Let us examine this distinction further using CFGs. Note that we can set up dependency links in a CFG. For example, consider the following grammar:

```
X0_2 -> X0_1* X2_1
X0_1 -> x0*
X2_1 -> X1_1 X2_2*
X1_1 -> x1*
X2_2 -> X2_3* X3_1
X2_3 -> x2*
X3_1 -> x3*
```

In this CFG, the terminal symbols are `x0, x1, x2, x3`, and the asterisk picks out a single symbol in the right-hand side of each rule that specifies the dependency links. We can view the asterisk as either a separate annotation on the nonterminal or simply as a new nonterminal in the probabilistic context-free grammar (PCFG). Abney [15] provides a detailed comparison of the PCFG form for projective dependency graphs and discusses their equivalence in detail. In this example, the dependency tree equivalent to the preceding CFG is as follows:

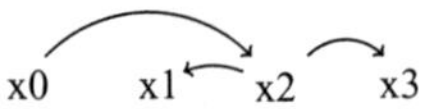

We can show that if we can convert a dependency tree into an equivalent CFG (using the notation used above), then the dependency tree must be projective. In a CFG converted from a dependency tree, we have only the following three types of rules with one type of rule to introduce the terminal symbols and two rules where Y is dependent on X or vice versa. The head word of X or Y can be traced by following the asterisk symbol.

```
Z -> X* Y
Z -> X Y*
A -> a*
```

Assume that we have a nonprojective dependency tree. For example,

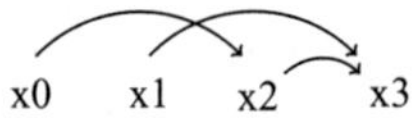

Converting such a dependency tree to a CFG with the asterisk notation gives us two options. Either we can capture that X3 depends on X2 but fail to capture that X1 depends on X3:

```
X2_3 -> X1_1 X2_2*
X1_1 -> x1
X2_2 -> X2_1* X3_1
X2_1 -> x2
X3_1 -> x3
```

or we can capture the fact that X1 depends on X3 but fail to capture that X3 depends on X2:

```
X2_3 -> X1_1 X3_2*
X1_1 -> x1
X3_2 -> X2_1 X3_1*
X2_1 -> x2
X3_1 -> x3
```

In fact, there is no CFG that can capture the nonprojective dependency. Recall that projectivity can be defined as follows: for each word in the sentence, its descendants form a contiguous substring of the sentence. Thus, nonprojectivity can be defined as follows: a nonprojective dependency means that there is a word in the sentence (or equivalently a nonterminal in the CFG created from the dependency tree) such that its descendants do not form a contiguous substring of the sentence. Put another way, there is a nonterminal Z such that Z derives spans (x_i, x_k) and (x_{k+p}, x_j) for some $p > 0$. This means there must be a rule $Z \rightarrow PQ$ where P derives (x_1, x_k) and Q derives (x_{k+p}, x_j). However, by definition, this is only valid in CFGs if $k = 0$ because P and Q *must* be contiguous substrings. Hence no dependency tree with nonprojective dependencies can be converted into an equivalent (asterisk-marked) CFG.

This gives a useful characterization of projective dependencies in terms of CFG. If we want a dependency parser to only produce projective dependencies, we can implicitly create an equivalent CFG that will ignore all nonprojective dependencies. We explore this topic further when we discuss parsing algorithms.

3.3.2 Syntax Analysis Using Phrase Structure Trees

A phrase structure syntax analysis of a sentence derives from the traditional sentence diagrams that partition a sentence into constituents, and larger constituents are formed by merging smaller ones. Phrase structure analysis also typically incorporate ideas from generative grammar (from linguistics) to deal with displaced constituents or apparent long-distance relationships between heads and constituents. A phrase structure tree can be viewed as implicitly having a predicate-argument structure associated with it. For example, the following phrase structure analysis of the sentence *Mr. Baker seems especially sensitive*, taken from the Penn Treebank, shows that the subject of the sentence is marked with the -SBJ marker and the predicate of the sentence is marked with the -PRD marker. The underlying predicate-argument structure is shown below the tree using an informal notation that captures the information implied by the phrase structure tree.

```
(S (NP-SBJ (NNP Mr.)
           (NNP Baker))
   (VP (VBZ seems)
       (ADJP-PRD (RB especially)
                 (JJ sensitive))))

Predicate-argument structure:
seems((especially(sensitive))(Mr. Baker))
```

The same sentence gets the following dependency tree analysis. Note how some of the information from the bracketing labels from the phrase structure analysis gets mapped onto the labeled arcs of the dependency analysis. Typically, dependency analysis would not link the subject with the predicate directly because it would create an inconvenient crossing dependency with the dependency between *seems* and the root symbol.

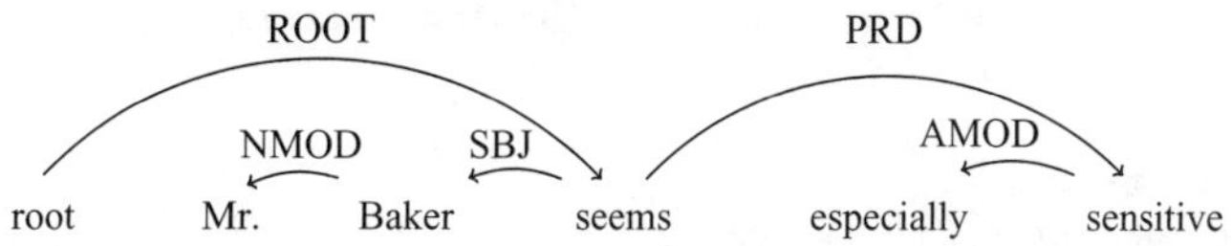

To explain some details of phrase structure analysis in treebanks, we use some examples of syntax analysis that show how null elements (constituents with no yield) are used to localize certain predicate-argument dependencies in the tree structure. The examples are taken from a paper [16] describing the annotation guidelines for the English Penn Treebank, which was a project that annotated 40,000 sentences from the *Wall Street Journal* with phrase structure trees. The POS tags for the words are omitted to simplify the tree.

In the first example, we see that an NP dominates a trace *T*, which is a null element, the same as an epsilon symbol in formal language theory, having no yield in the input. This empty trace has an index (here it is 1, but the actual value is not important) and is associated with the WHNP constituent with the same index. This co-indexation allows us to infer the predicate-argument structure shown below the tree.

```
(SBARQ (WHNP-1 What)
       (SQ is (NP-SBJ Tim)
              (VP eating (NP *T*-1)))
       ?)

Predicate-argument structure:
eat(Tim, what)
```

In the second example, the subject of the sentence, *The ball*, is actually not the logical subject of the predicate, which has been displaced due to the passive construction. The logical subject of the sentence, *Chris*, is marked as -LGS, enabling the recovery of the predicate argument structure for this sentence.

```
(S (NP-SBJ-1 The ball)
   (VP was (VP thrown)
           (NP *-1)
           (PP by (NP-LGS Chris))))

Predicate-argument structure:
throw(Chris, the ball)
```

The third example shows that different syntactic phenomena are often combined in the corpus, and both the analyses are combined to provide the predicate-argument structure in such cases.

```
(SBARQ (WHNP-1 Who)
       (SQ was (NP-SBJ-2 *T*-1)
               (VP believed (S (NP-SBJ-3 *-2)
                               (VP to (VP have
                                          (VP been
                                            (VP shot
                                              (NP *-3))))))))
       ?)

Predicate-argument structure:
believe(*someone*, shoot(*someone*, who))
```

The fourth pair of examples shows how null elements are used to annotate the presence of a subject for a predicate even if it is not explicit in the sentence. In the first case, the phrase structure annotation in the treebank marks the missing subject for *take back* as the object of the verb *persuaded.*

```
(S (NP-SBJ (PRP They))
   (VP (VP (VBD persuaded)
           (NP-1 (NNP Mr.)
                 (NNP Trotter))
           (S (NP-SBJ (-NONE- *-1))
              (VP (TO to)
                  (VP (VB take)
                      (NP (PRP it))
                      (PRT (RB back))))))))

Predicate argument structure:
persuade(they, Mr. Trotter, take_back(Mr. Trotter, it))
```

In the first case, the phrase structure annotation in the treebank marks the missing subject for *take back* as the subject of the verb *promised.*

```
(S (NP-SBJ-1 (PRP They))
   (VP (VP (VBD promised)
           (NP (NNP Mr.)
                 (NNP Trotter))
           (S (NP-SBJ (-NONE- *-1))
              (VP (TO to)
                  (VP (VB take)
                      (NP (PRP it))
                      (PRT (RB back))))))))

Predicate argument structure:
promise(they, Mr. Trotter, take_back(they, it))
```

The dependency analysis for *persuaded* and *promised* do not make such a distinction. The dependency analysis for the two sentences in the preceding pair of examples would be identical, as follows.

```
1 They      PRP 2 SBJ          1 They     PRP 2 SBJ
2 persuaded VBD 0 ROOT         2 promised VBD 0 ROOT
3 Mr.       NNP 4 NMOD         3 Mr.      NNP 4 NMOD
4 Trotter   NNP 2 IOBJ         4 Trotter  NNP 2 IOBJ
5 to        TO  6 VMOD         5 to       TO  6 VMOD
6 take      VB  2 OBJ          6 take     VB  2 OBJ
7 it        PRP 6 OBJ          7 it       PRP 6 OBJ
8 back      RB  6 PRT          8 back     RB  6 PRT
9 .         .   2 P            9 .        .   2 P
```

However, while pointing out these differences in annotation philosophy between dependency and phrase structure treebanks, it is important to note that most statistical parsers that are trained using phrase structure treebanks typically ignore these differences. The rich annotation of logical subjects, null elements, and so on, are all but ignored in modern statistical parsers. There has been some interest in recovering the null elements that were originally annotated in the Penn Treebank for English and discarded during training a statistical parser. For instance, a postprocessing step described by Johnson [17] recovers empty elements and identifies their antecedents. The evaluation scheme presented by Rimell, Clark, and Steedman [18] shows how to compare different parsers in terms of the recovery of the underlying predicate-argument structure of each sentence of the type shown in the previous examples.

In different treebanks for the same language, or in treebanks for different languages, there might be many differences in the phrase structure annotation. The differences could be in the choice of symbols and what they represent. In the following example from the Chinese treebank, the symbol *IP* is used instead of *S*, which reflects a move from the English Penn Treebank's predominantly transformational grammar–based phrase structure to government binding (GB)–based phrase structures. The differences could also be related to specific syntactic construction. In the following example, the possessive marker 的 is given a particular analysis that results in a fairly complex structural analysis with several null elements for 新 的, with a null WHNP even though Chinese has no relative pronouns. This structure is motivated by the perceived need for a uniform and consistent phrase structure for clauses and clause-like constituents throughout the treebank. Such differences mean that a phrase structure parser developed initially for English parsing and trained on the English treebank may not be easily portable to another language even though a phrase structure treebank exists for that language. Levy and Manning [19] discuss the many challenges in taking a CFG-based parser initially developed for English parsing and adapting it to Chinese parsing by training on the Chinese phrase structure treebank.

```
(IP (NP-SBJ (NP (NN 结售/settlement and sale)
                (NN 制度/system))
            (CC 和/and)
            (NP (CP (WHNP-2 (-NONE- *OP*))
                    (CP (IP (NP-SBJ (-NONE- *T*-2))
                            (VP (VA 新/new)))
                        (DEC 的)))
                (NP (NN 核销/verification and cancellation)
                    (NN 制度/system))))
    (VP (PP-LOC (P 在/in)
                (NP-PN (NR 西藏/Tibet)))
        (ADVP (AD 全面/fully))
        (VP (VV 实施/operating))))

English translation:
A (foreign exchange) settlement and sale system and a verification and
cancellation system that is newly created is fully operational in Tibet.
```

3.4 Parsing Algorithms

Given an input sentence, a parser produces an output analysis of that sentence, which we now assume is the analysis that is consistent with a treebank used to train a parser. Treebank parsers do not need to have an explicit grammar, but to make the explanation of parsing algorithms simpler we first consider parsing algorithms that assume the existence of a CFG.

Consider the following simple CFG G that can be used to derive strings such as *a and b or c* from the start symbol `N`.

```
N -> N 'and' N
N -> N 'or' N
N -> 'a' | 'b' | 'c'
```

An important concept for parsing is a **derivation**. For the input string *a and b or c*, the following sequence of actions separated by the `=>` symbol represents a sequence of steps called a derivation:

```
N
=> N 'or' N
=> N 'or c'
=> N 'and' N 'or c'
=> N 'and b or c'
=> 'a and b or c'
```

In this derivation, each line is called a **sentential form**. Furthermore, each line of the derivation applies a rule from the CFG to show that the input can, in fact, be derived from the start symbol `N`. In the above derivation, we restricted ourselves to only expand on the rightmost nonterminal in each sentential form. This method is called the **rightmost derivation** of the input using a CFG. An interesting property of a rightmost derivation is revealed if we arrange the derivation in reverse order:

```
'a and b or c'
=> N 'and b or c'         # use rule N -> a
=> N 'and' N 'or c'       # use rule N -> b
=> N 'or c'               # use rule N -> N and N
=> N 'or' N               # use rule N -> c
=> N                      # use rule N -> N or N
```

This derivation sequence exactly corresponds to the construction of the following parse tree from left to right, one symbol at a time.

```
(N (N (N a)
      and
      (N b))
   or
   (N c))
```

However, a unique derivation sequence is not guaranteed. There can be many different derivations, and as we saw before, the number of derivations can be exponential in the input length. For example, there is another rightmost derivation that results in the following parse tree:

```
(N (N a)
   and
   (N (N b)
      or
```

```
  (N c)))
'a and b or c'
=> N 'and b or c'       # use rule N -> a
=> N 'and' N 'or c'     # use rule N -> b
=> N 'and' N 'or' N     # use rule N -> c
=> N 'and' N            # use rule N -> N or N
=> N                    # use rule N -> N and N
```

3.4.1 Shift-Reduce Parsing

To build a parser, we need to create an algorithm that can perform the steps in the preceding rightmost derivation for any grammar and for any input string. Every CFG turns out to have an automaton that is equivalent to it, called a pushdown automaton (just like regular expressions can be converted to finite-state automata). A pushdown automaton is simply a finite-state automaton with some additional memory in the form of a stack (or pushdown). This is a limited amount of memory because only the top of the stack is used by the machine. This provides an algorithm for parsing that is general for any given CFG and input string. The algorithm is called **shift-reduce** parsing, which uses two data structures, a buffer for input symbols and a stack for storing CFG symbols, and is defined as follows:

1. Start with an empty stack and the buffer containing the input string.
2. Exit with success if the top of the stack contains the start symbol of the grammar and if the buffer is empty.
3. Choose between the following two steps (if the choice is ambiguous, choose one based on an oracle):
   - Shift a symbol from the buffer onto the stack.
   - If the top k symbols of the stack are $\alpha_1 \ldots \alpha_k$, which corresponds to the right-hand side of a CFG rule $A \rightarrow \alpha_1 \ldots \alpha_k$, then replace the top k symbols with the left-hand side nonterminal A.
4. Exit with failure if no action can be taken in previous step.
5. Else, go to step 2.

For the CFG G shown earlier in this section and for the input *a and b or c*, we show the individual steps in the shift-reduce parsing algorithm in Figure 3–4.

The same algorithm can also be applied for dependency parsing, as can be seen by the example in Figure 3–5 of using a shift-reduce parser for dependency parsing. At each step, the parser has a choice: either shift a new token into the stack or combine the top two elements of the stack with a head $\rightarrow$ dependent link or a dependent $\leftarrow$ head link. When using the shift-reduce algorithm in a statistical dependency parser, it helps to combine a shift and reduce action when possible. Other variants that vary the link between parser actions and statistical decisions are discussed by Nivre [20].

Parse Tree	Stack	Input	Action
		a and b or c	Init
a	a	and b or c	shift a
(N a)	N	and b or c	reduce `N -> a`
(N a) and	N and	b or c	shift and
(N a) and b	N and b	or c	shift b
(N a) and (N b)	N and N	or c	reduce `N -> b`
(N (N a) and (N b))	N	or c	reduce `N -> a`
(N (N a) and (N b)) or	N or	c	shift or
(N (N a) and (N b)) or c	N or c		shift c
(N (N a) and (N b)) or (N c)	N or N		reduce `N -> c`
(N (N (N a) and (N b)) or (N c))	N		reduce `N -> N or N`
(N (N (N a) and (N b)) or (N c))	N		Accept!

Figure 3–4: The individual steps of the shift-reduce parsing algorithm for the input *a and b or c* for the grammar G defined at the beginning of this section

Dependency Tree	Stack	Input	Action
root	root	a and b or c	Init
root a	root a	and b or c	shift a
root a and	root a and	b or c	shift and
root a and	root and	b or c	a ← and
root a and b	root and b	or c	shift b
root a and b	root and	or c	and → b
root a and b or	root and or	c	shift or
root a and b or	root or	c	and ← or
root a and b or c	root or c		shift c
root a and b or c	root or		or → c
root a and b or c	root		root → or

Figure 3–5: Steps of the shift-reduce parsing algorithm for dependency parsing

3.4.2 Hypergraphs and Chart Parsing

Shift-reduce parsing allows a linear time parse but requires access to an oracle. For general CFGs in the worst case, such a parser might have to resort to backtracking, which means reparsing the input, which leads to a time that is exponential in the grammar size in the worst case. On the other hand, CFGs do have a worst-case parsing algorithm that can run in $\mathcal{O}(n^3)$ where n is the length of the input. Variants of this algorithm are often used in statistical parsers that attempt to search the space of possible parse trees without the limitation of purely left-to-right parsing.

Our example CFG G:

```
N -> N 'and' N
N -> N 'or' N
N -> 'a' | 'b' | 'c'
```

is rewritten into a new CFG G_c where the right-hand side only contains up to two nonterminals. This is done by introducing two new nonterminals, `N^` and `Nv`:

```
N -> N N^
N^ -> 'and' N
N -> N Nv
Nv -> 'or' N
N -> 'a' | 'b' | 'c'
```

A key insight into this family of parsing algorithms is that we can specialize the above CFG G_c to a particular input string by creating a new CFG that represents a compact encoding of all possible parse trees that are valid in grammar G_c for this particular input sentence. For example, for input string *a and b or c*, this new CFG G_f that represents the **forest** of parse trees is shown below. Imagine that the input string is broken up into spans *0 a 1 and 2 b 3 or 4 c 5* so that *a* is span 0,1 and the string *b or c* is the span 2,5 in this string. The nonterminals in this forest grammar G_c include the span information. The different parse trees that can be generated using this grammar are the valid parse trees for the input sentence.

```
N[0,5] -> N[0,1] N^[1,5]
N[0,3] -> N[0,1] N^[1,3]
N^[1,3] -> 'and'[1,2] N[2,3]
N^[1,5] -> 'and'[1,2] N[2,5]
N[0,5] -> N[0,3] Nv[3,5]
N[2,5] -> N[2,3] Nv[3,5]
Nv[3,5] -> 'or'[3,4] N[4,5]
N[0,1] -> 'a'[0,1]
N[2,3] -> 'b'[2,3]
N[4,5] -> 'c'[4,5]
```

In this view, a parsing algorithm is defined as taking as input a CFG and an input string and producing a specialized CFG that is a compact representation of all legal parses for the input (see Figure 3–6). A parser has to create all the valid specialized rules or alternatively

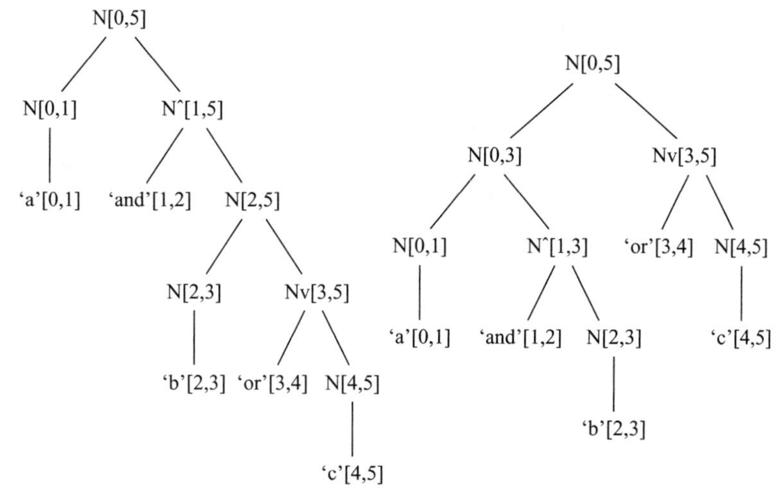

Figure 3–6: Parse trees embedded in the *specialized* CFG for a particular input string. The nodes with the same label, such as N[0,5], N[0,1], and [1,2], N[2,3], and Nv[3,5], can be merged to form a hypergraph representation of all parses for the input

create a path from the start symbol nonterminal that spans the entire string to the leaf nodes that are the input tokens.

Let us examine the steps the parser has to take to construct a specialized CFG. First let us consider the rules that generate only lexical items:

```
N[0,1] -> 'a'[0,1]
N[2,3] -> 'b'[2,3]
N[4,5] -> 'c'[4,5]
```

These rules can be constructed by simply checking for the existence of rules of the type $N \rightarrow x$ for any input token x and creating a specialized rule for token x. In pseudocode this step can be written as follows:

```
for i = 0...n do
  if N → x with score s for any x spanning i, i+1 exists then
    add specialized rule N[i, i+1] → x[i, i+1] with score s
    written as N[i, i+1] : s
  end if
end for
```

The next step recursively creates new specialized rules based on previously created specialized rules. If we see that $Y[i,k]$ and $Z[k,j]$ exist as left-hand sides of previously created specialized rules, then if there is a rule in the CFG of the type $X \rightarrow YZ$, we can infer that there should be a new specialized rule $X[i,j] \rightarrow Y[i,k]Z[k,j]$. Each nonterminal span is assigned a score s, $X[i,j] : s$. Only the highest scoring span for each nonterminal needs to be retained, so $X[i,j] = \max_s X[i,j] : s$.

```
for j = 2...n do
  for i = j − 1...0 do
    for k = i + 1...j do
      if Y[i,k] : s1 and Z[k,j] : s2 are in the specialized grammar then
        if X → YZ with score s exists in the original grammar then
          add specialized rule X[i,j] → Y[i,k]Z[k,j] with score s + s1 + s2
          keep only the highest scoring rule: X[i,j] → α
        end if
      end if
    end for
  end for
end for
```

This is called the CKY algorithm (named after Cocke, Kasami, and Younger who all discovered it independently). It considers every span of every length and splits up that span in every possible way to see if a CFG rule can be used to derive the span. Eventually we are guaranteed to find a rule that spans the entire input string if such a rule exists. Examining the loop structure of the algorithm shows that it takes n^3 time for an input of size n. However, exhaustively listing all trees from the specialized CFG will take exponential time in the worst case (by the reasoning we already covered about the number of trees possible in the worst case for CFGs). However, picking the most likely tree by using supervised machine learning will take no more than n^3 time.

Notice that for each span i, j and for each nonterminal X, we only keep the highest scoring way to reach $X[i,j]$. Thus, starting from the start symbol that spans the entire string $S[0][n]$ with the highest score, we can create the best-scoring parse tree by expanding the right-hand side of $S[0][n]$ and continue this process recursively to the terminal symbols. This gives us the best-scoring parse tree for a given sentence.

In a probabilistic setting, where the scores can be interpreted as log probabilities, this is called the Viterbi-best parse. Each cell contains the log probability of deriving the string $w[i,j]$ starting with nonterminal X, which can be written as $\Pr(X \Rightarrow^* w[i,j])$. Notice that the utility of a nonterminal X at a particular span i, j depends on reaching the start symbol S, which is captured by the outside probability $\Pr(S \Rightarrow^* w[0, i-1]Xw[j+1, N])$. Ideally we would like to use both the inside and the outside probabilities to compute the utility of each rule starting with $X[i,j]$.

There are ways to speed up the parser by throwing away less likely parts of the search space. For instance, we can compare the score of $X[i,j]$ with the score of the current highest scoring entry $Y[i,j]$ and throw away any rule starting with $X[i,j]$ if it is extremely unlikely compared to $Y[i,j]$. This could lead to a search error (where the highest scoring tree is missed), but it is very unlikely to happen, and we can trade off accuracy for a much faster parsing time. This technique is called beam thresholding. We can additionally augment this by looking at global ways to threshold entries. For instance, a rule starting with $X[i,j]$ cannot be viable if it does not have neighboring rules that can combine with it. Such a technique is called global thresholding. If we have a very complex set of nonterminals, such as the ones shown in Figure 3–7, then we could parse first with

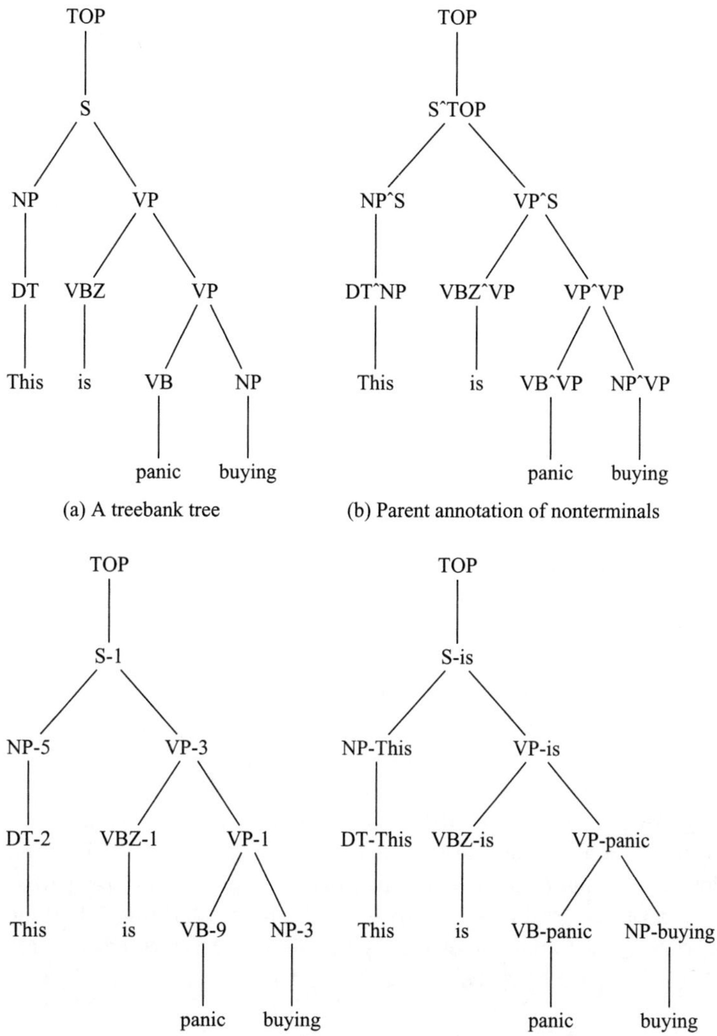

(a) A treebank tree

(b) Parent annotation of nonterminals

(c) Automatic split-merge of nonterminals into subcategories

(d) Lexicalization of the nonterminals

Figure 3–7: A treebank tree that is transformed in order to remove independence assumptions that hurt parsing performance: (a) is the original treebank tree, and a PCFG is easily extracted from that data; (b) grafts the parent node label onto each node label; (c) uses unsupervised learning to create subcategories for each nonterminal; and (d) uses lexical items percolated through the tree via lexicalizing nonterminals

a coarser nonterminal to prune the finer grained nonterminal (e.g., using simply a VP nonterminal instead of a VP^S nonterminal), and then use the scores associated with the coarse $VP[i, j]$ nonterminal to prune the finer grained nonterminals for the same span.

This approach is called coarse to fine parsing and it is particularly useful because the outside probability of the coarse step can be used in addition to the inside probability for more effective pruning. These three techniques, beam thresholding, global thresholding, and coarse to fine pruning, are all covered in a paper by Joshua Goodman on parsing PCFGs [21].

The parser can be sped up even further by using A^* search rather than the exhaustive search used in the algorithm shown previously [22]. A rich choice of heuristics can drive A^* search, which can be used to provide faster observed times for parsing while the asymptotic worst-case complexity remains the same as the CKY algorithm.

For projective dependency parsing, the same algorithm can be used by creating a CFG that produces dependency parses (as we showed in an earlier section). However, for dependency parsing, the above loop takes worst-case n^5 time because each Y and Z is lexicalized and in the worst case there can be n different Y nonterminals and n different Z nonterminals, giving us n^2 different possible combinations in the innermost loop of the CKY algorithm.

However, for dependency parsing, Eisner [23] observed that rather than using nonterminals augmented with words, it would be advantageous to represent compactly the set of different dependency trees for each span of the input string. The idea is to collect the left and the right dependents of each head independently and combine them at a later stage. This leads to the notion of a **split-head** where the head word is split into two: one for the left and the other for the right dependents. In addition to the head word, in each item we store for each span, we store whether the head is gathering left or right dependents and whether the item is complete (a complete item cannot be extended with more dependents). This provides an n^3 worst-case dependency parsing algorithm. This also reduces the number of intermediate states considered by not allowing any interleaving of left and right dependencies, unlike the CKY parser for dependency parsing.

The following pseudocode (from Ryan McDonald's thesis [24]) describes the Eisner algorithm in full detail. The spans are stored in a chart data-structure C, e.g. $C[i][j]$ refers to the dependency analysis of span i, j. Incomplete spans are referred to as C^i, complete spans are C^c. Spans that are being grown toward the left (adding left dependencies only) are referred to as $C_{\leftarrow}$, and spans growing to the right are referred to as $C_{\rightarrow}$. For $C_{\leftarrow}[i][j]$ the head must be j, and for $C_{\rightarrow}[i][j]$ the head must be i.

```
Initialize: for s = 1..n chart C^c_d[s][s] = 0.0 for d ∈ {←, →} and c ∈ {i, c}
for k = 1...n do
  for s = 1...n do
    t = s + k
    break if t > n
    first: create incomplete items
    C^i_←[s][t] = max_{s≤r<t} C^c_→[s][r] + C^c_←[r+1][t] + s(t, s)
    C^i_→[s][t] = max_{s≤r<t} C^c_→[s][r] + C^c_←[r+1][t] + s(s, t)
    second: create complete items
    C^c_←[s][t] = max_{s≤r<t} C^c_←[s][r] + C^i_←[r][t]
    C^c_→[s][t] = max_{s≤r<t} C^i_→[s][r] + C^c_→[r][t]
  end for
end for
```

We assume a unique root node as the leftmost token (as before). The score of the best tree for the entire sentence is in $C^{c}_{\rightarrow}[1][n]$. In addition to running in $\mathcal{O}(n^3)$, this algorithm can be extended to provide k-best parses with a complexity of $\mathcal{O}(n^3 k \log k)$.

3.4.3 Minimum Spanning Trees and Dependency Parsing

Finding the optimum branching in a directed graph is closely related to the problem of finding a minimum spanning tree in an undirected graph. The directed graph case is of interest because it corresponds to a dependency tree, which is always rooted and cannot have cycles. A prerequisite is that each potential dependency link between words should have a score. In NLP, the tradition is to use the term **minimum spanning tree** (MST) to refer to the optimum branching problem in directed graphs. In the case of parsing with a dependency treebank, we assume we have some model that can be used to provide such a score based on estimates of likelihood of each dependency link in the dependency tree. These scores can be used to find the MST, which is the highest scoring dependency tree. Because the linear order of the words in the input is not taken into account in the MST formulation, crossing or nonprojective dependencies can be recovered by such a parser. This can be an issue in languages that are predominantly projective, like English, but provide a natural way to recover the crossing dependencies in languages like Czech.

Rather than provide pseudocode for the MST algorithm for dependency parsing (which is provided in McDonald [24]), we show how the MST algorithm works using an example dependency parse using this algorithm.

Let us consider the following fully connected graph for the input sentence *John saw Mary.* The edges have weights based on some scoring function on edges (these scores come from various features that are computed on the edge, as explained in the next section).

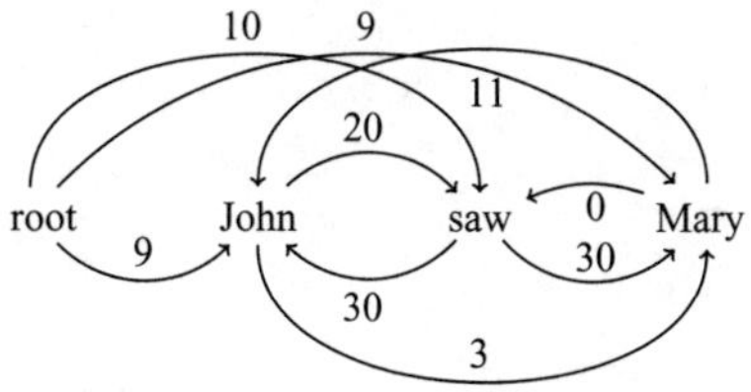

The first step is to find the highest scoring *incoming* edge. If this step results in a tree, then we report this as the parse because it would have to be an MST. In this example, however, after we pick only the highest scoring incoming edges from the graph, we do have a cycle.

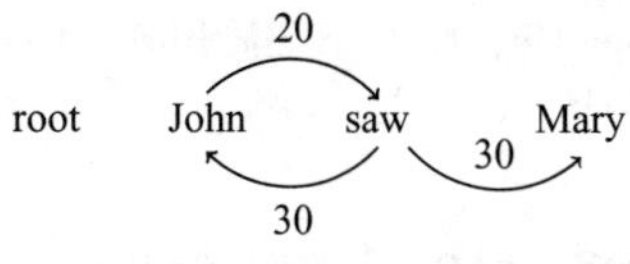

We can contract the cycle into a single node, and we recalculate the edge weights. When we compute the edge weights from each node to that contracted node, we also have to keep track of which component of the merged node is the one with maximum weight. For example, in the preceding graph, we compare the incoming edge: *root* $\rightarrow$ $\boxed{saw \rightarrow John}$: wt = 40 with *root* $\rightarrow$ $\boxed{John \rightarrow saw}$: wt = 29 and compare the incoming edge: *Mary* $\rightarrow$ $\boxed{saw \rightarrow John}$: wt = 30 with *Mary* $\rightarrow$ $\boxed{John \rightarrow saw}$: wt = 31 to obtain the ones with maximum weight shown below:

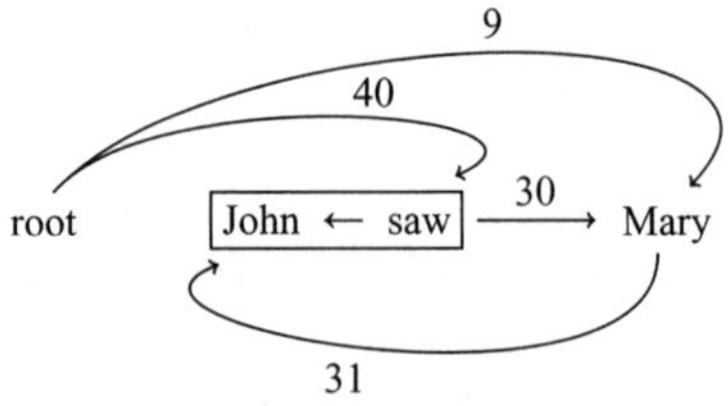

We now run the MST algorithm recursively on this graph, which means finding the graph with the best incoming edges to each word. In this case it means comparing *root* $\rightarrow$ *Mary* $\rightarrow$ $\boxed{John\text{-}saw}$: wt $= 9 + 31$ with *root* $\rightarrow$ $\boxed{John\text{-}saw}$ $\rightarrow$ *Mary:* wt $= 40 + 30$ which results in the following graph:

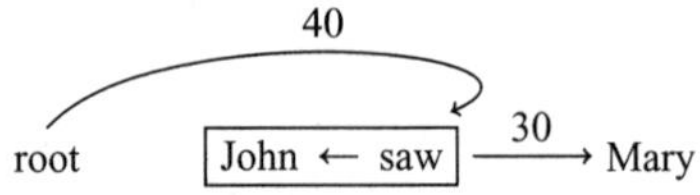

Unwinding the recursive step provides us with the MST that is the highest scoring dependency parse of the input:

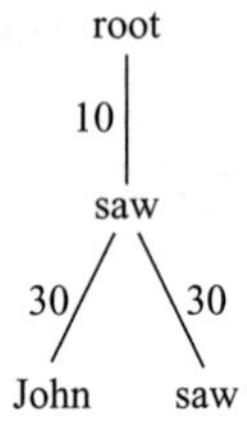

3.5 Models for Ambiguity Resolution in Parsing

In this section we focus on the modeling aspect of parsing: how to design features and ways to resolve ambiguity in parsing. Using these models to parse efficiently is covered in Section 3.4 when we discuss parsing algorithms. The algorithms from that section are used by the models described in this section to find the highest scoring parse tree or dependency analysis and sometimes to train the models as well.

3.5.1 Probabilistic Context-Free Grammars

Consider the ambiguity problem we discussed earlier, where we would like to choose between the following ambiguous parses for the sentence *John bought a shirt with pockets.*

```
(S (NP John)
   (VP (VP (V bought)
           (NP (D a)
               (N shirt)))
       (PP (P with)
           (NP pockets))))
```

```
(S (NP John)
   (VP (V bought)
       (NP (NP (D a)
               (N shirt))
           (PP (P with)
               (NP pockets)))))
```

We want to provide a model that matches the intuition that the second tree above is preferred over the first. The parses can be thought of as ambiguous (leftmost or rightmost) derivations of the following CFG.

```
S -> NP VP
NP -> 'John' | 'pockets' | D N | NP PP
VP -> V NP | VP PP
V -> 'bought'
D -> 'a'
N -> 'shirt'
PP -> P NP
P -> 'with'
```

We can add scores or probabilities to the rules in this CFG in order to provide a score or probability for each derivation. The probability of a derivation is the sum of scores or product of probabilities of all the CFG rules used in that derivation. Because scores can be viewed simply as log probabilities, we use the term probabilistic context-free grammar (PCFG) when scores or probabilities are assigned to CFG rules. To make sure the probability of the set of trees generated by a PCFG is well defined, we assign probabilities to the CFG rules such that for a rule $N \rightarrow \alpha$, the probability is $P(N \rightarrow \alpha \mid N)$; that is, each rule probability is conditioned on the left-hand side of the rule. This means that during the context-free expansion of a nonterminal, the probability is distributed among all the expansions of the nonterminals. In other words,

$$1 = \sum_{\alpha} P(N \rightarrow \alpha)$$

So in our example, we can assign probabilities to rules in the CFG to obtain the result we want—the more plausible parse gets the higher probability.

```
S -> NP VP (1.0)
NP -> 'John' (0.1) | 'pockets' (0.1) | D N (0.3) | NP PP (0.5)
VP -> V NP (0.9) | VP PP (0.1)
V -> 'bought' (1.0)
D -> 'a' (1.0)
N -> 'shirt' (1.0)
PP -> P NP (1.0)
P -> 'with' (1.0)
```

From these rule probabilities, the only deciding factor for choosing between the two parses for *John bought a shirt with pockets* is the two rules `NP -> NP PP` and `VP -> VP PP` because all the other rules in one parse also occur in the other. Because the probability for `NP -> NP PP` is set higher in the preceding PCFG, the most plausible analysis gets the higher probability.

The rule probabilities can be derived from a treebank, as we can observe from the following example. Consider a treebank with three trees t_1, t_2, and t_3:

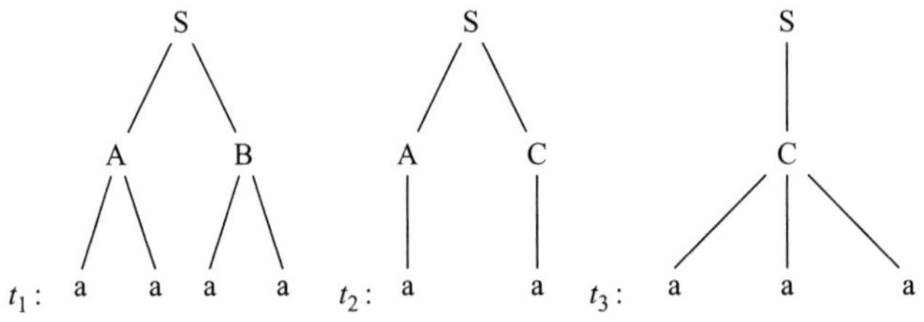

If we assume that tree t_1 occurred 10 times in the treebank, t_2 occurred 20 times, and t_3 occurred 50 times, then the PCFG we obtain from this treebank would be:

$$\begin{array}{lll}
\frac{10}{10+20+50} & = 0.125 & S \rightarrow A\ B \\
\frac{20}{10+20+50} & = 0.25 & S \rightarrow A\ C \\
\frac{50}{10+20+50} & = 0.625 & S \rightarrow C \\
\frac{10}{10+20} & = 0.334 & A \rightarrow a\ a \\
\frac{20}{10+20} & = 0.667 & A \rightarrow a \\
\frac{20}{20+50} & = 0.285 & B \rightarrow a\ a \\
\frac{50}{20+50} & = 0.714 & C \rightarrow a\ a\ a
\end{array}$$

For input $a\ a\ a\ a$ there are two parses using the above PCFG: The probability for

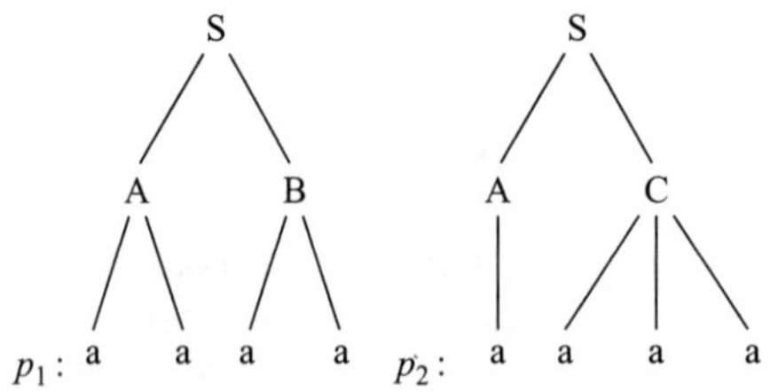

$p_1 = 0.125 \cdot 0.334 \cdot 0.285 = 0.01189$ and for $p_2 = 0.25 \cdot 0.667 \cdot 0.714 = 0.119$. The parse tree p_2 is the most likely tree for that input. The most likely parse tree does not even occur in the treebank! And the reason for this is the context-free nature of PCFGs, where a nonterminal can be expanded by any rule with that nonterminal in the left-hand side. To make appropriate independence assumptions, the usual approach in a statistical parser is to augment the node labels in order to avoid bad independence assumptions.

The Penn Treebank contains trees like those in Figure 3–7(a). The first approach was to remove some independence assumptions by annotating each nonterminal with the label of its parent [25]. The second approach [26] is to automatically learn these nonterminal splits by using an unsupervised learning algorithm (split-merge over trees using the expectation–maximization (EM) algorithm). The third approach [27] is to lexicalize the nonterminals, which leads to a better model because the words are included in the decision to attach an adjunct.

When each nonterminal is lexicalized, then the standard parsing algorithms have to be modified to work with heavily lexicalized rules. Lexicalized nonterminals have to be treated carefully in the model because sparsity is an issue with lexicalization. For lexicalized nonterminal PCFG, the unfolding history is created head outward: first predicting the head and producing the left siblings of the head and then the right siblings.

An alternative to finding the most likely tree for a given input is to find the most likely set of constituents. The idea is to find the best tree not with highest score but with the highest number of correct constituents. As shown in Goodman [28], the CKY algorithm (which we defined in §3.4.2) can be used to find the tree with the highest number of correct constituents by replacing the scoring function for each $X[i, j]$ to be the product of the inside and outside probability rather than just using the inside probability. This technique is often called max-rule parsing and can produce trees that are not valid PCFG parse trees, similar to the example we covered earlier. Max-rule parsing explicitly maximizes the recall at a per-constituent level and hence often gives higher recall scores in parser evaluations.

3.5.2 Generative Models for Parsing

To find the most plausible parse tree, the parser has to choose between the possible derivations each of which can be represented as a sequence of decisions. Let each derivation $D = d_1, \ldots, d_n$, which is the sequence of decisions used to build the parse tree. Then for input sentence x, the output parse tree y is defined by the sequence of steps in the derivation. We can introduce a probability for each derivation:

$$P(x, y) = P(d_1, \ldots, d_n) = \prod_{i=1}^{n} P(d_i \mid d_1, \ldots, d_{i-1})$$

The conditioning context in the probability $P(d_i \mid d_1, \ldots, d_{i-1})$ is called the **history** and corresponds to a partially built parse tree (as defined by the derivation sequence). We make a simplifying assumption that keeps the conditioning context to a finite set by grouping the histories into equivalence classes using a function Φ.

$$P(d_1, \ldots, d_n) = \prod_{i=1}^{n} P(d_i \mid \Phi(d_1, \ldots, d_{i-1}))$$

Using Φ, each history $H_i = d_1, \ldots, d_{i-1}$ for all x, y is mapped to some fixed finite set of feature functions of the history $\phi_1(H_i), \ldots, \phi_k(H_i)$. In terms of these k feature functions:

$$P(d_1, \ldots, d_n) = \prod_{i=1}^{n} P(d_i \mid \phi_1(H_i), \ldots, \phi_k(H_i))$$

However, the definition of PCFGs means that various other rule probabilities must be adjusted to obtain the right scoring of parses. Also, the independence assumptions in PCFG, which are dictated by the underlying CFG, often lead to bad models that cannot use information vital to the decision of rule scores, resulting in high-scoring plausible parses. We would like to model such ambiguities using arbitrary features of the parse tree. Discriminative methods provide us with such a class of models.

3.5.3 Discriminative Models for Parsing

Collins [29] extends the ideas from Freund and Schapire [30] to create a simple notation and framework that describes various discriminative approaches to learning for parsing (and also chunking or tagging). This framework is called a **global linear model** [29]. Let $\mathbf{x}$ be a set of inputs, and $\mathbf{y}$ be a set of possible outputs that can be a sequence of POS tags or a parse tree or a dependency analysis.

- Each $x \in \mathbf{x}$ and $y \in \mathbf{y}$ is mapped to a d-dimensional feature vector $\Phi(x,y)$, with each dimension being a real number, summarizing partial information contained in (x,y).
- A weight parameter vector $\mathbf{w} \in \Re^d$ assigns a weight to each feature in $\Phi(x,y)$, representing the importance of that feature. The value of $\Phi(x,y) \cdot \mathbf{w}$ is the score of (x,y). The higher the score, the more plausible it is that y is the output for x.
- The function $GEN(x)$ generates the set of possible outputs y for a given x.

Having $\Phi(x,y)$, $\mathbf{w}$, and $GEN(x)$ specified, we would like to choose the highest scoring candidate y^* from $GEN(x)$ as the most plausible output. That is,

$$F(x) = \operatorname*{argmax}_{y \in GEN(x)} p(y \mid x, \mathbf{w})$$

where $F(x)$ returns the highest scoring output y^* from $GEN(x)$. A **conditional random field** (CRF) [31] defines the conditional probability as a linear score for each candidate y and a *global* normalization term:

$$\log p(y \mid x, \mathbf{w}) = \Phi(x, y) \cdot \mathbf{w} - \log \sum_{y' \in GEN(x)} \exp(\Phi(x, y') \cdot \mathbf{w})$$

A simpler global linear model that ignores the normalization term is:

$$F(x) = \operatorname*{argmax}_{y \in GEN(x)} \Phi(x, y) \cdot \mathbf{w}$$

Many experimental results in parsing have shown that the simpler global linear model that ignores the normalization term (and is thus much faster to train) often provides the same accuracy when compared to the more expensively trained normalized models.

A perceptron [32] was originally introduced as a single-layered neural network. It is trained using online learning, that is, processing examples one at a time, during which it adjusts a weight parameter vector that can then be applied on input data to produce the corresponding output. The weight adjustment process awards features appearing in the truth and penalizes features not contained in the truth. After the update, the perceptron ensures that the current weight parameter vector is able to correctly classify the present training example.

Algorithm 3–1 The Original Perceptron Learning Algorithm

Inputs: Training Data $\langle (x_1, y_1), \ldots, (x_m, y_m) \rangle$; number of iterations T
Initialization: Set $\mathbf{w} = \mathbf{0}$
Algorithm:

```
for t = 1, ..., T do
  for i = 1, ..., m do
    Calculate y'_i, where y'_i = argmax_{y∈GEN(x)} Φ(x_i, y) · w
    if y'_i ≠ y_i then
      w = w + Φ(x_i, y_i) − Φ(x_i, y'_i)
    end if
  end for
end forOutput: The updated weight parameter vector w
```

Suppose we have m examples in the training set. The original perceptron learning algorithm [32] is shown in Algorithm 3–1.

The weight parameter vector $\mathbf{w}$ is initialized to $\mathbf{0}$. Then the algorithm iterates through those m training examples. For each example x, it generates a set of candidates $GEN(x)$, and picks the most plausible candidate, which has the highest score according to the current $\mathbf{w}$. After that, the algorithm compares the selected candidate with the truth, and if they are different from each other, $\mathbf{w}$ is updated by increasing the weight values for features appearing in the truth and by decreasing the weight values for features appearing in this top candidate. If the training data is linearly separable, meaning that it can be discriminated by a function that is a linear combination of features, the learning is proven to converge in a finite number of iterations [30].

This original perceptron learning algorithm is simple to understand and to analyze. However, the incremental weight updating suffers from overfitting, which tends to classify the training data better but at the cost of classifying the unseen data worse. Also, the algorithm is not capable of dealing with training data that is linearly inseparable.

Freund and Schapire [30] proposed a variant of the perceptron learning approach, the voted perceptron algorithm. Instead of storing and updating parameter values inside one weight vector, its learning process keeps track of all intermediate weight vectors, and these intermediate vectors are used in the classification phase to vote for the answer. The intuition is that good prediction vectors tend to survive for a long time and thus have larger weight in the vote. Algorithm 3–2 shows the voted perceptron training and prediction phases from Freund and Schapire, with slightly modified representation.

The voted perceptron keeps a count c_i to record the number of times a particular weight parameter vector $(\mathbf{w}_i, c_i)$ survives in the training. For a training example, if its selected top candidate is different from the truth, a new count c_{i+1}, being initialized to 1, is used, and an updated weight vector $(\mathbf{w}_{i+1}, c_{i+1})$ is produced; meanwhile, the original c_i and weight vector $(\mathbf{w}_i, c_i)$ are stored.

Compared with the original perceptron, the voted perceptron is more stable due to maintaining the list of intermediate weight vectors for voting. Nevertheless, to store those weight vectors is space inefficient. Also, the weight calculation, using all intermediate weight parameter vectors during the prediction phase, is time consuming.

Algorithm 3–2 The Voted Perceptron Algorithm

Training Phase

Input: Training data $\langle(x_1, y_1), \ldots, (x_m, y_m)\rangle$, number of iterations T

Initialization: $\mathrm{k} = 0$, $\mathbf{w}_0 = \mathbf{0}$, $c_1 = 0$

Algorithm:

```
for t = 1, ..., T do
  for i = 1, ..., m do
    Calculate y'_i, where y'_i = argmax_{y∈GEN(x)} Φ(x_i, y) · w_k
    if y'_i = y_i then
      c_k = c_k + 1
    else
      w_{k+1} = w_k + Φ(x_i, y_i) − Φ(x_i, y'_i)
      c_{k+1} = 1
      k = k + 1
    end if
  end for
end for
```

Output: A list of weight vectors $\langle(\mathbf{w}_1, c_1), \ldots, (\mathbf{w}_k, c_k)\rangle$

Prediction Phase

Input: The list of weight vectors $\langle(\mathbf{w}_1, c_1), \ldots, (\mathbf{w}_k, c_k)\rangle$, an unsegmented sentence x

Calculate:

$$y^* = \operatorname*{argmax}_{y \in GEN(x)} \left(\sum_{i=1}^{k} c_i \Phi(x, y) \cdot \mathbf{w}_i \right)$$

Output: The voted top ranked candidate y^*

The averaged perceptron algorithm [30] is an approximation to the voted perceptron that, on the other hand, maintains the stability of the voted perceptron algorithm but significantly reduces space and time complexities. In an averaged version, rather than using $\mathbf{w}$, the averaged weight parameter vector γ over the m training examples is used for future predictions on unseen data:

$$\gamma = \frac{1}{\mathrm{mT}} \sum_{i=1 \ldots m, t=1 \ldots T} \mathbf{w}^{i,t}$$

In calculating γ, an accumulating parameter vector σ is maintained and updated using $\mathbf{w}$ for each training example. After the last iteration, $\sigma/(\mathrm{mT})$ produces the final parameter vector γ. The entire algorithm is shown in Algorithm 3–3.

When the number of features is large, it is expensive to calculate the total parameter σ for each training example. To further reduce the time complexity, Collins [33] proposed

Algorithm 3–3 The Averaged Perceptron Learning Algorithm

Inputs: Training Data $\langle(x_1, y_1), \ldots, (x_m, y_m)\rangle$; number of iterations T
Initialization: Set $\mathbf{w} = \mathbf{0}$, $\gamma = \mathbf{0}$, $\sigma = \mathbf{0}$
Algorithm:

```
for t = 1, ..., T do
  for i = 1, ..., m do
    Calculate y'_i, where y'_i = argmax_{y∈GEN(x)} Φ(x_i, y) · w
    if y'_i ≠ y_i then
      w = w + Φ(x_i, y_i) − Φ(x_i, y'_i)
    end if
    σ = σ + w
  end for
end for
```

Output: The averaged weight parameter vector $\gamma = \sigma/(\mathrm{mT})$

a lazy update procedure that avoids the expensive update to the entire weight vector in each iteration. After processing each training sentence, not all dimensions of σ are updated. Instead, an update vector τ is used to store the exact location (p,t) where each dimension of the averaged parameter vector was last updated, and only those dimensions corresponding to features appearing in the current sentence are updated. p represents the training example index where this particular feature was last updated, and t represents its corresponding iteration number. For the last example in the final iteration, each dimension of τ is updated, no matter whether the candidate output is correct or not. Algorithm 3–4 shows the averaged perceptron with lazy update procedure.

3.6 Multilingual Issues: What Is a Token?[2]

3.6.1 Tokenization, Case, and Encoding

So far we have assumed that in a grammar or in a treebank, the notion of a word, or more specifically that of a word token, is well defined. However, this definition might be well defined given a treebank or parser but variable across different parsers or treebanks. One example is the possessive marker and copula verb *'s* (a variant of *be*) in English. In English, a token is typically separated from other tokens by a space character. However, in a parser/treebank for English, a word like *today's* or *There's* is treated as two independent tokens, *today* and *'s*, or *There* and *'s*. As the Penn Treebank annotation guidelines point out,

2. This section describes morphological and tokenization issues as they relate to the task of syntactic parsing. For a thorough review of morphological processing, please see Chapter 1.

Algorithm 3–4 The Averaged Perceptron Learning Algorithm with Lazy Update Procedure

Inputs: Training Data $\langle(x_1, y_1), \ldots, (x_m, y_m)\rangle$; number of iterations T
Initialization: Set $\mathbf{w} = \mathbf{0}$, $\gamma = \mathbf{0}$, $\sigma = \mathbf{0}$, $\tau = \mathbf{0}$
Algorithm:

```
for t = 1,..., T do
  for i = 1,..., m do
    Calculate y'_i, where y'_i = argmax_{y∈GEN(x)} Φ(x_i, y) · w
    if t ≠ T or i ≠ m then
      if y'_i ≠ y_i then
        // Update active features in the current sentence
        for each dimension s in (Φ(x_i, y_i) − Φ(x_i, y'_i)) do
          if s is a dimension in τ then
            // Include the total weight during the time
            // this feature remains inactive since last update
            σ_s = σ_s + w_s · (t · m + i − t_{τ_s} · m − i_{τ_s})
          end if
          // Also include the weight calculated from comparing y'_i with y_i
          w_s = w_s + Φ(x_i, y_i) − Φ(x_i, y'_i)
          σ_s = σ_s + Φ(x_i, y_i) − Φ(x_i, y'_i)
          // Record the location where the dimension s is updated
          τ_s = (i, t)
        end for
      end if
    else
      // To deal with the last sentence in the last iteration
      for each dimension s in τ do
        // Include the total weight during the time
        // each feature in τ remains inactive since last update
        σ_s = σ_s + w_s · (T · m + m − t_{τ_s} · m − i_{τ_s})
      end for
      // Update weights for features appearing in this last sentence
      if y'_i ≠ y_i then
        w = w + Φ(x_i, y_i) − Φ(x_i, y'_i)
        σ = σ + Φ(x_i, y_i) − Φ(x_i, y'_i)
      end if
    end if
  end for
end for
```

Output: The averaged weight parameter vector $\gamma = \sigma/(\mathrm{mT})$

the possessive marker can apply to some previous constituent and not just to the previous token:

```
(NP (NP (NP First)
        (PP of
            (NP America))
        's)
    operating results)
```

Similarly for the copula verb *'s*:

```
(S (NP-SBJ (EX There))
   (VP (VBZ 's)
       (NP-PRD (NP (NN nothing))
               (ADJP (RB very)
                     (JJ hot))))))
```

In some languages there are issues with uppercase and lowercase. It is tempting to lowercase all your treebank data and simply lowercase input texts for the parser. However, case can carry useful information. The token *Boeing* if it is previously unseen in the training data might look like a progressive verb like *singing*, but the initial uppercase character makes it more likely to be a proper noun. However, depending on the type and amount of data available for training, some case information, such as selective lowercasing of sentence initial tokens, might have to be done to obtain reasonable estimates from the treebank. Low-count tokens can be replaced with patterns that retain case information; for example, if *Patagonia* appears only twice in the corpus, then it can be replaced with *Xxx* to reflect that new unknown words that match the same pattern can be treated as known under this pattern. The same is true for cases such as dates, times, IP addresses, and URLs.

For language scripts that are not encoded in ASCII, the different encodings need to be managed. In particular, the data the parser will be used on should be converted to the encoding that the treebank uses, or vice versa. There are often issues with the sentence terminator period (.), which in some text corpora might be an ASCII character but in others may be encoded in UTF-8. Some languages, such as Chinese, are encoded in different formats depending on the place where the text originates—for example, GB, BIG5, and UTF-8 are all encodings you might find for Chinese text.

These are trivial issues, algorithmically speaking, compared to writing a parser, but in practice these issues can be quite challenging and time consuming, and while a full discussion of these issues is beyond the scope of this chapter, it does need to be pointed out that thinking about tokenization, case, and encoding are prerequisites for anyone wishing to write a parser or to get one working for a new language.

3.6.2 Word Segmentation

The written form of many languages, including Chinese, lack marks identifying words. Given the Chinese text 北京大学生比赛, a plausible segmentation would be "北京 (Beijing) /大学生 (university students) /比赛 (competition) 'competition among university students in Beijing'. However, if 北京大学 is taken to mean Beijing University, the segmentation for the character sequence might become 北京大学 (Beijing University) /生 (give birth to) /比赛 (competition) 'Beijing University gives birth to competition', which is less plausible.

Word segmentation is the process of demarcating blocks in a character sequence such that the produced output is composed of separated tokens and is meaningful. Only if we have identified each word in a sentence can POS tags (e.g., NNP or DT) then be assigned and the syntax tree for the whole sentence be built. In systems dealing with English or French, tokens are assumed to be already available because words have always been separated by spaces in these languages, whereas in Chinese, characters are written next to each other without marks identifying words.

Chinese word segmentation has a large community of researchers and has resulted in three SIGHAN bakeoffs [34, 35, 36]. Chapter 1 deals with these issues, so here we simply focus on the impact on parsing.

One interesting approach to Chinese parsing [37] is to parse the character sequence directly. The parser itself assigns word boundaries as part of the parsing process, where nonterminals in the tree that span a group of characters can be said to specify the word boundaries. However, this study found that immediate context was the most useful in predicting word boundaries. The global sentence context was not as useful in the discovery of word boundaries even though in some situations the ambiguity in word segmentation could need long-distance dependencies captured by the parse tree.

The use of a single best word segmentation from a word segmentation model creates a pipeline where the parser is unable to choose between different plausible segmentations. Using the result in Bar-Hillel, Perles, and Shamir [38], we know that a parser for CFGs can parse an input word lattice (which represents a finite language as a finite-state automata). The parser uses the states in the automata as indices, which generalizes the notion of indices into the input string. The input word lattice can be used to represent multiple segmentations of the Chinese input, and thus the parser can choose which of the ranked segmentation results lead to the most accurate parses.

3.6.3 Morphology

In many languages the notion of splitting up tokens using spaces is problematic because each word can contain several components, called morphemes, such that the meaning of a word can be thought of as composed of the combination of the meanings of the morphemes. A word must now be thought of as being decomposed into a stem combined with several morphemes.

For example, the following dependency analysis from the Turkish treebank shows that the syntactic dependencies need to be aware of the morphemes within words. In this example, morpheme boundaries within a word are shown using the + symbol. Morphemes, and not words, are used as heads and dependents.

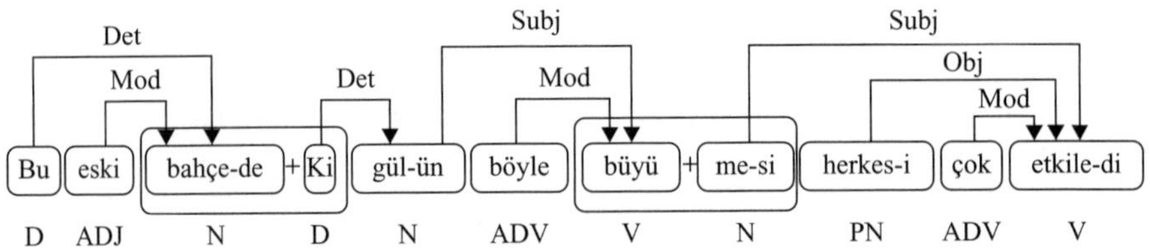

Turkish, Finnish, and other agglutinative languages have this property of entire clauses being combined with morphemes to create very complex words.

Inflectional languages like Czech and Russian are not as extreme but also suffer from the problem that many different morphemes are used to mark grammatical case, gender, and so on, and each type of morpheme can be orthogonal to the others (so they can independently co-occur). For instance, according to Hajic and Hladka [39], most adjectives in Czech can potentially form all four genders, all seven case markers, all three degrees of comparison, and can be either positive or negative in polarity. This results in 336 possible inflected word forms just for adjectives. In addition to a large number of word forms, each inflected word can be ambiguously segmented into morphemes with different analyses. Quite apart from syntactic ambiguity, the parser now also has to deal with morphological ambiguity.

To tackle the disambiguation problem for morphology, the problem of splitting a word into the most likely sequence of morphemes can be reduced to a (very complex) POS tagging task. Each word is to be tagged with a complex part of speech that encodes the various morphemes. For instance, a part of speech of `V--M-3----` can indicate that each word can have morphemes that inflect the word along 10 different dimensions, and in this case, the stem is a verb (V) with masculine gender (M) and in third person (3), and the other types of morphemes are assigned—which indicates that they do not occur in this analysis. The POS tagger has to produce this complex tag—and this is typically done by training separate subclassifiers for each component of the POS tag and combining the output for tagging each word [39]. The word itself is not split into morphemes, but each word is tagged with a POS tag that encodes a lot of information about the morphemes. This enriched tag set can be a rich source of features for a statistical parser for a highly inflected language.

Adding morphological awareness to statistical parsers can lead to improved accuracy. For example, in a language like Spanish [40], if we would like to create the following fragment of a parse tree, if the parser was morphologically aware then it might consider that plural nouns like *gatos* 'cats' are unlikely to modify the singular verb *corrió* 'ran'—even if it had not seen this particular bilexical dependency in the training data.

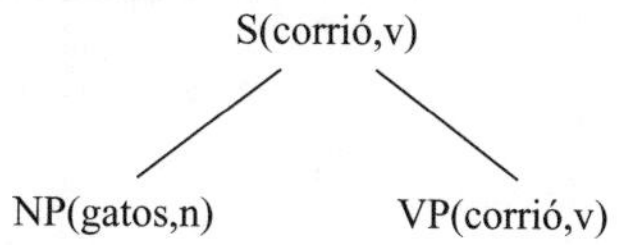

In discriminative models for statistical parsing (especially for dependency parsing), it has been fairly straightforward to include morphological information. Because discriminative models allow the inclusion of a large number of overlapping features, morphological information associated with the words can be used to build better statistical parsers by simply throwing them into the mix. As shown in the CoNLL 2007 shared task [13] and also in papers that explicitly looked at useful features per language in discriminative dependency parsing (e.g., [41, 42]), it was found that morphological information was helpful in improving the accuracy of statistical parsers especially for morphologically complex languages.

In phrase structure parsing, Cowan and Collins [40] provide a discriminative model for parsing Spanish that takes the k-best output from a generative model and uses morphological features to rerank the output. Various morphological information was included in the POS tags and in the reranking model, and it was shown that as long as the tagset was not expanded to a very large size, accuracy improved with the addition of morphological information. In Sarkar and Han [43], a generative model for parsing Korean was augmented with morphological information. The probabilities for dependencies were interpolated between full word forms and various morphologically decomposed forms of the words. It was found that, in this particular model, using the stems rather than suffixes helped the parser generalize over morphologically complex word forms and helped improve parsing accuracy.

3.7 Summary

This chapter covered the syntactic analysis of natural language and how parsers can be built that can efficiently and accurately parse natural language and provide syntactic trees. We covered the necessity of using a data-driven approach to parsing of natural language and introduced the notion of a treebank that can provide training data for parsing language. Parsing is also interesting from the perspective of machine learning because it is a complex, structured prediction task where the output labels are not simple class labels but rather decomposed into smaller units, and the number of structured output labels is exponential in the size of the input. We covered the use of phrase structure parsing and dependency parsing as different ways to represent the syntactic analysis of natural language. This chapter covered parsing algorithms that can efficiently parse input sentences, as well as machine learning models for ambiguity resolution in parsing. There are many issues with writing parsers for different languages. We covered a few of the issues that arise when parsing languages that are quite different from English: issues such as tokenization, case, encoding issues, and word segmentation and morphology. In each case, we discussed how solutions to these issues can be incorporated into statistical parsers for these languages.

Acknowledgments

Thanks to the School of Informatics at the University of Edinburgh for hosting me during my sabbatical year away from Simon Fraser University. Most this chapter was written in Edinburgh.

Bibliography

[1] K. Knight and D. Marcu, "Summarization beyond sentence extraction: A probabilistic approach to sentence compression," *Artificial Intelligence*, vol. 139, no. 1, pp. 91–107, 2002.

[2] C. Callison-Burch, "Syntactic constraints on paraphrases extracted from parallel corpora," in *Proceedings of the 2008 Conference on Empirical Methods in Natural Language Processing*, pp. 196–205, 2008.

[3] M. Galley, M. Hopkins, K. Knight, and D. Marcu, "What's in a translation rule?," in *Human Language Technology Conference of the North American Chapter of the Association for Computational Linguistics (HLT-NAACL 2004): Main Proceedings* (D. M. Susan Dumais and S. Roukos, eds.), pp. 273–280, 2004.

[4] S. Miller, H. Fox, L. Ramshaw, and R. Weischedel, "A novel use of statistical parsing to extract information from text," in *Proceedings of the 1st North American Chapter of the Association for Computational Linguistics Conference (NAACL 2000)*, pp. 226–233, 2000.

[5] R. Barzilay and K. R. McKeown, "Sentence fusion for multidocument news summarization," *Computational Linguistics*, vol. 31, no. 3, 2005.

[6] R. Barzilay, "Probabilistic approaches for modeling text structure and their application to text-to-text generation," in *Empirical Methods in Natural Language Generation* (E. Krahmer and M. Theune, eds.), Lecture Notes in Computer Science (LNAI 5790), Berlin: Springer, 2010.

[7] M. Lease, E. Charniak, and M. Johnson, "SS-11.4: Parsing and its applications for conversational speech," in *IEEE International Conference on Acoustics, Speech, and Signal Processing (ICASSP'05) 5: V-961-V964*, 2005.

[8] P. Pantel and D. Lin, "Concept discovery from text," in *Proceedings of Conference on Computational Linguistics (COLING-02)*, pp. 577–583, 2002.

[9] A. Rudnicky, C. Bennett, A. Black, A. Chotimongkol, K. Lenzo, A. Oh, and R. Singh, "Task and domain specific modeling in the Carnegie-Mellon communicator system," in *Proceedings of the 6th International Conference on Spoken Language Processing (ICSLP)*, 2000. Paper G4-01.

[10] M. Sipser, *Introduction to the Theory of Computation*, 2nd ed., Boston: PWS Publishing Co., 2005.

[11] J. Nivre, "Two notions of parsing," in *A Finnish Computer Linguist: Kimmo Koskenniemi. Festschrift on the 60th Birthday* (A. Arppe, L. Carlson, O. Heinämäki, K. Lindén, M. Miestamo, J. Piitulainen, J. Tupakka, H. Westerlund, and A. Yli-Jyrä, eds.), pp. 111–120, Stanford, CA: CSLI Publications, 2005.

[12] L. Tesnière, *Éléments de syntaxe structurale.* Paris: C. Klincksieck, 1959.

[13] J. Nivre, J. Hall, S. Kübler, R. McDonald, J. Nilsson, S. Riedel, and D. Yuret, eds., *Proceedings of the CoNLL Shared Task Session of Empirical Methods on Natural Language Processing-Conference on Natural Language Learning 2007*, 2007.

[14] H. Gaifman, "Dependency systems and phrase structure systems," Tech. Rep. P-2315, The RAND Corporation, Santa Monica, CA, May 1961.

[15] S. Abney, "Dependency grammars and context-free grammars," manuscript presented at meeting of Linguistic Society of America, Jan. 1995.

[16] M. Marcus, G. Kim, M. A. Marcinkiewicz, R. Macintyre, A. Bies, M. Ferguson, K. Katz, and B. Schasberger, "The Penn Treebank: Annotating predicate argument structure," in *Proceedings of the ARPA Human Language Technology Workshop*, pp. 114–119, 1994.

[17] M. Johnson, "A simple pattern-matching algorithm for recovering empty nodes and their antecedents," in *Proceedings of 40th Annual Meeting of the Association for Computational Linguistics*, pp. 136–143, 2002.

[18] L. Rimell, S. Clark, and M. Steedman, "Unbounded dependency recovery for parser evaluation," in *Proceedings of the Conference on Empirical Methods in Natural Language Processing (EMNLP-09)*, pp. 813–821, 2009.

[19] R. Levy and C. D. Manning, "Is it harder to parse Chinese, or the Chinese treebank?," in *Proceedings of the 41st Annual Meeting of the Association for Computational Linguistics*, pp. 439–446, 2003.

[20] J. Nivre, "Algorithms for deterministic incremental dependency parsing," *Computational Linguistics*, vol. 34, no. 4, pp. 513–553, 2008.

[21] J. Goodman, "Global thresholding and multiple-pass parsing," in *Proceedings of the 2nd Conference on Empirical Methods in Natural Language Processing*, 1997.

[22] P. F. Felzenszwalb and D. McAllester, "The generalized A* architecture," *Journal of Artificial Intelligence Research*, vol. 29, pp. 153–190, 2007.

[23] J. Eisner, "Three new probabilistic models for dependency parsing: An exploration," in *Proceedings of the 16th International Conference on Computational Linguistics (COLING-96)*, pp. 340–345, August 1996.

[24] R. McDonald, "Discriminative training and spanning tree algorithms for dependency parsing," PhD thesis, University of Pennsylvania, July 2006.

[25] M. Johnson, "PCFG models of linguistic tree representations," *Computational Linguistics*, vol. 24, no. 4, 1998.

[26] S. Petrov, L. Barrett, R. Thibaux, and D. Klein, "Learning accurate, compact, and interpretable tree annotation," in *Proceedings of the 21st International Conference on Computational Linguistics and 44th Annual Meeting of the Association for Computational Linguistics*, pp. 433–440, 2006.

[27] M. Collins, "Three generative, lexicalised models for statistical parsing," in *Proceedings of the 35th Annual Meeting of the Association for Computational Linguistics*, pp. 16–23, 1997.

[28] J. Goodman, "Parsing algorithms and metrics," in *Proceedings of the 34th Annual Meeting of the Association for Computational Linguistics*, pp. 177–183, 1996.

[29] M. Collins, "Discriminative training methods for hidden Markov models: Theory and experiments with perceptron algorithms," in *Proceedings of the Empirical Methods in Natural Language Processing (EMNLP)*, pp. 1–8, 2002.

[30] Y. Freund and R. E. Schapire, "Large margin classification using the perceptron algorithm," *Machine Learning*, vol. 37, no. 3, pp. 277–296, 1999.

[31] J. Lafferty, A. McCallum, and F. Pereira, "Conditional random fields: Probabilistic models for segmenting and labeling sequence data," in *Proceedings of the 18th International Conference on Machine Learning (ICML)*, pp. 282–289, 2001.

[32] F. Rosenblatt, "The perception: a probabilistic model for information storage and organization in the brain," *Psychological Review*, vol. 65, no. 6, pp. 386–408, 1958.

[33] M. Collins, "Ranking algorithms for named entity extraction: Boosting and the voted perceptron," in *Proceedings of Association for Computational Linguistics 2002*, pp. 489–496, 2002.

[34] R. Sproat and T. Emerson, "The 1st international Chinese word segmentation bakeoff," in *Proceedings of the 2nd SIGHAN Workshop on Chinese Language Processing*, pp. 123–133, 2003.

[35] T. Emerson, "The 2nd international Chinese word segmentation bakeoff," in *Proceedings of the 4th SIGHAN Workshop on Chinese Language Processing*, pp. 123–133, 2005.

[36] G.-A. Levow, "The 3rd international Chinese language processing bakeoff," in *Proceedings of the 5th SIGHAN Workshop on Chinese Language Processing*, pp. 108–117, 2006.

[37] X. Luo, "A maximum entropy chinese character-based parser," in *Proceedings of the 2003 Conference on Empirical Methods in Natural Language Processing, Volume 10*, pp. 192–199, 2003.

[38] Y. Bar-Hillel, M. Perles, and E. Shamir, "On formal properties of simple phrase structure grammars," in *Language and Information: Selected Essays on Their Theory and Application* (Y. Bar-Hillel, ed.), ch. 9, pp. 116–150, Reading, MA: Addison-Wesley, 1964.

[39] J. Hajic and B. Hladka, "Tagging inlective languages: Prediction of morphological categories for a rich structured tagset," in *Proceedings of the 36th Annual Meeting of the Association for Computational Linguistics and 17th International Conference on Computational Linguistics, Volume 1*, pp. 483–490, August 1998.

[40] B. Cowan and M. Collins, "Morphology and reranking for the statistical parsing of spanish," in *Proceedings of Human Language Technology Conference and Conference on Empirical Methods in Natural Language Processing*, pp. 795–802, 2005.

[41] J. Nivre, J. Hall, J. Nilsson, A. Chanev, G. Eryigit, S. Kübler, S. Marinov, and E. Marsi, "Maltparser: A language-independent system for data-driven dependency parsing," *Natural Language Engineering*, vol. 13, no. 2, pp. 95–135, 2007.

[42] G. Eryigit, J. Nivre, and K. Oflazer, "The incremental use of morphological information and lexicalization in data-driven dependency parsing," in *Proceedings of the 21st International Conference on the Computer Processing of Oriental Languages*, pp. 498–507, 2006.

[43] A. Sarkar and C. hye Han, "Statistical morphological tagging and parsing of Korean with an LTAG grammar," in *Proceedings of the Sixth Workshop on Tree Adjoining Grammars and Related Formalisms: TAG+6*, 2002.

Chapter 4

Semantic Parsing

Sameer Pradhan

Semantics by its dictionary definition is the study of meaning, and **parsing** is the examination of something in a minute way, that is, identifying and relating the pieces of information being parsed. When we put the two of these concepts together, we get **semantic parsing**, which, in the broadest sense of the phrase, is the process of identifying **meaning chunks** contained in an information signal in an attempt to transform it into some data structure that can be manipulated by a computer to perform higher level tasks. In our case, the information signal is human language text. Unfortunately, in the natural language processing community, the term semantic parsing is somewhat ambiguous. Over the years researchers have used it to represent various levels of granularity of meaning representation. Because semantics is such a vague term, it has been used to represent various depths of representations, from something as basic as identifying domain-specific relations between entities, to the more intermediate task of identifying the roles that various entities and artifacts play in an event, to converting a text to a series of specific logical expressions. Within the context of this chapter, we restrict its interpretation to the study of mapping naturally occurring text to some representation that is amenable to manipulation by computers for the purpose of achieving some goals, such as retrieving information, answering a question, populating a database, or taking an action.

4.1 Introduction

The holy grail of research in language understanding is the identification of a meaning representation that is detailed enough to allow reasoning systems to make deductions but, at the same time, is general enough that it can be used across many domains with little to no adaptation. It is not clear whether a final, low-level, detailed semantic representation covering various applications that use some form of language interface can be achieved or whether an ontology can be created that can capture the various granularities and aspects of meanings that are embodied in such a variety of applications—none has yet been created. Therefore, two compromise approaches have emerged in the natural language processing community for language understanding.

In the first approach, a specific, rich meaning representation is created for a limited domain for use by applications that are restricted to that domain, such as air travel reservations, football game simulations, or querying a geographic database. Systems are then crafted to generate output from text in this rich, domain-specific meaning representation. In the second approach, a related set of intermediate meaning representations is created, going from low-level analysis to a midlevel analysis, and the bigger understanding task is divided into multiple, smaller pieces that are more manageable, such as word sense disambiguation followed by predicate-argument structure recognition. By dividing the problem up this way, each intermediate representation is only responsible for capturing a relatively small component of overall meaning, thereby making the task of defining and modeling each representation easier. Unlike the first approach, each meaning representation, while covering only a small part of the overall meaning, is not tied to a specific domain, and so the data and methods created for it are similarly general purpose.

Unfortunately, we do not yet have the holy grail in the form of a detailed overall representation that would at once be easily learnable and have high coverage across domains. So, in this chapter, we treat the world as though it has exactly two types of meaning representations: a domain-dependent, deeper representation and a set of relatively shallow but general-purpose, low-level, and intermediate representations. The task of producing the output of the first type is often called **deep semantic parsing**, and the task of producing the output of the second type is often called **shallow semantic parsing**. We discuss algorithms for producing both kinds of output.

Both of these approaches are fraught with issues; the first approach is so specific that porting to every new domain can require anywhere from a few modifications to almost reworking the solution from scratch. In other words, the reusability of the representation across domains is very limited. The problem with the latter approach is that it is extremely difficult to construct a general-purpose ontology and create symbols that are shallow enough to be learnable but detailed enough to be useful for all possible applications. Therefore, an application-specific translation layer between the more general representation and the more specific representation becomes necessary. However, this translational component can be relatively small compared to the total effort required to adapt a more specific representation to a new domain. None of this even begins to consider the implications of using such systems across different languages or the role played by the structure of different languages in affecting these meaning representations or their learnability. For these reasons, over the history of language processing, the community has generally moved away from the more detailed, deep, domain-dependent representations to the more shallow ones.

4.2 Semantic Interpretation

Semantic parsing can be considered as part of a larger process, **semantic interpretation**, which involves various components that together let us define a representation of a text that can be fed into a computer to allow further computational manipulations and search, which are prerequisite for any language understanding system or application. The following sections talk about some of the main components of this process.

We begin this discussion with the seminal work by Chomsky, *Syntactic Structures* [1], which introduced the concept of a transformational phrase structure grammar to provide an operational definition for the combinatorial formations of meaningful natural language sentences by humans. Shortly after Chomsky's 1957 book, Katz and Fodor [2] published the first work treating semantics within the generative grammar paradigm. They found that Chomsky's transformational grammar was not a complete description of language because it did not account for meaning. In their 1963 paper "The Structure of a Semantic Theory," Katz and Fodor put forward what they thought were the properties a semantic theory should possess. A semantic theory should be able to:

1. Explain sentences having ambiguous meanings. For example, it should account for the fact that the word *bill* in the sentence *The bill is large* is ambiguous in the sense that it could represent money or the beak of a bird.
2. Resolve the ambiguities of words in context. For example, if the same sentence is extended to form *The bill is large but need not be paid*, then the theory should be able to disambiguate the monetary meaning of *bill*.
3. Identify meaningless but syntactically well-formed sentences, such as the famous example by Chomsky: *Colorless green ideas sleep furiously.*
4. Identify syntactically or transformationally unrelated paraphrases of a concept having the same semantic content.

In the following subsections we look at some requirements for achieving a semantic representation.

4.2.1 Structural Ambiguity

When we talk of structure, we generally refer to the syntactic structure of sentences. This is a sentence-level phenomenon and essentially means transforming a sentence into its underlying syntactic representation. Because syntax and semantics have such a strong interaction, most theories of semantic interpretation refer to the underlying syntactic representation. Conventionally, syntax has become the first stage of processing followed by various other stages in the process of semantic interpretation (see Chapter 3 for information on syntactic processing).

4.2.2 Word Sense

In any given language, it is almost certainly the case that the same word type, or word lemma, is used in different contexts and with different morphological variants to represent different entities or concepts in the world. For example, we use the word *nail* to represent a part of the human anatomy and also to represent the generally metallic object used to secure other objects. Humans are adept at identifying, through context, which sense of the word is intended by the author or speaker. Let's take the following four examples. The presence of words such as *hammer* and *hardware store* in sentences 1 and 2, and of *clipped* and *manicure* in sentences 3 and 4, enable humans to easily disambiguate the sense in which *nail* is used:

1. He *nailed* the loose arm of the chair with a hammer.
2. He bought a box of *nails* from the hardware store.

3. He went to the beauty salon to get his *nails* clipped.
4. He went to get a manicure. His *nails* had grown very long.

Resolving the sense of words in a discourse, therefore, constitutes one of the steps in the process of semantic interpretation. We discuss it in greater depth in Section 4.4.

4.2.3 Entity and Event Resolution

Any discourse inevitably consists of a set of entities participating in a series of explicit or implicit events over a period of time. The next important component of semantic interpretation is the identification of various entities that are sprinkled across the discourse using the same or different phrases. Reconciling what type of entity or event is being considered, along with disambiguating various ways in which the same entity is referred to over a discourse, is critical to creating a semantic representation. Two predominant tasks have become popular over the years: **named entity recognition** and **coreference resolution**. These two tasks fall under the umbrella of **information extraction** and are discussed in more detail in Chapter 8.

4.2.4 Predicate-Argument Structure

Once we have the word senses, entities, and events identified, another level of semantic structure comes into play: identifying the participants of the entities in these events. Resolving the argument structure of the predicates in a sentence is where we identify which entities play what part in which event. Generally, this process can be defined as the identification of *who* did *what* to *whom*, *when*, *where*, *why*, and *how*.

Figure 4–1 shows the participants of *say* and *acquire* events.

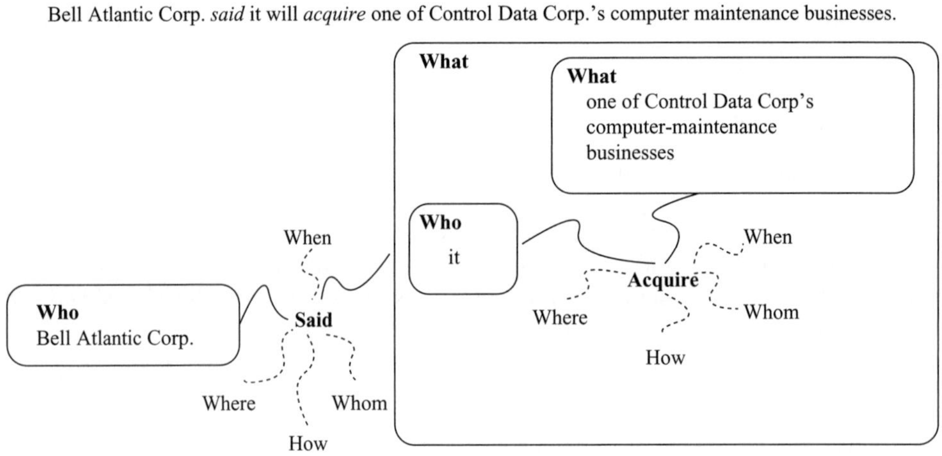

Figure 4–1: A representation of *who* did *what* to *whom*, *when*, *where*, *why*, and *how*

4.2.5 Meaning Representation

The final process of the semantic interpretation is to build a semantic representation or meaning representation that can then be manipulated by algorithms to various application ends. This process is sometimes called the **deep representation**. Unfortunately, as we mentioned earlier, due to the lack of a general-purpose representation that is also deep enough for any given application, most studies in this area have been application dependent, or dependent on the domain of particular applications. The following two examples show sample sentences and their meaning representations for the RoboCup and GeoQuery domains (described in §4.6.1):

(1) If our player 2 has the ball, then position our player 5 in the midfield.
`((bowner (player our 2)) (do (player our 5) (pos (midfield)))`

(2) Which river is the longest?
`answer(`x_1`, longest(`x_1` river(`x_1`)))`

This is a domain-specific approach; the remainder of this chapter focuses on domain-independent approaches.

4.3 System Paradigms

The problems discussed in this chapter are familiar to the computational linguistics and linguistics communities. Researchers from these communities have examined meaning representations and methods to recover them at different levels of granularity and generality, exploring the space of numerous languages. For many of the potential experimental conditions, no hand-annotated data is available. Therefore, it is important to get a perspective on the various primary dimensions on which the problem of semantic interpretation has been tackled. It is impossible to cover all these dimensions in this chapter, so while we mention many of the historic approaches, we try to focus on the more prevalent and successful approaches that lend themselves to practical applications. The approaches generally fall into the following three categories.

1. System Architectures
   (a) Knowledge based: As the name suggests, these systems use a predefined set of rules or a knowledge base to obtain a solution to a new problem.
   (b) Unsupervised: These systems tend to require minimal human intervention to be functional by using existing resources that can be bootstrapped for a particular application or problem domain.
   (c) Supervised: These systems involve the manual annotation of some phenomena that appear in a sufficient quantity of data so that machine learning algorithms can be applied. Typically, researchers create feature functions that allow each problem instance to be projected into a space of features. A model is trained to use these features to predict labels, and then it is applied to unseen data.

   (d) Semi-Supervised: Manual annotation is usually very expensive and does not yield enough data to completely capture a phenomenon. In such instances, researchers can automatically expand the data set on which their models are trained either by employing machine-generated output directly or by bootstrapping off of an existing model by having humans correct its output. In many cases, a model from one domain is used to quickly adapt to a new domain.

2. Scope
   (a) Domain Dependent: These systems are specific to certain domains, such as air travel reservations or simulated football coaching.
   (b) Domain Independent: These systems are general enough that the techniques can be applicable to multiple domains without little or no change.

3. Coverage
   (a) Shallow: These systems tend to produce an intermediate representation that can then be converted to one that a machine can base its actions on.
   (b) Deep: These systems usually create a terminal representation that is directly consumed by a machine or application.

4.4 Word Sense

In a compositional approach to semantics, where the meaning of the whole is composed of the meaning of the parts, the smallest parts under consideration in textual discourse are typically the words themselves: either tokens as they appear in the text or their lemmatized forms. Word sense has been examined and studied for a very long time [3, 4, 5], but its true nature still eludes researchers. It is not clear whether it is possible to identify a finite set of senses that each word in a language exhibits in various contexts. Even if it were possible to do so, it is not clear whether a given word evokes a single discrete sense in a given context or whether the word is associated with a distribution of some subset of all its senses.

Attempts to solve this problem range from rule based and knowledge based to completely unsupervised, supervised, and semi-supervised learning methods. Very early systems were predominantly rule based or knowledge based and used dictionary definitions of senses of words. Unsupervised word sense induction or disambiguation techniques try to induce the senses of a word as it appears in various corpora. These systems perform either a hard or soft clustering of words and tend to allow the tuning of these clusters to suit a particular application. Most recent supervised approaches to word sense disambiguation, on the other hand, primarily assume that a word can evoke only one particular sense in a given context and at a predefined—usually application-independent—level of granularity, although the output of supervised approaches can still be amenable to generating a ranking, or distribution, of membership of senses. In the case of supervised word sense disambiguation, where human annotation is necessary, a delicate balance often exists between making fine-grained distinctions between word senses and maintaining good interannotator agreements given the inventory of senses. The coarser the granularity of senses for a word, the more consistent the annotation and more learnable they become. However, there is an increased chance that this lower granularity might not identify nuances that are fine enough for the consuming application. An observed win in learning and annotation might not translate directly into the depth of representation of meaning expected by the application. Palmer, Dang, and Fellbaum [6] discussed this issue in great detail.

Although theoretically assumed to be an important aspect of language understanding, the applicability of word sense disambiguation seems to be an issue of much debate. The inherent difficulty of generating huge corpora of manually sense-tagged text, complicated in part by the prevailing agnostic or ambivalent status of applicability of word sense in various applications is also a probable cause of why few computational resources have been generated to support the creation of better automatic systems. Also, the absence of standard criteria has prevented the merging of various resources that have sense information. Some attempts are being made to create mappings between such resources.

One of the principle reasons for this ambivalence, as observed by Resnik and Yarowsky [7], is that in many of the more mature areas of language processing, such as information retrieval and speech recognition, either the sense disambiguation techniques tend to be redundant or cheaper and better alternatives are available. In information retrieval it is a well-accepted fact that the multiple words in a query matching with multiple words in the document context tend to provide an implicit disambiguation that is hard to beat with perfect word sense information [8]. In speech recognition, context classes [9, 10] have always proven to be more applicable than word classes [11]. Specific domains or genres of text tend to invoke a smaller subset, or even just one sense of a given content word. Therefore, in light of the fact that some semantic parsing systems are domain specific and some domain-independent, the disambiguation of sense is more necessary in the latter than in the former. Furthermore, in domain-specific applications, a word usually maps to a unique concept, and thus, finding a good mapping from words to the concepts is an easier problem, further diminishing the necessity for sense disambiguation. Resnik and Yarowsky [7] pointed out several reasons for the lack of progress in word sense disambiguation: a lack of standardized evaluations, the range of resources needed to provide required knowledge as compared to other tasks, and the difficulty of obtaining adequately large sense-tagged data sets. Following that study, the Special Interest Group on LEXicon (SIGLEX) has held several exercises called SENSEVAL 1, 2, and 3 and SEMEVAL 1 and 2. These competitions have been very successful in generating standard datasets and evaluation criteria, as well as identifying related tasks that have advanced the understanding of word sense disambiguation and its applications.

How to measure the performance of automatic word sense disambiguation systems is an important issue. Gale, Church, and Yarowsky [12] discussed it in great detail. Their proposal, which is still commonly followed, is that the lower bound on the performance of a system for disambiguating a word should be the one in which every instance of the lemma is assigned the most frequent sense it exhibits in a sufficiently large corpus. This is commonly known as the most frequent sense, or MFS, baseline. A good property of a gold-standard sense-tagged corpus is that it should be replicable to a high degree. In other words, multiple annotators should be able to annotate the same corpus with a sufficiently high agreement. Let's say this agreement is $x\%$. We would generally view $x\%$ as an upper bound on the performance of any automatic system.

Word sense ambiguities can be of three principal types: (i) homonymy, (ii) polysemy, and (iii) categorial ambiguity [13]. **Homonymy** indicates that the words share the same spelling, but the meanings are quite disparate. Each homonymous partition, however, may contain finer sense nuances that could be assigned to the word depending on the context, and this phenomenon is called **polysemy**. For example, these two senses of the word *bank* are orthogonal: *financial* bank and *river* bank. Further, *bank* has some other, somewhat finer, and related subsenses that indicate a collection of things: for example, financial bank and bank of clouds. To illustrate **categorial ambiguity**, the word *book* can mean a book such as the one in which this chapter appears or to enter charges against someone in a police register. The former belongs to the grammatical category of noun, and the latter, verb. Distinguishing between these two categories effectively helps disambiguate these two senses. Therefore, categorial ambiguity can be resolved with syntactic information (part of speech) alone, but polysemy and homonymy need more than syntax.

Traditionally, in English, word senses have been annotated for each part of speech separately, whereas in Chinese, the sense annotation has been done per lemma and so ranges across all parts of speech. Part of the reason is that the distinction between a noun or a verb is much more obscure in Chinese.

4.4.1 Resources

As with any language understanding task, the availability of resources is a key factor in the disambiguation of word senses in corpora. Unfortunately, the community has not seen the development of a significant amount of hand-tagged sense data—at least not until very recently. Early work on word sense disambiguation used machine-readable dictionaries or thesauruses as knowledge sources. Two prominent sources were the *Longman Dictionary of Contemporary English* (LDOCE) [14] and *Roget's Thesaurus* [15]. The late 1980s gave birth to a significant lexicographical resource, WordNet [16], which has been very influential. In addition to being a lexical resource with inventories of senses provided for most words in English across multiple parts of speech, it also has a rich taxonomy connecting words across many different relationships, such as hypernymy, homonymy, meronymy, and so on. In addition, to facilitate research in automatic sense disambiguation, a small portion of the Brown Corpus [17] has been annotated with WordNet senses to create a semantic concordance (SEMCOR) corpus [18]. More recently, WordNet has been extended by adding syntactic information on the glosses, disambiguating them with manual and automatic methods and generating logical forms to allow better incorporation in applications such as question answering [19]. Another corpus, the DSO Corpus of Sense-Tagged English, was created by tagging WordNet version 1.5 senses on the Brown and Wall Street Journal (WSJ) corpora for the 121 nouns and 70 verbs that are the most frequent and ambiguous words in English [20]. Further, the SENSEVAL [21] competitions held over the past decade have created many corpora for testing systems on word sense and related problems. The biggest sense annotation effort so far has been the OntoNotes corpus [22, 23, 24] released through the Linguistic Data Consortium (LDC), in which have been tagged a significant number of verb (~2,700) and noun (~2,200) lemmas covering roughly 85% of multiple corpora spanning multiple genres with coarse grained senses and with a very high interannotator agreement. Pradhan et al. [25] based a lexical sample task in SEMEVAL 2007 using this corpus.

Cyc [26] is another good example of a useful resource that creates a formalized representation of common sense knowledge about objects and events in the world to overcome the so-called knowledge bottleneck that is so crucial to word sense disambiguation and many other natural language tasks. Even after a couple of decades of handcrafting this knowledge base, it leaves much to be desired, which underscores the difficulty of such an endeavor.

Fortunately, English seems to have the most highly developed lexicons with various semantic features associated with words and words grouped together to form coherent semantic classes. Efforts are underway to create resources for other languages as well. For example, HowNet [27] is a network of words for Chinese similar to WordNet. The Global WordNet Association (http://www.globalwordnet.org) keeps track of WordNet development across various languages. Researchers are also using semiautomatic methods for expanding coverage of existing languages [28, 29, 30, 31] and for other languages such as Greek [32]. In addition to such corpora annotated with sense information, there are also many resources such as WordNet Domains (http://wndomains.fbk.eu/) that provide structured knowledge to help overcome the knowledge bottleneck in sense disambiguation.

4.4.2 Systems

Now that we have looked at the problem and some resources, we turn to some sense disambiguation systems. As mentioned earlier, researchers have explored various system architectures to address the sense disambiguation problem. We can classify these systems into four main categories: (i) rule based or knowledge based, (ii) supervised, (iii) unsupervised, and (iv) semisupervised.

In the following three sections, we look at each of these systems in order.

Rule Based

The first generation of word sense disambiguation systems was primarily based on dictionary sense definitions and glosses [33, 34]. Most of these techniques were handcrafted and used resources that are not necessarily accessible today. Also, access to the exact rules and systems was very limited, and most information was only available from archived publications and discussions of the specific lexical items and senses that were considered during those experiments. In short, much of this information is historical and cannot readily be translated and made available for building systems today. However, some valuable techniques and algorithms are still accessible, and we look at these in this section. Probably the simplest and oldest dictionary-based sense disambiguation algorithm was introduced by Lesk [35]. The first-generation word sense disambiguation algorithms were mostly based on computerized dictionaries; for example, see Calzolari and Picchi [33].

The first SENSEVAL evaluations [36] used a simplified version of the Lesk algorithm as a baseline for comparing word sense disambiguation performance. The pseudocode for the algorithm is shown in Algorithm 4–1. The core of the algorithm is that the sense of a word in a given context is most likely to be the dictionary sense whose terms most closely overlap with the terms in the context. There have since been further modifications to the algorithm to make it more robust to variation in term usages, context, and definition. Banerjee and Pedersen [37], for example, modified the Lesk algorithm so that synonyms, hypernyms, hyponyms, meronymns, and so on of the words in the context as well as in the dictionary definition are used to get a more accurate overlap statistic. The score

Algorithm 4–1 Pseudocode of the simplified Lesk algorithm
The function COMPUTEOVERLAP returns the number of words common to the two sets
Procedure: SIMPLIFIED_LESK(word, sentence) **returns** best sense of *word*

```
best-sense ← most frequent sense of word
max-overlap ← 0
context ← set of words in sentence
for all sense ∈ senses of word do
    signature ← set of words in gloss and examples of sense
    overlap ← COMPUTEOVERLAP(signature, context)
    if overlap gt max-overlap then
        max-overlap ← overlap
        best-sense ← sense
    end if
end for
return best-sense
```

associated with each match is measured as the square of the longest common subsequence between the context and the gloss.[1] Using a context window of five words (two on each side of the target, as well as the target itself), they report a twofold increase in performance from 16% to 32% over the vanilla Lesk algorithm when used on the SENSEVAL-2 lexical sample dataset. This performance improvement is considerable given the simplicity of the algorithm.

Another dictionary-based algorithm was suggested by Yarowsky [38]. This study used *Roget's Thesaurus* categories and classified unseen words into one of these 1,042 categories based on a statistical analysis of 100 word concordances for each member of each category, over a large corpus, in this case the 10-million-word *Grolier's Encyclopedia*. The method performed quite well on a set of 12 words for which there had been some previous quantitative studies. Although the instances and corpora used in this study were not the same as the ones reported previously, it still gives an idea of the success of a relatively simple method. The method consists of three steps, as shown in Figure 4–2. The first step is a collection of contexts. The second step computes weights for each of the salient words. One thing to note is that the amount of context used was 50 words on each side of the target word, which is much higher than the context windows found to be useful for this kind of broad topic classification by Gale et al. [12]. $P(w|RCat)$ is the probability of a word w occurring in the context of a *Roget's Thesaurus* category $RCat$. Finally, in the third step, the unseen words in the test set are classified into the category that has the maximum weight.

More recently, Navigli and Velardi [39, 40] suggested a knowledge-based algorithm that uses graphical representation of senses of words in context to disambiguate the term under

1. Multiple subsequences in the same gloss are allowable; however, subsequences of only noncontent words such as pronouns, prepositions, articles, and conjunctions are not considered. For example, the subsequence *of the* is not considered in the calculation of a score.

1. Collect contexts for each of the *Roget's Thesaurus* categories.
2. Determine weights for each of the salient words in the context.

$$\frac{P(w_i|RCat)}{P(w_i)}$$

3. Use the weights for predicting the appropriate category of the word in the test corpus.

$$\arg\max_{RCat} \sum_{W} \log \frac{P(w_i|RCat)P(RCat)}{P(w_i)}$$

Figure 4–2: Algorithm for disambiguating words into *Roget's Thesaurus* categories

consideration. This is called the structural semantic interconnections (SSI) algorithm. It uses various sources of information, including WordNet, domain labels [41], and all possible annotated corpora to form structural specifications of concepts, or semantic graphs. The algorithm consists of two steps: an initialization step and an iterative step, in which the algorithm attempts to disambiguate all the words in context iteratively until it cannot disambiguate any further or until all the terms are successfully disambiguated. Its performance is very close to that of supervised learning algorithms. Although it does not technically have a training phase, it surpasses the best unsupervised algorithm in the SENSEVAL-3 all-words task. Figure 4–3 shows the semantic graphs for two senses of the term *bus*. The first one is the *vehicle* sense, and the second one is the *connector* sense.

Notation:

- T (the **lexical context**) is the list of terms in the context of the term t to be disambiguated. $T = [t_1, t_2, \ldots, t_n]$.
- S_1^t, S_2^t, ... ,S_n^t are structural specifications of the possible concepts (or, senses) of t.
- I (the **semantic context**) is the list of structural specifications of the concepts associated with each of the terms in $T \setminus \{t\}$ (except t). $I = [S^{t_1}, S^{t_2}, \ldots, S^{t_n}]$, that is, the **semantic interpretation** of T.
- G is the grammar defining the various relations between the structural specifications (or **semantic interconnections**) among the graphs).
- Determine how well the structural specifications in I match that of S_1^t, S_2^t, ... ,S_n^t using G.
- Select the best matching S_i^t.

The algorithm works as follows. A set of pending terms in the context $P = \{t_i | S^{t_i} = null\}$ is maintained, and I is used in each iteration to disambiguate terms in P. The procedure iterates, and each iteration either disambiguates one term in P and removes it from the pending list or stops because no more terms can be disambiguated. The output I is updated with the sense of t. Initially I contains structures for monosemous terms in $T \setminus \{t\}$ and any

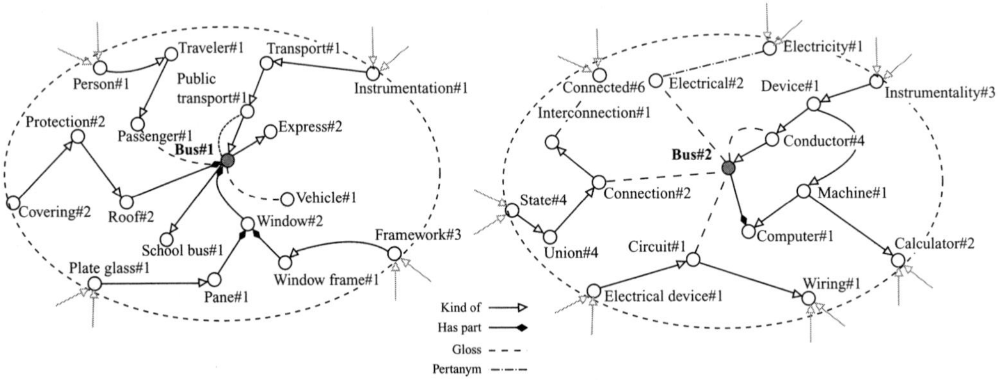

Figure 4–3: The graphs for sense 1 and 2 of the noun *bus* as generated by the SSI algorithm

possible disambiguated synsets (since we do use sense-tagged data)[2]. If this is a null set, then the algorithm makes an initial guess at what the most likely sense of the least ambiguous term in the context is. During an iteration, the algorithm selects those terms t in P that show semantic interconnections with at least one sense of S of t and one or more senses in I. A function $f_I(S,t)$ determines the likelihood of S being the correct interpretation of t and is defined as:

$$f_I(S,t) = \begin{cases} \rho(\{\varphi(S,S')|S' \in I\}), & \text{if } S \in Senses(t) \\ 0, & \text{otherwise} \end{cases} \tag{4.1}$$

where $Senses(t)$ are the senses associated with the term t, and

$$\varphi(S,S') = \rho'(\{w(e_1 \cdot e_2 \cdots e_n)|S \xrightarrow{e_1} S_1 \xrightarrow{e_2} \ldots \xrightarrow{e_{n-1}} S_{n-1} \xrightarrow{e_n} S'\}) \tag{4.2}$$

that is, a function (ρ') of the weights (w) of each path connecting S and S', where S and S' are semantic graphs, and edges e_1 to e_n are the edges connecting them. A good choice for ρ and ρ' would be a sum or average sum function.

Finally, a context-free grammar $G = (E, N, SG, PG)$ encodes all the meaningful semantic patterns, where:

$$E = \{e_{kind-of}, e_{has-kind}, e_{part-of}, \ldots\}$$

are the edge labels,

$$N = \{S_G, S_s, S_g, S_1, S_2, \ldots, E_1, E_2, \ldots\}$$

are nonterminal symbols that encode paths between the senses,

$$S_G$$

2. A *synset* is a set of lemmas that all have the same word sense. The term was coined by the creators of WordNet [16].

is the start symbol of the graph G, and

$$P_G = \{S_G \rightarrow S_s|S_g, S_s \rightarrow S_1|S_2|S_3, S_1 \rightarrow E_1S_1|E_1, E_1 \rightarrow e_{kind-of}|e_{part-of}, S_g \rightarrow e_{gloss}S_5|S_4|S_5, \ldots\}$$

are the productions (roughly 40 in the reported study).

The hierarchical concept information in WordNet has been successfully utilized by many approaches. Refer to Patwardhan, Banerjee, and Pedersen [42] for a comparison of several semantic similarity measures based on WordNet. Recent emergence of unstructured knowledge bases such as Wikipedia has led to a new generation of algorithms that extract the implicit knowledge encoded in them to assist generation of resources that previously relied mostly on WordNet-like resources to generate even wider coverage and multilingual knowledge bases that help further the state of the art in many tasks such as word sense disambiguation. Strube and Ponzetto [43, 44] provided an algorithm called WikiRelate! to estimate the distance between two concepts using the Wikipedia taxonomy. Even more recently, Navigli and Ponzetto [45] introduced a novel method for automatically creating a multilingual lexical knowledge base that establishes a mapping between the large multilingual resource Wikipedia and the English computational lexicon WordNet. It currently includes six languages (German, Spanish, Catalan, Italian, French, and English). The mapping to freely available WordNets in those languages can be easily generated using English WordNet as the interlingua. The continued growth of Wikipedia will enable the generation of resources for many other languages using this methodology. As a starting point, Ponzetto and Navigli [46] have already shown that the English information in BabelNet can be used to create a word sense disambiguation system that rivals previous methods on the task of coarse-grained sense dismabiguation as well as domain-specific sense disambiguation.

Supervised

Ironically, the simpler form of word sense disambiguating systems—the supervised approach, which tends to transfer all the complexity to the machine learning machinery while still requiring hand annotation—tends to be superior to unsupervised methods and performs best when tested on annotated data [21]. The downside to this approach is that the sense inventory has to be predetermined, and any change in the inventory might necessitate a round of expensive reannotation.

These systems typically consist of a machine learning classifier trained on various features extracted for words that have been manually disambiguated in a given corpus and the application of resulting models to disambiguate words in unseen test sets. A good feature of these systems is that the user can incorporate rules and knowledge in the form of features, and possibly semiautomatically generate training data to augment the set that has been manually annotated, in an attempt to achieve the best of all three approaches. Of course, a particular knowledge source and/or classifier combination may have issues that make it less amenable to deriving the most optimal feature representation, and the semiautomatically generated sense-tagged data could be noisy to varying degrees. Nevertheless, state-of-the-art systems usually tend to be a combination of rich features and exploitation of redundancy in language.

We look at some of the typical systems and features in this section. Brown et al. [47] were probably the first to use machine learning for word sense disambiguation using information in parallel corpora. Yarowsky [48] was among the first to use a rich set of features in a machine learning framework—decision lists—to tackle the word sense problem. Several other researchers, such as Ng and Lee [20, 49], have used and refined those features in several variations, including different levels of context and granularities: sentence, paragraph, microcontext, and so on. In this section, we look at some of the more popular methods and features that are relatively easy to obtain.

Classifier Probably the most common and high-performing classifiers are support vector machines (SVMs) and maximum entropy (MaxEnt) classifiers. Many good-quality, freely available distributions of each are available and can be used to train word sense disambiguation models. Typically, because each lemma has a separate sense inventory, it is almost always the case that a separate model is trained for each lemma and POS combination (i.e., if the language, as in the case of English, has separate sense inventories for various parts of speech).

Features We discuss a more commonly found subset of features that have been useful in supervised learning of word sense. These are not exhaustive by any means, but ones that have been time-tested, and provide a very good base that can be used to achieve nearly state-of-the-art performance.

Lexical context—This feature comprises the words and lemmas of words occurring in the entire paragraph or a smaller window of usually five words.

Parts of speech—This feature comprises the POS information for words in the window surrounding the word that is being sense tagged.

Bag of words context—This feature comprises using an unordered set of words in the context window. A threshold is typically tuned to include the most informative words in the larger context.

Local collocations—Local collocations are an ordered sequence of phrases near the target word that provide semantic context for disambiguation. Usually, a very small window of about three tokens on each side of the target word, most often in contiguous pairs or triplets, are added as a list of features. For example, if the target word is w, then $C_{i,j}$ would be a collocation where i and j refer to the start and offsets with respect to the word w. A positive sign indicates words on the right, and a negative sign indicates words on the left of the target.

The following set of 11 features is the union of the collocation features used in Ng and Lee [20, 50]. $C_{-1,-1}$, $C_{1,1}$, $C_{-2,-2}$, $C_{2,2}$, $C_{-2,-1}$, $C_{-1,1}$, $C_{1,2}$, $C_{-3,-1}$, $C_{-2,1}$, $C_{-1,2}$, $C_{1,3}$. To illustrate a few of these, let's take our earlier example for disambiguating *nail*: *He bought a box of <u>nails</u> from the hardware store*. In this example, the collocation $C_{1,1}$ would be the word *from*, and $C_{1,3}$ would be the string *from_the_hardware*, and so on. Usually, stop-words and punctuations are not removed before creating the collocations. Boundary conditions are treated by adding a null word in a collocation. Researchers could also experiment using root forms of the words and other variations that might help better generalize the context. A guideline on what criteria to consider in choosing the number and context of collocations is discussed by Gale et al. [12].

Syntactic relations—If the parse of the sentence containing the target word is available, then we can use syntactic features. One set of features that was proposed by Lee and Ng [49] is listed in Algorithm 4–2.

Topic features—The broad topic, or domain, of the article that the word belongs to is also a good indicator of what sense of the word might be most frequent.

Chen and Palmer [51] recently proposed some additional rich features for disambiguation:

Voice of the sentence—This ternary feature indicates whether the sentence in which the word occurs is a passive, semipassive,[3] or active sentence.

Presence of subject/object—This binary feature indicates whether the target word has a subject or object. Given a large amount of training data, we could also use the actual lexeme and possibly the semantic roles rather than the syntactic subject/objects.

Sentential complement—This binary feature indicates whether the word has a sentential complement.

Prepositional phrase adjunct—This feature indicates whether the target word has a prepositional phrase, and if so, selects the head of the noun phrase inside the prepositional phrase.

Algorithm 4–2 Rules for selecting syntactic relations as features

if w is a *noun* **then**
    select parent head word (h)
    select part of speech of h
    select voice of h
    select position of h (left, right)
else if w is a *verb* **then**
    select nearest word l to the left of w such that w is the parent head word of l
    select nearest word r to the right of w such that w is the parent head word of r
    select part of speech of l
    select part of speech of r
    select part of speech of w
    select voice of w
else if w is a *adjective* **then**
    select parent head word (h)
    select part of speech of h
end if

3. Verbs that are past participles and not preceded by *be* or *have* verbs are semipassive.

Named entity—This feature is the named entity of the proper nouns and certain types of common nouns.

WordNet—WordNet synsets of the hypernyms of head nouns of the noun phrase arguments of verbs and prepositions.

More recently, following research in semantic role labeling, Dligach and Palmer [52] proposed the following features for verb sense disambiguation:

Path—This feature is the path from the target verb to the verb's arguments.

Subcategorization—The subcategorization frame is essentially the string formed by joining the verb phrase type with that of its children.

Most likely, developers will have to perform a feature selection per-word to get the best set of features for a particular word.

Unsupervised

Progress in word sense disambiguation is stymied by the dearth of labeled training data to train a classifier for every sense of each word in a given language. There are a few solutions to this problem:

1. Devise a way to cluster instances of a word so that each cluster effectively constrains the examples of the word to a certain sense. This could be considered **sense induction** through clustering.
2. Use some metrics to identify the proximity of a given instance with some sets of known senses of a word and select the closest to be the sense of that instance.
3. Start with **seeds** of examples of certain senses, then iteratively grow them to form clusters.

We do not discuss in much detail the mostly clustering-based sense induction methods here. We assume that there is already a predefined sense inventory for a word and that the unsupervised methods use very few, if any, hand-annotated examples, and then attempt to classify unseen test instances into one of their predetermined sense categories.

We first look at the category of algorithms that use some form of distance measure to identify senses. Rada et al. [53] introduced a metric for computing the shortest distance between the two pairs of senses in WordNet. This metric assumes that multiple co-occurring words are likely to exhibit senses that would minimize the distance in a semantic network of hierarchical relations, for example, IS-A, from WordNet. Resnik [54] proposed a new measure of semantic similarity: **information content** in an IS-A taxonomy which produces much better results than the edge-counting measure. Agirre and Rigau [55] further refined this measure, calling it **conceptual density**, which not only depends on the number of separating edges but is also sensitive to the depth of the hierarchy and the density of its concepts and is independent of the number of concepts being measured. Conceptual density is defined for each of the subhierarchies in Figure 4–4. The sense that

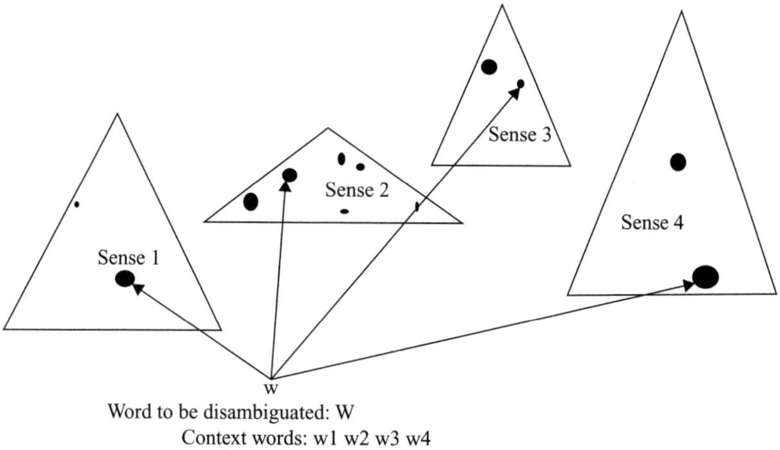

Figure 4–4: Conceptual density

falls in the subhierarchy with the highest conceptual density is chosen to be the correct sense.

$$CD(c,m) = \frac{\sum_{i=0}^{m-1} \text{hyponyms}^{i^{-0.20}}}{\text{descendants}_c} \tag{4.3}$$

In Figure 4–4, Sense 2 is the one with the highest conceptual density and is therefore the chosen sense.

Resnik [56] observed that selectional constraints and word sense are closely related and identified a measure by which to compute the sense of a word on the basis of predicate-argument statistics. Note that this algorithm is primarily limited to the disambiguation of nouns that are arguments of verb predicates.

Let A_R be the selectional association of the predicate p to the concept c with respect to argument R. A_R is defined as:

$$A_R(p,c) = \frac{1}{S_R(p)} P(c|p) \log \frac{P(c|p)}{P(c)}$$

If n is the noun that is in an argument relation R to predicate p, and $\{s_1, s_2, \ldots, s_k\}$ are its possible senses, then, for i from 1 to k, compute:

$$C_i = \{c | c \text{ is an ancestor of } s_i\} \tag{4.4}$$

$$a_i = \max_{c \in C_i} A_R(p,c) \tag{4.5}$$

where a_i is the score for sense s_i. The sense s_i which has the largest value of a_i is sense for the word. Ties are broken by random choice.

Leacock, Miller, and Chodorow [58] provide another algorithm that makes use of corpus statistics and WordNet relations, and show that monosemous relatives can be exploited for disambiguating words.

Algorithms Motivated by Crosslinguistic Evidence

There is a family of unsupervised algorithms based on crosslinguistic information or evidence. Brown et al. [47] were probably the first to make use of this information for purposes of sense disambiguation. They were particularly interested not only in the sense distinctions that were restricted to the ones made by monolingual dictionary resources but also in sense differences that required translating into other languages. They provide a method to use the context information for a given word to identify its most likely translation in the target language. This idea was further explored by Dagan and Itai [59], who use a bilingual lexicon paired with a monolingual corpus to acquire statistics on word senses automatically. They also propose that syntactic relations along with word co-occurrences statistics provide a good source to resolve lexical ambiguity. Further experiments were performed by Diab [60] using machine translated English-to-Arabic translations to extract sense information for training a supervised classifier. These experiments compared favorably with other purely unsupervised methods. The algorithm SALAAM, which requires a word-aligned parallel corpus, is described in Figure 4–5.

Semisupervised

The next category of algorithms we look at are those that start from a small seed of examples and an iterative algorithm that identifies more training examples using a classifier. This additional, automatically labeled data can then be used to augment the training data of the classifier to provide better predictions for the next selection cycle, and so on. The Yarowsky algorithm [61] is the classic case of such an algorithm and was seminal in introducing semisupervised methods to the word sense disambiguation problem. The algorithm is based on the assumption that two strong properties are exhibited by corpora:

1. **One sense per collocation:** Syntactic relationship and the types of words occurring nearby a given word tend to provide a strong indication as to the sense of that word.

1. L1 words that translate into the same L2 word are grouped into clusters.
2. SALAAM (Sense Assignment Leveraging Alignment and Multilinguality) identifies the appropriate senses for the words in those clusters according to the words senses' proximity in WordNet. The word sense proximity is measured in information theoretic terms on the basis of an algorithm by Resnik [57].
3. A sense selection criterion is applied to choose the appropriate sense label or set of sense labels for each word in the cluster.
4. The chosen sense tags for the words in the cluster are propagated back to their respective contexts in the parallel text. Simultaneously, SALAAM projects the propagated sense tags for L1 words onto their L2 corresponding translations.

Figure 4–5: SALAAM algorithm for creating training using parallel English-to-Arabic machine translations

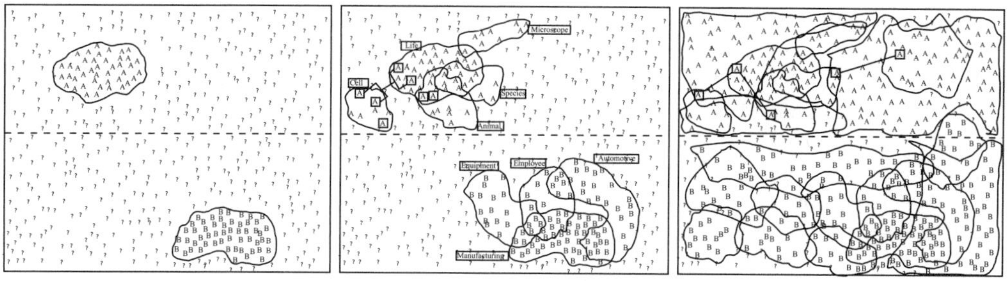

Figure 4–6: The three stages of the Yarowsky algorithm

2. **One sense per discourse:** Usually, in a given discourse, all instances of the same lemma tend to invoke the same sense.

Based on the assumption that these properties exist, the Yarowsky algorithm iteratively disambiguates most of the words in a given discourse.

Figure 4–6 shows the three stages of the algorithm. In the first box, *life* and *manufacturing* are used as collocates to identify the two senses of *plant*. Then, in the next iteration, a new collocate *cell* is identified, and the final block shows the small residual remaining at the end of the algorithm cycle. This algorithm, as described in Figure 4–7, has been shown to perform well on a small number of examples. For it to be successful, it is important to select a good way to identify seed examples and to devise a way to identify potential corruption of the labeled pool by wrong examples. More recently, Galley and McKeown [62] showed that the assumption of one sense per discourse assumption improves performance.

Another variation of semisupervised systems is the use of unsupervised methods for the creation of data combined with supervised methods to learn models for that data. The presumption is that the potential noise of wrong examples selected from a corpus during this process would be low enough so as not to affect learnability. Another presumption is that the overall discriminative ability of the model is superior to purely unsupervised methods or to situations in which not enough hand-annotated data is available to train a purely supervised system. Mihalcea and Moldovan [63] describe one such system in which the algorithm in Figure 4–8 is used to obtain examples from large corpora for particular senses in WordNet.

Mihalcea [64] proposes the following method using Wikipedia for automatic word sense disambiguation.

- **Extract** all the sentences in Wikipedia in which the word under consideration is a link. There are two types of links: a simple link, such as `[[bar]]`, or a piped link, such as `[[musical_notation|bar]]`.

- **Filter** those links that point to a disambiguation page. This means that we need further information to disambiguate the word. If the word does not point to a disambiguation page, then the word itself can be the label. For all piped links, the string before the pipe serves as the label.

- **Collect** all the labels associated with the word, and then map them to possible WordNet senses. Sometimes they might all map to the same sense, essentially making the

Step 1. In a sufficiently large corpus, identify all the instances of a particular polysemous word that needs to be disambiguated, storing its context alongside.
Step 2. Identify a small set of instances that are strongly representative of one of the senses of the word. This can either be done in a completely unsupervised fashion by identifying collocations that give a strong indication of the sense usage for the word under consideration or by manually tagging a small portion of the data. In this example, we assume a polysemous word with only two senses, but this algorithm can be extended to n senses.
Step 3.

Step 3a. Train a supervised classifier on this set of examples.

Step 3b. Using these classifiers, classify the remaining instances of the word in the corpus and select those that are classified above a certain level of confidence.

Step 3c. Filter out the possible misclassifications using one sense per discourse constraint, and identify possible new collocations to be added to the list of seed collocations.

Step 3d. Repeat step 3 iteratively, thereby slowly shrinking the residual.

Step 4. Stop. At some point, a small, stable residual will remain.
Step 5. The trained classifier can now be used to classify new data, and that in turn can be used to annotate the original corpus with sense tags and probabilities.

Figure 4–7: The Yarowsky algorithm

verb monosemous and not useful for this purpose. Often, the categories can be mapped to a significant number of WordNet categories, thereby proving sense-disambiguated data for training. The manual mapping is a relatively inexpensive process.

This algorithm provides a cheap way of extracting sense information for many words that display the required properties, and it can alleviate the manually intensive process of sense tagging. Depending on how many words in the entire Wikipedia exhibit this property, it could be very useful for generating sense-tagged data. A rough idea of the coverage of this method can be gleaned from the fact that roughly 30 of 49 nouns that were used for SENSEVAL-2 and SENSEVAL-3 were found to have more than two senses for which data could be extracted from Wikipedia. The average disambiguation accuracy on these senses was in the mid-80% range. The interannotator agreement for mapping the senses to WordNet was around 91%.

4.4.3 Software

Several software programs are made available by the research community for word sense disambiguation, ranging from similarity measure modules to full disambiguation systems. It is not possible to list all of them here, so we list a selected few.

Step 1. *Preprocessing*

- For each sense of a word W, determine the synsets of WordNet in which it appears. For each such synset, determine monosemous words included in that synset. Parse the gloss definition attached to each synset.

Step 2. *Search*

- Form search phrases using the following procedures in order of preference
  1. If they exist, extract monosemous synonyms from the synsets selected in step 1.
  2. Select each of the unambiguous parsed constituents in the gloss as a search phrase.
  3. After parsing the gloss, replace all stop-words with a NEAR operator and create a query from the words in the current synset. For example, if the synset for *produce#6* is *grow, raise, farm, produce*, and the gloss is *cultivate by growing*, then the query will look like: *cultivate* NEAR *growing* AND (*grow* OR *raise* OR *farm* OR *produce*).
  4. Use only the head phrase combined by words in the synset using the AND operator. For example, if the definition for *company#5* is *band of people* and its synset is (*party, company*), then the query becomes: *band of people* AND (*party* OR *company*).
- Search the Internet with the phrases determined in the previous step and gather matching documents
- From these documents, extract the sentences containing these words

Step 3. *Postprocessing*

- Keep only those sentences in which the word under consideration belongs to the same part of speech as the selected sense, and delete the others.

Figure 4–8: Mihalcea and Moldovan [63] algorithm for generating examples for words tagged with particular senses by querying a very large corpus

- **IMS** (It Makes Sense) http://nlp.comp.nus.edu.sg/software
  This is a complete word sense disambiguation system.
- **WordNet-Similarity-2.05** http://search.cpan.org/dist/WordNet-Similarity
  These WordNet Similarity modules for Perl provide a quick way of computing various word similarity measures.
- **WikiRelate**!
  http://www.h-its.org/english/research/nlp/download/wiki pediasimilarity.php
  This is a word similarity measure based on the categories in Wikipedia.

4.5 Predicate-Argument Structure

Shallow semantic parsing, or what is popularly known today as **semantic role labeling**, is the process of identifying the various arguments of predicates in a sentence. The linguistic community has been debating for a few decades over what constitutes the set of arguments and what the granularity of such argument labels should be for various predicates, which in turn can be the verbs, nouns, adjectives, and prepositions in a sentence [65, 66].

4.5.1 Resources

The late 1990s saw the emergence of two important corpora that are semantically tagged. One is FrameNet[4] [67, 68, 69, 70] and the other is PropBank[5] [71]. These resources have begun a transition from a long tradition of predominantly rule-based approaches toward more data-oriented approaches. These approaches focus on transforming linguistic insights into features, rather than into rules, and letting a machine learning framework use those features to learn a model that helps automatically tag the semantic information encoded in such resources. FrameNet is based on the theory of **frame semantics**, where a given predicate invokes a **semantic frame**, thus instantiating some or all of the possible semantic roles belonging to that frame [72]. PropBank, on the other hand, is based on Dowty's [73] prototype theory and uses a more linguistically neutral view in which each predicate has a set of core arguments that are predicate dependent, and all predicates share a set of non-core, or adjunctive, arguments. It builds on the syntactic Penn Treebank corpus. We now discuss these approaches in more detail.

FrameNet

FrameNet contains frame-specific semantic annotation of a number of predicates in English. It contains tagged sentences extracted from the British National Corpus (BNC). The process of FrameNet annotation consists of identifying specific semantic frames and creating a set of frame-specific roles called **frame elements**. Then, a set of predicates that instantiate the semantic frame, irrespective of their grammatical category, are identified, and a variety of sentences are labeled for those predicates. The labeling process entails identifying the frame that an instance of the predicate lemma invokes, then identifying semantic arguments for that instance, and tagging them with one of the predetermined set of frame elements for that frame. The combination of the predicate lemma and the frame that its instance invokes is called a lexical unit (LU). This is therefore the pairing of a word with its meaning. Each sense of a polysemous word tends to be associated with a unique frame. For example, the verb *break* can mean *fail to observe (a law, regulation, or agreement)* and can belong to a COMPLIANCE frame along with other word meanings such as *violation, obey, flout*; or it can mean *cause to suddenly separate into pieces in a destructive manner* and can belong to a CAUSE_TO_FRAGMENT frame along with other meanings such as *fracture, fragment, smash.*

4. http://framenet.icsi.berkeley.edu/
5. http://verbs.colorado.edu/~mpalmer/projects/ace.html

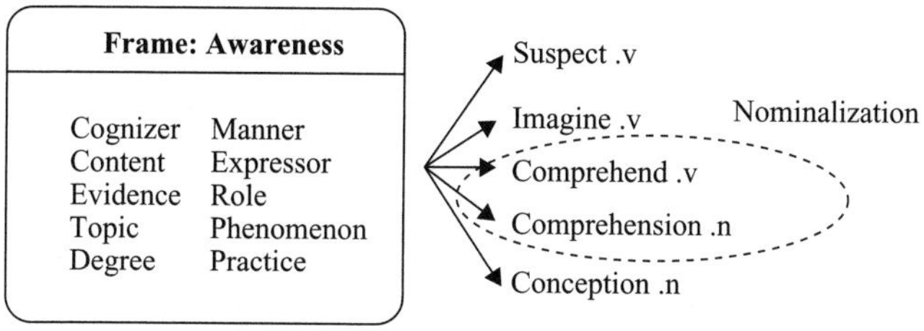

Figure 4–9: FrameNet example

The following example illustrates the general idea. Here, the frame AWARENESS is instantiated by the verb predicate *believe* and the noun predicate *comprehension*. Figure 4–9 shows the AWARENESS frame along with the frame-elements and a sample set of predicates that involve it—including verbs and nominalizations.

1. [$_{Cognizer}$ We] [$_{Predicate:verb}$ *believe*] [$_{Content}$ it is a fair and generous price]
2. No doubts existed as to [$_{Cognizer}$ our] [$_{Predicate:noun}$ *comprehension*] [$_{Content}$ of it]

FrameNet encompasses a wide variety of nominal predicates. They include ultra-nominals [74, 73], nominals, and nominalizations. FrameNet also contains some adjective and preposition predicates.

To get an idea of the amount of data we are talking about as of this writing, the latest release of FrameNet, R1.5, contains about 173,000 predicate instances covering about 8,000 frame elements from roughly 1,000 frames over the BNC. Although the number of frame elements seems very large, many share the same meaning across the 11,000 lexical units. For example, the frame element BODY_PART in frame CURE has the same meaning as the same element in the frame GESTURE or in WEARING.

PropBank

PropBank only includes annotations of arguments of verb predicates. All the noncopular verbs in the WSJ part of the Penn Treebank [75] have been labeled with their semantic arguments. PropBank restricts the argument boundaries to that of a syntactic constituent, as defined in the Penn Treebank. It uses a linguistically neutral terminology to label the arguments. The arguments are tagged as either **core arguments**, with labels of the type ARGN, where N takes values from 0 to 5, or **adjunctive arguments** (listed in Table 4–2), with labels of the type ARGM-X, where *X* can take values such as TMP for temporal, LOC for locative, and so on. Adjunctive arguments share the same meaning across all predicates, whereas the meaning of core arguments has to be interpreted in connection with a predicate. ARG0 is the PROTO-AGENT (usually the subject of a transitive verb), ARG1 is the PROTO-PATIENT (usually its direct object of the transitive verb) [73]. Table 4–1 shows a list of core arguments for the predicates *operate* and *author*. Note that some core arguments, such as ARG2 and ARG3, do not occur with *author*. This is explained by the fact that not all core arguments can be instantiated by all senses of all predicates. A list of core arguments that can occur with a particular sense of the predicate, along with their real-world meaning, is present in a file called the *frames* file. One frames file is associated with each predicate.

Table 4–1: Argument labels associated with the predicate *operate.01* (sense: work), and for *author.01* (sense: to write or construct) in the PropBank corpus

Predicate	Argument	Description
operate.01		
	ARG0	Agent, operator
	ARG1	Thing operated
	ARG2	Explicit patient (thing operated on)
	ARG3	Explicit argument
	ARG4	Explicit instrument
author.01		
	ARG0	Author, agent
	ARG1	Text authored

Table 4–2: List of adjunctive arguments in PropBank—ARGMs

Tag	Description	Examples
ARGM-LOC	Locative	*the museum, in Westborough, Mass.*
ARGM-TMP	Temporal	*now, by next summer*
ARGM-MNR	Manner	*heavily, clearly, at a rapid rate*
ARGM-DIR	Direction	*to market, to Bangkok*
ARGM-CAU	Cause	*In response to the ruling*
ARGM-DIS	Discourse	*for example, in part, Similarly*
ARGM-EXT	Extent	*at $38.375, 50 points*
ARGM-PRP	Purpose	*to pay for the plant*
ARGM-NEG	Negation	*not, n't*
ARGM-MOD	Modal	*can, might, should, will*
ARGM-REC	Reciprocals	*each other*
ARGM-PRD	Secondary Predication	*to become a teacher*
ARGM	Bare ARGM	*with a police escort*
ARGM-ADV	Adverbials	*(none of the above)*

An example extracted from the PropBank corpus along with its syntax tree representation and argument labels is shown in Figure 4–10.

Most Treebank-style trees have **trace nodes** that refer to another node in the tree but have no words associated with them. These can also be marked as arguments. Because traces are not reproduced by a usual syntactic parser, the community has disregarded them from most standard experiments. PropBank also contains arguments that are coreferential. As with any strategy that integrates multiple layers of annotation, there exist some disagreements between the Treebank and PropBank annotation. Sometimes the PropBankers strongly believed an error existed in the tree or the tree structure was not amenable to a

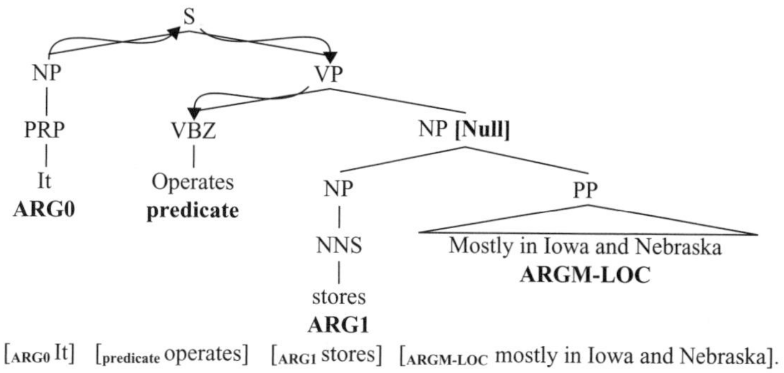

Figure 4–10: Syntax tree for a sentence illustrating the PropBank tags

one-to-one mapping between the argument and a tree node. In such cases, they annotated a sequence of nodes in the tree as the argument. These are called **discontiguous arguments**, and very few (~1%–2%) cases exist in the data. There are around 115,000 predicate instances instantiating about 250,000 instances of the roughly 20 argument types over about 5,000 frames in the WSJ portion of the PropBank release. There are about 18,000 more predicates annotated with arguments from the Brown Corpus. More recently, the OntoNotes project [22, 23, 24] has annotated more corpora from various genres with predicate-argument structures using the PropBank guidelines. This has led to modifications to the Penn Treebank and PropBank guidelines to generate a better, more aligned resource [76]. Most experiments discussed in this chapter use the WSJ annotation from PropBank v1.0.

An important distinction to note between the FrameNet and PropBank corpora is that in FrameNet there exist lexical units, which are words paired with their meanings or the frames that they invoke, whereas in PropBank each lemma has a list of different **framesets** that represent all the senses for which there is a different argument structure. These are akin to word senses but tend to be coarser grained [77].

Other Resources

Other resources have been developed to aid further research in predicate-argument recognition. NomBank [78] was inspired by PropBank. In the process of identifying and tagging the arguments of nouns, the NOMLEX (NOMinalization LEXicon) [79] dictionary was expanded to cover about 6,000 entries. Along with this, the frames from PropBank were used to generate the frame files for NomBank. Another resource that ties PropBank frames with more predicate-independent thematic roles and also provides a richer representation associating the framesets with Levin classes [80] is VerbNet [81]. In fact the PropBank frames have a strong connection with the Levin verb classes, specifically the intersective Levin classes [82]. FrameNet frames are also somewhat related in the sense that FrameNet's generation of verb classes is more data driven than theoretical. Baker and Ruppenhofer [83] present an interesting discussion on how the FrameNet frames relate to Levin classes.

Although FrameNet and PropBank started with annotating predicate-argument structures in English, it was not long before their philosophy propagated to other languages. Because FrameNet was based on frame semantics with coarse-grained semantic frames, and the nature of semantics is lingua independent, it was apparent that these frames could be reused to annotate data in other languages. The SALSA project [84, 85] was the first to put this into practice. FrameNet tags both literal and metaphorical interpretations of text, but that can lead to ambiguity and lower consistency, so the SALSA project remained close to the literal meaning. It reused all possible, preexisting FrameNet frames, and when linguistic semantic parallelism did not propagate across languages, they created more frames. Subsequently, there exist FrameNets in Japanese [86, 87], Spanish [88], and Swedish [89]. As of this writing, there are FrameNet projects underway in more than 10 languages [90].

PropBank has inspired the creation of similar resources in Chinese [91], Arabic [92, 93], Korean [94], Spanish, Catalan [95], and most recently, Hindi [96]. Many of these involve the same core researchers. Unlike FrameNet, every new PropBank requires the creation of a new set of frame files.

Although the FrameNet and PropBank philosophies have inspired similar projects in other languages, they are not the only styles used in practice. For example, the Prague Dependency Treebank [97] takes a different approach, tagging the predicate-argument structure in its tectogrammatic layer on top of the dependency structure. It also makes a distinction similar to that of core and adjunctive arguments called **inner participants** and **free modifications**. The NAIST Text Corpus [98] is strongly influenced by the traditions in Japanese linguistics.

4.5.2 Systems

Unlike word sense disambiguation, little research has gone into learning predicate-argument structures from unannotated corpora, perhaps because it is closer to the actual applications and has been more or less absorbed in the area of information extraction. Most early systems, such as KL-ONE [99] and others [100, 101], were based primarily on heuristics on syntax trees, which were in turn rule based until the Penn Treebank was available as a training resource for supervised syntactic parsers. Most of these systems dealt with (predicate-independent) thematic roles. There has been a great deal of linguistic inquiry into the nature of argument structure, but most of it did not directly apply to domain-independent understanding systems. Until corpora were available, the main resources were rules based on syntactic trees. One significantly useful resource, mentioned earlier in context of PropBank, was the classification of verbs and their alternations by Levin [80]. The Absity parser [102, 13] is one of the first rule-based semantic parsers. Also notable was the parser used in the PUNDIT understanding system [103, 104]. Efforts were later made to use a hybrid method for thematic role tagging [105, 106] using WordNet as a resource for domain-specific interpretation [107]. Other notable efforts are the corpus-based studies by Manning [108] and Briscoe and Carroll [109], which seek to derive the subcategorization information from large corpora, and by Pustejovsky [110], which tries to acquire lexical semantic knowledge from corpora.

A major leap forward in semantic role labeling research happened after the introduction of FrameNet and PropBank. One big problem with the FrameNet philosophy, and also partly with that of PropBank, is that significant work goes into creating the frames, that is, in classifying verbs into the framesets in preparation for manual annotation. Therefore, providing coverage for all possible verbs in one or more languages requires significant manual effort upfront. Green, Dorr, and Resnik [111] propose a way to learn the frame structures automatically, but the result is not accurate enough to replace the manual frame creation. Swier and Stevenson [112] represent one of the more recent approaches to handling this problem in an unsupervised fashion.

Let us now review the more recent and common approaches since the advent of these corpora. The process of semantic role labeling can be defined as identifying a set of word sequences, each of which represents a semantic argument of a given predicate. For example, for the sentence in Figure 4–10, for the predicate *operates*, the word *I* fills the role ARG0, the word *stores* fills the role ARG1, and the sequence of words *mostly in Iowa and Nebraska* fills the role ARGM-LOC. Recall that PropBank is largely agnostic to any generalizations made across predicates; an ARGN for one predicate need not have similar semantics compared to another predicate.[6]

FrameNet was the first project that used hand-tagged arguments of predicates in data, and Gildea and Jurafsky [113] were the first to formulate semantic role labeling as a supervised classification problem that assumes the arguments of a predicate and the predicate itself can be mapped to a node in the syntax tree for that sentence. They introduced three tasks that could be used to evaluate the system and that have become standard since:

Argument identification—This is the task of identifying all and only the parse constituents that represent valid semantic arguments of a predicate.

Argument classification—Given constituents known to represent arguments of a predicate, assign the appropriate argument labels to them.

Argument identification and classification—This task is a combination of the previous two tasks, where the constituents that represent arguments of a predicate are identified, and the appropriate argument label is assigned to them.

Once the sentence has been parsed using a syntactic parser, each node in the parse tree can be classified as either one that represents a semantic argument (i.e., non-null node) or one that does not represent any semantic argument (i.e., a null node). The non-null nodes can then be further classified into the set of argument labels.

For example, in the tree of Figure 4–10, the noun phrase that encompasses *stores mostly in Iowa and Nebraska* is a null node because it does not correspond to a semantic argument. The node NP that encompasses *stores* is a non-null node because it does correspond to a semantic argument: ARG1.

The pseudocode for a generic semantic role labeling (SRL) algorithm is shown in Algorithm 4–3.

Syntactic Representations

As we have seen, PropBank was created as a layer of annotation on top of Penn Treebank–style phrase structure trees, and in some of the early work in recovering PropBank annotations, Gildea and Jurafsky [113] added argument labels to parses obtained from a parser trained on Penn Treebank. In subsequent years, researchers have used various other types of

6. The PropBank project did not haphazardly assign argument role numbers, either. For instance, in practice, ARG0 tends to have the role *Agent* and ARG1 tends to have the role *Patient*, to borrow the terminology from θ-roles.

Algorithm 4–3 The semantic role labeling (SRL) algorithm

Procedure: SRL(sentence) **returns** best *semantic role labeling*

Input: *syntactic parse* of the *sentence*

generate a full syntactic parse of the *sentence*
identify all the *predicates*
for all *predicate* ∈ *sentence* **do**
    extract a set of features for each node in the tree relative to the *predicate*
    classify each feature vector using the *model* created in training
    select the class of highest scoring classifier
    return best *semantic role labeling*
end for

sentence representations, either directly or as an independent source of evidence, to tackle the semantic role labeling problem. We look at each of these sentence representations in turn and at the features that were used to tag text with PropBank arguments.

Phrase Structure Grammar (PSG) FrameNet marks word spans in sentences to represent arguments, whereas PropBank tags nodes in a treebank tree with arguments. Because several high-quality statistical parsers existed that could produce phrase structure trees, and because the phrase structure representation is amenable to tagging, Gildea and Jurafsky [113] used it. They introduced the following features, some of which were extracted from the parse tree of the sentence:

Path—This feature is the syntactic path through the parse tree from the parse constituent to the predicate being classified. For example, in Figure 4–10, the path from ARG0 *It* to the predicate *operates* is represented by the string NP↑S↓VP↓VBZ. ↑ and ↓ represent upward and downward movement in the tree respectively.

Predicate—The identity of the predicate lemma is used as a feature.

Phrase type—This feature is the syntactic category (NP, PP, S, etc.) of the constituent to be labeled.

Position—This feature is a binary feature identifying whether the phrase is before or after the predicate.

Voice—This feature indicates whether the predicate is realized as an active or passive construction. A set of handwritten `tgrep2`[7] expressions on the syntax tree are used to identify the passive-voiced predicates.

Head word—This feature is the syntactic head of the phrase. It is calculated using a head word table described by Magerman [114] and modified by Collins [115].

7. See http://tedlab.mit.edu/~dr/Tgrep2/.

Subcategorization—This feature is the phrase structure rule expanding the predicate's parent node in the parse tree. For example, in Figure 4–10, the subcategorization for the predicate *operates* is VP→VBZ-NP.

Verb clustering—The predicate is one of the most salient features in predicting the argument class. Given various syntactic/semantic constructions that a predicate can appear in, any amount of hand-tagged training data would be relatively limited for estimating the parameters of a model, and any real-world test set will contain predicate sense/frames that have not been seen in training. In these cases, researchers can benefit from some information about the predicate by creating clusters or classes and using them as features. Gildea and Jurafsky [113] used a distance function for clustering that is based on the intuition that verbs with similar semantics will tend to have similar direct objects. For example, verbs such as *eat*, *devour*, and *savor* will tend to all occur with direct objects describing food. The clustering algorithm uses a database of verb–direct object relations extracted by Lin [116]. The verbs were clustered into 64 classes using the probabilistic co-occurrence model of Hofmann and Puzicha [117].

Surdeanu et al. [118] suggested the following additional features:

Content word—Because the head word feature of some constituents, such as PP and SBAR, is not very informative, they defined a set of heuristics for some constituent type. A different set of rules was used to identify a so-called **content** word instead of using the usual head word–finding rules. This was used as an additional feature. The rules that they used are shown in Figure 4–11.

Part of speech of the head word and content word—Adding part of speech of the head word and content word of a constituent as a feature to help generalize in the

H1: if phrase type is PP **then** select the rightmost child
  Example: phrase = "in Texas," content word = "Texas"
H2: if phrase type is SBAR **then** select the leftmost sentence (S*) clause
  Example: phrase = "that occurred yesterday," content word = "occurred"
H3: if phrase type is VP **then**
    if there is a VP child **then**
      select the leftmost VP child
    else
      select the head word
  Example: phrase = "had placed," content word = "placed"
H4: if phrase type is ADVP **then** select the rightmost child, not IN or TO
  Example: phrase = "more than," content word = "more"
H5: if phrase type is ADJP **then** select the rightmost adjective, verb, noun, or ADJP
  Example: phrase = "61 years old," content word = "61"
H6: for all other phrase types select the head word
  Example: phrase = "red house," content word = "red"

Figure 4–11: List of content word heuristics

task of argument identification gave a significant performance boost to their decision tree-based system.

Named entity of the content word—Certain roles, such as ARGM-TMP and ARGM-LOC, tend to contain TIME or PLACE named entities. This information was added as a set of binary-valued features.

Boolean named entity flags—Surdeanu et al. also added named entity information as a feature. They created indicator functions for each of the seven named entity types: PERSON, PLACE, TIME, DATE, MONEY, PERCENT, ORGANIZATION.

Phrasal verb collocations—This feature comprises frequency statistics related to the verb and the immediately following preposition.

Fleischman, Kwon, and Hovy [119] added the following features to their system:

Logical function—This is a feature that takes three values—external argument, object argument, and other argument—and is computed using some heuristics on the syntax tree.

Order of frame elements—This feature represents the position of a frame element relative to other frame elements in a sentence.

Syntactic pattern—This feature is also generated using heuristics on the phrase type and the logical function of the constituent.

Previous role—This is a set of features indicating the nth previous role that had been observed/assigned by the system for the current predicate.

Pradhan et al. [120] suggested using the following additional feature variations:

Named entities in constituents—Surdeanu et al. [118] reported a performance improvement on classifying the semantic role of the constituent by using the presence of a named entity in the constituent. Some of these entities, such as location and time, are particularly important for the adjunctive arguments ARGM-LOC and ARGM-TMP. Entity tags should also help in cases where the head words are not common or for a closed set of locative or temporal cues, such as *in Mexico*, or *in 2003*. They also tagged seven named entities in the corpus using IdentiFinder [121] and added them via seven binary features. Each of these features is true if its respective type of named entity is contained in the constituent.

Verb sense information—The arguments that a predicate can take depend on the sense of the predicate. Each predicate tagged in the PropBank corpus is assigned a separate set of arguments depending on the sense in which it is used. This is also known as the **frameset ID**. Table 4–3 illustrates the argument sets for a word. Depending on the sense of the predicate *talk*, either ARG1 or ARG2 can identify the *hearer*. Absence of this information can be potentially confusing to the learning mechanism.

Verb sense information extracted from PropBank is added by treating each sense of a predicate as a distinct predicate, which helps performance. The disambiguation of PropBank framesets can be performed at a very high accuracy [122].

Table 4–3: Argument labels associated with the two senses of predicate *talk* in PropBank corpus

talk.01		talk.02	
Tag	Description	Tag	Description
ARG0	Talker	ARG0	Talker
ARG1	Subject	ARG1	Talked to
ARG2	Hearer	ARG2	Secondary action

Noun head of prepositional phrases—Many adjunctive arguments, such as temporals and locatives, occur as prepositional phrases in a sentence, and the head words of those phrases, which are always prepositions, often are not very discriminative. For instance, *in the city* and *in a few minutes* both share the same head word *in*, and neither contains a named entity, but the former is ARGM-LOC, whereas the latter is ARGM-TMP. Therefore, Pradhan et al. [120] replaced the head word of a prepositional phrase with that of the first noun phrase inside the prepositional phrase. The preposition information was retained by appending it to the phrase type; for example, the head word of the prepositional phrase *for about 20 minutes* was originally the preposition *for*. After the transformation, the head word was changed to *minutes*, and the phrase PP was changed to PP-FOR. The head word was used in its surface form as well as a lemmatized form. The lemmatization was performed automatically using the XTAG morphology database [123].[8]

First and last word/POS in constituent—Some arguments tend to contain discriminative first and last words, so these were used along with their part of speech as four new features.

Ordinal constituent position—This feature avoids false positives where constituents far away from the predicate are spuriously identified as arguments. It is a concatenation of the constituent type and its ordinal position from the predicate.

Constituent tree distance—This is a finer way of specifying the already present position feature, where the distance of the constituent from the predicate is measured in terms of the number of nodes that need to be traversed through the syntax tree to go from one to the other.

Constituent relative features—These are nine features representing the constituent type, head word and head word part of speech of the parent, and left and right siblings of the constituent in focus. These were added on the intuition that encoding the tree context this way might add robustness and improve generalization.

Temporal cue words—Several temporal cue words are not captured by the named entity tagger and were therefore added as binary features indicating their presence.

8. ftp://ftp.cis.upenn.edu/pub/xtag/morph-1.5/morph-1.5.tar.gz

The BOW (Bag of words) toolkit[9] was used to identify words and bigrams that had highest average mutual information with the ARGM-TMP argument class.

Dynamic class context—In the task of argument classification, these are dynamic features that represent the hypotheses of, at most, the previous two non-null nodes belonging to the same tree as the node being classified.

Path generalizations—As will be seen in Section 4.5.2, for the argument identification task, the path is one of the most salient features. However, it is also the most data-sparse feature. To overcome this problem, the path was generalized in several different ways:

Clause-based path variations—Position of the clause node (S, SBAR) seems to be an important feature in argument identification [124]. Accordingly, Pradhan et al. [120] experimented with four clause-based path feature variations.

- Replacing all the nodes in a path other than clause nodes with an (*). For example, the path NP↑S↑VP↑SBAR↑NP↑VP↓VBD becomes NP↑S↑*S↑*↑*↓VBD. SBAR is replaced with S.
- Retaining only the clause nodes in the path, which for the above example would produce NP↑S↑S↓VBD.
- Adding a binary feature that indicates whether the constituent is in the same clause as the predicate,
- Collapsing the nodes between S nodes, which gives NP↑S↑NP↑VP↓VBD.

Path *n*-grams—This feature decomposes a path into a series of trigrams. For example, the path NP↑S↑VP↑SBAR↑NP↑VP↓VBD becomes NP↑S↑VP, S↑VP↑SBAR, VP↑SBAR↑NP, SBAR↑NP↑VP, and so on. Shorter paths were padded with nulls.

Single-character phrase tags—Each phrase category is clustered to a category defined by the first character of the phrase label.

Path compression—Compressing sequences of identical labels into following the intuition that successive embedding of the same phrase in the tree might not add additional information.

Directionless path—Removing the direction in the path, thus making insignificant the point at which it changes direction in the tree.

Partial path—Using only that part of the path from the constituent to the lowest common ancestor of the predicate and the constituent. For example, the partial path for the path illustrated in Figure 4–10 is NP↑S.

Another work that deals with paths in an orthogonal fashion is that of Vickrey and Koller [125]. They perform a rule-based sentence simplification in an attempt to automatically accrue path generalizations.

---

9. http://www.cs.cmu.edu/˜mccallum/bow/

Predicate context—This feature captures predicate sense variations. Two words before and two words after were added as features. The part of speech of the words were also added as features.

Punctuations—For some adjunctive arguments, punctuation plays an important role. This set of features captures whether punctuation appears immediately before and after the constituent.

Feature context—Features of constituents that are parent or siblings of the constituent being classified were found useful. Traditionally, each constituent is classified independently; however, in reality, there is a complex interaction between the types and number of arguments that a constituent can have. In other words, the classification of each argument is dependent on the classifications of other nodes. As we will see later, the method of Pradhan et al. performs a postprocessing step using the argument sequence information, but that does not cover all possible constraints. One way of trying to capture those best in the current architecture would be to take into consideration the feature vector compositions of all the non-null constituents for the sentence. This is exactly what this feature does. It uses all the other feature vector values of the constituents that are likely to be non-null, as an added context.

Combinatory Categorial Grammar (CCG) As we learned, although the path feature is very important for the argument identification task, it is one of the most sparse features and may be difficult to train or generalize [126, 127]. A dependency grammar should generate shorter paths from the predicate to dependent words in the sentence and could be a more robust complement to the phrase structure grammar paths extracted from the PSG parse tree. Gildea and Hockenmaier [128] report that using features extracted from a CCG representation improves semantic role labeling performance on core arguments (ARG0-5). Because CCG trees are binary trees and the constituents have poor alignment with the semantic arguments of a predicate, the researchers performed experiments using head words rather than the entire span. Later, Pradhan et al. (2005) [129] used these features to augment the original phrase structure tree-based algorithm to accrue further benefits.

Figure 4–12 shows the CCG parse of the sentence *London denied plans on Monday*. Gildea and Hockenmaier [128] introduced three features:

Phrase type—This is the category of the maximal projection between the two words, the predicate and the dependent word.

London denied plans on Monday

w_h	w_a	c_h	i
denied	*London*	$(S[dcl]\backslash NP_1)/NP_2$	1
denied	*plans*	$(S[dcl]\backslash NP_1/NP_2$	2
on	*denied*	$((S\backslash NP_1\backslash (S\backslash NP)_2/NP)_3$	2
on	*Monday*	$((S\backslash NP_1\backslash (S\backslash NP)_2/NP)_3$	3

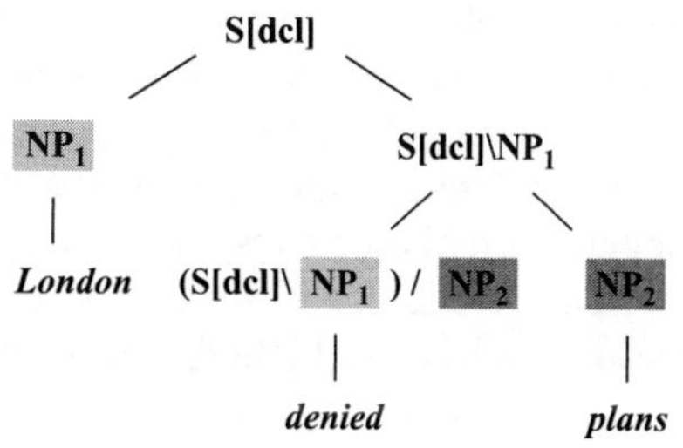

Figure 4–12: Combinatory categorial grammar parse

Categorial path—This is a feature formed by concatenating the following three values: (i) category to which the dependent word belongs, (ii) the direction of dependence, and (iii) the slot in the category filled by the dependent word. For example, for the tree in Figure 4–12, the path between *denied* and *plans* would be (S[dcl]\NP)/NP.2.←.

Tree Path—This is the categorial analogue of the path feature in the Charniak parse-based system, which traces the path from the dependent word to the predicate through the binary CCG tree.

Tree-Adjoining Grammar (TAG) Chen and Rambow [130] report results using two different sets of features: (i) surface syntactic features much like the Gildea and Palmer [131] system and (ii) additional features that result from the extraction of a TAG from the Penn Treebank. They chose a TAG because of its ability to address long-distance dependencies in text. The additional features they introduced are:

Supertag path—This feature is the same as the path feature seen earlier except that in this case it is derived from a TAG rather than from a PSG.

Supertag—This feature is the tree frame corresponding to the predicate or the argument.

Surface syntactic role—This feature is the surface syntactic role of the argument.

Surface subcategorization—This feature is the subcategorization frame.

Deep syntactic role—This feature is the deep syntactic role of an argument, whose values include *subject* and *direct object.*

Deep subcategorization—This is the deep syntactic subcategorization frame. For example, for a transitive verb, it would be NP0_NP1. When available, the preposition modifying the NP is used to lexicalize the feature. So, in case of the predicate *load*, a possible frame would be NP0_NP1_NP2(into).

Semantic subcategorization—Gildea and Palmer also used a semantic subcategorization frame where, in addition to the syntactic categories, the feature includes semantic role information.

While many researchers were constructing various features manually, Moschitti, Pighin, and Basili [132] tried a different approach. They used a tree kernel that identified and selected subtree patterns from a large number of automatically generated patterns to capture the tree context. Unfortunately, for this application, the performance was somewhat inferior to the manually selected features. It is possible that for some other machine learning problem where handcrafting of features is not as intuitive, this technique could prove valuable.

Dependency Trees One issue in the formulations so far is that the performance of a system depends on the exact span of the arguments annotated according to the constituents in the Penn Treebank. Labels are scored as correct only if they match the PropBank annotation exactly; both the bracketing and the label must match. Because PropBank and most syntactic parsers are developed on the Penn Treebank corpus and are therefore based on the same syntactic structures, they would be expected to match the PropBank labeling better than the other representations. But does a better score here imply that the output is more usable for any applications built on the role labels? It may often be the case that the specific bracketing is not really important; rather, the critical information is the relation of the argument head word to the predicate. Scoring the output of the algorithm using this strategy gives a much higher performance with an F-score of about 85 (vs. 79).

Hacioglu [133] formulated the problem of semantic role labeling on a dependency tree by converting the Penn Treebank trees to a dependency representation using a script by Hwa, Lopez, and Diab [134] and creating a dependency structure labeled with PropBank arguments. The performance on this system seemed to be about 5 F-score points better than the one trained on the phrase structure trees. One possible shortcoming of this and other approaches is that all the parsers are trained on the same Penn Treebank, and when evaluated on sources other than WSJ, seem to degrade in performance. Pradhan et al. [129] experimented to find how well a rule-based dependency parser might fare. Minipar [135, 136] is the rule-based dependency parser that was used. It outputs dependencies between a word called **head** and another called **modifier**. Each word can modify at most one word. The dependency relationships form a dependency tree. The set of words under each node in Minipar's dependency tree form a contiguous segment in the original sentence and correspond to the constituent in a constituent tree. Figure 4–13 shows how the arguments of the predicate *kick* map to the nodes in a phrase structure grammar tree as well as the nodes in a Minipar parse tree. The nodes that represent head words of constituents are the targets of classification. They used the same features as Hacioglu [133] (see Table 4–4).

Minipar performance on the PropBank corpus is substantially worse than the Charniak-based system (47.2 if computed using the strict span criteria). This is expected, as Minipar is not designed to produce constituents that exactly match the constituent segmentation

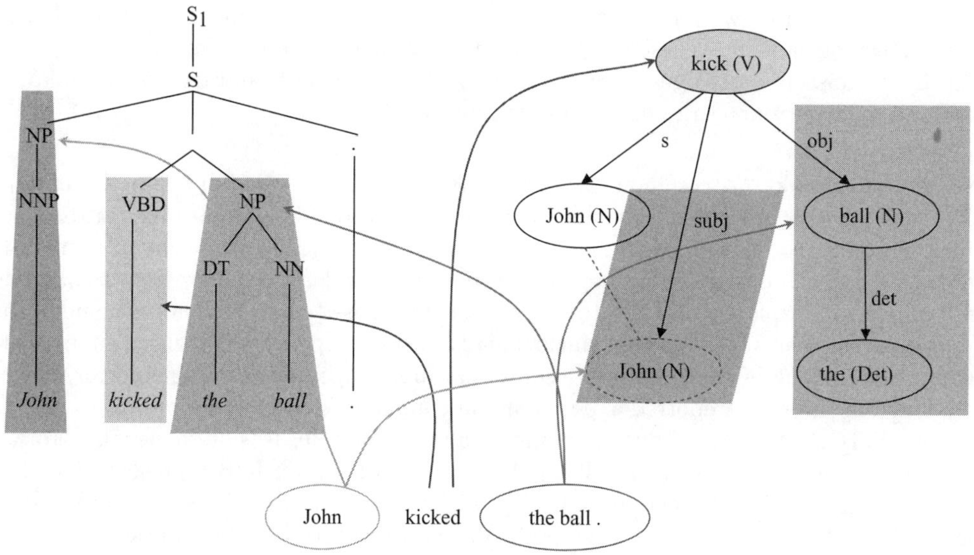

Figure 4–13: New architecture

Table 4–4: Features used in the baseline system using Minipar parses

Head word	The word representing the node in the dependency tree.
Head word POS	Part of speech of the head word.
POS path	The path from the predicate to the head word through the dependency tree connecting the part of speech of each node in the tree.
Dependency path	Each word that is connected to the head word has a dependency relationship to the word. These are represented as labels on the arc between the words. This feature comprises the dependencies along the path that connects two words.
Voice	Voice of the predicate.
Position	Whether the node is before or after the predicate.

used in the Penn Treebank. In experiments reported by Hacioglu [133], a mismatch of about 8% was introduced in the transformation from Treebank trees to dependency trees. Using an errorful automatically generated tree, a still higher mismatch would be expected. In the case of the CCG parses, as reported by Gildea and Hockenmaier [128], the mismatch was about 23%. A more realistic way to score the performance is to score tags assigned to head words of constituents, rather than considering the exact boundaries of the constituents. This score turns out to be an F-score of about 61.7, which is much better and provides orthogonal benefits. These results are a compelling argument for the integration of dependency trees with phrase structure predicate-argument structure.

Since then, there was significant work done on dependency parsing, which led to a series of experiments in this vein. Two Computational Natural Language Learning (CoNLL) shared tasks [137, 138] were held to further research ways to combine dependency parsing and semantic role labeling. These included the use of a richer syntactic dependency representation by Johansson and Nugues [139], which considers tree gaps and traces, and mapping PropBank predicates and arguments to that representation.

Base Phrase Chunks A common question is, How much does the full syntactic representation help the task of semantic role labeling? In other words, how important is it to create a full syntactic tree before classifying the arguments of a predicate? A chunk representation can be faster and more robust to phrase reordering as happens in speech data. Gildea and Palmer [131] explored this question using a chunk-based approach and concluded that syntactic parsing helps fill a big gap. Hacioglu [124] further experimented with a chunk-based semantic labeling method and reached a somewhat more optimistic conclusion. Punyakanok, Roth, and Yih [140] also reported experiments in chunking. Generally, chunk-based systems classify each base phrase as the B(eginning) of a semantic role, I(nside) a semantic role, or O(utside) any semantic role (i.e., null). This is referred to as an IOB representation [141]. This system uses SVM classifiers to first chunk input text into flat chunks or base phrases, each labeled with a syntactic tag. A second SVM is trained to assign semantic labels to the chunks. Figure 4–14 shows a schematic of the chunking process. Table 4–5 lists the features used by the semantic chunker.

Sales declined 3% to $ 524.5 million from 539.4 million.

⇩ Chunk into syntactic base phrases

[$_{NP}$ Sales] ($_{VP}$ declined) [$_{NP}$ 3 %] [$_{PP}$ to] [$_{NP}$ $ 524.5 million] [$_{PP}$ from] [$_{NP}$ $ 539.4 million]

⇩ Extract features

Phrase	Head word	POS	BP	Path	Position	
NP	Sales	NNS	B-NP	NNS→NP→PRED→VBD	b	B-A1
PRED	declined	VBD	B-VP	-	t	B-V
NP	%	NN	I-NP	NN→NP→PRED→VBD	a	B-A2
PP	to	TO	B-PP	TO→PP→NP→PRED→VBD	a	O
NP	million	CD	I-NP	CD→NP→PP→NP→PRED→VBD	a	B-A4
PP	from	IN	B-PP	IN→PP→NP→PP→NP→PRED→VBD	a	O
NP	million	CD	I-NP	CD→NP→PP→NP→PP→NP→PRED→VBD	a	B-A3

⇩ Generate parse

[$_{ARG1}$ Sales] ($_{B\text{-}V}$ declined) [$_{ARG2}$ 3 %] to [$_{ARG4}$ $ 524.5 million] from [$_{ARG3}$ $ 539.4 million]

Figure 4–14: Semantic chunker

For each token (base phrase) to be tagged, a set of features is created from a fixed-size context that surrounds each token. In addition to the above features, the chunker uses previous semantic tags that have already been assigned to the tokens contained in the linguistic context. A five-token sliding window is used for the context. The performance on the task of identification and classification was an F-score of about 70.

Classification Paradigms

In the previous section, we looked at sentence-level structural representations that have been used to tackle the problem of semantic role labeling and the features in each of those representations that were identified to capture those characteristics that would help train a model to identify them automatically. In this section, we focus on the ways in which machine learning has been brought to bear on the problem. The approaches range widely in their complexity. The simplest approaches are those that view semantic role labeling as a pure classification problem, where each argument of a predicate may be classified independently of the others. Other researchers have adopted this basic paradigm but added a simple postprocessor that removes implausible analysis, such as when two arguments overlap. A few more complicated approaches augment the postprocessing step to use argument-specific language models or frame-element group statistics. These postprocessors tend to take care of a significant portion of the problems introduced by the original independence assumption.

There have also been more sophisticated approaches to performing joint decoding of all the arguments, trying to capture the arguments' interdependence. Unfortunately, these

Table 4–5: Features used by chunk-based classifier

Words	Words in the chunk.
Predicate lemma	The predicate lemma.
POS tags	Part of speech of the words in the chunk.
BP positions	The position of a token in a base phrase (BP) using the IOB2 representation (e.g., B-NP, I-NP, O).
Clause tags	The tags that mark token positions in a sentence with respect to clauses.
Named entities	The IOB tags of named entities.
Token position	The position of the phrase with respect to the predicate. It has three values: "before," "after," and "-" (for the predicate).
Path	Defines a flat path between the token and the predicate.
Clause bracket patterns	
Clause position	A binary feature that identifies whether the token is inside or outside the clause containing the predicate.
Headword suffixes	Suffixes of head words of length 2, 3, and 4.
Distance	Distance of the token from the predicate as a number of base phrases and the distance as the number of VP chunks.
Length	The number of words in a token.
Predicate POS tag	The part of speech category of the predicate.
Predicate frequency	Frequent or rare using a threshold of 3.
Predicate BP context	The chain of BPs centered at the predicate within a window of size $-2/+2$.
Predicate POS context	POS tags of words immediately preceding and following the predicate.
Predicate-argument frames	Left and right core argument patterns around the predicate.
Number of predicates	This is the number of predicates in the sentence.

sophisticated approaches have so far yielded only slight gains, partly because the performance with a pure classifier followed by a simple postprocessor is already quite high. In this section, rather than provide detailed descriptions of all previous approaches, we concentrate on a current high-performing approach that effectively utilizes multiple knowledge sources and uses a combined architecture that degrades gracefully when run on out-of-genre text.

To begin with, Gildea and Jurafsky's [113] variation of the SRL algorithm involves two steps. In the first step, the system calculates maximum likelihood probabilities that the constituent is an argument, based on these two features, $P(\text{argument}|\text{Path, Predicate})$ and $P(\text{argument}|\text{Head, Predicate})$, and interpolates them to generate the probability that the constituent under consideration represents an argument. In the second step, it assigns each constituent that has a nonzero probability of being an argument a normalized probability calculated by interpolating distributions conditioned on various sets of features, and selects

Table 4–6: Distributions used for semantic argument classification, calculated from the features extracted from a Charniak parse

Distributions
P(argument|Predicate)
P(argument|Phrase Type, Predicate)
P(argument|Phrase Type, Position, Voice)
P(argument|Phrase Type, Position, Voice, Predicate)
P(argument|Phrase Type, Path, Predicate)
P(argument|Phrase Type, Path, Predicate, Subcategorization)
P(argument|Head Word)
P(argument|Head Word, Predicate)
P(argument|Head Word, Phrase Type, Predicate)

Table 4–7: Argument classification using same features but different classifiers

Classifier	Accuracy (%)
SVM (Pradhan et al.) [120]	88
Decision Tree (Surdeanu et al.) [118]	79
Gildea and Palmer [131]	77

the most probable argument sequence. Some of the distributions they used are shown in Table 4–6.

Surdeanu et al. [118] used a decision tree classifier algorithm, C5 [142, 143] on the same features as Gildea and Jurafsky [113]. The built-in boosting capabilities of this classifier gave a slight improvement in performance. Chen and Rambow [130] also report results using a decision tree classifier, C4.5 [142]. Fleischman and Hovy [144] report results on the FrameNet corpus using a maximum entropy framework. Pradhan et al. [120] used SVM for the same and got even better performance on the PropBank corpus. Nonetheless, the difference between a maximum entropy classifier and SVM turned out to be small.

Pradhan et al. [120] report results using the same set of features on the same data and compare the classifiers with each other. Gildea and Palmer's [131] system estimates the posterior probabilities using several different feature sets and interpolates the estimates—exactly like the Gildea and Jurafsky [113] system—whereas Surdeanu et al. [118] use a decision tree classifier. Table 4–7 shows compares the three systems for the task of argument classification.

For our discussion, we use TinySVM[10] along with YamCha[11] as the SVM training and test software [145, 146]. The SVM parameters, such as the type of kernel, and the values of various parameters was empirically determined using the development set. A polynomial

10. http://chasen.org/~taku/software/TinySVM/
11. http://chasen.org/~taku/software/yamcha/

kernel of degree 2 was selected with the cost per unit violation of the margin $C = 1$ and tolerance of the termination criterion $e = 0.001$.

SVMs perform well on text classification tasks where data are represented in a high-dimensional space using sparse feature vectors [147, 148]. Inspired by the success of using SVMs for tagging syntactic chunks [145], Pradhan et al. [149, 126, 120] formulated the semantic role labeling problem as a multiclass classification problem using SVMs.

SVMs are inherently binary classifiers, but multiclass problems can be reduced to a number of binary-class problems using either the pairwise approach or the one versus all (OVA) approach [150]. For an N class problem, in the pairwise approach, a binary classifier is trained for each pair of the possible $\frac{N(N-1)}{2}$ class pairs, whereas, in the OVA approach, N binary classifiers are trained to discriminate each class from a metaclass created by combining the rest of the classes. Comparing these two approaches, there is a trade-off between the number of classifiers to be trained and the data used to train each classifier. Although some experiments have reported that the pairwise approach outperforms the OVA approach [151], Pradhan et al.'s [120] initial experiments show better performance for OVA. Therefore, they chose the OVA approach.

SVM outputs the distance of a feature vector from the maximum margin hyperplane. To facilitate probabilistic thresholding and generate an n-best hypotheses lattice, they convert the distances to probabilities by fitting a sigmoid to the scores, as described in Platt [152].

The system can be viewed as comprising two stages: the training stage and the testing stage. We first discuss how the SVM is trained for this task. Because the training time taken by SVMs scales exponentially with the number of examples, and about 90% of the nodes in a syntactic tree have null argument labels, it is efficient to divide the training process into two stages:

1. Filter out the nodes that have a very high probability of being null. A binary null/non-null classifier is trained on the entire dataset. Fit a sigmoid function to the raw scores to convert the scores to probabilities, as described by Platt [152]. All the training examples are run through this classifier, and the respective scores for null and non-null assignments are converted to probabilities using the sigmoid function. Nodes that are most likely null (probability >0.90) are pruned from the training set. This reduces the number of null nodes by about 90% and the total number of nodes by about 80%. This is accompanied by a negligible (about 1%) pruning of nodes that are non-null.

2. The remaining training data are used to train OVA classifiers for all the classes along with a null class.

With this strategy, only one classifier (null or non-null) has to be trained on all of the data. The remaining OVA classifiers are trained on the nodes passed by the filter (approximately 20% of the total), resulting in a considerable savings in training time.

In the testing stage, all the nodes are classified directly as null or one of the arguments using the classifier trained in step 2. They observe a slight decrease in recall if we filter the test examples using a null/non-null OVA classifier in a first pass, as we do in the training process. This small performance gain is obtained at little or no cost of computation because SVMs are very fast in the testing phase. Pseudocode for the testing algorithm is shown earlier in Figure 4–3. A variation in this strategy would be to filter all the examples that are null in the first pruning stage instead of just pruning out the high-probability ones. This strategy, however, has a statistically significant performance degradation associated with it.

On gold-standard Treebank parses, the performance of such a system on the combined task of argument identification and classification is in the low 90s, whereas on automatically generated parses, the performance tends to be in the high 70s.

Overcoming the Independence Assumption

As mentioned earlier, various postprocessing stages have been proposed to overcome the limitations of treating semantic role labeling as a series of independent argument classification steps. We now look at some of these strategies.

Disallowing Overlaps Since each constituent is classified independently of the other, it is possible that two constituents that overlap get assigned an argument type. Because we are dealing with parse tree, nodes overlapping in words always have an ancestor-descendant relationship, and therefore the overlaps are restricted to subsumptions only as shown in Example 4–1.

EXAMPLE 4–1: But [$_{ARG0}$ nobody] [$_{predicate}$ knows] [$_{ARG1}$ at what level [$_{ARG1}$ the futures and stocks will open today]]

This is a problem because overlapping arguments were not allowed in PropBank (or, more specifically, any two arguments of a verb predicate even in FrameNet cannot overlap). One way to deal with this issue is to choose among overlapping constituents by retaining the one for which the SVM has the highest confidence based on the classification probabilities and labeling the others Null. The probabilities obtained by applying the sigmoid function to the raw SVM scores are used as the measure of confidence.

Argument Sequence Information Another way makes use of the fact that a predicate is likely to instantiate a certain set of argument types as done by Gildea and Jurafsky (2002) [113] to improve the performance of their statistical argument tagger. A similar but more principled approach involves imposing additional constraints in which argument ordering information is retained and the predicate is considered as an argument and is part of the sequence. This can be achieved by training a trigram language model on the argument sequences by first converting the raw SVM scores to probabilities, as described earlier. Then, for each sentence being parsed, an argument lattice is generated using the n-best hypotheses for each node in the syntax tree. Then a Viterbi search is performed through the lattice using the probabilities assigned by the sigmoid as the observation probabilities, along with the language model probabilities, to find the maximum likelihood path through the lattice such that each node is assigned a value belonging to the PropBank arguments or null.

The search is constrained in such a way that no two non-null nodes overlap. To simplify the search, Pradhan et al. [120] allowed only null assignments to nodes having a null likelihood above a threshold. While training the language model, we can use the actual predicate to estimate the transition probabilities in and out of the predicate, or we can perform a joint estimation over all the predicates. Pradhan et al. found that there was an improvement in the core arguments accuracy on the combined task of identifying and assigning semantic arguments, whereas the accuracy of the adjunctive arguments slightly deteriorated. This seems logical considering that the adjunctive arguments have looser constraints on their ordering and even their quantity. It is therefore beneficial to use this strategy only for the core arguments. Some other strategies have been used to incorporate argument context information. Toutanova, Haghighi, and Manning [153] report performance on using a more global model to predict semantic roles for a given predicate using log-linear models, whereas Punyakanok et al. [154] use an integer linear programming–based inference framework to improve the performance of semantic role labeling. Both show small gains over the Viterbi approach.

Feature Performance

Not all features are equally useful in each task. Some features add more noise than information in one context than in another, and features can vary in efficacy depending on the classification paradigm in which they are used. Table 4–8 shows the effect each feature has on the argument classification and argument identification tasks when added individually to the baseline. Addition of named entities to the null/non-null classifier degraded its performance in this particular configuration of classifier and features. This effect can be attributed to a combination of two things: (i) a significant number of constituents contain named entities but are not arguments of a predicate (the parent of an argument node also contains the same named entity), resulting in a noisy feature for null/non-null classification; and (ii) SVMs don't seem to handle irrelevant features very well [155]. When this feature was solely used in the task of classifying constituents known to represent arguments, using features extracted from Treebank parses, the overall classification accuracy increased from 87.9% to 88.1%, whereas adding head word POS as a feature significantly improves both the argument classification and the argument identification tasks.

Feature Salience

In analyzing the performance of the system, it is useful to estimate the relative contribution of the various feature sets used. Table 4–9 shows the argument classification accuracies for combinations of features on the training and test set for all PropBank arguments, using Treebank parses.

In the upper part of Table 4–9 we see the degradation in performance by leaving out one feature at a time. The features are arranged in the order of increasing salience. Removing all head word-related information has the most detrimental effect on performance. The lower part of the table shows the performance of some feature combinations by themselves. Table 4–10 shows the feature salience on the task of argument identification. As opposed to the argument classification task, where removing the path has the least effect on performance, on the task of argument identification, removing the path causes the convergence in SVM training to be very slow and has the most detrimental effect on performance.

Feature Selection

The fact that adding the named entity features to the null/non-null classifier had a detrimental effect on the performance of the argument identification task, while the same feature set showed significant improvement to the argument classification task, indicates that a feature

Table 4–8: Effect of each feature on the argument classification task and argument identification task when added to the baseline system. An asterisx indicates that the improvement is statistically significant

FEATURES	ARGUMENT CLASSIFICATION	ARGUMENT IDENTIFICATION		
	A	P	R	F_1
Baseline [120]	87.9	93.7	88.9	91.3
+ Named entities	**88.1**	93.3	88.9	91.0
+ Head POS	* **88.6**	94.4	90.1	* **92.2**
+ Verb cluster	**88.1**	94.1	89.0	**91.5**
+ Partial path	**88.2**	93.3	88.9	91.1
+ Verb sense	**88.1**	93.7	89.5	**91.5**
+ Noun head PP (only POS)	* **88.6**	94.4	90.0	* **92.2**
+ Noun head PP (only head)	* **89.8**	94.0	89.4	**91.7**
+ Noun head PP (both)	* **89.9**	94.7	90.5	* **92.6**
+ First word in constituent	* **89.0**	94.4	91.1	* **92.7**
+ Last word in constituent	* **89.4**	93.8	89.4	**91.6**
+ First POS in constituent	**88.4**	94.4	90.6	* **92.5**
+ Last POS in constituent	**88.3**	93.6	89.1	91.3
+ Ordinal const. pos. concat.	87.7	93.7	89.2	**91.4**
+ Const. tree distance	**88.0**	93.7	89.5	**91.5**
+ Parent constituent	**87.9**	94.2	90.2	* **92.2**
+ Parent head	85.8	94.2	90.5	* **92.3**
+ Parent head POS	* **88.5**	94.3	90.3	* **92.3**
+ Right sibling constituent	**87.9**	94.0	89.9	**91.9**
+ Right sibling head	**87.9**	94.4	89.9	* **92.1**
+ Right sibling head POS	**88.1**	94.1	89.9	**92.0**
+ Left sibling constituent	* **88.6**	93.6	89.6	**91.6**
+ Left sibling head	86.9	93.9	86.1	89.9
+ Left sibling head POS	* **88.8**	93.5	89.3	**91.4**
+ Temporal cue words	* **88.6**	-	-	-
+ Dynamic class context	**88.4**	-	-	-

selection strategy would be beneficial. One strategy would be to perform a leave-one-out experiment whereby one feature is left out of the full set of features at a time, and depending on the degradation in performance, it is either kept of pruned out. This is a very naïve feature-selection strategy that assumes the features are independent of each other. We could use a more complicated feature-selection strategy instead. One downside of feature selection based on each argument type in the SVM paradigm is that SVMs output distances, not probabilities. These distances may not be comparable across classifiers, especially if different features are used to train each binary classifier. A solution is to use the algorithm described by Platt [152] to convert the SVM scores into probabilities by fitting to a sigmoid. Foster and Stine [156] show that the pool-adjacent-violators (PAV) algorithm [157] provides a better

Table 4–9: Performance of various feature combinations on the task of argument classification

FEATURES	ACCURACY
All features [120]	91.0
All except Path	90.8
All except Phrase Type	90.8
All except HW and HW-POS	90.7
All except All Phrases	*83.6
All except Predicate	*82.4
All except HW and FW and LW info.	*75.1
Only Path and Predicate	74.4
Only Path and Phrase Type	47.2
Only Head Word	37.7
Only Path	28.0

Table 4–10: Performance of various feature combinations on the task of argument identification

FEATURES	P	R	F_1
All features [120]	95.2	92.5	93.8
All except HW	95.1	92.3	93.7
All except Predicate	94.5	91.9	93.2
All except HW and FW and LW info.	91.8	88.5	*90.1
All except Path and Partial Path	88.4	88.9	*88.6
Only Path and HW	88.5	84.3	86.3
Only Path and Predicate	89.3	81.2	85.1

method for converting raw classifier scores to probabilities when Platt's algorithm fails. The probabilities resulting from either conversion may not be properly calibrated, in which case the probabilities can be binned, and a warping function can be trained to calibrate them.

Size of Training Data

One important concern in any supervised learning method is the amount of training examples required for decent performance of a classifier. To check the behavior of this learning problem, Pradhan et al. [129] trained the classifiers on varying amounts of training data. The resulting plots are shown in Figure 4–15. The first curve from the top indicates the change in F_1 score on the task of argument identification alone. The third curve indicates the F_1 score on the combined task of argument identification and classification. It can be seen that after about 10,000 examples, the performance starts to plateau, which indicates that simply tagging more data might not be a good strategy. A better strategy is to tag only appropriate new data. Also, the fact that the first and third curves—the first being the

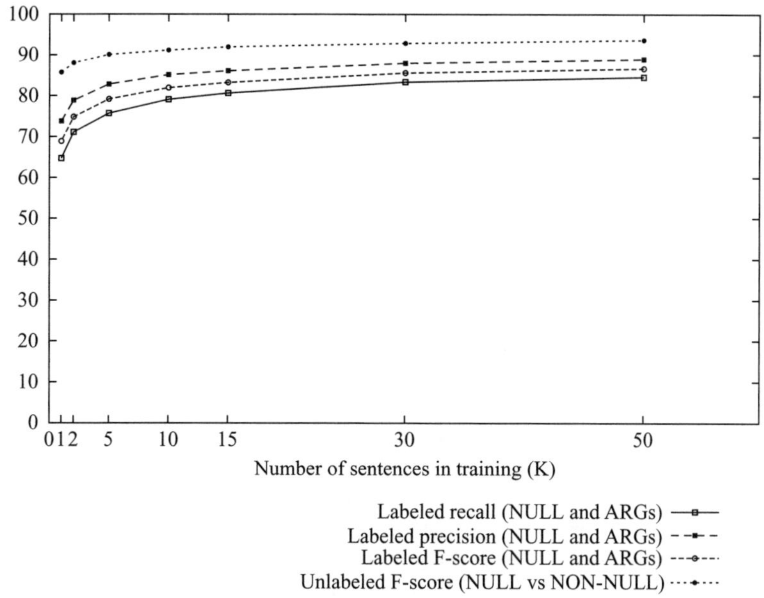

Figure 4–15: Learning curve for the tasks of identifying and classifying arguments using Treebank parses

F-score on the task of argument identification task and the third being the F-score on the combined task of identification and classification—run almost parallel to each other tells us that a constant loss occurs due to classification errors throughout the data range. One way to bridge this gap could be to identify better features.

Overcoming Parsing Errors

After performing a detailed error analysis, Pradhan et al. [129] found that the identification problem poses a significant bottleneck to improving overall system performance. The baseline system's accuracy on the task of labeling nodes known to represent semantic arguments is 90%. On the other hand, the system's performance on the identification task is quite a bit lower, achieving only 80% recall with 86% precision. The two sources of these identification errors are failures by the system to identify all and only those constituents that correspond to semantic roles, *when those constituents are present in the syntactic analysis*, and failures by the syntactic analyzer to provide the constituents that align with correct arguments. Classification performance using Charniak parses is about 3 F-score points worse than when using treebank parses. On the other hand, argument identification performance using Charniak parses is about 12.7 F-score points worse. Half of these errors—about 7 points—are due to missing constituents, and the other half—about 6 points—are due to misclassifications.

This severe degradation in argument identification performance for automatic parses was the motivation for examining two techniques for improving argument identification: combining parses from different syntactic representations and using n-best parses or a parse forest in the same representation.

Multiple Views Pradhan et al. [129] report on experiments that address the problem of arguments missing from a given syntactic analysis. They investigate ways to combine hypotheses generated from semantic role taggers trained using different syntactic views: one trained using the Charniak parser [158]; another on a rule-based dependency parser, Minipar [135]; and a third based on a flat, shallow syntactic chunk representation [159]. They showed that these three views complement each other to improve performance.

Some of the systems we have discussed use features based on syntactic constituents produced by a syntactic parser [149, 126], and others use only a flat syntactic representation produced by a syntactic chunker [160, 159, 124]. The latter approach lacks the information provided by the hierarchical syntactic structure, and the former imposes the limitation that the possible candidate roles should be one of the nodes already present in the syntax tree. Although the chunk-based systems are very efficient and robust, the systems that use features based on full syntactic parses are generally more accurate. Analysis of the source of errors for the parse constituent–based systems showed that incorrect parses were a major source of error. The syntactic parser often did not produce any constituent that corresponded to the correct segmentation for the semantic argument. Pradhan et al. [129] report on a first attempt to overcome this problem by combining semantic role labels produced from different syntactic parses. The hypothesis is that the syntactic parsers will make different errors, and combining their outputs will be an improvement over any one system. This initial attempt used features from the Charniak parser, the Minipar parser, and a chunk-based parser. It did show some improvement from the combination, but the method for combining the information was heuristic and suboptimal. The researchers proposed an improved framework for combining information from different syntactic views. The goal was to preserve the robustness and flexibility of the segmentation of the phrase-based chunker but to take advantage of features from full syntactic parses. They also wanted to combine features from different syntactic parses to gain additional robustness. To this end, they used features generated from the Charniak parser and the Collins parser. The main contribution of combining both the Minipar-based and the Charniak-based semantic role labeler was significantly improved performance on ARG1 in addition to slight improvements to some other arguments. See Figure 4–16.

The semantic parses were combined as follows. Scores for arguments were converted to calibrated probabilities, and arguments with scores below a threshold value were deleted. Separate thresholds were used for each semantic role labeler. For the remaining arguments, if any set of arguments overlapped, the least probable among them were removed until no overlaps remained. In the chunk-based system, an argument could consist of a sequence of chunks. The probability assigned to the BEGIN tag of an argument was used as the probability of the sequence of chunks forming an argument.

The general framework is to train separate semantic role labeling systems for each of the parse tree views, and then to use the role arguments output by these systems as additional features in a semantic role classifier using a flat syntactic view. The constituent-based classifiers walk a syntactic parse tree and classify each node as null (no role) or as one of the set of semantic roles. As we saw in Section 4.5.2, chunk-based systems classify each base phrase using the IOB representation. The constituent level roles are mapped to the IOB representation used by the chunker. The IOB tags are then used as features for a separate base-phrase semantic role labeler (chunker), in addition to the standard set of features used

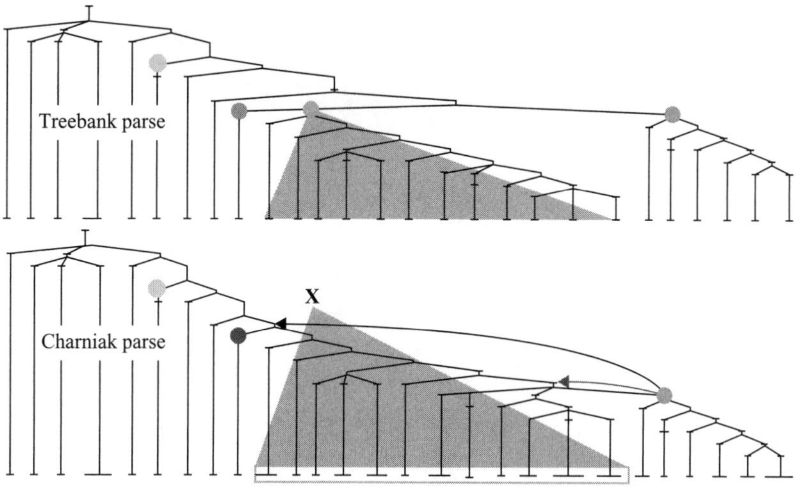

Figure 4–16: Argument deletions owing to parse error

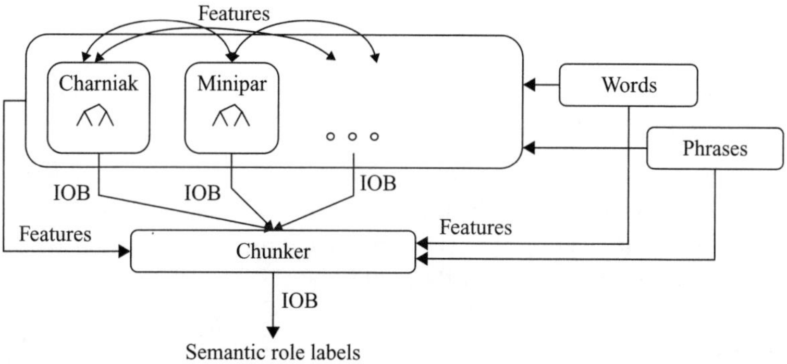

Figure 4–17: New architecture

by the chunker. An n-fold cross-validation paradigm is used to train the constituent-based role classifiers and the chunk-based classifier. See Figure 4–17.

The chunking system for combining all features is trained using a fourfold paradigm. In each fold, separate SVM classifiers are trained using 75% of the training data. The other 25% of the training data are then labeled by each of the systems. Iterating this process four times creates the training set for the chunker. After the chunker is trained, the PSG- and Minipar-based semantic labelers are retrained using all of the training data. Once the retraining is complete, SVMs are trained for begin (B) and inside (I) classes of all arguments and an outside (O) class. One particular advantage of this architecture, as depicted in Figure 4–18, is that the final segmentation does not necessarily have to adhere to one of the input segmentations. Depending on the information provided in terms of features, the classifier can generate a new, better segmentation.

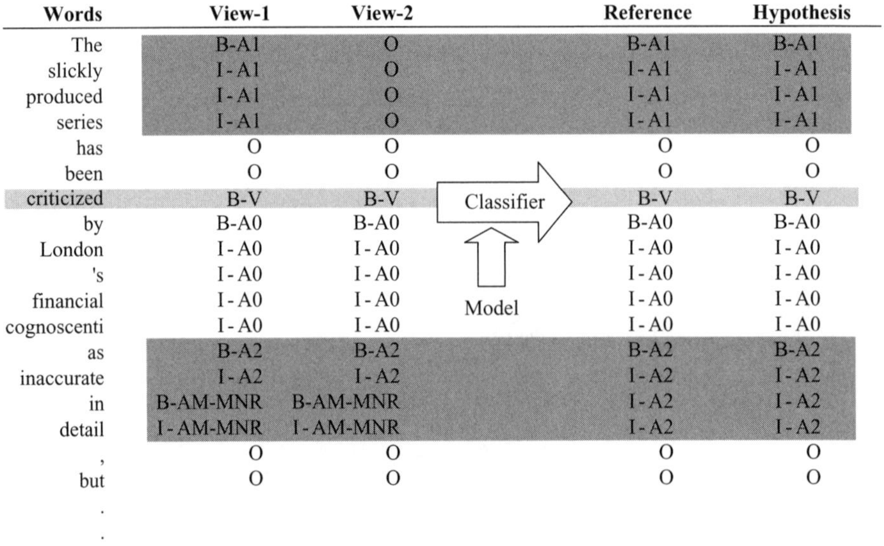

Figure 4–18: Example classification using the new architecture

This is just one way of combining various views. Another combination strategy by Surdeanu et al. [161] also shows improvement over using a single view.

Broader Search Another approach is to broaden the search by selecting constituents in n-best parses [153, 154] or using a packed forest representation [162], which more efficiently represents variations over much larger n. Using a parse forest shows an absolute improvement of 1.2 points over single best parses and 0.5 points over n-best parses.

Noun Arguments

Until now we have only dealt with the task of identification and classification of arguments of verb predicates in a sentence. To generate a sentence-level semantic representation, it is necessary to identify arguments of other possible predicates in a sentence, such as nominal predicates, adjectival predicates, and prepositional predicates. This chapter discusses the task of semantic role labeling as applied to a class of nominal predicates, or nominalizations. A simple linguistic definition of nominalization is "the process of converting a verb into an abstract noun." Take, for example, the two sentence pairs in Figure 4–19, where the second sentence in each pair is a nominalized version of the first. One important thing to note is that the verbs in the nominalized sentences are *make* and *took* respectively. A semantic analyzer that parses these sentences for the arguments of these verbs will miss the events—*complaining* and *walking*—that are central to understanding the meaning of the sentences and that are represented by the nominal predicates *complain* and *walk* respectively.

Of the vast literature on automatic semantic role labeling, very little deals with assigning the semantic role properties of nouns. Of what does, most deal with nominalizations. However, because of the lack of a corpus annotated with nominal predicates and their arguments, there have been no investigations into applying statistical algorithms that can automatically

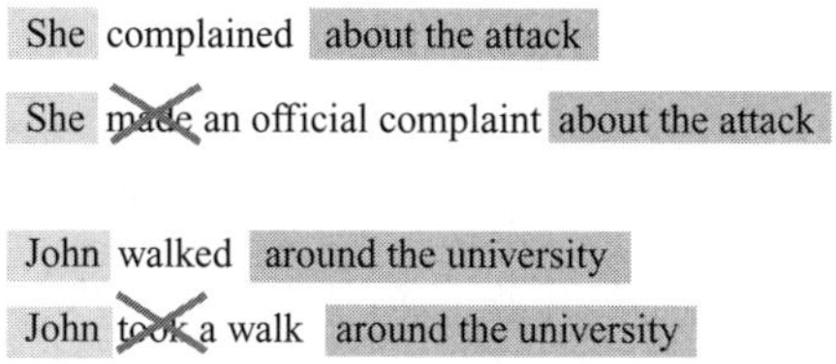

Figure 4–19: Example of nominalization

identify and label the arguments of nouns. To our knowledge, the only works that come close are the rule-based system described by Hull and Gomez [163] and the work of Lapata [164] on interpreting the relationship between the head of a nominalized compound and its modifier noun. With the availability of hand-labeled argument information for nominal predicates from the FrameNet project, an investigation into the feasibility of automatically identifying nominal predicates using this data can be performed.

In this section, we look at the adaptation to nouns of features that were originally derived for verbs; most of these adaptations are quite straightforward. We also investigate how well these transformed features identify the semantic properties of noun arguments. In other words, how good are these features at identifying and classifying nominal arguments? Furthermore, can any new sets of features specific to nominalizations be added to good effect?

Following are some new features that were identified by Pradhan et al. [165] along with a justification. Some of these features don't exist for some constituents. In those cases, the respective feature values are set to UNK. Almost all the new features that we used for the verb predicates, except the CCG features, were added to the baseline system.

Intervening verb features—Support verbs play an important role in realizing the arguments of nominal predicates. Three classes of intervening verbs were used: (i) verbs of being, (ii) light verbs (a small set of verbs such as *make, take, have*), and (iii) other verbs with part of speech starting with the string VB. Three features were added for each: (i) a binary feature indicating the presence of the verb between the predicate and the constituent, (ii) the actual word as a feature, and (iii) the path through the tree from the constituent to the verb. The following example illustrates the intuition behind these intervening verb features:

[$_{Speaker}$ Leapor] *makes* general [$_{Predicate}$ assertions] [$_{Topic}$ about marriage]

Predicate NP expansion rule—This is the noun equivalent of the verb subcategorization feature used by Gildea and Jurafsky [113]. It represents the expansion rule instantiated by the syntactic parser, for the lowermost NP in the tree, encompassing the predicate. This feature tends to cluster noun phrases with a similar internal structure and thus helps find argument modifiers.

Is predicate plural—This binary feature indicates whether the predicate is singular or plural, as these tend to have different argument selection properties.

Genitives in constituent—This is a binary feature that is true if there is a genitive word (one with the part of speech POS, PRP, PRP$, or WP$) in the constituent, as these tend to be subject/object markers for nominal arguments. The following example helps clarify this notion:

[$_{Speaker}$ Burma 's] [$_{Phenomenon}$ oil] [$_{Predicate}$ search] hits virgin forests

Verb dominating predicate—The head word of the first VP ancestor of the predicate.

More recently, Jiang and Ng [166] use additional features in a maximum entropy framework to perform argument tagging on the NomBank corpus. Also, NomBank arguments have been added to an integrated syntax-semantic dependency representation in the recent CoNLL evaluations [137, 138].

Multilingual Issues

Because early research on semantic role labeling was performed on English corpora, various core features and learning mechanisms were explored specifically for English. Apparently, most of the core features for English translate well for other languages [167, 168]. Some special cases of language-specific features turned out to be important for a specific language but also improved performance for English systems; for example, the predicate frame feature that was introduced by Xue and Palmer [127] for Chinese also shows some features improvement in English. Some features are so language specific that they have no parallels in English, and those usually are unique to a particular language; for example, Chinese requires a much more complex word segmentation process—something that can be performed quite accurately in English using very simple rules. Therefore, special word segmentation models have to be trained in the case of Chinese before parsing or semantic role labeling can begin.

On the other hand, fortunately, the morphology-poor nature of Chinese blurs the difference between verbs, nouns, and adjectives, forming a closer connection between these predicates and their arguments. This allows the training of a unified model across all types of predicates. Yet another property of Chinese that impacts automatic semantic role labeling is that Chinese has many more verb types than English—at least a factor of four—and so in a similarly sized corpus, the number of instances per verb is much smaller for Chinese, which exacerbates an already critical issue of data sparsity. At the same time, this means that there is less polysemy to deal with, which is a preferred property from a performance perspective. The creation of a specific clustering feature helps overcome this problem to some degree. So, in some sense, although a similar set of features are useful across languages, the specific instantiation of some can differ greatly, and the relative benefit of each varies with language as well. These new features were introduced by Xue [167] to improve the performance of the Chinese semantic role labeling system. Another thing to note about Chinese is that the syntactic parsing performance is inferior to that of English, and so systems based on shallow syntactic chunking [169] achieved quite competitive results with those based on a full syntactic parse.

In contrast to Chinese, a particular characteristic of Arabic is its morphological richness. What this means in parsing is that there are many more syntactic POS categories for Arabic than there are for English or Chinese—almost an order of magnitude. So far, results reported in the literature on Arabic semantic role labeling systems have not exploited its specific morphologically rich nature [168].

Another notable difference from English is that both Arabic and Chinese have many more implicit (or dropped) subjects. The Penn Treebank marks them with a trace, and they are tagged with an argument in PropBank. Unlike English, Chinese and Arabic require the training of special models to identify dropped subjects before the predicate-argument structure can be fully realized [170].

Robustness across Genre

One possible shortcoming of this and other approaches is that all the parsers are trained on the same Penn Treebank, which, when evaluated on sources other than WSJ, seems to degrade in performance. Carreras and Màrquez [171] show that the drop in performance on test data from the Brown corpus was 10 F-score points lower than the test data from WSJ. When trained and tested on WSJ propositions the syntactic parser's performance is the main source of error, and the classification performance is quite good. However, Pradhan, Ward, and Martin [172] report that when we train the system on WSJ data and test on the Brown propositions, the classification performance and the identification performance are affected to the same degree. This provides some evidence that more lexical semantic features are needed to bridge the performance gap across genres. Zapirain [173] shows that incorporating features based on selectional preferences provides one way of effecting more lexico-semantic generalization.

4.5.3 Software

Following is a list of software packages available for semantic role labeling.

- **ASSERT** (Automatic Statistical SEmantic Role Tagger)
  [http:://www.cemantix.org/assert.html]
  A semantic role labeler trained on the English PropBank data.
- **C-ASSERT** [http://hlt030.cse.ust.hk/research/Pc-assert/]
  An extension of ASSERT for the Chinese language.
- **SwiRL** [http://www.surdeanu.name/mihai/swirl/]
  Another semantic role labeler trained on PropBank data.
- **Shalmaneser** (A *Shal*low Se*man*tic Par*ser*)
  [http://www.coli.uni-saarland.de/projects/salsa/shal/]
  A toolchain for shallow semantic parsing based on the FrameNet data.

4.6 Meaning Representation

We now turn to the third, deeper level of semantic interpretation whose objective is to take natural language input and transform it into an unambiguous representation that a machine can act on. This is the form that would be more likely to be as incomprehensible to humans as it would be comprehensible to machines. We can think of a parallel between programming languages that are much closer to the way humans manipulate information and the low-level machine code that the computer executes. Although compilers and interpreters impose various specific syntactic and semantic restrictions on a program written in a high-level programming language, no such restrictions are imposed on the form that natural language can take; whereas precision in artificial languages is necessary to define scope and eliminate ambiguity, natural language relies on the recipient to disambiguate it using context and general world knowledge. Researchers have spent decades figuring out how to interpret and/or encode context and use world knowledge so that we can make machines understand what humans seem to understand so effortlessly. However, there is still a lot of progress to be made, and so far the techniques that have been developed only work within specific domains and problems instead of being scalable to arbitrary domains. This is often termed **deep semantic parsing**, as opposed to shallow semantic parsing that comprises word sense disambiguation and semantic role labeling.

4.6.1 Resources

A number of projects have created representations and resources that have promoted experimentation in this area. Let us look at a few of those resources.

ATIS

Though not quite focused on formal knowledge representation, the Air Travel Information System (ATIS) project [174] is considered one of the first concerted efforts to build systems to transform natural language into a representation that could be used by an end application to make decisions. The task involved a machine to transform a user query in spontaneous speech, using a restricted vocabulary, about flight information. It then formed a representation that was compiled into a SQL query, which was used to extract answers from a flight database. A hierarchical frame representation was used to encode the intermediate semantic information. Figure 4–20 shows a sample user query and the corresponding frame representation. The training corpus includes over 774 scenarios completed by 137 subjects, yielding a total of over 7,300 utterances. All utterances are transcribed, and 2,900 of them have been categorized and annotated with canonical reference answers.[12] Roughly 600 of these have also been treebanked.[13]

Communicator

The Communicator program was the follow-on to ATIS. While ATIS was more focused on **user-initiated dialog** (i.e., the user asked questions to the machine, which provided answers), Communicator involved a **mixed-initiative dialog**, whereby the human and machine had a dialog with each other with the computer presenting users with real-time travel information and helping them negotiate a preferred itinerary. Over the period of the program, many thousands of dialogs were collected and are available through the Linguistic Data Consortium. Carnegie-Mellon University collected more data, a portion of which is available for research.[14] Roughly a million words and ~1,600 dialogs have been annotated with dialog acts.[15]

---

12. http://www.ldc.upenn.edu/Catalog/CatalogEntry.jsp?catalogId=LDC95S26
13. http://www.ldc.upenn.edu/Catalog/CatalogEntry.jsp?catalogId=LDC99T42
14. http://www.speech.cs.cmu.edu/Communicator/Corpus/
15. http://www.ldc.upenn.edu/Catalog/CatalogEntry.jsp?catalogId=LDC2002S56

FRAME Representation

```
SHOW:
 FLIGHTS:
  TIME:
   PART-OF-DAY:
  ORIGIN:
   CITY: Boston
  DEST:
   CITY: San Francisco
  DATE:
   DAY-OF-WEEK: Tuesday
```

Natural langauge representation

Please show me morning flights from Boston to San Francisco on Tuesday

Figure 4–20: A sample user query and its *frame* representation in the ATIS program

GeoQuery

In the domain of U.S. geography, there is a natural language interface (NLI) to a geographic database called Geobase [175], which has about 800 Prolog facts stored in a relational database with geographic information such as population, neighboring states, major rivers, and major cities. Some sample queries and their representations are as follows:

(1) What is the capital of the state with the largest population?
`answer(C, (capital(S, C), largest(P, (state(S), population(S, P)))))`

(2) What are the major cities in Kansas?
`answer(C, (major(C), city(C), loc(C, S), equal(S, stateid(kansas))))`

This is the GeoQuery corpus, which has also been translated into Japanese, Spanish, and Turkish.

Robocup: CLang

RoboCup (www.robocup.org) is an international initiative by the artificial intelligence community that uses robotic soccer as its domain. There is a special formal language, CLang, which is used to encode the advice from the team coach, and the behaviors are expressed as if-then rules. Following is an example representation in this domain:

(1) If the ball is in our penalty area, all our players except player 4 should stay in our half.
`((bpos (penalty-area our)) (do (player-except our 4) (pos (half our))))`

4.6.2 Systems

As we can see in these examples, depending on the consuming application, the meaning representation can be a SQL query, a Prolog query, or a domain-specific query representation.

Now we look at the various ways the problem of mapping the natural language to such meaning representation has been tackled.

Rule Based

Some of the semantic parsing systems that performed very well for both the ATIS and Communicator projects were rule-based systems in the sense that they used an interpreter whose semantic grammar was handcrafted to be robust to speech recognition errors. The underlying philosophy was that the traditional syntactic explanation of a sentence is much more complex than the underlying semantic information, so parsing the meaning units in the sentence into semantics proved to be a better approach. Furthermore, especially in dealing with spontaneous speech, the system has to account for ungrammatical instructions, stutters, filled pauses, and so on. Word order therefore becomes less important, which leads to meaning units scattered in the sentences/utterances and not necessarily in the order that would make sense to a syntactic parser. Ward's [176, 177, 178] system, Phoenix, uses recursive transition networks (RTNs) [179] and a handcrafted grammar to extract a hierarchical frame structure, and reevaluates and adjusts the values of these frames with each new piece of information obtained. This system had an error rate of 13.2% for spontaneous speech input with a speech recognition word-error rate of 4.4%, and a 9.3% error for transcript input.

Supervised

Although rule-based techniques are relatively easy to craft in the beginning and serve a good purpose to formulate solutions to various tasks, they have several downsides: (i) they need some effort upfront to create the rules, (ii) the time and specificity required to write rules usually restricts the development to systems that operate in limited domains, (iii) they are hard to maintain and scale up as the problem becomes more complex and more domain independent, and (iv) they tend to be brittle. The alternative is to use statistical models derived from hand-annotated data. However, unless some hand-annotated data is available, statistical models cannot be used to deal with unknown phenomena. During the ATIS evaluations, some data was hand-tagged for semantic information. Schwartz et al. [180] used this as an opportunity to create what was probably the first end-to-end supervised statistical learning system for the ATIS domain. They had four components in their system: (i) semantic parse, (ii) semantic frame, (iii) discourse, and (iv) backend. This system used a supervised learning approach combined with quick training augmentation through a human-in-the-loop corrective approach to generate slightly lower quality but more data for improved supervision. Miller et al. [181] described the algorithm in more detail. Their system achieved an error rate of 14.5% on the entire test set and 9.5% on the subset of sentences that were context independent. Since then, various improvements have been made, such as by He and Young [182].

Continuing on the line of research that is today commonly known as natural language interface for databases (NLIDB), Zelle and Mooney [183] tackled the task of retrieving answers from a Prolog database by converting natural language questions into Prolog queries in the domain of GeoQuery. They introduced a system called CHILL (Constructive Heuristics Induction for Language Learning), based on the relational learning techniques of inductive logic programming. It uses a shift-reduce parser to map the input sentence into parses expressed as a Prolog program. They preferred a representation closer to formal logic rather than SQL, because once achieved, it can easily be translated into other equivalent representations. They tested the system performance with the rule-based system Geobase that comes with the GeoQuery dataset over a varying number of queries as inputs. It took CHILL roughly 175 training queries to match the performance of Geobase. Additional queries made it surpass Geobase, achieving an accuracy of 84% on novel queries, at times inducing 1,100 lines of Prolog code.

Since then, advances have been made in machine learning and syntactic parsing, and researchers have identified new approaches and refined existing approaches. The SCISSOR (Semantic Composition that Integrates Syntax and Semantics to get Optimal Representation) system, for example, uses a statistical syntactic parser to create a **semantically augmented parse tree** (SAPT) [184, 185]. Training for SCISSOR consists of a (natural language, SAPT, meaning representation) triplet. It uses a standard syntactic parser augmented with semantic tags, then a recursive procedure is used to compositionally construct the meaning representation for each node in the tree given the representations of its children. SCISSOR shows significant performance improvement over earlier approaches. KRISP (Kernel-based Robust Interpretation for Semantic Parsing) [186] uses string kernels and SVMs to improve the underlying learning techniques. WASP (Word Alignment-based Semantic Parsing) [187] takes a radical approach to semantic parsing by using state-of-the-art machine translation techniques to learn a semantic parser. Wong and Mooney treat the meaning representation language as an alternative form of natural language and use GIZA++ to produce an alignment between the natural language and a variation of the meaning representation language. Complete meaning representations are then formed by combining these aligned strings using a synchronous CFG (SCFG) framework. SCISSOR is somewhat more accurate than WASP and KRISP, which can themselves benefit from the information in SAPTs [188]. KRISP, CHILL, and WASP have also learned semantic parsers for Spanish, Turkish, and Japanese with similar accuracies. Yet another approach comes from Zettlemoyer and Collins [189], who trained a structured classifier for natural language interfaces by learning probabilistic combinatory categorial grammar (PCCG) along with a log-linear model that represents the distribution over the syntactic and semantic analysis conditioned on the natural language input.

4.6.3 Software

Not a lot of software programs are available for the older, more rule-based systems, but the following are available for download.

- **WASP** [http://www.cs.utexas.edu/~ml/wasp/]
- **KRISPER** [http://www.cs.utexas.edu/~ml/krisp/]
- **CHILL** [http://www.cs.utexas.edu/~ml/chill.html]

4.7 Summary

In this chapter we looked at the problem of semantic parsing through various lenses. There is no silver bullet to the problem of meaning representation and language understanding, so over the years, researchers have come up with tasks that either solve parts of the bigger problem in a more domain-independent fashion or solve the complete problem but for a very restricted domain. The first case, shallow semantic interpretation, deals separately with the four main aspects of language: structural ambiguity (which is syntactic in nature and is the subject of a separate chapter), word sense, entity and event recognition, and predicate-argument structure recognition. The latter three are components of what has widely come to be known as shallow semantic parsing. As we have seen, syntax plays a very important role in this process, and cannot be considered completely divorced from semantics. The second, deep parsing, or semantic parsing, comprises taking natural language input and transforming it into a meaning representation, which tends to be task specific and something that the end application can unambiguously execute.

We learned that developments on various fronts have been made in all these methods. In the early era of the field, few hand-labeled corpora and few well-developed learning techniques were avaliable. Even now, in the case of resource-poor languages, there is not much data to train sophisticated learning algorithms. In these cases, researchers resort to encoding the domain information in a rule-based system, which is usually domain specific. For languages for which there is enough human-annotated data available, more statistical approaches became predominant. Given the sparseness of data even when there is sufficient annotation (any amount of realistic human annotation would never be enough to learn all the various nuances of language), researchers have resorted to semisupervised or unsupervised methods, the latter being usually much less accurate than supervised or rule-based methods.

4.7.1 Word Sense Disambiguation

Word sense disambiguation is an integral part of language understanding. In information retrieval, speech understanding, and applications restricted to certain domains, it has not been very important, because of limited sense usability or implicit disambiguation. However, for applications that deal with a deeper understanding of text, sense disambiguation may be critical. Research in this area started with senses that were defined in dictionaries, because they were the primary resource in the beginning. Lesk's algorithm is generally recognized as the first dictionary-based word sense algorithm, where sense disambiguation is performed using the overlap between the context in which a word appears in the discourse and its dictionary gloss. The creation of *Roget's Thesaurus* led to more English-specific algorithms to classify words into the categories defined in it. The notion of one sense per discourse led to an important semisupervised algorithm: the Yarowsky algorithm. With the advent of a much richer lexicon like WordNet and corpora annotated with senses defined in it (SEMCOR)—interestingly, in parallel with the advances in machine learning—most of the research community shifted to using them as the standard until later studies showed that the granularity of senses in WordNet might be too fine. If humans cannot agree on sense distinctions to a certain degree, then machines should not be expected to either. This led to the folding of word senses in WordNet into coarser units that are more amenable to human agreement and at the same time provide a better means of achieving high-accuracy automatic disambiguation. WordNet has continued to be an important resource that has significantly improved the field, and it is still used in state-of-the-art disambiguation systems.

In a separate vein, with the growth of the Internet, the availability of resources such as Wikipedia, which served as a surrogate annotation resource, exploiting Internet resources became one of the mainstream pursuits. An increasing number of areas in language understanding are making use of this resource in novel ways. Active learning is another direction that is still probably more an art than a science but has been quite useful for amassing annotations for words that are either rare (low-frequency), high sense perplexity (many senses), or do not have enough annotation for some reason or other, including, but not limited to, low-resource languages [190]. In languages where there was no hand-annotated data available, various unsupervised approaches were developed, some of which exploited the differing sense granularities and instantiations across parallel corpora.

4.7.2 Predicate-Argument Structure

Unlike word sense disambiguation, there were far fewer rule-based systems that tagged thematic roles in text. With the advent of corpora such as FrameNet and PropBank labeled with a predicate-argument structure, there was a giant wave of research focused on building systems to tag these structures in text, primarily for verb and noun predicates. Many new features were introduced in various syntactic frameworks, some of them not even conducting a full syntactic analysis and resorting only to the base phrase chunks. It turns out that, at least for the genres that have treebanks, the contribution of a syntactic parser is invaluable. When lexicalization is the only way in which a syntactic representation is informed by semantics, a semantic role labeler tends to make errors that could be avoided using a more bottom-up approach. Also, using richer features in the first pass can be prohibitive, so a combination of producing n-best hypotheses and reranking them based on a more global feature set is the approach that generally performs better. Furthermore, a combination of a top-down and bottom-up approach by combining the information from various syntactic and nonsyntactic views improves performance as well. One big bottleneck at present is that performance on genres of text that exhibit even somewhat different syntactic styles, word usage, or entity and event structures tends to be much worse than if you have matched training and test corpora. We are at a point where structural information has been utilized to a significant degree to the benefit of semantic analysis, but the lexical- and sense-level generalization is significantly lacking, thereby making the existing approaches much less robust across genres or domains of text. We also saw that the fundamental techniques developed for English—which happens to be the language for which the hand-tagged corpora were first created—translate very well to other languages. Of course, each new language has its own idiosyncrasies that lead to the identification of new features. These new features may in turn improve the original English system. Many annotation efforts are underway across the world, and we have much more to learn.

4.7.3 Meaning Representation

Finally, we looked at meaning representation. This is a much less researched topic and especially so across languages. Meaning representation is the process of converting natural language input into a format that is unambiguous and easily understandable by a machine or end application, which can take actions based on the input. So far, there is no one universally accepted representation, so these systems and their representations tend to be domain specific.

New research programs are stretching the possibilities of existing techniques and creating novel ones that will eventually let us bring these pieces together into a richer, deeper representation that would also be independent of domain.

Bibliography

[1] N. Chomsky, *Syntactic Structures.* The Hague: Mouton, 1957.

[2] J. Katz and J. Fodor, "The structure of a semantic theory," *Language*, vol. 39, pp. 170–210, 1963.

[3] V. H. Yngve, "Syntax and the problem of multiple meaning," in *Machine Translation of Languages* (W. N. Locke and A. D. Booth, eds.), pp. 208–226, Cambridge, MA: MIT Press, 1955.

[4] N. Ide and J. Véronis, "Introduction to the special issue on word sense disambiguation: The state of the art," *Computational Linguistics*, vol. 24, no. 1, pp. 2–40, 1998.

[5] E. Agirre and P. Edmonds, eds., *Word Sense Disambiguation: Algorithms and Applications.* Dordrecht: Springer, 2006.

[6] M. Palmer, H. Dang, and C. Fellbaum, "Making coarse-grained and fine-grained sense distinctions, both manually and automatically," *Natural Language Engineering Journal*, vol. 13, no. 2, pp. 137–163, 2007.

[7] P. Resnik and D. Yarowsky, "Distinguishing systems and distinguishing senses: New evaluation methods for word sense disambiguation," *Journal of Natural Language Engineering*, vol. 5, no. 2, pp. 113–133, 1999.

[8] R. Krovetz and W. B. Croft, "Lexical ambiguity and information retrieval," *ACM Transactions on Information Systems*, vol. 10, no. 2, pp. 115–141, 1992.

[9] S. Katz, "Estimation of probabilities from sparse data for the language model component of a speech recognizer," *IEEE Transactions on Acoustics, Speech and Signal Processing*, vol. 35, no. 3, pp. 400–401, 1987.

[10] L. Bahl, F. Jelinek, and R. Mercer, "A maximum likelihood approach to continuous speech recognition," *PAMI—IEEE Transactions on Pattern Analysis and Machine Intelligence*, vol. 5, no. 2, pp. 179–190, 1983.

[11] P. F. Brown, V. J. Della Pietra, P. V. deSouza, J. C. Lai, and R. L. Mercer, "Class-based n-gram models of natural language," *Computational Linguistics*, vol. 18, no. 4, pp. 467–479, 1992.

[12] W. Gale, K. W. Church, and D. Yarowsky, "Estimating upper and lower bounds on the performance of word-sense disambiguation programs," in *Proceedings of the*

30th annual meeting on Association for Computational Linguistics, pp. 249–256, 1992.

[13] G. Hirst, *Semantic Interpretation and the Resolution of Ambiguity.* Cambridge: Cambridge University Press, 1987.

[14] P. Procter, *Longman Dictionary of Contemporary English (LDOCE).* Harlow: Longman Group, 1978.

[15] R. Chapman, *Roget's International Thesaurus.* New York: Harper and Row, 1977.

[16] G. A. Miller, "WordNet: An on-line lexical database," *International Journal of Lexicography*, vol. 3, no. 4, pp. 235–312, 1990.

[17] H. Kučera and W. N. Francis, *Computational Analysis of Present-Day American English.* Providence, RI: Brown University Press, 1967.

[18] G. A. Miller, C. Leacock, R. Tengi, and R. T. Bunker, "A semantic concordance," in *Proceedings of the Workshop on Human Language Technology*, pp. 303–308, 1993.

[19] D. I. Moldovan and V. Rus, "Logic form transformation of WordNet and its applicability to question answering," in *Proceedings of the Association for Computational Linguistics*, pp. 394–401, 2001.

[20] H. T. Ng and H. B. Lee, "Integrating multiple knowledge sources to disambiguate word sense: An exemplar-based approach," in *Proceedings of the 34th annual meeting on Association for Computational Linguistics*, pp. 40–47, 1996.

[21] SIGLEX, "SENSEVAL: Evaluation Exercises for the Semantic Analysis of Text," 2011. http://www.senseval.org.

[22] R. Weischedel, E. Hovy, M. Palmer, M. Marcus, R. Belvin, S. Pradhan, L. Ramshaw, and N. Xue, "OntoNotes: A large training corpus for enhanced processing," in *Handbook of Natural Language Processing and Machine Translation* (J. Olive, C. Christianson, and J. McCary, eds.) New York: Springer, 2011.

[23] S. Pradhan, E. Hovy, M. Marcus, M. Palmer, L. Ramshaw, and R. Weischedel, "OntoNotes: A unified relational semantic representation," *International Journal of Semantic Computing*, vol. 1, no. 4, pp. 405–419, 2007.

[24] E. Hovy, M. Marcus, M. Palmer, L. Ramshaw, and R. Weischedel, "OntoNotes: The 90% solution," in *Proceedings of the Human Language Technology Conference of the North American Chapter of the Association for Computational Linguistics*, pp. 57–60, 2006.

[25] S. Pradhan, E. Loper, D. Dligach, and M. Palmer, "Semeval-2007 task-17: English lexical sample, srl and all words," in *Proceedings of the 4th International Workshop on Semantic Evaluations (SemEval-2007)*, pp. 87–92, 2007.

[26] D. Lenat, "Cyc: A large-scale investment in knowledge infrastructure," *Communications of the ACM*, vol. 38, no. 11, pp. 33–35, 1995.

[27] Z. Dong and Q. Dong, *HowNet and the Computation of Meaning.* Hackensack, NJ: World Scientific, 2006.

[28] A. D. de Ilarraza, A. Mayor, and K. Sarasola, "Semiautomatic labeling of semantic features," in *Proceedings of the International Conference on Computational Linguistics*, 2002.

[29] M. A. Hearst, "Automatic acquisition of hyponyms from large text corpora," in *Proceedings of the 14th conference on Computational linguistics*, pp. 539–545, 1992.

[30] R. Snow, D. Jurafsky, and A. Y. Ng, "Semantic taxonomy induction from heterogenous evidence," in *ACL-44: Proceedings of the 21st International Conference on Computational Linguistics and the 44th Annual Meeting of the Association for Computational Linguistics*, pp. 801–808, 2006.

[31] T. Chklovski and P. Pantel, "Verbocean: Mining the web for fine-grained semantic verb relations," in *Proceedings of the Conference on Empirical Methods in Natural Language Processing*, 2004.

[32] A. Thanopoulos, N. Fakotakis, and G. Kokkinakis, "Automatic extraction of semantic relations from specialized corpora," in *Proceedings of the International Conference on Computational Linguistics*, pp. 836–842, 2000.

[33] N. Calzolari and E. Picchi, "Acquisition of semantic information from an on-line dictionary," in *Proceedings of the 12th Conference on Computational Linguistics*, pp. 87–92, 1988.

[34] S. McRoy, "Using multiple knowledge sources for word sense disambiguation," *Computational Linguistics*, vol. 18, no. 1, pp. 1–30, 1992.

[35] M. E. Lesk, "Automatic sense disambiguation using machine readable dictionaries: How to tell a pine cone from an ice cream cone," in *Proceedings of the SIGDOC Conference*, 1986.

[36] A. Kilgarriff and J. Rosenzweig, "English framework and results," *Computers and the Humanities*, vol. 34, no. 1–2, 2000.

[37] S. Banerjee and T. Pedersen, "An adapted lesk algorithm for word sense disambiguation using wordnet," in *Proceedings of the 3rd International Conference on Computational Linguistics and Intelligent Text Processing (CICLing-02)*, pp. 136–145, 2002.

[38] D. Yarowsky, "Word-sense disambiguation using statistical models of Roget's categories trained on large corpora," in *Proceedings of the 14th Conference on Computational Linguistics (COLING-92)*, pp. 454–460, 1992.

[39] R. Navigli and P. Velardi, "Learning domain ontologies from document warehouses and dedicated web sites," *Computational Linguistics*, vol. 30, no. 2, 2004.

[40] R. Navigli and P. Velardi, "Structural semantic interconnections: A knowledge-based approach to word sense disambiguation," *IEEE Transactions on Pattern Analysis and Machine Intelligence*, vol. 27, no. 7, pp. 1075–1086, 2005.

[41] B. Magnini and G. Cavaglia, "Integrating subject field codes into wordnet," in *Proceedings of the 2nd International Conference on Language Resources and Evaluation*, 2000.

[42] S. Patwardhan, S. Banerjee, and T. Pedersen, "Using measures of semantic relatedness for word sense disambiguation," in *Proceedings of the 4th International Conference on Intelligent Text Processing and Computational Linguistics (CICLing-03)*, 2003.

[43] M. Strube and S. P. Ponzetto, "Wikirelate! Computing semantic relatedness using Wikipedia," in *Proceedings of the 21st National Conference on Artificial Intelligence (AAAI'06)*, pp. 1419–1424, 2006.

[44] S. P. Ponzetto and M. Strube, "Knowledge derived from Wikipedia for computing semantic relatedness," *Journal of Artificial Intelligence Research*, vol. 30, pp. 181–212, 2007.

[45] R. Navigli and S. P. Ponzetto, "Babelnet: Building a very large multilingual semantic network," in *Proceedings of the 48th Annual Meeting of the Association for Computational Linguistics*, pp. 216–225, 2010.

[46] S. P. Ponzetto and R. Navigli, "Knowledge-rich word sense disambiguation rivaling supervised systems," in *Proceedings of the 48th Annual Meeting of the Association for Computational Linguistics*, pp. 1522–1531, 2010.

[47] P. F. Brown, S. A. D. Pietra, V. J. D. Pietra, and R. L. Mercer, "Word-sense disambiguation using statistical methods," in *Proceedings of the 29th annual meeting on Association for Computational Linguistics*, pp. 264–270, 1991.

[48] D. Yarowsky, "Homograph disambiguation in text-to-speech synthesis," in *Progress in Speech Synthesis* (J. Hirschberg, R. Sproat, and J. van Santen, eds.), pp. 159–175, New York: Springer, 1996.

[49] Y. K. Lee and H. T. Ng, "An empirical evaluation of knowledge sources and learning algorithms for word sense disambiguation," in *Proceedings of the ACL-02 Conference on Empirical Methods in Natural Language Processing (EMNLP '02)*, pp. 41–48, 2002.

[50] H. T. Ng, "Exemplar-based word sense disambiguation: Some recent improvements," in *Proceedings of the 2nd Conference on Empirical Methods in Natural Language Processing*, pp. 208–213, 1997.

[51] J. Chen and M. S. Palmer, "Towards robust high performance word sense disambiguation of english verbs using rich linguistic features," in *Proceedings of 2nd International Joint Conference on Natural Language Processing*, pp. 933–944, 2005.

[52] D. Dligach and M. Palmer, "Novel semantic features for verb sense disambiguation," in *Proceedings of the Conference of Association of Computational Linguistics*, pp. 29–32, 2008.

[53] R. Rada, H. Mili, E. Bicknell, and M. Blettner, "Development and application of a metric on semantic nets," *IEEE Transactions on Systems, Man, and Cybernetics*, vol. 19, no. 1, pp. 17–30, Jan 1989.

[54] P. Resnik, "Using information content to evaluate semantic similarity in a taxonomy," in *Proceedings of the 14th International Joint Conference on Artificial Intelligence*, pp. 448–453, 1995.

[55] E. Agirre and G. Rigau, "Word sense disambiguation using conceptual density," in *Proceedings of the 16th conference on Computational linguistics*, pp. 16–22, 1996.

[56] P. Resnik, "Selectional preference and sense disambiguation," in *Proceedings of the ACL SIGLEX Workshop on Tagging Text with Lexical Semantics: Why, What, and How?*, 1997.

[57] P. Resnik, "Disambiguating noun groupings with respect to WordNet senses," in *Proceedings of the 3rd Workshop on Very Large Corpora*, pp. 27–38, 1995.

[58] C. Leacock, G. A. Miller, and M. Chodorow, "Using corpus statistics and WordNet relations for sense identification," *Computational Linguistics*, vol. 24, no. 1, pp. 147–165, 1998.

[59] I. Dagan and A. Itai, "Word sense disambiguation using a second-language monolingual corpus," *Computational Lingustics*, vol. 20, no. 4, 1994.

[60] M. T. Diab, "An unsupervised approach for bootstrapping Arabic sense tagging," in *Proceedings of the Workshop on Computational Approaches to Arabic Script-based Languages*, pp. 43–50, 2004.

[61] D. Yarowsky, "Unsupervised word sense disambiguation rivaling supervised methods," in *Proceedings of the 33rd Annual Meeting of the ACL*, 1995.

[62] M. Galley and K. McKeown, "Improving word sense disambiguation in lexical chaining," in *Proceedings of the 18th International Joint Conference on Artificial Intelligence (IJCAI'03)*, pp. 1486–1488, 2003.

[63] R. Mihalcea and D. I. Moldovan, "An automatic method for generating sense tagged corpora," in *Proceedings of the 16th National Conference on Artificial Intelligence and the 11th Conference on Innovative Applications of Artificial Intelligence (AAAI '99/IAAI '99)*, pp. 461–466, 1999.

[64] R. Mihalcea, "Using Wikipedia for automatic word sense disambiguation," in *Human Language Technologies 2007: The Conference of the North American Chapter of the Association for Computational Linguistics; Proceedings of the Main Conference*, pp. 196–203, 2007.

[65] J. Grimshaw, *Argument Structure.* Cambridge, MA: MIT Press, 1990.

[66] M. Baker, "Thematic roles and syntactic structure," in *Elements of Grammar: Handbook of Generative Syntax* (L. Haegeman, ed.), New York: Springer, 1997.

[67] C. F. Baker, C. J. Fillmore, and J. B. Lowe, "The Berkeley FrameNet project," in *Proceedings of the International Conference on Computational Linguistics (COLING/ACL-98)*, pp. 86–90, 1998.

[68] C. J. Fillmore and C. F. Baker, "FrameNet: Frame semantics meets the corpus," poster presentation at the *74th Annual Meeting of the Linguistic Society of America*, Chicago, Jan. 6–9, 2000.

[69] C. Fillmore, C. Johnson, and M. R. L. Petruck, "Background to FrameNet," *International Journal of Lexicography*, vol. 16, no. 3, 2003.

[70] C. J. Fillmore, C. Wooters, and C. F. Baker, "Building a large lexical databank which provides deep semantics," in *Proceedings of the Pacific Asian Conference on Language, Information and Computation*, 2001.

[71] M. Palmer, D. Gildea, and P. Kingsbury, "The Proposition Bank: An annotated corpus of semantic roles," *Computational Linguistics*, pp. 71–106, 2005.

[72] C. J. Fillmore, "Frame semantics," in *Linguistics in the Morning Calm*, pp. 111–138, Seoul: Hanshin; Linguistics Society of Korea, 1982.

[73] D. R. Dowty, "Thematic proto-roles and argument selction," *Language*, vol. 67, no. 3, pp. 547–619, 1991.

[74] C. Barker and D. Dowty, "Non-verbal thematic proto-roles," in *Proceedings of North-Eastern Linguistics Conference (NELS-23)*, pp. 49–62, 1992.

[75] M. Marcus, G. Kim, M. A. Marcinkiewicz, R. MacIntyre, A. Bies, M. Ferguson, K. Katz, and B. Schasberger, "The Penn Treebank: Annotating predicate argument structure," 1994. http://clair.si.umich.edu/clair/anthology/query.cgi?type=Paper&id=H94-1020.

[76] O. Babko-Malaya, A. Bies, A. Taylor, S. Yi, M. Palmer, M. Marcus, S. Kulick, and L. Shen, "Issues in synchronizing the English treebank and PropBank," in *Proceedings of the Workshop on Frontiers in Linguistically Annotated Corpora 2006*, July 2006.

[77] M. Palmer, O. Babko-Malaya, and H. T. Dang, "Different sense granularities for different applications," in *Proceedings of the HLT-NAACL 2004 Workshop: 2nd Workshop on Scalable Natural Language Understanding*, pp. 49–56, 2004.

[78] A. Meyers, R. Reeves, C. Macleod, R. Szekely, V. Zielinska, B. Young, and R. Grishman, "The nombank project: An interim report," in *Proceedings of the NAACL/HLT Workshop on Frontiers in Corpus Annotation*, 2004.

[79] C. Macleod, R. Grishman, A. Meyers, L. Barrett, and R. Reeves, "Nomlex: A lexicon of nominalizations," http://citeseerx.ist.psu.edu/viewdoc/summary?doi=10.1.1.12.1452, 1998.

[80] B. Levin, *English Verb Classes And Alternations: A Preliminary Investigation*. Chicago: University of Chicago Press, 1993.

[81] K. Kipper, A. Korhonen, N. Ryant, and M. Palmer, "A large-scale classification of English verbs," *Language Resources and Evaluation*, vol. 42, no. 1, pp. 21 – 40, 2000.

[82] H. T. Dang, K. Kipper, M. Palmer, and J. Rosenzweig, "Investigating regular sense extensions based on intersective Levin classes," in *COLING/ACL-98: Proceedings of the 20th Conference on Computational Linguistics*, pp. 293–299, ACL, 1998.

[83] C. F. Baker and J. Ruppenhofer, "FrameNet's frames vs. Levin's verb classes," in *Proceedings of the 28th Annual Meeting of the Berkeley Linguistics Society*, 2002.

[84] K. Erk and S. Pado, "Towards a resource for lexical semantics: A large German corpus with extensive semantic annotation," in *Proceedings of Association for Computational Linguistics*, 2003.

[85] A. Burchardt, K. Erk, A. Frank, A. Kowalski, S. Pado, and M. Pinkal, "Using FrameNet for the semantic analysis of German: Annotation, representation, and automation," in *Multilingual FrameNets in Computational Lexicography: Methods and Applications* (H. C. Boas, ed.), New York: Mouton de Gruyter, 2009.

[86] K. H. Ohara, "Lexicon, grammar, and multilinguality in the Japanese FrameNet," in *Proceedings of the 6th International Conference on Language Resources and Evaluation*, 2008.

[87] C. Subirats, "Spanish FrameNet: A frame-semantic analysis of the Spanish lexicon," in *Multilingual FrameNets in Computational Lexicography: Methods and Applications* (H. C. Boas, ed.), pp. 135–162, Mouton de Gruyter, 2009.

[88] C. Subirats and H. Sato, "Spanish FrameNet and FrameSQL," in *Proceedings of the 4th International Conference on Language Resources and Evaluation, Workshop on Building Lexical Resources from Semantically Annotated Corpora*, 2004.

[89] L. D. Borin, F. Dana, T. G. Markus, and K. D. Maria, "The past meets the present in the Swedish FrameNet++," in *Proceedings of the 14th Euralex International Congress*, (Leeuwarden), 2010.

[90] H. C. Boas, ed., *Multilingual FrameNets in Computational Lexicography: Methods and Applications.* New York: Mouton de Gruyter, 2009.

[91] N. Xue and M. Palmer, "Adding semantic roles to the Chinese treebank," *Natural Language Engineering*, vol. 15, no. 1, pp. 143–172, 2009.

[92] M. Palmer, O. Babko-Malaya, A. Bies, M. Diab, M. Maamouri, A. Mansouri, and W. Zaghouani, "A pilot Arabic propbank," in *Proceedings of the International Conference on Language Resources and Evaluation (LREC)*, 2008.

[93] W. Zaghouani, M. Diab, A. Mansouri, S. Pradhan, and M. Palmer, "The revised Arabic propbank," in *Proceedings of the 4th Linguistic Annotation Workshop*, pp. 222–226, July 2010.

[94] M. Palmer, S. Ryu, J. Choi, S. Yoon, and Y. Jeon, "Korean propbank," 2006.

[95] M. Taulé, M. Martí, and M. Recasens, "Ancora: Multilevel annotated corpora for Catalan and Spanish," in *Proceedings of Language, Resources and Evaluation, LREC*, 2008.

[96] M. Palmer, R. Bhatt, B. Narasimhan, O. Rambow, D. M. Sharma, and F. Xia, "Hindi syntax: Annotating dependency, lexical predicate-argument structure, and phrase structure," in *Proceedings of the 7th International Conference on Natural Language Processing (ICON-2009)*, 2009.

[97] J. Hajic, B. Vidova-Hladka, and P. Pajas, "The Prague Dependency Treebank: Annotation structure and support," in *Proceedings of the IRCS Workshop on Linguistic Databases*, pp. 105–114, 2001.

[98] R. Iida, M. Komachi, K. Inui, and Y. Matsumoto, "Annotating a Japanese text corpus with predicate-argument and coreference relations," in *Proceedings of ACL Linguistic Annotation Workshop*, 2007.

[99] N. Sondheimer, R. Weischedel, and R. Bobrow, "Semantic interpretation using KL-ONE," in *Proceedings of the 10th International Conference on Computational Linguistics and 22nd Annual Meeting of the Association for Computational Linguistics*, pp. 101–107, 1984.

[100] N. Calzolari, "Acquiring and representing semantic information in a lexical knowledge base," in *Proceedings of the ACL SIGLEX Workshop on Lexical Semantics and Knowledge Representation*, pp. 188–197, 1992.

[101] R. long Liu and V. wun Soo, "An empirical study on thematic knowledge acquisition based on syntactic clues and heuristics," in *Proceedings 31st Annual Meeting of the ACL*, pp. 243–250, 1993.

[102] G. Hirst, "A foundation for semantic interpretation," in *Proceedings of the 21st Annual Meeting of the Association for Computational Linguistics*, pp. 64–73, 1983.

[103] D. Dahl, M. Palmer, and R. Passonneau, "Nominalizations in PUNDIT," in *Proceedings of the 25th Annual Meeting of the Association for Computational Linguistics*, 1987.

[104] M. Palmer, C. Weir, R. Passonneau, and T. Finin, "The kernel text understanding system," *Artificial Intelligence*, vol. 63 (Special Issue on Text Understanding), pp. 17–68, October 1993.

[105] J. L. G. Rosa and E. Francozo, "Hybrid thematic role processor: Symbolic linguistic relations revised by connectionist learning," in *Proceedings of the 16th International Joint Conference on Artificial Intelligence (IJCAI)*, pp. 852–861, 1999.

[106] C. Rose, "A framework for robust semantic interpretation," in *Proceedings of the 1st Meeting of the North American Chapter of the Association for Computational Linguistics*, pp. 311–318, 2000.

[107] L. S. Peh and H. T. Ng, "Domain-specific semantic class disambiguation using wordnet," in *Proceedings of the ACL Workshop on Very Large Corpora*, pp. 56–65, 1997.

[108] C. D. Manning, "Automatic acquisition of a large subcategorization dictionary from corpora," in *Proceedings of the 31st Meeting of the Association for Computational Linguistics*, pp. 235–242, 1993.

[109] T. Briscoe and J. Carroll, "Automatic extraction of subcategorization from corpora," in *Proceedings of the 5th Conference on Applied Natural Language Processing*, March 31 – April 3 1997.

[110] J. Pustejovsky, "The acquisition of lexical semantic knowledge from large corpora," in *Proceedings of Speech and Natural Language Workshop*, pp. 311–315, 1992.

[111] R. Green, B. J. Dorr, and P. Resnik, "Inducing frame semantic verb classes from WordNet and LDOCE," in *Proceedings of the 42nd Meeting of the Association for Computational Linguistics (ACL'04), Main Volume*, pp. 375–382, 2004.

[112] R. S. Swier and S. Stevenson, "Unsupervised semantic role labelling," in *Proceedings of the Conference on Empirical Methods on Natural Language Processing*, pp. 95–102, 2004.

[113] D. Gildea and D. Jurafsky, "Automatic labeling of semantic roles," *Computational Linguistics*, vol. 28, no. 3, pp. 245–288, 2002.

[114] D. Magerman, "Natural language parsing as statistical pattern recognition," PhD thesis, Stanford University, 1994.

[115] M. J. Collins, "Head-driven statistical models for natural language parsing," PhD thesis, University of Pennsylvania, Philadelphia, 1999.

[116] D. Lin, "Automatic retrieval and clustering of similar words," in *Proceedings of the 17th International Conference on Computational Linguistics and 36th Annual Meeting of the Association of Computational Linguistics (COLING/ACL)*, 1998.

[117] T. Hofmann and J. Puzicha, "Statistical models for co-occurrence data" (memo), Massachusetts Institute of Technology Artificial Intelligence Laboratory, Feb. 1998.

[118] M. Surdeanu, S. Harabagiu, J. Williams, and P. Aarseth, "Using predicate-argument structures for information extraction," in *Proceedings of the 41st Annual Meeting of the Association for Computational Linguistics (ACL)*, 2003.

[119] M. Fleischman, N. Kwon, and E. Hovy, "Maximum entropy models for framenet classification," in *Proceedings of the Conference on Empirical Methods in Natural Language Processing*, 2003.

[120] S. Pradhan, K. Hacioglu, V. Krugler, W. Ward, J. Martin, and D. Jurafsky, "Support vector learning for semantic argument classification," *Machine Learning Journal*, vol. 60, no. 1, pp. 11–39, 2005.

[121] D. M. Bikel, R. Schwartz, and R. M. Weischedel, "An algorithm that learns what's in a name," *Machine Learning*, vol. 34, pp. 211–231, 1999.

[122] R. Girju, D. Roth, and M. Sammons, "Token-level disambiguation of VerbNet classes," in *Proceedings of the Interdisciplinary Workshop on the Identification and Representation of Verb Features and Verb Classes*, 2005.

[123] K. Daniel, Y. Schabes, M. Zaidel, and D. Egedi, "A freely available wide coverage morphological analyzer for English," in *Proceedings of the 14th International Conference on Computational Linguistics (COLING-92)*, 1992.

[124] K. Hacioglu, S. Pradhan, W. Ward, J. Martin, and D. Jurafsky, "Semantic role labeling by tagging syntactic chunks," in *Proceedings of the 8th Conference on Computational Natural Language Learning (CoNLL)*, May 2004.

[125] D. Vickrey and D. Koller, "Applying sentence simplification to the CoNLL-2008 shared task," in *Proceedings of the 12th Conference on Computational Natural Language Learning (CoNLL 2008)*, pp. 268–272, 2008.

[126] S. Pradhan, W. Ward, K. Hacioglu, J. Martin, and D. Jurafsky, "Shallow semantic parsing using support vector machines," in *Proceedings of the Human Language Technology Conference/North American Chapter of the Association of Computational Linguistics (HLT/NAACL)*, 2004.

[127] N. Xue and M. Palmer, "Calibrating features for semantic role labeling," in *Proceedings of the Conference on Empirical Methods in Natural Language Processing (EMNLP)*, 2004.

[128] D. Gildea and J. Hockenmaier, "Identifying semantic roles using combinatory categorial grammar," in *Proceedings of the Conference on Empirical Methods in Natural Language Processing*, 2003.

[129] S. Pradhan, W. Ward, K. Hacioglu, J. Martin, and D. Jurafsky, "Semantic role labeling using different syntactic views," in *Proceedings of the 43rd Annual Meeting of the Association for Computational Linguistics (ACL)*, 2005.

[130] J. Chen and O. Rambow, "Use of deep linguistics features for the recognition and labeling of semantic arguments," in *Proceedings of the Conference on Empirical Methods in Natural Language Processing*, 2003.

[131] D. Gildea and M. Palmer, "The necessity of syntactic parsing for predicate argument recognition," in *Proceedings of the 40th Annual Conference of the Association for Computational Linguistics (ACL-02)*, 2002.

[132] A. Moschitti, D. Pighin, and R. Basili, "Tree kernels for semantic role labeling," *Computational Linguistics*, vol. 34, no. 2, 2008.

[133] K. Hacioglu, "Semantic role labeling using dependency trees," in *Proceedings of Coling 2004*, pp. 1273–1276, 2004.

[134] R. Hwa, A. Lopez, and M. Diab, "`engconst2dep` program for converting Treebank trees to dependency trees," 2011.

[135] D. Lin, "Dependency-based evaluation of MINIPAR," in *Workshop on the Evaluation of Parsing Systems*, 1998.

[136] D. Lin and P. Pantel, "Discovery of inference rules for question answering," *Natural Language Engineering*, vol. 7, no. 4, pp. 343–360, 2001.

[137] M. Surdeanu, R. Johansson, A. Meyers, L. Màrquez, and J. Nivre, "The CoNLL 2008 shared task on joint parsing of syntactic and semantic dependencies," in *CoNLL 2008: Proceedings of the 12th Conference on Computational Natural Language Learning*, pp. 159–177, 2008.

[138] J. Hajič, M. Ciaramita, R. Johansson, D. Kawahara, M. A. Martí, L. Màrquez, A. Meyers, J. Nivre, S. Padó, J. Štěpánek, P. Straňák, M. Surdeanu, N. Xue, and Y. Zhang, "The CoNLL-2009 shared task: Syntactic and semantic dependencies in multiple languages," in *Proceedings of the 13th Conference on Computational Natural Language Learning (CoNLL 2009): Shared Task*, pp. 1–18, 2009.

[139] R. Johansson and P. Nugues, "Extended constituent-to-dependency conversion for English," in *Proceedings of 16th Nordic Conference on Computational Linguistics (NODALIDA)*, pp. 105–112, 2007.

[140] V. Punyakanok, D. Roth, and W. tau Yih, "The necessity of syntactic parsing for semantic role labeling," in *Proceedings of the 19th International Joint Conference on Artificial Intelligence (IJCAI)*, 2005.

[141] L. A. Ramshaw and M. P. Marcus, "Text chunking using transformation-based learning," in *Proceedings of the 3rd Annual Workshop on Very Large Corpora*, pp. 82–94, 1995.

[142] J. R. Quinlan, "Induction of decision trees," *Machine Learning*, vol. 1, no. 1, pp. 81–106, 1986.

[143] R. Quinlan, "Data Mining Tools See5 and C5.0," 2003. http://www.rulequest.com.

[144] M. Fleischman and E. Hovy, "A maximum entropy approach to framenet tagging," in *Proceedings of the Human Language Technology Conference*, 2003.

[145] T. Kudo and Y. Matsumoto, "Use of support vector learning for chunk identification," in *Proceedings of the 4th Conference on Computational Natural Language Learning (CoNLL)*, 2000.

[146] T. Kudo and Y. Matsumoto, "Chunking with support vector machines," in *Proceedings of the 2nd Meeting of the North American Chapter of the Association for Computational Linguistics (NAACL)*, 2001.

[147] T. Joachims, "Text categorization with support vector machines: Learning with many relevant features," in *Proceedings of the European Conference on Machine Learning (ECML)*, 1998.

[148] H. Lodhi, C. Saunders, J. Shawe-Taylor, N. Cristianini, and C. Watkins, "Text classification using string kernels," *Journal of Machine Learning Research*, vol. 2, no. Feb, pp. 419–444, 2002.

[149] S. Pradhan, K. Hacioglu, W. Ward, J. Martin, and D. Jurafsky, "Semantic role parsing: Adding semantic structure to unstructured text," in *Proceedings of the International Conference on Data Mining (ICDM 2003)*, 2003.

[150] E. L. Allwein, R. E. Schapire, and Y. Singer, "Reducing multiclass to binary: A unifying approach for margin classifiers," in *Proceedings of the 17th International Conference on Machine Learning*, pp. 9–16, 2000.

[151] U. H. G. Kressel, "Pairwise classification and support vector machines," in *Advances in Kernel Methods* (B. Scholkopf, C. Burges, and A. J. Smola, eds.), Cambridge, MA: MIT Press, 1999.

[152] J. Platt, "Probabilities for support vector machines," in *Advances in Large Margin Classifiers* (A. Smola, P. Bartlett, B. Scholkopf, and D. Schuurmans, eds.), Cambridge, MA: MIT press, 2000.

[153] K. Toutanova, A. Haghighi, and C. D. Manning, "A global joint model for semantic role labeling," *Computational Linguistics*, vol. 34, no. 2, 2008.

[154] V. Punyakanok, D. Roth, and W. tau Yih, "The importance of syntactic parsing and inference in semantic role labeling," *Computational Linguistics*, vol. 34, no. 2, 2008.

[155] J. Weston, S. Mukherjee, O. Chapelle, M. Pontil, T. Poggio, and V. Vapnik, "Feature selection for svms," *Advances in Neural Information Processing Systems (NIPS)*, vol. 13, pp. 668–674, 2001.

[156] D. P. Foster and R. A. Stine, "Variable selection in data mining: Building a predictive model for bankruptcy," *Journal of American Statistical Association*, vol. 99, pp. 303–313, 2004.

[157] R. E. Barlow, D. J. Bartholomew, J. M. Bremmer, and H. D. Brunk, *Statistical Inference under Order Restrictions*. New York: Wiley, 1972.

[158] E. Charniak, "A maximum-entropy-inspired parser," in *Proceedings of the 1st Annual Meeting of the North American Chapter of the Association for Computational Linguistics (NAACL)*, pp. 132–139, 2000.

[159] K. Hacioglu, "A lightweight semantic chunking model based on tagging," in *Proceedings of the Human Language Technology Conference/North American Chapter of the Association of Computational Linguistics (HLT/NAACL)*, 2004.

[160] K. Hacioglu and W. Ward, "Target word detection and semantic role chunking using support vector machines," in *Proceedings of the Human Language Technology Conference*, 2003.

[161] M. Surdeanu, L. Màrquez, X. Carreras, and P. R. Comas, "Combination strategies for semantic role labeling," *Journal of Artificial Intelligence Research*, vol. 29, pp. 105–151, 2007.

[162] X. Hao, H. Mi, Y. Liu, and Q. Liu, "Forest-based semantic role labeling," in *Proceedings of the Association for the Advancement of Artificial Intelligence (AAAI) Conference*, 2010.

[163] R. D. Hull and F. Gomez, "Semantic interpretation of nominalizations," in *Proceedings of the 13th National Conference on Artificial Intelligence*, pp. 1062–1068, 1996.

[164] M. Lapata, "The disambiguation of nominalizations," *Computational Linguistics*, vol. 28, no. 3, pp. 357–388, 2002.

[165] S. Pradhan, H. Sun, W. Ward, J. Martin, and D. Jurafsky, "Parsing arguments of nominalizations in English and Chinese," in *Proceedings of the Human Language Technology Conference/North American Chapter of the Association of Computational Linguistics (HLT/NAACL)*, 2004.

[166] Z. P. Jiang and H. T. Ng, "Semantic role labeling of nombank: A maximum entropy approach," in *Proceedings of the 2006 Conference on Empirical Methods in Natural Language Processing* (EMNLP '06), pp. 138–145, 2006.

[167] N. Xue, "Labeling chinese predicates with semantic roles," *Computational Linguistics*, vol. 34, no. 2, pp. 225–255, 2008.

[168] M. Diab, A. Moschitti, and D. Pighin, "Semantic role labeling systems for Arabic language using kernel methods," in *Proceedings of Association for Computational Linguistics (ACL)*, 2008.

[169] W. Sun, Z. Sui, M. Wang, and X. Wang, "Chinese semantic role labeling with shallow parsing," in *Proceedings of the 2009 Conference on Empirical Methods in Natural Language Processing*, pp. 1475–1483, 2009.

[170] Y. Yang and N. Xue, "Chasing the ghost: Recovering empty categories in the Chinese Treebank," in *Proceedings of the 23rd International Conference on Computational Linguistics (COLING 2010)*, pp. 1382–1390, 2010.

[171] X. Carreras and L. Màrquez, "Introduction to the CoNLL-2005 shared task: Semantic role labeling," in *Proceedings of the 9th Conference on Computational Natural Language Learning (CoNLL)*, 2005.

[172] S. Pradhan, W. Ward, and J. H. Martin, "Towards robust semantic role labeling," *Computational Linguistics*, vol. 34, no. 2, 2008.

[173] B. n. Zapirain, E. Agirre, L. Màrquez, and M. Surdeanu, "Improving semantic role classification with selectional preferences," in *Proceedings of the 2010 Annual Conference of the North American Chapter of the Association for Computational Linguistics*, pp. 373–376, 2010.

[174] P. J. Price, "Evaluation of spoken language systems: The ATIS domain," in *Proceedings of the 3rd DARPA Speech and Natural Language Workshop*, 1990.

[175] Borland, *Turbo Prolog 2.0 Reference Guide*, 1988.

[176] W. Ward, "Understanding spontaneous speech," in *Proceedings of the Workshop on Speech and Natural Language*, pp. 137–141, 1989.

[177] W. Ward, "The CMU Air Travel Information Service: Understanding spontaneous speech," in *Proceedings of the Workshop on Speech and Natural Language*, pp. 127–129, 1990.

[178] W. Ward and S. Issar, "Recent improvements in the CMU spoken language understanding system," in *Proceedings of the Workshop on Human Language Technology*, pp. 213–216, 1994.

[179] W. A. Woods, "Transition network grammars for natural language analysis," *Communications of the ACM*, vol. 13, no. 10, pp. 591–606, 1970.

[180] R. Schwartz, S. Miller, D. Stallard, and J. Makhoul, "Hidden understanding models for statistical sentence understanding," in *Proceedings of the IEEE International Conference on Acoustics, Speech, and Signal Processing (ICASSP-97)*, pp. 1479–1482, 1997.

[181] S. Miller, R. Bobrow, R. Ingria, and R. Schwartz, "Hidden understanding models of natural language," in *Proceedings of the 32nd Meeting of the Association for Computational Linguistics*, pp. 25–32, ACL, 1994.

[182] Y. He and S. Young, "Semantic processing using the hidden vector state model," *Computer Speech and Language*, vol. 19, pp. 85–106, 2005.

[183] J. Zelle and R. Mooney, "Learning to parse database queries using inductive logic programming," in *Proceedings of the Association for the Advancement of Artificial Intelligence*, pp. 1050–1055, 1996.

[184] R. Ge and R. Mooney, "A statistical semantic parser that integrates syntax and semantics," in *Proceedings of the 9th Conference on Computational Natural Language Learning (CoNLL-2005)*, pp. 9–16, 2005.

[185] R. Ge and R. Mooney, "Learning a compositional semantic parser using an existing syntactic parser," in *Proceedings of the Joint Conference of the 47th Annual Meeting of the ACL and the 4th International Joint Conference on Natural Language Processing of the AFNLP*, pp. 611–619, 2009.

[186] R. J. Kate and R. J. Mooney, "Using string-kernels for learning semantic parsers," in *Proceedings of the 21st International Conference on Computational Linguistics and 44th Annual Meeting of the Association for Computational Linguistics*, pp. 913–920, 2006.

[187] Y. W. Wong and R. Mooney, "Learning synchronous grammars for semantic parsing with lambda calculus," in *Proceedings of the 45th Annual Meeting of the Association of Computational Linguistics*, pp. 960–967, 2007.

[188] R. J. Mooney, "Learning for semantic parsing," in *Proceedings of the 8th International Conference on Computational Linguistics and Intelligent Text Processing*, 2007.

[189] L. Zettlemoyer and M. Collins, "Online learning of relaxed CCG grammars for parsing to logical form," in *Proceedings of the 2007 Joint Conference on Empirical Methods in Natural Language Processing and Computational Natural Language Learning (EMNLP-CoNLL)*, pp. 678–687, 2007.

[190] J. Chen, A. Schein, L. Ungar, and M. Palmer, "An empirical study of the behavior of active learning for word sense disambiguation," in *Proceedings of the main conference on Human Language Technology Conference of the North American Chapter of the Association of Computational Linguistics*, pp. 120–127, 2006.

Chapter 5

Language Modeling

Katrin Kirchhoff

5.1 Introduction

Many applications in human language technology involve the use of a statistical language model—a model that specifies the a priori probability of a particular word sequence in the language of interest. Given an alphabet or inventory of units Σ and a sequence $W = w_1 w_2 \ldots w_t \in \Sigma^*$, a language model can be used to compute the probability of W based on parameters previously estimated from a training set. Most commonly, the inventory Σ (also called **vocabulary**) is the list of unique words encountered in the training data; however, as we will see in this chapter, selecting the units over which a language model should be defined can be a rather difficult problem, particularly in languages other than English.

A language model is usually combined with some other model or models that hypothesize possible word sequences. In speech recognition, a speech recognizer combines acoustic model scores (and possibly other scores, such as pronunciation model scores) with language model scores to decode spoken word sequences from an acoustic signal. In machine translation, a language model is used to score translation hypotheses generated by a translation model. Language models have also become a standard tool in information retrieval [1], authorship identification [2], and document classification [3]. In several related fields, language models are used that are defined not over words but over acoustic units or isolated text characters. One of the core approaches to language identification, for example, relies on language models over phones or phonemes [4]; in optical character recognition, language models predicting character sequences are used [5, 6]. In this chapter, however, the focus is on language models over natural language words or wordlike units, which we define for now as units delimited by whitespace. We first present the fundamental n-gram modeling approach to statistical language modeling, as well as a range of more advanced modeling techniques, before discussing problems arising from the characteristics of particular languages, such as morphologically rich languages or languages without explicit word segmentation. The chapter concludes with a presentation of multilingual and crosslingual language modeling approaches.

5.2 *n*-Gram Models

The probability of a word sequence W of nontrivial length cannot be computed directly because unrestricted natural language permits an infinite number of word sequences of variable lengths. The probability $P(W)$ can be decomposed into a product of component probabilities according to the chain rule of probability:

$$P(W) = P(w_1 \ldots w_t) = P(w_1) \prod_{i=1}^{t} P(w_i | w_{i-1} w_{i-2} \ldots w_2 w_1) \tag{5.1}$$

Because the individual terms in this product are still too difficult to be computed directly, statistical language models make use of the ***n*-gram approximation**, which is why they are also called n-gram models. The assumption is that all previous words except for the $n-1$ words directly preceding the current word are irrelevant for predicting the current word, or, alternatively, that they are equivalent. Given this assumption of "history equivalence classes," the n-gram model is defined as:

$$P(W) \approx \prod_{i=1}^{t} P(w_i | w_{i-1}, \ldots w_{i-n+1}) \tag{5.2}$$

Depending on the length of n, we can distinguish between unigrams ($n=1$), bigrams ($n=2$), trigrams ($n=3$), or 4-grams, 5-grams, and so on. An n-gram model is also often called an ($n-1$)-th order Markov model, because the approximation in Equation 5.2 embodies the Markov assumption of the independence of the current word given all other words except the $n-1$ preceding words.

5.3 Language Model Evaluation

Before describing parameter estimation methods and further refinements of the basic n-gram modeling approach, let us consider the problem of judging the performance of a language model. According to the basic definition given previously, a language model computes the probability of a word sequence W. How can we tell whether a language model is successful at estimating word sequence probabilities? Typically, two criteria are used: **coverage rate** and **perplexity** on a held-out test set that does not form part of the training data. The coverage rate measures the percentage of n-grams in the test set that are represented in the language model. A special case of this is the out-of-vocabulary rate (or OOV rate), which is 100 minus the unigram coverage rate, or, in other words, the percentage of unique word types *not* covered by the language model. The second criterion, perplexity, is an information-theoretic measure. Given a model p of a discrete probability distribution, perplexity can be defined as 2 raised to the entropy of p:

$$PPL(p) = 2^{H(p)} = 2^{-\sum_x p(x) log_2 p(x)} \tag{5.3}$$

In language modeling, we are often more interested in the performance of a language model q on a test set of a fixed size, say t words $(w_1 w_2 \ldots w_t)$. Then, language model perplexity can be computed as

$$PPL(p, q) = 2^{H(p,q)} = 2^{-\sum_{i=1}^{t} p(w_i) log_2 q(w_i)} \tag{5.4}$$

or simply

$$2^{-\frac{1}{t}\sum_{i=1}^{t} log_2 q(w_i)} \tag{5.5}$$

where $q(w_i)$ computes the probability of the $i'th$ word. If $q(w_i)$ is an n-gram probability, the equation becomes

$$2^{-\frac{1}{t}\sum_{i=1}^{t} log_2 p(w_i|w_{i-1},\ldots,w_{i-n+1})} \tag{5.6}$$

When comparing different language models, especially models based on different ways of decomposing a text into language modeling units (e.g., words vs. morphemes), care must be taken to normalize their perplexities with respect to the same number of units in order to obtain a meaningful comparison.

Perplexity can be thought of as the average number of equally likely successor words when transitioning from one position in the word string to the next. If the model has no predictive power at all, perplexity is equal to the vocabulary size. A model achieving perfect prediction, by contrast, has a perplexity of one. The goal in language model development is most often to minimize the perplexity on a held-out data set representative of the domain of interest.

However, it should be noted that sometimes the goal of language modeling is not to predict word sequence probabilities but to distinguish between "good" and "bad" word sequence hypotheses generated by some frontend such as a machine translation system or a speech recognizer. In this case, the language model should assign maximally distinct scores to word sequences that are errorful, ungrammatical, or otherwise unacceptable, as opposed to those that are correct. Optimizing for minimum perplexity does not necessarily achieve this goal; we return to this point in Section 5.6.3.

5.4 Parameter Estimation

5.4.1 Maximum-Likelihood Estimation and Smoothing

The standard procedure in training n-gram models is to estimate n-gram probabilities using the maximum-likelihood criterion in combination with parameter smoothing. The maximum-likelihood estimate is obtained by simply computing relative frequencies:

$$P(w_i|w_{i-1}, w_{i-2}) = \frac{c(w_i, w_{i-1}, w_{i-2})}{c(w_{i-1}, w_{i-2})} \tag{5.7}$$

where $c(w_i, w_{i-1}, w_{i-2})$ is the count of the trigram $w_{i-2}w_{i-1}w_i$ in the training data. It is obvious that this method fails to assign nonzero probabilities to word sequences that have not been observed in the training data; on the other hand, the probability of sequences that were observed might be overestimated. The process of redistributing probability mass such that peaks in the n-gram probability distribution are flattened and zero estimates are floored to some small nonzero value is called **smoothing**. The most common smoothing technique is **backoff**. Backoff involves splitting n-grams into those whose counts in the training data fall below a predetermined threshold τ and those whose counts exceed the threshold. In the former case, the maximum-likelihood estimate of the n-gram probability is replaced with an estimate derived from the probability of the lower-order $(n-1)$-gram and a backoff weight. In the latter case, n-grams retain their maximum-likelihood estimates, discounted by a factor that redistributes probability mass to the lower-order distribution. Thus, the backed-off probability P_{BO} for w_i given w_{i-1}, w_{i-2} is computed as follows:

$$P_{BO}(w_i|w_{i-1}, w_{i-2}) = \begin{cases} d_c P(w_i|w_{i-1}, w_{i-2}) \text{ if } c > \tau \\ \alpha(w_{i-1}, w_{i-2}) P_{BO}(w_i|w_{i-1}) \text{ otherwise} \end{cases} \tag{5.8}$$

where c is the count of (w_i, w_{i-1}, w_{i-2}), and d_c is a discounting factor that is applied to the higher-order distribution. The normalization factor $\alpha(w_{i-1}, w_{i-2})$ ensures that the entire distribution sums to one and is computed as

$$\alpha(w_{i-1}, w_{i-2}) = \frac{1 - \sum_{w_i:c(w_i,w_{i-1},w_{i-2})>\tau} d_c P(w_i|w_{i-1}, w_{i-2})}{\sum_{w_i:c(w_i,w_{i-1},w_{i-2})\leq\tau} P_{BO}(w_i|w_{i-1})} \tag{5.9}$$

The way in which the discounting factor is computed determines the precise smoothing technique. Well-known techniques include Good-Turing, Witten-Bell, Kneser-Ney, and others; see the study by Chen and Goodman [7] for an in-depth description and comparison of various smoothing techniques. For example, in Kneser-Ney smoothing, a fixed discounting parameter D is applied to the raw n-gram counts before computing the probability estimates:

$$P_{KN}(w_i|w_{i-1}, w_{i-2}) = \begin{cases} \frac{max\{c(w_i,w_{i-1},w_{i-2})-D,0\}}{\sum_{w_i} c(w_i,w_{i-1},w_{i-2})} \text{ if } c > \tau \\ \alpha(w_{i-1}, w_{i-2}) P_{KN}(w_i|w_{i-1}) \text{ otherwise} \end{cases} \tag{5.10}$$

In modified Kneser-Ney smoothing, which is one of the most widely used techniques, different discounting factors D_1, D_2, D_{3+} are used for n-grams with exactly one, two, or three or more counts:

$$Y = \frac{n_1}{n_1 + 2 * n_2} \tag{5.11}$$

$$D_1 = 1 - 2Y\frac{n_2}{n_1} \tag{5.12}$$

$$D_2 = 2 - 3Y\frac{n_3}{n_2} \tag{5.13}$$

$$D_{3+} = 3 - 4Y\frac{n_4}{n_3} \tag{5.14}$$

where $n_1, n_2, \ldots$ are the counts of n-grams with one, two, $\ldots$, counts.

Another common way of smoothing language model estimates is linear model interpolation [8]. In linear interpolation, M models are combined by

$$P(w_i|w_{i-1}, w_{i-2}) = \sum_{m=1}^{M} \lambda_m P(w_i|h_m) \tag{5.15}$$

where λ is a model-specific weight. The component models may use different conditioning variables, such as histories of different lengths, or they may have been estimated from different data sets, such as a large set of general data or a smaller set of domain-specific data (see Section 5.5). The following constraints hold for the model weights: $0 \leq \lambda \leq 1$, and $\sum_m \lambda_m = 1$. Weights are estimated by maximizing the log-likelihood (minimizing the perplexity) on a held-out data set that is different from the training set for the component models (and also different from the final evaluation or test set). This is typically done using the expectation-maximization (EM) procedure [9].

5.4.2 Bayesian Parameter Estimation

Bayesian probability estimation is an alternative parameter estimation method whereby the set of parameters of a model is itself viewed as a random variable governed by a prior statistical distribution. Given a training sample S and a set of parameters θ, $P(\theta)$ denotes a prior distribution over different possible values of θ, and $P(\theta|S)$ is the posterior distribution, which can be expressed using Bayes's rule as

$$P(\theta|S) = \frac{P(S|\theta)P(\theta)}{P(S)} \tag{5.16}$$

In language modeling, the set of parameters is the vector of word probabilities, that is, $\theta = \langle P(w_1), \ldots, P(w_K)\rangle$ (where K is the vocabulary size) for a unigram model, or, more generally, $\theta = \langle P(w_1|h_1), \ldots, P(w_K|h_K)\rangle$ for an n-gram model with K n-grams and history h of a specified length. The training sample S is a sequence of words, $w_1 \ldots w_t$. We require a point estimate of θ given the constraints expressed by the prior distribution and the training sample. This can be done using either the maximum a posteriori (MAP) criterion or the Bayesian criterion. The former finds the value that maximizes the posterior probability given in Equation 5.16:

$$\theta^{MAP} = \underset{\theta\in\Theta}{\operatorname{argmax}}\, P(\theta|S) = \underset{\theta\in\Theta}{\operatorname{argmax}}\, P(S|\theta)P(\theta) \tag{5.17}$$

where Θ is the space of all possible assignments for θ. The Bayesian criterion finds the *expected* value of θ given the sample S:

$$\theta^{B} = E[\theta|S] = \int_{\Theta} \theta P(\theta|S)d\theta \tag{5.18}$$

$$= \frac{\int_{\Theta} \theta P(S|\theta)P(\theta)d\theta}{\int_{\Theta} P(S|\theta)P(\theta)d\theta} \tag{5.19}$$

Under the assumption that the prior distribution is a uniform distribution, the MAP estimate of the probability for a given word w is equivalent to the maximum-likelihood estimate, whereas the Bayesian estimate is equivalent to the maximum-likelihood estimate with Laplace smoothing:

$$\theta_w^B = \frac{c(w) + 1}{\sum_w c(w) + K} \tag{5.20}$$

Different choices for the prior distribution lead to different estimation functions. The most commonly used prior distribution in language model is the Dirichlet distribution. The Dirichlet distribution is the conjugate prior to the multinomial distribution (i.e., prior and posterior distribution have the same functional form). It is defined as

$$p(\theta) = D(\alpha_1, \ldots, \alpha_K) = \frac{\Gamma(\sum_{k=1}^K \alpha_k)}{\prod_{k=1}^K \Gamma(\alpha_k)} \prod_{k=1}^K \theta_k^{\alpha_k - 1} \tag{5.21}$$

where Γ is the gamma function and $\alpha_1, \ldots, \alpha_K$ are the parameters of the Dirichlet distribution (or hyperparameters), which can also be thought of as counts derived from an a priori training sample. The MAP estimate under the Dirichlet prior is

$$\theta^{MAP} = \operatorname*{argmax}_{\theta \in \Theta} \frac{\Gamma(\sum_{k=1}^K \alpha_k)}{\prod_{k=1}^K \Gamma(\alpha_k)} \prod_{k=1}^K \theta_k^{n_k + \alpha_k - 1} \tag{5.22}$$

where n_k is the number of times word k occurs in the training sample. The result is another Dirichlet distribution, parameterized by $n_k + \alpha$. The MAP estimate of $P(\theta|W, \alpha)$ thus is equivalent to the maximum-likelihood estimate with add-m smoothing, where $m_k = \alpha_k - 1$; that is, pseudocounts of size $\alpha_k - 1$ are added to each word (or n-gram) count. Hyperparameters offer a convenient way of integrating different information sources into the language model estimation process. This approach has most successfully been used for language model adaptation (e.g., [10]), where the prior is computed from a large out-of-domain data set and the observed counts are computed from a small in-domain data set; see Section 5.5 for further details on Bayesian language model adaptation. Early approaches to building language models entirely based on Bayesian estimation [11] did not perform as well as standard n-gram models estimated with the techniques described in Section 5.4.1. However, with recent progress in Bayesian statistics, alternative models have been developed that yield results comparable to those of Kneser-Ney smoothed n-gram models. In particular, this includes models that assume a latent topic structure of documents and use Bayesian estimation techniques to model this structure. These models are discussed more fully in Section 5.6.8.

5.4.3 Large-Scale Language Models

Recently, there has been much interest in scaling language models to very large data sets. The amount of available monolingual data increases daily, and for many languages, models can now be built from sets as large as several billions or trillions of words. Scaling language models to data sets of this size requires modifications to the ways in which language models are trained, stored, and integrated into real-world systems (e.g., speech recognition decoders). It also affects parameter estimation in that exact probability computations may no longer be feasible.

Several sites [12, 13] have proposed distributed approaches to large-scale language modeling. Their common feature is that the entire language model training data is subdivided into several partitions, and counts or probabilities derived from each partition are stored in separate physical locations (i.e., they are distributed over a cluster of independent compute nodes in a client-server architecture). During runtime, clients can request statistics from a set of data partitions through a language model server, thus producing (possibly interpolated) probability estimates on demand. The advantage of distributed language modeling is that it scales to very large amounts of data and large vocabulary sizes and allows new data to be added dynamically without having to recompute static model parameters. Desired parameters, such as the n-gram model order or the specific mixture of different data partitions, can be chosen and requested at runtime, which allows dynamic decoding approaches to be used. The drawback of distributed approaches, however, is the slow speed of networked queries.

In Brants et al. [13], a nonnormalized form of backoff is introduced that differs from standard backoff (Equation 5.8) in that it uses the raw relative frequency estimate instead of a discounted probability if the n-gram count exceeds the minimum threshold (in this case 0):

$$S(w_i|w_{i-1}, w_{i-2}) = \begin{cases} P(w_i|w_{i-1}, w_{i-2}) \text{ if } c > 0 \\ \alpha S(w_i|w_{i-1}) \text{ otherwise} \end{cases} \quad (5.23)$$

The α parameter is fixed for all contexts rather than being dependent on the lower-order n-gram, as in Equation 5.8. The result is no longer a normalized probability distribution but a set of unnormalized scores (denoted by S rather than P for probabilities) that are used in the same manner as standard probabilities. The advantage of this scheme is that unnormalized scores are easier to compute in a distributed framework because summing over all n-gram contexts (which are stored in different physical locations and are therefore expensive to query) is no longer required. Interestingly, the authors found that the model performs almost as well as a model trained with standard Kneser-Ney smoothing on large amounts of data.

An alternative possibility is to use large-scale distributed language models at a second-pass rescoring stage only, after first-pass hypotheses have been generated using a smaller language model [14, 15]. Yet another approach is to store large-scale language models in the working memory of a single machine but to use efficient though possibly lossy data structures. Talbot and Osborne [16] investigate the use of Bloom filters for this purpose. Under this approach, corpus statistics (n-gram frequency counts, context counts, etc.) are represented in a highly memory-efficient, randomized data structure (a Bloom filter) in a quantized fashion. If $c(w_1 \dots w_n)$ is the count of n-gram $w_1 \dots w_n$, the quantized count $q(w_1 \dots w_n)$ is defined as

$$q(w_1 \dots w_n) = 1 + [log_b c(w_1 \dots w_n)] \quad (5.24)$$

At test time, the necessary statistics are queried from the filter, and the true frequency is approximated by the expected count given the quantized count:

$$E[c(w_1 \ldots w_n)|q(w_1 \ldots w_n) = j] = \frac{b^{j-1} + b^j - 1}{2} \tag{5.25}$$

In this framework, frequencies will never be underestimated but may possibly be overestimated, although the probability of overestimation decreases exponentially with the size of the estimation error. The advantage of this method is that, although the raw frequency counts may be inaccurate, querying the data structure is fast, thus enabling the model to compute smoothed probabilities on the fly. In practice, it was found that the performance of a Bloom filter language model on a machine translation task was close to that of a language model based on exact parameter estimation while providing memory savings of a factor of 4 to 6 [16].

The overall trend in large-scale language modeling is to abandon exact parameter estimation of the type described in the previous section in favor of approximate techniques. This development is likely to continue, leading to more powerful and refined approximation techniques as the number and size of text data collections continue to increase.

5.5 Language Model Adaptation

It is often the case that the amount of language model training data is insufficient, particularly when porting a speech or language processing system to a new domain, topic, or language. For this reason, much effort has been invested in **language model adaptation**, that is, designing and tuning a language model such that it performs well on a new test set for which little equivalent training data is available.

The most commonly used adaptation method is that of mixture language models, or model interpolation. Usually, an in-domain language model is trained using a small amount of in-domain data, and a larger background or generic model is trained using a large amount of out-of-domain data. These models are then interpolated according to Equation 5.15, optimizing the interpolation weights on a small development set. Naturally, this approach generalizes to more than two models, and several variations of basic model interpolation have been developed.

One popular method is topic-dependent language model adaptation. Seymour and Rosenfeld [17] show how documents can first be clustered into a large number of different topics, and individual language models can be built for each topic cluster. The desired final model is then fine-tuned by choosing and interpolating a smaller number of topic-specific language models.

A form of dynamic self-adaptation of a language model is provided by **trigger models**. The idea is that, in accordance with the underlying topic of the text, certain word combinations are more likely than others to co-occur; some words are said to "trigger" others—for example, the words *stock* and *market* in a financial news text. For clustering words according to topic and using them as trigger pairs, latent semantic analysis (LSA) [18] and probabilistic latent semantic analysis (PLSA) [19] have also been been used [20, 21, 22]. LSA, originally formulated for information retrieval, represents a collection of texts as a document-word co-occurrence matrix, where rows correspond to words, columns correspond to documents, and individual cells represent the (possibly weighted) frequency of the word in the document. Singular-value decomposition applied to this matrix maps words to a low-rank continuous vector space. The semantic similarity within this space can then be computed using, for example, the cosine similarity of the corresponding word vectors. A language model can be adapted dynamically as follows:

$$P(w_i|h_i, \widetilde{h}_i) = \frac{P(w_i|h_i)\rho(w_i, \widetilde{h}_i)}{Z(h_i, \widetilde{h}_i)} \tag{5.26}$$

Here, $\widetilde{h}_i$ represents the global document history in LSA space up to word i, and ρ represents the similarity function measuring the compatibility between the current word and the semantic history. The idea is that the probabilities of semantically similar words get boosted by a factor proportional to their similarity with the global document history. Trigger relationships can also be incorporated into a language model in the form of constraints within constraint-based modeling frameworks (such as the maximum entropy [MaxEnt] model discussed in Section 5.6.5 [23] or the discriminative language model discussed in Section 5.6.3 [24]).

PLSA extends the basic, nonprobabilistic LSA approach by assuming a more sophisticated latent class model to decompose the word-document co-occurrence matrix instead of using simple singular-value decomposition. Given a latent class c, the probability of each word-document co-occurrence (w, d) can be expressed as:

$$P(w, d) = \sum_c P(c)P(w|c)P(d|c) = P(d)\sum_c P(c|d)P(w|c) \tag{5.27}$$

However, a potential concern with PLSA is its tendency to overfit to the training data. A more recent form of topic-based clustering is latent Dirichlet allocation (LDA) [25], which can be interpreted as a regularized version of PLSA. Topic models based on LDA and its extensions are described in Section 5.6.8.

A further variant of the standard adaptation framework is **unsupervised adaptation**, which is primarily relevant for speech recognition applications. Rather than using written text or perfectly transcribed speech as adaptation data, it is possible to directly use the output of a speech recognizer instead [26]. Several studies (e.g., [27, 28]) have shown that this method achieves roughly half of the improvement obtained by using perfect transcriptions for adaptation.

Recently, it has become common to utilize the Internet as a resource for additional language model data. If available text data for a given topic, domain, or language is insufficient, the web can be queried and additional domain-related data can be retrieved. After preprocessing and possibly filtering the data, it is added to the pool of existing data, or a separate model is trained on the web data and is subsequently interpolated with an existing baseline language model. Several rapid adaptation methods based on this general procedure have been described [29, 30, 31, 32].

Finally, alternative probability estimation schemes for language model adaptation have also been investigated. One of these is **maximum a posteriori (MAP) adaptation** [10].

Here, the counts collected separately from the generic out-of-domain (OD) and the in-domain adaptation (ID) data are combined as follows:

$$P(w|h) = \frac{c_{OD}(w,h) \cdot \varepsilon c_{ID}(w,h)}{c_{OD}(h) \cdot \varepsilon c_{ID}(h)} \tag{5.28}$$

where h and w are the history and predicted word respectively, c_{OD} is the count obtained from the out-of-domain data, and c_{ID} is the count from the in-domain data. The ε parameter ranges between 0 and 1 and represents the weight assigned to the adaptation data: because the amount of out-of-domain data is usually going to outweigh the amount of available adaptation data, the contributions from both sets can be balanced by appropriately setting the ε parameter, which is done empirically. A comparison of MAP and mixture models [33] has shown that mixture models are less robust than MAP adaptation toward variability in the adaptation data.

Although much of the work on language model adaptation has been performed in the context of speech recognition, several studies have also been done on adapting language models for machine translation. In Eck, Vogel, and Waibel [34] and Zhao, Eck, and Vogel [35], queries constructed from first-pass translation hypotheses are used to select additional sentences from a large corpus of target language data, which are then used as additional training data. Models built from this data are interpolated with the baseline language model and are used to retranslate the source language input text. Additional techniques for adapting language models using crosslingual data are described in Section 5.8.2.

5.6 Types of Language Models

Although n-gram models are still the most widely used type of statistical language model by far, a range of alternative models have been developed that have shown additional benefits in practical applications, often when used in combination with n-gram models.

5.6.1 Class-Based Language Models

Class-based language models [36] are a simple way of addressing data sparsity in language modeling. Words are first clustered into classes, either by automatic means [37] or based on linguistic criteria, for example, using part-of-speech (POS) classes. The statistical model makes the assumption that words are conditionally independent of other words given the current word class. If c_i is the class of word w_i, a class-based bigram model can be defined as follows:

$$P(w_i|w_{i-1}) = \sum_{c_i, c_{i-1}} P(w_i|c_i)p(c_i|c_{i-1}, w_{i-1})P(c_{i-1}|w_{i-1}) \tag{5.29}$$

$$= \sum_{c_i, c_{i-1}} P(w_i|c_i)P(c_i|c_{i-1})P(c_{i-1}|w_{i-1}) \tag{5.30}$$

under the assumption that c_i is independent of w_{i-1} given c_{i-1}. Usually, a class will contain more than one word, such that the model simplifies to

$$P(w_i|w_{i-1}) = P(w_i|c_i)P(c_i|c_{i-1}) \tag{5.31}$$

Goodman [38] compared this decomposition to the following model:

$$P(w_i|w_{i-1}) \approx P(w_i|c_i, c_{i-1})P(c_i|c_{i-1}) \tag{5.32}$$

where the current word is conditioned not only on the current word class but also on the preceding word classes. Experiments on the North American Business News Corpus (with the training size ranging between 100,000 and 284 million words), using 20,000 test sentences and a vocabulary of 58,000 words showed that the model in Equation 5.32 worked better unless the training data size was at the lower end. Class-based models have been successful in reducing perplexity as well as practical performance in a wide range of language processing systems; however, they typically need to be interpolated with a word-based language model.

5.6.2 Variable-Length Language Models

In standard language modeling, vocabulary units are defined by simple criteria, such as whitespace delimiters, and the prediction of the probability of the next word is based on an invariable fixed-length history (save for backoff). Several modifications to this basic approach have been developed that aim at redefining vocabulary units in a data-driven way, resulting in merged units composed out of a variable number of basic units. These approaches are termed **variable-length** n-gram models. The challenge in these models is to find the best segmentation of the word sequence $w_1w_2 \ldots w_t$ into language modeling units in addition to estimating the language model probabilities. Deligne and Bimbot [39] model the segmentation as a hidden variable and use an ME procedure to find the best segmentation. A variable-length model of order 7 yielded slight improvements in perplexity compared to a standard word-based bigram model, but no application results were reported.

A simpler approach is to start with the initial whitespace-based segmentation suggested by the standard orthography of the language and to merge selected units, rather than attempting to rederive the entire vocabulary segmentation from scratch. A limited number of merged units corresponding to frequently observed short phrases can thus be added to the language model vocabulary. A common criterion for identifying potential phrasal candidate units is the mutual information between adjacent words (e.g., [40]). The actual selection of phrasal units is then made using a greedy iterative algorithm: in each iteration, those candidates are selected that reduce the perplexity of a development corpus the most [41, 42]. In Zitouni, Smaili, and Haton [42], word class information is used to identify candidate phrasal units in that mutual information is computed over pairs of classes rather than pairs of words, which was shown to reduce perplexity by roughly 10% compared to word-based selection of candidate pairs. This model also achieved an 18% relative reduction in word-error rate on a medium-scale French automatic speech recognition (ASR) task.

5.6.3 Discriminative Language Models

Standard n-gram models embody a generative model for assigning a probability to a given word sequence W. However, in practical applications like machine translation or speech recognition, the task of a language model is often to separate good sentence hypotheses from bad sentence hypotheses. For this reason, it would be desirable to train language model parameters discriminatively, such that word strings of widely differing quality receive maximally distinct probability estimates. Recent attempts at such **discriminative**

language modeling include Roark et al. [43], Collins, Saraçlar, and Roark [44], Shafran and Hall [45], and Arisoy et al. [46]. Here, the language model is applied to an existing set of competing sentence hypotheses $\mathcal{Y}$ generated for an input x (e.g., an acoustic sequence in the case of speech recognition, or the source language string in the case of machine translation) by some generation function GEN(x). Arbitrary feature functions $\phi(x, y)$ can be defined jointly over the input and each output $y \in \mathcal{Y}$. These are then used in a global linear model that selects the best hypothesis:

$$F(x) = \underset{y \in \text{GEN}(x)}{\text{argmax}} \ \phi(x, y)\alpha \tag{5.33}$$

where α is a weight vector. In the most basic case, the feature functions are the raw n-gram counts obtained from the training data. However, additional feature functions representing statistics over word classes or subword units may be integrated (see §5.7.1). The parameter vector α can be trained by the perceptron algorithm [47] or a conditional log-linear model [43]. The perceptron algorithm, for example, iterates through all training samples (for several epochs) and selects the currently best-scoring hypothesis for each sample. If it differs from the true reference hypothesis, it updates the current weights by adding the counts of the features in the correct hypothesis and subtracting their counts in the chosen hypothesis. Such a training procedure directly minimizes the desired objective function, such as word-error rate in a speech recognition system. Thus, the weights with which the counts of different n-grams contribute to the final model are trained to optimize system performance rather than minimize the perplexity criterion described in Section 5.3. Roark, Saraçlar, and Collins [48] reported a 1.8% absolute improvement in word-error rate (from 39.2% to 37.4%) on a large-vocabulary speech recognition task for a one-pass system and a 0.9% reduction in word-error rate for a multipass recognizer. Recently, discriminative language modeling has also been applied to statistical machine translation [49], where it yielded an improvement of 1 to 2 BLEU points over a state-of-the-art baseline system. As we shall see, a discriminative language model also offers a convenient way of integrating additional linguistic information, such as morphological features.

5.6.4 Syntax-Based Language Models

A well-known drawback of n-gram language models is that they cannot take into account relevant words in the history that fall outside the limited window of the directly preceding $n-1$ words. However, natural language exhibits many types of **long-distance dependencies**, where the choice of the current word is dependent on words that are relatively far removed in terms of sentence position. In the following example, the plural noun *Investors* triggers the plural verb *were* but is not taken into account as a conditioning variable by an n-gram model, where n is usually no larger than 4 or 5.

Investors, *who still showed confidence in financial markets last week,* **were** *responsible for today's downturn.*

To address this problem, several approaches to syntax-based language modeling have been developed, whose goal is to explicitly model such syntactic relationships and use them to estimate better probabilities. Most of these approaches use a statistical parser to construct the syntactic representation S of the sentence and define a probability model that incorporates S. Chelba and Jelinek's **structured language model** [50] computes the joint probability of a word sequence and its parse S, $P(W, S)$ and decomposes it into a product of component probabilities involving various elements of the the word sequence proper, the head words from the parse structure, and the POS tags in the parse structure. Results reported in [50] indicate that a structured language model interpolated with a trigram model achieved a relative reduction in perplexity of 8% on the Wall Street Journal Continuous Speech Recognition (CSR) and Switchboard corpora. When used for lattice rescoring in a speech recognition system, it yielded a 6% relative reduction on the Wall Street Journal corpus and a 0.5% absolute reduction (41.1% to 40.6%) on Switchboard.

Another syntax-based model is the "almost-parsing" language model by Wang and Harper [51] (also called SuperARV model), which is based on a constraint-dependency grammar. Here, sentences are annotated with so-called SuperARVs, which are rich tags combining lexical features and syntactic information pertaining to a word (entry in the lexicon). A joint language model (the SuperARV language model) is defined over the word sequence and the sequence of tags as follows:

$$P(w_1, \ldots, w_N, t_1, \ldots, t_N) = \prod_{i=1}^{N} P(w_i t_i | w_1 \ldots, w_{i-1}, t_1 \ldots t_{i-1}) \quad (5.34)$$

$$= \prod_{i=1}^{N} P(t_i | w_1 \ldots, w_{i-1}) P(w_i | w_1 \ldots w_{i-1}, t_1 \ldots t_{i-1}) \quad (5.35)$$

$$\approx \prod_{i=1}^{N} P(t_i | w_{i-2}, w_{i-1}, t_{i-1}, t_{i-1}) P(w_i | w_{i-2}, w_{i-1}, t_{i-2}, t_{i-1}) \quad (5.36)$$

The model is smoothed by recursive linear interpolation of higher-order and lower-order models. The SuperARV model was evaluated on the Wall Street Journal Penn Treebank and CSR tasks and was compared to other parser-based language models, including the structured language model described previously, as well as to standard trigram and POS-based models. It was found that the SuperARV achieved the lowest perplexity scores out of all. When used for lattice rescoring on the CSR task, the SuperARV model yielded relative word-error rate reductions between 3.1% and 13.5% and again outperformed all other models.

5.6.5 MaxEnt Language Models

One shortcoming of maximum-likelihood-based probability estimation for language models is that the constraints imposed by estimates solely derived from the training data are too strong. MaxEnt models represent an alternative where these constraints are relaxed. Rather than setting the probability of a given n-gram to its relative frequency in the training data (modulo smoothing), the requirement of MaxEnt modeling is that the model agree, on average, with the observed counts of events in the training data. The MaxEnt model is formulated as follows:

$$P(y|x) = \frac{1}{Z(x)} \exp\left(\sum_k \lambda_k f_k(x,y)\right) \tag{5.37}$$

where $f(x,y)$ is a feature function defined both on the input and the predicted variables, λ is a feature function specific weight, and $Z(x)$ is a normalization factor, computed as

$$Z(x) = \sum_{y \in Y} \exp\left(\sum_k \lambda_k f_k(x,y)\right) \tag{5.38}$$

Once appropriate feature functions have been defined, the expected value of f_k is

$$E(f_k) = \sum_{x \in X, y \in Y} \widetilde{p}(x) p(y|x) f_k(x,y) \tag{5.39}$$

where $\widetilde{p}(x)$ is the empirical distribution of x in the training data. The empirical expectation of f_k (derived from the training data) is

$$\widetilde{E}(f_k) = \sum_{x \in X, y \in Y} \widetilde{p}(x,y) f_k(x,y) \tag{5.40}$$

The model is then trained such that expected values match empirical expected values

$$E(f_k) = \widetilde{E}(f_k) \qquad \forall k \tag{5.41}$$

while simultaneously maximizing the entropy of the distribution $p(y|x)$. This is equivalent to maximizing the conditional log-likelihood of the training data.

The MaxEnt framework was first applied to language modeling by Rosenfeld [52]. In the context of language modeling, y represents the predicted word and x the history or, more generally, the conditioning variables used for prediction. Note that in this case, a much larger context than the $n-1$ directly preceding words may be included: feature functions may be defined over the entire sentence [53] or over an even larger domain. Most commonly, however, feature functions are simply defined over n-grams; for example, for a given word w_i and history h_i, a bigram feature function would be defined as follows:

$$f_{w_1,w_2}(h_i, w_i) = \begin{cases} 1 & \text{if } h_i \text{ ends in } w_1 \text{ and } w_i = w_2 \\ 0 & \text{otherwise} \end{cases} \tag{5.42}$$

The model can be trained using iterative methods, such as generalized iterative scaling [54] or improved iterative scaling [55], or by the faster quasi-Newton approaches (see [56]). Nevertheless, training of MaxEnt language models can be computationally demanding: in principle, the normalization factor in Equation 5.38 needs to be computed for all different values of x, and computing the feature expectations requires summation over all (x,y) pairs for which the feature is defined. Wu and Khudanpur [57] presented efficient training methods that result in considerable speedups during training. First the vocabulary is partitioned according to whether words are subject to marginal or conditional constraints, and the summation required for the normalization factor is computed separately for both sets. Second, a hierarchical normalization computation procedure is proposed where partial sums (e.g., for histories ending in the same suffix) are reused. Together, these modifications led to speedups ranging between 15x and 30x.

Another potential problem of MaxEnt models is that they are prone to overfitting, especially when a large number of feature functions is used in relation to the number of samples. Possible solutions to this problem are feature selection [58], regularization [59], or incorporating priors on the feature functions. Using a Gaussian prior was proposed by Chen and Rosenfeld [59], for example. Rather than simply maximizing the conditional log-likelihood of the training data,

$$\underset{\Lambda}{\operatorname{argmax}} \sum_{i=1}^{M} logP_{\Lambda}(y_i|x_i) \tag{5.43}$$

this approach maximizes the conditional log-likelihood modulo a penalty term composed of a product of zero-mean Gaussians for all feature functions:

$$\underset{\Lambda}{\operatorname{argmax}} \sum_{i=1}^{M} \log P_{\Lambda}(y_i|x_i) \times \prod_{k=1}^{K} \frac{1}{\sqrt{2\pi\sigma_k^2}} \exp\left(\frac{\lambda^2}{2\sigma_k^2}\right) \tag{5.44}$$

where σ_k^2 is the variance of the kth Gaussian. Goodman [60] suggests exponential priors as an alternative, which can sometimes yield better performance.

Wu and Khudanpur [61] report on a MaxEnt model for speech recognition on the Switchboard task that incorporates topic constraints. The model achieved a 7% perplexity reduction and an absolute word-error rate reduction of 0.7% (38.5% to 37.8%). Integration of syntactic constraints independently yielded a 7% perplexity reduction and a 0.8% reduction in word-error rate. The combination of both types of constraints was shown to be additive, yielding a 12% relative perplexity reduction and an absolute word-error rate improvement of 1.3%.

5.6.6 Factored Language Models

The factored language model (FLM) approach [62, 63] builds on the observations that the prediction of words is dependent on the surface form of the preceding words and that better generalizations can be made when additional information, such as the word's POS or morphological class, is taken into account. In particular, word n-gram counts might be insufficient to robustly estimate the probability of word w_i given word w_{i-1}, but if we know that word w_{i-1} is of a particular class, say a determiner, we might be able to obtain a good probability estimate for $P(w_i|\text{determiner})$. This is reminiscent of the class-based models described previously; however, in an FLM, many such class-based estimates are combined and structured hierarchically through the use of a **generalized backoff** strategy. FLMs assume a factored word representation, where words are considered feature vectors rather than individual surface forms; that is, $W \equiv f_{1:K}$. An example is shown here:

WORD:	*Stock*	*prices*	*are*	*rising*
STEM:	Stock	price	be	rise
TAG:	Nsg	N3pl	V3pl	Vpart

The word surface form itself can be one of the features. A statistical model over this representation can be defined as follows (using a trigram approximation):

$$p\left(f_1^{1:K}, f_2^{1:K}, \ldots, f_t^{1:K}\right) \approx \prod_{i=3}^{t} p\left(f_i^{1:K} | f_{i-1}^{1:K}, \ldots, f_{i-2}^{1:K}\right) \tag{5.45}$$

Thus, each word is dependent not only on a single stream of temporally ordered word variables but also on additional parallel (i.e., simultaneously occurring) feature variables.

In the definition of standard backoff (Equation 5.8), the model backs off from the higher-order to the next lower-order distribution. In an FLM, however, it is not immediately obvious how backoff should proceed because conditioning variables are not only temporally ordered but also occur in parallel. Thus, a decision must be made as to which subset of features the model should back off to in which order. In principle, there are several different ways of choosing among different backoff "paths":

1. Choose a fixed, predetermined backoff path based on linguistic knowledge (e.g., always drop syntactic before morphological variables).
2. Choose the path at runtime based on statistical criteria.
3. Choose multiple paths and combine their probability estimates.

The last option, called **parallel backoff**, is implemented via a new, generalized backoff function (here shown for a trigram):

$$P_{GBO}(f|f_1, f_2) = \begin{cases} d_c P_{ML}(f|f_1, f_2) \text{ if } c > \tau \\ \alpha(f_1, f_2) g(f, f_1, f_2) \text{ otherwise} \end{cases} \tag{5.46}$$

where, similar to Equation 5.8, c is the count of (f, f_1, f_2), $P_{ML}(f|f_1, f_2)$ is the maximum likelihood estimate, τ is the count threshold, and $\alpha(f_1, f_2)$ is the normalization factor that ensures that the resulting scores form a probability distribution. The function $g(f, f_1, f_2)$ determines the backoff strategy. In a typical backoff procedure, $g(f, f_1, f_2)$ equals $P_{BO}(f|f_1)$. In generalized parallel backoff, however, g can be any nonnegative function of f, f_1, f_2 and can be instantiated to, for example, the mean, weighted mean, product, or maximum functions. For example, the mean function would take the average of the individual estimates:

$$g_{\text{mean}}(f, f_1, f2) = 0.5 P_{BO}(f|f_1) + 0.5 P_{BO}(f|f_2) \tag{5.47}$$

In addition to different choices for g, different discounting parameters can be chosen at different levels in the backoff graph.

It is not a priori obvious which backoff strategy works best; the optimal strategy is highly dependent on the particular language modeling task. Because the space of possible factored language model structures and backoff parameters is very large, it is advisable to use an automatic, data-driven procedure to find the best settings. An automatic FLM optimization procedure based on genetic algorithms was proposed by Duh and Kirchhoff [64].

FLMs have been implemented as an add-on to the widely used SRILM (Stanford Research Institute Language Modeling) toolkit [65] and have been used successfully for morpheme-based language modeling [62], multispeaker language modeling [66], dialog act tagging [67], and speech recognition [68, 63], especially in sparse data scenarios such as highly inflecting languages (see also §5.7.2).

5.6.7 Other Tree-Based Language Models

Several other language modeling approaches make use of tree structures; one, for example, is the hierarchical class-based backoff model proposed by Zitouni [69]. Here, backoff proceeds along a hierarchy of word classes arranged in a tree structure, with more general classes at the top and more specific classes at the bottom. Backoff proceeds along the class hierarchy from bottom to top; that is, more specific backoff classes are utilized before more general ones. The main differences from FLMs are that the backoff path is fixed and predefined in advance, whereas FLMs permit the combination of probability estimates from different paths in the backoff graph, as well as the dynamic choice of a path at runtime. Zitouni found that a hierarchical class-based language model yields gains primarily when the test set contains a large number of unseen events: on a speech recognition language modeling task with a 5,000-word vocabulary, the unseen word perplexity was reduced by 10%, whereas on a task with a 20,000-word vocabulary, it was reduced by 26% and the word-error rate decreased by 12%. Some extensions to this hierarchical class n-gram language model were proposed by Wang and Vergyri [70]. Specifically, POS information was integrated into the word clustering process, and separate hierarchical class trees were defined for different POS categories. On an Egyptian Colloquial Arabic speech recognition task (a test set of 18,000 words), the model achieved 8% relative improvement in perplexity over a standard n-gram model and a 3% relative improvement over the model described by Zitouni [69].

Random forest language models (RFLMs), proposed by Xu and Jelinek [71], model all word histories seen in the training data as a collection of randomly grown decision trees (a random forest). Nodes in the decision trees are associated with sets of histories, with the root node containing all histories. Trees are grown by dividing the set of histories into two subsets according to the word identity at a particular position in the history. Out of a number of possible splits, the split that maximizes the log-likelihood of the training data is chosen. Two steps are taken to introduce randomness into this process: first, the set of histories from a parent node are initially assigned randomly to the two subnodes; second, the set of splits chosen to undergo the log-likelihood test is selected randomly as well. After the growing process has stopped, each leaf node in a decision tree can be viewed as a cluster of similar word histories forming an equivalence class. Rather than defining equivalence classes deterministically by the most recent $n-1$ words (as done by conventional n-gram models), equivalence classes are now defined based on the set membership of the words in the history.

The decision tree–growing procedure is run multiple times, and the decision trees resulting from each run are added to the random forest. Supposing that M decision trees have been obtained, the RFLM probabilities are computed as averages of the individual decision tree probabilities:

$$P_{RF}(w_i|w_{i-n+1}, \ldots w_{i-1}) = \frac{1}{M}\sum_{j=1}^{M} P_{DT_j}(w_i|\phi_{DT_j}(w_{i-n+1}, \ldots, w_{i-1})) \tag{5.48}$$

Here, ϕ_{DT_j} is the $j'th$ is a function mapping the history $w_{i-1+n+1}, \ldots, w_{i-1}$ to a leaf node in the j'th decision tree. The number of decision trees M usually ranges in the dozens or hundreds. Perplexity and word-error rate tests on the Penn Treebank portion of the Wall Street Journal corpus showed that the perplexity of a random forest trigram was reduced by 10.6% relative to a trigram with interpolated Kneser-Ney smoothing. Interpolation of the RFLM with a Kneser-Ney model did not improve perplexity any further. N-best list rescoring with RFLMs yielded a relative word-error rate improvement of 11% on the Wall Street Journal DARPA'93 HUB1 benchmark task. Since their inception, RFLMs have been applied to structured language modeling [71] and prosodic modeling [72]. In the context of multilingual language modeling, they have also been applied to morphologically rich languages (see §5.7.1).

5.6.8 Bayesian Topic-Based Language Models

A significant recent trend in statistical language modeling is Bayesian modeling of latent topic structure in documents. One of the first models of this type was the latent Dirichlet allocation model proposed by Blei, Ng, and Jordan [25]. The LDA model assumes that a document is composed of K topics, denoted as $z_1, \ldots, z_K$. Each topic generates words according to a topic-specific distribution over individual words (i.e., a topic is modeled as a bag of words; n-grams are not taken into account). The probability vector over words is denoted by $\phi_{\mathbf{k}}$ for each topic $k = 1, \ldots, K$. Each topic has a prior probability, denoted by θ_k. The topic priors $\theta_1, \theta_2, \ldots, \theta_K$ are themselves distributed according to the Dirichlet distribution with hyperparameters $\alpha_1, \ldots, \alpha_K$ (see §5.4.2 for an explanation of the Dirichlet distribution):

$$P(\theta_1, \ldots, \theta_k) = \frac{\Gamma(\sum_k \alpha_k)}{\prod_k \Gamma(\alpha_k)} \prod_{k=1}^{K} \theta_k^{\alpha_k - 1} \tag{5.49}$$

The generative model underlying this approach is that a set of priors $\theta_1, \ldots, \theta_K$ is sampled from the Dirichlet distribution. A given topic z_k is chosen with probability θ_k, then a word w is generated from the topic with probability $\phi_k(w)$. The probability of an entire document consisting of a sequence W of t words is modeled as

$$p(W|\alpha, \phi) = \int p(\theta|\alpha) \left(\prod_{i=1}^{t} \sum_{z_i} p(z_i|\theta) p(w_i|z_i, \phi) \right) d\theta \tag{5.50}$$

The challenging aspect of LDA is computing the posterior distribution of the latent variables θ and $\mathbf{z}$, $p(\theta, \mathbf{z}|W, \alpha, \phi)$, which is not amenable to exact inference. Sampling techniques such as Markov chain Monte Carlo (e.g., [73]) or variational inference [25] need to be used.

Because the LDA model is a unigram model, it also needs to be combined with an n-gram model for practical purposes. Wang et al. [74] combined LDA with a trigram and a probabilistic context-free grammar, yielding perplexity reductions of 9% to 23% on the Wall Street Journal corpus relative to a Kneser-Ney smoothed trigram model. Hsu and Glass [75] used LDA combined with a hidden Markov model for a spoken lecture recognition task. A combination of language models trained with the topic labels provided by this model yielded a 16.1% perplexity reduction and a 2.4% word-error rate reduction over an already adapted trigram model.

The LDA model has been extended in various ways: first, LDA can be generalized to utilize Dirichlet processes [76], a prior for nonparametric models that can handle an infinite number of topics. Thus, rather than assuming a fixed set of K topics, the number can be adjusted on the basis of training data properties. Second, the latent topic variables can be structured hierarchically: each topic can have a number of subtopics, and individual topics can be shared between different data clusters. This is modeled by a hierarchical Dirichlet process (HDP) [77]. Huang and Renals exploited HDPs for integrating topic and participant role into language models for meeting-style conversational speech recognition. HDP-adapted language models yielded slight word-error-rate reductions (0.3% absolute) compared to standard adaptation methods, for baseline systems ranging around 39% word-error rate. Teh [78] reports on a Bayesian language model based on a Pitman-Yor process that by itself achieves perplexities comparable to those of a Kneser-Ney smoothed trigram model (without requiring interpolation with the baseline model).

5.6.9 Neural Network Language Models

With the exception of LSA-based language models, all of the language modeling approaches described previously estimate probabilities for events in a discrete space. Neural network language models (NNLMs) [79] take a different approach: discrete word sequences are first mapped into a continuous representation, and n-gram probabilities are then estimated within this continuous space. The assumption is that words having similar distributional properties will receive similar continuous representations, which will in turn result in smoother probability estimates.

The neural network is typically a multilayer perceptron with an input layer, a projection layer, a hidden layer, and an output layer of nodes. A graphical representation of the architecture of an NNLM is shown in Figure 5–1. Adjacent layers are fully interconnected by weights. For a vocabulary of V words, the input consists of a concatenation of $n-1$ V-dimensional binary feature vectors representing the history of $n-1$ words (e.g., the first two words in a trigram). The projection layer i of a given fixed dimensionality d encodes the shared continuous representation of the words, which is learned during training. The hidden layer h also has a fixed number of J nodes, each of which computes a thresholded, nonlinear combination of incoming activations, for example, using the tangent function:

$$h_j = \tanh\left(\sum_{k=1}^{d} w_{jk}^h i_k + b_j^h\right) \qquad \forall j, i = 1, \ldots, J \tag{5.51}$$

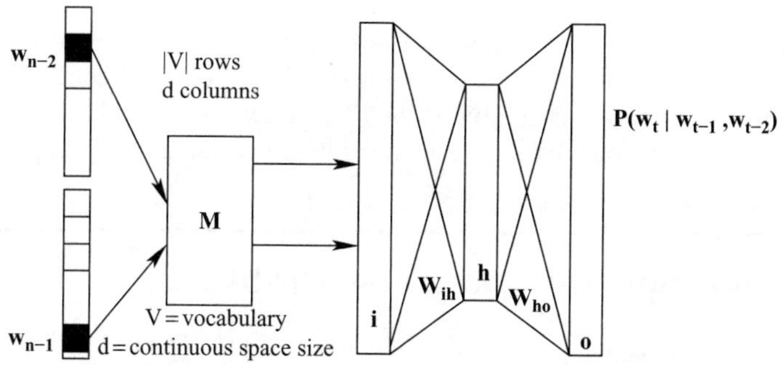

Figure 5–1: Neural network language model

where w^h denotes the weights connecting the projection, and the hidden layers and b^h are the biases on the hidden layer nodes. Finally, the output layer o computes a posterior probability distribution over V by

$$o_j = \frac{a_j}{\sum_{k=1}^{V} a_k} \qquad \forall j, j = 1, \ldots, V \tag{5.52}$$

and

$$a_j = \sum_{k=1}^{J} w^o_{jk} h_k + b^o_j \tag{5.53}$$

During training, binary target labels are associated with the output layer, 1 for the predicted word and 0 for all other words. The network is trained (e.g., using backpropagation) to maximize the log-likelihood of the training data, possibly enriched with a regularization term R to constrain the parameter values θ:

$$L = \frac{1}{T} \sum_{i=1}^{T} log(P(w_i|h_i); \theta) - R(\theta) \tag{5.54}$$

The regularization term can take various forms; a common approach is to use the sum of the squared weights: $\sum_w w^2$. This limits the complexity of the network and reduces the chance of overfitting by preventing the weights from becoming too large. Thus, a particular word in the history is first projected into a continuous representation shared among all words, which is then used as the basis for estimating the probability of the predicted word given its history.

NNLMs have been successfully used for speech recognition by Schwenk and Gauvain [80], Schwenk [81], and Schwenk, Déchelotte, and Gauvain [82], for example, and for machine translation by Alexandrescu and Kirchhoff [83]. Although they typically use a truncated vocabulary consisting of the m most frequent words only, they have yielded significant improvements when used in combination with standard n-gram models. Schwenk [81] reported an 8% relative reduction in perplexity and a 0.5% absolute improvement in word-error rate on a French broadcast news recognition task. Emami and Mangu [82] obtained a 0.8% absolute (3.8% relative) improvement in word-error rate on an Arabic speech recognition task.

Emami and Jelinek [84] used neural network–based probability estimation in combination with a structured language model; Alexandrescu and Kirchhoff [85] combined NNLMs with a factored word representation for Arabic to be able to exploit word similarities derived not only from distributional properties but from morphological and POS classes.

5.7 Language-Specific Modeling Problems

The majority of language modeling research has focused on the English language. However, speech and language processing technology has been ported to a range of other languages, some of which have highlighted problems with the standard n-gram modeling approach and have necessitated modifications to the traditional language modeling framework. In this section, we look at three types of language-specific problems: morphological complexity, lack of word segmentation, and spoken versus written languages.

5.7.1 Language Modeling for Morphologically Rich Languages

A morphologically rich language is characterized by a large number of different unique word forms (types) in relation to the number of word tokens in a text that is due to productive morphological (word-formation) processes in the language. A morpheme is the smallest meaning-bearing unit in a language. Morphemes can be either free (i.e., they can occur on their own), or they are bound (i.e., they must be combined with some other morpheme). Morphological processes include compounding (forming a new word out of two independently existing free morphemes), derivation (combination of a free morpheme and a bound morpheme to form a new word), and inflection (combination of a free and a bound morpheme to signal a particular grammatical feature).

Germanic languages, for example, are notorious for their high degree of compounding, especially for nominals. Turkish, an agglutinative language, combines several morphemes into a single word; thus, the same material that would be expressed as a syntactic phrase in English can be found as a single whitespace-delimited unit in a Turkish sentence, such as: *görülmemeliydik* = 'we should not have been seen'.

As a result, Turkish has a huge number of possible words. Many languages have rich inflectional paradigms. In languages like Finnish and Arabic, a root (base form) may have thousands of different morphological realizations. Table 5–1 shows two Modern Standard Arabic (MSA) inflectional paradigms, one for present tense verbal inflections for the root *skn* (basic meaning: 'live'), one for pronominal possessive inflections for the root *ktb* (basic meaning 'book').

Morphological complexity causes problems for language modeling due to the high ratio of types to tokens, which results in a lack of training data: many n-grams in the test data are not seen at all in the training data or are not observed frequently enough, leading to unreliable probability estimates. Another effect is a high OOV rate. To some extent, this effect can be mitigated by simply collecting more training data; however, depending on the

Table 5–1: MSA inflectional paradigms for present tense verb forms and possessive pronouns (affixes are separated from the word stem by hyphens)

Word	Meaning	Word	Meaning
'a-skun(u)	I live	kitaab-iy	my book
ta-skun(u)	you (MASC) live	kitaabu-ka	your (MASC) book
ta-skun-iyna	you (FEM) live	kitaabu-ki	your (FEM) book
ya-skun(u)	he lives	kitaabu-hu	his book
ta-skun(u)	she lives	kitaabu-haa	her book
na-skun(u)	we live	kitaaabu-na	our book
ta-skun-uwna	you (MASC-PL) live	kitaabu-kum	your book
ya-skun-uwna	they live	kitaabu-hum	their book

Table 5–2: Number of word tokens, word types, and OOV rates for different languages in non-decomposed form

Language	Style	# Tokens	# Types	OOV Rate at (N) Words	Source
English	news text	19M	105k	1% (60k)	[86]
Arabic	news text	19M	690k	11% (60k)	[86]
Czech	news text	16M	415k	8% (60k)	[87]
Korean	news text	15.5M	1.5M	25% (100k)	[88]
Turkish	mixed text	9M	460k	12% (460k)	[89]
Finnish	news text, books	150M	4M	1.5% (4M)	[90]

morphological complexity of the language, the vocabulary growth does not slow down as sharply as for morphologically poor languages as more and more running text is taken into account. Table 5–2 shows examples of the relationship between word types and word tokens for different languages, as well as typical OOV rates for different languages on held-out test sets.

When processing morphologically rich languages, it must be determined whether the vocabulary needed for a given application can be expressed as a list of full word forms (e.g., the most frequent forms occurring in the training data) or whether smaller subword units need to be chosen as basic language modeling units. The choice depends on the constraints imposed by available computing resources, such as the efficiency of the decoder in a speech recognition application, memory, and desired speed, as well as on the amount of training data. The advantage of decomposing words into smaller units lies in the reduction of the vocabulary size, which in turn reduces the number of distinct n-grams. In addition to improving speed and reducing memory consumption, subword units occur in multiple words; therefore, training data can be shared across words, and the number of training tokens per unit increases, which leads to more robust probability estimation. Finally, modeling based on subword units might also allow the language model to assign probabilities to words that were not seen in the training data. On the other hand, if a word is decomposed linearly, a fixed n-gram context provides only information about the relationship between different parts of a word but not about interword dependencies. Thus, the predictive power of the language model is diminished. Moreover, when the language modeling vocabulary is identical to the vocabulary used in a speech recognizer, care must be taken to define units that do not become too short and hence acoustically confusable.

Arabic, generally recognized as a morphologically rich language, is an interesting example highlighting different situations where decomposition may or may not be required. Several studies [68, 63, 91] have shown that integrating morphological information into the language model is helpful for modeling dialectal Arabic. Although the dialects of Arabic exhibit morphological simplifications compared to MSA (the written standard), they have very sparse training data because they are essentially spoken languages and need to be transcribed manually to obtain language modeling data. Large amounts of data are available for MSA, and significant improvements through morphological decomposition in the language model have not been observed for this variety when large training sets were used [91]. Moreover, the vocabulary size needed for large-scale applications such as speech recognition of MSA is around 600,000 to 800,000 words, which is within the range that current decoders can accommodate [92].

It is obvious, however, that for languages with particularly high type to token ratios (e.g., Finnish or Turkish), some form of decomposition is required: for large tasks, the size of the vocabulary needed to achieve sufficient coverage of the test data is likely to exceed current decoder capabilities, and the corresponding language model would not be able to be estimated reliably. In the following section, we discuss several recent approaches to the problem of word decomposition.

5.7.2 Selection of Subword Units

The identification of subword units can be performed in a data-driven, unsupervised way; it can be based on linguistic information (e.g., a morphological analyzer); or it can be a combination of both. Linguistically based methods typically involve a handcrafted morphological analysis tool, such as the Buckwalter Morphological Analyzer developed for Arabic [93], which analyzes each word form into its morphological components. In the case where several possible analyses are provided for each word form, statistical disambiguation needs to be performed in a subsequent step (e.g., [94]). Data-driven approaches may incorporate varying degrees of information about the specific language in question, and they may vary with respect to the optimization criterion. Some approaches are intended to discover units corresponding to linguistically defined morphemes, whereas others are aimed at selecting an inventory of units that is best suited to the task or application at hand.

Automatic algorithms for identifying linguistic morphemes are as old as Zellig Harris's 1955 approach of estimating the perplexity of different letters following each letter in a word [95]. If the perplexity at a certain transition is high (i.e., the following letters are not easily predictable) a morpheme boundary can be hypothesized at that point. Adda-Decker and Lamel [96] show how a modified version of this approach can be used to decompose German compounds, thus reducing the OOV rate by a relative amount of 23% to 50%, in a German corpus of 300 million words and a fixed vocabulary ranging from 65,000 to 100,000.

In general, simple frequency-based approaches are prone to overfitting to the training data and hypothesizing more morphemes than desired, because the fit to the data is not balanced against the total size of the inventory. This shortcoming is addressed by models that include explicit penalty terms for the size of the morpheme inventory. The more recently developed Morfessor package [97] is one such example. It attempts to derive a morpheme inventory M from a corpus C by maximizing its posterior probability:

$$M = \underset{M}{\operatorname{argmax}}\, P(M|C) = P(C|M)P(M) \tag{5.55}$$

which is equivalent to a minimum description length approach. The search over possible morphemes proceeds by way of a greedy algorithm that recursively splits each word into two subparts, trying out all possible positions. Those splits that improve the probability $P(M|C)$ (reduce the code length) are chosen. Later versions of this approach [98, 99] include a stochastic morphological category model and different probability estimation techniques. Morfessor models outperformed most other automatic segmentation algorithms in a benchmark evaluations task involving Finnish, Turkish, and English [100]. Language models using Morfessor to decompose words have been applied to Finnish, Estonian, Turkish, and Arabic speech recognition and achieved good results on the first three languages, which are highly agglutinative [90].

An alternative to trying to match a predefined linguistic inventory is to derive a unit inventory that directly optimizes a criterion related to language model performance, such as perplexity or OOV rate. This may be preferable in cases where languages are not strictly agglutinative but contain some amount of fusion, such as nontransparent changes in the word form produced by the combination of two or more morphemes. This approach has been pursued by Whittaker and Woodland [101], for example, for Russian language modeling. Here, a particle-based model was developed, defined as

$$P(w_i|h) = \frac{1}{Z(h)} P\left(u^{w_i}_{L(w_i)} | u^{w_i}_{L(w_i)-1}\right) P\left(u^{w_i}_{L(w_i)-1} | u^{w_i}_{L(w_i)-2}\right), \ldots, P(u^{w_i}_1) \,\Big|\, u^{w_{i-1}}_{L(w_{i-1})}\Big) \tag{5.56}$$

where word w_i is decomposed by some decomposition function L into $L(w_i)$ particles $u_1, \ldots, u_{L(w_i)}$. The particle language model then computes the probability of a particle given its history consisting of all particles up to the last particle in the preceding word. Two data-driven methods for deriving particles were compared: a greedy search over possible units of a fixed length, retaining those particles that maximizing the likelihood of the data, and a particle-growing technique whereby particles are initialized to all single-character units and are successively extended by adding surrounding characters such that the resulting units minimize perplexity.

Kiecza, Schultz, and Waibel [88] proposed an approach to Korean language modeling whereby elementary syllable units are combined into units larger than syllables but smaller than Korean words (called *eojols*), which are of a complexity similar to Turkish words. Syllable combination was done by minimizing OOV rate. In both these approaches, significant improvements in perplexity/OOV rate, but only limited gains if any in the final system evaluation (speech recognition word-error rate), were reported.

More recently, the choice of subword units has been optimized with respect to the final system performance, usually by trying different segmentation schemes and evaluating each with respect to its effect on the performance metric. An example is presented by Arisoy, Sak, and Saraçlar [102], where words, statistically derived units, linguistically defined morphemes, and stems plus endings were compared for the purpose of Turkish language modeling for speech recognition, with the result that stems plus endings yielded the best word-error rate out of all four choices.

5.7.3 Modeling with Morphological Categories

Most of the work on language modeling with subword units has focused on linear decomposition of words, primarily for agglutinative languages. As a consequence, the resulting subword units are most frequently used in a standard n-gram model. As mentioned earlier, one problem is that the n-gram context needs to be increased in order to be able to model interword dependencies in addition to dependencies between subword units. This in turn places demands on the amount of training data needed.

However, several alternative approaches have been developed wherein the word remains the basic modeling unit but the probability assignment takes into account statistics over subword components or morphological classes. Arisoy et al. [46] proposed a discriminative language model (see §5.6.3) for Turkish that incorporates feature functions defined over morphemes, such as root n-gram counts or inflectional group counts. The language model assigns probabilities to sequences of entire words (undecomposed n-best hypotheses), but does so by taking into account the constraints provided by morpheme-based feature functions. This model was shown to provide slightly better results (0.3% absolute word-error rate reduction on a Broadcast News recognition task) than a discriminative language model using only word-based features. The same approach was taken by Shafran and Hall [45] for Czech, with similar results.

Kirchhoff et al. [63] and Vergyri et al. [68] used both morphological classes (stem, root, etc.) and words as conditioning variables in a factored language model for Arabic. Although the model predicts probabilities for entire word forms, the probabilistic backoff procedure makes use of morphological constituents. On a dialectal Arabic speech recognition task with a limited amount of training data, FLMs yielded slight reductions in word error rate (0.5%–1.5% absolute). FLMs have also been used successfully for speech recognition of other highly inflected languages, such as Estonian [103], and for machine translation [104].

Morphological features were also used as additional input features (beyond words) to a neural language model (see §5.6.9) for both Arabic and Turkish [85], thus creating a factored neural language model. Perplexity was shown to improve substantially over a word-based neural language model (up to 10% for Arabic and 40% for Turkish), but no application results were reported.

Sarikaya and Deng [105] proposed a joint morphological-lexical language model for Arabic. Here, a sentence is annotated with a rich parse tree representing morphological, syntactic, semantic, and other attribute information. The language model predicts the probability of the word string and the associated tree jointly, using MaxEnt probability estimation (see §5.6.5). The model was evaluated on an English-to-Arabic translation task and improved the BLEU score by 0.3 points (absolute) over a word trigram model and 0.6 points over a morpheme trigram model.

RFLMs (see §5.6.7) were applied to morphological language modeling by Oparin et al. [106]. The difference from standard word-based RFLMs is that the decision trees used in the random forest model can ask questions not only about the set membership of words but also about morphological features (inflections or morphological tags), stems, lemmas, and parts of speech. Morphological RFLMs were evaluated on a Czech spoken lecture recognition task with a 240,000-word vocabulary. Whereas word-based RFLMs did not show any substantial gain over Kneser-Ney-style trigram language models, morphological RFLMs yielded a relative gain in perplexity of up to 10.4% and a relative improvement in word accuracy of up to 3.4%. Unlike previous studies' results, it was also found that interpolation of RFLMs and standard n-gram models yielded an improvement (of up to 15.6% in perplexity). In addition to producing different word history clusters (induced by morphological features rather than words), a morphological RFLM offers more possibilities for randomization because the set of potential splits at each decision tree node is greatly enlarged, which may contribute to the superior performance of morphological RFLMs in this case.

5.7.4 Languages without Word Segmentation

Although agglutination produces a large number of long and complex word forms in many languages, other languages do not possess any explicit segmentation of character strings into words at all. In languages such as Chinese and Japanese, sentences are written as sequences of characters delimited by punctuation signs but without any intervening whitespaces to indicate word boundaries. Readers with knowledge of the language can immediately decompose character sequences into the word segmentation that corresponds to the most plausible interpretation of the sentence. Although statistical language models for such languages can be constructed over characters, it is preferable to first segment sentences into words automatically and then train the language model over the resulting words. Similar to the situation in which words are decomposed into subword units (§5.7.1), a language model using characters as the basic modeling units may fail to express important interword relationships. Moreover, the word segmentation may determine how characters are pronounced, which is important if the same modeling units are intended to be used in the language model and the acoustic model of a speech recognition system. Finally, it has been shown experimentally that a language model built on automatically segmented text outperforms a character-based language model in terms of perplexity for both Japanese [107] and Chinese [108].

Automatic segmentation algorithms typically use a combination of dictionary information, statistical search, and additional features such as nonnative letters, character co-occurrence counts, and character positions. Generating the most likely segmentation follows a statistical decoding framework that uses, for example, Viterbi search. Other modeling approaches that have been explored recently include conditional random fields [109, 110, 111], MaxEnt modeling [112, 113], and discriminative modeling using perceptrons [114]. Much of the work on Chinese word segmentation has been performed in the context of the SIGHAN Chinese word segmentation competitions that have been taking place since 2003, organized by the Association for Computational Linguistics. This competition serves as a benchmark comparing different word segmentation systems. Automatic word segmentations are compared against a linguistically segmented gold standard and are evaluated in terms of precision (P), that is, the percentage of correct cases out of all hypothesized boundaries, recall R (the percentage of identified boundaries out of all possible boundaries), and their combination in the form of F-measure, $F = 2PR/(P+R)$. These measures can be calculated separately on the OOV words versus in-vocabulary words. The best-performing systems in the most recent evaluation achieved an F-measure of 0.96; however, performance on OOV words was much lower with F-measures around 0.76 [115].

Rather than trying to match linguistically defined words, it is also possible to optimize segmentation directly for language model performance. Sproat et al. [108] showed that the dictionary used for Chinese word segmentation significantly influences the perplexity of a bigram language model trained on the segmented text and that it is possible to iteratively optimize the dictionary by merging frequent word co-occurrences, such that the perplexity is reduced at each iteration. Note that such approaches are similar to the data-driven algorithms for deriving morpheme-like subword units described earlier in Section 5.7.1. Another example of a data-driven approach, in this case for Japanese, uses chunks of characters for language modeling [107]. Chunks are derived from the training data by selecting the highest-frequency n-grams and additional patterns with close similarity to them. Thus, the basic modeling units are neither characters nor words but intermediate units.

5.7.5 Spoken versus Written Languages

Statistical language modeling crucially relies on large amounts of written text data, and a significant trend within language modeling research is the development of methods for scaling current language modeling techniques to ever-larger databases. However, many of the world's 6,900 languages are spoken languages, that is, languages without a writing system. They are either indigenous languages without a literary tradition, or they are linguistic varieties such as regional dialects that are used in everyday spoken communication but are rarely put into writing. This is the case, for example, with the many dialects of Arabic, which are used in everyday conversation but are almost never found in written form. Other languages may be spoken as well as written but may not have a standardized orthography.

Both cases represent difficulties for language modeling. In the first case, the only way of obtaining language model training data is to manually transcribe the language or dialect. This is a costly and time-consuming process because it involves (i) the development of a writing standard, (ii) training native speakers to use the writing system consistently and accurately, and (iii) the actual transcription effort. In the second case, those text resources that can be obtained for the language in question (e.g., from the web) will need to be normalized, which can also be a laborious process. As a consequence, very little work has been carried out on language model development for such underresourced languages. Most studies have concentrated on how to rapidly collect corpora for underresourced languages using web resources. Some of the challenges inherent in this process are described by Le et al. [116] and Ghani, Jones, and Mladenic [117]. Possible methods for rapid language model bootstrapping for spoken languages and languages characterized by a lack of standardization might include grammar-based or class-based approaches in combination with a limited amount of transcribed material. For a constrained application, such as the development of a dialog system, the structure of possible utterances could be predefined by a task grammar or a class-based language model, whereas more fine-grained word sequence probabilities, or probabilities of words given their classes, are modeled by a language model trained from a small amount of data. An interesting research direction is the possible use of data from language that is closely related to the language in question or from a language that is unrelated but resource rich. The following section describes some of these approaches.

5.8 Multilingual and Crosslingual Language Modeling

5.8.1 Multilingual Language Modeling

Up to this point we have discussed problems that arise when tailoring statistical language models to a particular language or language type, such as agglutinative languages or languages without word segmentation. The tacit assumption has been that the resulting language model is used in an application where only the language of interest is encountered. However, in many situations, a system can be presented with multiple languages sequentially (e.g., different users speaking different languages, without advance indication of which language will be encountered next), or simultaneously, as happens in the case of **code switching**. Here, speakers may use several languages or dialects side by side, often within the same utterance. The phenomenon of code switching exists in a variety of bilingual and multilingual communities or where diglossia exists, such as where a formal standard language is used in addition to colloquial or dialectal varieties. The use of "Spanglish" (mixed Spanish/English) in the United States is one example of code switching, as demonstrated by the following example from Franco and Solorio [118]:

I need to tell her que no voy a poder ir.
'I need to tell her that I won't be able to make it.'

To handle multilingual input where language can be switched dynamically between utterances, separate language models can be constructed from monolingual corpora, and a system using these models (e.g., a speech-based information kiosk or telephone-based dialog system) can access them dynamically based on the output from a first-step language identification module or based on which language model (possibly combined with an acoustic model in the case of speech recognition) yields the highest scores after the first processing steps.

Fügen et al. showed how several such monolingual models can be combined into a single multilingual language model by means of a context-free grammar whose nonterminal states can encode language information and whose terminal states correspond to monolingual n-gram models. Explicit grammar rules can be leveraged to expand current states with n-grams from the matching language only, thus preventing language switching at inappropriate times. Alternative ways of constructing a single multilingual language model are to combine monolingual corpora and train a single model on the pooled data or to interpolate several monolingual language models. The first technique has been shown to degrade performance, especially when the sizes of the corpora are unbalanced [120, 121]. The second technique may fare slightly better yet was shown to be inferior to the grammar-based combination method described earlier [119].

Building a language model for the second case (intrasentential language switching) is more difficult because little or no relevant training material is available. Weng et al. [122] built a four-lingual language model by introducing a common backoff node in the form of a pause unit; that is, language switches are allowed with some probability after a pause has occurred.

5.8.2 Crosslingual Language Modeling

Another question that might be asked is whether data in one language can be leveraged to improve a language model for a different language, provided that the style or domain are closely related. If insufficient data is available for the language of interest, inaccurate probability estimation might be improved if sufficient information can be extracted from a large amount of foreign-language text.

The most straightforward way of applying this idea is to automatically translate the foreign-language text into the desired language and to use the translated text (though errorful) as additional language training data. This approach was chosen, for example, by Khudanpur and Kim [123] and Jensson et al. [124].

In the former study, training data for a Mandarin news text language model intended for speech recognition was enriched with training data obtained by automatically translating English text from the same domain. A unigram extracted from the translated text was interpolated with a trigram baseline language model trained on the available Mandarin data. The selection of English text for translation, and the determination of the interpolation parameter λ were specific to each news story, thus providing at the same time an implicit form of topic adaptation. The resulting model improved character perplexity by about 10% relative and the word-error rate of the speech recognizer by 0.5% absolute (for various different systems ranging around 26% baseline character-error rate). The authors also noted that the English text was more recent than the Chinese text, which may have contributed to the improved performance. This is an important consideration when investigating potential out-of-language data resources.

Jensson et al. [124] developed a language model for weather reports in Icelandic using a small amount of in-language data and a limited amount of parallel English–Icelandic data for training a machine translation system. A language model trained on a larger set of automatically translated data was then interpolated with the baseline language model, with positive effects on perplexity (9.20% improvement) and word-error rate (1.9–9.5% relative improvement) of an Icelandic speech recognition system.

The use of machine translation technology for processing out-of-language data is likely to fail when the desired language does not have sufficient data to train a machine translation system in the first place, although the abovementioned experiments on Icelandic show that a limited amount of parallel data may still be sufficient if the domain is very constrained. An alternative to using a fully fledged machine translation system is to rely on a high-quality word-based translation dictionary only. Kim and Khudanpur [125] showed that a good-quality translation dictionary can be extracted by simply computing mutual information statistics on word pairs from document-aligned parallel corpora, eliminating the need for sentence-aligned parallel text. In their experiments on Mandarin broadcast news recognition, they found that a unigram model built from the resulting dictionary-based translations and interpolated with a baseline language model achieved a performance similar to that of a crosslingual language model. Another possibility for constructing a translation dictionary from document-aligned data is to use crosslingual latent semantic analysis [126]. Under this approach, words in both languages are projected into a common semantic space, and a measure of similarity between words from different languages in this space is used to construct word translation probabilities.

A drawback of the previous approaches is that the quality of the resulting model is heavily dependent on the translation accuracy. Tam et al. [127] recently presented an alternative model in which bilingual latent semantic analysis (bLSA) is used for adaptation before translation. The approach uses one LSA model each for the source and the target languages; it thus requires a parallel training corpus. The LSA models incorporate Dirichlet-style prior distributions over topics (see §5.6.8). Topic mixture weights are determined from the source LSA model and are projected onto the target LSA model, where they can be used to compute target-language marginal distributions. Assuming that the source language is Chinese (Ch) and the target language is English (En), the marginal word probability distribution in English is

$$P_{\text{En}}(w) = \sum_k \phi_k^{\text{En}}(w)\theta_k^{\text{Ch}} \tag{5.57}$$

where θ_k is the prior for the kth topic and $\phi_k(w)$ is the probability assigned to word w by the kth latent topic. As we can see, topic priors are determined by the source language, whereas the topic-dependent word probability distribution is determined by the target language. The target-language marginals are then incorporated into the target-language model as follows:

$$P_{\text{target}}(w|h) \propto \left(\frac{P_{b\text{LSA}}(w)}{P_{\text{base}}(w)}\right)^{\beta} P_{\text{base}}(w|h) \tag{5.58}$$

where $P_{b\text{LSA}}$ is the adapted probability and P_{base} is the baseline probability. This approach enforces a one-to-one topic correspondence across languages. Evaluation on a Chinese–English statistical machine translation task in the news domain showed that the bLSA-adapted language model reduced perplexity by 9% to 13% and improved the BLEU score by up to 0.3 points.

5.9 Summary

Statistical language modeling has undergone drastic developments in recent years. Although the classical n-gram model in combination with smoothed maximum-likelihood estimation is still the predominant approach, many novel models, ranging from neural network models to discriminative language models, are now being used side by side with standard n-gram models.

Many language modeling techniques, such as language model adaptation, have proven applicable to languages of vastly different types, and the core techniques can be said to be language independent. Crucial differences exist in those cases where languages have a rich morphology, in particular in highly agglutinative languages that can produce a very large number of different word forms per lexeme. In these cases, word decomposition prior to n-gram language modeling or the integration of statistics over subword components into discriminative, factored, or neural language models has been helpful.

A relatively recent trend is the use of very large-scale, distributed language models, which do not follow the traditional probability estimation scheme but use approximate scores or counts. Given that the amount of language modeling data is increasing daily, this trend will certainly become very influential in the near future. It also has significance for languages with large vocabularies (e.g., morphologically rich languages) because it facilitates the use of large language models in practical systems.

Comparatively little research has been carried out on languages that can be characterized as resource poor, that is, languages that do not have a large amount of text data. This includes most of the spoken languages and dialects in the world. At this point, the standard way of obtaining data for these linguistic varieties is to transcribe them manually, which will yield only a limited amount of data. The use of speech recognition technology in combination with a bootstrapping technique could be used to automatically transcribe more data in an incremental fashion. However, there is a chicken-and-egg problem in that the development of sufficiently accurate speech recognition systems requires a sufficient amount of both text and acoustic data to train initial models. The further development of crosslingual adaptation techniques for language models is an important future research direction, which would make a significant contribution toward applying human language technology to resource-poor languages.

Bibliography

[1] J. Ponte and B. Croft, "A language modeling approach to information retrieval," in *Proceedings of the ACM Special Interest Group on Information Retrieval (SIGIR)*, pp. 275–281, 1998.

[2] F. Peng, D. Schuurmans, S. Wang, and V. Keselj, "Language independent authorship attribution using character level language models," in *Proceedings of the European Chapter of the Association for Computational Linguistics (EACL)*, pp. 267–274, 2003.

[3] F. Peng, D. Schuurmans, and S. Wang, "Language and task independent text categorization with simple language models," in *Proceedings of the Human Language Technology Conference of the North American Chapter of the Association for Computational Linguistics (HLT/NAACL)*, pp. 110–117, 2003.

[4] M. Zissman, "Comparison of four approaches to automatic language identification of telephone speech," *IEEE Transactions on Speech and Audio Processing*, vol. 4(1), pp. 31–44, 1996.

[5] M. Nagata, "Japanese OCR error correction using character shape similarity and statistical language model," in *Proceedings of the Association for Computational Linguistics*, pp. 922–928, 1998.

[6] I. Bazzi, R. Schwartz, and J. Makhoul, "An omnifont open-vocabulary OCR system for English and Arabic," *IEEE Transactions on Pattern Analysis and Machine Intelligence*, vol. 21, pp. 495–504, 1999.

[7] S. Chen and J. Goodman, "An empirical study of smoothing techniques for language modeling," Tech. Rep. TR-10-98, Harvard University, 1998.

[8] F. Jelinek and R. Mercer, "Interpolation estimation of Markov source parameters from sparse data," in *Proceedings of the Workshop on Pattern Recognition in Practice*, 1980.

[9] A. Dempster, N. Laird, and D. Rubin, "Maximum likelihood from incomplete data via the EM algorithm," *Journal of the Royal Statistical Society*, vol. 39(1), pp. 1–38, 1977.

[10] M. Federico, "Bayesian estimation methods for n-gram language model adaptation," in *Proceedings of the 4th International Conference on Spoken Language Processing (ICSLP)*, pp. 240–243, 1996.

[11] A. Nadas, "Estimation of probabilities in the language model of the IBM speech recognition system," in *Proceedings of the International Conference on Acoustics, Speech, and Signal Processing (ICASSP)*, pp. 859–861, 1984.

[12] A. Emami, K. Papineni, and J. Sorensen, "Large-scale distributed language modeling," in *Proceedings of the International Conference on Acoustics, Speech, and Signal Processing (ICASSP)*, pp. 37–40, 2007.

[13] T. Brants, A. Popat, P. Xu, F. Och, and J. Dean, "Large language models in machine translation," in *Proceedings of the Conference on Empirical Methods on Natural Language Processing (EMNLP)*, pp. 858–867, 2007.

[14] Y. Zhang, A. Hildebrand, and S. Vogel, "Distributed language modeling for n-best list reranking," in *Proceedings of the Conference on Empirical Methods on Natural Language Processing (EMNLP)*, pp. 216–223, 2006.

[15] H. Schwenk and P. Koehn, "Large and diverse language models for machine translation," in *Proceedings of the International Joint Conference on Natural Language Processing (IJCNLP)*, pp. 661–666, 2008.

[16] D. Talbot and M. Osborne, "Smoothed Bloom filter language models: tera-scale LMs on the cheap," in *Proceedings of the Conference on Empirical Methods on Natural Language Processing (EMNLP)*, pp. 468–476, 2007.

[17] K. Seymour and R. Rosenfeld, "Using story topics for language model adaptation," in *Proceedings of Eurospeech: European Conference on Speech Communication and Technology*, pp. 1987–1990, 1997.

[18] S. Deerwester, S. Dumais, G. Furnas, T. Landauer, and R. Harshman, "Indexing by latent semantic analysis," *Journal of the American Society for Information Science*, vol. 41, pp. 391–407, 1990.

[19] T. Hoffmann, "Probabilistic latent semantic analysis," in *Proceedings of the 22nd Annual International SIGIR Conference on Research and Development in Information Retrieval (SIGIR-99)*, pp. 35–44, 1999.

[20] J. Bellegarda, "Exploiting latent semantic information in statistical language modeling," *Proceedings of the IEEE*, vol. 88(8), pp. 1279–1296, 2000.

[21] D. Mrva and P. Woodland, "A PLSA-based language model for conversational telephone speech," in *Proceedings of the 8th International Conference on Spoken Language Processing (ICSLP)*, pp. 2257–2260, 2004.

[22] S. Bai and H. Li, "PLSA based topic mixture language modeling approach," in *Proceedings of the 6th International Symposium on Chinese Spoken Language Processing*, pp. 1–4, 2008.

[23] R. Lau, R. Rosenfeld, and S. Roukos, "Trigger-based language models: a maximum-entropy approach," in *Proceedings of International Conference on Acoustics, Speech, and Signal Processing (ICASSP)*, pp. 45–48, 1993.

[24] N. Singh-Miller and M. Collins, "Trigger-based language modeling using a loss-sensitive perceptron algorithm," in *Proceedings of International Conference on Acoustics, Speech, and Signal Processing (ICASSP)*, pp. 25–28, 2007.

[25] D. Blei, A. Ng, and M. Jordan, "Latent Dirichlet allocation," *Journal of Machine Learning Research*, vol. 3, pp. 993–1022, 2003.

[26] R. Gretter and G. Riccardi, "On-line learning of language models with word error probability distributions," in *Proceedings of International Conference on Acoustics, Speech, and Signal Processing (ICASSP)*, pp. 557–560, 2001.

[27] M. Bacchiani and B. Roark, "Unsupervised language model adaptation," in *Proceedings of International Conference on Acoustics, Speech, and Signal Processing (ICASSP)*, pp. 224–227, 2003.

[28] G. Tür and A. Stolcke, "Unsupervised language model adaptation for meeting recognition," in *Proceedings of International Conference on Acoustics, Speech, and Signal Processing (ICASSP)*, pp. 173–176, 2007.

[29] I. Bulyko, M. Ostendorf, and A. Stolcke, "Getting more mileage from web text sources for conversational speech language modeling using class-dependent mixtures," in *Proceedings of the Human Language Technology Conference of the North American Chapter of the Association for Computational Linguistics (HLT/NAACL)*, pp. 7–9, 2003.

[30] T. Ng, M. Hwang, M. Siu, I. Bulyko, and M. Ostendorf, "Web-data augmented language models for Mandarin conversational speech recognition," in *Proceedings of International Conference on Acoustics, Speech, and Signal Processing (ICASSP)*, pp. 589–592, 2005.

[31] A. Sethy, P. Georgiou, and S. Narayanan, "Building topic-specific language models from webdata using competitive models," in *Proceedings of Eurospeech: European Conference on Speech Communication and Technology*, pp. 1293–1296, 2005.

[32] V. Wan and T. Hain, "Strategies for language model web-data collection," in *Proceedings of International Conference on Acoustics, Speech, and Signal Processing (ICASSP)*, pp. 1069–1072, 2006.

[33] L. Chen, J. Gauvain, L. Lamel, G. Adda, and M. Adda, "Language model adaptation for broadcast news transcription," in *Proceedings of the ISCA ITR Workshop on Adaptation Methods for Speech Recognition*, 2001.

[34] M. Eck, S. Vogel, and A. Waibel, "Language model adaptation for statistical machine translation based on information retrieval," in *Proceedings of the 4th International Conference on Language Resources and Evaluation (LREC)*, pp. 26–28, 2004.

[35] B. Zhao, M. Eck, and S. Vogel, "Language model adaptation for statistical machine translation with structured query models," in *Proceedings of the 20th International Conference on Computational Linguistics (COLING)*, pp. 411–417, 2004.

[36] P. Brown, V. D. Pietra, P. de Souza, J. Lai, and R. Mercer, "Class-based n-gram models of natural language," *Computational Linguistics*, vol. 18(4), pp. 467–479, 1992.

[37] S. Martin, J. Liermann, and H. Ney, "Algorithms for bigram and trigram word clustering," in *Speech Communication*, pp. 1253–1256, 1998.

[38] J. Goodman, "A bit of progress in language modeling," *Computer Speech and Language*, pp. 403–434, 2001.

[39] S. Deligne and F. Bimbot, "Language modeling by variable length sequences: Theoretical formulation and evaluation of multigrams," in *Proceedings of International Conference on Acoustics, Speech, and Signal Processing (ICASSP)*, pp. 169–172, 1995.

[40] F. Jelinek, "Self-organized language modeling," in *Readings in Speech Recognition* (A. Waibel and K.-F. Lee, eds.), pp. 450–506, San Mateo, CA: Morgan Kaufman, 1990.

[41] K. Ries, F. Buo, and A. Waibel, "Class phrase models for language modeling," in *Proceedings of the 4th International Conference on Spoken Language Processing (ICSLP)*, pp. 389–401, 1996.

[42] I. Zitouni, K. Smaili, and J.-P. Haton, "Statistical language modelling based on variable length sequences," *Computer Speech and Language*, vol. 7, pp. 27–41, 2003.

[43] B. Roark, M. Saraçlar, M. Collins, and M. Johnson, "Discriminative language modeling with conditional random fields and the perceptron algorithm," in *Proceedings of the Association for Computational Linguistics*, pp. 47–54, 2004.

[44] M. Collins, M. Saraçlar, and B. Roark, "Discriminative syntactic language modeling for speech recognition," in *Proceedings of Association for Computational Linguistics*, pp. 507–514, 2005.

[45] I. Shafran and K. Hall, "Corrective models for speech recognition of inflected languages," in *Proceedings of the Conference on Empirical Methods on Natural Language Processing (EMNLP)*, pp. 390–398, 2006.

[46] E. Arisoy, B. Roark, Z. Shafran, and M. Saraçlar, "Discriminative n-gram modeling for Turkish," in *Proceedings of Interspeech: Annual Conference of the International Speech Communication Association*, pp. 825–828, 2008.

[47] M. Collins, "Discriminative training methods for hidden Markov models: Theory and experiments with perceptron algorithms," in *Proceedings of the Conference on Empirical Methods on Natural Language Processing (EMNLP)*, pp. 1–8, 2002.

[48] B. Roark, M. Saraçlar, and M. Collins, "Discriminative n-gram language modeling," *Computer, Speech and Language*, vol. 21(2), pp. 373–392, 2007.

[49] Z. Li and S. Khudanpur, "Large-scale discriminative n-gram models for statistical machine translation," in *Proceedings of the Association for Machine Translation in the Americas (AMTA)*, pp. 133–142, 2008.

[50] C. Chelba and F. Jelinek, "Structured language modeling," *Computer, Speech and Language*, vol. 14, pp. 283–332, 2000.

[51] W. Wang and M. Harper, "The SuperARV language model: Investigating the effectiveness of tightly integrating multiple knowledge sources," in *Proceedings of the Conference on Empirical Methods on Natural Language Processing (EMNLP)*, pp. 238–247, 2002.

[52] R. Rosenfeld, "A maximum entropy approach to adaptive statistical language modeling," *Computer, Speech and Language*, vol. 10, pp. 187–228, 1996.

[53] R. Rosenfeld, "A whole sentence maximum entropy language model," in *Proceedings of the IEEE Workshop on Automatic Speech Recognition and Understanding*, pp. 230–237, 1997.

[54] J. Darroch and G. Ratcliff, "Generalized iterative scaling for log-linear models," *Annals of Mathematical Statistics*, vol. 43(5), pp. 1470–1480, 1972.

[55] S. D. Pietra, V. D. Pietra, and J. Lafferty, "Inducing features on random fields," *IEEE Transactions on Pattern Analysis and Machine Intelligence*, vol. 19, pp. 380–393, 1997.

[56] R. Malouf, "A comparison of algorithms for maximum entropy parameter estimation," in *Proceedings of the Conference on Computational Linguistics (COLING)*, pp. 1–7, 2002.

[57] J. Wu and S. Khudanpur, "Efficient training methods for maximum entropy language modeling," in *Proceedings of the 6th International Conference on Spoken Language Processing (ICSLP)*, pp. 114–118, 2000.

[58] S. D. Pietra, V. D. Pietra, and J. Lafferty, "Inducing features of random fields," *IEEE Transactions on Pattern Analysis and Machine Intelligence*, vol. 19(4), pp. 1–13, 1997.

[59] S. Chen and R. Rosenfeld, "A survey of smoothing techniques for ME models," *IEEE Transactions on Speech and Audio Processing*, vol. 8, pp. 37–50, 2000.

[60] J. Goodman, "Exponential priors for maximum entropy models," in *Proceedings of the North American Chapter of the Association for Computational Linguistics*, pp. 305–312, 2004.

[61] J. Wu and S. Khudanpur, "Maximum entropy techniques for exploiting syntactic, semantic and collocational dependencies in language modeling," *Computer, Speech and Language*, vol. 14, pp. 355–372, 2000.

[62] J. Bilmes and K. Kirchhoff, "Factored language models and generalized parallel backoff," in *Proceedings of the Human Language Technology Conference of the North American Chapter of the Association for Computational Linguistics (HLT/NAACL)*, pp. 4–6, 2003.

[63] K. Kirchhoff, D. Vergyri, K. Duh, J. Bilmes, and A. Stolcke, "Morphology-based language modeling for Arabic speech recognition," *Computer, Speech and Language*, vol. 20(4), pp. 589–608, 2006.

[64] K. Duh and K. Kirchhoff, "Automatic learning of language model structure," in *Proceedings of the Conference on Computational Linguistics (COLING)*, pp. 148–154, 2004.

[65] A. Stolcke, "SRILM - an extensible language modeling toolkit," in *Proceedings of the 7th International Conference on Spoken Language Processing (ICSLP)*, pp. 901–904, 2002.

[66] G. Ji and J. Bilmes, "Multi-speaker language modeling," in *Proceedings of the Human Language Technology Conference of the North American Chapter of the Association for Computational Linguistics (HLT/NAACL)*, pp. 137–140, 2004.

[67] G. Ji and J. Bilmes, "Dialog act tagging using graphical models," in *Proceedings of International Conference on Acoustics, Speech, and Signal Processing (ICASSP)*, 2005.

[68] D. Vergyri, K. Kirchhoff, K. Duh, and A. Stolcke, "Morphology-based language modeling for Arabic speech recognition," in *the 8th International Conference on Spoken Language Processing (ICSLP)*, pp. 2245–2248, 2004.

[69] I. Zitouni, "Backoff hierarchical class n-gram language models: effectiveness to model unseen events," *Computer Speech and Language*, vol. 21, pp. 88–104, 2007.

[70] W. Wang and D. Vergyri, "The use of word n-grams and parts of speech for hierarchical cluster language modeling," in *Proceedings of International Conference on Acoustics, Speech, and Signal Processing (ICASSP)*, pp. 321–324, 2006.

[71] P. Xu and F. Jelinek, "Random forests in language modeling," in *Proceedings of the Conference on Empirical Methods on Natural Language Processing (EMNLP)*, pp. 325–332, 2004.

[72] Y. Su and F. Jelinek, "Exploiting prosodic breaks in language modeling with random forests," in *Proceedings of the ISCA Workshop on Speech Prosody*, pp. 91–94, 2008.

[73] C. Andrieu, N. de Freitas, A. Doucet, and M. Jordan, "An introduction to MCMC for machine learning," *Machine Learning*, vol. 50, pp. 5–42, 2003.

[74] S. Wang, R. Greiner, D. Schuurmans, L. Cheng, and S. Wang, "Integrating trigram, PCFG and LDA for language modeling via directed Markov random fields," in *Proceedings of the NIPS Workshop on Bayesian Methods for Natural Language Processing*, 2005.

[75] B. Hsu and J. Glass, "Style and topic adaptation using HMM-LDA," in *Proceedings of the Conference on Empirical Methods on Natural Language Processing (EMNLP)*, pp. 373–381, 2006.

[76] T. Ferguson, "A Bayesian analysis of some nonparameteric problems," *Annals of Statistics*, vol. 1(2), pp. 209–230, 1973.

[77] Y. Teh, M. Jordan, M. Beal, and D. Blei, "Hierarchical Dirichlet processes," *Journal of the American Statistical Association*, vol. 101, pp. 1566–1581, 2006.

[78] Y. Teh, "A hierarchical Bayesian language model based on Pitman-Yor process," in *Proceedings of the Association for Computational Linguistics*, pp. 985–992, 2006.

[79] Y. Bengio, R. Ducharme, and P. Vincent, "A neural probabilistic language model," in *Proceedings of Neural Information Processing Systems (NIPS) Conference*, vol. 13, 2000.

[80] H. Schwenk and J. Gauvain, "Neural network language models for conversational speech recognition," in *Proceedings of Interspeech: Annual Conference of the International Speech Communication Association*, pp. 2253–2256, 2004.

[81] H. Schwenk, "Training neural network language models on very large corpora," in *Proceedings of Human Language Technology Conference on Empirical Methods in Natural Language Processing (HLT/EMNLP)*, pp. 201–208, 2005.

[82] A. Emami and L. Mangu, "Empirical study of neural network language models for Arabic speech recognition," in *Proceedings of IEEE Automatic Speech Recognition and Understanding (ASRU) Workshop*, pp. 147–152, 2007.

[83] H. Schwenk, D. Déchelotte, and J. Gauvain, "Continuous space language models for statistical machine translation," in *Proceedings of the COLING/ACL 2006 Main Conference Poster Sessions*, pp. 723–730, 2006.

[84] A. Emami and F. Jelinek, "A neural syntactic language model," *Machine Learning*, pp. 195–227, 2005.

[85] A. Alexandrescu and K. Kirchhoff, "Factored neural language models," in *Proceedings of the Human Language Technology Conference of the North American Chapter of the Association for Computational Linguistics (HLT/NAACL)*, pp. 1–4, 2006.

[86] S. Khudanpur, "Multilingual language modeling," in *Multilingual Speech Processing*, pp. 169–205, 2006.

[87] W. Byrne, J. Hajic, P. Ircing, and F. Jelinek, "Large vocabulary speech recognition for read and broadcast Czech," in *Text, Speech and Dialog. Lecture Notes in Computer Science*, vol. 1692, pp. 235–240, 1999.

[88] D. Kiecza, T. Schultz, and A. Waibel, "Data-driven determination of appropriate dictionary units for Korean LVCSR," in *Proceedings of the International Conference on Speech Processing (ICSP)*, pp. 323–327, 1999.

[89] H. Dutağacı, *Language Models for Large Vocabulary Turkish Speech Recognition.* PhD thesis, Boğaçizi University, 1999.

[90] M. Creutz, T. Hirsimäki, M. Kurimo, A. Puurula, J. Pylkkönen, V. Siivola, M. Varjokallio, E. Arisoy, M. Saraçlar, and A. Stolcke, "Analysis of morph-based speech recognition and language modeling of out-of-vocabulary words across languages," in *Proceedings of the Human Language Technology Conference of the North American Chapter of the Association for Computational Linguistics (HLT/NAACL)*, pp. 380–387, 2007.

[91] G. Choueiter, D. Povey, S. Chen, and G. Zweig, "Morpheme-based language modeling for Arabic LVCSR," in *Proceedings of International Conference on Acoustics, Speech, and Signal Processing (ICASSP)*, pp. 1053–1056, 2006.

[92] H. Soltau, G. Saon, D. Povey, L. Mangu, B. Kingsbury, J. Kuo, M. Omar, and G. Zweig, "The IBM 2006 GALE Arabic ASR system," in *Proceedings of International Conference on Acoustics, Speech, and Signal Processing (ICASSP)*, pp. 329–352, 2007.

[93] T. Buckwalter, "Buckwalter Arabic morphological analyzer version 2.0." Linguistic Data Consortium (LDC) catalog number LDC2004L02, ISBN 1-58563-324-0, 2004.

[94] O. Rambow and N. Habash, "Arabic diacritization through full morphological tagging," in *Proceedings of the Human Language Technology Conference of the North American Chapter of the Association for Computational Linguistics (HLT/NAACL)*, pp. 117–120, 2007.

[95] Z. Harris, "From phoneme to morpheme," *Language*, vol. 31(2), pp. 190–222, 1955.

[96] M. Adda-Decker and L. Lamel, "Multilingual dictionaries," in *Multilingual Speech Processing*, pp. 305–322, Amsterdam: Elsevier, 2006.

[97] M. Creutz and K. Lagus, "Unsupervised models for morpheme segmentation and morphology learning," *ACM Transactions on Speech and Language Processing*, vol. 4, no. 1, pp. 1–34, 2007.

[98] M. Creutz and K. Lagus, "Induction of a simple morphology for highly-inflecting languages," in *Proceedings of the 7th Meeting of the ACL Special Interest Group in Computational Phonology (SIGPHON)*, pp. 43–51, 2004.

[99] M. Creutz and K. Lagus, "Inducing the morphological lexicon of a natural language from unannotated text," in *Proceedings of the International and Interdisciplinary Conference on Adaptive Knowledge Representation and Reasoning (AKRR'05)*, pp. 106–113, 2005.

[100] M. Kurimo, M. Creutz, M. Varkalljo, E. Arisoy, and M. Saraçlar, "Unsupervised segmentation of words into morphemes: Challenge 2005. An introduction and evaluation report," in *PASCAL Challenge Workshop on Unsupervised Segmentation of Words into Morphemes*, 2006.

[101] E. Whittaker and P. Woodland, "Particle-based language modeling," in *Proceedings of the 6th International Conference on Spoken Language Processing (ICSLP)*, 2000.

[102] E. Arisoy, H. Sak, and M. Saraçlar, "Language modeling for automatic Turkish broadcast news transcription," in *Proceedings of Interspeech: Annual Conference of the International Speech Communication Association*, pp. 2381–2384, 2007.

[103] T. Alumae, "Sentence-adapted factored language model for transcribing Estonian speech," in *Proceedings of International Conference on Acoustics, Speech, and Signal Processing (ICASSP)*, 2006.

[104] K. Kirchhoff, M. Yang, and K. Duh, "Statistical machine translation of parliamentary proceedings using morpho-syntactic knowledge," in *Proceedings of the TC-STAR Workshop on Speech-to-Speech Translation*, pp. 57–62, 2006.

[105] R. Sarikaya and Y. Deng, "Joint morphological-lexical language modeling for SMT," in *Proceedings of the Human Language Technology Conference of the North American Chapter of the Association for Computational Linguistics (HLT/NAACL)*, pp. 145–148, 2007.

[106] I. Oparin, O. Glembek, L. Burger, and J. Cernocky, "Morphological random forests for language modeling of inflectional languages," in *Proceedings of the IEEE Spoken Language Technology Workshop*, pp. 189–192, 2008.

[107] A. Ito and M. Kohda, "Language modeling by string pattern n-gram for Japanese speech recognition," in *Proceedings of the 4th International Conference on Spoken Language Processing (ICSLP)*, pp. 490–493, 1996.

[108] R. Sproat, T. Zheng, L. Gu, J. Li, Y. Zheng, Y. Su, H. Zhou, P. Bramsen, D. Kirsch, I. Shafran, S. Tsakalidis, R. Starr, and D. Jurafsky, "Dialectal speech recognition: Final report," Tech. Rep., CLSP, Johns Hopkins University, 2004.

[109] H. Tseng, P. Chang, G. Andrew, D. Jurafsky, and C. Manning, "A conditional random field word segmenter for SIGHAN bakeoff 2005," in *Proceedings of the 4th SIGHAN Workshop on Chinese Language Processing*, pp. 168–171, 2005.

[110] H. Zhao, C.-N. Huang, and M. Li, "An improved Chinese word segmentation system with conditional random field," in *Proceedings of the 5th SIGHAN Workshop on Chinese Language Processing*, pp. 162–165, 2006.

[111] X. Mao, Y. Dong, S. He, S. Bao, and H. Wang, "Chinese word segmentation and named entity recognition based on conditional random fields," in *Proceedings of the 6th SIGHAN Workshop on Chinese Language Processing*, pp. 90–93, 2008.

[112] Y. Song, J. Guo, and D. Cai, "Chinese word segmentation based on an approach of maximum entropy modeling," in *Proceedings of the 5th SIGHAN Workshop on Chinese Language Processing*, pp. 201–204, 2006.

[113] A. Jacobs and Y. Wong, "Maximum entropy word segmentation of Chinese text," in *Proceedings of the 5th SIGHAN Workshop on Chinese Language Processing*, pp. 185–188, 2006.

[114] D. Song and A. Sarkar, "Training a perceptron with local and global features for Chinese word segmentation," in *Proceedings of the 6th SIGHAN Workshop on Chinese Language Processing*, pp. 143–146, 2008.

[115] G. Jin and X. Chen, "The fourth international Chinese language processing bakeoff: Chinese word segmentation, named entity recognition and Chinese POS tagging," in *Proceedings of the 6th SIGHAN Workshop on Chinese Language Processing*, pp. 69–81, 2008.

[116] V. B. Le, B. Bigi, L. Besacier, and E. Castelli, "Using the web for fast language model construction in minority languages," in *Proceedings of Eurospeech: European Conference on Speech Communication and Technology*, pp. 3117–3120, 2003.

[117] R. Ghani, R. Jones, and D. Mladenic, "Building minority language corpora by learning to generate web search queries," *Knowledge Information Systems*, vol. 7, no. 1, pp. 56–83, 2005.

[118] J. Franco and T. Solorio, "Baby steps towards a language model for Spanglish," in *Proceedings of the 8th International Conference on Intelligent Text Processing and Computational Linguistics (CICLing-2007)*, 2007.

[119] C. Fügen, S. Stüker, H. Soltau, and F. Metze, Efficient handling of multilingual language models," in *Proceedings of the IEEE Automatic Speech Recognition and Understanding (ASRU) Workshop*, pp. 441–446, 2003.

[120] T. Ward, S. Roukos, C. Neti, M. Epstein, and S. Dharanipragada, "Towards speech understanding across multiple languages," in *Proceedings of the 5th International Conference on Spoken Language Processing (ICSLP)*, 1998.

[121] Z. Wang, U. Topkara, T. Schultz, and A. Waibel, "Towards universal speech recognition," in *Proceedings of the IEEE International Conference on Multimodal Interfaces (ICMI)*, pp. 14–16, 2002.

[122] F. Weng, H. Bratt, L. Neumeyer, and A. Stolcke, "A study of multilingual speech recognition," in *Proceedings of the Eurospeech: European Conference on Speech Communication and Technology*, pp. 359–362, 1997.

[123] S. Khudanpur and W. Kim, "Contemporaneous text as side information in statistical language modeling," *Computer Speech and Language*, vol. 18(2), pp. 143–162, 2004.

[124] A. Jensson, E. Whittaker, K. Iwano, and S. Furui, "Language model adaptation for resource deficient languages using translated data," in *Proceedings of Interspeech: Annual Conference of the International Speech Communication Association*, pp. 1329–1332, 2005.

[125] W. Kim and S. Khudanpur, "Cross-lingual lexical triggers in statistical language modeling," in *Proceedings of the Conference on Empirical Methods on Natural Language Processing (EMNLP)*, pp. 17–24, 2003.

[126] W. Kim and S. Khudanpur, "Cross-lingual latent semantic analysis for language modeling," in *Proceedings of International Conference on Acoustics, Speech, and Signal Processing (ICASSP)*, pp. 257–260, 2004.

[127] Y. Tam, I. Lane, and T. Schultz, "Bilingual-LSA based LM adaptation for spoken language translation," in *Proceedings of the Association for Computational Linguistics*, pp. 520–527, 2007.

Chapter 6

Recognizing Textual Entailment

Mark Sammons, V.G.Vinod Vydiswaran, and Dan Roth

6.1 Introduction

Since 2005, researchers have worked on a broad task called **recognizing textual entailment** (RTE), which is designed to focus efforts on general textual inference capabilities but without constraining participants to use a specific representation or reasoning approach. There have been promising developments in this subfield of natural language processing (NLP), with systems showing steady improvement and investigations of a range of approaches to the problem. A number of researchers appear to have converged on some defining characteristics of the problem and on characteristics of practical approaches to solving it. RTE solutions have been shown to be of practical use in other NLP applications, and other grand natural language understanding (NLU) challenges, such as **Learning by Reading** [1] and **Machine Reading** [2] have emerged that will require similar problems to be solved. It is an exciting time to be working in this area.

Textual inference is a key capability for improving performance in a wide range of NLP tasks, particularly those that can benefit from integrating background knowledge. Performance of question answering systems, which can be thought of as potentially the next generation of search engines, is limited, especially outside the class of factoid questions. Furthermore, the task of extracting facts of interest (such as "people who have worked for Company X") from a collection of plain-text documents (such as newspaper articles) may require significant abstraction, synthesis, and application of world knowledge on the part of a human reader—and therefore of software required to perform the same task.

In this chapter, we specify a framework within which we can design and build an RTE system. First, we define the problem of RTE and outline its applications to other tasks in NLP. We then define a framework for an RTE system and show how it accommodates techniques used by successful RTE systems, describing key research in the RTE field (with a focus on system development), and showing how each system relates to the framework we have defined. We finish by addressing the pressing challenges in RTE research and pointing to useful resources.

We assume that readers are already familiar with the fundamental ideas of machine learning and its methodology of training, development, and testing; our focus is on the practical difficulties of developing an application for RTE.

We provide simple algorithms for all the key steps of the RTE framework. Although they are deliberately simplified, and as a result not particularly efficient, these are sufficient to build a basic RTE system designed to allow expansion along multiple dimensions. In Section 6.4, where we discuss key research investigating different approaches to RTE, we map each line of research to our framework at a high level (for full implementation details beyond the scope of this chapter, refer to the cited works). This mapping allows us to develop the relevant aspects of the system to pursue those approaches that interest us most.

6.2 The Recognizing Textual Entailment Task

In this section, we define the task of RET, explain the pros and cons of this formulation, and show why the problem is nontrivial. We show how RTE can be applied to a range of NLP tasks and present some concrete examples of such applications.

6.2.1 Problem Definition

The RTE task in the form we address in this chapter is defined by Dagan, Glickman, and Magnini [3] as:

> **Definition 6–1. Textual entailment** is defined as a directional relationship between pairs of text expressions, denoted by T, the entailing text, and H, the entailed hypothesis. We say that T entails H if the meaning of H can be inferred from the meaning of T, as would typically be interpreted by people.

The researchers note that this somewhat informal definition is based on (and assumes) common human understanding of language as well as common background knowledge.

An **entailment pair** is composed of a text T and a hypothesis H; usually, H is a short statement, and T is a longer span of text. Figure 6–1 shows a sample text and three hypotheses. The label of each entailment pair is determined by multiple human annotators; the background knowledge required is not specified and remains a latent factor in the labeling process. Often, when such knowledge is required, it is **static**—such as cause-effect relations or locations of well-known cities or landmarks (which do not change over time)—rather than facts like the name of the current president of the United States, which changes over time.

The specification of the RTE task also requires that the text be an inherent part of the reasoning for inferring the truth of the hypothesis: although background knowledge may augment that represented by the text, it may not replace it. If, for example, an RTE system uses facts extracted from Wikipedia, it might have a statement that ascertains the nationality of a popular film star, which could be equivalent to a hypothesis statement. However, if evidence for this fact is not present in the text, the entailment label is Not Entailed even though the hypothesis alone states a "true" fact.

The two-way RTE task requires that systems label each entailment pair as either Entailed or Not Entailed—that is, either T entails H, or T does not entail H. In Figure 6–1, the text entails Hyp 1, but not Hyp 2, or Hyp 3.

Text: The purchase of Houston-based LexCorp by BMI for $2Bn prompted widespread sell-offs by traders as they sought to minimize exposure. LexCorp had been an employee-owned concern since 2008.

Hyp 1: BMI acquired an American company.
Hyp 2: BMI bought employee-owned LexCorp for $3.4Bn.
Hyp 3: BMI is an employee-owned concern.

Figure 6–1: Some representative RTE examples

The three-way RTE task introduces the concept of contradiction. We define contradiction in entailment based on de Marneffe, Rafferty, and Manning [4]:

Definition 6–2. The hypothesis H of an entailment pair contradicts the text T if a human reader would say that the relations/events described by H are highly unlikely to be true given the relations/events described by T.

The three-way RTE task requires that systems label each entailment pair as either Entailed, Contradicted, or Unknown—that is, either T entails H, or H contradicts T, or it is unknown whether H is true given T. In Figure 6–1, the text T entails Hyp 1; Hyp 2 contradicts T; and the truth value of Hyp 3 is unknown given the information in T.

The difficulty of the task depends on the entailment pairs selected, and designing a suitable corpus is nontrivial. The corpora produced by PASCAL (Pattern Analysis, Statistical Modelling and Computational Learning)[1] and the National Institute of Standards and Technology (NIST)[2] are challenging. All corpora except RTE 4 have separate development and test components, each having between 600 and 800 entailment pairs; RTE 4 has a single component of 1,000 pairs. All these corpora are balanced, with approximately 50% having Entailed and 50% Not Entailed labels. In RTE 4 and RTE 5, the Not Entailed examples were further divided into two categories: Unknown and Contradicted (35% and 15% of total examples respectively).

Each corpus defines a set of three to seven tasks that further divide the data. Each task corresponds to the domain from which its examples were drawn (examples: QA for question answering, IE for information extraction; see the publications describing each challenge for more detail, e.g., Bentivogli et al. [5]). Performance of systems varies across tasks, indicating significant qualitative differences between the examples in each; but because the task label is not available to deployed RTE applications, we do not consider it here. (If task information is present, it is trivial to extend the implementation of the framework described here to take advantage of it, either by introducing a feature representing the task or by using separately tuned and trained inference components for each task.)

In addition, some pilot tasks were introduced in RTE 3 (explanation, contradiction) and RTE 5 (search). The contradiction task was made part of the main task for RTE 4 and

1. http://pascallin.ecs.soton.ac.uk/Challenges/RTE3/
2. http://www.nist.gov/tac/2010/RTE/index.html

RTE 5. RTE 5 also introduced a search pilot task, which we do not pursue further here (see Bentivogli et al. [5] for further details).

A system that performs well on these corpora could be said to have achieved a good "understanding" of natural language text.[3] State-of-the-art systems had accuracies of about 74% on the two-way task (Entailed vs. Not Entailed) and about 68% on the three-way task on the two most recent challenges (RTE 4 and RTE 5).

In the rest of this chapter, we identify the challenges involved in the RTE task, define a general framework to tackle it, and describe relevant research in RTE, showing how it fits into this framework.

6.2.2 The Challenge of RTE

It is informative to consider the different steps a human reader must go through to determine the entailment labels of the entailment pairs shown in Figure 6–1.

To recognize that hypothesis 1 is entailed by the text, a human reader must recognize that (i) *company* in the hypothesis can match *LexCorp* and that (ii) *based in Houston* implies *American*. She must also (iii) identify the nominalized relation *purchase* and (iv) determine that "A purchased by B" implies "B acquires A."

To recognize that hypothesis 2 contradicts the text, similar steps are required, with the difference that the reader must integrate the information that LexCorp is employee-owned and must then infer that because the stated purchase price is different in the text and hypothesis, but with high probability refers to the same transaction, hypothesis 2 contradicts the text.

Hypothesis 3 consists entirely of words from the text but asserts a relation that cannot be discerned from the available evidence, and so its label is Unknown: it is possible that BMI is employee owned, but it may not be.

Some of these steps, such as named entity recognition (recognizing that LexCorp and BMI are companies), coreference (different mentions of LexCorp refer to the same underlying entity), and semantic role labeling (BMI did the buying, not LexCorp), relate to other tasks defined by the NLP/computational linguistics community. Others may not; the relevant tasks have not yet been well developed in isolation, though they may be related to recognized problem definitions. Perhaps hardest of all are textual inference steps that require us to apply our understanding of the world to identify cause-effect relations, entailment relations, and abstraction over multiple statements to a general principle.

Although it is not required that a computerized solution to the RTE challenge follow such steps or emulate such capabilities, the limited success of approaches not informed by the human process has encouraged researchers to try a divide-and-conquer approach motivated by intuitions of the human process. Researchers have had some success isolating specific capabilities such as normalizing numerical quantities (dates, rates, proportions, counts) and have leveraged solutions to linguistically motivated problems like syntactic parsers and shallow semantic analytical tools like named entity recognizers.

It could be argued that the examples in Figure 6–1 might be resolved by simple lexical matching; but it should be evident that the text can be made lexically very dissimilar to

3. This assumption is based on the standard machine learning practice of evaluating the performance of a system on held-out data that was not used in training or development.

hypothesis 1 while maintaining the entailment relation and that, conversely, the lexical overlap between the text and hypothesis 2 can be made very high while maintaining the contradiction relation. This intuition is borne out by the results of the RTE challenges, which show that lexical similarity-based systems are outperformed by systems that use other, more structured analysis, as shown in Section 6.2.3.

6.2.3 Evaluating Textual Entailment System Performance

Definition 6–1 was used as the basis of six research challenges by PASCAL [3] and then NIST [5]. These corpora are available to the public, the first three without restrictions, the second three subject to a user agreement (see the websites noted earlier). Definition 6–2 motivated a pilot study in the third challenge, RTE 3; the corpora for the main task in both RTE 4 and RTE 5 incorporated contradiction and so were labeled for both the two-way and three-way prediction tasks.[4]

These research challenges have generated a lot of interest and significant progress on the RTE problem. We describe some informative examples in Section 6.4; for now, we present a general sense of the performance of state-of-the-art systems.

Figure 6–2 shows the summary of the results of the two-way entailment task for all five RTE challenges through 2009. For each data set, the performance of a lexical baseline (due to Mehdad and Magnini [6]) is also shown for comparison.

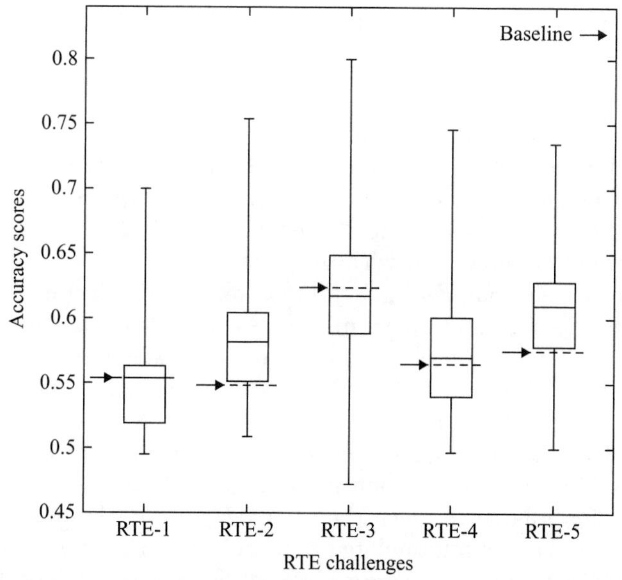

Figure 6–2: Results in PASCAL Recognizing Textual Entailment Challenges two-way task 2005–2009. For each year's challenge, the five-point statistics of participant systems' accuracy is shown. In addition, the performance of a lexical baseline system is also shown

4. At the time of writing, RTE 6 was underway.

It is difficult to compare results from different years because each year's corpus is different (drawn from different domains and/or according to different guidelines). RTE 4 and RTE 5 saw a significant increase in the average length of text, to about 40 and 100 words respectively, and are considered more challenging than entailment pairs with shorter texts. The lexical baseline, which uses a threshold based on the overlap between hypothesis and text words, indicates a fairly consistent baseline difficulty level of between 55% and 58% for four of the five challenges so far. The result for RTE 3 (2007) is markedly higher, and all system entries appear correspondingly higher than in other years, suggesting an "easier" entailment corpus. In all cases, the baseline score is at or below the median score for each challenge.

The upper range of system performance has also been fairly consistent. The longer texts in RTE 4 and RTE 5 increase the difficulty of the task by introducing more irrelevant signals (additional words, phrases, and sentences that are often irrelevant to the entailment decision), increasing the processing burden on RTE systems, and broadening the scope for entailment examples that require the integration of information from multiple sentences.

Due to the noncomparability of the RTE data sets, it is hard to draw strong conclusions from the numbers themselves other than to gauge the difficulty of the task on the basis of the relatively strong performance of the lexical baseline and to observe that some systems are significantly outperforming this baseline.

6.2.4 Applications of Textual Entailment Solutions

Many NLP problems can be formulated in terms of recognizing textual entailment. RTE clearly has relevance to summarization [7], in which systems are required to generate human-readable summaries of one or more documents. The subtask of identifying whether a new sentence contains information already expressed by a summary-in-progress (redundancy detection) can be thought of as an entailment pair with the present summary as the text and the new sentence as hypothesis. If T does not entail H, the sentence contains new information and should be integrated with the summary.

Information extraction comprises the task of recognizing instances of a fixed set of relations such as "works for" and "born in" in a set of natural language text documents. If we express the relations as short sentences, like *A person works for an organization,*" and *A person was born in a location,*" text spans from the source documents become the texts of entailment pairs with the reformulated relations as hypotheses, and an RTE system can be directly applied. Similarly, question answering, which requires automated systems to find candidate answers (sections of documents from a fixed document collection) to a set of questions, can be reformulated in much the same way: a question like *What is the largest city in South America?* can be reformulated as a short statement: *The largest city in South America is a city.* This statement becomes a hypothesis, and sections of the document set—typically, paragraphs—become the texts of a set of entailment pairs with this hypothesis. An RTE system can be directly applied to identify actual answers.

Of course, these naïve reformulations of the information extraction and question answering tasks are not in themselves sufficient because RTE solutions are generally resource intensive. However, the intuition is practical, as shown by research that applies RTE to other NLP tasks.

Question Answering

Harabagiu and Hickl [8] directly apply an RTE solution to rerank candidate answers in a question answering system. The underlying idea is simple: a preexisting question answering system returns the best candidate answers. Although the top candidate may not be the correct answer, in many cases the correct answer is in the set of returned candidates.

Harabagiu and Hickl use an RTE system to assess each candidate answer. Their system first applies a rule-based implementation to transform the input question into a short statement, as illustrated earlier. A set of entailment pairs is created by combining each candidate answer in the set returned by the system as a text, with the transformed question as the hypothesis. The RTE system is then applied to each pair in turn: those candidates that entail the transformed question are moved to the top of the list, and those that did not are moved to the bottom. The study shows that including the textual entailment component improves system accuracy from 30.6% to 42.7%.

Celikyilmaz, Thint, and Huang [9] use an entailment-like component to extract a feature-based representation of candidate question–answer pairs after transforming the query in a similar way to Harabagiu and Hickl. They use the real-valued feature vectors derived from the entailment comparison to compute similarity values between members of a large set of question–answer pairs. These values are used as edge weights linking nodes representing individual question–answer pairs in a graph. A (small) subset of the question–answer pairs have gold-standard labels; the labels of the remaining nodes are then inferred using a semisupervised learning method.

Exhaustive Search for Relations

In many information foraging tasks, such as patent search, accident report mining, and detecting confidential information in documents that must be shared with partners lacking appropriate clearance, there is a need to find all text snippets relevant to a given concept. This involves finding all passages that talk about the concept directly or indirectly while screening out passages that are superficially similar but have a different meaning.

This information need maps directly to recognizing entailed passages from large text corpora. However, it requires scaling up textual entailment systems to move from pairwise text–hypothesis decision to a search-based entailment framework. Because most successful RTE systems apply a lot of NLP resources and computationally expensive inference algorithms, a naïve approach (for every paragraph of each document, test whether it entails any one of a set of statements representing the target information) is impractical.

Roth, Sammons, and Vydiswaran [10] define a focused textual entailment approach, SERR (scalable entailment relation recognition), that consists of two stages: semantic retrieval and entailment recognition. Figure 6–3 shows the schematic diagram of the approach.

The algorithm is outlined in Figure 6–4. In this approach, the text corpus is first preprocessed to find semantic components such as named entities (people, location, organizations, numeric quantities, etc.). These are indexed as semantic units to facilitate quick retrieval. The user expresses the information need as a relation query, which is enriched with synonyms, alternative names, and other semantically similar keywords. This query is then used

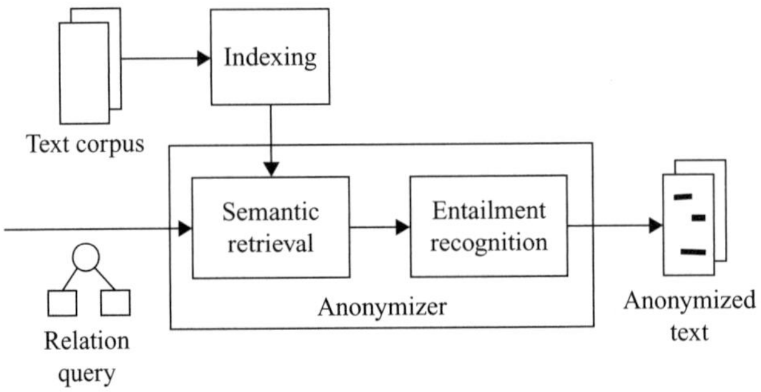

Figure 6–3: SERR framework [10]

SERR Algorithm
SETUP:
Input: Text set D
Output: Indices $\{I\}$ over D
for each text $d \in D$
Annotate d with local semantic content
Build Search Indices $\{I\}$ over D
Input: Information need S

EXPANDED LEXICAL RETRIEVAL (ELR)(s):
$R \leftarrow \emptyset$
Expand s with semantically similar words
Build search query q_s from s
$R \leftarrow k$ top-ranked texts for q_s using indices $\{I\}$
return R

SERR:
Answer set $A \leftarrow \emptyset$
for each query $s \in S$
$R \leftarrow$ ELR(s)
Answer set $A_s \leftarrow \emptyset$
for each result $r \in R$
Annotate s, r with NLP resources
if r entails s
$A_s \leftarrow A_s \cup r$
$A \leftarrow A \cup \{A_s\}$

Figure 6–4: SERR algorithm [10]

to retrieve text passages from the corpus. The results are processed by the textual entailment module to decide if the text entails the given query, and the entailed text snippets are then output as the results. The semantic retrieval helps improve the recall of entailing passages, and the RTE module filters the results to improve the overall precision.

The experimental evaluation was conducted using a corpus derived by taking all the hypotheses from the information retrieval and information extraction subtasks of RTE 1, 2, and 3 as defining the information needs, with all texts from the same entailment pairs forming a "document" set. The retrieval component found the most relevant documents (texts) for each hypothesis, and the RTE module labeled this returned set as Entailed or Not Entailed to identify the relevant documents.

When evaluated on the overall classification performance for the hypothesis–text pairs corresponding to actual examples from the RTE challenges, the system achieved performance in the top three ranks of published results for each challenge. The architecture also reduced the number of computationally intensive comparisons from about 3,800,000 for a naïve approach (compare all hypotheses to all texts using the RTE module) to only about 40,000 for the SERR system.

Machine Translation

Techniques developed by RTE researchers have also been applied to the task of evaluation in machine translation (MT). Padó et al. [11] use insights from textual entailment to propose a new automated measure of candidate translation quality. MT evaluation uses statistical measures to evaluate the similarity of translations proposed by MT systems to reference translations produced by human annotators, as human evaluation of a large number of MT outputs is too resource intensive to allow rapid evaluation of systems on large corpora. The dominant similarity metric is n-gram–based; while this measure has reasonable correlation with human judgments, it is far from perfect, not least because it takes no account of nonlocal structure in the translations to be compared.

Padó et al. propose a new metric that also accounts for structural characteristics; the metric based on features similar to those used in the textual entailment system developed by Chambers et al. [12]. Their intuition is that the candidate translation should be a paraphrase of the reference translation, and therefore the two translations should entail each other. Missing information in the candidate means it does not entail the reference, and additional information in the candidate means the reference does not entail the candidate. Bad translations will cause entailment to fail in both directions. They use features based on the alignment score; modality, polarity, and tense mismatches; semantic relations; entity and date compatibility; and others.

To evaluate their new metric, they use data from MT workshops. Their comparison shows a significant improvement in Spearman's correlation coefficient with human judgments over the standard metric.

Mirkin et al. [13] use entailment to translate unknown terms. When a term is relatively rare, or when translating from a language with scarce linguistic resources, that term may not appear in the phrase tables used by MT systems. Mirkin et al. tackle this problem by transforming the source translation into a more general form by applying lexical entailment rules. They demonstrate the feasibility of this approach using an MT model trained on a parallel French/English corpus. They then apply this model to sentences from news articles in English, which have many unknown terms, being drawn from a different domain than that used to train the model.

Using English as the source language allows them to use WordNet [14], a large English-language ontology relating words via synonymy, hypernymy, and many other lexical relations. They use synonymy to generate paraphrases for unknown words and hypernymy to generate entailed (more general) texts from the English sentences. They then compare the quality of the French translations of these different versions of sentences with unknown words and the quality of French translations using only the more standard paraphrase resources.

Their results show that the coverage of unknown terms over the paraphrase-based approach is improved by as much as 50% by the textual entailment-based approach; translation quality is also much higher than when unknown words are omitted, with an additional 15.6% of translations produced by the system being judged acceptable by human judges, with only a 2.7% drop in the number of correct translations.

6.2.5 RTE in Other Languages

As yet, few entailment corpora are available in languages other than English. The two known sources of non-English RTE data are EVALITA[5] and the Cross-Language Evaluation Forum (CLEF).[6] EVALITA, an Italian NLP evaluation program run by FBK-Irst of Trento, Italy, assesses NLP technologies for the Italian language on a range of problems that includes RTE. CLEF's Answer Validation Exercise uses the RTE formalism to push question answering technology. CLEF develops corpora that pair candidate answers with questions reformulated as statements, with the idea that an RTE system can detect valid answers by determining whether each candidate answer entails the reformulated question; CLEF has corpora for German, English, Spanish, French, Italian, Dutch, and Portuguese.

The NLP community has made steady progress in developing NLP resources comparable to those available for English in other languages: some good sources of information are the European Language Resources Association[7] and the Asian Federation of Natural Language Processing.[8] However, there are languages for which resources such as named entity taggers and syntactic parsers have not yet been developed, requiring developers to use shallower cues for entailment.

One specific assumption we make in the framework we describe in Section 6.3 is that when a language has multiple resources, those resources are consistent in their determination of word boundaries. In reality, even English resources may be inconsistent in their tokenization of raw input text. Morphologically rich languages like Arabic may result in resources that segment individual words differently by separating affixes and/or clitics. Languages like German that combine words to form unsegmented compounds also pose challenges to recognizing word boundaries. Chinese characters are not whitespace separated and are grouped into word equivalents by NLP applications such as machine translation systems.

There is no one-size-fits-all solution; in the proposed framework, developers must determine the tokenization scheme that best suits their needs and ensure that their different levels of representation respect the chosen tokenization; if different resources use conflicting tokenization schemes, it is the developer's task to satisfactorily resolve them. However, provided

5. http://evalita.fbk.eu/te.html
6. http://nlp.uned.es/clef-qa/ave/
7. http://www.elra.info/
8. http://www.afnlp.org/

this requirement is satisfied, the framework we describe allows developers to implement a solution appropriate to the resources available to them.

6.3 A Framework for Recognizing Textual Entailment

In this section, we define a flexible framework as the basis of an RTE application; we draw on insights from Roth and Sammons [15]. To extensively define a single implementation of any real RTE system would easily fill a chapter by itself; instead, we describe a system, giving sample algorithms where appropriate. In Section 6.4, we describe some relevant research publications that provide details of specific implementations, and we show how they fit into our framework.

The framework we specify here is designed to incorporate existing (and new) NLP resources in a uniform way and to allow systematic development of both straightforward and complex RTE systems. It is also intended to directly support implementation of a wide range of approaches to RTE that have been described by researchers such as those in Section 6.4.

At the end of the chapter, we provide an incomplete list of resources that are available for download (most of which have a license for noncommercial use). However, here we avoid committing to any specific implementation; we focus on applications that perform well-established tasks and therefore expect these applications to produce consistent output, so you should be able to use the specific applications that best suit your needs.

6.3.1 Requirements

Before designing an framework for an RTE system, it is instructive to consider the preexisting NLP components that could be useful for determining entailment. We focus on components for well-known NLP tasks that clearly contribute to good performance on the RTE task or that intuitively form the basis of useful RTE functionality. Furthermore, we consider only NLP components that have a broadly agreed-upon output format.

Two main kinds of resources are of immediate interest: resources that enrich raw text with semantic information—such as named entity taggers and syntactic parsers—and resources that compare spans of text—such as individual words, or names, or phrases—and indicate some measure of similarity. We refer to the former as **annotators** (or, equivalently, **analytics**), and the latter as **comparators** or **metrics** (see §6.3.3).

Consider again the illustrative example in Figure 6–1, and the steps a human reasoner must follow, as a guide to the capabilities our system must support. In step 1, it is necessary to identify the entities BMI and LexCorp and to recognize that they are companies. This information, or something like it, can be provided by a named entity recognizer (see Chapter 8). Step 2 involves mapping *based in Houston* to *American*. One possible route to attain this connection is to infer *in America* from *in Houston*. This requires a factoid knowledge base that operates at least at the lexical level. To recognize the nominalized relation *purchase* in step 3 first requires that this word be identified as a noun (provided by a part-of-speech [POS] tagger). To map arbitrary nominalized verbs to their regular forms requires a lexicon; one possibility is the popular lexical ontology WordNet [16], using the relation "derivationally related form" to identify the verb *purchase*. The next step requires interpretation of the syntactic structure to identify the subject, object, and direct object—the **arguments** of the nominalized verb—in order to allow comparison with the structure *BMI acquired an American company.* This structure could be obtained using a syntactic or dependency parser (see Chapter 3); alternatively, these steps might be resolved by a shallow semantic parser, or semantic role labeler (see Chapter 4). Finally, in step 4, the two syntactic (or shallow semantic) structures must be compared in order to recognize that the text entails the hypothesis.

Other resources could be useful; successful RTE systems also use resources that

- identify and normalize numeric quantities,
- identify different ways of expressing a given named entity (for example, International Business Machines might be referred to as IBM but not as BMI) and
- determine which entities in a span of text refer to the same underlying entity (also known as coreference resolution, as described in Chapter 8).

Individual implementations generally use a mixture of off-the-shelf applications and custom-built modules but attack the same set of underlying problems.

The implications for a general-purpose RTE framework are that it must support a range of annotations of the text of the entailment pair at multiple granularities (from words to phrases to verb-argument structures) and must support comparison of these annotations using specialized resources.

6.3.2 Analysis

The range of NLP resources described earlier presuppose that natural language understanding is (largely) compositional: we can isolate individual phenomena and solve the task of recognizing each phenomenon. We see a similar intuition at work in the way human annotators describe solving entailment problems, as in Section 6.2.2. Experience in a range of other fields of computer science give testimony to the power of the divide-and-conquer approach. We therefore seek a way to apply this strategy to the RTE problem.

6.3.3 Useful Components

We define here some components that are broadly useful in our generic RTE framework.

A Multiview Representation for NLP Analysis

We consider the output of all analytics to define **constituents** over the underlying text, which may optionally be linked by **relations**. We refer to any pattern over constituents and/or relations as a **structure**. Each constituent is trivially a structure.

We consider each analytic resource to define its own **view** of the underlying text, with the most fundamental view being the Word view. We require that the Word view represent tokens rather than the raw text and that all other views be normalized with respect to this view; that is, the word tokens used to generate every view must be the same as those in the word view. Consequently, every constituent must correspond precisely to a set of word indices, which is convenient when detecting correspondences across different views (e.g., recognizing that a semantic role labeling argument is also a named entity).

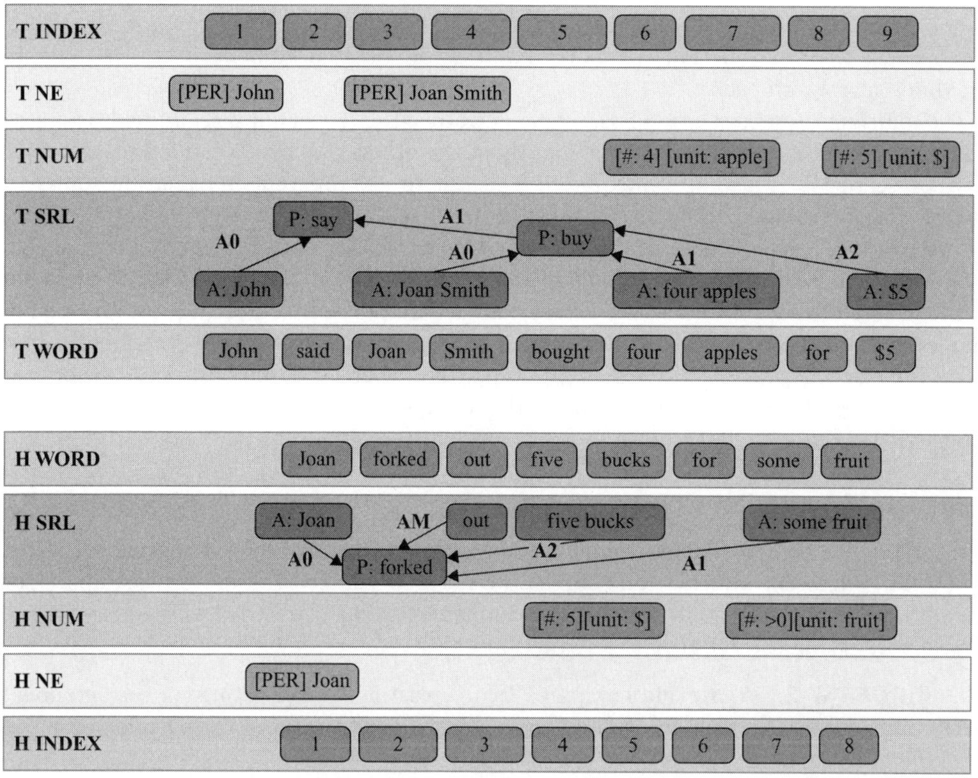

Figure 6–5: Example of a multiview representation of a textual entailment pair

Figure 6–5 illustrates the data structure generated from input of a system that combines named entities (NE), numerical quantities (NUM), and semantic role label (SRL) analysis, in addition to the words and their indices. Each constituent corresponds to words in the original text and contains the list of indices to which it corresponds.

In general, constituents specify a type (used to select from available similarity metrics); one or more attribute-value pairs specifying information of interest—such as part of speech and lemma for words—and which may be used by the relevant similarity metrics; and the set of indices of words in the original text to which the constituent corresponds. In the example shown, the NE constituents have a type and a value derived from the output of a named entity recognizer.

The NUM constituents have a normalized representation of the number and its unit, together with the indices of the corresponding tokens in the original text.

The SRL view contains predicate (P) and argument (A) constituents; these are joined by relations representing the roles of the arguments related to the predicate (A0 is *agent*, or semantic subject; A1 is *patient*, or semantic object). These roles are distinct from syntactic subject and object roles, as they are not affected by, for example, passive constructions (for a full explanation of semantic role labeling, see Chapter 4). Note that nesting is allowed in our representation: a predicate may take another predicate as its argument (in this case, *say* has the predicate *buy* as its semantic object). The argument constituents are not assigned roles because they may be part of more than one predicate-argument structure and could have different roles in each.

The multiview representation has several key advantages over simpler, unified representations. Each resource is handled independently of the others and can be added incrementally. The representation is also very flexible: if we want to use different information sources for different purposes—as in the case of filtering (see §6.3.7)—it is straightforward. It is also possible to write generic algorithms for processing multiple views without knowing what views will be present. Finally, the multiview representation defers **canonization**: combining the different views into a single data structure may require resolving disagreements in boundaries and relation structure, and it may be desirable to make these decisions at a later stage—for example, during the inference step, when there may be additional evidence to support one decision over another. If desired, the many views can be collapsed into a single graph structure as the final step of the preprocessing stage.

Comparing Annotation Constituents

A crucial step in RTE is that of comparing the hypothesis with the text. Given our integration of many different information sources, we need specialized resources to compare some types of constituents. We will simplify our implementation if we treat these resources in a uniform way, so we use the metric abstraction:

> **Definition 6–3.** A **metric** compares two constituents and returns a real number in the interval $[-1, 1]$, with the value 1 indicating identity, -1 indicating opposition, and 0 indicating irrelevance.

The metric is a specialization of the concept of **comparator**. A comparator compares two structures and returns arbitrary information; a metric compares two constituents and returns only a score. Comparators tend to be more specialized, being designed to work with specific structures (such as predicate-argument structures derived from semantic role label annotation).

Note that this definition of metric limits consideration of the context except for the knowledge of the type of constituents being compared and whatever information is encoded by the analytical resource that generates the input used to create the constituents and by the algorithm that parses that input into the constituents. We think of metrics as fairly simple, focused resources, and we chose the metric abstraction to allow us to specify a simple interface and thereby simplify graph generation code.

One reason for this design choice becomes clear when we consider what happens when a new information source is added to an existing, possibly complex, RTE system: ideally, we want to avoid rewriting our graph generation and alignment algorithms. If the new comparators we write to handle the new annotation follow the same specification as the others we have already written, we should not have to change these algorithms. Another reason for this localization is to promote the encapsulation of domain-specific knowledge in a convenient form.

To give a concrete example of a metric, we describe the behavior of a word metric (see Algorithm 6–1). Given the pair of word constituents with the lemmas *rise* and *increase*, our word metric should return a high positive score such as 0.8, as these words are synonymous

Algorithm 6–1 Algorithm for a word metric. The function levenshteinDistance() computes the edit distance between two strings. The function isSynonym() consults WordNet and returns true if the two words are synonyms, false otherwise. isHypernym() consults WordNet and returns the number of hypernym links separating the two words (infinity if there is no link)

```
// Assume: words both set to lowercase

compare( firstWordC, secondWordC )
  score ← 0
  firstWord ← getAttribute( firstWordC, WORD )
  secondWord ← getAttribute( secondWordC, WORD )

  if ( firstWord == secondWord )
      score ← 1.0
  else
      levDistance ← levenshteinDistance( firstWord, secondWord )
      numChars ← max( firstWord.length, secondWord.length )

      if ( ( numChars – levDistance ) / numChars > 0.9 )
          score ← 0.8
      else if ( isSynonym( firstWord, secondWord ) )
          score ← 0.9
      else if ( isAntonym( firstWord, secondWord ) )
          score ← −0.7
      else
          numHypernymLinks ← isHypernym( firstWord, secondWord ) )
          if ( numHypernymLinks < 4 )
              score ← (0.9/numHypernymLinks)
  return score
```

in some contexts. Given *paper* and *exterminate*, it should return a value near 0, as these two words are generally unrelated. If called with *rise* and *fall*, it should return a negative value close to -0.7, as these are antonymous. (We use a smaller magnitude negative score so that our alignment step will prefer positive matches over negative ones, but this decision is based on our intuition of desired behavior rather than empirical knowledge.)

The determination of scores is presently more of an art than a science; we leave them as real values to retain flexibility in inference. We have found, for example, that the lexical baseline we use in our experiments performs better when using an admittedly imperfect real-valued word similarity score than when the word similarity metric is thresholded to assign either 1.0 or 0.0.

In the general case, some metric scores may need to be adjusted. For example, some named entity similarity metrics use variations on string edit distance; these tend to return moderate positive scores for very dissimilar names. A word similarity metric based on WordNet, however, might return a relatively low positive score for two words related by several steps of hypernymy; yet this is more likely to coincide with a case in which an entailment relationship holds between the two words than with a case in which the two entities have a similar score via a string edit distance.

Generally, metrics are not symmetric, because the entailment relation is not symmetric. Consider the case of a metric that compares noun phrases being applied in the entailment example in Figure 6–1. One of the phrase pairs that must be compared comprises *a company* from the text, and *an American company* from the hypothesis: in this case, the text does not contain sufficient information, so the noun phrase metric should return a score of zero. However, if *an American company* were from the text and *a company* from the hypothesis, the metric should return a score close to 1.0, as the first entails the second.[9]

A named entity metric should recognize that *John Q. Smith* entails *John Smith* and *Mr. J. Smith* with high likelihood but not *Ms. J. Smith*; again, this relationship is not always symmetric, as *John Smith* does not necessarily entail *John Q. Smith*.

6.3.4 A General Model

A block diagram of a typical RTE system is presented in Figure 6–6. Entailment pairs are processed either one at a time or as a batch; for simplicity, we describe the process per pair except in specific contexts that require a batch-processing mode. We describe the system in terms of its **evaluation** (which corresponds to the behavior of a deployed RTE system). We handle the process of training machine learning components separately, though this process usually uses many of the same steps.

Preprocessing

We assume that as the first step in the RTE process, our system must apply a suite of off-the-shelf[10] annotators to the text of the entailment pair. While the list of resources is open-ended, typical resources include sentence and word segmentation (identify sentence boundaries, word and punctuation tokens), POS tagging, dependency parsing or syntactic parsing, named entity recognition, coreference resolution, and semantic role labeling. These different resources are used to enrich the text.[11]

We describe a data structure suited to integrating such diverse annotations in Section 6.3.3, and where appropriate, we show how it can be mapped to the types of representations used in some specific RTE systems.

Depending on the off-the-shelf components used, you may also need to clean up the input prior to applying these resources, but we know of no prepackaged solutions. Some older packages may not handle multibyte characters, for example: these must be replaced or omitted. A cleanup step could also normalize spelling, which may have a significant impact on, for example, syntactic parsers and POS taggers.

---

9. The effect of additional modifiers (in this case, *American*) on entailment is called *monotonicity*; for a discussion of entailment and monotonicity, see MacCartney and Manning [17].

10. Packages or components that are readily available from one or more open-source/academic sources.

11. The terminology of RTE is overloaded. We use text *span* to describe generic sentences, paragraphs, or portions of same, and *text* to refer to the larger component of an entailment pair.

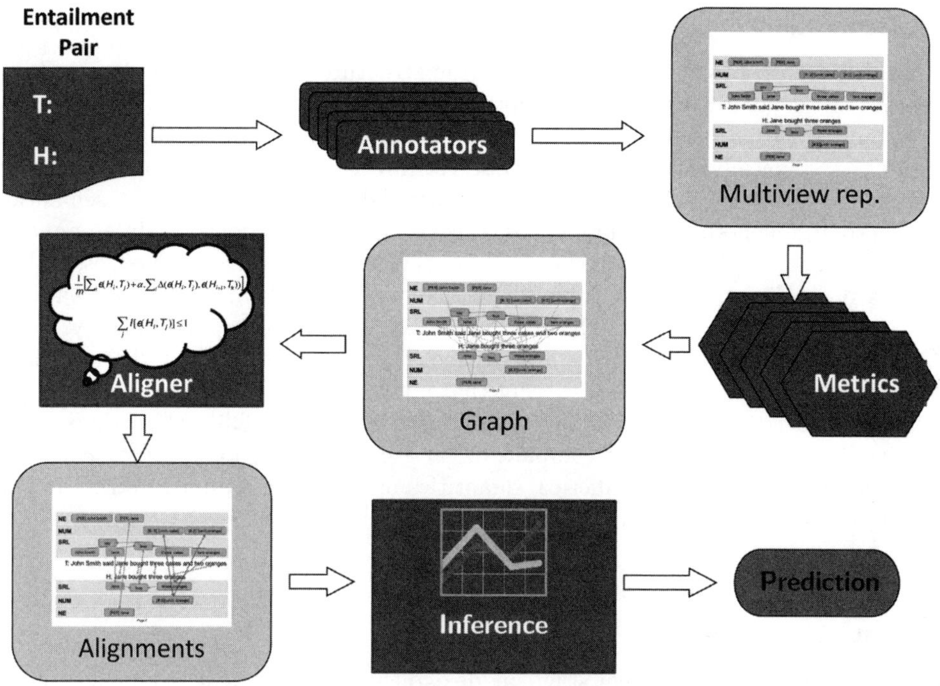

Figure 6–6: Block diagram for generic RTE framework

Enrichment

We use the term **enrichment**, as distinct from preprocessing, to refer to resources that operate on (combinations of) preexisting views to either augment existing views or generate new views. This is in contrast to analytical resources that process text and generate an annotated form that is directly parsed into constituents, relations, and views. Enrichment resources serve one of two functions: to abstract over some text/annotation patterns by mapping them to a closed set of structures or to augment the existing annotation by recognizing implicit content in the input text/annotation and making it explicit as new structure.

An example of abstraction would be to represent modifiers of verbs such as *failed to* in the sentence *Attackers failed to enter the building* or *said that* in the example shown in Figure 6–5, by using an attribute in the verb or relation node in the corresponding predicate-argument structure. In the latter case, we could write code to identify such structures and mark embedded predicates like *buy* with an attribute indicating uncertainty.

An example of augmentation is that of rule application (see §6.4.3), to make implicit content of the underlying text more explicit or to generate explicit paraphrases of the text. The RTE system may use them to generate additional syntactic parse trees representing paraphrases of the underlying text or predicate-argument structures like those encoding semantic role labeling information.

Graph Generation

After identifying various syntactic and semantic structures in the text and hypothesis, it is necessary to compare those in the hypothesis with those in the text. In the simplest systems, only words are compared. In more successful systems, a range of annotation types are compared. Typically, the text and hypothesis are represented as graphs whose nodes correspond to annotation units (such as words, named entities, parse subtrees, semantic role labeling verb arguments), and whose edges correspond to connections within an annotation type (e.g., connecting different mentions of a single entity via coreference edges, or linking words in a dependency tree with typed dependency edges). Then, the constituents in the hypothesis are linked to those in the text based on some measure of similarity (possibly simple equality) to form a bipartite graph distinct from the text and hypothesis structures.

We assume that each type of constituent that must be compared in the graph generation step has an associated comparator (or metric, as defined in §6.3.3). More than one type of constituent may use the same comparator, and comparators for complex constituents (those with structure, such as numerical quantities or predicate argument structures) may themselves call other, more basic comparators.

Alignment

The intuition behind the alignment stage, made explicit by de Marneffe et al. [4], is that only a relatively small portion of the text is relevant to the hypothesis. The goal of alignment is to identify that relevant portion and thereby simplify the inference step.

Many RTE systems have an explicit alignment step; others have an integrated alignment/inference process. In general, alignments map each constituent in the hypothesis to a single constituent in the text. This is a heuristic based on the observation that the hypothesis tends to be much shorter than the text, and that in positive entailment examples, a human reader can often generate a "piecewise" explanation of the hypothesis using portions of the text.

Most RTE systems first integrate all constituents into a single graph structure—a single view in our terminology—and align each constituent in this representation. Others perform an alignment using only words and, in the inference step, analyze the structure in other views that corresponds to the aligned words. In our own work [18] (described in §6.4.6), our system performs multiple alignments for different groups of views, and the inference step compares them to discern cues for entailment/nonentailment.

Inference

All RTE systems must use a decision component to label each entailment pair. This may be a relatively simple measure of overlap plus a threshold, or it may be significantly more complex, such as extracting features from the alignment graph and applying a machine-learned classifier to determine the final label. Some use theorem-provers over a logical representation induced from the entailment pair and the analysis from the preprocessing step. We discuss some different approaches in Section 6.4.

Text: John said Joan Smith bought three apples for five dollars.
Hyp: Joan Smith forked out $5 for three apples.

Figure 6–7: A textual entailment pair for implementation examples

6.3.5 Implementation

In this section, we fill out the explanation of the different parts of the RTE system with a focus on functionalities common to a range of successful RTE systems. The case studies we consider in Section 6.4—drawn from recent RTE challenges—are mapped onto these descriptions. For this general framework, we use as our running example a simple lexical entailment algorithm (LEA) that uses a WordNet-based similarity measure for word constituents and a simple named entity–based filtering rule.

We use as our sample input the (slightly contrived) entailment pair shown in Figure 6–7. This example allows us to illustrate each step of the RTE framework in the context of the LEA system.

Preprocessing

We need to write the modules to control the flow of data through the various analytical resources and to translate from the output of each resource to the constituent/relation/view data structures. Word-level annotation like parts of speech and lemmas can be integrated into Word constituents. Shallow annotation like named entities are straightforward to parse into constituents in their own view; structured annotation like coreference, and semantic role predicates and arguments, require some decisions about representation, such as whether to have separate views for predicates and arguments, or whether to create additional constituents that each correspond to a complete semantic role labeling structure.

A typical order for preprocessing is:

1. sentence splitting
2. word boundary detection
3. POS tagging
4. dependency or syntactic parsing
5. named entity recognition
6. coreference resolution (identify referents of pronouns and possibly other entity mentions)
7. semantic role labeling (verbs and nominalized verbs)

This ordering reflects some typical dependencies: for example, many NLP applications require POS tags as an information source, and most semantic role labeling systems require syntactic or dependency parse information. Some tools may allow or even expect the user to provide these inputs, and others handle everything internally. Providing such inputs yourself can improve efficiency by avoiding repeated application of tools with comparable functionality. For convenience, word-level annotations like parts of speech and lemma can be added to word constituents.

Note that if you use resources from different sources, they may have different expectations about input. For example, many applications take unsegmented text as input and segment the text internally. The problem here is that there is no clear set of guidelines for "correct" segmentation, so the output from different sources may disagree about some word and sentence boundaries. For example, should hyphenated words be separated (e.g., *American-led* or *American - led*)? Should symbols representing currency remain with the corresponding number (e.g., $*12M* or $ *12 M*)? In such cases you must resolve the differences yourself. Of course, you could use an integrated tool set that provides all the different kinds of annotation you need or restrict yourself to tools that accept presegmented input. However, it is seldom the case that the tools with the highest performance in each task all come from the same source, and if a specific tool has been developed using a specific segmentation scheme, it may not perform as well when it is given input that uses a different segmentation scheme.

Running Example: Lexical Entailment Algorithm

For our LEA RTE system, we need two views: a Word view and an NE view. The Word view will contain a word constituent for each token in the corresponding entailment pair member (i.e., either the text or the hypothesis), which will include the original word and its lemma (if it has one). The NE view will contain one constituent for each named entity in the corresponding entailment pair member, containing the entity's original representation (the sequence of tokens from the original text) and its type. We do not initially use all this information, but it enables us to suggest possible extensions to the original algorithm. The resulting multiview data structure is the same as that in Figure 6–5, without the SRL and NUM views.

Some NLP applications provide a programmatic interface, but many do not; however, almost all generate marked-up text output. For those unfamiliar with the task of parsing NLP tool outputs, we outlined an algorithm to parse the named entity recognition (NER) output in Algorithm 6–2, which also shows a sample NER output. We assume that either the NER segments the input text in the same way as that used to induce the Word view or that the NER takes tokenized text as input. We also assume that there is no overlap of named entities in the NER output, an assumption that holds for the NER taggers we have used, though it is not hard to extend the algorithm to handle outputs of tools allowing tagged entities to overlap.

Enrichment

To extend our LEA system, we enrich our underlying text by adding simpler expressions equivalent to idiomatic usage. This simplistic resource uses a hand-generated mapping from simple idiomatic phrases to simpler equivalent expressions, such as from *kick the bucket* to *die*. Provided we consider only those expressions that can be mapped to the same number or fewer of replacement words, we can simply add alternative word constituents that correspond to the same indexes as the original idiomatic expression (a single replacement

Algorithm 6–2 Algorithm to parse NER-style annotations. The function getNextWord(nerOutput) splits the first word from nerOutput at the first noninitial whitespace character and returns it; peekNextChar(aWord) returns the first character of aWord; and concatenate(startString, nextWord) appends nextWord to startString separated by a single whitespace character.

```
// sample nerOutput: "[PER Joan Smith ] bought apples."

// ASSUME: no overlapping entities, and that square brackets
// in input have been replaced.

CreateViewFromNerOutput( String nerOutput )

  neView ← ∅
  neType ← null
  neValue ← null
  indexSet ← ∅
  isInNe ← false

  while ( nextWord ← getNextWord( nerOutput ) )

      firstChar ← peekNextChar( nextWord )
      if ( firstChar == '[' )
          isInNe ← true
          getFirstChar( nextWord )
          neType ← nextWord
      else if ( firstChar == ']' )
          neConstituent ← { neType, neValue, indexSet}
          neView ← neView ∪ neConstituent
          indexSet ← ∅
          neType ← null
          neValue ← null
          isInNe ← false
      else if ( isInNe )
          wordIndex ← wordIndex + 1
          indexSet ← indexSet ∪ index
          neValue ← concatenate( neValue, nextWord )
      else
          continue

  return neView
```

Algorithm 6–3 Simple algorithm for generating Idiom view

```
// ASSUME: annotationGraph already has word view;
// idiomList is a map from idiom strings to single words
// such as "forked out → buy"

AddIdiomView( annotationGraph )
  maxWordsInIdiom ← 3
  indices ← getOrderedWordIndices( annotationGraph )

  foreach index ( indices )
      indexSet ← ∅
      offset ← 0
      sequence ← ""
      replacement ← null

      do
          offsetIndex ← index + offset
          word ← findWordWithIndex( annotationGraph, offsetIndex )
          sequence ← concatenate( sequence, word )
          replacement ← findIdiomMatch( sequence )
          indexSet ← indexSet ∪ offsetIndex
          offset ← offset + 1
      while ( ( replacement != null ) AND ( offset < maxWordsInIdiom ) );

      if ( replacement != null )
          idiomConstituent ←generateIdiomConstituent( replacement, indexSet )
          idiomView ← idiomView ∪ idiomConstituent

  if ( idiomView != ∅ )
      addView( annotationGraph, idiomView )

  return
```

word constituent may cover more than one of the original sentence indexes). A naïve algorithm for the IdiomMapper is shown in Algorithm 6–3.

The enriched multiview data structure is presented in Figure 6–8. The original hypothesis text is *Mr. Smith forked out $5 for three oranges.* The multiview representation has a word constituent for each token, including the period.

The IdiomMapper has added the new word constituent *pay.* Note that this constituent covers both of the indices that the original idiom *forked out* covered. This is important when determining optimal alignments (see §6.3.6).

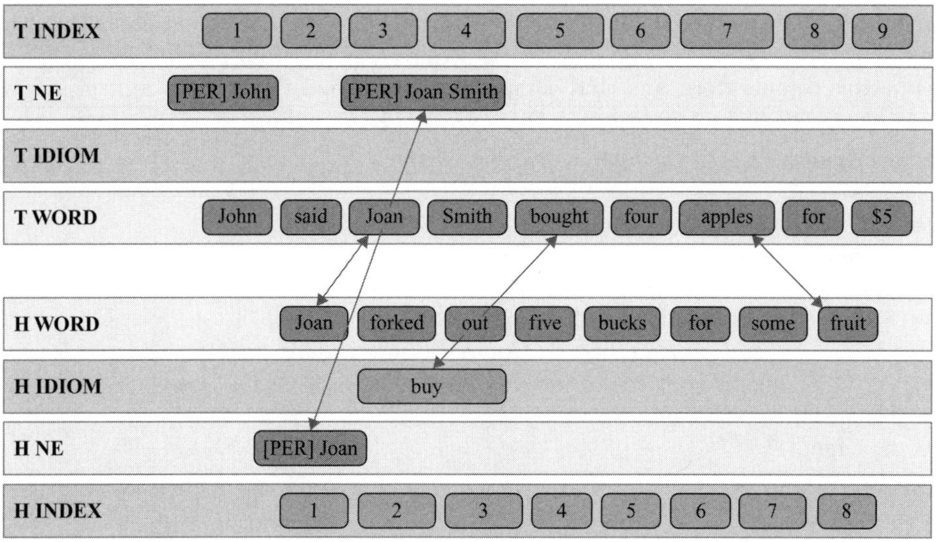

Figure 6–8: Best alignment by LEA for sample entailment pair; aligned components are connected by green arrows

Graph Generation

In the graph-generation step, the comparison resources (metrics) are applied to the relevant constituent pairs drawn from the text and hypothesis. This can be implemented in a straightforward way: iterate over views in the hypothesis and text, iterate over the constituents in each, and apply the appropriate metrics.

The metric code may itself be complicated, however, for highly structured constituents like dependency parse (sub)trees. We provide a simple graph-generation algorithm in Algorithm 6–4.

Running Example

In our example, we have the named entities *John* and *Joan Smith* in the text and *Joan* in the hypothesis. *John* and *Joan* have a very low edit distance (of 1), but a human reader knows that unless there is a typographical error, these two names refer to different people. We assume that our named entity metric is smart enough to know this too and that it will return a similarity score of -0.7.

The two strings *Joan Smith* and *Joan*, our other text-hypothesis named entity pair, should return a high score even though their edit distance (of 6) is relatively high. We assume our NER metric returns a score of 0.9 because the strings are not identical but are highly likely to refer to the same individual.

We assume that our word similarity metric uses WordNet and applies the following heuristic: if words are linked by synonymy or one level of hypernymy, the score is 0.9. If they are linked by two levels of hypernymy, the score is 0.6. If they are linked by three levels

Algorithm 6–4 Algorithm for the graph-generation step (comparing entailment pair member graphs). It is assumed that the system stores a mapping from paired constituent types to compatible comparators, and that comparators behave like metrics in returning a score.

```
CompareHypothesisToText( hypGraph, textGraph )
  edgeList ← ∅
  foreach view hypV in hypGraph
      viewEdgeList ← ∅
      foreach view textV in textGraph
          if ( isCompatible( hypV, textV ) )
              viewPairEdgeList ← CompareViews( hypV, textV )
              viewEdgeList ← viewEdgeList ∪ viewPairEdgeList
      edgeList ← edgeList ∪ viewEdgeList
  return edgeList


CompareViews( hypView, textView )
  edgeList ← ∅
  foreach constituent hypC in hypView
      hypEdgeList ← ∅
      hypId ← getIdentifier( hypC )
      foreach constituent textC in textView
          textId ← getIdentifier( textC )
          score ← CompareConstituents( hypC, textC )
          matchEdge ← { ViewType, hypId, textId, score }
          hypEdgelist ← hypEdgeList ∪ matchEdge
      edgeList ← edgeList ∪ hypEdgeList
  return edgeList


CompareConstituents( hypC, textC )
  hypType ← getType( hypC )
  textType ← getType( textC )
  comparatorSet ← getCompatibleComparator( hypType, textType )
  matchScore ← 0
  foreach ( comparator ∈ comparatorSet )
      score ← comparator → compare( hypC, textC )
      if ( score > matchScore )
          matchScore ← score
  return matchScore
```

of hypernymy, the score is 0.3. If the words are linked by antonymy, the score is −0.5. This behavior is specified in the algorithm shown in Algorithm 6–1.

6.3.6 Alignment

The fundamental idea behind most alignment algorithms is the notion that some alignments are better than others and that simply picking the most similar text constituent for each hypothesis constituent is too simplistic, as it does not account for sentence structure.

Given our formulation of comparators (metrics) and the method for generating the entailment graph, we can frame the task of finding an optimal alignment as an optimization problem. We will align **groups** of views together: for example, we could combine NE and NUM views in a single alignment. We may align all views together simultaneously, or we may align each separately, depending on the type of inference we want to perform.

We constrain the alignment to allow each index in the hypothesis to be mapped to, at most, *one* target in the text, so constituents covering more than one token may not overlap. The goal is to identify parts of the text that *explain* the tokens of the hypothesis and to simplify the inference problem.

In general, our intuition is that some views should compete: when there are several alternative representations of the same token(s)—such as substitutions for idioms—we may wish these to be considered as mutually exclusive choices, in which case these views should be grouped before alignment; we wish other views to be handled separately, because they may give us useful information that would be lost if they were grouped. For example, suppose a named entity metric returns only scores in the range $[0, 1]$, and no entity constituents match. If we combine the NE view with the Word view, we may get spurious matches of parts of entities that share a title, or a surname, or that have a regular noun as either a forename or surname that happens to appear in the other entailment pair member. A similar problem arises when we combine views using metrics that do not have compatible output (i.e., their scores cannot be interpreted in the same way). Again, combining named entities and words may result in problems because the word similarity metric consistently returns lower scores for positive matches.

Constituents at different granularities may both have alignment edges in an optimal solution, provided they do not overlap.

Because metrics may return negative scores, the objective function must account for these. Negative scores indicate contradiction: in the absence of a better positive match, this information may be highly relevant to the subsequent entailment decision. In the objective function, therefore, the **magnitude** of the edge weight is used. The edge retains a label indicating its negativity, which is used in the inference stage.

For alignments over shallow constituents, we must guess at the deep structure; we therefore include locality in the objective function by penalizing alignments where neighboring constituents in the hypothesis are paired with widely separated constituents in the text. We ignore crossing edges, as we do not believe these are reliably informative of entailment.

The objective function is then:

$$\frac{\sum_i e(H_i, T_j) + \alpha . \sum_i \Delta(e(H_i, T_j), e(H_{i+1}, T_k))}{m} \tag{6.1}$$

and the constraint:

$$\sum_j I[e(H_i, T_j)] \leq 1 \tag{6.2}$$

where m is the number of tokens in the hypothesis; $e(H_i, T_j)$ is the magnitude of the score of a metric comparing hypothesis token i and text token j; and α is a parameter weighting the distance penalty. $\Delta(e(H_i, T_j), e(H_{i+1}, T_k))$ measures the distance between the text constituent aligned to hypothesis token i and the text constituent aligned to hypothesis token $i+1$. For constituents covering multiple tokens, this value is the minimum distance between any token covered by the constituent covering T_j and any token covered by T_k. This distance function could be measured in a variety of ways: for example, in tokens or by edges in a path through a dependency parse tree. $I[e(H_i, T_j)]$ is an indicator function indicating that token i in the hypothesis is mapped to token j in the text.

For alignments that combine constituents of different granularities, the preceding formulation uses as token-level edge weights the magnitude of the edge score for the mapped constituents covering the pair of tokens in question. For example, an edge between two named entities with a score of 1.0 would count as 1.0 for each token covered by the named entity in the hypothesis; a named entity covering two indices would therefore generate an edge with the value 2.0. This avoids penalizing matches of constituents larger than a single token.

In our own RTE system [18], we did not have alignment training data, so we selected the alignment parameter α by hand (a positive value close to zero, sufficient to break ties) and used brute-force search to find the optimal alignment. The search time has an upper limit, after which a greedy left-to-right alignment is used in place of the optimal solution. We used the number of tokens as the distance measure Δ.

The search algorithm we used is shown in Algorithm 6–5. EdgeSetList is populated as follows: for each index in the text span of the hypothesis, all edges from constituents *starting* at that index are collected in a set, which is added to the EdgeSetList. All possible alignments are considered and scored, and the highest scoring alignment returned.

The function *getNextAlignment* is used to iterate over all possible sets of edges that respect the "one edge per hypothesis token" constraint. To do this, it uses a CounterSet: this object stores the total number of edges from constituents covering each index of the hypothesis and an index indicating which edge in the EdgeSetList for the corresponding index was used in the previous alignment. To generate the next alignment, it increments the first EdgeSet index not already at the last edge in the set of edges for the corresponding hypothesis index. If an individual counter is at the maximum index, it is reset to the first index, and the next counter is processed. If all counters are at the maximum index, all alignments have been considered.

To generate the alignment corresponding to the current CounterSet values, the EdgeSetList is traversed. Starting from the set of edges from constituents starting at the lowest index, the edge corresponding to the index in the corresponding counter is selected. The last index of that edge's hypothesis constituent is found, and intermediate indices are skipped. The next index not covered by the hypothesis constituent is then processed, and so on until the hypothesis indices have been traversed.

(As written, the algorithm may generate duplicate alignments when the CounterSet is incremented, but the incremented counter is in the interval covered by a constituent corresponding to an edge selected by a counter for a lower hypothesis index. In the interests of clarity and space, the duplicate detection has been omitted. The algorithm presented is nonetheless correct—just not as efficient as it could be.)

Algorithm 6–5 Algorithm for finding the best alignment for a set of views. The function `getIndices()` returns a sorted list of word indices for a graph.

```
findBestAlignment( edgeSet, hypGraph, textGraph )
  bestScore ← 0.0
  edgeSetList ← ∅
  foreach index ( getIndices( hypGraph ) )
      currentEdgeSet ← findEdgesWithStartIndex( hypGraph, index )
      edgeSetList ← edgeSetList ∪ currentEdgeSet
  counterSet ← getCounterSet( edgeSetList )
  bestAlignment ← ∅
  do
      currentAlignment ← getNextAlignment( edgeSetList, hypGraph, textGraph,
      counterSet )
      score ← scoreAlignment( currentAlignment )
      if ( score > bestScore )
          bestAlignment ← currentAlignment
          bestScore ← score
  while ( currentAlignment != ∅ );
  return bestAlignment

getNextAlignment( edgeSetList, hypGraph, textGraph, edgeSetCounters )
  currentAlignment ← ∅
  if ( incrementCounters( edgeSetCounters ) )
      position ← 0
      maxPosition ← sizeOf( edgeSetCounters )
      nextUncoveredIndex ← 0
      while ( position < maxPosition )
          position ← position + 1
          if ( nextUncoveredIndex <= position )
              currentEdgeSet ← edgeSetList[ position ]
              currentPositionCounter ← edgeSetCounters[ position ]
              currentEdge ← currentEdgeSet[ currentPositionCounter ]
              currentAlignment ← currentAligment ∪ currentEdge
              hypConstituentId ← getHypConstituentId( currentEdge )
              hypConstituent ← findConstituent( hypGraph, hypConstituentId )
              lastIndex ← getLastIndex( hypConstituent )
              nextUncoveredIndex ← lastIndex + 1
  return currentAlignment

incrementCounters( edgeSetCounters, edgeSetList )
  index ← 0
  while ( index < sizeOf( edgeSetList ) )
      counter ← edgeSetCounters[ index ]
      edgeSet ← edgeSetList[ index ]
```

Algorithm 6–5 (*Continued*)

```
    maxCount ← sizeOf( edgeSet )
    if ( counter < maxCount )
        counter ← counter + 1
        return true
    counter ← 0
    index ← index + 1
return false
```

Running Example

In the alignment step of our LEA system, we combine the Word and Idiom views and align the NE view separately. The rationale is that we can use the same word metric for the Idiom constituent as for the Word constituents, and we believe that the idiom replacement effectively generates a new sentence, where the replacement term competes with the original idiomatic term; it does not make sense to partially match the idiom. The alignment generated by the LEA system is shown in Figure 6–8.

LEA's implementation of the distance function shown in Equation 6.1, for simplicity, always returns 0, though it is possible to specify a penalty for distance that will tend to group edges when the text is very long, and there are multiple matching words in the text for certain words in the hypothesis.

The simple LEA uses a greedy alignment approach, taking the maximum value match for each individual hypothesis word. In the Idiom and Word views alignment, the idiom replacement counts twice, as it covers two word indices. Function words like articles (*a*, *the*, etc.) and prepositions (*on*, *of*, etc.) generally carry much less semantic content than nouns, verbs, and adjectives; LEA therefore uses a list of stopwords containing such terms and ignores their edge scores.

The total alignment score for the best alignment (shown in the figure) is 0.43.

The NE view is also aligned. There is only one NE constituent in the hypothesis view, and it is aligned using its highest-scoring edge.

6.3.7 Inference

The Inference component of RTE systems makes the final decision about the label (and score) assigned to each entailment pair. Although we present it as distinct from the alignment step, there are approaches in which the two are closely coupled.

In some systems, inference is a simple comparison of the alignment score to a threshold. In the two-way RTE task, if the score is higher than the threshold, the entailment pair is labeled Entailed; otherwise, it is labeled Not Entailed. In the three-way task, some systems perform two sequential classifications: one to distinguish between Unknown examples and the rest, and a second classification step to split the rest into Entailed and Contradicted (see Wang, Zhang, and Neumann [19]). Others apply two thresholds to the single alignment score: the second, lower threshold distinguishes between Unknown and Contradicted (see Iftene and Moruz [20]).

Other systems apply a feature extraction step after the alignment step (such as Chambers et al. [12]). For example, these features could characterize the correspondence between dependency parse connections linking each pair of hypothesis words with the corresponding connections for the aligned text words. These features would then be used as input to a machine-learned classifier that would use them to predict the label of the entailment pair.

Some systems may alter the alignment score based on global features. Such features might be filter rules: for example, if there is a named entity in the hypothesis and no match is found in the text, it is very likely that the example is Not Entailed. Other examples are negation features: usually, negations or other terms/structures affecting polarity, such as "failed to," are identified in the preprocessing or enrichment steps and encoded in the graph structure. They may then be used to affect the final decision, perhaps by switching Entailment to Contradiction if there is a negation in the text and none in the hypothesis, or vice versa, when other factors indicate the text entails the hypothesis. In allowing metrics to return negative scores, and tracking this via edge labels but using the magnitude of the edge score for determining alignments, such a feature is already accommodated in the proposed framework: it is possible to do the abstraction in the enrichment step, account for the enriched representation in the relevant similarity metric (by allowing it to return a negative score), then determine if negative edges are present in the final alignment.

Running Example

The named entity alignment is used as a filter: if there is any named entity in the hypothesis that does not match anything in the text, LEA automatically says no. We can achieve this by thresholding the individual edge scores and setting the predicted label to Not Entailed if all edges for any single hypothesis NE constituent have scores lower than the threshold.

If the hypothesis named entities are all matched, it consults the Word and Idiom alignment.

Because the hypothesis contains a single named entity and is aligned with a positive score to an entity in the text, LEA does not set the label to No Entailment and consults the Word and Idiom alignment.

For the Word and Idiom alignment, the LEA system applies a simple threshold, as it is applied only to the two-label task. Let us assume the Word threshold is 0.67; LEA therefore predicts the label Not Entailed for this example based on the Word and Idiom alignment.

Note that LEA got this example wrong; to do better, it would need to be able to identify that *$5* and *five bucks* are equivalent—functionality provided by numerical quantity analysis and the corresponding similarity metric. Such a resource might also identify a mapping between *some fruit* and *four apples*, especially if it makes use of the word similarity metric.

If there had been antonymous terms in the text and hypothesis, such as *love* and *hate*, our word metric would have returned a negative score. Had there been no better (nonantonymous) match for *hate* in the text, the aligner would select the antonymous match edge because it ignores the sign of the edge value. In the inference step, the negative value would remain and would automatically penalize the score. We could enhance the inference algorithm by changing the scoring function to use rules (such as "if two aligned verbs from the text and hypothesis are antonymous, predict Contradicted") or by making the alignment score aggregation multiplicative (a single negative edge will result in a negative overall score). Such heuristics are sometimes effective but generally introduce new sources of error;

nevertheless, such effects are taken into account and used by successful RTE systems to improve performance.

6.3.8 Training

In most successful systems, the alignment and/or inference components must be tuned to the entailment corpus using the development data set. In systems using machine learning components, this process is called **training**: the machine learning algorithm processes the entailment examples in the development corpus, computes relevant statistics, and generates a model of the problem based on characteristics of the inputs it receives, usually expressed as **features**: expressions or functions that take a specific part of the input and compute a value for each example.

In non–machine-learning–based components, there may be a process of tuning similarity functions using the development corpus, possibly by trial and error or by brute-force search over a parameter space.

We discuss the training procedures for some of the systems presented in Section 6.4.

Running Example

For the LEA system, we need to compute the threshold used by the inference step to determine the entailment label. We do this by computing the best alignment for each example in the development corpus, sorting the examples by alignment score, and then testing each score as a possible threshold. We pick the threshold that correctly classifies the most examples.

You may have observed that in Equation 6.1, we normalize the sum of the alignment edge scores by the number of tokens in the hypothesis. We do this so that in the inference step (and training), the decision is not biased by the length of the hypothesis. (Consider, for example, two different examples, one with a hypothesis of length 4 and another of length 12. If there are four similar components for each example, we intuitively desire different entailment labels, as the first is more likely than the second to be labeled Entailed.)

6.4 Case Studies

In this section we present a summary of a number of state-of-the-art systems as case studies. For each case, we define the key characteristics of the approach, the preprocessing modules used, and the method used to predict the entailment decision (where relevant). A number of open-source resources are used by multiple systems; rather than give multiple, repeated citations for each such resource, we simply name them here and collect all this information at the end of the chapter (see §6.6). Our goal here is to describe interesting research in RTE and to relate the different approaches to our framework. For specific details of implementation, refer to the original publications.

Note that where possible, we have included systems that were evaluated on the RTE 5 dataset. However, some interesting systems were only evaluated on earlier RTE data sets, so their accuracy results are not directly comparable.

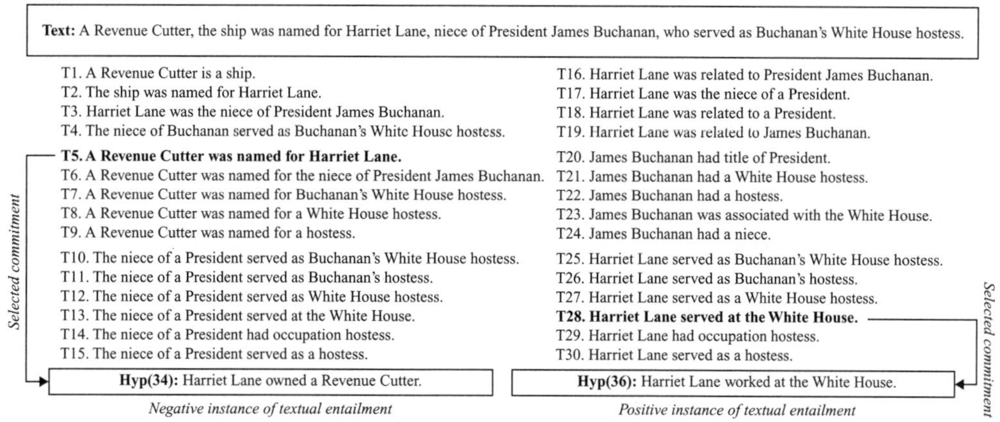

Figure 6–9: Example of discourse commitments from text [21]

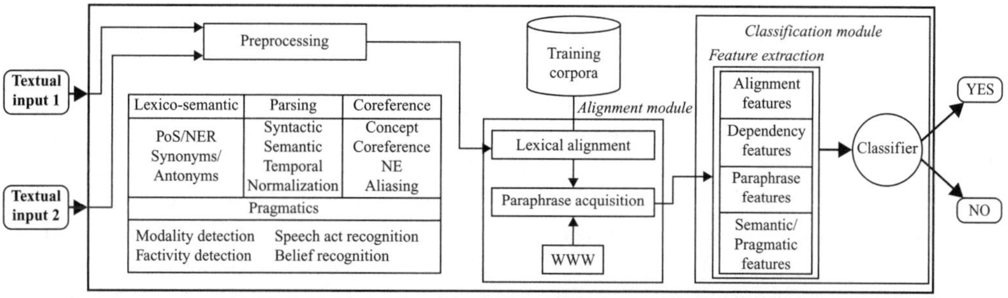

Figure 6–10: Textual entailment framework [22]

6.4.1 Extracting Discourse Commitments

Hickl and Bensley [21] propose a framework for recognizing textual entailment based on extraction of implicit beliefs or discourse commitments. The assumption is that the text consists of many simpler constructs that are true even if the particular Text-Hypothesis pair does not entail. Figure 6–9 shows a sample entailment pair with all discourse commitments; the block diagram of the system is shown in Figure 6–10.

The preprocessing step includes syntactic parsing and semantic-dependency parsing, named entity recognition, coreference resolution, and numeric quantity recognition. The outputs of these systems are unified in a single graph representation.

In the enrichment step, the text and hypothesis sentences are decomposed into sets of simpler sentences that are themselves true, irrespective of the truth value of the pair. A relation extractor is used to recognize known relations, such as owner-of, location-near, employee-of, and supplemental expressions, such as parenthesis, as-clauses, and appositives.

In the alignment step, a token-based aligner is applied that uses multiple similarity metrics such as WordNet-based word similarity, Levenshtein string-edit distance, and named entity similarity (equality) metrics. These metrics are used to align words from hypothesis commitments to text commitments.

In the inference step, the system extracts features based on entity and argument matches, and a decision-tree classifier is used to decide if a commitment pair represents a valid entailment instance.

The classifier is trained in the standard way, using features extracted for each example in the development corpus.

The system achieves an accuracy of 80.4% on the RTE 3 test set, and a modified version of the system scored 74.6% on the RTE 4 data set (see Hickl [23]).

While the performance of this system is very strong, it depends on a large corpus of proprietary supplemental training data, and the preprocessing tools it uses are also mostly proprietary. However, the underlying concept is similar to numerous other approaches, breaking the surface text down into simpler units and matching them rather than the original words and sentences.

6.4.2 Edit Distance-Based RTE

To the best of our knowledge, tree edit distance (typically based on dependency parse structure) was first used for textual inference by Punyakanok, Roth, and Yih [24] to select answers in the task of question answering. Several teams later applied tree edit distance to the task of recognizing textual entailment (e.g., Kouylekov and Magnini [25] in RTE 1).

Mehdad et al. [26] propose an open-source framework for textual entailment called the Edit Distance Textual Entailment Suite (EDITS) [27], which provides a basic, customizable framework for systematic development and evaluation of edit distance–based approaches to RTE. The framework allows the computation of edit distance to transform the text into the hypothesis using edit operations at the string, token, and tree levels. In addition, it allows specification of entailment and contradiction rules that associates a score with the transformation rule of an element from the text to an element from the hypothesis.

The EDITS framework also defines a common text-annotation format to represent the input Text-Hypothesis pair and the entailment and contradiction rules. The training data is used to learn a distance model. The EDITS workflow is shown in Figure 6–11.

In the system submitted to TAC RTE 5, the preprocessing step used dependency parsing, POS tagging, lemmatization, and morphological analysis.

The graph-generation and alignment steps are integrated. The lowest cost edit distance is determined using a set of operations (insertion, deletion, and substitution), each of which has an associated cost. These costs are learned using an optimization algorithm, together with a threshold score that maximizes performance on the development set. Word-level substitution resources were derived from VerbOcean [28], WordNet [14], and Latent Semantic Analysis of Wikipedia.

The inference step compares the computed edit distance with the learned threshold score: if the pair's edit distance is greater than the threshold, the system assigns the label Not Entailed; otherwise, it assigns the label Entailed.

The EDITS-based RTE system achieved a score of 60.2% in RTE 5 but could probably be improved by investigating new substitution resources and possibly by enriching the input structures with, for example, named entity information (and using a specialized similarity measure in the inference step).

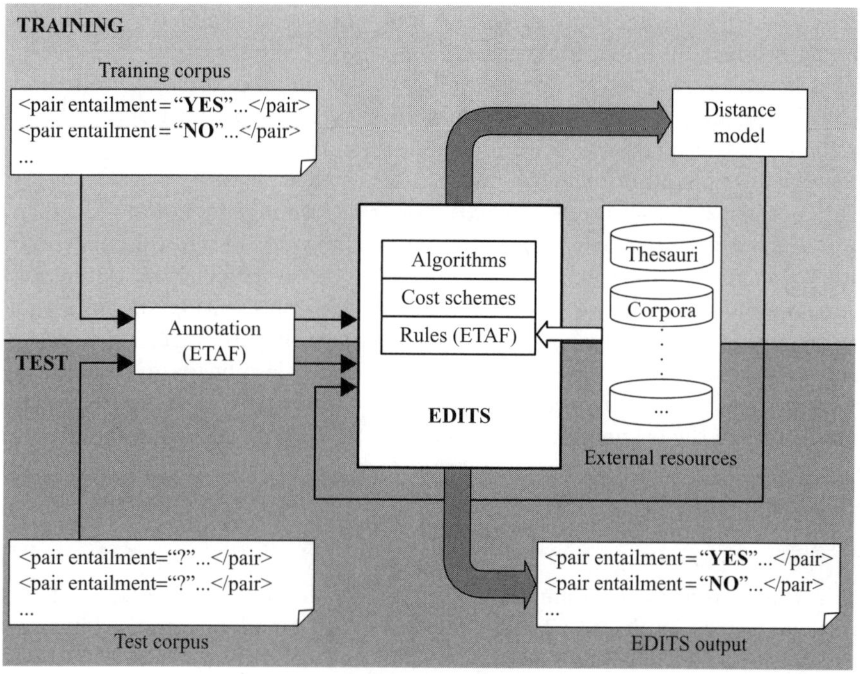

Figure 6–11: EDITS workflow [27]

6.4.3 Transformation-Based Approaches

Braz et al. [30] describe an RTE system based on the augmentation of a graph-based representation of the entailment pair's text and hypothesis using hand-coded rules designed to capture alternative expressions of information at the lexical, phrasal, syntactic, and predicate-argument levels. They provide a model-theoretic justification of their approach: when a rule is applied to the entailment pair text, the augmented representation makes explicit one possible (valid) interpretation of that text (ideally, in a way that makes the text more closely resemble the hypothesis, when the text entails the hypothesis). If any such representation of the text subsumes the hypothesis, the text entails the hypothesis.

The subsumption is formulated as an integer linear programming problem, which is used to find a minimum-cost subsumption of the hypothesis by the text. Rules have associated costs, and these costs are further weighted depending on the level of the representation at which the rule is expressed (the intuition being that it is more important to match relations—and therefore verbs—than individual terms like determiners).

The preprocessing step of this system annotates the entailment pair with shallow parse, syntactic parse, named entity, and semantic role labels. The enrichment step attempts to match the left-hand side of each rule to the text graph; if the rule matches, the right-hand side of the rule is used to augment the text graph. Several iterations are run, allowing limited chaining of rule applications.

There is no explicit alignment step; the inference step formulates the integer linear programming problem and determines the minimum cost of subsumption of the hypothesis by the text. If the cost is too high, the entailment pair is labeled Not Entailed; otherwise, it is labeled Entailed. This system was shown to outperform a smart lexical baseline on a subset of the RTE 1 development set and achieved an accuracy of 56.1% on the RTE 1 test set (the two best systems both achieved accuracies of 58.6%).

Bar-Haim et al. [29] describe a framework for transforming a syntactic-parse–based representation of the entailment pair text, using rules expressed as fragments of syntactic parse trees. Hand-coded rules are used to abstract over a range of syntactic alternations. The rules pair two syntax tree fragments with placeholders representing subtrees that remain unchanged in the transformation. An example is given in Figure 6–12.

In the enrichment step of their RTE process, the rules' heads are compared to the structure of the text. If they match, a new syntactic parse tree is generated with the rule body; the subtrees in the original text structure identified by the rule placeholders are copied to the corresponding positions in the new parse tree.

The inference step extracts features from the most closely matching pair of text-hypothesis representations (as defined by a distance metric), and these are used by a classifier to predict the entailment label.

To train the classifier, the same steps are run, the features extracted, and the feature representation of each entailment pair together with the pair's label are used in the standard supervised machine learning paradigm. A version of this system achieved an accuracy of 60.5% on RTE 4 (Bar-Haim et al. [31]).

The disadvantage of these approaches is the need for many rules to capture a large range of possible syntactic alternations; the high cost of producing such rules by hand makes such an effort problematic. However, the straightforward mechanism for incorporating world knowledge is appealing, as the problem of incorporating background knowledge must be overcome to make significant progress in RTE.

6.4.4 Logical Representation and Inference

The Boeing Language Understanding Engine (BLUE) system by Clark and Harrison [33] is based on a formal logical approach to RTE. It transforms the text into a logic-based representation and then tries to infer the hypothesis using a theorem-prover over this representation.

The BLUE system consists of a two-stage pipeline, as shown in Figure 6–13. Initially, the text and hypothesis are parsed into a logical representation, using a bottom-up chart parser [34]. The logical form is a simplified tree structure with logic-type elements. It incorporates some preprocessing steps such as dependency parsing, POS tagging, and pronoun and reference resolution. Modality attributes, such as plurality, tense, and negation, are represented by special predicates in the logical form. This logical representation is used to infer entailment, based on subsumption and equivalence using WordNet and discovery of inference rules from text (DIRT). If the logical inference step fails to decide entailment or contradiction, a bag-of-words alignment model is used (in conjunction with WordNet and DIRT) as a backoff inference module.

BLUE tries to find an explanation for the entailment decision using the logical theorem-prover to search for a chain of reasoning from text to hypothesis. It is, however, limited by

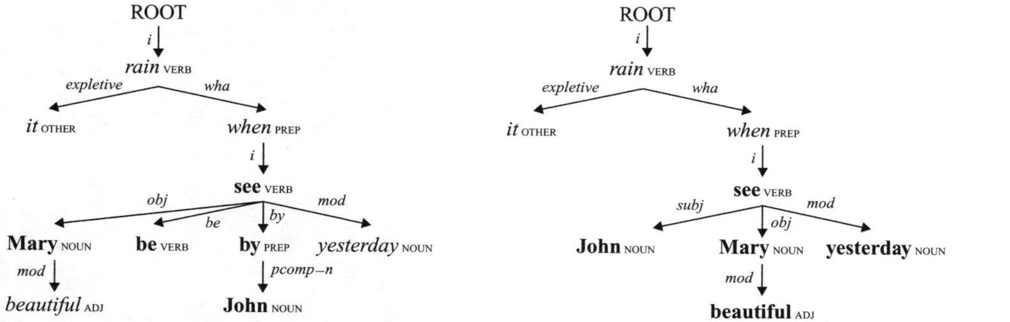

Source: It rained when beautiful Mary was seen by John yesterday

Derived: It rained when John saw beautiful Mary yesterday

(a) Application of passive to active transformation

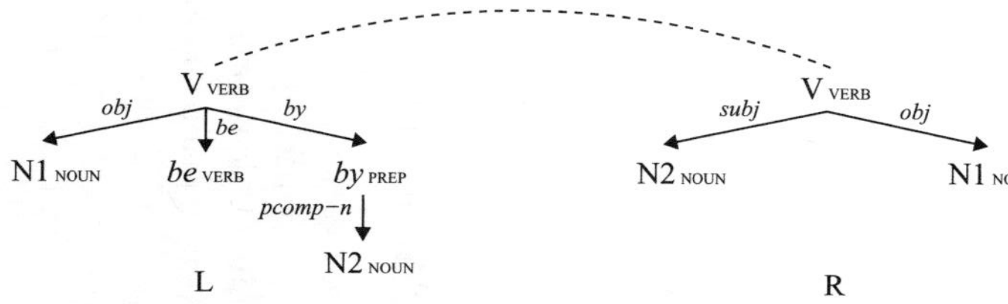

(b) Passive to active transformation (substitution rule). The dotted arc represents alignment.

Figure 6–12: Example of an application of inference rules, as given in Bar-Haim et al. [29]

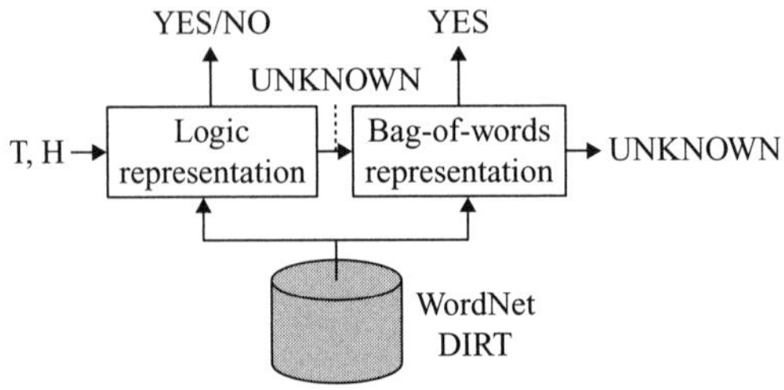

Figure 6–13: BLUE system architecture [32]

errors in the knowledge sources and the preprocessing stages such as parsing and semantic analysis. Further, according to the analysis presented in Clark and Harrison [33], the presence of some implicit knowledge in text, combined with lack of knowledge to bridge the semantic gap between the text and hypothesis, presently limits the performance of the system (61.5% on RTE 5).

One strong positive characteristic of this system is that it produces an explanation of its label, which allows us to identify sources of errors and to assess the reliability of the system: if the explanation is plausible for a given set of entailment examples, we may be more confident that this system will perform well on unseen examples from a similar domain.

6.4.5 Learning Alignment Independently of Entailment

De Marneffe et al. [35] investigate alignment independently of RTE, proposing that alignment be thought of as identifying *relevant* portions of the text, with the idea that it is simpler than determining which portions of the text entail portions of the hypothesis. They formalize alignment as an optimization problem that accounts for alignments of individual tokens in the hypothesis and of pairs of hypothesis tokens connected by a dependency edge. They use human-annotated alignment data to train their aligner, which they evaluate in its own right. This automatic aligner is the basis of the alignment step in the entailment system described in MacCartney, Grenager, and de Marneffe [36], where it is used as a source of features for a global classifier. They present a useful formulation of alignment in terms of an objective function. One drawback of their approach is that they require annotated alignment data to train their system, which is time- and resource-intensive to produce.

MacCartney, Galley, and Manning [37] generalize the alignment problem to the phrase level (where *phrase* simply means contiguous text span) and formalize the alignment score in terms of equality, substitution, insertion, and deletion of phrases in the text with respect to the hypothesis. They train this model using lexical alignment labelings generated by Brockett [38]. Although they report an improvement over two lexical-level alignment baselines, they did not observe significant differences in performance between the phrase-level system and a token-level alignment by the same system (i.e., where the phrase size is fixed at one token).

One limitation of this approach is that it appears to disregard known constituent boundaries and does not seem to offer a clean mechanism for applying specialized similarity resources in ways other than uniformly across all contiguous text spans. Moreover, it requires labeled alignment data, of which only a limited amount is available, and that too only at the token level. However, their solutions to the problems of training an aligner and of exploring the possible space of alignments at runtime are elegant and clearly described.

6.4.6 Leveraging Multiple Alignments for RTE

Two difficulties faced by RTE system developers who wish to use deeper NLP analytics are the integration of NLP analyses operating at different granularities (word, phrase, syntax, and predicate-argument levels) and the application of similarity metrics or other knowledge resources (such as rules) in a consistent way across these different layers of representation. In both alignment- and global similarity–based approaches to RTE, problems arise when trying to incorporate multiple knowledge resources because resources developed for different tasks may have incompatible outputs even when they all return real-valued scores. For example, a named entity metric may return a score of 0.6 that indicates relatively low similarity, while a WordNet-based metric may return the same value to indicate relatively high similarity: their scores are not compatible, because the same returned score does not have an equivalent meaning.

Sammons et al. [18] attempt to address both these problems, describing a multiview approach in which different sources of NLP analysis are represented in separate views of the data, though comparable levels of representation may be combined in the same view. Specialized knowledge resources are encoded as metrics operating on these individual views. Their system uses multiple alignments of the text and hypothesis in each entailment pair, separating views with incompatible metrics into separate alignments.

Features are defined over individual alignments, and also between alignments, on the basis of the observation that (for example) if lexical-level alignments or semantic role–based predicate-argument structure alignments indicate entailment, but alignments using numerical quantity metrics do not, this is a good indication that the text does not entail the hypothesis. These features are used to train a classifier.

The multiview, multialignment model allows a modular approach to integrating new NLP analytics and knowledge resources, and the machine learning–based inference component allows the system to determine the reliability of cues from different sources of analysis.

The system performs competitively with other alignment-based systems, scoring 66.6% on the RTE 5 two-way task.

6.4.7 Natural Logic

MacCartney and Manning [17] propose a framework based on a natural logic-based representation and inference process to address the textual entailment challenge. In this approach, valid inference patterns are characterized in terms of syntactic forms that are close to the original surface form without involving the full semantic interpretation.

The underlying idea is to break down the entailment process into a sequence of smaller entailment decisions, whereby portions of the text are compared to portions of the hypothesis and related by one of a closed set of operations that indicate the semantic relationship between the two. For example, semantic containment identifies when one concept generalizes another, whereas semantic exclusion indicates when one concept, if true, precludes the other being true.

They also classify context structures that affect the validity of a given relationship in admitting entailment of the hypothesis by the text. This is expressed in terms of polarity and monotonicity. Polarity must be compatible to permit entailment and accounts for negation and modal modifiers of predicates expressed in the entailment pair. Monotonicity specifies whether a text concept must be more general or more specific than its counterpart in the hypothesis and typically arises in specific types of construction such as universally quantified statements.

To determine entailment, the text is first represented as basic semantic relations (premises), and then a sequence of edit operations is applied to transform the premise to the hypothesis. For each edit operation, a lexical entailment relation is predicted using a statistical classifier, and these relations are propagated upward through a syntax tree, according to semantic properties of intermediate nodes. The final step composes the resulting entailment relations across the edit sequence.

This approach works well on simple sentences, such as those in the FraCaS corpus (Cooper et al. [39]), but it becomes much harder to reliably extract the basic premises from the texts in entailment pairs because world knowledge is often required to infer relations more closely reflecting the structure of those in the hypothesis. To apply the natural logic inference to the RTE task, Padó et al. [40] combine the alignment system described previously with a simple NatLog edit distance via a straightforward linear function and achieve a score of 62.7% on RTE 4.

6.4.8 Syntactic Tree Kernels

The SemKer system, proposed by Mehdad, Zanzotto, and Moschitti [41], uses syntactic tree kernels to define similarity between pairs of text trees and pairs of hypothesis trees drawn from each pair of entailment examples and extends the model with a similarity measure based on Wikipedia. The system uses a dependency tree—based representation, with abstraction of nodes via lexical/semantic match. SemKer computes the similarity between terms using the Syntactic Semantic Tree Kernel (SSTK) [42], which encodes lexical similarity in the fragment (subtree) matching.

The system has a preliminary lexical alignment stage, which establishes potential subtree-matching locations, called **anchors**. These focus the application of the subtree-matching component, which determines the final alignment between text and hypothesis for each entailment pair.

To train the inference model, these anchors are then abstracted into generic placeholders, and a second tree-kernel-based similarity function is applied to compare patterns of alignments between entailment pairs. The goal is to learn more general structural correspondences that apply over multiple entailment pairs. A support vector model is trained using this interpair distance metric and the entailment example labels; this model is applied at the inference step of their RTE system.

The system performed well on RTE 5, with 66.2% accuracy on the two-way labeling task (one of the top five scores). To capture the large variety of syntactic variations permitted in natural language text, and thereby improve its performance and capacity to generalize, this approach appears to need a lot more training data. It would be interesting to see how it performed if it were trained using the proprietary corpus described by Hickl [23].

6.4.9 Global Similarity Using Limited Dependency Context

Iftene and Moruz [20] developed the system that performed best in both the two- and three-way entailment tasks in RTE 5. The structure of their system, like that of many other successful systems, closely matches the one we described in Section 6.3.

In the preprocessing step, the text of the entailment pair is first normalized to expand contractions (e.g., *is not* instead of *isn't*) and replace some punctuation characters. This improves the performance of the off-the-shelf packages they use. The induced representation of the entailment pair is based on a dependency parse tree, enriched with named entity information. The preprocessing step also applies some custom resources that annotate specific relations (such as "work-for"), numerical quantities, and languages.

The alignment step comprises local and global scoring functions. First, each hypothesis constituent is mapped to the best candidate text constituent. This process includes the application of rules derived from WordNet, Wikipedia, VerbOcean, and other custom resources to identify possible mappings between dissimilar text—hypothesis term pairs; these mappings have associated scores. These local fitness scores also account for the parents of the nodes being compared and the types of dependency edges connecting them.

These local alignment scores are then integrated, and some adjustments are made on the basis of global characteristics of the alignment, such as whether the named entities in the hypothesis are matched by entities in the text and whether an aligned predicate is negated in one of the text and hypothesis but not the other.

The inference step applies two thresholds to the resulting score: a higher threshold that distinguishes between Entailed and Not Entailed, and a lower threshold that distinguishes between Unknown and Contradicted. These thresholds are tuned to maximize performance on the three-way task for the development set; the two-way labeling score is derived directly from the three-way labeling by combining the Unknown and Contradicted labels to generate Not Entailed labels.

This system achieved accuracies of 68.5% on the RTE 5 three-way task and 73.5% on the RTE 5 two-way task.

6.4.10 Latent Alignment Inference for RTE

Chang et al. [43] developed a joint learning approach that learns to make entailment decisions along with learning an intermediate representation that aligns texts and hypotheses. No supervision is assumed at the intermediate alignment level. They propose a general learning framework for RTE and other problems that require learning over intermediate representations.

The framework uses the declarative integer linear programming (ILP) inference formulation (see Chang, Ratinov, and Roth [44]), where the intermediate representation can be easily defined in terms of binary variables and knowledge can be injected as constraints in the model. The model assumes that all positive examples have *at least one* good intermediate representation (alignment), while negative examples have *no* good intermediate representation.

During training, if the model generates a good (valid) alignment—in the sense that the resulting entailment decision based on the features activated by this alignment is correct—the learning stage uses this as a positive example for the entailment classifier and also to provide feedback to the alignment model.

The text and hypothesis are represented as graphs, where the words and phrases are nodes and dependency relations between words form the edges. In addition, directed edges link verbs to the head words of their semantic-role-labeled arguments. The mappings between the nodes and edges in the text graph and the hypothesis graph define the alignment. These alignment variables are constrained using relations between word mappings and edge mappings: for instance, an edge mapping is active only if the corresponding word mappings are active.

One key aspect of this approach is that the alignment step is not specified as a separate, standalone task; rather, a space of alignment structures is defined, and the gold-standard training labels of the target application are used together with an optmization approach to determine the **optimal intermediate representation** for the target task, that is, the representation that maximizes performance on the target task. This obviates the need for expensive annotation efforts on the intermediate structure.

Chang et al. [43] apply their framework to transliteration discovery, paraphrase identification, and recognizing textual entailment. For the RTE task, the preprocessing step uses named entity, dependency parse, semantic role labeling, and coreference analysis and collapses them into a single, canonical graph structure. The graph-generation step uses similarity metrics for words and named entities (see Do et al. [45]) but also computes alignment edges between edges in the text and the hypothesis, where the edges' sources and sinks are also aligned.

The alignment and inference steps are integrated, with the optimal alignment and optimal entailment decisions based on the feature weights learned in the training process. Chang et al.'s system achieved an accuracy of 66.8% in the two-way task for the RTE 5 corpus.

6.5 Taking RTE Further

The results in Figure 6–2 show that there is still a long way to go before RTE can be considered a solved problem. From the various examples given throughout this chapter, it should be evident that reliably recognizing textual entailment requires many smaller entailment phenomena to be handled—such as identifying when two strings refer to the same underlying entity or applying background knowledge to infer something not explicitly stated in the text. In this section, we present some particularly important capabilities that are not yet (sufficiently) developed, to provide a possible focus for ongoing research.

6.5.1 Improve Analytics

All successful RTE approaches depend on input from other NLP tools. The more complex the annotation, the poorer the performance of the corresponding tool tends to be. Improving the performance of resources such as named entity recognizers and syntactic parsers will tend to improve the performance of RTE components that depend on them. This is particularly true of RTE systems like that of Bar-Haim et al. [29] that enrich the input using rules based on parse structure.

One functionality commonly identified as crucial to textual inference is coreference resolution. Although coreference systems achieve reasonable performance on purpose-built corpora, they (like other NLP applications) tend to perform significantly less well on raw text from other domains. This performance decrease is partly due to overfitting to the evaluation domain and partly due to assumptions made in the evaluations themselves. In particular, systems perform badly linking coreference of phrasal (i.e., nonpronominal) mentions to the correct entity.

6.5.2 Invent/Tackle New Problems

There are many linguistic phenomena that seem relevant to RTE but have no existing NLP resource; they may not even be widely recognized as necessary tasks by the NLP community. Such problems may lack relevant corpora even if they are recognized as potentially useful.

One example that seems particularly relevant is trace or parasitic gap recovery: identifying places in sentences where the writer implicitly refers to something, relying on the reader to fill in a gap on the basis of the context: for example, in the sentence *John sold apples, Jane oranges*, a human reader infers that the *sold* relation holds between *Jane* and *oranges*. Attempts at training syntactic parsers to recover traces, such as Dienes and Dubey [46], have had only limited success, in part because syntactic parsers are not error free and in part because the original annotation (see Marcus, Santorini, and Marcinkiewicz [47]) is not consistent.

A related problem is zero anaphora resolution. For example, in the sentence *One rainy day is bad enough, but three in a row are intolerable*, a human reader recognizes the *three* as referring to *three rainy days*. There are publications addressing this problem, but so far, no application has been made available that has been widely used by the community.

NLP tools typically tag only explicit content, and significant additional processing is required to solve the problems described here. If these problems were solved—for example, by identifying the places where content is missing, or better yet, by adding the missing content—some NLP analytics would generate more useful output from the perspective of RTE and also of other NLP tasks.

Another topic deserving long-term attention is discourse structure. The harder RTE examples require synthesis of information spread across multiple sentences; in the search task piloted in RTE 5, Mirkin et al. [48] observed that in some news articles, information from the headline is needed throughout the article to fully understand sentences. Certain relations between events, such as causality and timing, may be expressed by structures that are not restricted to single sentences—the boundary of many NLP tools. These very long-distance dependencies are signified by discourse structure, which is very much an open topic in NLP research. With the publication of the Penn Discourse Treebank [49], there is a resource suited to developing analysis of some classes of long-range dependencies.

6.5.3 Develop Knowledge Resources

There are many recognized entailment phenomena that are not strongly represented in the RTE corpora but are clearly needed for systems to achieve natural language understanding.

In particular, certain types of reasoning that human readers do without conscious effort are extremely challenging for an automated system. Some examples are causal and spatial reasoning (examples from the RTE 5 corpus are presented in Figures 6–14 and 6–15).

Causal reasoning relates to world knowledge a human can bring to bear that expresses domain-specific cause-and-effect relationships: for example, that bombs can explode and that explosions can cause injury and/or death to people.

In the entailment pair in Figure 6–14, a reader must infer that people exert force (weight) on structures they stand on and that too much weight on a bridge implies too many people; it is therefore valid to conclude that the cause of the bridge collapse can be expressed in the hypothesis as a result of *too much weight* instead of *too many people.*

In the entailment pair in Figure 6–15, the text states that political leaders in Baghdad and Washington are concerned about bombings, and then it gives details of three bombings. The reader must infer that *south of Baghdad* implies *in the Baghdad area* and that Abu Gharib, if only by virtue of being located in Iraq (which itself might be known via background geographical knowledge), can also be considered to be *in the Baghdad area*, at least in the given context.

Other types of reasoning, such as recognizing various kinship relations in order to identify strong connections in entailment pairs like that in Figure 6–16, are less generic but seem

Text: Local health department officials were quoted as saying that the bridge over the Santa Barbara river, in southern Peru's Ayacucho province, "broke in two" as students and teachers from four rural schools were crossing it while going home... Local police said the 120-meter bridge, made of wooden boards and slats held together by steel cables, collapsed because too many people were on it.

Hyp: The Peruvian bridge in Ayachuco province broke because of the weight on it.

Figure 6–14: RTE5 example (development set, text truncated) requiring understanding of causal relations

Text: Three major bombings in less than a week will be causing some anxiety among political leaders in Baghdad and Washington. Last Thursday 10 people were killed by a car bomb at a crowded cattle market in Babel province, south of Baghdad. On Sunday more than 30 died when a suicide bomber riding a motorbike blew himself up at a police academy in the capital. Tuesday's bombing in Abu Ghraib also killed and wounded a large number of people—including journalists and local officials.

Hyp: Some journalists and local officials were killed in one of the three bombings in the Baghdad area.

Figure 6–15: RTE5 example (development set, text truncated) requiring understanding of spatial relations

> **Text:** British newsreader Natasha Kaplinsky gave birth to a baby boy earlier this morning at around 08:30 BST. She had been on maternity leave since August 21. Kaplinsky had only been working with Five News just over a month when she announced she was pregnant. Her husband of three years, investment banker Justin Bower announced "We're absolutely thrilled."
>
> **Hyp:** Natasha Kaplinsky and Justin Bower got married three years ago.

Figure 6–16: RTE5 example (development set, text truncated) requiring understanding of kinship relations

well represented in NLP tasks. Here, the challenge is to specify the necessary knowledge in a consistent, sufficiently unambiguous way that is also accessible to RTE systems. The CYC database [50] is a vast repository of knowledge, painstakingly encoded in a consistent logical form; but it is not widely used precisely because its representation constrains its use. Lin and Pantel's DIRT rules [51], however, are widely considered to be in a usable form (dependency tree paths with slots for entities) but too noisy to be of practical use (see Clark and Harrison [33] and the ablation study in Bentivogli et al. [5] for some examples). The kinds of "facts" identified by OpenIE approaches like TextRunner [52] are also noisy and have yet to be proven useful in RTE.

Noise-free sets of rules for common domains, in an appropriate representation, would be a valuable asset; Szpektor et al. [53] propose a promising representation.

6.5.4 Better RTE Evaluation

The current evaluation of RTE focuses mainly on absolute performance, reporting the accuracy of a given system in predicting one of two labels (Entailed and Not Entailed) for the two-way task or one of three labels (Entailed Contradicted, and Unknown) for the three-way task. One problem for RTE researchers is that from the human reasoning perspective, predicting this label requires many other entailment decisions to be made, and another is that the single final label does not tell us anything about the way the system handles those smaller decisions. In the example in Figure 6–15, a human reader must reason that there are three bombing events reported in the text, that the phrase *including journalists and local officials* represents entities specified by *a large number of people*, and that the three separate locations mentioned in the text are all in the Baghdad area. Without knowing what the system actually did to handle each of these problems, we cannot reliably predict how the approach used by the system will handle new entailment problems requiring similar kinds of inference: a system might incorrectly predict the entailment label but might be reliably resolving inferences requiring spatial reasoning, for example. If reliable solutions for entailment subproblems are developed, it is in the interest of the RTE community to recognize and reuse them to avoid duplication of effort and focus attention on other needed capabilities.

There are two obvious solutions to this problem: require systems to generate explanations of their answers and/or annotate RTE examples with more information than the present binary or ternary label.

At least one RTE system (Clark and Harrison [33]) already generates explanations that are useful in identifying flaws in its knowledge resources, though it is strongly dependent on its formal logical inference process, which is brittle in the face of noisy inputs. But even with this, the steps in the explanation are not always clear, and it is not self-evident that the kinds of steps made by a human reasoner can all be accommodated in a transparent way in this formalism.

A standard format for explanation—and a corresponding annotation of entailment examples—would be a step forward to making it possible for RTE system builders to work on explanation generation in a systematic, coordinated way rather than each following an independent direction.

A second option is to annotate RTE examples more fully but without committing to a particular representation for explanations. As a partial measure, an annotation standard for determining and recording the entailment phenomena that are required to predict the entailment label for an entailment pair would allow at least an approximate understanding of which capabilities a given RTE system has by checking the correlations between correctly labeled examples and the active entailment phenomena.

In addition, such labeling would allow researchers to quickly extract entailment corpora with specific characteristics, allowing evaluation of phenomena-specific resources in the context of RTE performance. These questions are raised, and an annotation standard proposed, in Sammons, Vydiswaran, and Roth [54].

6.6 Useful Resources

This section gives some information about resources used by some of the RTE systems evaluated in the RTE challenges.

6.6.1 Publications

Many RTE researchers participate in the NIST TAC RTE challenge, which publishes data sets and descriptions of participating RTE systems at its website.[12] You can find pointers to additional research publications on RTE at the ACL RTE portal.[13] Other publications relating to RTE appear in conferences such as ACL, EMNLP, COLING, and AAAI; ACL and EMNLP papers are available online via the ACL anthology.[14]

6.6.2 Knowledge Resources

The ACL RTE portal also has pointers to some useful knowledge resources,[15] such as collections of rules, some of which are mentioned in the case studies in Section 6.4.

12. http://www.nist.gov/tac/
13. http://www.aclweb.org/aclwiki/index.php?title=Textual_Entailment
14. http://aclweb.org/anthology-new/
15. http://www.aclweb.org/aclwiki/index.php?title=RTE_Knowledge_Resources

The ACL RTE portal also has several complete RTE systems available for download.

6.6.3 Natural Language Processing Packages

Some popular NLP frameworks are LingPipe,[16] UIMA,[17] NLTK,[18] and GATE,[19] though there are other publicly available frameworks. Some of these frameworks also offer NLP modules for named entity recognition, coreference, segmentation, and so on. We have also found Thrift[20] and XML RPC libraries (such as that of Apache[21]) to be useful resources for distributing NLP tools across multiple computers.

A number of research groups make NLP annotation tools available. Stanford[22] offers a POS tagger, syntactic parser, and named entity recognizer, together with some resources to simplify some NLP programming tasks. The Cognitive Computation group[23] offers a large suite of NLP tools, including the state-of-the-art Illinois named entity tagger, coreference resolver, POS tagger, chunker (shallow parser), and semantic role labeler. They have also released their Named Entity and Lexical similarity metrics (Illinois-NESim and Illinois-WNSim). They also offer Learning-Based Java (LBJ), an extension to the Java programming language, which simplifies development and deployment of machine learning techniques as integral parts of Java applications and includes some useful NLP tools such as a sentence-level and word-level segmenter. Many researchers use syntactic parsers by Michael Collins,[24] Dan Bikel,[25] and Eugene Charniak.[26]

There are many more implementations of these and other NLP tools and even more publications describing unpublished applications. Those listed in this section are a popular subset that should help you to get started.

6.7 Summary

The RTE task provides a general, representation-agnostic framework for semantic inference in text processing, allowing researchers to entertain a wide range of approaches to solve the problem. The approach of the NLP community to other textual inference problems like named entity recognition and resolution has been to tackle "component" inference tasks that can be thought of as part of some unspecified, comprehensive inference process. A popular approach to RTE is to think of it as a framework that integrates (subsets of) these components in a way that fills in the gaps of this overarching process; it is in this spirit that we have proposed the RTE framework described in this chapter.

16. http://alias-i.com/lingpipe/
17. http://incubator.apache.org/uima/
18. http://www.nltk.org/
19. http://gate.ac.uk/
20. http://incubator.apache.org/thrift/
21. http://ws.apache.org/xmlrpc/
22. http://nlp.stanford.edu
23. http://L2R.cs.uiuc.edu/cogcomp
24. http://people.csail.mit.edu/mcollins/code.html
25. http://www.cis.upenn.edu/~dbikel/software.html
26. ftp://ftp.cs.brown.edu/pub/nlparser/

We sought to address several distinct requirements that are in tension with each other:

- The ability to incorporate an arbitrary selection of existing NLP resources, which may not be consistent in granularity (word vs. phrase vs. predicate-argument structure), formalism, or availability across languages.
- The flexibility to accommodate developer constraints such as engineering effort and runtime complexity.
- The capacity to add new NLP analytics and knowledge resources in a modular way.
- The versatility to allow developers to use a range of approaches to inference.

The concept of alignment is a natural way to think about the RTE problem because it allows the modularization of knowledge resources via a multiview representation of enriched text in tandem with specialized, constituent-level similarity metrics. At the system level, this allows straightforward extension of the different stages to accommodate new resources.

The framework we propose is designed with respect to dominant approaches to developing NLP resources in various languages and is intended to allow development in any language for which appropriate resources are available. It also allows for a trade-off between representational expressivity and computational speed: if shallower (less structured) knowledge resources and NLP analytics are used, a simpler inference algorithm and swifter processing will result. This also accommodates users working in languages with fewer NLP resources: although sophisticated inference may be limited by availability of NLP resources, it is still possible to develop an RTE system working at a shallower level of representation.

In our survey of promising research in the field, we have illustrated different approaches to various aspects of the RTE problem, including representation, application of background knowledge resources, approaches to alignment, and inference techniques. To allow readers to incorporate insights from these works into their own RTE systems, we indicated how the execution of each approach matches the framework we specified.

RTE is a complex problem, and solutions require significant planning and effort. Our goal has been to provide you with the tools to quickly get started within a model that can be extended to accommodate improvements in specific subtasks and a roadmap of relevant research and useful resources.

Bibliography

[1] E. Hovy, "Learning by reading: An experiment in text analysis," in *Text, Speech and Dialog*, vol. 4188 of *Lecture Notes in Computer Science*, pp. 3–12, Berlin: Springer, 2006.

[2] Homeland Security Newswire, "DARPA awards BBN $30 million in machine reading project," 2009. http://www.homelandsecuritynewswire.com/darpa-awards-bbn-30-million-machine-reading-project.

[3] I. Dagan, O. Glickman, and B. Magnini, "The PASCAL Recognising Textual Entailment Challenge," *Lecture Notes in Computer Science*, no. 3944, pp. 177–190, 2006.

[4] M.-C. de Marneffe, A. N. Rafferty, and C. D. Manning, "Finding contradictions in text," in *Proceedings of ACL-08: HLT*, pp. 1039–1047, 2008.

[5] L. Bentivogli, I. Dagan, H. T. Dang, D. Giampiccolo, and B. Magnini, "The fifth PASCAL Recognizing Textual Entailment Challenge," in *Proceedings of the 2nd Text Analysis Conference (TAC)*, 2009.

[6] Y. Mehdad and B. Magnini, "A word overlap baseline for the recognizing textual entailment task," 2009. http://hlt.fbk.eu/sites/hlt.fbk.eu/files/baseline.pdf.

[7] H. Dang and K. Owczarzak, "Overview of the TAC 2009 summarization track," in *Proceedings of the 2nd Text Analysis Conference (TAC)*, 2009.

[8] S. Harabagiu and A. Hickl, "Methods for using textual entailment in open-domain question answering," in *Proceedings of the 21st International Conference on Computational Linguistics and 44th Annual Meeting of the Association for Computational Linguistics*, pp. 905–912, 2006.

[9] A. Celikyilmaz, M. Thint, and Z. Huang, "A graph-based semi-supervised learning for question-answering," in *Proceedings of the Annual Meeting of the Association of Computational Linguistics*, pp. 719–727, 2009.

[10] D. Roth, M. Sammons, and V. Vydiswaran, "A framework for entailed relation recognition," in *Proceedings of the Annual Meeting of the Association of Computational Linguistics (ACL)*, 2009.

[11] S. Padó, M. Galley, D. Jurafsky, and C. D. Manning, "Robust machine translation evaluation with entailment features," in *Proceedings of the 47th Annual Meeting of the Association for Computational Linguistics and the 4th International Joint Conference on Natural Language Processing of the AFNLP*, pp. 297–305, 2009.

[12] N. Chambers, D. Cer, T. Grenager, D. Hall, C. Kiddon, B. MacCartney, M.-C. de Marneffe, D. Ramage, E. Yen, and C. D. Manning, "Learning alignments and leveraging natural logic," in *Proceedings of the ACL-PASCAL Workshop on Textual Entailment and Paraphrasing*, pp. 165–170, 2007.

[13] S. Mirkin, L. Specia, N. Cancedda, I. Dagan, M. Dymetman, and I. Szpektor, "Source-language entailment modeling for translating unknown terms," in *Proceedings of the 47th Annual Meeting of the Association for Computational Linguistics and the 4th International Joint Conference on Natural Language Processing of the AFNLP*, pp. 791–799, 2009.

[14] C. Fellbaum, *WordNet: An Electronic Lexical Database.* Cambridge, MA: MIT Press, 1998.

[15] D. Roth and M. Sammons, "A unified representation and inference paradigm for natural language processing," Tech. Rep. UIUCDCS-R-2008-2969, UIUC Computer Science Department, 2008.

[16] G. Miller, R. Beckwith, C. Fellbaum, D. Gross, and K. Miller, "Wordnet: An on-line lexical database," *International Journal of Lexicography*, vol. 3, no. 4, pp. 235–312, 1990.

[17] B. MacCartney and C. D. Manning, "An extended model of natural logic," in *The 8th International Conference on Computational Semantics (IWCS-8)*, 2009.

[18] M. Sammons, V. Vydiswaran, T. Vieira, N. Johri, M.-W. Chang, D. Goldwasser, V. Srikumar, G. Kundu, Y. Tu, K. Small, J. Rule, Q. Do, and D. Roth, "Relation alignment for textual entailment recognition," in *Proceedings of the 2nd Text Analysis Conference (TAC)*, 2009.

[19] R. Wang, Y. Zhang, and G. Neumann, "A joint syntactic-semantic representation for recognizing textual relatedness," in *Notebook Papers and Results, Text Analysis Conference (TAC)*, pp. 133–139, 2009.

[20] A. Iftene and M.-A. Moruz, "Uaic participation at RTE5," in *Notebook Papers and Results, Text Analysis Conference (TAC)*, pp. 367–376, 2009.

[21] A. Hickl and J. Bensley, "A discourse commitment-based framework for recognizing textual entailment," in *Proceedings of the ACL-PASCAL Workshop on Textual Entailment and Paraphrasing*, pp. 171–176, 2007.

[22] S. Harabagiu and A. Hickl, "Methods for using textual entailment in open-domain question answering," in *Proceedings of the 21st International Conference on Computational Linguistics and 44th Annual Meeting of the Association for Computational Linguistics*, pp. 905–912, 2006.

[23] A. Hickl, "Using discourse commitments to recognize textual entailment," in *Proceedings of the 22nd International Conference on Computational Linguistics (COLING)*, 2008.

[24] V. Punyakanok, D. Roth, and W. Yih, "Natural language inference via dependency tree mapping: An application to question answering," 2004. http://hdl.handle.net/2142/11100.

[25] M. Koulyekov and B. Magnini, "Recognizing textual entailment with tree edit distance algorithms," in *Proceedings of RTE 2005*, 2005.

[26] Y. Mehdad, M. Negri, E. Cabrio, M. Kouylekov, and B. Magnini, "Edits: An open source framework for recognizing textual entailment," in *Notebook Papers and Results, Text Analysis Conference (TAC)*, pp. 169–178, 2009.

[27] Y. Mehdad, M. Negri, E. Cabrio, M. Kouylekov, and B. Magnini, "EDITS: An open source framework for recognizing textual entailment," in *Proceedings of the 2nd Text Analysis Conference (TAC)*, pp. 169–178, 2009.

[28] T. Chklovski and P. Pantel, "VerbOcean: Mining the web for fine-grained semantic verb relations," in *Proceedings of Conference on Empirical Methods in Natural Language Processing (EMNLP-04)*, pp. 33–40, 2004.

[29] R. Bar-Haim, I. Dagan, I. Greental, I. Szpektor, and M. Friedman, "Semantic inference at the lexical-syntactic level for textual entailment recognition," in *Proceedings of the ACL-PASCAL Workshop on Textual Entailment and Paraphrasing*, pp. 131–136, 2007.

[30] R. Braz, R. Girju, V. Punyakanok, D. Roth, and M. Sammons, "An inference model for semantic entailment in natural language," in *Proceedings of the National Conference on Artificial Intelligence (AAAI)*, pp. 1678–1679, 2005.

[31] R. Bar-Haim, I. Dagan, S. Mirkin, E. Shnarch, I. Szpektor, J. Berant, and I. Greenthal, "Efficient semantic deduction and approximate matching over compact parse forests," in *Proceedings of the 1st Text Analysis Conference (TAC)*, 2008.

[32] P. Clark and P. Harrison, "An inference-based approach to recognizing entailment," in *Proceedings of the 2nd Text Analysis Conference (TAC)*, pp. 63–72, 2009.

[33] P. Clark and P. Harrison, "An inference-based approach to recognizing entailment," in *Notebook Papers and Results, Text Analysis Conference (TAC)*, pp. 63–72, 2009.

[34] P. Harrison and M. Maxwell, "A new implementation of GPSG," in *Proceedings of the 6th Canadian Conference on AI (CSCSI'86)*, pp. 78–83, 1986.

[35] M.-C. de Marneffe, T. Grenager, B. MacCartney, D. Cer, D. Ramage, C. Kiddon, and C. D. Manning, "Aligning semantic graphs for textual inference and machine reading," in *AAAI Spring Symposium at Stanford 2007*, 2007.

[36] B. MacCartney, T. Grenager, and M. de Marneffe, "Learning to recognize features of valid textual entailments," in *Proceedings of RTE-NAACL 2006*, 2006.

[37] B. MacCartney, M. Galley, and C. D. Manning, "A phrase-based alignment model for natural language inference," in *Proceedings of the Conference on Empirical Methods in Natural Language Processing (EMNLP-2008)*, 2008.

[38] C. Brockett, "Aligning the RTE 2006 corpus," Tech. Rep. MSR-TR-2007-77, Microsoft Research, 2007.

[39] R. Cooper, D. Crouch, J. V. Eijck, C. Fox, J. V. Genabith, J. Jaspars, H. Kamp, D. Milward, M. Pinkal, M. Poesio, and S. Pulman, "Using the framework," Tech. Rep., The FRACAS Consortium, 1996.

[40] S. Padó, M.-C. de Marneffe, B. MacCartney, A. N. Rafferty, E. Yeh, and C. D. Manning, "Deciding entailment and contradiction with stochastic and edit distance-based alignment," in *Proceedings of the 1st Text Analysis Conference (TAC)*, 2008.

[41] Y. Mehdad, F. M. Zanzotto, and A. Moschitti, "SemKer: Syntactic/semantic kernels for recognizing textual entailment," in *Notebook Papers and Results, Text Analysis Conference (TAC)*, pp. 259–265, 2009.

[42] S. Bloehdorn and A. Moschitti, "Combined syntactic and semantic kernels for text classification," in *Proceedings of the 29th European Conference on IR Research (ECIR)*, 2007.

[43] M.-W. Chang, D. Goldwasser, D. Roth, and V. Srikumar, "Discriminative learning over constrained latent representations," in *Proceedings of the Human Language Technology Conference of the North American Chapter of the Association for Computational Linguistics (HLT/NAACL)*, pp. 429–437, 2010.

[44] M. Chang, L. Ratinov, and D. Roth, "Constraints as prior knowledge," in *ICML Workshop on Prior Knowledge for Text and Language Processing*, pp. 32–39, July 2008.

[45] Q. Do, D. Roth, M. Sammons, Y. Tu, and V. Vydiswaran, "Robust, lightweight approaches to compute lexical similarity," Computer Science Research and Technical Reports, University of Illinois, 2010. http://L2R.cs.uiuc.edu/~danr/Papers/DRSTV10.pdf.

[46] P. Dienes and A. Dubey, "Antecedent recovery: Experiments with a trace tagger," in *Proceedings of the 2003 Conference on Empirical Methods in Natural Language Processing*, pp. 33–40, 2003.

[47] M. P. Marcus, B. Santorini, and M. A. Marcinkiewicz, "Building a large annotated corpus of English: The Penn Treebank," *Computational Linguistics*, vol. 19, no. 2, pp. 313–330, 1994.

[48] S. Mirkin, R. Bar-Haim, E. Shnarch, A. Stern, and I. Szpektor, "Addressing discourse and document structure in the RTE search task," in *Proceedings of the 2nd Text Analysis Conference (TAC)*, 2009.

[49] R. Prasad, N. Dinesh, A. Lee, E. Miltsakaki, L. Robaldo, A. Joshi, and B. Webber, "The Penn Discourse Treebank 2.0," in *Proceedings of the 6th International Conference on Language Resources and Evaluation (LREC 2008)*, 2008.

[50] C. Matuszek, J. Cabral, M. Witbrock, and J. DeOliveira, "An introduction to the syntax and content of CYC," in *Proceedings of the 2006 AAAI Spring Symposium on Formalizing and Compiling Background Knowledge and Its Applications to Knowledge Representation and Question Answering*, 2006.

[51] D. Lin and P. Pantel, "DIRT: Discovery of inference rules from text," in *Proceedings of ACM SIGKDD Conference on Knowledge Discovery and Data Mining 2001*, pp. 323–328, 2001.

[52] A. Yates, M. Banko, M. Broadhead, M. Cafarella, O. Etzioni, and S. Soderland, "TextRunner: Open information extraction on the web," in *Proceedings of Human Language Technologies: The Annual Conference of the North American Chapter of the Association for Computational Linguistics (NAACL-HLT)*, pp. 25–26, 2007.

[53] I. Szpektor, I. Dagan, R. Bar-Haim, and J. Goldberger, "Contextual preferences," in *Proceedings of the Annual Meeting of the Association for Computational Linguistics (ACL) with the Human Language Technology Conference (HLT) of the North American Chapter of the ACL*, pp. 683–691, 2008.

[54] M. Sammons, V. Vydiswaran, and D. Roth, ""Ask not what Textual Entailment can do for you..."," in *Proceedings of the 48th Annual Meeting of the Association for Computational Linguistics*, pp. 1199–1208, 2010.

Chapter 7

Multilingual Sentiment and Subjectivity Analysis

Carmen Banea, Rada Mihalcea, and Janyce Wiebe

7.1 Introduction

Subjectivity and sentiment analysis focuses on the automatic identification of private states, such as opinions, emotions, sentiments, evaluations, beliefs, and speculations in natural language. While subjectivity classification labels text as either subjective or objective, sentiment classification adds an additional level of granularity by further classifying subjective text as either positive, negative, or neutral.

To date, a large number of text-processing applications have already used techniques for automatic sentiment and subjectivity analysis, including automatic expressive text-to-speech synthesis [1], tracking sentiment timelines in online forums and news [2, 3], and mining opinions from product reviews [4]. In many natural language processing tasks, subjectivity and sentiment classification have been used as a first-phase filtering to generate more viable data. Research that benefited from this additional layering ranges from question answering [5] to conversation summarization [6] and text semantic analysis [7, 8].

Much of the research work to date on sentiment and subjectivity analysis has been applied to English, but work on other languages, including Japanese [9, 10, 11, 12], Chinese [13, 14], German [15], and Romanian [16, 17], is growing. In addition, several participants in the Chinese and Japanese opinion-extraction tasks of NTCIR-6 [18] performed subjectivity and sentiment analysis in languages other than English.[1]

As only 29.4% of Internet users speak English,[2] the construction of resources and tools for subjectivity and sentiment analysis in languages other than English is a growing need. In this chapter, we review the main directions of research focusing on the development of resources and tools for multilingual subjectivity and sentiment analysis. Specifically, we identify and overview three main categories of methods: (i) those focusing on word- and phrase-level annotations, overviewed in Section 7.4, (ii) methods targeting the labeling of sentences, described in Section 7.5, and (iii) methods for document-level annotations, presented in Section 7.6.

1. NTCIR is a series of evaluation workshops sponsored by the Japan Society for the Promotion of Science, targeting tasks such as information retrieval, text summarization, information extraction, and others. NTCIR-6, 7 and 8 included an evaluation of multilingual opinion analysis on Chinese, English, and Japanese.
2. www.internetworldstats.com/stats.htm, June 30, 2008.

We address both multilingual and crosslingual methods. For multilingual methods, we review work concerned with languages other than English, where the resources and tools have been specifically developed for a given target language. In this category, in Section 7.3, we also briefly overview the main directions of work on English data, highlighting the methods that can be easily ported to other languages. For crosslingual approaches, we describe several methods that have been proposed to leverage on the resources and tools available in English by using crosslingual projections.

7.2 Definitions

An important kind of information conveyed in many types of written and spoken discourse is the mental or emotional state of the writer or speaker or some other entity referenced in the discourse. News articles, for example, often report emotional responses to a story in addition to the facts. Editorials, reviews, weblogs, and political speeches convey the opinions, beliefs, or intentions of the writer or speaker. A student engaged in a tutoring session may express his or her understanding or uncertainty. Quirk et al. give us a general term, **private state**, for referring to these mental and emotional states [19]. In their words, a private state is a state that is not open to objective observation or verification: "a person may be observed to assert that God exists, but not to believe that God exists. Belief is in this sense 'private'." A term for the linguistic expression of private states, adapted from literary theory [20], is **subjectivity**. **Subjectivity analysis** is the task of identifying when a private state is being expressed and identifying attributes of the private state. Attributes of private states include who is expressing the private state, the type(s) of attitude being expressed, about whom or what the private state is being expressed, the polarity of the private state (i.e., whether it is positive or negative), and so on. For example, consider the following sentence:

> The choice of Miers was praised by the Senate's top Democrat, Harry Reid of Nevada.

In this sentence, the phrase *was praised by* indicates that a private state is being expressed. The private state, according to the writer of the sentence, is being expressed by Reid, and it is about the choice of Miers, who was nominated to the Supreme Court by President Bush in October 2005. The type of the attitude is a sentiment (an evaluation, emotion, or judgment), and the polarity is positive [21].

This chapter is primarily concerned with detecting the presence of subjectivity, and further, identifying its polarity. These judgments may be made along several dimensions. One dimension is context. On the one hand, we may judge the subjectivity and polarity of words, out of context: *love* is subjective and positive, while *hate* is subjective and negative. At the other extreme, we have "full" contextual interpretation of language as it is being used in a text or dialog. In fact, there is a continuum from one to the other, and we can define several natural language processing tasks along this continuum.

The first is developing a word-level subjectivity lexicon, a list of keywords that have been gathered together because they have subjective usages; polarity information is often added to such lexicons. In addition to *love* and *hate*, other examples are *brilliant* and *interest* (positive polarity) and *alarm* (negative polarity).

We can also classify word **senses** according to their subjectivity and polarity. Consider, for example, the following two senses of *interest* from WordNet [22]:

- Interest, involvement—(a sense of concern with and curiosity about someone or something; "an interest in music")
- Interest—a fixed charge for borrowing money; usually a percentage of the amount borrowed; "how much interest do you pay on your mortgage?"

The first sense is subjective, with positive polarity. But the second sense is not (nonsubjective senses are called **objective** senses)—it does not refer to a private state. For another example, consider the senses of the noun *difference*:

- difference—(the quality of being unlike or dissimilar) "there are many differences between jazz and rock"
- deviation, divergence, departure, difference (a variation that deviates from the standard or norm) "the deviation from the mean"
- dispute, difference, difference of opinion, conflict (a disagreement or argument about something important) "he had a dispute with his wife"
- difference (a significant change) "his support made a real difference"
- remainder, difference (the number that remains after subtraction)

The first, second, and fifth of these definitions are objective. The others are subjective. Interestingly, the third sense has negative polarity (referring to conflict between people), while the fourth sense has positive polarity.

Word- and sense-level subjectivity lexicons are important because they are useful resources for **contextual subjectivity analysis** [23]—recognizing and extracting private state expressions in an actual text or dialog. We can judge the subjectivity and polarity of texts at several different levels. At the document level, we can ask if a text is opinionated and, if so, whether it is mainly positive or negative. We can perform a more fine-grained analysis and ask if a sentence expresses any subjectivity. For instance, consider the following examples from Wilson [23]. The first sentence is subjective (and has positive polarity), but the second one is objective, because it does not contain any subjective expressions:

- He spins a riveting plot which grabs and holds the reader's interest.
- The notes do not pay interest.

Even further, individual expressions may be judged: for example, *spins, riveting,* and *interest* in the first sentence may be judged as subjective expressions. A more interesting example appears in this sentence: *Cheers to Timothy Whitfield for the wonderfully horrid visuals.* While *horrid* would be listed as having negative polarity in a word-level subjectivity lexicon, in this context, it is being used positively: *wonderfully horrid* expresses a positive sentiment toward the visuals (similarly, *Cheers* expresses a positive sentiment toward *Timothy Whitfield*).

7.3 Sentiment and Subjectivity Analysis on English

Before we describe the work that has been carried out for multilingual sentiment and subjectivity analysis, we briefly overview the main lines of research carried out on English, along with the most frequently used resources that have been developed for this language. Several of these English resources and tools have been used as a starting point to build resources in other languages, via crosslingual projections or monolingual and multilingual bootstrapping. As described in more detail shortly, in crosslingual projection, annotated data in a second language is created by projecting the annotations from a source (usually major) language across a parallel text. In multilingual bootstrapping, in addition to the annotations obtained via crosslingual projections, monolingual corpora in the source and target languages are also used in conjunction with bootstrapping techniques such as cotraining, which often lead to additional improvements.

7.3.1 Lexicons

One of the most frequently used lexicons is perhaps the subjectivity and sentiment lexicon provided with the OpinionFinder distribution [24]. The lexicon was compiled from manually developed resources augmented with entries learned from corpora. It contains 6,856 unique entries, out of which 990 are multiword expressions. The entries in the lexicon have been labeled for part of speech as well as for reliability: those that appear most often in subjective contexts are *strong* clues of subjectivity, while those that appear less often, but still more often than expected by chance, are labeled *weak*. Each entry is also associated with a polarity label, indicating whether the corresponding word or phrase is positive, negative, or neutral. To illustrate, consider the following entry from the OpinionFinder lexicon: *type=strongsubj word1=agree pos1=verb mpqapolarity=weakpos*, which indicates that the word *agree* when used as a *verb* is a strong clue of subjectivity and has a polarity that is weakly positive.

Another lexicon that has been often used in polarity analysis is the General Inquirer [25]. It is a dictionary of about 10,000 words grouped into about 180 categories, which have been widely used for content analysis. It includes semantic classes (e.g., animate, human), verb classes (e.g., negatives, becoming verbs), cognitive orientation classes (e.g., causal, knowing, perception), and others. Two of the largest categories in the General Inquirer are the valence classes, which form a lexicon of 1,915 positive words and 2,291 negative words.

SentiWordNet [26] is a resource for opinion mining built on top of WordNet, which assigns each synset in WordNet with a score triplet (positive, negative, and objective), indicating the strength of each of these three properties for the words in the synset. The SentiWordNet annotations were automatically generated, starting with a set of manually labeled synsets. Currently, SentiWordNet includes an automatic annotation for all the synsets in WordNet, totaling more than 100,000 words.

7.3.2 Corpora

Subjectivity and sentiment annotated corpora are useful not only as a means to train automatic classifiers, but also as resources to extract opinion mining lexicons. For instance, a large number of the entries in the OpinionFinder lexicon mentioned in the previous section were derived based on a large opinion-annotated corpus.

The MPQA corpus [27] was collected and annotated as part of a 2002 workshop on Multi-Perspective Question Answering (thus the MPQA acronym). It is a collection of 535 English-language news articles from a variety of news sources manually annotated for opinions and other private states (beliefs, emotions, sentiments, speculations, etc.). The corpus was originally annotated at clause and phrase levels, but sentence-level annotations associated with the data set can also be derived via simple heuristics [24].

Another manually annotated corpus is the collection of newspaper headlines created and used during the recent SEMEVAL task on affective text [28]. The data set consists of 1,000 test headlines and 200 development headlines, each of them annotated with the six Eckman emotions (anger, disgust, fear, joy, sadness, surprise) and their polarity orientation (positive, negative).

Two other data sets, both of them covering the domain of movie reviews, are a polarity data set consisting of 1,000 positive and 1,000 negative reviews and a subjectivity data set consisting of 5,000 subjective and 5,000 objective sentences. Both data sets were introduced in Pang and Lee [29] and have been used to train opinion-mining classifiers. Given the domain-specificity of these collections, they were found to lead to accurate classifiers for data belonging to the same or similar domains.

7.3.3 Tools

A large number of approaches have been developed to date for sentiment and subjectivity analysis in English. The methods can be roughly classified into two categories: rule-based systems, relying on manually or semiautomatically constructed lexicons, and machine learning classifiers, trained on opinion-annotated corpora.

Among the rule-based systems, one of the most frequently used is OpinionFinder [24], which automatically annotates the subjectivity of new text based on the presence (or absence) of words or phrases in a large lexicon. Briefly, the OpinionFinder high-precision classifier relies on three main heuristics to label subjective and objective sentences: (i) if two or more strong subjective expressions occur in the same sentence, the sentence is labeled Subjective; (ii) if no strong subjective expressions occur in a sentence, and at most two weak subjective expressions occur in the previous, current, and next sentence combined, then the sentence is labeled Objective; (iii) otherwise, if none of the previous rules apply, the sentence is labeled Unknown. The classifier uses the clues from a subjectivity lexicon and the rules mentioned previously to harvest subjective and objective sentences from a large amount of unannotated text; this data is then used to automatically identify a set of extraction patterns, which are then used iteratively to identify a larger set of subjective and objective sentences.

In addition to the high-precision classifier, OpinionFinder includes a high-coverage classifier. This high-precision classifier is used to automatically produce an English-labeled data set, which can then be used to train a high-coverage subjectivity classifier.

When evaluated on the MPQA corpus, the high-precision classifier was found to lead to a precision of 86.7% and a recall of 32.6%, whereas the high-coverage classifier has a precision of 79.4% and a recall of 70.6%.

Another unsupervised system worth mentioning, this time based on automatically labeled words or phrases, is the one proposed by Turney [30], which builds on earlier work by Hatzivassiloglou and McKeown [31]. Starting with two reference words, *excellent* and *poor*, Turney classifies the polarity of a word or phrase by measuring the fraction between its pointwise mutual information (PMI) with the positive reference (excellent) and the PMI with the negative reference (poor).[3] The polarity scores assigned in this way are used to automatically annotate the polarity of product, company, or movie reviews. Note that this system is completely unsupervised and thus particularly appealing for application to other languages.

Finally, when annotated corpora is available, machine learning methods are a natural choice for building subjectivity and sentiment classifiers. For example, Wiebe, Bruce, and O'Hara [32] used a data set manually annotated for subjectivity to train a machine learning classifier, which led to significant improvements over the baseline. Similarly, starting with semiautomatically constructed data sets, Pang and Lee [29] built classifiers for subjectivity annotation at sentence level as well as a classifier for sentiment annotation at document level. To the extent that annotated data is available, such machine learning classifiers can be used equally well in other languages.

7.4 Word- and Phrase-Level Annotations

The development of resources and tools for sentiment and subjectivity analysis often starts with the construction of a lexicon, consisting of words and phrases annotated for sentiment or subjectivity. Such lexicons are successfully used to build rule-based classifiers for automatic opinion annotation by primarily considering the presence (or absence) of the lexicon entries in a text.

Three main directions have been considered so far for word- and phrase-level annotations: (i) manual annotations, which involve human judgment of selected words and phrases, (ii) automatic annotations based on knowledge sources such as dictionaries, and (iii) automatic annotations based on information derived from corpora.

7.4.1 Dictionary-Based

One of the simplest approaches that have been attempted for building opinion lexicons in a new language is the translation of an existing source language lexicon by using a bilingual dictionary. Mihalcea, Banea, and Wiebe [16] generated a subjectivity lexicon for Romanian by starting with the English subjectivity lexicon from OpinionFinder (described in §7.3.1) and translating it using an English-Romanian bilingual dictionary.

Several challenges were encountered in the translation process. First, although the English subjectivity lexicon contains inflected words, the lemmatized form is required in order to be able to translate the entries using the bilingual dictionary. However, words may lose their subjective meaning once lemmatized. For instance, the inflected form of *memories* becomes *memory*. Once translated into Romanian (as *memorie*), its main meaning is objective, referring to the ability of retaining information.

3. The PMI of two words w_1 and w_2 is defined as the probability of seeing the two words together divided by the probability of seeing each individual word: $PMI(w_1, w_2) = \frac{p(w_1, w_2)}{p(w_1)p(w_2)}$

Table 7–1: Examples of entries in the Romanian subjectivity lexicon

Romanian	English	Attributes
înfrumuseţa	beautifying	strong, verb
notabil	notable	weak, adj
plin de regret	full of regrets	strong, adj
sclav	slaves	weak, noun

Second, neither the lexicon nor the bilingual dictionary provides information concerning the sense of the individual entries, and therefore the translation has to rely on the most probable sense in the target language. Fortunately, some bilingual dictionaries list the translations in reverse order of their usage frequencies, which is a heuristic that can be used to partly address this problem. Moreover, the lexicon sometimes includes identical entries expressed through different parts of speech; for example, *grudge* has two separate entries, for its noun and verb roles respectively.

Using this direct translation process, Mihalcea et al. obtained a subjectivity lexicon in Romanian containing 4,983 entries. Table 7–1 shows examples of entries in the Romanian lexicon, together with their corresponding original English form. The table also shows the reliability of the expression (weak or strong) and the part of speech—attributes that are provided in the English subjectivity lexicon.

To evaluate the quality of the lexicon, two native speakers of Romanian annotated the subjectivity of 150 randomly selected entries. Each annotator independently read approximately 100 examples of each drawn from the Web, including a large number from news sources. The subjectivity of a word is consequently judged in the contexts where it most frequently appears, accounting for its most frequent meanings on the Web. After the disagreements were reconciled through discussions, the final set of 123 correctly translated entries included 49.6% (61) subjective entries, but as many as 23.6% (29) entries were found to have primarily objective uses (the other 26.8% were mixed).

The study from Mihalcea et al. [16] suggests that the Romanian subjectivity clues derived through translation are less reliable than the original set of English clues. In several cases, the subjectivity is lost in the translation, mainly due to word ambiguity in either the source or target language, or both. For instance, the word *fragile* correctly translates into Romanian as *fragil*, yet this word is frequently used to refer to breakable objects, and it loses its subjective meaning of *delicate*. Other words completely lose subjectivity once translated. For example, *one-sided* becomes in Romanian *cu o singura latură*, meaning "with only one side" (as of objects).

Using a similar translation technique, Kim and Hovy [15] built a lexicon for German starting with a lexicon in English, this time focusing on polarity rather than subjectivity. They used an English polarity lexicon semiautomatically generated starting with a few seeds and using the WordNet structure [22]. Briefly, for a given seed word, its synsets and synonyms are extracted from WordNet, and then the probability of the word belonging to one of the three classes is calculated on the basis of the number and frequency of seeds from a particular class appearing within the word's expansion. This metric thus represents the closeness of a word to the seeds. Using this method, Kim and Hovy generated an English lexicon of about 1,600 verbs and 3,600 adjectives, classified as positive or negative according to their polarity.

The lexicon was then translated into German by using an automatically generated translation dictionary obtained from the European Parliament corpus via word alignment [33]. To evaluate the quality of the German polarity lexicon, the entries in the lexicon were used in a rule-based system that was applied to the annotation of polarity for 70 German emails. Overall, the system obtained an F-measure of 60% for the annotation of positive polarity and 50% for the annotation of negative polarity.

Another method for building subjectivity lexicons was proposed by Banea, Mihalcea, and Wiebe [34], by **bootstrapping** from a few manually selected seeds. At each iteration, the seed set is expanded with related words found in an online dictionary, which are filtered by using a measure of word similarity. The bootstrapping process is illustrated in Figure 7–1.

Starting with a seed set of subjective words, evenhandedly sampled from verbs, nouns, adjectives, and adverbs, new related words are added on the basis of the entries found in the dictionary. For each seed word, all the open-class words appearing in its definition are collected, as well as synonyms and antonyms if available. Note that word ambiguity is not an issue, as the expansion is done with all the possible meanings for each candidate word. The candidates are subsequently filtered for incorrect meanings by using a measure of similarity with the seed words, calculated using a latent semantic analysis system trained on a corpus in the target language.

In experiments carried out on Romanian, starting with 60 seed words, Banea et al. built a subjective lexicon of 3,900 entries. The quality of the lexicon was evaluated by embedding

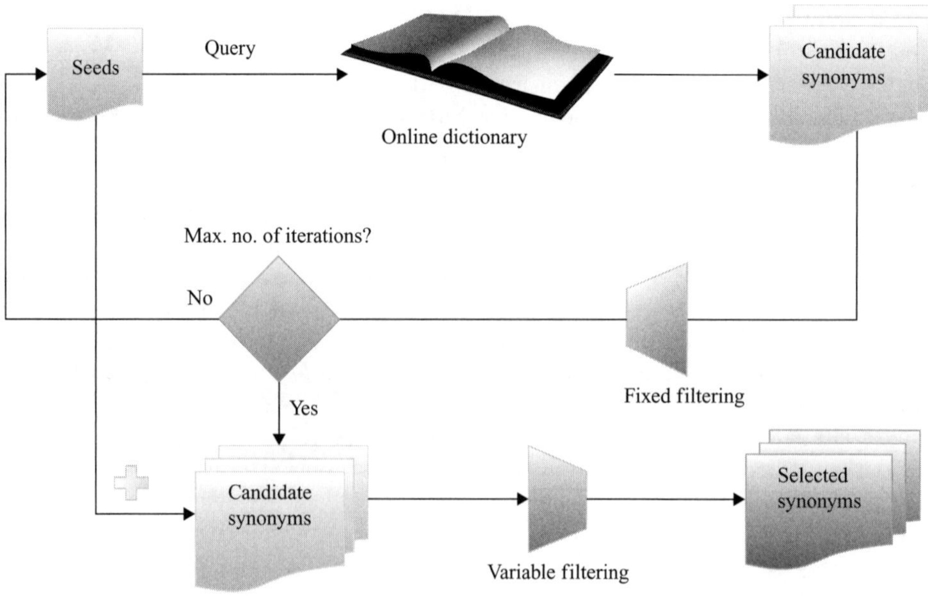

Figure 7–1: Bootstrapping process

it into a rule-based classifier used for the classification of subjectivity for 504 manually annotated sentences. The classifier led to an F-measure of 61.7%, which is significantly higher than a simple baseline of 54% that can be obtained assigning a majority class by default.

A similar bootstrapping technique was used by Pitel and Grefenstette [35], for the construction of affective lexicons for French. They classified words into 44 affect classes (e.g., morality, love, crime, insecurity), each class being in turn associated with a positive or negative orientation. Starting with a few seed words (two to four seed words for each affective dimension), they used synonym expansion to automatically add new candidate words to each affective class. The new candidates were then filtered according to a measure of similarity calculated with latent semantic analysis and machine learning trained on seed data. Using this method, Pitel and Grefenstette generated a French affective lexicon of 3,500 words, which was evaluated against a gold-standard data set consisting of manually annotated entries. As more training samples became available in the training lexicon, the F-measure classification increased from 12% to 17% up to a maximum of 27% F-measure for a given class.

7.4.2 Corpus-Based

In addition to dictionaries, textual corpora were also found useful to derive subjectivity and polarity information associated with words and phrases. Much of the corpus-based research carried out to date follows the work of Turney [30] (see §7.3.3), who presented a method to measure the polarity of a word on the basis of its PMI association with a positive or a negative seed (e.g., excellent and poor).

Kaji and Kitsuregawa [36] proposed a method to build sentiment lexicons for Japanese, by measuring the strength of association with positive and negative data automatically collected from Web pages. First, using structural information from the layout of HTML pages (e.g., list markers or tables that explicitly indicate the presence of the evaluation sections of a review, such as *pros, cons, minus, plus*, etc.), as well as Japanese-specific language structure (e.g., particles used as topic markers), a corpus of positive and negative statements was automatically mined from the Web. Starting with 1 billion HTML documents, about 500,000 polar sentences were collected, with 220,000 being positive and the rest negative. Manual verification of 500 sentences, carried out by two human judges, indicated an average precision of 92%, which shows that reasonable quality can be achieved using this corpus construction method.

Next, Kaji and Kitsuregawa used this corpus to automatically acquire a set of polar phrases. Starting with all the adjectives and adjectival phrases as candidates, they measured the chi-squared and the PMI between these candidates and the positive and negative data, followed by a selection of those words and phrases that exceed a certain threshold. Through experiments, the PMI measure was found to work better than the chi-squared. The polarity value of a word or phrase based on PMI is defined as:

$$PV_{PMI}(W) = PMI(W, pos) - PMI(W, neg)$$

where

$$PMI(W, pos) = log_2 \frac{P(W,pos)}{P(W)P(pos)} \qquad PMI(W, neg) = log_2 \frac{P(W,neg)}{P(W)P(neg)}$$

pos and *neg* representing the positive and negative sentences automatically collected from the Web.

Using a data set of 405 adjective phrases, consisting of 158 positive phrase, 150 negative, and 97 neutral, Kaji and Kitsuregawa built a lexicon ranging from 8,166 to 9,670 entries, depending on the value of the threshold used for the candidate selection. The precision for the positive phrases was 76.4% (recall 92.4%) when a threshold of 0 was used and went up to 92.0% (recall 65.8%) when the threshold was raised to 3.0. For the same threshold values, the negative phrases had a precision ranging from 68.5% (recall 84.0%) to 87.9% (recall 62.7%).

Another corpus-based method for the construction of polarity lexicons in Japanese, this time focusing on domain-specific propositions, was proposed by Kanayama and Nasukawa [12]. The researchers introduced a novel method for performing domain-dependent, unsupervised sentiment analysis through the automatic acquisition of polar atoms in a given domain by building on a domain-independent lexicon. In their work, a polar atom is defined as "the minimum human-understandable syntactic structures that specify the polarity of clauses," and it typically represents a tuple of polarity and a verb or an adjective along with its optional arguments. The system uses both intrasentential and intersentential coherence as a way to identify polarity shifts and automatically bootstraps a domain-specific polarity lexicon.

First, candidate propositions are identified by using the output of a full parser. Next, sentiment assignment is performed in two stages. Starting from a lexicon of preexisting polar atoms based on an English sentiment lexicon, the method finds occurrences of the entries in the propositions extracted earlier. These propositions are classified as either positive or negative depending on the label of the atom they contain, or its opposite if a negation is encountered. The next step involves the extension of the initial sentiment labeling to those propositions that are not labeled. To this end, context coherency is used, which assumes that in a given context the polarity will not shift unless an adversative conjunction is encountered, either between sentences and/or within sentences. Finally, the confidence of each new polar atom is calculated on the basis of its total number of occurrences in positive and negative contexts.

The method was evaluated on Japanese product reviews extracted from four domains: digital cameras, movies, mobile phones, and cars. The number of reviews in each corpus ranged from 155,130 (mobile phones) to 263,934 (digital cameras). Starting with these data sets, the method can extract 200 to 700 polar atoms per domain, with a precision evaluated by human judges ranging from 54% for the mobile phones corpus to 75% for the movies corpus.

Kanayama and Nasukawa's method is similar to some extent to an approach proposed earlier by Kobayashi et al., which extracts opinion triplets from Japanese product reviews mined from the Web [9]. An opinion triplet consists of the following fields: product, attribute, and value. The process involves a bootstrapping process consisting of two steps. The first step consists of the generation of candidates based on a set of co-occurrence patterns, which are applied to a collection of web reviews. Three dictionaries that are updated at the end of each bootstrapping iteration are also provided (dictionaries of subjects, attributes, and values). Once a ranked list of candidates is generated, a human judge is presented with the top-ranked candidates for annotation. The manual step involves identifying the attributes and their values and updating their corresponding dictionaries with the newly extracted entities.

For the experiments, Kobayashi et al. used two data sets, consisting of 15,000 car reviews and 10,000 game reviews respectively. The bootstrapping process starts with a subject dictionary of 389 car names and 660 computer games names, an initial attribute list with seven generic descriptors (e.g., cost, price, performance), and a value list with 247 entries (e.g., good, beautiful, high). Each extraction pattern is scored according to the frequency of the extracted expressions and their reliability. For the evaluation, a human annotator tagged 105 car reviews and 280 computer game reviews and identified the attributes and their corresponding values. Overall, using the semiautomatic system, Kobayashi et al. found that lexicons of opinion triplets can be built eight times faster than can a fully manual setup. Moreover, the semiautomatic system is able to achieve a coverage of 35% to 45% with respect to the manually extracted expressions, which represents a significant coverage.

The semantic orientation of phrases in Japanese is also the goal of the work of Suzuki, Takamura, and Okumura [10] and Takamura, Inui, and Okumura [11], both using an expectation maximization model trained on annotated data. Takamura et al. considered the task of finding the polarity of phrases such as "light laptop," which cannot be directly obtained from the polarity of individual words (since, in this case, both "light" and "laptop" are neutral). On a data set of 12,000 adjective-noun phrases drawn from a Japanese newspaper, they found that a model based on triangle and U-shaped graphical dependencies leads to an accuracy of approximately 81%.

Suzuki et al. targeted instead evaluative expressions, similar to those addressed by Kobayashi et al. [9]. They used an expectation maximization algorithm and a naïve Bayes classifier to bootstrap a system to annotate the polarity of evaluative expressions consisting of subjects, attributes, and values. Using a data set of 1,061 labeled examples and 34,704 unlabeled examples, they obtained an accuracy of 77%, which represents a significant improvement over the baseline of 47% obtained by assigning the majority class from the set of 1,061 labeled examples.

Finally, another line of work concerned with the polarity analysis of words and phrases is presented by Bautin, Vijayarenu, and Skiena [37]. Instead of targeting the derivation of subjectivity or sentiment lexicon in a new language, the goal of Bautin et al.'s work measured the polarity of given entities (e.g., George Bush, Vladimir Putin) in a text written in a target language. Their approach relies on the translation of documents (e.g., newswire, European parliament documents) from the given language into English, followed by a calculation of the polarity of the target entity by using association measures between the occurrence of the entity and positive/negative words from a sentiment lexicon in English.

Their experiments focused on nine different languages (Arabic, Chinese, English, French, German, Italian, Japanese, Korean, Spanish) and 14 entities covering country and city names. They showed that large variations can be achieved in the measures of polarity or subjectivity of an entity across languages, ranging from very weak correlations (close to 0) to strong correlations (0.60 and higher). For instance, an aggregation of all the polarity scores measured for all 14 entities in different languages leads to a low correlation of 0.08 between mentions of such entities in Japanese and Chinese text, but as high as 0.63 when the mentions are collected from French and Korean texts.

7.5 Sentence-Level Annotations

Corpus annotations are often required either as an end goal for various text-processing applications (e.g., mining opinions from the Web, classification of reviews into positive and negative), or as an intermediate step toward building automatic subjectivity and sentiment classifiers. Work in this area has considered annotations at either sentence or document level, depending mainly on the requirements of the end application (or classifier). The annotation process is typically done following one of two methods: dictionary-based, consisting of rule-based classifiers relying on lexicons built with one of the methods described in the previous section, or corpus-based, consisting of machine learning classifiers trained on preexisting annotated data.

7.5.1 Dictionary-Based

Rule-based classifiers, such as the one introduced by Riloff and Wiebe in [38], can be used in conjunction with any opinion lexicon to develop a sentence-based classifier. These classifiers mainly look for the presence (or absence) of lexicon clues in the text and correspondingly decide on the classification of a sentence as subjective/objective or positive/negative.

One of the lexicons described in the previous section that has been evaluated in a rule-based classifier is the Romanian subjectivity lexicon built by translating an English lexicon [16] (see §7.4.1). The classifier relied on three main heuristics to label subjective and objective sentences: (i) if two or more strong subjective expressions occur in the same sentence, the sentence is labeled subjective; (ii) if no strong subjective expressions occur in a sentence, and at most three weak subjective expressions occur in the previous, current, and next sentence combined, then the sentence is labeled objective; (iii) otherwise, if none of the previous rules applied, the sentence is labeled unknown.

The quality of the classifier was evaluated on a Romanian gold-standard corpus annotated for subjectivity, consisting of 504 sentences from the Romanian side of an English-Romanian parallel corpus, annotated according to the annotation scheme in [27]. The classifier had an overall precision of 62% and a recall of 39%; the precision for the subjective annotations only was evaluated at 80%, for a recall of 21%.

Another subjectivity lexicon that was evaluated in a rule-based approach is the one from Banea et al. [34] (§7.4.1). Using a lexicon of 3,900 entries in Romanian, obtained after several bootstrapping iterations, Banea et al. built a rule-based classifier with an overall precision and recall of 62% when evaluated on the same data set of 504 manually annotated Romanian sentences. This is significantly higher than the results obtained on the basis of the translated lexicons, indicating the importance of language-specific information for subjectivity analysis.

Besides Romanian, a lexicon approach is also used for the classification of polarity for sentences in Japanese [39]. Kanayama et al. use a machine translation system based on deep parsing to extract "sentiment units" with high precision from Japanese product reviews, where a sentiment unit is defined as a tuple between a sentiment label (positive or negative) and a predicate (verb or adjective) with its argument (noun). The sentiment analysis system uses the structure of a transfer-based machine translation engine, where the production rules and the bilingual dictionary are replaced by sentiment patterns and a sentiment lexicon respectively.

The system is ultimately able not only to mine product reviews for positive/negative product attributes but also to provide a user-friendly interface to browse product reviews. The sentiment units derived for Japanese are used to classify the polarity of a sentence, using the information drawn from a full syntactic parser in the target language. Using about 4,000 sentiment units, when evaluated on 200 sentences, the sentiment annotation system was found to have high precision (89%) at the cost of low recall (44%).

7.5.2 Corpus-Based

Once a corpus annotated at sentence level is available, with either subjectivity or polarity labels, a classifier can be easily trained to automatically annotate additional sentences.

This is the approach taken by Kaji and Kitsuregawa [40, 36], who collect a large corpus of sentiment-annotated sentences from the Web, and subsequently use this data set to train sentence-level classifiers. Using the method described in Section 7.4.2, which relies on structural information from the layout of HTML pages as well as Japanese-specific language structure, Kaji and Kitsuregawa collected a corpus of approximately 500,000 positive and negative sentences from the Web. The quality of the annotations was estimated by two human judges, who found an average precision of 92% as measured on a randomly selected sample of 500 sentences.

A subset of this corpus, consisting of 126,000 sentences, was used to build a naïve Bayes classifier. Using three domain-specific data sets (computers, restaurants, and cars), automatically collected by selecting manually annotated reviews consisting of only one sentence, the precision of the classifier was found to have an accuracy ranging between 83% (computers) and 85% (restaurants), which is comparable to the accuracy obtained by training on in-domain data. These results demonstrate the quality of the automatically built corpus that can be used to train reliable sentence-level classifiers with good portability to new domains.

Another corpus-based approach is explored by Mihalcea et al. [16], where a Romanian corpus annotated for subjectivity at sentence level is built via crosslingual projections across parallel texts. Mihalcea et al. used a parallel corpus consisting of 107 documents from the English SemCor corpus [41] and their manual translation into Romanian. The corpus consists of roughly 11,000 sentences, with approximately 250,000 tokens on each side. It is a balanced corpus covering a number of topics in sports, politics, fashion, education, and others.

To annotate the English side of the parallel corpus, the two OpinionFinder classifiers (described in §7.3.3) are used to label the sentences in the corpus. Next, the OpinionFinder annotations are projected onto the Romanian training sentences, which are then used to develop a naïve Bayes classifier for the automatic labeling of subjectivity in Romanian sentences. The quality of the classifiers was evaluated on a corpus of 504 sentences manually annotated for subjectivity (the same gold-standard corpus used in the experiments described in the previous sections). When the high-precision classifier was used to produce the annotations for the English corpus, the overall accuracy was measured at 64%. When the high-coverage classifier was used, the accuracy rose to 68%. In both cases, the accuracy was found to be significantly higher than the majority-class baseline of 54%, indicating that crosslingual projections represent a reliable technique for building subjectivity annotated corpora in a new language.

Following the same idea of using crosslingual projections across parallel texts, Banea et al. [17] proposed a method based on machine translation to generate the required parallel texts. The English sentence-level subjectivity annotations are projected across automatically translated texts to build subjectivity classifiers for Romanian and Spanish. Using first Romanian as a target language, several translation scenarios were considered, with various results as measured on the same gold-standard data set of 504 sentences described before. First, a classifier was trained on annotations projected across the automatic translation of an English manually annotated corpus (MPQA; see §7.3.2); this resulted in an accuracy of 66% using an SVM classifier [42]. Second, an English corpus was automatically annotated with the high-coverage OpinionFinder classifier, and the annotations were projected across machine translated text. Again, an SVM classifier was trained on the resulting annotations in the new language, this time resulting in an accuracy of 69%. Finally, a Romanian corpus was automatically translated into English, followed by an annotation of the English version using the OpinionFinder classifier, and a projection of the subjectivity labels back into Romanian. The SVM classifier trained on this data had an accuracy of 67%.

The same experiments were replicated on Spanish, which led to 68% accuracy when the source language text had manual subjectivity annotations and 63% when the annotations were automatically generated with OpinionFinder. Overall, the results obtained with machine translated text were found to be just a few percentages below the results obtained with manually translated text, which shows that machine translation can be effectively used to generate the required parallel texts for crosslingual projections.

7.6 Document-Level Annotations

Natural language applications, such as review classification or web opinion mining, often require corpus-level annotations of subjectivity and polarity. In addition to sentence-level annotations, described in the previous section, several methods have been proposed for the annotation of entire documents. As before, the two main directions of work have considered: dictionary-based annotations, which assume the availability of a lexicon, and corpus-based annotations, which mainly rely on classifiers trained on labeled data.

7.6.1 Dictionary-Based

Perhaps the simplest approach for document annotations is to use a rule-based system based on the clues available in a language-specific lexicon. One of the methods proposed by Wan [43] consists of annotating Chinese reviews by using a polarity lexicon, along with a set of negation words and intensifiers. The lexicon contains 3,700 positive terms, 3,100 negative words, and 148 intensifier terms, all of them collected from a Chinese vocabulary for sentiment analysis released by HowNet, as well as 13 negation terms collected from related research. Given this lexicon, the polarity of a document is annotated by combining the polarity of its constituent sentences, where in turn the polarity of a sentence is determined as a summation of the polarity of the words found in the sentence. When evaluated on a data set of 886 Chinese reviews, this method was found to give an overall accuracy of 74.3%.

The other method proposed by Wan [43] is to use machine translation to translate the Chinese reviews into English, followed by the automatic annotation of the English reviews using a rule-based system relying on English lexicons. Several experiments were run with two commercial machine translation systems, using the OpinionFinder polarity lexicon (see §7.3.1). For the same test set mentioned before, the translation method achieved an accuracy of up to 81%, significantly higher than the one achieved by directly analyzing the reviews using a Chinese lexicon. Moreover, an ensemble combining different translations and methods leads to an even higher accuracy of 85%, demonstrating that a combination of different knowledge sources can exceed the performance obtained with individual resources.

Another approach, proposed by Zagibalov and Carroll [14], consists of a bootstrapping method to label the polarity of Chinese text by iteratively building a lexicon and labeling new text. The method starts by identifying "lexical items" in text, which are sequences of Chinese characters that occur between noncharacter symbols and include a negation and an adverbial; a small hand-picked list of six negations and five adverbials is used, which increases the portability of the method to other languages. In order to be considered for candidacy in the seed list, the lexical item should appear at least twice in the data that is being considered.

Next, "zones" are identified in the text, where a zone is the sequence of characters occurring between punctuation marks. The sentiment associated with an entire document is calculated as the difference between the number of positive and negative zones that the review entails. In turn, the sentiment of a zone is computed by summing the polarity scores of their component lexical items. Finally, the polarity of a lexical item is proportional with the square of its length (number of characters) and with its previous polarity score, while being inversely proportional to the length of the containing zone. This score is multiplied by -1 in case a negation precedes the lexical item.

The bootstrapping process consists of iterative steps that result in an incrementally larger set of seeds and an incrementally larger number of annotated documents. Starting with a seed set consisting initially of only one adjective (*good*), new documents are annotated as positive and negative, followed by the identification of new lexical items occurring in these documents that can be added to the seed set. The addition to the seed set is determined on the basis of the frequency of the lexical item, which has to be at least three times larger in the positive (negative) documents for it to be considered. The bootstrapping stops when in over two runs no new seeds are found.

The method was evaluated over a balanced corpus of Chinese reviews compiled from ten different domains. The average accuracy at document level was measured at 83%. Moreover, the system was also able to extract a set of 50 to 60 seeds per domain, which may be helpful for other sentiment annotation algorithms.

Another method, used by Kim and Hovy [15], consists of the annotation of German documents using a lexicon translated from English. A lexicon construction method, described in detail in Section 7.4.1, is used to generate an English lexicon of about 5,000 entries. The lexicon is then translated into German by using an automatically generated translation dictionary obtained from the European Parliament corpus using word alignment. The German lexicon is used in a rule-based system that is applied to the annotation of polarity for 70 German emails. Briefly, the polarity of a document is decided on the basis of heuristics: a number of negative words above a particular threshold renders the document negative, whereas a majority of positive words triggers a positive classification. Overall, the system obtained an F-measure of 60% for the annotation of positive polarity and 50% for the annotation of negative polarity.

7.6.2 Corpus-Based

The most straightforward approach for corpus-based document annotation is to train a machine learning classifier, assuming that a set of annotated data already exists. Li and Sun [44] use a data set of Chinese hotel reviews on which they apply several classifiers, including SVM, naïve Bayes, and maximum entropy. Using a training set consisting of 6,000 positive reviews and 6,000 negative reviews and a test set of 2,000 positive reviews and 2,000 negative reviews, they obtain an accuracy of up to 92%, depending on the classifier and on the features used. These experiments demonstrate that if enough training data are available, it is relatively easy to build accurate sentiment classifiers.

A related yet more sophisticated technique is proposed by Wan [45], who uses a cotraining approach to leverage resources from both a source and a target language. The technique is tested on the automatic sentiment classification of product reviews in Chinese. For a given product review in the target language (Chinese), an alternative view is obtained in another language (English) via machine translation. The algorithm then uses two SVM classifiers, one in Chinese and one in English, to start a cotraining process that iteratively builds a sentiment classifier. Initially, the training data set consists of a set of labeled examples in Chinese and their English translations. Next, the first iteration of cotraining is performed, and a set of unlabeled instances is classified and added to the training set if the labels assigned in the models built on the languages agree. The newly labeled instances are used to retrain the two classifiers at the next iteration. Reviews with conflicting labels are not considered. As expected, the performance initially grows with the number iterations, followed by a degradation when the number of erroneously labeled instances exceeds a certain threshold. The best results are reported at the 40th iteration, for an overall F-measure of 81%, after adding five negative and five positive reviews at each iteration. The method is successful because it makes use of both crosslanguage and within-language knowledge.

7.7 What Works, What Doesn't

When faced with a new language, what is the best method that we can use to create a sentiment or subjectivity analysis tool for that language? The answer largely depends on the monolingual resources and tools available for that language, such as dictionaries, large corpora, natural language processing tools, and/or the crosslingual connections that can be made to a major language[4] such as English (e.g., bilingual dictionaries or parallel texts).

7.7.1 Best Scenario: Manually Annotated Corpora

The best scenario is when a corpus manually annotated for sentiment or subjectivity exists in the target language. Unfortunately, this is rarely the case, as large, manually annotated corpora exist only for a handful of languages (e.g., the MPQA corpus that is available for English [27]).

4. That is, a language for which many resources and tools are already available.

The alternative is to derive such corpora from online data, such as collections of product or movie reviews. This is a viable solution for languages where a significant number of online reviews exist. For instance, a number of methods rely on online review repositories, including movie or product reviews in English [29, 4], product reviews in Japanese [12, 9], and hotel reviews in Chinese [44].

Once a large, annotated data set is available, either manually annotated or mined from publicly available websites, a tool for automatic annotation can be easily constructed by training a machine learning system. The task can be thus regarded as a text classification problem, and learning algorithms such as naïve Bayes, decision trees, and SVMs[5] can be used to annotate the subjectivity or the sentiment of new text.

7.7.2 Second Best: Corpus-Based Cross-Lingual Projections

The second-best option is to construct an annotated data set by doing crosslingual projections from a major language that has such annotations readily available. This assumes that a bridge can be created between the target language and a major language such as English in the form of parallel texts constructed via manual or automatic translations. By using this bridge, the corpus annotations available in the major language can be automatically transferred into the target language. This method was first introduced by Mihalcea et al. [16], for the projection of subjectivity labels across parallel Romanian-English texts, and was later used in conjunction with machine translation for the projection of subjectivity labels onto Romanian [17] or sentiment annotations onto Chinese [43].

The translation can be performed in two directions. First, researchers can take a collection of texts in the major language and manually or automatically translate it into the target language. In this case, if the source text is already manually annotated for subjectivity or sentiment (e.g., MPQA), then the manual labels can be projected into the target language. Alternatively, the text in the major language can be automatically annotated by using subjectivity or sentiment analysis tools such as OpinionFinder [24]. The other option is to start with texts in the target language and translate them into the major language. Again, the translation can be done either by hand or by using a machine translation system.

Regardless of the direction of the translation, and regardless of the use of manually created parallel corpora or machine translated text, the result is a data set in the target language annotated for subjectivity or sentiment, which can be used to train an automatic classifier as described in the previous section.

7.7.3 Third Best: Bootstrapping a Lexicon

A number of methods rely on the availability of subjectivity and sentiment lexicons to build rule-based classifiers for the annotation of new text. For instance, one of the most frequently used subjectivity annotation tools for English is OpinionFinder [24], which is based on a large subjectivity lexicon [47]. Similarly, the method suggested by Turney [30] relies on a dictionary of sentiment words to automatically annotate the polarity of text.

---

5. Usually available in off-the-shelf packages such as Weka [46].

One of the most successful approaches for the construction of subjectivity or sentiment lexicons is to bootstrap from a few manually selected seeds. If language processing tools such as part-of-speech taggers and parsers are available for the language at hand, the bootstrapping process can rely on information extraction patterns [48]. The alternative is to perform the bootstrapping using the synonyms and definitions found in an electronic dictionary [34]. In this case, no advanced language processing tools are required, only a dictionary in the target language. Starting with a set of seeds covering all open-class words, all the related words found in the dictionary are collected, including the synonyms, antonyms, and words found in the definitions. From this set of candidates, only those that are closely related to the seeds are kept for the next bootstrapping iteration, with the relatedness being measured with a similarity metric such as latent semantic analysis [49]. The bootstrapping process is illustrated in Figure 7–1. Running the process for several iterations can result in large lexicons with several thousands entries.

The typical use of a subjectivity or sentiment lexicon is within rule-based classifiers for sentence-level or document-level annotations. For instance, the classifier used by Banea et al. [34] labels a sentence as subjective if it contains three or more entries that appear in the subjective lexicon and as objective if it has two or fewer entries. Document-level annotations can also be performed by determining the frequency of subjective or sentiment words in the document.

7.7.4 Fourth Best: Translating a Lexicon

If none of the previous methods is applicable to the target language, the last resort is to construct a lexicon by automatically translating an already existing lexicon from a major language. The only requirements for this approach are a sentiment or subjectivity lexicon in a source language and a bilingual dictionary used to automatically translate the lexicon into the target language. The method was first used for building a sentiment lexicon in German [15] and later was applied to the construction of a subjectivity lexicon in Romanian [16].

Although very simple and efficient (a lexicon of over 5,000 entries can be created in seconds), the accuracy of the method is rather low, mainly due to the challenges that are typical to a context-free translation process: difficulty in selecting the most appropriate translation for words that are ambiguous, small coverage for phrase translations, mismatch between the inflected forms appearing in the lexicon and the lemmatized forms from the bilingual dictionary. Even so, a lexicon constructed this way can be easily corrected by hand and may therefore provide a building block for the generation of subjectivity or sentiment resources in a given target language.

7.7.5 Comparing the Alternatives

It is difficult to make a full comparison among the four methods presented because there is no single language on which all four alternatives have been applied. There are, however, several experiments that were run for the construction of a subjectivity annotation tool for Romanian, which were all evaluated on a common data set, thus allowing for a partial comparison.

Table 7–2 shows the results of these experiments, which were run on a data set of 504 sentences manually annotated for subjectivity (see §7.4.1). The only method that is not

Table 7–2: Comparison of several subjectivity annotation methods for Romanian

	Precision	Recall	F-measure	Accuracy
parallel texts	**69.35**	78.75	73.76	**69.64**
machine translation, source-target	67.76	**83.15**	**74.57**	69.44
machine translation, target-source	76.06	59.34	66.67	67.86
lexicon bootstrapping	68.98	61.90	65.25	64.29
lexicon translation	65.84	38.83	48.85	55.95

included in this comparison is the one relying on manually annotated corpora, because no manually annotated data set is available for Romanian. Not surprisingly, the highest accuracy is obtained when the corpus annotations are projected across manually constructed parallel texts, followed closely by the methods that rely on source-target or target-source machine translation. When no annotated data is available, a rule-based classifier can be built on the basis of subjectivity lexicons. In this case, the best results are obtained using a bootstrapping method, followed by the projection of the lexicon based on a bilingual dictionary.

7.8 Summary

Sentiment and subjectivity analysis is a rapidly growing area. Although most of the work to date has focused on English, work targeting other languages is growing, with resources or tools for subjectivity or sentiment analysis currently available in Chinese, German, Japanese, Romanian, Spanish, and others.

This chapter described some of the most recent methods for multilingual sentiment and subjectivity analysis. The methods differ in the approach they take: supervised corpus-based algorithms or unsupervised rule-based approaches, as well as in the span of text they target: single words or phrases, entire sentences, or entire documents. Although it is difficult to draw a comparison encompassing all the methods that have been proposed to date, the chapter also attempted to provide an overview of the most commonly used techniques and showed how they compare to each other when applied on the specific task of subjectivity analysis in Romanian.

Although still far from the performance that can be obtained on rich-resource languages such as English, the growing body of work on multilingual methods promises to lead to resources and tools in a continuously increasing number of languages.

Acknowledgments

This material is based in part on work supported by National Science Foundation awards #0917170 and #0916046. Any opinions, findings, and conclusions or recommendations expressed in this material are those of the authors and do not necessarily reflect the views of the National Science Foundation.

Bibliography

[1] C. O. Alm, D. Roth, and R. Sproat, "Emotions from text: Machine learning for text-based emotion prediction," in *Proceedings of the Human Language Technologies Conference/Conference on Empirical Methods in Natural Language Processing (HLT/EMNLP-2005)*, pp. 347–354, 2005.

[2] L. Lloyd, D. Kechagias, and S. Skiena, "Lydia: A system for large-scale news analysis," in *String Processing and Information Retrieval (SPIRE 2005)*, 2005.

[3] K. Balog, G. Mishne, and M. de Rijke, "Why are they excited? Identifying and explaining spikes in blog mood levels," in *Proceedings of the 11th Meeting of the European Chapter of the Association for Computational Linguistics (EACL-2006)*, 2006.

[4] M. Hu and B. Liu, "Mining and summarizing customer reviews," in *Proceedings of ACM SIGKDD Conference on Knowledge Discovery and Data Mining 2004 (KDD 2004)*, pp. 168–177, 2004.

[5] H. Yu and V. Hatzivassiloglou, "Towards answering opinion questions: Separating facts from opinions and identifying the polarity of opinion sentences," in *Proceedings of the Conference on Empirical Methods in Natural Language Processing (EMNLP-2003)*, pp. 129–136, 2003.

[6] G. Carenini, R. Ng, and X. Zhou, "Summarizing emails with conversational cohesion and subjectivity," in *Proceedings of the Association for Computational Linguistics: Human Language Technologies (ACL-HLT 2008)*, 2008.

[7] J. Wiebe and R. Mihalcea, "Word sense and subjectivity," in *Proceedings of the Annual Meeting of the Association for Computational Linguistics*, 2006.

[8] A. Esuli and F. Sebastiani, "Determining term subjectivity and term orientation for opinion mining," in *Proceedings the 11th Meeting of the European Chapter of the Association for Computational Linguistics (EACL-2006)*, pp. 193–200, 2006.

[9] N. Kobayashi, K. Inui, K. Tateishi, and T. Fukushima, "Collecting evaluative expressions for opinion extraction," in *Proceedings of International Joint Conference on Natural Language Processing (IJCNLP)*, pp. 596–605, 2004.

[10] Y. Suzuki, H. Takamura, and M. Okumura, "Application of semi-supervised learning to evaluative expression classification," in *Proceedings of the 7th International Conference on Intelligent Text Processing and Computational Linguistics*, 2006.

[11] H. Takamura, T. Inui, and M. Okumura, "Latent variable models for semantic orientations of phrases," in *Proceedings of the 11th Meeting of the European Chapter of the Association for Computational Linguistics*, 2006.

[12] H. Kanayama and T. Nasukawa, "Fully automatic lexicon expansion for domain-oriented sentiment analysis," in *Proceedings of the Conference on Empirical Methods in Natural Language Processing*, 2006.

[13] Y. Hu, J. Duan, X. Chen, B. Pei, and R. Lu, "A new method for sentiment classification in text retrieval," in *Proceedings of the International Joint Conference on Natural Language Processing*, pp. 1–9, 2005.

[14] T. Zagibalov and J. Carroll, "Automatic seed word selection for unsupervised sentiment classification of chinese text," in *Proceedings of the Conference on Computational Linguistics*, 2008.

[15] S.-M. Kim and E. Hovy, "Identifying and analyzing judgment opinions," in *Proceedings of the Human Language Technology Conference of the North American Chapter of the Association for Computational Linguistics*, 2006.

[16] R. Mihalcea, C. Banea, and J. Wiebe, "Learning multilingual subjective language via cross-lingual projections," in *Proceedings of the Association for Computational Linguistics*, 2007.

[17] C. Banea, R. Mihalcea, J. Wiebe, and S. Hassan, "Multilingual subjectivity analysis using machine translation," in *Proceedings of the Conference on Empirical Methods in Natural Language Processing (EMNLP 2008)*, 2008.

[18] N. Kando, T. Mitamura, and T. Sakai, "Introduction to the NTCIR-6 special issue," *ACM Transactions on Asian Language Information Processing (TALIP)*, vol. 7, no. 2, 2008.

[19] R. Quirk, S. Greenbaum, G. Leech, and J. Svartvik, *A Comprehensive Grammar of the English Language.* New York: Longman, 1985.

[20] A. Banfield, *Unspeakable Sentences.* Boston: Routledge and Kegan Paul, 1982.

[21] T. Wilson, "Fine-grained subjectivity and sentiment analysis: Recognizing the intensity, polarity, and attitudes of private states," PhD thesis, University of Pittsburgh, 2007.

[22] G. Miller, "WordNet: A lexical database," *Communication of the ACM*, vol. 38, no. 11, 1995.

[23] T. Wilson, "Fine-grained subjectivity and sentiment analysis: Recognizing the intensity, polarity, and attitudes of private states," PhD thesis, University of Pittsburgh, 2008.

[24] J. Wiebe and E. Riloff, "Creating subjective and objective sentence classifiers from unannotated texts," in *Proceedings of the 6th International Conference on Intelligent Text Processing and Computational Linguistics (CICLing-2005)*, 2005.

[25] P. Stone, *General Inquirer: Computer Approach to Content Analysis.* Cambridge, MA: MIT Press, 1968.

[26] A. Esuli and F. Sebastiani, "SentiWordNet: A publicly available lexical resource for opinion mining," in *Proceedings of the 5th Conference on Language Resources and Evaluation (LREC 2006)*, 2006.

[27] J. Wiebe, T. Wilson, and C. Cardie, "Annotating expressions of opinions and emotions in language," *Language Resources and Evaluation*, vol. 39, no. 2-3, pp. 165–210, 2005.

[28] C. Strapparava and R. Mihalcea, "Semeval-2007 task 14: Affective text," in *Proceedings of the 4th International Workshop on the Semantic Evaluations (SemEval 2007)*, 2007.

[29] B. Pang and L. Lee, "A sentimental education: Sentiment analysis using subjectivity summarization based on minimum cuts," in *Proceedings of the 42nd Meeting of the Association for Computational Linguistics*, 2004.

[30] P. Turney, "Thumbs up or thumbs down? Semantic orientation applied to unsupervised classification of reviews," in *Proceedings of the 40th Annual Meeting of the Association for Computational Linguistics (ACL 2002)*, pp. 417–424, 2002.

[31] V. Hatzivassiloglou and K. McKeown, "Predicting the semantic orientation of adjectives," in *Proceedings of the Conference of the European Chapter of the Association for Computational Linguistics*, pp. 174–181, 1997.

[32] J. Wiebe, R. Bruce, and T. O'Hara, "Development and use of a gold-standard data set for subjectivity classifications," in *Proceedings of the 37th annual meeting of the Association for Computational Linguistics on Computational Linguistics*, pp. 246–253, 1999.

[33] F. Och and H. Ney, "Improved statistical alignment models," in *Proceedings of the 38th Annual Meeting of the Association for Computational Linguistics*, 2000.

[34] C. Banea, R. Mihalcea, and J. Wiebe, "A bootstrapping method for building subjectivity lexicons for languages with scarce resources," in *Proceedings of the Learning Resources Evaluation Conference (LREC 2008)*, 2008.

[35] G. Pitel and G. Grefenstette, "Semi-automatic building method for a multidimensional affect dictionary for a new language," in *Proceedings of the 6th International Language Resources and Evaluation (LREC'08)*, 2008.

[36] N. Kaji and M. Kitsuregawa, "Building lexicon for sentiment analysis from massive collection of HTML documents," in *Proceedings of the Conference on Empirical Methods in Natural Language Processing*, 2007.

[37] M. Bautin, L. Vijayarenu, and S. Skiena, "International sentiment analysis for news and blogs," in *Proceedings of the International Conference on Weblogs and Social Media*, 2008.

[38] E. Riloff and J. Wiebe, "Learning extraction patterns for subjective expressions," in *Conference on Empirical Methods in Natural Language Processing (EMNLP-03)*, pp. 105–112, 2003.

[39] H. Kanayama, T. Nasukawa, and H. Watanabe, "Deeper sentiment analysis using machine translation technology," in *International Conference on Computational Linguistics*, 2004.

[40] N. Kaji and M. Kitsuregawa, "Automatic construction of polarity-tagged corpus from HTML documents," in *Proceedings of the International Conference on Computational Linguistics / Association for Computational Linguistics*, 2006.

[41] G. Miller, C. Leacock, T. Randee, and R. Bunker, "A semantic concordance," in *Proceedings of the 3rd DARPA Workshop on Human Language Technology*, 1993.

[42] V. Vapnik, *The Nature of Statistical Learning Theory.* New York: Springer, 1995.

[43] X. Wan, "Using bilingual knowledge and ensemble techniques for unsupervised Chinese sentiment analysis," in *Proceedings of the 2008 Conference on Empirical Methods in Natural Language Processing*, 2008.

[44] J. Li, , and M. Sun, "Experimental study on sentiment classification of Chinese review using machine learning techniques," in *International Conference on Natural Language Processing and Knowledge Engineering*, 2007.

[45] X. Wan, "Co-training for cross-lingual sentiment classification," in *Proceedings of the Joint Conference of the Association of Computational Linguistics and the International Joint Conference on Natural Language Processing*, 2009.

[46] I. Witten and E. Frank, *Data Mining: Practical Machine Learning Tools and Techniques.* Boston: Morgan Kaufmann, 2005.

[47] T. Wilson, J. Wiebe, and P. Hoffmann, "Recognizing contextual polarity in phrase-level sentiment analysis," in *Proceedings of Human Language Technologies Conference/Conference on Empirical Methods in Natural Language Processing (HLT/EMNLP 2005)*, 2005.

[48] E. Riloff, J. Wiebe, and T. Wilson, "Learning subjective nouns using extraction pattern bootstrapping," in *Proceedings of the Seventh Conference on Natural Language Learning (CoNLL-2003)*, 2003.

[49] T. K. Landauer, P. Foltz, and D. Laham, "Introduction to latent semantic analysis," *Discourse Processes*, vol. 25, 1998.

Part II

In Practice

Chapter 8, "Entity Detection and Tracking," discusses methods for determining whether types of real-world entities, such as people, organizations, and locations, are mentioned in text, what the boundaries of those referring expressions are, and methods for determining when those entity mentions *corefer*.

Chapter 9, "Relations and Events," focuses on extracting from a corpus of text relevant entities, their relevant properties, and the relationships among them, then storing the information in a structured way.

Chapter 10, "Machine Translation," describes methods for automatically translating from one human language to another.

Chapter 11, "Multilingual Information Retrieval," explores the problem of retrieving documents, or parts of documents, on the basis of a user's search query.

Chapter 12, "Multilingual Automatic Summarization" discusses the problem of automatically summarizing a document.

Chapter 13, "Question Answering" explores ways to answer questions automatically on the basis of information contained in a corpus of documents.

Chapter 14, "Distillation," describes a relatively new area of answering, on the basis of information in a corpus of documents, complex queries that have multiple answers.

Chapter 15, "Spoken Dialog Systems," describes how to build a system that can handle a dialog between a human and a computer system.

Chapter 16, "Combining Natural Language Processing Engines," discusses the way in which multiple natural language processing engines may be combined using a common infrastructure.

Chapter 8

Entity Detection and Tracking

Xiaoqiang Luo and Imed Zitouni

8.1 Introduction

Information extraction (IE) is the task of identifying and extracting useful textual information from natural language documents. While "usefulness" is user- and application-dependent, we often care about "*who* did *what* to *whom* at *when* and/or for what reason (*why*)" from the input document. Clearly, the scope of information extraction can be arbitrarily broad, and sometimes it may even require world knowledge. To make problems tractable, we focus on two subtasks in this chapter:

1. detecting mentions from a document and identifying mentions' attributes: a **mention** is a text chunk identifying a physical object (e.g., a person or an organization);
2. grouping mentions referring the same object into entities; an **entity** is the collection of mentions that refer to the same object.

These two subtasks are crucial steps toward document understanding, as they identify the important conceptual objects and relations among them in a discourse.

The first problem is called **mention detection**, which consists of detecting the boundary of a mention and optionally identifying the semantic type (e.g., PERSON or ORGANIZATION) and other attributes (e.g., named, nominal, or pronominal). The second problem is termed **coreference resolution**, which clusters mentions referring to the same entity into equivalence classes. Because solving the two problems would identify entities and their attributes throughout a document, this chapter is titled "Entity Detection and Tracking," the same jargon used in the ACE [1] program.

A mention can be either named, nominal, or pronominal. For instance, the sentence

President Ford said that he has no comments.

contains three PERSON mentions: *President*, *Ford*, and *he*. Note that *Ford* is a named mention, *President* a nominal mention, and *he* a pronominal mention. Clearly, *President* and *Ford* refer to the same person, and we say that they are mentions belonging to the same entity. However, with the limited context, it is ambiguous that *he* may or may not refer to *President Ford*. Taken in isolation, *Ford* could also be an organization, as in "Ford sold

10 million cars in the first quarter." Like many other problems in natural language processing (NLP), such ambiguities are the major difficulties for entity detection and tracking (EDT).

The most successful approach for both mention detection and coreference resolution has been a data-driven, statistical one. Using this approach, a set of training data is annotated by humans, and statistical models are learned automatically from the data. The learned model can then be applied to unseen documents. Compared with a rule-based system, the statistical approach enjoys many benefits:

- A data-driven approach makes it possible to rapidly test different algorithms and features.
- A statistical system can be continually improved when new data become available by adding the new data to the training set.
- A statistical system can be easily ported to other languages.

Approaches discussed in this chapter are structured to separate the core EDT algorithms from idiosyncrasies specific to a language. In fact, the algorithms to be presented have been used to build systems for multiple languages without major modification. This is not to say that we should ignore the language issue. Instead, language-dependent phenomena are handled by either a preprocessing step or a configurable module that extracts features from data. For example, for highly inflected languages such as Arabic, space-delimited words may not be a good unit for EDT, and a **morph** is often chosen to counter the data-sparseness problem. For written languages without spaces, such as Chinese, Korean, and Japanese, it is necessary to segment input text into words. Another example is Chinese "acronyms": new words in Chinese can be formed by concatenating either first, last, or sometimes mixed characters of multiple contiguous words. Computationally, the phenomenon can be captured by expanding the definition of acronyms to include these cases.

In terms of system architecture, there are two kinds EDT systems:

1. Cascading system: in such systems, a mention detection component is followed by a coreference resolution component. One advantage of this architecture is that a clear boundary exists between the two subsystems, and the two can be independently developed and improved. For example, the mention detection system can be trained on one data set and the coreference resolution on a totally different set. Because of the separation, it is easier to identify and correct the mistakes made by such a system. The drawback of the cascading architecture is that the two problems are solved in isolation, although they are highly interconnected.
2. Joint system: an alternative architecture to solve the two problems jointly [2]. In other words, the system tries to detect mentions and find coreference chains simultaneously: it proposes a hypothetical mention, then finds its antecedent; in other words, mention detection operation and coreference operation are interleaved. This architecture has the benefit of having "globally" optimal system parameters, but it typically has higher time, space, and algorithm complexity than its cascading counterpart.

We present a sample cascading system in this chapter for the following reasons: first, mention detection and coreference resolution are complex enough that they deserve separate treatment; second, a cascading system makes debugging and error analysis a lot easier than lumping two system components into one; third, the cascading approach presented here has shown remarkably good performance in practice [3].

8.2 Mention Detection

The mention detection task has close ties to named entity recognition (NER), which has been the focus of much investigation in the recent past [3, 4, 5, 6] and has been at the center of several evaluations: MUC-6, MUC-7, CoNLL'02, and CoNLL'03 shared tasks. In the NLP literature, a named entity represents an instance of a name, such as a location, a person, or an organization, and the NER task consists of identifying each individual occurrence of such an entity.[1] In this chapter, we call instances of textual references to objects or abstractions **mentions**, which can be either named (e.g., *John Mayor*), nominal (e.g., *the president*), or pronominal (e.g., *she, it*). This task has been of particular interest since it was introduced in the ACE 2003 competition.

During the CoNLL'03 shared task, the system with the best performance was described by Florian et al. [7]. This system uses a linear interpolation of three different classifiers: (i) hidden Markov model (HMM), (ii) maximum entropy (MaxEnt), and (iii) robust risk minimization (RRM). Their final results were 88.76F for English and 72.41F for German, the best results in both languages. The system described in [8] was ranked second in CoNLL'03. It is a fully maximum entropy–based approach that uses different types of features: contextual and lexical features as well as capitalization. Another approach for NER in CoNLL'03, described by Klein et al. [9], uses a character-based HMM approach. This method relies heavily on internal evidence for the named entities. Recently, Tran et al. [10] showed that using a support vector machine (SVM) approach outperforms a conditional random field (CRF)-based model ($F_{\beta=1} = 87.75$ versus 86.48) on the NER task in Vietnamese. The comparison is based on the average F-measure obtained by using the same feature set with both SVMs and CRFs. Benajiba and Rosso [11] and Benajiba, Diab, and Rosso show how a CRF-based technique is effective for mention detection and NER. They report results for Arabic on different feature sets including contextual, morphological, and lexical features, together with gazetteer-based features. There are also several papers that present results on automatic content extraction (ACE) data. As an example, Florian et al. [12] show a two-step approach, boundary detection and then classification, for mention detection. This technique leads to better performance when compared to a model that jointly predicts the boundary and the mention type. We present in the following a data-driven approach to mention detection that uses the MaxEnt framework. This approach showed very competitive results at the ACE evaluation campaigns [1].

8.2.1 Data-Driven Classification

The mention detection problem can be formulated as a classification problem by assigning a label to each token in the text. These labels encode whether a token starts a specific mention, is inside a specific mention, or is outside any mentions. Under this formulation, mention detection is similar to many other NLP tasks such as base noun phrase chunking [13], text chunking [14], and NER [15].

1. In the 1995 Message Understanding Conference (MUS-6), for example, the set of named entity types consisted of PERSON, ORGANIZATION, LOCATION, TIME, PERCENT, MONEY.

Past results show that a modeling framework capable of integrating many sources of information [3, 4, 5] is critical for obtaining good performance. In this section, we present a MaxEnt mention detection system that can integrate arbitrary types of information when making a classification decision. You can of course replace the MaxEnt model with your favorite machine learning methods, so long as the information can be effectively used in the system.

Formally, let $x_1^L = (x_1, x_2, \ldots x_L)$ be a sequence of contiguous tokens (i.e., a sentence or a document). The mention detection problem can be cast into a sequential classification problem by assigning a label y_i to each token x_i, where y_i takes value from a finite set: $\mathcal{Y} = \{l_1, \ldots, l_n\}$. For example, if we are interested in finding PER (for person) and ORG (for organization), a possible label set encoding mention would be $\mathcal{Y} = \{\text{PER-B}, \text{PER-I}, \text{ORG-B}, \text{ORG-I}, \text{O}\}$, where a token labeled PER-B and PER-I denotes the beginning or inside of a person mention; a token labeled ORG-B and ORG-I denotes the beginning or inside of an organization mention, and a token labeled O signifies that the token is not a mention. Note that although a legitimate mention detection result can be encoded with a unique -B,-I,-O sequence, care has to be taken to rule out illegal tag sequence at the decoding phase; for instance, a PER-I tag is not allowed unless it follows a PER-B tag.

With this setup, the goal of a mention detection system is to find the most likely sequence of labels, given a sentence x_1^L, or

$$\widehat{y}_1^L = \arg\max_{y_1^L} P\left(y_1^L | x_1^L\right). \tag{8.1}$$

In practice, the number of parameters in the model $P\left(y_1^L | x_1^L\right)$ is often so large that it is impractical to get a good estimate from limited training data. So the model is factorized by chain rule, and modeling assumptions are made to drop long-range conditions:

$$\begin{aligned} P\left(y_1^L | x_1^L\right) &= P\left(y_1 | x_1^L\right) P\left(y_2 | x_1^L, y_1\right) \ldots P\left(y_L | x_1^L, y_1^{L-1}\right) \\ &\approx P\left(y_1 | x_1^L\right) P\left(y_2 | x_1^L, y_1\right) \ldots P\left(y_L | x_1^L, y_{L-k+1}^{L-1}\right). \end{aligned} \tag{8.2}$$

Note that only the most recent $k-1$ labels are kept in the basic modeling building block, $P\left(y_i | x_1^L, y_{i-k+1}^{i-1}\right)$.

In this chapter, the MaxEnt model is adopted to compute $P\left(y_i | x_1^L, y_{i-k+1}^{i-1}\right)$:

$$P\left(y_i | x_1^L, y_{i-k+1}^{i-1}\right) = \frac{1}{Z\left(x_1^L, y_{i-k+1}^{i-1}\right)} \exp\left[\sum_{j=1}^{m} \lambda_j f_j\left(x_1^L, y_{i-k+1}^{i-1}, y_i\right)\right], \tag{8.3}$$

where $Z\left(x_1^L, y_{i-k+1}^{i-1}\right)$ is a normalization factor, λ_j is a weight associated with the feature function $f_j\left(x_1^L, y_{i-k+1}^{i-1}, y_i\right)$. Given a set of labeled data, there are well-studied training algorithms [16, 17, 18, 19] to find the optimal parameters that maximize the log-likelihood of the training data.[2]

2. Describing these methods is beyond the scope of this chapter. Please refer to the cited material for in-depth descriptions.

The MaxEnt method can nicely integrate multiple feature types seamlessly, but it can overestimate its confidence in especially low-frequency features. The problem surfaces when we enforce a hard constraint on a feature whose estimation is not reliable enough. Several adjustments can be made to the model to address this issue, such as regularization by adding Gaussian priors [20] or exponential priors [21] to the model, using fuzzy MaxEnt boundaries [22], or using MaxEnt with inequality constraints [23].

Of the various methods for estimating the optimal λ_j values, one that has shown itself to be both fast and robust for mention detection (as well as for a wide range of NLP problems) is the **sequential conditional generalized iterative scaling** (SCGIS) technique [18]. To overcome the problem of overestimating confidence in low-frequency features especially, we recommend starting with the regularization method based on adding Gaussian priors as described in [20].[3] Intuitively, this measure models parameters as being close to 0 in value unless the data suggests otherwise. After computing the class probability distribution, the chosen criterion is the one with the most a posteriori probability. The decoding algorithm, described in Section 8.2.2, performs sequence classification through dynamic programming.

8.2.2 Search for Mentions

Now that we have our model, we are interested in using it to find the mentions in a sentence. These mentions have strong interdependencies that cannot be properly modeled if the classification is performed independently for each token.

In Equation 8.2, we restricted the conditioning on the classification tag sequence to the previous $k-1$ tags, but we do not impose any restrictions on the conditioning on the tokens: the probability is computed using the entire token sequence x_1^L. In practical situations, though, features examine only a limited context of the particular token of interest, but they are allowed to "look ahead"—that is, to examine features of the tokens succeeding the current token.

Under the constraint described in Equation 8.2, the sequence in Equation 8.1 can be efficiently identified. To obtain it, we create a **classification tag lattice** (also called a **trellis**), as follows:

- Let x_1^L be the token input sequence and $S = \{s_1, s_2, \ldots, s_m\}$ be an enumeration of $\mathcal{Y}^k$ ($m = |\mathcal{Y}|^k$). We call an element s_j a state. Every such state corresponds to the labeling of k successive tokens. We find it useful to think of an element s_i as a vector with k elements. We use the notations $s_i[j]$ for j^{th} element of such a vector (the label associated with the token $x_{i-k+j+1}$) and $s_i[j_1 \ldots j_2]$ the sequence of elements between indices j_1 and j_2.
- We conceptually associate every character $x_i, i = 1, \ldots, L$ with a copy of S, $S^i = \{s_1^i, \ldots, s_m^i\}$; this set represents all the possible labeling of characters x_{i-k+1}^i at the stage where x_i is examined.

3. Note that the resulting model cannot really be called a MaxEnt model, as it does not yield the model that has the maximum entropy (the second term in the product) but rather is a maximum a posteriori model.

- We then create links from the set S^i to the set S^{i+1} for all $i = 1 \ldots L-1$, with the property that

$$w\left(s_{j_1}^i, s_{j_2}^{i+1}\right) = \begin{cases} p\left(s_{j_1}^{i+1}[k]\,|x_1^L, s_{j_2}^{i+1}[1..k-1]\right) \\ \quad if\ s_{j_1}^i[2..k] = s_{j_2}^{i+1}[1..k-1] \\ 0 \qquad\qquad\qquad \text{otherwise} \end{cases}$$

These weights correspond to probability of a transition from the state $s_{j_1}^i$ to the state $s_{j_2}^{i+1}$. If the states are not compatible (i.e., there is no possible tag sequence Y such that $Y[i-k+1,\ldots,i]$ is the sequence of labels associated with the tokens x_{i-k+1}^i and $Y[i-k+2, i+1]$ is the sequence of classification tags associated with the token sequence x_{i-k+2}^{i+1}), then the weight is 0. If the two states are compatible, the weight is proportional to predicting the tag $s_{j_2}^{i+1}[k]$ in the tag context $s_{j_2}^{i+1}[1\ldots k-1]$ and observed token sequence x_1^L.

- For every token x_i, we compute recursively[4]

$$\begin{aligned} \alpha_0(s_j) &= 0, j = 1,\ldots,k \\ \alpha_i(s_j) &= \max_{j_1=1,\ldots,M} \alpha_{i-1}(s_{j_1}) + \log w\left(s_{j_1}^{i-1}, s_j^i\right) \\ \gamma_i(s_j) &= \arg\max_{j_1=1,\ldots,M} \alpha_{i-1}(s_{j_1}) + \log w\left(s_{j_1}^{i-1}, s_j^i\right) \end{aligned}$$

Intuitively, $\alpha_i(s_j)$ represents the log-probability of the most probable path through the lattice that ends in state s_j after i steps, and $\gamma_i(s_j)$ represents the state just before s_j on that particular path.[5]

- Having computed the $(\alpha_i)_i$ values, the algorithm for finding the best path, which corresponds to the solution of Equation 8.1, is

1. Identify $\widehat{s}_L^L = \arg\max_{j=1\ldots L} \alpha_L(s_j)$
2. For $i = L-1\ldots 1$, compute $\widehat{s}_i^i = \gamma_{i+1}\left(\widehat{s}_{i+1}^{i+1}\right)$
3. The solution for Equation 8.1 is given by

$$\widehat{y} = \left\{\widehat{s}_1^1[k], \widehat{s}_2^2[k], \ldots, \widehat{s}_L^L[k]\right\}$$

The full algorithm is presented in Algorithm 8–1. The time complexity of the algorithm is $\Theta\left(|\mathcal{Y}|^k \cdot L\right)$, linear in the size of the sentence L but exponential in the size of the Markov dependency, k. To reduce the search space, we use **beam search**.

---

4. For convenience, the index i associated with state s_j^i is moved to α; the function $\alpha_i(s_j)$ is in fact $\alpha(s_j^i)$.
5. For numerical reasons, the values α_i are computed in log space because computing them in normal space will result in underflow for even short sentences. Alternatively, we can compute a normalized version of the α_i coefficients, where they are normalized at each stage by the sum of all coefficients in the trellis column.

Algorithm 8–1 Viterbi search

Input: tokens w_1^L.
Output: the most probable sequence of tags (i.e., mentions) $\widehat{y}_1^L = \arg\max_{y_1^L} P\left(y_1^L|x_1^L\right)$
Create $S = \{s_1, \ldots, s_M\}$, an enumeration of $\mathcal{Y}^k$
for $j = 1, M$ **do** $a_j \leftarrow 0$
for $i = 1-k, L+k$ **do**
    for $j = 1, M$ **do**
        $\gamma_{ij} = 1,\ b_j = -\infty$
        for $j' = 1, M$ **such that** $s_{j'}[2..k] = s_j[1..k-1]$ **do**
            $v \leftarrow a_{j'} - \log w\left(s_{j'}^{i-1}, s_j^i\right)$
            if $(v > b_j)$ **then**
                $b_j \leftarrow v,\ \gamma_{ij} \leftarrow j'$
    $a \leftarrow b$
$\widehat{s}_{L+k} = \arg\max_{j=1\ldots m} a_j$
$j = \arg\max_j \gamma_{L+k,j}$
for $i = L+k-1 \ldots 1$ **do** $\widehat{s}_i \leftarrow s_j,\ j \leftarrow \gamma_{i+1,j}$
$\widehat{y}_1^L \leftarrow (\widehat{s}_1[1], \widehat{s}_2[1], \ldots, \widehat{s}_L[1])$

Beam Search

Anyone implementing Algorithm 8–1 faces a practical challenge: even for small values of k, the space $\mathcal{Y}^k$ can be quite large, especially if the classification space is large. This problem arises because the algorithm's search space size is proportional to $|\mathcal{Y}|^k$. This is the reason why, in practice, for many NLP tasks, a beam search algorithm is preferred instead. This algorithm is constructed around the idea that many of the nodes in the trellis have such small α values that they will not be included in any "good" paths and therefore can be skipped from computation without any loss in performance. To achieve this, the algorithm keeps only a few of the $M = |\mathcal{Y}|^k$ states alive at any trellis stage i. Then, after computing the expansion of those nodes for stage $i+1$, it eliminates some of the resulting states on the basis of their α_i values. We can use a variety of filtering techniques, among which the two most commonly used are:

- fixed beam: keep only the n top-scoring candidates at each stage i for expansion.
- variable beam: keep only the candidates that are within a specified relative distance (in terms of α_i) from the top-scoring candidate at stage i.

Both options are good choices. Experience shows that a beam of 5 and a relative beam of 30% can be used to speed up the computation significantly (20–30 times) with almost no drop in performance. These parameter values should be optimized on a held-out development data set for a specific task, and may also vary depending on how the researcher wants to trade off speed for accuracy.

8.2.3 Mention Detection Features

As mentioned previously within the MaxEnt framework, any type of feature can be used. This enables the system designer to experiment with interesting feature types rather than worry about specific feature interactions. In contrast, in a rule-based system, the system designer would have to consider how, for instance, information derived from a dictionary for a particular example interacts with part-of-speech (POS)–based information and chunking information. That is not to argue that, ultimately, rule-based systems are in some aspect inferior to statistical models. Rule-based systems are built using valuable insight, which is hard to obtain if we limit ourselves to the approach of statistical modeling. In fact, the output of such a rule-based system can be easily integrated into the MaxEnt framework as one of the input features; this usually leads to performance greater than could be achieved by either type of system on its own.

The particular features used in a typical mention detection system can be divided into four categories: lexical; syntactic; information obtained from other named entity classifiers (with different semantic tag sets); and gazetteers-based features and features obtained using crosslanguage mention propagation. We also use the two previously assigned classification tags as an additional feature.

1. **Lexical features**
   The identity and context of a current token (segment) x_i is clearly one of the most important features in predicting whether or not x_i is a mention [3, 5]. Lexical features are implemented as token n-grams spanning the current token, both preceding and following it. For a token x_i, token n-gram features will contain the previous $n-1$ tokens $(x_{i-n+1}, \ldots, x_{i-1})$ and the following $n-1$ tokens $(x_{i+1}, \ldots, x_{i+n-1})$. A number of n equal to 3 turned out to be a good choice.

   In a case of languages with high morphology, such as Arabic, we may think of implementing features that look to stem n-grams spanning the current stem, both preceding and following it [4]. If the current token x_i is a stem, stem n-gram features contain the previous $n-1$ stems and the following $n-1$ stems. Stem n-gram features represent a lexical generalization that reduces data sparseness, introduced by attaching prefixes and suffixes to the base form (i.e., stem) of words. In our experiments, n is set to 3 (stem trigram features).

2. **Syntactic features**
   Syntactic features include POS tags and shallow parsing information. They introduce another level of abstraction and generality when predicting the mentions. We have found it effective to use POS and shallow parsing information within a short window of the current token. For example, for each token in a window of five (current, two previous, and two next), we can compute features based on POS and chunking information.[6] The POS information helps disambiguate some tokens. The shallow parsing information, or text-chunks, helps define the boundary of a mention. As an example, if two contiguous tokens x_i, x_{i+1} belong to two different groups (e.g., nominal phrase and verbal phrase respectively), and if x_i is part of some mention m_j, then x_{i+1} is unlikely to be part of the same mention m_j.

3. **Features from other named entity classifiers**
   In addition to using rich lexical and syntactic features, it is often useful to leverage different mention taggers. These taggers are trained on data sets different from the

6. A **chunk** is a short sequence of words that typically corresponds to a syntactic phrase, usually one that does not have any subphrases.

"primary" tagger. Furthermore, these taggers may identify types of mentions different from the mentions of interest in our task. Suppose we are focused on the ACE task. One of these alternative taggers may identify dates or occupation references (which are not part of ACE), among other types. It might identify a class called PERSON, but under the respective annotation guidelines, it may not match exactly the notion of the PERSON type in our task. One hypothesis—the **combination hypothesis**—is that combining mention/named entity classifiers from diverse sources will boost performance by injecting complementary information into the mention detection models. Indeed, as shown by Borthwick et al. [24], the output of a diverse set of taggers can be quite effective as additional feature streams for the mention detection models. This approach allows the system to automatically correlate the different mention types to the desired output; no manual mapping is required.

4. **Gazetteer-based features**
A **gazetteer** is a special type of dictionary containing lexical items of a particular type.[7] Gazetteers for mention detection systems typically comprise person names, country names, and company names. A name gazetteer usually contains single-token names, such as Daniel or Gafsa, as well as phrases, such as Ben Ali, Barak Obama, or United States. Mention detection systems can benefit from simple feature functions that return whether a particular token is a member of a name in a gazetteer. More formally, when processing a token x_i, we check if the token itself x_i or its surrounding tokens $(x_{i-n}, \ldots, x_{i+m})$ belong to one of the gazetteers.

5. **Crosslanguage mention propagation features**
Few languages other than English have large and high-quality data resources available. Most languages, however, do have smaller data resources available. We can mitigate this difference by using the large resources in one language to improve a mention detection system in another language. The approach requires a mention detection system built in the resource-rich language and a translation from the source language to the resource-rich language together with **word alignment**. We first use a statistical machine translation (SMT) system to translate the source unit (document or sentence) x_1^N into the resource-rich language, yielding the sequence $\xi_1^M = (\xi_1, \xi_2, \ldots, \xi_M)$. Taking the sequence of tokens ξ_1^M as input, the mention detection system built in a resource-rich language assigns a mention label to each token, building the label sequence $\psi_1^M = (\psi_1, \psi_2 \ldots \psi_M)$. Using the SMT-produced word alignment between source text x_1^N and translated text ξ_1^M [25], we propagate the target labels ψ_1^M to the source language, building the label sequence $\widetilde{y}_1^N = (\widetilde{y}_1, \widetilde{y}_2 \ldots \widetilde{y}_N)$.[8] As an example, if a sequence of tokens in the resource-rich language $\xi_i \xi_{i+1} \xi_{i+2}$ is aligned to $x_j x_{j+1}$ in the source language, and if $\xi_i \xi_{i+1} \xi_{i+2}$ is tagged as a location mention, then the sequence $x_j x_{j+1}$ can be labeled as a location mention: B-LOC, I-LOC. Hence, each token x_i in x_1^N is tagged with a corresponding propagated label $\widetilde{y}_i$ in $\widetilde{y}_1^N$, $\widetilde{y}_i = \phi\left(i, A, \psi_1^M\right)$, where A is the alignment between the source and resource-rich languages. Once we use SMT word alignment to propagate label sequence ψ_1^M of ξ_1^M to the corresponding text x_1^N in the target language, we end up with a sequence of labels $\widetilde{y}_1^N$ where for each token x_i

7. Technically, the term *gazetteer* specifically refers to a list of place names, but the term has been applied more broadly by those in the NLP community.
8. Or by using Giza++ if your favorite engine does not give you word alignment.

in x_1^N we attach its label $\widetilde{y}_i$ in $\widetilde{y}_1^N$. This sequence of labels can be used as an additional feature in the MaxEnt framework or can be used to build gazetteer-based features. For more details about crosslanguage mention propagation for mention detection, refer to Zitouni and Florian [26] and Benajiba and Ztouni [27].

8.2.4 Mention Detection Experiments

Experiments are conducted on the ACE 2007 data sets[9] in four languages: Arabic, Chinese, English, and Spanish. This data is selected from a variety of sources (broadcast news, broadcast conversations, newswires, blogs, conversational telephony) and is labeled with seven types: PERSON, ORGANIZATION, LOCATION, FACILITY, GPE (geopolitical entity), VEHICLE, and WEAPON. Besides mention-level information, also labeled are coreferences between the mentions, relations, events, and time resolution.

Because the evaluation test sets are not publicly available, we split the publicly available training corpus into an 85%/15% data split. To facilitate future comparisons with work presented here, and to simulate a realistic scenario, the splits are created on the basis of article dates: the test data is selected as the latest 15% of the data in chronological order in each of the covered genres. This way, the documents in the training and test data sets do not overlap in time, and the content of the test data is more recent than the training data. Table 8–1 presents the number of documents in the training/test data sets for each of the four languages.

Although performance on the ACE data is usually evaluated using a special-purpose measure, the ACE value metric [1], given that we are interested in the mention detection task only, we use here the more intuitive and popular (unweighted) F-measure, the harmonic mean of precision and recall.

Table 8–2 shows the performance of mention detection systems in all four languages that can be obtained by using all available resources in that language, including lexical (words and morphs in a three-word window, prefixes and suffixes of length up to four, WordNet [28] for English), syntactic (POS tags, text chunks), and the output of other information extraction models.

Results show that the English mention detection system has a better performance when compared to systems dealing with other languages such as Arabic, Chinese, and Spanish.

Table 8–1: The sizes of data sets in number of documents

Language	Training	Test
Arabic	323	56
Chinese	538	95
English	499	100
Spanish	467	52

9. Same data as for ACE 2008.

Table 8–2: Performance of Arabic, Chinese, English, and Spanish mention detection systems. Performance is presented in terms of precision (P), recall (R), and F-measure (F). The column (N) displays the number of mentions in the test set.

	N	P	R	F
Arabic	3566	83.6	76.8	**80.0**
Chinese	4791	81.1	71.3	**75.8**
English	8170	84.6	80.8	**82.7**
Spanish	2487	79.1	73.5	**76.2**

These results are expected because the English model has access to a larger training data set and uses a richer set of information such as WordNet [28] and the output of a larger set of information extraction models.

Another experiment is to use the high-performance English mention detection system and study the impact of the crosslanguage mention propagation feature to improve systems in other languages; specifically, we look at improving systems in Arabic, Chinese, and Spanish. For this, we use three SMT systems with very competitive performance in terms of BLEU [29].[10] The Arabic-to-English SMT system is similar to the one described by Huang and Papineni [30]; it has 0.55 BLEU score on the National Institute of Standards and Technology (NIST) 2003 Arabic-English machine translation evaluation test set. The Chinese-to-English SMT system has similar architecture to the one described by Al-Onaizan and Papineni [31]. This system obtains a score of 0.32 cased BLEU on the NIST 2003 Arabic-English machine translation evaluation test set. The Spanish-to-English SMT system is similar to the one described by Lee et al. [32]; it has a 0.55 BLEU score on the final text edition of the European Parliament Plenary Speech corpus in TC-STAR 2006 evaluation. Table 8–3 presents the performance of mention detection systems on Arabic, Chinese, and Spanish when they benefit from features extracted from the English mention detection system. The performance of mention detection systems is improved by 0.9F for Arabic (80.9 vs. 80.0), 2.3F for Chinese (78.1F vs. 75.8F), and 1.9F for Spanish (78.1 vs. 76.2F). Results show that the use of crosslanguage mention propagation information is effective in improving the performance even in this case. Zitouni and Florian [26] show that the improvement in performance has a decreasing tendency as more resources are available in the language to improve. Obtained results help answer an important question: When trying to improve mention detection systems in a resource-poor language, should we invest in building resources, or should we use propagation from a resource-rich language to (at least) bootstrap the process? The answer seems to be the latter.

10. BLEU is an automatic measure for the translation quality that makes good use of multiple reference translations.

Table 8–3: Performance of Arabic, Chinese, and Spanish mention detection systems using lexical, syntactic, output of other information extraction models, and crosslanguage mention propagation features: full-blown systems. Performance is presented in terms of precision (P), recall (R), and F-measure (F). The column displays the number of mentions in the test set.

	Crosslanguage Mention Propagation			
	N	P	R	F
Arabic	3,566	84.2	77.8	**80.9**
Chinese	4,791	81.7	74.8	**78.1**
Spanish	2,487	80.1	76.2	**78.1**

8.3 Coreference Resolution

Knowing individual mentions in a document may not be sufficient for some natural language applications. For example, consider the problem of answering the question *When was John F. Kennedy assassinated?* based on the following passage:

> *John F. Kennedy* was the thirty-fifth President of the United States. He was later assassinated on Friday, November 22, 1963.

The answer is found in the last sentence where *John F. Kennedy* is referred to by a pronominal mention, *He*. Thus it is crucial to know that *He* refers to *John F. Kennedy* in order to answer the question correctly.

The process of chaining mentions referring to the same physical object into an entity is called **coreference resolution**. Coreference resolution is closely related to anaphora resolution, which concerns finding the correct antecedent for a pronoun. We use *coreference resolution* because the scope of the problem to be discussed in the section is broader than that of anaphora resolution in that it includes resolving the referential relationships of all kinds of noun phrases.

While there is much work with rule-based approaches [33, 34, 35, 36] to coreference resolution, we concentrate here on the machine learning-based approaches. We find plenty of published work for building learnable coreference resolution systems [37, 38, 39, 40, 41, 42, 43]. Early systems [37, 38] learn a model from training data that assigns a score to a pair of mentions indicating the likelihood that the two mentions refer to the same entity. Mentions are then clustered into entities on the basis of mention-pair scores. One technical difficulty associated with this type of system is the transitivity. For instance, if mention A is linked[11] with mention B, mention B is linked with mention C, but mention A is not linked with

11. That is, when the score is above a preset threshold.

mention C, the system will not be able to enforce the transitivity. In practice, mention-pair-based systems often go around this problem by linking a mention to either the first candidate antecedent whose score is above the threshold or the best one among a group of candidate antecedents. To overcome this shortcoming, some researchers [40, 44, 42] employ entity-mention models where a score is computed on a candidate entity and the current mention. Ng [45] provides an excellent account of the research community's progress in the past 10 to 15 years in machine learning-based coreference resolution. Ng's work also contains pointers to resources such as annotated coreference corpora and results of various shared tasks. In the rest of this chapter, we concentrate on one coreference resolution system based on the Bell tree algorithm [40]. Our goal is that practitioners can implement the presented algorithm after reading the chapter.

8.3.1 The Construction of Bell Tree

Bell tree is a data structure representing the hypothesis space of entity outcomes from mentions in a document. It is well known that the number of ways partitioning n objects into disjoint nonempty subsets is the Bell number [46], $B(n)$. The Bell number has a "closed" formula $B(n) = \frac{1}{e}\sum_{k=0}^{\infty}\frac{k^n}{k!}$ and it increases rapidly as n grows; for example, $B(20) \approx 5.2 \times 10^{13}$, which is already an intractable number! It is out of the question to search exhaustively the entire space, and so an efficient search strategy is needed.

But before we tackle the search issue, we first describe the process of constructing the Bell tree from mentions in a document and the coreference models. We imagine that entities in a document are created from mentions in an incremental and synchronous fashion by constructing a Bell tree. The first mention is used to create the root of this tree. Each subsequent mention either *starts* a new entity or is *linked* with one of the existing entities. At the end of this process, each leaf node represents a possible coreference outcome. The process is **mention-synchronous** in that each layer of tree nodes is created by adding one new mention. Because the number of tree leaves is the number of possible coreference outcomes and it is equal to the Bell number ([46]), this tree is called Bell tree.

Figure 8–1 illustrates how the Bell tree is created for three mentions in the following sentence:

> *President* Ben Ali said that his minister, Mohammed Ghannouchi, will present the case.

The initial node consists of the first partial entity *[President]* (i.e., node (a) in Figure 8–1). Next, mention *Ben Ali* becomes active (see the top line of Figure 8–1) and can either link with the partial entity *[President]* and result in a new node (b1), or start a new entity and create another node (b2). The partial entity that the active mention considers linking with is said to be *in-focus*. Similarly, mention *his* will be active in the next stage and can take five possible actions, which create five possible coreference results shown in nodes (c1) through (c5).

Under the derivation illustrated in Figure 8–1, each leaf node in the Bell tree corresponds to a possible coreference outcome, and there is no other possible entity outcome. Therefore, the Bell tree fully represents the search space of the coreference resolution problem. The coreference resolution can thus be cast equivalently as finding the "best" leaf node. Because the search space is large, even for a document with a moderate number of mentions, it is difficult to estimate a distribution over leaves directly. Instead, we choose to model the

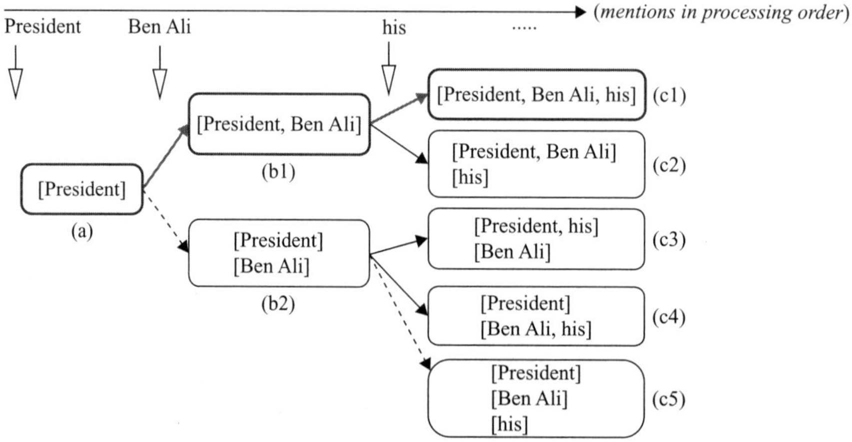

Figure 8–1: Bell tree representation of the process of forming entities from mentions. Mentions in [ ] denote a partial entity. Solid arrows signify that a mention is linked with an in-focus partial entity, and dashed arrows indicate starting a new entity. Mentions here are processed in the order they appear in the text

process from mentions to entities. By taking a dynamic view of the entity creation, the coreference resolution problem is naturally cast into scoring the competing paths in the Bell tree.

A nice property of the Bell tree representation is that the number of linking or starting steps is the same for all the hypotheses. This makes it easy to rank them using the "local" linking and starting probabilities because the number of factors is the same.

The Bell tree representation is also incremental in that mentions are added sequentially. This makes it easy to design a decoder and search algorithm: coreference models are presented in Section 8.3.2, but let us assume for the time being that there are models to score linking and starting branches. Then decoding a document is nothing but constructing the Bell tree with mentions in it, as just described, and scoring the paths in the tree. After processing n mentions, we get a depth-(n-1) tree. We then prune all partial paths whose cumulative scores fall below a threshold (relative to the highest score) before extending the tree with the next mention; in other words, we perform a breadth-first search on the Bell tree with pruning.

8.3.2 Coreference Models: Linking and Starting Model

We use a binary conditional model to compute the probability that an active mention links with an in-focus partial entity. The conditions include all the partially formed entities before, the focus entity index, and the active mention.[12]

Formally, let $\{m_i : 1 \leq i \leq n\}$ be n mentions in a document. Mention index i represents the order by which mentions are processed in the document (not necessarily the document order). Let e_j be an entity, and $g : i \mapsto j$ be the (many-to-one) map from mention index i

12. The document itself is always part of the context or conditioning. It is omitted to simplify typesetting.

to entity index j. For an active mention index $k (1 \leq k \leq n)$, define

$$I_k = \{t : t = g(i), \quad \text{for some} \quad 1 \leq i \leq k-1\}, \tag{8.4}$$

the set of indices of the partially established entities prior to m_k (note that $I_1 = \emptyset$), and

$$E_k = \{e_t : t \in I_k\},$$

the set of the partially established entities. The link probability is then

$$P(L|E_k, m_k, A_k = t), \tag{8.5}$$

the probability linking the active mention m_k with the in-focus entity e_t. The random variable A_k takes value from the set I_k and signifies which entity is in focus; L takes binary value and is 1 if m_k links with e_t, and 0 otherwise.

As an example, for the branch from (b2) to (c4) in Figure 8–1, the active mention is *his*, the set of partial entities prior to processing `his` is $E_3 = \{[\text{President}], [\text{Ben Ali}]\}$, and the active entity is the second partial entity *[Ben Ali]*. Probability $P(L = 1|E_3, \text{his}, A_3 = 2)$ measures how likely mention *his* links with the entity *[Ben Ali]*.

$P(L|E_k, m_k, A_k = t)$ only measures how likely m_k links with e_t. It does not say anything about the possibility that m_k starts a new entity. Fortunately, the starting probability can be computed using link probabilities (Equation 8.5), as shown now.

Because starting a new entity means that m_k does not link with any entities in E_k, the probability of starting a new entity, $P(L = 0|E_k, m_k)$, can be computed as

$$\begin{aligned} & P(L = 0|E_k, m_k) && (8.6) \\ & \quad = \sum_{t \in I_k} P(L = 0, A_k = t|E_k, m_k) \\ & \quad = 1 - \sum_{t \in I_k} P(A_k = t|E_k, m_k) P(L = 1|E_k, m_k, A_k = t). && (8.7) \end{aligned}$$

Equation 8.7 indicates that the probability of starting an entity can be computed using the linking probabilities $P(L=1|E_k, m_k, A_k=t)$, provided that the marginal $P(A_k=t|E_k, m_k)$ is known. The model component $P(A_k=t|E_k, m_k)$ can also be interpreted as the candidate entity selection model: given the current mention m_k and the set of entities created so far E_k, $P(A_k = t|E_k, m_k)$ is then the probability of e_t being the candidate entity.

Training directly a model for $P(A_k = t|E_k, m_k)$ is difficult because I_k increases in size as mentions are processed. Instead, we approximate $P(A_k = t|E_k, m_k)$ as follows:

$$P(A_k = t|E_k, m_k) = \begin{cases} 1 & \text{if } t = \arg\max_{i \in I_k} \\ & \quad P(L = 1|E_k, m_k, A_k = i) \\ 0 & \text{otherwise} \end{cases} \tag{8.8}$$

Equation 8.8 is not the only way $P(A_k = t|E_k, m_k)$ can be approximated. For example, we could use a uniform distribution over I_k. We experimented with several schemes of approximation, including a uniform distribution, and Equation 8.8 worked the best, so it is adopted here. We may consider training $P(A_k = t|E_k, m_k)$ directly and using it to score paths in the Bell tree. The problem is that the size of I_k from which A_k takes value is variable, and the start action depends on all entities in E_k, which makes it difficult to train $P(A_k = t|E_k, m_k)$ directly.

With the approximation Equation 8.8, the starting probability in Equation 8.7 becomes

$$\begin{aligned} P(L = 0|E_k, m_k) & \\ &= 1 - \max{}_{t \in I_k} P(L = 1|E_k, m_k, A_k = t). \end{aligned} \tag{8.9}$$

The linking probability (see Equation 8.5) and approximated starting probability (Equation 8.9) are used to score paths in the Bell tree. For example, the score for the path (a)-(b2)-(c4) in Figure 8–1 is the product of the start probability from (a) to (b2) and the linking probability from (b2) to (c4).

Because Equation 8.9 is only an approximation, we also introduce a constant α to balance the linking probability and starting probability, and the actual starting score then becomes:

$$P_\alpha(L = 0|E_k, m_k) = \alpha P(L = 0|E_k, m_k). \tag{8.10}$$

If $\alpha < 1$, it penalizes creating new entities; therefore, α is called **start penalty**. The start penalty α is often tuned on a development test and can be used to balance entity miss and false alarm.

The model $P(L|E_k, m_k, A_k = t)$ depends on all partial entities E_k, which is still very expensive. When linking a mention m_k with the in-focus entity e_t, it is reasonable to assume that it does not depend on other entities. Thus,

$$\begin{aligned} P(L = 1|E_k, m_k, A_k = t) & \qquad (8.11)\\ \approx P(L = 1|e_t, m_k) & \qquad (8.12)\\ \approx \max_{m \in e_t} P(L = 1|e_t, m, m_k). & \qquad (8.13) \end{aligned}$$

From Equation 8.11 to 8.12, entities other than the one in focus, e_t, are assumed to have no influence on the decision of linking m_k with e_t. Equation 8.13 further assumes that the entity-mention score can be obtained by the score of the maximum mention pair. The model in Equation 8.13 is very similar to the model used by Morton [47], Soon, Ng, and Lim [37], and Ng and Cardie [38], except that Equation 8.13 can incorporate entity-level features because e_t is part of conditioning.

8.3.3 A Maximum Entropy Linking Model

A MaxEnt model is adopted for the model in Equation 8.13:

$$\begin{aligned} P(L|e_t, m, m_k) & \\ = \frac{1}{Z(e_t, m, m_k)} & \exp\left[\sum_i \lambda_i g_i(m, m_k, L) + \sum_j \lambda_j h_j(e_t, m_k, L)\right] \end{aligned} \tag{8.14}$$

where $g_i(m, m_k, L)$ is a mention-pair feature, and $h_j(e_t, m_k, L)$ is an entity-level feature because it is computed over entity e_t and mention m_k. The entity-level features can be used to implicitly capture things such as gender and number agreement between an entity e_t and the current mention m_k; mention-pair features, on the other hand, are useful when encoding lexical features, such as whether or not surface strings of m and m_k match. Once features are selected in a MaxEnt model, optimal feature weights $\{\lambda_i\}$ and $\{\lambda_j\}$ can be found efficiently, as described by Berger, Della Pietra, Della Pietra [17].

Because the relationship between an entity and a mention (or a pair of mentions) is characterized by features, a good set of features are crucial for a system's performance. The features used in the coreference model are organized by groups, and most features are general and portable across languages, while some other features, such as stem-matching features, are designed to capture the morphological similarity in Arabic:

1. Lexical features are specific to nonpronominal mentions only. They include exact or partial matching surface strings of two mentions, and acronyms, and actual pairing of mention spellings.

2. Attribute features are computed from training data, if available. For example, ACE training data includes entity type, entity subtype, and mention type information which can be used to characterize which mentions are in the same entity. Because pronouns are a closed category, we extract the gender, number, possessiveness, and reflexivity of a pronoun and propagate it to the entity where it belongs.

3. Edit distance is a feature that computes the editing distance of two strings (i.e., spellings of two mentions) and quantizes the distance. It is another way to characterize the similarity of two mentions.

4. Distance features characterize how far apart the two mentions are, either by the number of tokens, by the number of sentences, or by the number of mentions in between.

5. Stem-matching features try to compare stems of two mentions. These features are designed specifically for language such as Arabic.

6. Agreement features are computed over a pair of mention and entity. They are meant to check the gender and number agreement between a mention and an entity. Notice that this set of features is different from the gender and number attributes of pronouns.

7. Syntactic features are derived from parse trees generated automatically by a MaxEnt parser [48] trained on the Arabic Penn Treebank [49]. The POS tags of mention heads are also extracted from the parse trees. We also test if two mentions in the same sentence are appositive by examining their structural relationship in the parse tree. Because binding theory [50] has a very good account of pronoun resolution, a group of features are computed for pronoun mentions to characterize whether or not a within-sentence candidate antecedent of the pronoun is in or out of the governing category. Luo and Zitouni [44] provide details of this set of features.

Apart from these basic features, composite features are generated by taking a conjunction of selected basic features. For example, a distance feature together with reflexiveness of a pronoun mention can help to capture that the antecedent of a reflexive pronoun is often closer than that of a nonreflexive pronoun.

8.3.4 Coreference Resolution Experiments

We report the experimental results on the most recent ACE data [51].[13] The data set consists of 599 documents from rich and diversified sources, which include newswire articles, blogs, Usenet posts, transcriptions of broadcast news, broadcast conversations, and telephone conversations. We reserve the last 16% documents of each source as the test set and use the rest of the documents as the training set. Statistics such as the number of documents, words, mentions, and entities of this data split are tabulated in Table 8–4.

The 2008 ACE-value is the official score reported in the ACE task and is used to report our coreference system's performance. Its detailed definition can be found in the official evaluation document.[14] Because ACE-Value is a weighted metric measuring a coreference system's relative value, and because weights and its formula changed from year to year in the course of the ACE program, it is important to know what year's scorer is used when comparing two systems. It is also worth noting that ACE-value is not sensitive to certain type of errors because they are heavily down-weighted (e.g., pronoun errors are weighted one-tenth of that of named errors).

Table 8–5 contains the results on the aforementioned test set, which are computed with the latest ACE08 scorer: http://www.itl.nist.gov/iad/mig//tests/ace/2008/software/ace08-eval-v17.pl. The second column is the F-measure based on ACE08-value, and the last column is the official ACE-value. The second row contains the results when gold mentions are used as the input to the coreference system, and the last row corresponds to the results for mentions

Table 8–4: Statistics of ACE data: number of documents, words, mentions, and entities in the training and test set

Data Set	Docs	Words	Mentions	Entities
Training	499	253,771	46,646	16,102
Test	100	45,659	8,178	2,709
Total	599	299,430	54,824	18,811

Table 8–5: Coreference results measured by ACE08 scorer: the second column is the value-based B3-F measure, and ACE08-Value is the official metric

Mention	valB3-F	ACE08-Value
Gold	89.1	79.8
System	80.2	60.3

13. In ACE 2007 and 2008 evaluations, no new training data was released; in other words, the same training data was used in 2005, 2007, and 2008.

14. The official evaluation document can be found at http://www.itl.nist.gov/iad/mig/tests/ace/2008/doc/ace08-evalplan.v1.2d.pdf.

detected by system. As can be seen, when gold mentions are given, the coreference system can achieve fairly high ACE-value. However, noisy system mentions degrade considerably the performance, lowering the ACE-value from 79.8% to 60.3%.

8.4 Summary

In this chapter, we discussed two important tasks in information extraction: mention detection and coreference resolution. An example cascaded system implementation was presented in detail. The system consists of a MaxEnt-based mention detection component followed by a coreference system based on the Bell tree algorithm. The mention detection component detects mentions by treating it as a sequential tagging problem, which makes use of a variety of lexical, syntactic, and semantic features extracted automatically from training data. The Bell tree-based coreference system searches the best coreference result for a document by finding a path from the root to one of the leaf nodes in the Bell tree, which is used to represent the hypothesis space. An entity-mention binary model is used to score every branch on the path. The strength of such statistical systems is that they are data driven and can be quickly ported to other languages while capturing language-specific idiosyncrasies as features.

We pointed out that mention detection and coreference resolution can be solved in a joint fashion because they are closely related in that some mention decisions need coreference resolution (and vice versa). In practice, though, the complexity of a joint system often overshadows its benefit, and this is an area worthy of further research. The output of mention detection and coreference forms the basis for further deeper analysis, such as relation and event extraction, discussed in Chapter 9. It can also be used directly by downstream applications such as question answering (discussed in Chapter 13) or machine translation (discussed in Chapter 10) systems.

Bibliography

[1] NIST (National Institute of Standards and Technology), "The ACE evaluation plan," 2007. www.nist.gov/speech/tests/ace/index.htm.

[2] H. Daumé III and D. Marcu, "A large-scale exploration of effective global features for a joint entity detection and tracking model," in *Proceedings of the Conference on Human Language Technology and Empirical Methods in Natural Language Processing*, pp. 97–104, 2005.

[3] R. Florian, H. Hassan, A. Ittycheriah, H. Jing, N. Kambhatla, X. Luo, N. Nicolov, and S. Roukos, "A statistical model for multilingual entity detection and tracking," in *Proceedings of the Human Language Technology Conference of the North American Chapter of the Association for Computational Linguistics (HLT-NAACL 2004)*, pp. 1–8, 2004.

[4] I. Zitouni, J. Sorensen, X. Luo, and R. Florian, "The impact of morphological stemming on Arabic mention detection and coreference resolution," in *Proceedings of the ACL Workshop on Computational Approaches to Semitic Languages*, pp. 63–70, 2005.

[5] I. Zitouni, X. Luo, and R. Florian, "A cascaded approach to mention detection and chaining in Arabic," *IEEE Transactions on Audio, Speech and Language Processing*, vol. 17, pp. 935–944, 2009.

[6] Y. Benajiba, M. Diab, and P. Rosso, "Arabic named entity recognition: A feature-driven study," *In the special issue on Processing Morphologically Rich Languages of the IEEE Transaction on Audio, Speech and Language*, 2009.

[7] R. Florian, Abe Ittycheriah, H. Jing, and T. Zhang, "Named entity recognition through classifier combination," in *Conference on Computational Natural Language Learning*, 2003.

[8] H.-L. Chieu and H. Ng., "Named entity recognition with a maximum entropy approach," in *Conference on Computational Natural Language Learning*, 2003.

[9] D. Klein, Joseph Smarr, H. Nguyen, and C. Manning, "Named entity recognition with character-level models," in *Conference on Computational Natural Language Learning*, 2003.

[10] Q. T. Tran, T. T. Pham, Q. Hung-Ngo, D. Dinh, and N. Collier, "Named entity recognition in Vietnamese documents," *Progress in Informatics Journal*, no. 4, 2007.

[11] Y. Benajiba and P. Rosso, "Arabic named entity recognition using conditional random fields," in *Workshop on HLT and NLP within the Arabic world. Arabic Language and local languages processing: Status Updates and Prospects, 6th International Conference on Language Resources and Evaluation* (LREC), 2008.

[12] R. Florian, H. Jing, N. Kambhatla, and I. Zitouni, "Factorizing complex models: A case study in mention detection," in *Proceedings of the 21st International Conference on Computational Linguistics and 44th Annual Meeting of the Association for Computational Linguistics*, pp. 473–480, 2006.

[13] L. Ramshaw and M. Marcus, "Exploring the statistical derivation of transformational rule sequences for part-of-speech tagging," in *The Balancing Act: Proceedings of the ACL Workshop on Combining Symbolic and Statistical Approaches to Language*, pp. 128–135, 1994.

[14] L. Ramshaw and M. Marcus, "Text chunking using transformation-based learning," in *Proceedings of the Third Workshop on Very Large Corpora*, pp. 82–94, 1995.

[15] E. F. Tjong Kim Sang, "Introduction to the CoNLL-2002 shared task: Language-independent named entity recognition," in *Proceedings the Conference on Natural Language Learning*, pp. 155–158, 2002.

[16] J. N. Darroch and D. Ratcliff, "Generalized iterative scaling for log-linear models," *The Annals of Mathematical Statistics*, vol. 43, no. 5, pp. 1470–1480, 1972.

[17] A. Berger, S. Della Pietra, and V. Della Pietra, "A maximum entropy approach to natural language processing," *Computational Linguistics*, vol. 22, no. 1, pp. 39–71, 1996.

[18] J. Goodman, "Sequential conditional generalized iterative scaling," in *Proceedings of the Association for Computational Linguistics*, 2002.

[19] D. C. Liu and J. Nocedal, "On the limited memory BFGS method for large scale optimization," *Mathematical Programming*, vol. 45, no. 3 (Ser. B), pp. 503–528, 1989.

[20] S. Chen and R. Rosenfeld, "A survey of smoothing techniques for me models," *IEEE Transactions on Speech and Audio Processing*, 2000.

[21] J. Goodman, "Exponential priors for maximum entropy models," in *Proceedings of the Human Language Technology Conference of the North American Chapter of the Association for Computational Linguistics*, pp. 305–312, 2004.

[22] S. Khudanpur, "A method of maximum entropy estimation with relaxed constraints," in *1995 Johns Hopkins University Language Modeling Workshop*, 1995.

[23] J. Kazama and J. Tsujii, "Evaluation and extension of maximum entropy models with inequality constraints," in *Proceedings of the 2003 Conference on Empirical Methods in Natural Language Processing*, pp. 137–144, 2003.

[24] A. Borthwick, J. Sterling, E. Agichtein, and R. Grishman, "Exploiting diverse knowledge sources via maximum entropy in named entity recognition," in *Proceedings of the 6th Workshop on Very Large Corpora*, 1998.

[25] P. Koehn, "Pharaoh: A beam search decoder for phrase-based statistical machine translation models," in *Proceedings of the Association for Machine Translation in the Americas*, 2004.

[26] I. Zitouni and R. Florian, "Mention detection crossing the language barrier," in *Proceedings of the Conference on Empirical Methods on Natural Language Processing*, 2008.

[27] Y. Benajiba and I. Zitouni, "Using parallel corpora to enhance mention detection," in *Proceedings of the Conference on Empirical Methods on Natural Language Processing*, 2010.

[28] G. A. Miller, "WordNet: A lexical database," *Communications of the ACM*, vol. 38, no. 11, 1995.

[29] K. Papineni, S. Roukos, T. Ward, and W.-J. Zhu, "BLEU: A method for automatic evaluation of machine translation," in *Proceedings of the 40th Annual Meeting of the Association for Computational Linguistics*, pp. 311–318, 2002.

[30] F. Huang and K. Papineni, "Hierarchical system combination for machine translation," in *Proceedings of the 2007 Joint Conference on Empirical Methods in Natural Language Processing and Computational Natural Language Learning (EMNLP-CoNLL)*, pp. 277–286, 2007.

[31] Y. Al-Onaizan and K. Papineni, "Distortion models for statistical machine translation," in *Proceedings of the 21st International Conference on Computational Linguistics and 44th Annual Meeting of the Association for Computational Linguistics*, pp. 529–536, 2006.

[32] Y.-S. Lee, Y. Al-Onaizan, K. Papineni, and S. Roukos, "IBM spoken language translation system," in *TC-STAR Workshop on Speech-to-Speech Translation*, pp. 13–18, 2006.

[33] J. Hobbs, "Pronoun resolution," Tech. Rep., Dept. of Computer Science, City University of New York, Technical Report TR76-1, 1976.

[34] S. Lappin and H. J. Leass, "An algorithm for pronominal anaphora resolution," *Computational Linguistics*, vol. 20, no. 4, 1994.

[35] R. Mitkov, "Robust pronoun resolution with limited knowledge," in *Proceedings of the 17th Internaltional Conference on Computational Linguistics*, pp. 869–875, 1998.

[36] R. Stuckardt, "Design and enhanced evaluation of a robust anaphor resolution algorithm," *Computational Linguistics*, vol. 27, no. 4, 2001.

[37] W. M. Soon, H. T. Ng, and C. Y. Lim, "A machine learning approach to coreference resolution of noun phrases," *Computational Linguistics*, vol. 27, no. 4, pp. 521–544, 2001.

[38] V. Ng and C. Cardie, "Improving machine learning approaches to coreference resolution," in *Proceedings of the Association for Computational Linguistics*, pp. 104–111, 2002.

[39] X. Yang, G. Zhou, J. Su, and C. L. Tan, "Coreference resolution using competition learning approach," in *Proceedings of the Association for Computational Linguistics*, 2003.

[40] X. Luo, A. Ittycheriah, H. Jing, N. Kambhatla, and S. Roukos, "A mention-synchronous coreference resolution algorithm based on the Bell tree," in *Proceedings of the Association for Computational Linguistics*, 2004.

[41] D. Zelenko, C. Aone, and J. Tibbetts, "Coreference resolution for information extraction," in *ACL 2004: Workshop on Reference Resolution and Its Applications*, pp. 24–31, 2004.

[42] X. Yang, J. Su, J. Lang, C. L. Tan, T. Liu, and S. Li, "An entity-mention model for coreference resolution with inductive logic programming," in *Proceedings of the Association for Computational Linguistics: Human Language Technology*, pp. 843–851, 2008.

[43] A. Rahman and V. Ng, "Supervised models for coreference resolution," in *Proceedings of the 2009 Conference on Empirical Methods in Natural Language Processing*, pp. 968–977, 2009.

[44] X. Luo and I. Zitouni, "Multi-lingual coreference resolution with syntactic features," in *Proceedings of Human Language Technology (HLT)/Empirical Methods in Natural Language Processing (EMNLP)*, 2005.

[45] V. Ng, "Supervised noun phrase coreference research: The first fifteen years," in *Proceedings of the 48th Annual Meeting of the Association for Computational Linguistics*, pp. 1396–1411, 2010.

[46] E. Bell, "Exponential numbers," *American Mathematical Monthly*, pp. 411–419, 1934.

[47] T. S. Morton, "Coreference for NLP applications," in *Proceedings of the 38th Annual Meeting of the Association for Computational Linguistics*, 2000.

[48] K. Toutanova, D. Klein, C. Manning, and Y. Singer, "Feature-rich part-of-speech tagging with a cyclic dependency network," in *Proceedings of the Human Language Technology Conference of the North American Chapter of the Association for Computational Linguistics*, 2003.

[49] M. Maamouri and A. Bies, "Developing an Arabic treebank: Methods, guidelines, procedures, and tools," in *Proceedings of the Workshop on Computational Approaches to Arabic Script-based Languages*, 2004.

[50] L. Haegeman, *Introduction to Government and Binding*, 2nd ed., Oxford: Basil Blackwell, 1994.

[51] NIST (National Institute of Standards and Technology), "ACE 2005 evaluation," 2005. www.nist.gov/speech/tests/ace/ace05/index.htm.

Chapter 9

Relations and Events

Daniel M. Bikel and Vittorio Castelli

9.1 Introduction

The world is awash in words. These words are increasingly being stored electronically: as of 2008, the world surpassed more than 1 trillion unique web pages, all of which contain at least some text, and this number has been growing at more than 1 billion pages per day [1]. As we learned in previous chapters, natural language text is rife with ambiguity *and* loaded with information. In fact, these two properties are quite complementary. With so many electronic text documents, humans have an ever-increasing need for computer systems that can automatically synthesize the free-form, ambiguous text documents into more precise, more compact, structured representations. Such systems are essential for humans to be able to access and process this deluge of documents in an efficient and effective manner. For example, a company may want to follow the public's reaction to its products; a politician may need to follow the sentiment of his or her constituents; an intelligence analyst may want to keep track of the activities or speech attributed to a particular person, group of people, or organization.

For a computer to have something resembling a full understanding of natural language text, it should have a model of syntax, semantics, pragmatics, and/or world knowledge, as well as an appropriately rich representation of meaning. Such a complete notion of understanding is beyond the scope of this chapter. We explore the more limited problem of extracting relevant bits of information to populate a "database" of facts, where what is relevant is specific to each task. More concretely, we define the problem as finding all relevant entities in a corpus of text (explored in detail in Chapter 8), finding all relevant properties of those entities and all relevant relationships among entities, and storing these bits of information in a structured way. Intuitively, once it is populated with facts, our database should allow us to answer the following types of questions via a rather simple database lookup:

- Who are the people or entities mentioned in a particular document or set of documents?
- How many people work at a particular company, and what are their names?
- What are the relationships among a set of people or entities?
- What events, if any, are mentioned in a document or in a range of documents?

- When did a particular set of events happen?
- Where did a particular type of event take place?

Even this seemingly modest goal of populating a database with facts from a set of documents is a daunting challenge, as evinced by the limited success of two widespread information extraction projects: Message Understanding Conference (MUC) [2, 3] and Automatic Content Extraction (ACE) [4, 5, 6, 7].

9.2 Relations and Events

In Chapter 8, we saw how to identify and find the type of mentions in text (mention detection, §8.2), as well as how to find which mentions corefer (coreference resolution, §8.3). This chapter focuses on finding **semantic relations** among entities; systems capable of performing this task are often called **relation extraction systems**. The term relation extraction is somewhat overloaded in the NLP literature. In broad strokes, we can distinguish between two main lines of investigation. The first ([8, 9]) is concerned with three rather specific forms of relation extraction:

- extracting relations typically associated with lexical ontologies, such as meronymy, hyponymy, and troponymy;
- extracting relations similar in nature, such as detecting that `verb1` expresses the same concept as `verb2` but in a stronger fashion; and
- finding **similarity enablement**, that is, detecting that the action expressed by `verb1` is a prerequisite for the action expressed by `verb2`.

The second line of investigation addresses the problem of identifying more general semantic links between potentially heterogeneous entities, such as employment relations between people and companies, cause of death relations between diseases and people, or ownership of one entity (such as a company) by another. This chapter focuses on this second, broader class of relation extraction.

For example, suppose we want to build a multilingual system that identifies every time a PERSON is described as the *owner of* some other entity in the text. This and many other types of semantic relationships are often fully expressed within a single sentence; thus, the most common approach in the literature consists of building systems that find **within-sentence** relations. In this vein, we would like to build a system capable of analyzing a sentence whose entity mentions have already been identified, and then identify an "owner of" relation mention between a pair of mentions when it exists. As a more ambitious goal, we really would like to have a system identify relations between entities regardless of whether the two entities are mentioned—are *mentions*—in the same sentence; for the purposes of this chapter, however, we assume that the two entities have mentions in the same sentence as the evidence of a relation between them, even if one or both entity mentions is pronominal (e.g., "*he owns it*," where "*he*" refers to some PERSON entity and *it*, say, refers to a company owned by that PERSON).

In a very real way, we have already encountered a relation extraction system: a **coreference resolution system** finds the relation "is the same entity as" between coreferent entity mentions in a document. But what about when there is some relationship that holds among more than two entities? When that relationship involves a change of state of one or more of the entities, we call it an **event**. An **event extraction system** is one that identifies the set of entities involved in some change of state. For example, the sentence *Mary bought apples for $20* involves the event of "buying" where there are three entities participating in the event: `Mary`, `apples`, and `$20`. Using predicate calculus, we might notate such an event using a three-place predicate, as in `bought(Mary, apples, $20)` or as a (related) pair of two-place predicates `bought(Mary, apples)` and `paid(Mary, $20)`. This distinction becomes important when we discuss the design of an event extraction system in §9.6, below.

9.3 Types of Relations

Just as with mention detection and coreference resolution, much of the recent work on relation extraction has been due to the National Institute of Standards and Technology (NIST) ACE evaluations [7]. As discussed in Section 8.2, the ACE task involved seven main types of entities: FAC (facility), GPE (geopolitical entity), LOC (location), ORG (organization), PER (person), VEH (vehicle), and WEA (weapon), each with several subtypes, for a total of 45 entity categories. The ACE competition required the systems to produce a rich set of relations, divided into seven main classes and eighteen subclasses:

- PHYS (physical): A spatial relation denoting that a person is located at or near a facility, a location, or a GPE; that a facility is located at or near a location or a GPE; that a location is located at a larger location, a GPE, or, potentially, a facility; and that a GPE is located at or near another GPE. Its subtypes are LOCATED and NEAR.
- PART-WHOLE: A spatial relation denoting that a facility, a location, a GPE, or an organization is a part of another facility, location, GPE, or organization. The relation subtype GEOGRAPHICAL captures a PART-WHOLE relation between locations, facilities, and GPEs; for organizations and GPEs with role organization, the subtype SUBSIDIARY captures an organizational PART-WHOLE relation between the arguments.
- PER-SOC (personal-social): Personal-social relations capture links between people. Relations can be BUSINESS-related, can be FAMILY-based, or can be a LASTING PERSONAL relations, such as friendship. Thus, the PER-SOC has three subtypes to distinguish between these three cases. Occasional personal-social relations were not considered in ACE.
- ORG-AFF (organization-affiliation): This type of relation pertains to connections between persons and organizations. A person could be EMPLOYED by an organization or could be a MEMBER. A specific kind of membership or employment is the

affiliation with a sport organization (SPORT-AFFILIATION). People can be linked to organizations of which they are neither members nor employees; this is the case of FOUNDERS, OWNERS, and INVESTORS-SHAREHOLDERS in companies. Finally, people can be affiliated with an educational institution when they are students or alumns (captured by the STUDENT-ALUMN subtype).

- GEN-AFF (general affiliation): Some affiliations between people and organizations/GPEs or organizations and GPEs do not fall in the previous categories. Among such relations we identify citizenship, residence in a country, religious affiliation, and ethnicity (all of these are clumped in the CITIZEN-RESIDENT-RELIGION-ETHNICITY ACE subtype). Similarly, a company might be doing business in a certain location or in a specific country; this is captured by the ORG-LOCATION ACE subtype.
- ART (artifact): A relation between a user, inventor, or manufacturer of some physical artifact and the artifact itself.
- METONYMY: A relation between two different aspects of the same underlying entity. The most common example is when an organization name is used to refer to a facility of that organization.

Internally, of course, systems might produce an even richer array of relations that might be mappable to the required set, and in later years of the ACE evaluations, this was often the case. In addition to the type of subtype of the relation, ACE defined several other properties, such as modality (e.g., whether the relation was asserted or negated), and tense (whether a relation was asserted as being true in the past, present, or future, or whether its tense was not specified).

9.4 Relation Extraction as Classification

9.4.1 Algorithm

In this section, we view relation extraction as a multiclass classification problem, as shown very succinctly in Algorithm 9–1.

Algorithm 9–1 Initial version of a relation extraction algorithm, viewing it as a classification problem

```
procedure RelExtract d                 // d is a document
R ← ∅                                  // R is the set of relations output by this procedure
foreach sentence s ∈ d with mentions m_1 ... m_n do
    foreach pair of mentions m_i, m_j, 1 ≤ i < j ≤ n, do
        R ← R ∪ CLASSIFY(m_i, m_j)
    end
end
return R
```

In such a simplistic scenario, we would have the possible classification labels be

$$S = \{\texttt{NONE, Phys.located, Phys.near, } \ldots\}$$

With this design, we might also need to expand the set of outputs of our classifier to be the cross product of S with the set of possible modalities M and the set of possible tenses T, that is, one of $S \times M \times T$. While such a joint model might be possible, it may overly fragment the data, making it difficult to model highly correlated labels. Recognizing this potential data sparsity problem, systems from IBM [10] and elsewhere employ a **factored** or **cascaded model**, implementing the CLASSIFY function (line 5 of Algorithm 9–1) via a sequence of binary or multiclass classifications:

Existence	binary	Does a relation of *any* type hold between m_i and m_j?
Type	multi	Given that a relation holds, what type is it?
Subtype	multi	Given that a relation of some type holds, what subtype is it?
Modality	multi	Asserted, negative, possible, unspecified?
Tense	multi	Past, present, future, or unspecified?
Order	binary	For relation as predicate p, is the order $p(m_i, m_j)$ or $p(m_j, m_i)$?

If the `Existence` classifier returns false, then the entire pipeline of classifiers, as one might expect, is short-circuited.

The last classifier determines the order of two mentions as though they were arguments to a predicate. This is because the semantics of some relations, such as BUY, depend on the order of their arguments, which can be different than the order in which mentions appear in text. Consider the pair of sentences

- `Mary bought apples.`
- `Apples were bought by Mary.`

In both cases, the relation is `bought(Mary, apples)`, where `Mary` is the buyer and `apples` is the thing bought, regardless of the order of the mentions in text. For many types of relations, however, argument order is irrelevant, such as with the MEETING relation, which is true whenever two people have met.

Structuring this problem as a cascade is certainly an expedient approach, but is it the only one? One problem with propagation of the first-best output of each classifier is the propagation of errors. For example, if the `Type` classifier misclassifies a SUBSIDIARY relation then the `Subtype` classifier has no hope of correcting the error. One solution to this problem, short of implementing a true joint model, is to propagate the k-best hypotheses at each stage of the pipeline, picking the highest-scoring hypothesis at the end.

9.4.2 Features

There are several main classes of features for classification-based relation extractors, including structural, lexical, entity-based, syntactic, amd semantic. Features for relation classification typically capture specific characteristics of the mention pair being analyzed or describe how the pair occurs in the context of the sentence.

Structural features. Consider the following sentence:

> In 1860 there was a four-way race between the Republican Party with Abraham Lincoln, the Democratic Party with Stephen Douglas, the Southern Democratic Party with John Breckenridge, and the Constitutional Union Party with John Bell.

There are four ORG-AFF ACE relations between the candidates and their respective party. A (non-ACE) `TimeOf` relation also exists between *race* and *1860.* The example illustrates the intuitive concept that pairs of mentions that are far from each other in some sense are rarely connected by a relation, while pairs of mentions that are close to each other often partake the same relation. A first class of structural features captures the distance between mentions, measured in some appropriate way such as the number of intervening tokens, the number of intervening mentions, or the length of the shortest path between the mentions in the parse tree. Another class of structural features fire when one or both mentions in the pair being considered take part in relations with other mentions. To be usable in a one-pass decoding algorithm, these features need to be causal; that is, they can only fire in the presence of other relations that can be detected by the decoder before any relation between the current mention pair. For instance, consider the sentence *Mary bought apples and pears*; let the decoder analyze the pair (`Mary, apples`) first and (`Mary, pears`) second. When decoding the latter pair, the feature `FirstArgAppearsInBoughtRelation` would fire, but no corresponding feature would fire when decoding the former pair.

Lexical features. The two sentences *Bob married Mary* and *Bob called Mary* are structurally identical and yet convey very different information. Specifically, the first sentence contains an instance of the ACE relation PER-SOC.FAMILY, while the second does not support any of the PER-SOC.FAMILY, PER-SOC.BUSINESS, or PER-SOC.LASTING-PERSONAL ACE relations. In order to detect a relation and classify it appropriately, more information is needed that is not part of the short sentence. Structural features are not sufficient to discriminate between the two cases; however, including lexical information would give the system a chance to make the right decisions. Lexical features encode some or all of the words of the mentions being analyzed, often with a special feature just for the head word of an entity if it is a named entity. Other features in this class encode words that appear in a small window on either side of each mention being classified, as well as any verb between, to the left, or to the right of the two mentions. Unlike structural features, lexical features dramatically increase the dimensionality of the feature space. As a consequence, for languages with rich morphology—and even for English—it is often crucial to use a morphological analyzer or stemmer to ensure that affixes are ignored.

Entity-based features. Consider the two sentences *I went to France* and *I went to IBM*: the first contains a PHYS-LOCATED relation, and the second does not. Unless France and IBM both appear in the training set in sentences similar to these, a relation detector would have a hard time discriminating between the sentences using just structural and lexical features. However, in the first sentence, the mention *France* has type GPE and role LOCATION, while *IBM* has type ORG and no specific role. The example hints at the usefulness of features that capture properties of the mentions in the pair, such as the types, subtype, and role of the corresponding entities and the level of the mentions (name, nominal, or pronoun). These features would also discourage the system from finding LOC relations in the sentence *France was ousted during the first round of the World Cup*, where the GPE *France* plays the role of a team.

Syntactic features. These features are often fairly similar to those employed by coreference resolution systems. Such features can themselves be divided into two subcategories: label-based and path-based. Label-based features look at various nonterminal labels associated with words in the mentions being classified, up to and including part-of-speech tags, which are often the nonterminals that immediately dominate words. Path-based features are much more fine-grained in that they represent various encodings of the nonterminals found along the shortest path between the head words of the two mentions being classified. Examples of path-based features include:

- the constituent label of the root of the smallest subtree covering the pair.
- the list of the labels of the children of the root; the list of all or of selected constituent labels along the shortest path between the two mentions.
- indicator functions that fire when the mentions are in the same phrase, noun phrase, sentence, and so on.
- indicator functions that detect specific patterns, such as `Mention1-PP`, where the `PP` contains `Mention2`.
- the indicator of whether one of the mentions is or contains the head of the smallest covering subtree.

An important class of syntactic features are those derived from dependency trees; they typically consist of full or reduced paths along the dependency tree connecting the mention extents or the mention heads, where the paths are represented in terms of constituent labels, can be lexicalized, or can be decorated with additional labels.

Semantic features. In the sentence *Both have since left the embattled company*, evidence that the mentions *both* and *company* are related by the ORG-AFF ACE relation is concisely captured by their semantic roles [11]: the first mention is ARG0 of the verb *left*, while the second is ARG1. Semantic features rely on semantic role labels to capture this type of connection between mentions: for instance, some would fire when the mentions are (covered by parse tree nodes labeled as) arguments of the same verb; others would fire if one of the mentions is an argument of a verb but the second is not.[1]

Additional features can be designed that fall simultaneously into multiple categories. The head word of the smallest subtree covering the mention pair is an example of a lexical feature based on syntactic information, as is the head word of the smallest VP covering the mention pair. Knowing that `Mention1` is the closest mention of an entity of type `Type1` to `Mention2` is a hybrid structural-entity-based feature useful in predicting existence and attributes of relations.

It is natural to ask how useful these features are to detect and label relations. Although the answer appears to be dependent on the specific taxonomy of relations and on the application domain, entity-based features and syntactic features are consistently very useful both for relation detection and for relation classification. In particular, dependency features

1. Please see Chapter 4 for a thorough review of semantic role labeling.

have found broad applications in relation extraction even beyond the realm of discriminative classification, as described later. Jiang and Zhai [12] describe a systematic evaluation of the usefulness of several categories of features for detecting and classifying relations in the English language.

9.4.3 Classifiers

The features defined in the previous section define a remarkably large feature space, which can cause a curse-of-dimensionality effect when learning a statistical classifier. It is wise to choose a classifier that is impervious to large feature spaces and data sparsity, and as a consequence, recent work on relation extraction has overwhelmingly relied on methods such as maximum entropy (MaxEnt) [13], support vector machines (SVM) [14], conditional random fields (CRF) [15], and, to a lesser degree, naïve Bayes [16] and rote extractors [17].

MaxEnt classifiers are simple exponential models.[2] Let (x, y) denote a training instance, where x is the evidence (e.g., a pair of mentions together with their document) and y is the independent variable (e.g., the indicator function of whether a relation exists between the mention, when detecting relations, or the value of a relation attribute, such as the relation type). Let $f(x, y)$ denote a binary feature function: for example, $f(x, y) = 1$ if the entity type of the first mention is PERSON, the entity type of the second mention is ORGANIZATION, and there is no relation between the two mentions. We can create a huge number of binary feature functions using the features described in the previous section: one for *each value* of *each feature* extracted from the training set and *each value* of the *attribute* being predicted observed in conjunction with the feature value. Index these feature function in an arbitrary way, using the running index i. The MaxEnt model estimates the conditional probability of y given x as

$$p(y|x) = \frac{1}{Z_\lambda(x)} \exp\left(\sum_i \lambda_i f_i(x, y)\right)$$

where the denominator is a normalizing constant called the **partition function**, which ensures that for every x the sum over all y's of the right-hand side is equal to 1, and the weights λ_i are obtained by maximizing the probability of the training set under the constraints that the marginals of the individual counts are equal to the empirical marginals (i.e., the normalized counts).

MaxEnt classifiers are appealing for two main reasons: first they are log-linear models, and their extremely simple functional form makes them robust to data sparsity in general and to the curse of dimensionality in particular; second, learning a MaxEnt classifier can be cast in terms of a constrained optimization problem on the probability symplex, which is a well-understood problem for which efficient solutions exist. MaxEnt classifiers were successfully used, for instance, by Kambhatla [10, 18], in each stage of the cascaded mode. Kambhatla [18] further remarks that the main source of errors in extracting relations from the ACE corpus are misses; the error rate of the relation attribute classifiers is much smaller than that of the detection stage. In our experience, this is not an uncommon problem and probably

2. This is a brief description of using MaxEnt models as classifiers. Please see Section 8.2 for a longer overview of MaxEnt modeling as applied to sequence classification problems.

occurs because most mention pairs indeed do not partake a relation. The author addresses the problem by adding a bagging layer [19] on top of the MaxEnt classifiers: 25 MaxEnt classifiers are learned from different training sets obtained by independently sampling with replacement from the original training set. When analyzing a mention pair, all classifiers are invoked, and their results polled. If at least five existence classifiers fire, the system accepts the presence of a relation. The study shows that bagging yields a 7% improvement in ACE score. We conclude our brief discussion of MaxEnt classifiers for multilanguage relation extraction by remarking that the feature functions f_i are not limited to capturing values of individual features; it is common practice to write feature functions that fire in correspondence of combinations of the features described, for example, in Section 9.4.2.

An SVM is a binary classifier that uses a hyperplane in the feature space to separate samples of different classes; if the training data is linearly separable (i.e., separable by means of a hyperplane), there are typically infinitely many hyperplanes that partition the data. A distinguishing characteristic of SVMs is that they choose the hyperplane that is at maximum distance from the nearest samples of both classes; this property gives them provable optimality properties over other support vector–based methods. SVMs are appealing for relation extraction for two main reasons. The first is that the problem of learning an SVM can be cast into a dual space–constrained optimization problem that can be efficiently solved even in high-dimensional spaces; the second is that SVMs can learn very complex decision surfaces (much more complex than hyperplanes) by *implicitly* mapping the feature space into a higher-dimensional space, learning a separating hyperplane in this space, and projecting the hyperplane back onto the original space. The mapping relies on **kernel** functions, which are essentially similarity metrics of points in the original space that satisfy a few mathematical properties. By using kernel functions, the classifier can implicitly account for interactions between the features; for example, a quadratic kernel enables the SVM to account for all pairwise interactions between the features.

9.5 Other Approaches to Relation Extraction

9.5.1 Unsupervised and Semisupervised Approaches

Supervised discriminative feature-based approaches are by no means the only viable approach to relation extraction. We devote this section to an overview of techniques suitable for multilingual relation extraction.

An obvious limitation of supervised approaches is the need for large, manually constructed training sets. Public training sets for relation extraction are available for selected languages; for instance, annotated corpora for English, Chinese, and Arabic were produced for the ACE evaluations. The cost of creating an annotated corpus makes unsupervised and semisupervised approaches appealing.

Few purely unsupervised approaches to the relation extraction problem have emerged so far. González and Turmo [20] describe an approach to relation detection based on ensemble clustering methods applied to binary features. The ensemble clustering method produces a mixture of multivariate Bernoulli distributions; each distribution is assigned a score, which is higher for more "compact" as measured by the sum of the eigenvalues of the covariance matrix; each training instance is assigned a score computed as the sum of the scores of the clusters weighted by the probability that the instance comes from the cluster; the histogram of the scores of the training instance is analyzed to find a change point (a knee in the histogram), which is used as a threshold; new pairs of mentions are analyzed in the same fashion, and those with a score better than the threshold are deemed to be connected by a relation. This conceptually simple approach yields an F-measure of 56 on the gold-standard mentions of the ACE corpus for a selected subset of the ACE relations, which is surprisingly high given how the F-measure of the supervised method of [21] is 63.2.

While purely unsupervised methods have the potential of being successfully used for relation detection, they are unsuitable for relation classification. If a small amount of labeled data is available, then researchers can attempt to leverage it together with unlabeled data by means of semisupervised learning algorithms [22]. A common approach to semisupervised learning is **bootstrapping**, the process of using the labeled samples to guess the labels of nearby unlabeled samples, which are subsequently added to the training set. An example of bootstrapping applied to relations can be found in Chen et al. [23]. The authors use the label propagation algorithm [24], a graph-based algorithm where mention pairs are represented as nodes, and edges are labeled by the similarity between the two mention pairs it connects. Labels are iteratively propagated from the labeled samples to the nearest vertices, ensuring that the original labeled samples are never relabeled. The performance of the method for relation detection ranges from F = 58.5 when only 1% of the data is labeled all the way to 71.1% when all the data is labeled, with F = 63.2 when the fraction of labeled data is 10%. For relation detection and classification, F ranges from 39.0 when the labeled samples are 1% of the training set to 54.6 when all the data is labeled, with F = 43.6 when 10% of the data is labeled.

A similar approach is described in Greenwood and Stevenson [25], who rely on patterns derived from dependency trees (the use of dependency tree-based patterns is discussed in more details shortly), which are represented as chains of triples, where each triple consists of a word, its POS tag, and its relation to its parent verb, as defined by the dependency tree. The authors advocate an approach consisting of extracting a large number of patterns from a corpus and having annotators provide an initial seed set of meaningful annotated patterns. These labeled patterns are then used in conjunction with a similarity function to find a set of unlabeled patterns that are very similar to the labeled patterns; the selected unlabeled patterns are labeled with the label of their closest labeled sample, and the process is repeated. The experimental results on the MUC-6 dataset [2] show that the semisupervised approach substantially improves the F-measure over the use of the seed-labeled training set and that the F-measure keeps increasing for a substantial number of iterations (190, in the specific case); however, the results are not as good as those obtained with large labeled training sets.

Ravichandran and Hovy [17] suggest an intuitive procedure for learning surface patterns that capture relations using the web. They issue queries consisting of entity pairs for which a desired relation is known to hold, identify sentences containing mentions of both entities, assume that the sentences are likely to describe the relation, and identify lexical patterns involving these mentions using a suffix tree constructor. To evaluate the performance of the algorithm for question-answering tasks, the authors propose a procedure consisting of issuing queries consisting of entity pairs, one of which plays the role of question argument and the other of question answer. The authors count the number occurrences of the pattern with both query arguments and the number of occurrences of the pattern with the question argument, irrespective of whether the question answer occurs in the pattern; the precision of the approach is measured as the ratio of these two numbers. Alfonseca et al. [26] describe an alternative method for evaluating the performance of rote extractors trained using the unsupervised procedure described by Ravichandran and Hovy.

9.5.2 Kernel Methods

The system described in Section 9.4 is based on MaxEnt classifiers or other generative or discriminative classifiers. A different class of methods that have recently gained popularity for relation extraction and that are potentially suitable for multilingual relation extraction are kernel-based algorithms. The gist of these approaches consists of describing a relation by extracting an appropriate pattern and computing the similarity between patterns by counting how many subpatterns match. The intuition is that the pattern describing a relation is likely to be simple if the mentions that take part in the relation are very close to each other in the sentence, and the complexity grows quickly with the distance between the mentions. Matching the entire pattern might therefore not work well for "long-distance" relations involving mentions that are even at moderate distance. However, there might be revealing subpatterns that occur frequently enough to be useful indicators of relations, and matching these subpatterns might be sufficient to detect and classify relations. Kernel methods provide efficient means for describing the similarity of patterns in terms of the number of matching subpatterns. Their main appeals are the ability to compute the number of matching subtypes in a computationally efficient fashion (the brute-force approach is exponential in the length of the pattern) and the ease of use in conjunction with powerful discriminative classifiers, such as SVMs [14] and related methods like the voted perceptron [27]. These methods are appealing especially for resource-poor languages because they typically rely on a limited number of features, unlike more conventional classification-based approaches that might require a broad spectrum of heterogeneous features.

Zelenko, Aone, and Richardella [28] describe a kernel over shallow parses [29] of the text for learning PERSON-AFFILIATION and ORGANIZATION-LOCATION relations from text. Nodes in the shallow parse have Type and Role attributes, as well as a variable number of other attributes. The relation kernel is defined in terms of a matching function, which determines whether or not two nodes are matchable, and of a similarity function, which recursively computes the similarity between two nodes using the attributes of these nodes and of their descendants.

Culotta and Sorensen [21] represent relation instances in the training set as augmented dependency trees; they extend the work of Zelenko et al. by enriching the sentence representation, proposing a more general framework for weighting features, and adopting composite kernels. Composite kernels are combinations of tree kernels and bag-of-word kernels that treat trees as vector of features over nodes.

Bunescu and Mooney [30] propose a relation kernel that computes the number of common subsequences of tokens between two sequences, weighted by the distances between the first and last tokens. The authors use the kernel in conjunction with an SVM learning package and show improvements over existing rule-based systems on two different data sets, AImed and ACE. The authors extend the kernel methods to a weakly supervised setting in a follow-on paper [31].

9.5.3 Joint Entity and Relation Detection

A recent area of investigation in NLP is joint inference, where multiple problems are addressed simultaneously. In particular, emerging efforts are aimed at extracting mentions and relations simultaneously. The intuition is that text commonly conveys information on entities that can be captured by relations or events; the existence of relations involving candidate entity mention is therefore an indication supporting the existence of that mention; conversely, given the detection of a relation mention between a pair of entity mentions can be influenced by attributes of the entity mentions, including the posterior probabilities produced by the mention detection algorithm. While this area is in its infancy, it is nevertheless appealing for multilanguage relation extraction, especially for resource-poor languages where the state of the art of mention detection and relation extraction yields unsatisfactory results and where joint inference can improve the performance in the absence of additional resources.

9.6 Events

In its broadest sense, an **event** denotes any change of state in the world that is described using natural language text. Event extraction is the use of any algorithm to extract a structured representation of that change of state, crucially including the entities involved. Typically, a single word, often a verb, indicates a change of state, and the arguments of that verb are often the entities involved in the event. In this way an event can be viewed as a generalization of a relation in that it is a set of relations between entities and a single trigger (again, typically a verb).

In 2004 in the DARPA ACE evaluation [32], participating systems were asked to find five major types of events, identifying up to seven different types of entities involved, as shown in Table 9–1. Crucially, there could be multiple entities of the same type involved in the same event. For example, in the sentence *The criminal destroyed the car and the building*, both *car* and *building* should be labeled *Object*.

The concept of an event was refined in the 2005 ACE evaluation [6]. The notion of an event trigger was reified (although trigger detection was never part of the evaluation metric), and the types of events to be extracted were made more concrete, as were the types of the entities involved, as shown in Table 9–2. The guidelines restricted events to be only those mentioned explicitly within a single sentence using a verb. In this way, ACE event extraction is very similar to the task of semantic parsing, described in detail in Chapter 4. In fact, it can be considered a targeted, real-world application of semantic parsing.

9.7 Event Extraction Approaches

There have been two main approaches to the problem of within-sentence event extraction. The first main approach, explored, for example, by IBM, New York University [33], and David Ahn of the University of Amsterdam [34], is that of a pipeline: first there is a trigger

Table 9–1: Types associated with the ACE 2004 event extraction task

Destruction/Damage (BRK)
Creation/Improvement (MAK)
Transfer of Possession or Control (GIV)
Movement (MOV)
Interaction of Agents (INT)

(a) Event types.

Role	Description
Agent	The cause of the event
Object	The entity acted upon by the event
Source	The original location (for MOV and GIV only)
Target	The resultant location (for MOV and GIV only)
Time	The time of the event
Location	The location of the event
Other	Other event participants

(b) Event participant roles.

Table 9–2: Types and subtypes of events in the ACE 2005 task

Type	Subtype
Life	Be-Born, Marry, Divorce, Injure, Die
Movement	Transport
Transaction	Transfer-Ownership, Transfer-Money
Business	Start-Org, Merge-Org, Declare-Bankruptcy, End-Org
Conflict	Attack, Demonstrate
Contact	Meet, Phone-Write
Personnel	Start-Position, End-Position, Nominate, Elect
Justice	Arrest-Jail, Release-Parole, Trial-Hearing, Charge-Indict, Sue, Convict, Sentence, Fine, Execute, Extradict, Acquit, Appeal

detection system looking for verbs that correspond to the eight targeted event types, and then there are systems that attempt to find mentions that correspond to the roles of the event. More concretely, a typical pipeline of classifiers would be as follows:

1. trigger identification
2. argument identification
3. argument attribute assignment
4. event coreference

In the case of NYU's system, there were a combination of handwritten heuristics along with some machine learning components. Ahn compared the use of memory-based learning [35] with a MaxEnt classifier [36] for the first of the three tasks, finding nearly identical overall performance. The IBM system used MaxEnt models for the first three tasks and heuristics for the fourth task.

The features used by IBM, NYU, Ahn, and others all bore great similarity to the features used to capture relations—and for good reason, given how the overall pipelining approach is similar to relation finding, where one end of each relation is the event trigger. Most of these feature types are language-independent, with the notable of exception of features based on a lexical ontology for English, WordNet.[3] Finding triggers, however, is more like mention detection than relation detection, and as such, the most common approach is to use a mention detection system with its stock set of position and lexical features. IBM, for example, simply employed annotated trigger data and ran its mention detection system, which treats mention detection as a multiclass tagging problem using the BIO (begin, inside, outside) tag set [37, 38].

Argument identification and classification may be viewed as two factored problems, as performed by Ahn's system, or as a single classification step, as in the case of IBM's approach. In either case, each mention is considered independently as a possible argument to a trigger. IBM refined this approach by classifying mentions in a left-to-right manner (mentions earlier in the sentence were classified before mentions later in the sentence), conditioning later classifications on previous ones. This is known as a **greedy best-first** decoding strategy.

The second major approach, employed by BBN [39], is to use an initial process (trained using machine learning, heuristics, or both) to propose entire events—triggers with their labeled arguments—and then use a classifier to determine which of the proposed events to output, if any. This approach was inspired by and is very similar to reranking for structured prediction problems [40], as described in detail in Chapter 3, Section 3.5.3. The whole-event classifier is trained in a supervised manner by using the first-pass event "proposal" algorithm to generate many event candidates for a given trigger in a given sentence. This first-pass process produces each event candidate with a score. If the event candidate with the top score is not the "true" event for that trigger, then the truth is added as a positive training instance (typically with a label of 1.0) and the top-scoring candidate is added as a negative training instance (typically with a label of -1.0). In this way, a hyperplane may be learned that separates the event candidates proposed by the first-pass system. As per much of the structured prediction reranking literature, BBN employed a perceptron-style classifier to learn this hyperplane.

The advantage of this approach is that it can consider features related to the entirety of the event—the trigger and all of its labeled arguments. By contrast, the pipeline approach must either consider each argument independently or else look only at previously generated arguments, and usually only the first-best output of the classifier. A disadvantage of this second approach is that is has a slightly more complicated decoding strategy.

3. Resources similar to WordNet are available for a handful of languages other than English. If you are developing a relation or event extraction system, it is advisable to search for all such lexical resources pertinent to the languages in which your system will operate.

9.8 Moving Beyond the Sentence

The initial work on extracting events focused on processing each sentence independently. Resolving event mentions into events was generally a simple process solved via heuristics looking at matching the triggers and arguments, making ample use of the fact that coreference resolution had already been performed. Subsequently, a line of research emerged pursuing two strategies to help aid event extraction by looking beyond the single sentence.

Ji and Grishman [41] extrapolated from the one-sense-per-discourse constraint [42] a one-sense-per-topic-cluster constraint, where a topic cluster is a collection of documents all on the same topic. The idea is that the words used to express an event tend to be unambiguous in the set of documents that mention that event or are otherwise related by the same topic. So, each event mention to be classified—both triggers and arguments—should be consistent with other triggers and arguments in the same topic cluster. Ji and Grishman used an open-source document retrieval engine, INDRI [43], to gather documents related to the topic of the target document, and then applied a series of hand-tuned weights to cross-document statistics to promote the consistency of the local decision. The use of these consistency statistics showed an absolute improvement of 7.6% F-measure in trigger classification over their baseline system and a 6% F-measure absolute gain for argument classification in the ACE event extraction task.

In a related effort to move beyond the sentence, Liao and Grishman [44] found not only that event triggers have consistency within a document and in the document's topic cluster but that other event types strongly correlate with a target event type. That is, the presence of other events in a document provide a strong cue for a given event type. As an example, the authors found that *Attack*, *Transport*, and *Injure* events appear often with the event *Die*, all having correlation coefficients greater than 0.3. Making use of this kind of cross-event consistency, they achieved a 9.0% absolute improvement in F-measure in trigger classification and more than an 8% absolute F-measure gain in argument classification over their baseline system.

9.9 Event Matching

Often, the goal of information extraction—and event extraction in particular—is the population of a database with records of events of interest, but that is not the only use for information extraction techniques. For question-answering systems that attempt to answer open-ended questions, particularly those with more than one answer, the aim of an information extraction system can be to produce valuable sentence-level information. This type of system is described more fully in Chapter 14, but here we describe the subproblem of having a description of an event and finding out which sentences in a corpus also contain descriptions of that event.

Bikel and Castelli [45] developed a binary classifier that takes a description of an event and a sentence as input and returns true if the sentence contains a description of that event, false otherwise.[4] They chose to use the averaged perceptron algorithm [27], and trained it with two classes of features.

The first class of features were **low-level features**. The low-level features comprised **lexical features** and **mention-matching features**. The lexical features measured the percentage of lexical items present in the event description that were also present in the sentence. In order to stick to binary feature functions, this percentage was binned into five intervals, $[0, 0]$, $(0, 0.33]$, $(0.33, 0.66]$, $(0.66, 0.99]$, $(0.99, 1.0]$, and a binary feature function was created for each interval. The mention-matching features were binary functions returning true if, say, a PERSON mention detected in the event decription was also detected in the sentence. One such binary feature was created for each mention type (see Chapter 8 for more information about mention detection).

The second class of features, the **high-level features**, made use of dependency parses (as discussed in Chapter 3) of both sentences in the corpora as well as of the query. For our purposes here, we formally define a dependency tree for a sentence $\mathbf{w} = \langle \omega_1, \omega_2, \ldots, \omega_k \rangle$ as a rooted tree $\tau = \langle V, E, r \rangle$, where $V = \{1, \ldots, k\}$, $E = \{(i, j) : \omega_i \text{ is the child of } \omega_j\}$ and $r \in \{1, \ldots, k\} : \omega_r$ is the root word. Instead of using a standard dependency tree where the nodes are simply the lexical items of the sentence, for each word w_i the model associated a POS tag t_i, a morph (or stem) m_i (which is w_i itself if w_i has no variant), a set of nonterminal labels N_i, a set of synonyms S_i for that word, and a canonical mention $cm(i)$. More formally, we let each element of the sentence be a sextuple $\omega_i = \langle w_i, t_i, m_i, N_i, S_i cm(i) \rangle$. The dependency trees in this case were derived from head-lexicalized constituent trees, which meant that a single head word could be associated with multiple nonterminal labels, which is why N_i is a set and not a single nonterminal. The canonical mention $cm(i)$ for a word w_i is the longest named mention for that word in case that word is, say, a pronoun coreferent with other mentions in its document.

The high-level features of the model crucially made use of the transitive closure of **dependency relations**, that is, the head-modifier relations produced by a dependency parser. We can view such head-modifier relations as a relation in the set-theoretic sense, where aRb if word a is a modifier of head b in a sentence, and R is the relation denoting modification. For example, in the short sentence *John saw Mary*, we would have `Mary` R `saw`. Just as in set theory, we can then view the **transitive closure** of any relation, where $\forall a, b, c : (aRb \wedge bRc) \Rightarrow aRc$. Suppose we have the slightly longer sentence *John saw someone talking to Mary*. In this case, with the parse

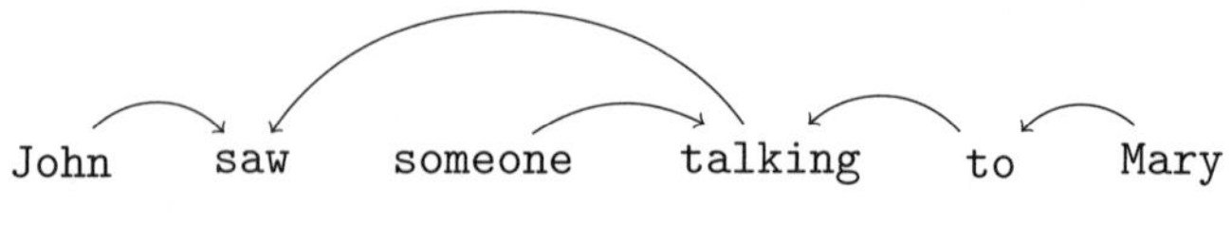

we would have the head-modifier relations

- `talking` R `saw`
- `to` R `talking`
- `Mary` R `to`

4. Bikel and Castelli are also the authors of the chapter you are presently reading.

among others, but using the transitive closure,

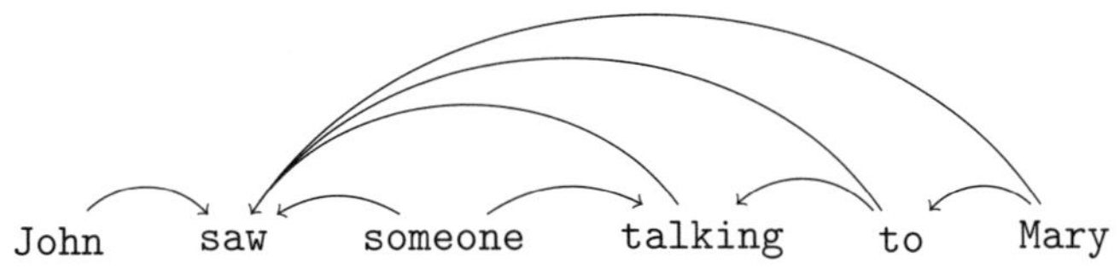

we would also include $\texttt{Mary}\,R\,\texttt{saw}$.[5] In both sentences, the relation $\texttt{John}\,R\,\texttt{saw}$ exists, since *John* is also a modifier of the main verb *saw*.

More formally, if E is the child-of relation in a dependency parse, then we let E' be the transitive closure of E, the descendant-of relation. Because we are ultimately trying to build a model that determines whether an event description e is mentioned within a sentence s, we let E'_e be the descendant-of relation in an event description and E'_s be the descendant-of relation in a sentence. The higher-level features essentially compute the overlap between E'_e and E'_s. To do this, we define a pair of matching functions that allow us to determine if a dependency pair $d_e = (d_e.d, d_e.a) \in E'_e$ is equivalent to $d_s = (d_s.d, d_s.a) \in E'_s$, where $d_x.d$ denotes the (index of a) descendant of a dependency pair and $d_x.a$ denotes an ancestor. The first matching function match_d checks that the two descendants of a pair of dependencies d_e and d_s are equivalent and the second matching function match_a does the same for ancestors:

$$\text{match}_d(d_e, d_s) = (m_{d_e.d} = m_{d_s.d}) \vee (cm(d_e.d) = cm(d_s.d))$$

$$\text{match}_a(d_e, d_s) = (m_{d_e.a} = m_{d_s.a}) \vee (cm(d_e.a) = cm(d_s.a))$$

These two matching functions essentially say that two descendants (resp. ancestors) are equivalent if they have identical morphs *or* if they have string-equal canonical mentions. Finally, we can define the overall matching function for d_e and d_s:

$$\text{match}(d_e, d_s) = \text{match}_d(d_e, d_s) \wedge \text{match}_a(d_e, d_s).$$

If $\text{match}(d_e, d_s)$ returns false, then d_e, d_s are tested for a weaker type of equivalence based on overlapping synonym sets:

$$\text{synmatch}(d_e, d_s) = (S_{d_e.d} \cap S_{d_s.d} \neq \varnothing) \wedge (S_{d_e.a} \cap S_{d_s.a} \neq \varnothing)$$

Table 9–3, taken from Bikel and Castelli [45], shows the types of features used in the model for an example event description e = *Abdul Halim Khaddam resigns as Vice President of Syria* and s = *The resignation of Khaddam was abrupt.*

One final class of features in the model was based on quantizing the value of a kind of kernel function on the two sets of dependencies E'_e and E'_s:

$$K(E'_e, E'_s) = \sum_{(d_e,d_s)\in E'_e \times E'_s:\text{match}(d_e,d_s)} (\Delta(d_e)\cdot\Delta(d_s))^{-1},$$

5. This type of relation is also known to linguists as a simple **dominance relation**.

Table 9–3: Types of dependency-matching features; in example features, $\mathtt{x} \in \{\mathtt{m}, \mathtt{s}\}$, depending on whether the dependency match was due to $\text{match}(d_e, d_s)$ returning true or due to synonym set matching via $\text{synmatch}(d_s, d_s)$

Feature type	Example	Comment
Morph bigram	`x-resign-Khaddam`	Sparse but helpful.
Tag bigram	`x-VBZ-NNP`	
Nonterminal	`x-VP-NP`	All pairs from $N_i \times N_j$ for $(i, j) \in E'_e$.
Depth	`x-eventArgHeadDepth=0`	Depth is 0 because *resigns* is root of event.

where $\Delta((i, j))$ is the path distance in the dependency tree τ from node i to node j. This kernel function essentially measures the overall distance among the set of matching dependencies between E'_e and E'_s.

By using the transitive closure of dependency relations, the model obtained a much more powerful and general way of matching descriptions of events to the way they might appear in sentences. Bikel and Castelli trained this model on a small training set of 3,546 instances and found that their technique performed with an F-measure of 66.5% on a small held-out development test set of 465 instances. Crucially, they could tune the model to trade off precision for recall, or vice versa.

9.10 Future Directions for Event Extraction

As mentioned at the beginning of this chapter, event extraction bears strong similarity to semantic parsing, specifically to semantic role labeling. Both tasks are interested in extracting predicate-argument structures, but in the case of event extraction, the goal is typically limited to a predefined set of possible predicate types. With the advent of ever-more sophisticated semantic parsing systems, we are likely to see a greater confluence of these two approaches to predicate-argument extraction. In particular, the availability of annotated resources such as PropBank [46] and NomBank [47] mean we can model generalized predicate-argument extraction, where the extraction of specific events can be cast as a filtering problem rather than a standalone modeling problem. Furthermore, if the goal is answering questions, then such filtering could be done on demand, as we saw in the previous section.

9.11 Summary

In this chapter, we reviewed the primary ways in which relations and events are extracted from text. We saw how relations and events form the higher-level components in an information extraction toolkit, in that they rely on features derived from lower-level components, such as POS taggers, parsers, a mention detection component, and a coreference resolution system. Both event and relation extraction systems typically rely on lexical features, which provide a rich but potentially sparse form of usefully discriminative information, and features based on paths in a parse tree, which can often generalize better and can deal with long-distance dependencies. Furthermore, both types of systems typically rely on mention detection as a crucial way to identify the participants in relations and events and provide features that generalize well, because there are only a small, fixed number of mention types.

One of the main reasons event extraction bears such a strong semblance to relation extraction is that events themselves can be thought of as collections of relations centered around a particular anchor. In this way, events also bear great similarity to semantic role labeling systems, as we have seen.

One of the primary goals of relation and event extraction is the structured representation of information in text, such that it may be entered into a database and searched with greater ease and more utility than, say, simple keyword search. We also saw how lower-level information extraction processing can help provide the basis for event matching. This type of approach, as we will see in Chapter 14, can form the basis for open-ended question-answering systems as well.

Bibliography

[1] J. Alpert and N. Hajaj, "We knew the web was big," Blog post: http://googleblog.blogspot.com/2008/07/we-knew-web-was-big.html, July 2008.

[2] *Proceedings of the 6th conference on Message Understanding (MUC-6)*, Association for Computational Linguistics, 1995.

[3] *Proceedings of the 7th Message Understanding Conference (MUC-7)*, Association for Computational Linguistics, 1998.

[4] *Proceedings of ACE 2003 Workshop*, 2003.

[5] *Proceedings of ACE 2004 Workshop*, 2004.

[6] NIST (National Institute of Standards and Technology), "The ACE 2005 (ACE05) evaluation plan." http://www.itl.nist.gov/iad/mig/tests/ace/2005/doc/ ace05 evalplan.v2a.pdf, 2005.

[7] NIST, "The ACE evaluation plan." www.nist.gov/speech/tests/ace/index.htm, 2007.

[8] T. Chklovski and P. Pantel, "Verbocean: Mining the web for fine-grained semantic verb relations," in *Proceedings of Conference on Empirical Methods in Natural Language Processing (EMNLP-04)*, 2004.

[9] T. Chklovski and P. Pantel, "Large-scale extraction of fine-grained semantic relations between verbs," in *International Workshop on Mining for and from the Semantic Web*, p. 12, 2004.

[10] N. Kambhatla, "Combining lexical, syntactic, and semantic features with maximum entropy models for extracting relations," in *Proceedings of the ACL 2004 on Interactive Poster and Demonstration Sessions*, p. 22, 2004.

[11] D. Gildea and D. Jurafsky, "Automatic labeling of semantic roles," *Computational Linguistics*, vol. 28, no. 3, pp. 245–288, 2002.

[12] J. Jiang and C. Zhai, "A systematic exploration of the feature space for relation extraction," in *Proceedings of the Human Language Technology Conference of the North American Chapter of the Association for Computational Linguistics*, pp. 113–120, 2007.

[13] A. Berger, S. Della Pietra, and V. Della Pietra, "A maximum entropy approach to natural language processing," *Computational Linguistics*, vol. 22, no. 1, pp. 39–71, 1996.

[14] C. J. C. Burges, "A tutorial on support vector machines for pattern recognition," *Data Mining and Knowledge Discovery*, vol. 2, no. 2, pp. 121–167, 1998.

[15] J. D. Lafferty, A. McCallum, and F. C. N. Pereira, "Conditional random fields: Probabilistic models for segmenting and labeling sequence data," in *ICML '01: Proceedings of the Eighteenth International Conference on Machine Learning*, pp. 282–289, 2001.

[16] P. Domingos and M. Pazzani, "On the optimality of the simple bayesian classifier under zero-one loss," *Machine Learning*, vol. 29, no. 2-3, pp. 103–130, 1997.

[17] D. Ravichandran and E. Hovy, "Learning surface text patterns for a question answering system," in *ACL '02: Proceedings of the 40th Annual Meeting on Association for Computational Linguistics*, pp. 41–47, 2002.

[18] N. Kambhatla, "Minority vote: at-least-n voting improves recall for extracting relations," in *Proceedings of the COLING/ACL on Main Conference Poster Sessions*, pp. 460–466, 2006.

[19] L. Breiman, "Bagging predictors," in *Machine Learning*, vol. 24, p. 123, 1996.

[20] E. González and J. Turmo, "Unsupervised relation extraction by massive clustering," *Data Mining, IEEE International Conference on*, vol. 0, pp. 782–787, 2009.

[21] A. Culotta and J. Sorensen, "Dependency tree kernels for relation extraction," in *ACL '04: Proceedings of the 42nd Annual Meeting on Association for Computational Linguistics*, p. 423, 2004.

[22] O. Chapelle, B. Schölkopf, and A. Zien, eds., *Semi-Supervised Learning.* Cambridge, MA: MIT Press, 2006.

[23] J. Chen, D. Ji, C. L. Tan, and Z. Niu, "Relation extraction using label propagation based semi-supervised learning," in *ACL-44: Proceedings of the 21st International Conference on Computational Linguistics and the 44th annual meeting of the Association for Computational Linguistics*, pp. 129–136, 2006.

[24] D. Zhou, O. Bousquet, T. N. Lal, J. Weston, and B. Schölkopf, "Local and global consistency," in *Advances in Neural Information Processing Systems 16*, pp. 321–328, Cambridge, MA: MIT Press, 2004.

[25] M. Greenwood and M. Stevenson, "Improving semi-supervised acquisition of relation extraction patterns," in *Workshop on Information Extraction beyond the Document*, pp. 29–35, 2006.

[26] E. Alfonseca, M. Ruiz-Casado, M. Okumura, and P. Castells, "Towards large-scale non-taxonomic relation extraction: Estimating the precision of rote extractors," in *Proceedings of the 2nd Workshop on Ontology Learning and Population: Bridging the Gap between Text and Knowledge*, pp. 49–56, 2006.

[27] Y. Freund and R. E. Schapire, "Large margin classification using the perceptron algorithm," in *COLT' 98: Proceedings of the 11th Annual Conference on Computational Learning Theory*, (New York, NY, USA), pp. 209–217, ACM, 1998.

[28] D. Zelenko, C. Aone, and A. Richardella, "Kernel methods for relation extraction," *Journal of Machine Learning Research*, vol. 3, pp. 1083–1106, 2003.

[29] S. Abney, "Parsing by chunks," in *Principle-Based Parsing* (R. Berwick, S. Abney, and C. Tenny, eds.), pp. 257–278, Boston: Kluwer Academic Publishers, 1991.

[30] R. Bunescu and R. Mooney, "Subsequence kernels for relation extraction," *Advances in Neural Information Processing Systems*, vol. 18, p. 171, 2006.

[31] R. C. Bunescu and R. J. Mooney, "Learning to extract relations from the web using minimal supervision," in *Proceedings of the 45th Annual Meeting of the Association for Computational Linguistics (ACL'07)*, 2007.

[32] NIST, "The ACE 2004 evaluation plan." http://www.itl.nist.gov/iad/mig/tests/ace/ace04/doc/ace04-evalplan-v7.pdf, 2004.

[33] R. Grishman, D. Westbrook, and A. Meyers, "NYU's English ACE 2005 system description," Tech. Rep., New York University, 2005.

[34] D. Ahn, "The stages of event extraction," in *Proceedings of the Workshop on Annotating and Reasoning about Time and Events (ARTE '06)*, pp. 1–8, 2006.

[35] W. Daelemans, J. Zavrel, K. van Der Sloot, and A. van Den Bosch, "TiMBL: Tilburg memory-based learner, verson 5.1," Tech. Rep., University of Tilburg, 2004.

[36] H. Daumé III, "Notes on CG and LM-BFGS optimization of logistic regression." Paper available at http://pub.hal3.name#daume04cg-bfgs; implementation available at http://hal3.name/megam/, August 2004.

[37] L. Ramshaw and M. Marcus, "Exploring the statistical derivation of transformational rule sequences for part-of-speech tagging," in *The Balancing Act: Proceedings of the ACL Workshop on Combining Symbolic and Statistical Approaches to Language*, pp. 128–135, 1994.

[38] E. Sang and J. Veenstra, "Representing text chunks," in *Proceedings of the 9th Conference of the European Chapter of the Association for Computational Linguistics*, pp. 173–179, 1999.

[39] L. Ramshaw, E. Boschee, M. Freedman, J. MacBride, R. Weischedel, and A. Zamanian, *Handbook of Natural Language Processing and Machine Translation.* New York: Springer, 2011.

[40] M. Collins and N. Duffy, "New ranking algorithms for parsing and tagging: Kernels over discrete structures, and the voted perceptron," in *Proceedings of the 40th Annual Meeting on Association for Computational Linguistics*, pp. 263–270, 2002.

[41] H. Ji and R. Grishman, "Refining Event Extraction through Cross-document Inference," in *Proceedings of ACL-08: HLT*, pp. 254–262, 2008.

[42] D. Yarowsky, "Unsupervised word sense disambiguation rivaling supervised methods," in *Proceedings of the 33rd Annual Meeting of the Association for Computational Linguistics*, pp. 189–196, 1995.

[43] T. Strohman, D. Metzler, H. Turtle, and W. B. Croft, "INDRI: A language-model-based search engine for complex queries," in *Proceedings of the International Conference on Intelligent Analysis*, 2005.

[44] S. Liao and R. Grishman, "Using document-level cross-event inference to improve event extraction," in *Proceedings of the 48th Annual Meeting of the Association for Computational Linguistics*, pp. 789–797, 2010.

[45] D. M. Bikel and V. Castelli, "Event matching using the transitive closure of dependency relations," in *Proceedings of the 46th Annual Meeting of the Association for Computational Linguistics on Human Language Technologies: Short Papers*, HLT '08, pp. 145–148, 2008.

[46] M. Palmer, P. Kingsbury, and D. Gildea, "The proposition bank: An annotated corpus of semantic roles," *Computational Linguistics*, vol. 31, 2005.

[47] A. Meyers, R. Reeves, C. Macleod, R. Szekely, V. Zielinska, B. Young, and R. Grishman, "Annotating noun argument structure for NomBank," in *Proceedings of the 4th International Conference on Language Resources and Evaluation (LREC-2004)*, 2004.

Chapter 10

Machine Translation

Philipp Koehn

Machine translation is one of the holy grails of natural language processing. It is a seemingly well-defined task: converting text in one language into another while preserving its meaning. It mirrors a human activity that is done by amateur bilingual speakers and professionals on a daily basis. But at the same time, it is fraught with difficulties so that most researchers do not expect to reach human quality anytime soon. The goal is more modest: producing translations that are *good enough* or *useful*.

In recent years, with the advent of the world wide web and the emergence of data-driven methods, machine translation research has received a jolt of new activity and much more visibility. An expanding number of research groups have taken on the problem. Everybody has access to machine translation by visiting popular websites such as Google Translate and Systran's Babelfish.[1]

The prominence of machine translation research signifies two things: machine translation systems have matured to the point that they offer a useful service for a large number of people. But the visible lack of accuracy also shows that much work remains to be done, maybe not to reach perfect translation but to reach ever higher levels of quality.

10.1 Machine Translation Today

The most profound recent change in the long history of machine translation can be dated back to 1988. Although machine translation research started in the 1940s, a group of researchers at IBM proposed to radically change the approach to machine translation. A **statistical** approach to language translation [1] would eliminate the need for a large group of linguists toiling away at defining the transformations and lexicons that powered traditional systems up to that point. Instead, large corpora of translated texts, typically many millions of words, would provide the answer, and a clever statistical model would help to learn the rules of translation and provide the basis for a decoding algorithm that finds the best translation for a given input sentence.

The rather simple models proposed by IBM at that time (we will discuss them in some detail in §10.3) have evolved over the last two decades into the phrase-based model (§10.4) and tree-based model (§10.5).

1. http://translate.google.com/ and http://babelfish.yahoo.com/

Current research pursues several directions, most notably

- the development of models that more closely mirror linguistic understanding of language,
- the application of novel machine learning methods to the estimation problem of learning translation rules from the data, and
- the attempts to exploit various types of data sources, which are often not in the desired domain or may not be even proper sentence-by-sentence translations at all.

Machine translation is being integrated into various applications: crosslingual information retrieval, speech translation, tools for translators, to name a few.

This chapter focuses on the basic methods that underlay modern machine translation systems. But first, let us make first sure we know what our goal is and how we evaluate that we are coming closer.

10.2 Machine Translation Evaluation

We defined machine translation as converting text in one language into another while preserving its meaning—and there it is, the word **meaning**. While it may inspire the minds of philosophers, it is a dreaded word for the engineer. What is meaning? How can we measure it? How do we know that two words, phrases, or sentences have the same meaning? And if they are close, how close?

The fact that there are almost as many metrics for machine translation as there are research groups working in the field [2, 3, 4] is testament to how this is, indeed, not a trivial problem. Figure 10–1 shows what happens when we ask 10 different human translators to translate one sentence, here from Chinese to English. Even for such a short sentence, each translator comes up with a different translation. This disparity is not due to the nature of Chinese—the same can be demonstrated for other languages.

Consequently, if we translate a Chinese sentence into a machine translation system, the result very likely would not match a human translation, even if it were a perfectly fine translation. So, how do we know whether it is a correct translation?

Because we cannot expect that it matches one of the references, we need to have some measure that matches the meaning of the system output against the meaning of the source, or as it is more commonly done, against the meaning of human reference translations.

10.2.1 Human Assessment

Because we do not trust computers to deal with problems of meaning, a common retreat is to assign the task to human judges. Given the source and the system output, we may ask them if the output constitutes a correct translation.

Figure 10–2 shows how four different human judges assessed translations of a French sentence into English in a recent study [5]. While the judges agreed on some translations, for most there is disagreement. So, even a simple task such as the assessment of correctness of translation does not lead to clear answers.

这个 机场 的 安全 工作 由 以色列 方面 负责 .

Israeli officials are responsible for airport security.
Israel is in charge of the security at this airport.
The security work for this airport is the responsibility of the Israel government.
Israeli side was in charge of the security of this airport.
Israel is responsible for the airport's security.
Israel is responsible for safety work at this airport.
Israel presides over the security of the airport.
Israel took charge of the airport security.
The safety of this airport is taken charge of by Israel.
This airport's security is the responsibility of the Israeli security officials.

Figure 10–1: Ten different translations of the same Chinese sentence, created by different human translators (a typical example from the 2001 NIST evaluation set)

correct	Sans se démonter, il s'est montré concis et précis.
1/3	Without fail, he has been concise and accurate.
4/0	Without getting flustered, he showed himself to be concise and precise.
4/0	Without falling apart, he has shown himself to be concise and accurate.
1/3	Unswayable, he has shown himself to be concise and to the point.
0/4	Without showing off, he showed himself to be concise and precise.
1/3	Without dismantling himself, he presented himself consistent and precise.
2/2	He showed himself concise and precise.
3/1	Nothing daunted, he has been concise and accurate.
3/1	Without losing face, he remained focused and specific.
3/1	Without becoming flustered, he showed himself concise and precise.

Figure 10–2: Human judgments on translations. Four different human evaluators often disagree if a translation is correct; for instance, the first translation of the French sentence was judged as correct by one judge and wrong by three others

Is this a problem? No. In the probabilistic view of the world that we adopt in statistical machine translation, there are no clear answers. Some answers are just more likely than others. For each translation, there is a probability distribution over possible judgments. If we have enough samples, our statistics converge to the true distribution and hence to valid assessments. In the world of meaning, there is no true black and white. There will always be someone who finds fault with a translation.

In practice, machine translation systems will produce translations that have some mistakes. Especially for long sentences of, say, 30 words, we cannot expect flawless output. Moreover, we are often not interested in absolute assessments (How many sentences are translated correctly?) but in comparisons of systems (Is system A better than system B?). So, instead of asking if a translation is correct, we more often ask if one translation is better than another.

See Figure 10–3 for an artificial example of five different systems that produce five different translations, each of them with a different mistake, be it a missing word, mistranslation of a word, insertion of the word *not*, wrong punctuation, or spelling errors. Which translation do you prefer?

Reference:	Israeli officials are responsible for airport security.
System A:	Israeli officials are responsible for security.
System B:	Israeli officials are responsible for rail security.
System C:	Israeli officials are not responsible for airport security.
System D:	Israeli officials are responsible. For airport security.
System E:	Israeli officials are responsible for arport sequrity.

Figure 10–3: Five different translation with mistakes. How would you rank them?

Again, not a straightforward task. Human judges have different preferences. Some may be obsessed with punctuation [6], while others could not care less. How bad is the insertion of a simple function word? What if the word is *not*?

We may want to break up the simple question of **correctness** into more fine-grained distinctions. Is the translation **fluent**—that is, is the output well-formed in the target language? Is the translation **adequate**—that is, is the meaning preserved regardless of output language quality? Even with such categories, different human judges may have different preferences.

And here we are getting a bit more concerned. We are setting up a very artificial task for a human judge. Nobody except for language teachers who are grading exams would look at translations and assess their quality in isolation. Humans use translations to fill an information need. If the translation of a foreign text gives them the answers they were looking for, then it was successful.

To truly test machine translation quality, we need to place it in a setting that involves its use. There have been some recent efforts to create **task-based** evaluation methods. For instance, we may give a human assessor a translated text and then ask her questions about the content. If she was able to answer them, the translation was successful [7]. In a variation of this method, we may ask a human assessor to edit the translation to produce fluent output without access to the source. Then, we check if the edited translation is correct, hence testing her understanding [3].

10.2.2 Automatic Evaluation Metrics

The development of machine translation systems requires frequent evaluation—too frequent for costly manual evaluation. One of the turning points of statistical machine translation research was the establishment of a regime of automatic evaluation that is commonly accepted. In fact, papers on improvements in machine translation rarely include human evaluation, but they pretty much have to include improvements in the current most popular automatic evaluation metric, BLEU.

How can we trust a computer program that computes a metric score to give us reliable assessment of machine translation quality? If a computer program could tell us if a translation is correct or incorrect, why could it not produce a correct translation in the first place? Well, it uses one trick and one copout.

The trick is to not only use the source and system output but also to use one or more reference translations that were produced by reliable human translators. We have already discussed at length that human and machine translation may lead to translations that are different from existing reference translations but are still correct. But, and here is where the copout comes in and the argument gets a bit murky: if the machine translation is similar to existing reference translations, then it is more likely to be correct. Although it is easy to defeat this argument with a single sentence example, the case for automatic metrics is built on the use of a large test set of hundreds or even thousands of sentences. Over a large test set, better translations are expected to be more similar to references.

Developers of machine translation evaluation metrics do not just appeal to such an argument, they validate this claim by carrying out correlation studies showing that their metrics rank systems in pretty much the same way as human judges would do. There are even evaluation campaigns for evaluation metrics, where different metric developers compete for the highest correlation with human judges [2, 3, 4].

We have now established a regime to test performance during development of a machine translation system. We first select a test set. We give it to human translators to produce one or more translations. We then run our machine translation system and measure how similar the output is to the reference translations. Then, we make a change to our machine translation system, run it again over the same test data, measure similarity again, and see if it has improved.

We are left with the task to define a measure of **similarity** between machine translation output and reference translations. This is, again, one of these dreaded words that are in the same sphere as *meaning*, but we will start simply.

10.2.3 WER, BLEU, METEOR, ...

Language is made up out of words, so two sentences are similar if they share a lot of words. So, when comparing machine translation output and a reference translation, we can count (i) **matches**, words that are both in the reference and in the output; (ii) **insertions**, words that are only in the output; and (iii) **deletions**, words that are only in the reference.

Given these three statistics, we can compute a number of metrics:

$$\text{precision} = \frac{\text{matches}}{\text{matches} + \text{insertions}} \tag{10.1}$$

$$\text{recall} = \frac{\text{matches}}{\text{matches} + \text{deletions}} \tag{10.2}$$

$$\text{PER} = 1 - \frac{\text{matches}}{\text{matches} + \max(\text{insertions}, \text{deletions})} \tag{10.3}$$

$$\text{F-score} = \frac{2 \times \text{precision} \times \text{recall}}{\text{precision} + \text{recall}} \tag{10.4}$$

$$\text{weighted F-score} = \frac{(1+\alpha) \times \text{precision} \times \text{recall}}{\alpha \times \text{precision} + \text{recall}} \tag{10.5}$$

All these metrics are the basis of machine translation metrics that have been proposed over the last years. There is some debate whether precision or recall is more important, which is related to the question of how to penalize too-short and too-long translations. PER, **position-independent errror rate**, is one of the earliest metrics to have been proposed.

Let us now look at a number of refinements that have been applied to this simple idea of matching words between machine translation output and reference translations.

The first refinement is the use of **multiple reference translations**. Given the allowable variation in translation, it may be too constraining to use only a single reference translation as the gold standard. If we have multiple translations, the chances that correct machine translation output matches one of them very closely increases. This should reduce the problem of correct but badly scoring translations. In terms of integrating multiple reference translations into a metric, we may always choose the best score with any of the reference translations or come up with more elaborate schemes. For instance, we may count as a match if an output word matches in any of the reference translations.

Second, we may match not only words, but also n-grams of words. This is an attempt to take word order into account. We may not expect that all the matching words in output and reference are in the same order, but if neighboring words in the output match neighboring words in the reference translation, then this is certainly a plus.

These two refinements are the basis of the BLEU score [8]. It is the most commonly used metric in the field, so it is worth taking a closer look. The formal definition is:

$$\begin{aligned} \text{BLEU} &= \text{brevity–penalty} \times \exp\left(\frac{1}{4}\sum_{i=1}^{4} \log \text{precision}_i\right) \\ \text{brevity–penalty} &= \min\left(1, \frac{\text{output–length}}{\text{reference–length}}\right) \end{aligned} \tag{10.6}$$

BLEU is in essence the geometric mean of n-gram precisions, typically using n-grams of length 1 to 4 (precision_i is precision for n-grams of size i). Because it is a precision-based metric, there is a need to hedge against too-short translations. This is done with a brevity penalty, which is applied only if the output length is shorter than the reference length. Multiple reference translations are incorporated by allowing n-gram matches against any of the reference translations. If an n-gram occurs multiple times in the output, it is counted as correct only as many times as the maximum number of times it occurs in one of the reference translations. The reference length for multiple references is chosen by selecting the closest length to the output length.

The BLEU score is computed over entire documents or test sets, not for single sentences. In fact, it is not a very good metric for single sentences because the four-gram precision is often zero or otherwise has too strong of an impact. When using BLEU on the sentence level, the precision is typically smoothed by adding 1 to the number of actual matches.

Since the BLEU score was proposed in 2002, a number of further refinements have been proposed. One is to relax the restriction of matches to exact surface form matches. We may also want to give at least partial credit for words that differ only in their morphological variation but derive from the same **lemma**. We may also give credit to **synonym** matches utilizing resources such as WordNet [9]. A metric that recently gained some prominence, METEOR (metric for evaluation of translation with explicit ordering) [10], allows for such matches and also relies more heavily on recall than on precision.

An old idea is to not only treat sentences as bags of words or n-grams, but to compute an explicit word alignment between the machine translation output and the reference translation. A metric borrowed from speech recognition, word-error rate (WER), enforces such an alignment and does not allow for any reordering between the sentences. Because a significant amount of allowable variation in word order occurs without change in meaning,

WER has been refined into metrics that do allow movements but penalize them as additional errors (similar to insertions and deletions). TER, which is known as translation-error rate or translation-edit rate, computes the minimal cost alignment between output and reference allowing for moves. Unfortunately, finding the optimal alignment is a computationally hard problem, so this metric is slow in practice and usually an approximation is computed.

Finally, we have all the ingredients for setting up machine translation evaluation as a machine learning problem. Over the years, evaluation campaigns have created training data in terms of system translations and their human assessment. We have a well-defined goal: optimizing correlation of an automatic metric with the human judgments. So, we can use any kind of features in a machine learning approach. In recent years, researchers have incorporated linguistic features such as syntactic relationships or semantic roles.

10.3 Word Alignment

The idea of statistical machine translation is to learn translation rules from a sentence-aligned parallel corpus. Let us start with the extraction of word translations from such a corpus. Detecting word translations provides the basis for establishing a word alignment, a fundamental step in any statistical machine translation model.

10.3.1 Co-occurrence

We assume that we have a sentence-aligned parallel corpus, where each foreign sentence $\mathbf{f}$ is paired with its English translation $\mathbf{e}$. Such corpora are available on the Internet (e.g., Europarl[2] or from the Linguistic Data Consortium [LDC][3]) or are collected by translation agencies who call them translation memories. Raw corpora require some basic preprocessing, typically tokenization (separating out punctuation), data cleaning (throwing out very long sentences or sentences mismatched due to their relative length), and normalizing uppercase and lowercase (e.g., by lowercasing all words), and we are ready to go.

We would like to learn which words in one language translate into words of the other language. We want to learn this in the form of a probability distribution $t(e|f)$ that gives for each foreign word f and each English word e the probability that e is a translation of f. For instance, for the German word *Haus* we expect to learn something like this:

$$t(e|Haus) = \begin{cases} 0.8 & \text{if } e = \textit{house}, \\ 0.16 & \text{if } e = \textit{building}, \\ 0.02 & \text{if } e = \textit{home}, \\ 0.015 & \text{if } e = \textit{household}, \\ 0.005 & \text{if } e = \textit{shell}. \end{cases} \tag{10.7}$$

As the name statistical machine translation implies, we learn such a model from the statistics of the data, that is, the counts we see in our parallel corpus. We can go over all sentence pairs that contain a specific foreign word f (like *Haus*), and see what English

2. http://www.statmt.org/europarl/
3. http://www.ldc.upenn.edu/

words occur on the English side. Based on these counts, we can estimate the conditional probability distribution:

$$\hat{t}(e|f) = \frac{\text{count}(f, e)}{\sum_{e'} \text{count}(f, e')} \tag{10.8}$$

We have to be a bit careful with the counting. Let us say, we have foreign sentence **f** that contains the German word f in question. On the English side, there are five words. Can we now treat each co-occurrence of f with each of the five words $e \in \mathbf{e}$ as one count?

We could, but it would lead to different count collections for short and long sentences. In a sentence pair with five English words, we would collect five counts for the foreign word f. But if there are ten English words, we would collect ten counts. But in fact, the foreign word f occurs in each instance only once.

So, instead, we are resorting to fractional counting: if there are five English words, and since we do not know which of them is the translation of f, we count each word as $\frac{1}{5}$.

How well will this work? Intuitively, an English word e that is a common translation of f will co-occur frequently with that word, so we would expect to estimate a relatively high $\hat{t}(e|f)$. But, then, the English period at the end of the sentence will occur in nearly every English sentence, so it will likely co-occur more frequently with f than any of its true translations individually. But is the most likely translation of every foreign word really the period?

Something has gone awry. We normalize the co-occurrence counts (f, e) with the frequency of f but not with the frequency of e. There are now several other statistical measures we could use to do our estimation. For instance, we could look at mutual information. In fact, several such measures have been used in the literature to massage co-occurrence statistics.

10.3.2 IBM Model 1

The very first model of machine translation, IBM Model 1, tackles the estimation problem in a different way. Instead of changing the conditional probability model, it forces us to find for each sentence pair a word alignment. The probability of a foreign sentence **f** to translate into an English sentence **e** with an alignment a is defined as:

$$p(\mathbf{e}, a|\mathbf{f}) = \frac{1}{Z} \prod_{j=1}^{l_e} t(e_j|f_{a(j)}) \tag{10.9}$$

The formula includes the alignment function a, which is straightforward to explain: it matches each English position j to a foreign word position $a(j)$. Note that the formula is a slight simplification of the original IBM Model 1. We avoid the introduction of the noisy channel model[4] at this point. We are also glossing over the normalization Z that ensures that $p(\mathbf{e}, a|\mathbf{f})$ is a proper probability distribution.

Let us say that we went through the estimation process as in the previous section. We ended up with a conditional distribution $t(e|f)$. We now look at the first sentence pair of the parallel corpus again and would like to find the most likely word alignment.

4. The noisy channel approach employs the Bayes rule $\text{argmax}_{\mathbf{e}} p(\mathbf{e}|\mathbf{f}) = p(\mathbf{e})\, p(\mathbf{f}|\mathbf{e})$ to integrate a language model $p(\mathbf{e})$, and hence reverses the direction of the translation model from $p(\mathbf{e}|\mathbf{f})$ to $p(\mathbf{f}|\mathbf{e})$.

A closer look at Equation 10.9 reveals that maximizing $p(\mathbf{e}, a|\mathbf{f})$ means that we independently maximize each $t(e_j|f_{a(j)})$. In other words, we need to find the one foreign word f in the sentence $\mathbf{f}$ that best explains e.

You may still have in mind the mess we got ourselves into in the previous section. Each foreign word f would prefer to produce the English period. But this is not the question we are asking here. Only one foreign word gets to produce the period. But we also need to explain the other English words. What is the foreign word that best explains an occurrence of the English *house*? It is certainly not the foreign period, which is a very confused word that spreads its probability mass over many words. We would expect that the German *Haus* has a fighting chance to be chosen to align to *house*. Yes, it is also confused and may have an odd preference for producing periods, but we would expect $p(house|Haus)$ to be bigger than $p(house|.)$.

Let us go one step further: if we go through each sentence pair of the parallel corpus, find the most likely word alignment for each, and then use only aligned words for count collection, we would expect to obtain better statistics for estimating the word translation probability distribution $t(e|f)$. In the next section, we do one better: we invoke the magic of the EM algorithm.

10.3.3 Expectation Maximization

To learn word translation probabilities from a parallel corpus, we are suffering from the curse of incomplete data. Yes, we have a parallel corpus, where English sentences are matched up with their foreign translations. But while we have aligned sentences, we do not have aligned words.

If we had the true word alignment, it would be straightforward to collect counts and estimate word translation probabilities $t(e|f)$. On the other hand, if someone gave us the true word translation probabilities $t(e|f)$, then we could find for each sentence pair the most likely word alignment. But we have neither. So, what can we do?

The basic idea of the expectation maximization (EM) algorithm is the following: let us just pretend that we have a probability distribution $t(e|f)$. Then we can find the best word alignments. And with those word alignments, we can estimate a better model. Now we have a new model and can repeat the process.

The EM algorithm, in a nutshell, is the following process:

1. Initialize the model, typically with a uniform distribution.
2. Apply the model to the data: compute probabilities for each possible word alignment.
3. Learn the model from the data, based on collected counts from the word alignments, and estimate a new word translation probability distribution.
4. Repeat steps 2 and 3 until convergence.

In fact, in the previous section, we already went through two iterations of the EM algorithm with slight simplifications. In the EM algorithm, we have to consider each possible alignment—not just the most likely alignment—and collect counts based on the conditional probability of the alignment given the sentence pair (we implicitly did this in the first iteration by collecting fractional counts).

Going over each possible alignment is quite a daunting task: because each English word is aligned to any of the foreign words, there is an exponential number of possible word alignments for a sentence pair. For IBM Model 1, there is a trick that allows us to do exact estimation in polynomial time, but in further refinements of the model, this is no longer possible. Instead, we have to sample the alignment space to find the most likely alignments and restrict our count collection to this subset.

10.3.4 Alignment Model

IBM Model 1 is a simplistic model for word alignment or statistical machine translation, and even the original researchers at IBM used it only as a stepping stone to more sophisticated models. It does not work very well with rare words because there are just too many choices. It also does not work if a foreign word occurs multiple times in the foreign sentence. Which one of them should an English word pick for alignment? They all have the same probability.

One way to extend the model is to include a component for alignment probabilities. IBM Model 2 introduces a model based on absolute word positions: $a(i|j, l_e, l_f)$. Based on the length of the English and foreign sentences l_e, l_f and the English word position j, we predict the foreign word position i.

Putting it all together, we have IBM Model 2:

$$p(\mathbf{e}, a|\mathbf{f}) = \frac{1}{Z} \prod_{j=1}^{l_e} t(e_j|f_{a(j)}) \; a(a(j)|j, l_e, l_f) \tag{10.10}$$

Instead of mapping absolute word positions, it is preferable to condition the alignment of a word on the alignment of its preceding word. After all, words typically move in phrases. Such a relative alignment model is used in IBM Model 4 and also in the hidden Markov model (HMM) for word alignment [11].

One more extension: although we restrict each English word to align to a single foreign word, foreign words may align to any number of English words. To reign in, IBM Model 3 introduces the concept of **fertility** and adds another conditional probability that predicts how many English words a foreign word generates.

10.3.5 Symmetrization

We have come to the point to admit to the most shameful secret in statistical machine translation. The IBM models, although they are still commonly used for word alignment, are fundamentally flawed. The trick that makes EM training work so well is to enforce that each English word aligns to exactly one foreign word.[5]

Linguistically, this makes very little sense, and the restriction to one-to-many alignments is also oddly asymmetrical. So, what can be done? Well, we run the EM training with the IBM models in both directions (resulting in a one-to-many and a many-to-one alignment), and then force an agreement between the two resulting word alignments. We call this crude hack **symmetrization** [12].

5. Actually, we also allow an English word to align to the artificial null word, but we do not allow an English word to align to multiple foreign words.

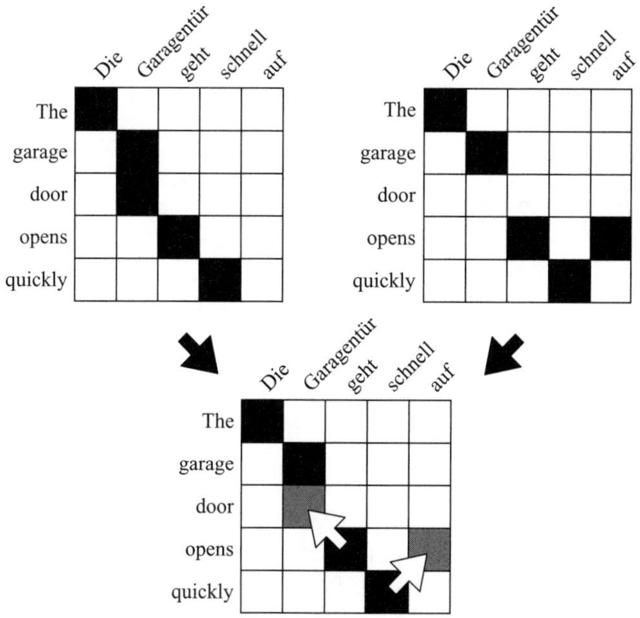

Figure 10–4: Overcoming the flaw in IBM models, which assume one-to-many alignments (or many-to-one if run in reverse). A heuristic such as grow-diag-final starts with the alignment points from the intersection of two alignments obtained by running the model in both directions (black arrows). Then, it adds neighboring alignment points from the union (white arrows)

Once we obtain the two word alignments, we can take the union and the intersection between their alignment points. In a common method, we use all alignment points in the intersection and add some of the alignment points in the union. Usually, alignment-points in the union that neighbor already-established alignment points are added. See Figure 10–4 for an illustration.

For instance, in the commonly used **grow-diag-final** method that ships with the open source Moses system, alignment points that directly and diagonally neighbor existing alignment points are added until convergence. Then, in a desperate final step, alignment points for words that are hitherto unaligned are added. The pseudocode for the heuristic is given in Algorithm 10–1.

There are a number of refinements of this symmetrization process; for instance, symmetrization can be done after each iteration of EM training [13]. Also, machine learning methods have been developed to either iteratively add alignment points to the intersection [14, 15] or to delete alignment points from the union [16].

10.3.6 Word Alignment as Machine Learning Problem

As with evaluation metrics, once the natural language community manages to properly define a problem, it does not take long before the hordes of machine learning researchers come in and attack it with all their favorite algorithms. This has also happened with word alignment, increasingly so in recent years.

Algorithm 10–1 Pseudocode for a symmetrization heuristic that settles on a set of alignment points between the intersection and the union of two IBM model alignments

Input: sentence pair $(\mathbf{e}, \mathbf{f})$, with alignments $e2f$ and $f2e$
Output: word alignment $\mathbf{a}$

```
grow-diag-final(e2f,f2e):
neighboring = ((-1,0),(0,-1),(1,0),(0,1), (-1,-1),(-1,1),(1,-1),(1,1))
alignment = intersect(e2f,f2e);
GROW-DIAG();
FINAL(e2f);
FINAL(f2e);

function GROW-DIAG():
while iterate until no new points added do
   for all english words e ∈ {e_1...e_n} do
      for all foreign words f ∈ {f_1...f_m} do
         if e aligned with f then
            for all neighboring points e_new, f_new do
               if (e_new unaligned | f_new unaligned)
               & (e_new, f_new) ∈ union(e2f, f2e) then
                  add alignment point (e_new, f_new)
               end if
            end for
         end if
      end for
   end for
end while

function FINAL(a):
for all english words e_new ∈ {e_1...e_n} do
   for all foreign words f_new ∈ {f_1...f_m} do
      if (e_new unaligned | f_new unaligned) & (e_new, f_new) ∈ union(e2f, f2e) then
         add alignment point (e_new, f_new)
      end if
   end for
end for
```

For machine learning, word alignment is an interesting unsupervised learning problem. It would be futile to list all methods that have been recently applied. You have your usual suspects, such as the perceptron algorithm [17, 18], maximum entropy models [19], neural networks [20], max-margin methods [21], boosting [22, 23], support vector machines [24], conditional random fields [25, 26], and the margin infused relaxed algorithm (MIRA) [27].

One ingredient for a successful onslaught of machine learning was the establishment of test sets, in this case gold-standard word alignments that were created by human annotators. There are several such sets for a number of language pairs, usually available through the LDC.[6]

6. http://www.ldc.upenn.edu/

There is some debate over how to best evaluate alignment quality. One early metric, alignment-error rate (AER), has come under heavy criticism [28]. Because word alignment is mostly done in the context of statistical machine translation, the ultimate evaluation metric is the machine translation quality that can be obtained using the word alignment. Of course, this is a very costly metric to compute.

10.4 Phrase-Based Models

Currently, the dominant approach in statistical machine translation is a model based on the mapping of short text chunks (typically only one to three words long), which are somewhat misleadingly called phrases albeit they are not necessarily *linguistic* phrases (i.e., constituents in a syntactic analysis).

Compared to word-based models, phrase-based models overcome the fundamental flaw of insisting on the lexical mapping of a one-to-one correspondence of words. Of course, word-based models do confront reality and introduce components such as fertility or null-word generation. But these complications make training and decoding algorithms much more cumbersome. Phrase-based models also have the advantage that with more training data, longer and longer phrases can be learned. In the limit, a sentence may be translated by looking it up in its entirety in the training corpus.

10.4.1 Model

The phrase-based model has the advantage that it is quite easy, which allows for straightforward training methods and efficient decoding algorithms. See Figure 10–5 for an illustration. The input sentence is segmented into phrases, and each phrase is mapped one-to-one into an English phrase. Phrases may be reordered.

Let us now define the phrase-based statistical machine translation model mathematically. First, we apply the Bayes rule, so we can integrate a language model p_{LM} by inverting the translation direction. The best English translation $\mathbf{e}_{\text{best}}$ for a foreign input sentence $\mathbf{f}$ is defined as

$$\begin{aligned}\mathbf{e}_{\text{best}} &= \text{argmax}_{\mathbf{e}}\, p(\mathbf{e}|\mathbf{f}) \\ &= \text{argmax}_{\mathbf{e}}\, \frac{p(\mathbf{f}|\mathbf{e})\, p_{\text{LM}}(\mathbf{e})}{p(\mathbf{f})} \\ &= \text{argmax}_{\mathbf{e}}\, p(\mathbf{f}|\mathbf{e})\, p_{\text{LM}}(\mathbf{e})\end{aligned} \tag{10.11}$$

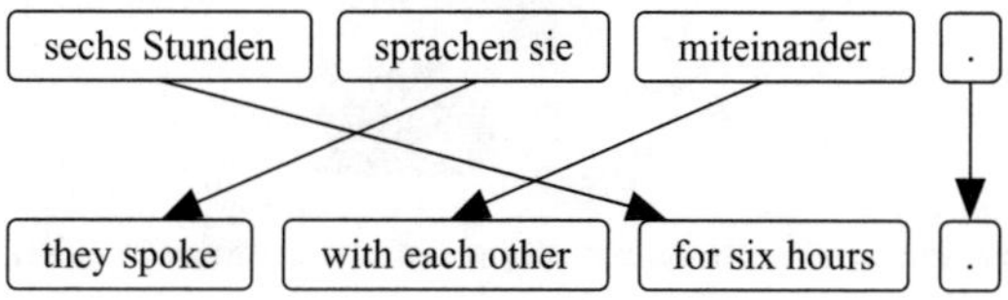

Figure 10–5: Phrase-based machine translation. The input is segmented into phrases (not necessarily linguistically motivated), translated one-to-one into phrases in English, and possibly reordered

Note that we can ignore $p(\mathbf{f})$ because it is constant for all possible translations $\mathbf{e}$. We decompose $p(\mathbf{f}|\mathbf{e})$ further into

$$p(\mathbf{f}|\mathbf{e}) = \prod_{i=1}^{I} \phi(\bar{f}_i|\bar{e}_i)\ d(start_i - end_{i-1} - 1) \tag{10.12}$$

The foreign sentence $\mathbf{f}$ is broken up into I phrases $\bar{f}_i$. Each foreign phrase $\bar{f}_i$ is translated into an English phrase $\bar{e}_i$. Because we mathematically inverted the translation direction, the phrase translation probability $\phi(\bar{f}_i|\bar{e}_i)$ is modeled as a translation from English to foreign.

Reordering is handled by a **distance-based reordering model**. We consider reordering relative to the previous phrase. We define $start_i$ as the position of the first word of the foreign input phrase that translates to the ith English phrase, and end_i as the position of the last word of that foreign phrase. Typically, this model is not estimated from the data but rather is a fixed cost relative to the movement distance is applied: $d(x) = \frac{1}{Z}\alpha^{|x|}$.

There are other components that we may want to add. Typically, a word penalty $\omega^{|e_i|}$ is factored in that adds a factor ω for each produced word. This allows us to adjust the model to produce shorter or longer output.

10.4.2 Training

The main knowledge source in phrase-based models is a massive phrase translation table. It contains input phrases, their possible translations, and corresponding probability scores.

The table is learned from a word-aligned parallel corpus. Given a sentence pair and a word alignment, we extract all phrase pairs that are consistent with the word alignment. By consistent we mean that all the words in the phrases align to each other and not to words outside the phrase pair.

See Figure 10–6 for an example. Given the word alignment points between *(opens, geht)*, *(opens, auf)*, and *(quickly, schnell)*, we can extract the phrase pair *(opens quickly, geht schnell auf)*.

Some subtle decisions must be made in phrase extraction, such as a maximum phrase length (typically 5–7), whether phrases may have unaligned words at the boundaries (typically yes, but sometimes limited), and whether partial counts are assigned or multiple target phrases are found for a source phrase (done either way).

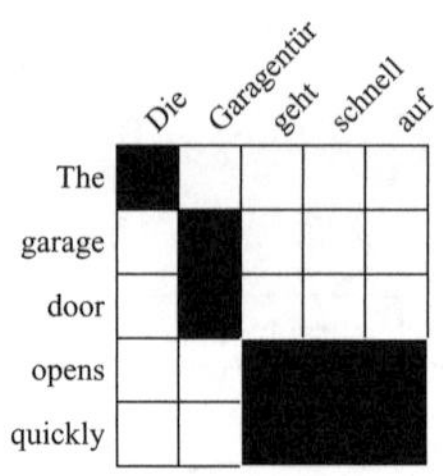

Figure 10–6: Phrase extraction: given the word alignment, the phrase pair *(opens quickly, geht schnell auf)* is extracted

When extracting all phrase pairs, count collection leads to a straightforward definition of conditional phrase translation probability based on relative frequency:

$$\widehat{\phi}(\bar{f}|\bar{e}) = \frac{\text{count}(\bar{e}, \bar{f})}{\sum_{\bar{f}'} \text{count}(\bar{e}, \bar{f}')} \tag{10.13}$$

The conditional phrase translation probabilities are often estimated from very sparse counts. In the extreme case, for an English phrase $\bar{e}$ that only occurs once, its lone foreign correspondent $\bar{f}$ receives a phrase translation probability of $\widehat{\phi}(\bar{f}|\bar{e}) = 1$.

There are several ways to remedy this. Commonly, additional scoring functions based on the lexical translation probabilities are added, for instance, IBM Model 1. Discounting the raw counts using Good-Turing smoothing have also been shown to be effective [29].

We refine the model in Section 10.4.5, where we reformulate it as a log-linear model that allows for the easier integration of additional scoring functions, but let us first turn to the practical issue of producing translations for a new, previously unseen input sentence.

10.4.3 Decoding

Let us say we would like to translate the German sentence

Sechs	*Stunden*	*sprachen*	*sie*	*miteinander*	.
six	*hours*	*spoke*	*they*	*with each other*	.

An English sentence typically starts with the subject, so when creating a translation into English, we would pick out the subject *sie* and start the translation with *They*. Then we would pick out the verb *sprachen* and continue the translation with *spoke*. By building the translation from left to right, we reach the English translation:

They spoke with each other for six hours.

With our decoding algorithm, we want the machine also to translate from left to right. However, this is not so simple. There are many options in our phrase translation table to choose from. See Figure 10–7 for an excerpt of the options from a real example (using a phrase translation table aquired from the Europarl [European Parliament] corpus). Only when we have the full sentence translation we can compute its full translation probability.

At the beginning, the algorithm may pick any of the translation options displayed in the figure. In the second step, we cannot translate the same input word or phrase again, but

Sechs	Stunden	sprachen	sie	miteinander	.
six	hours	it would be		with each other .	
six ,	hours ,	it would		to each other .	
6	hours of	they spoke		together	.
for six	few hours	spoke	they	with	
	time	talked	she	each other	

Figure 10–7: Translation options for a short German sentence

Algorithm 10–2 Pseudocode for the stack decoding heuristic

Input: Foreign sentence $\mathbf{f} = f_1, ...f_{l_f}$

Output: English translation **e**

```
place empty hypothesis into stack 0
for all stacks 0...n − 1 do
   for all hypotheses in stack do
      for all translation options do
         if applicable then
            create new hypothesis
            place in stack
            recombine with existing hypothesis if possible
            prune stack if too big
         end if
      end for
   end for
end for
```

we are still left with almost as many options. A naïve algorithm that tries all possible combinations of translation options to translate the sentence has a runtime that is exponential with respect to sentence length. In fact, machine translation decoding has been proven to be NP-complete [30].

In the commonly used beam-search stack decoding algorithm, we explore the space of possible translations by keeping the promising partial translations and extending them with new translation options until we have covered the entire input sentence.

The partial translations (called **hypotheses**) are organized in **stacks** according to the number of input words they cover. So, for instance, stack 1 contains all hypotheses that have already translated one input word. We keep a limited number of hypotheses in a stack, so we have to prune out some that do not look promising.

We proceed through the expansions of all hypotheses in a stack, which generates new hyoptheses that are placed in stacks farther down the road. Then, we move on to the next stack. The pseudocode for the algorithm is displayed in Algorithm 10–2. For a graphical illustration, see Figure 10–8.

The term **beam search** implies that we search through the most promising part of the search space, using a "beam of light" that illuminates a number of alternatives but that is not bright enough to explore all possible paths.

We mentioned that we have to sort out the less promising hypotheses in each stack. Note that when generating a partial translation, we can already compute all the probability costs implied by Equation 10.13 that have been incurred by the translation options so far. We can then sort the hypotheses according to the costs-so-far and drop the worst ones.

Especially because hypotheses may cover different words, pruning based on costs-so-far is unfair to the translations that already tackled the harder part of the sentence. So, in addition to the cost-so-far, we include a **future cost estimate**.

There is one more, very important twist: **recombination**. There may be two different decoding paths that lead to pretty much the same state in the search. For instance, we

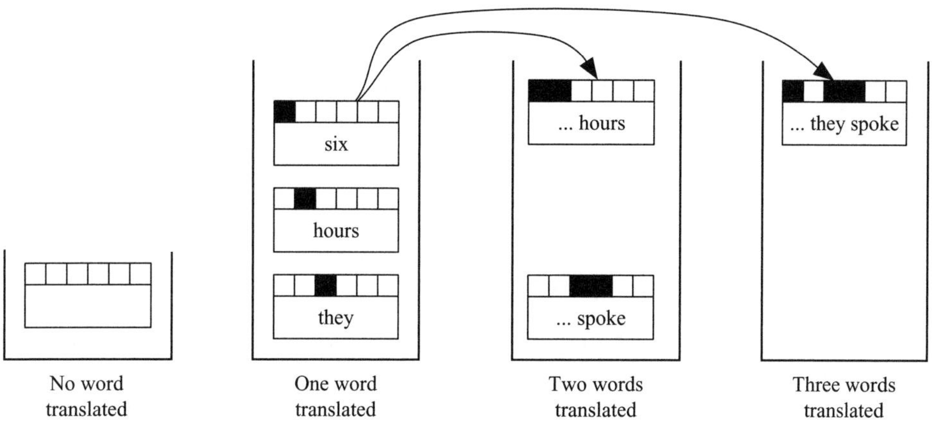

Figure 10–8: Illustration of the stack decoding heuristic

may start translation with the one-word phrase mapping *sie* → *they* and then continue with *sprachen* → *spoke*. But we may have simply used the two-word phrase mapping *sprachen sie* → *they spoke*. One of the two resulting hypotheses will have a higher cost-so-far (depending on the translation costs of the phrase translations), so we can safely drop the worse one.

Note that hypotheses do not have to match exactly for recombination, they only have to be undistinguishable in terms of their continuation. Although they have to match in the foreign word coverage (this affects future search), they may differ in the output words that they have produced so far if these are outside the window of the n-gram language model.

10.4.4 Cube Pruning

A popular new variation of the decoding heuristic is called **cube pruning**, although in phrase-based decoding it has nothing to do with cubes or pruning. A better name would be **sorted expansion**. Because most hypotheses that are generated are discarded, cube pruning focuses on expanding hypotheses that are most promising. To this end, hypotheses that are translation options are sorted, and only the most probable hypotheses are combined with the most probable translation options. See Figure 10–9 for an illustration.

Let us say that we want to expand hypotheses that covered the first word already with translation options that cover the second word. In the example, there are four such hypotheses and five such translation options—in practice the numbers are easily a magnitude bigger. The original beam-search algorithm generates all four by five expansions—we now want to focus on just a subset of these.

The most promising new hypothesis is the combination of the best old hypothesis with the best translation option. So, we start in the top left corner.

We could proceed by creating the top n hypotheses based on the old hypothesis cost and the estimated translation option cost. However, the cost of the new hypothesis is not simply the combination of the cost of the hypothesis and the cost of the expansion. Only once we put them together can we compute the true language model cost and know the true hypothesis cost.

	1.5 hours	1.7 hours	2.6 hours of	3.2 few hours	3.9 time
six 1.0	2.1	2.5			
6 1.3	2.9				
six, 2.2					
for six 2.6					

Figure 10–9: Cube pruning: sorting hypotheses (y-axis) and options (x-axis) allows for the expansion of only the most promising hypotheses

Instead, we proceed in a way that takes into account that some hypotheses and some translation options turn out to be more promising that their costs suggest. We always expand the hypotheses neighboring the best hypothesis that we have expanded so far and that still has unexpanded neighbors.

In the example, the most promising hypothesis in the top left corner has a true cost of 2.1. We explore its neighbors, which have costs of 2.5 and 2.9. Next we, explore the neighbors of the hypothesis with cost 2.5, and so on.

10.4.5 Log-Linear Models and Parameter Tuning

We already mentioned a number of components that may improve our translation model: lexical translation probabilities or a word penalty. It would be awkward to derive a model that includes such components mathematically from the sentence translation probability $p(\mathbf{e}|\mathbf{f})$, including interpolation, independence assumptions, and backoff, so we may as well throw in the towel and clearly state that our model is a combination of feature functions h_i that are weighted (λ_i) according to their importance:

$$\begin{aligned} p(\mathbf{e}|\mathbf{f}) &= \prod_i h_i(\mathbf{e},\mathbf{f})^{\lambda_i} \\ \log p(\mathbf{e}|\mathbf{f}) &= \sum_i \lambda_i \log h_i(\mathbf{e},\mathbf{f}) \end{aligned} \tag{10.14}$$

The feature functions are the components of the phrase-based model we introduced in Section 10.4.1: for instance, the language model $h_{\text{LM}}(\mathbf{e},\mathbf{f}) = p_{\text{LM}}$ or the phrase translation model $h_\phi(\mathbf{e},\mathbf{f}) = \sum_i \phi(\bar{f}_i|\bar{e}_i)$.

Now that we introduced weights λ_i for the feature functions h_i, how do we set them? Each of the feature functions has something to say about the English sentence $\mathbf{e}$ being a good translation of $\mathbf{f}$. We would like to weight these functions so that we optimize overall translation quality.

Here is where we close the circle to the discussion of automatic evaluation metrics: for a given **tuning set** of foreign input sentences and their reference translations, we can—under any given weight setting $\{\lambda_i\}$—translate the set with our model and decoder and compute the resulting automatic BLEU score. We then change the weight setting, decode again, and see if we have an improvement. What we have here is a well-defined multi-dimensional optimization problem, which is called **parameter tuning** or **minimum error rate training** (MERT).

Because decoding is very expensive, we use a shortcut of generating n-best translations for each input sentence and carry out optimization on these n-best lists first. A common method [31] optimizes one parameter at a time. It is possible to find the optimal value for one parameter when leaving all others fixed. However, we are limiting ourselves to a grid search that may get stuck in local optima. So, random restarts are needed. Also, we rerun the decoder to avoid optima on the n-best lists that are unrepresentative of the full search space.

10.4.6 Coping with Model Size

It is not entirely intuitive, but the phrase translation tables we build for phrase-based models are much larger than the parallel corpus itself. Consider that a sentence with n contains $O(n^2)$ phrases.

Typically, training corpora have millions of sentence pairs, and resulting phrase translation tables are often measured in gigabytes. Moore's law has gone a long way to make the practical use of phrase-based models feasible, but even today we cannot store large models in memory. Efforts to run translation systems in handheld devices exacerbate the situation.

A number of solutions have been suggested, ranging from efficient storage of the translation table to filtering and pruning. Let us take a look.

We already mentioned that a table is larger than the corpus we extract it from. A compelling solution is to not store the table at all but to store only the corpus. Of course, we need to quickly look up source phrases (and their translations) that match a given input sentence. Here, the use of suffix arrays has been proposed [32].

A suffix array is a data structure that contains a sorted list of all suffixes of the corpus. Think of suffixes as very long phrases starting anywhere in the corpus and going to the end. The number of suffixes is identical to the number of words in the corpus, and hence the sorted index is of the same size as well. When we look up a suffix of the input sentences, we can find arbitrarily large matches using the index. We then we refer to the (also stored) word alignment and target side of the corpus to extract phrases on the fly.

However, if even the corpus size is too large, then we need even more constraint on what we store in memory. Note that, for the translation of a single sentence, only a tiny fraction of the phrase translation table is used. Instead of loading all of it into memory, we can filter it down to the fraction that is needed. Filtering is common in experimental work, where the same test set of typically one or two thousand sentences is used.

If we want to deploy a machine translation system in an online setting, we do not have the time to filter through gigabytes of data unless we organize the table on-disk in an efficient data structure that lends itself to quick lookups of phrases, such as a prefix tree [33].

Finally, we can take a hard look at the translation table and realize that much of it is junk: either long phrase pairs that are unlikely to ever be useful or low-probability phrases such as thousands of translations for the period (there are even more for the comma). So, why not just clean up the table? Phrase pairs may be discarded on the basis of significance tests on their more-than-random occurrence [34] or log-likelihood ratios [35]. Such considerations may also be taken into account in a second-pass phrase extraction stage that does not extract bad phrase pairs [36].

We may only need to extract the shortest phrase pairs that explain each training sentence pair [37]. This is also the basis of the n-gram translation model [38, 39], a variant of the phrase-based model. Or, we may prune the translation table on the basis of how often a phrase pair was considered during decoding and how often it was used in the best translation [40, 41]. Finally, Kutsumi et al. [42] use a support vector machine for cleaning phrase tables.

10.5 Tree-Based Models

Any reader with some background in linguistics will view our models as hopelessly naïve. One of the fundamental properties of language is recursion. A sentence is made up of clauses, which are made up of verbs, noun phrases, and alike. Noun phrases may include relative clauses that again are made up of verbs, and so on. Virtually all modern theories of grammar look at a sentence and do not see a string of words but a hierarchical tree structure.

None of this is a revelation to researchers in statistical machine translation. The use of syntactic trees—either using syntactic parsers or automatically learning tree structures from the data—within the paradigm of statistical machine translation has been an ongoing focus of attention since the mid-1990s. However, until very recently, such approaches have not been successful in head-to-head comparisons with simpler phrase-based models.

One reason is that operations on tree structures are more complex and thus require computationally more expensive learning methods and also make the search during decoding much harder. This led to simplifications such as requiring some form of isomorphism between source and target syntax trees (e.g., allowing only reordering of children nodes and no major restructuring) that turned out to be too harsh a restriction.

Another problem for syntax-based approaches is that talking about syntax in all its glory is fine, but at the end of day we have to use available syntactic parsing tools that just may not be not good enough.

Current tree-based approaches build on the success of phrase-based models and can be seen as extensions of that approach.

10.5.1 Hierarchical Phrase-Based Models

A limitation of phrase-based models, as we defined them, is that they do not allow for discontinuous phrases with gaps. For instance, we may want to map between English and French:

$$\textit{does not } X \rightarrow \textit{ne } X \textit{ pas}$$

Such a mapping may be expressed, however, by a synchronous context-free grammar, which distinguishes between terminal symbols (words) and nonterminals (X). A grammar rule may also have multiple nonterminals:

$$X_1 \textit{ of } X_2 \rightarrow X_2\ X_1$$

Coming from phrase-based models, we may view such rules as phrase mappings from which subphrase pairs have been subtracted. Allowing for such rules, we obtain a better

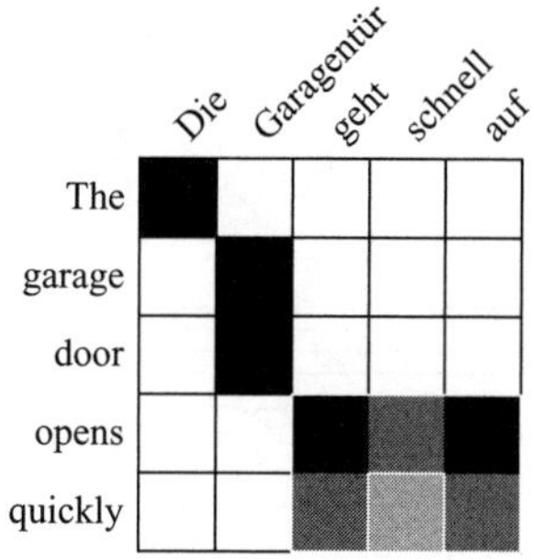

Figure 10–10: Learning hierarchical phrase translation rules: Starting with the phrase pair *(geht schnell auf, opens quickly)*, we extract the subphrase pair *(schnell, quickly)* and arrive at the translation rule *(geht x auf, opens x)*

explanation for certain reordering phenomena, roles of function words such as *of*, and discontinuous phrases.

The extraction of such **hierarchical phrase pairs** [43] from a word-aligned parallel corpus is straightforward. In addition to the fully lexicalized phrase pairs, we have to look at each phrase pair to see if we can subtract subphrase pairs and replace them with nonterminals. Then, we add these hierarchical phrase pairs to our translation table. See Figure 10–10 for an example.

The process of extracting subphrase pairs has the potential to blow up the number of phrase pairs, so we must introduce some reasonable constraints, such as that rules must include at least one word and rules must span at most a maximum number of words.

Adding hierarchical phrase pairs seems to be an obvious win, except that it breaks the decoding algorithm we presented in Section 10.4.3, which required that we construct the translation left to right. How can we build a sentence left to right when we have to add phrases such as *ne X pas*?

Coming from syntactic grammars, there is a straightforward answer: this is a parsing problem, and we have to apply a parsing algorithm, such as chart parsing.

10.5.2 Chart Decoding

Instead of decoding from left to right, we decode bottom up. First we find translations for all single words, then for all spans of two words, then for all spans of three words, and so on until we cover the entire sentence. See Figure 10–11 for an illustration.

For instance, when translating the sentence

Je ne parle pas anglais.

into English, we may first apply a number of traditional phrase translation rules that give us the chart entries:

I		*speak*		*English*
je	*ne*	*parle*	*pas*	*anglais*

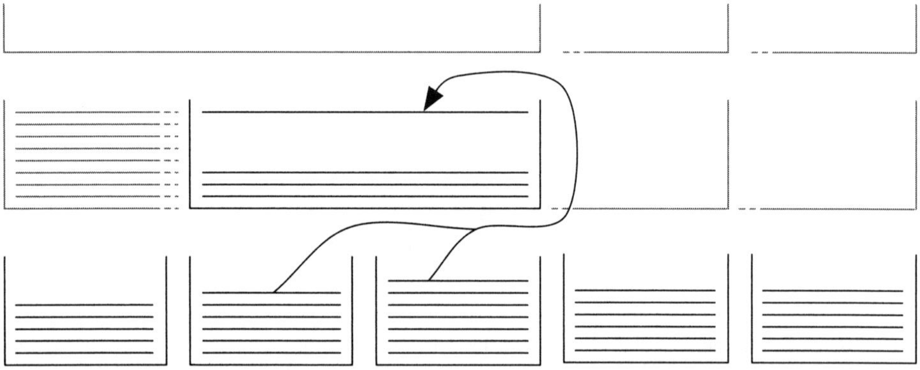

Figure 10–11: Decoding with tree-based model: one stack for each input word (bottom row), and higher level stacks for each contiguous span

We can then apply hierarchical phrase rule (where X matches *speak*):

$$ne\ X\ pas \rightarrow do\ not\ X$$

This adds the chart entry *do not speak*:

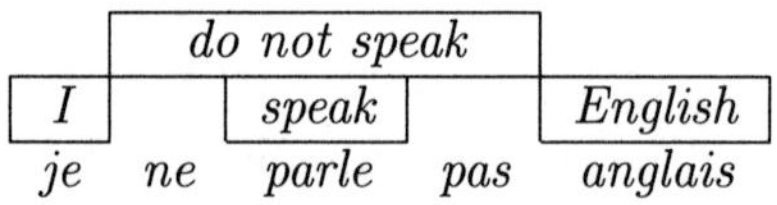

Finally, we can apply the glue rule:

$$X_1\ X_2 \rightarrow X_1\ X_2$$

Using it twice gives us the complete output:

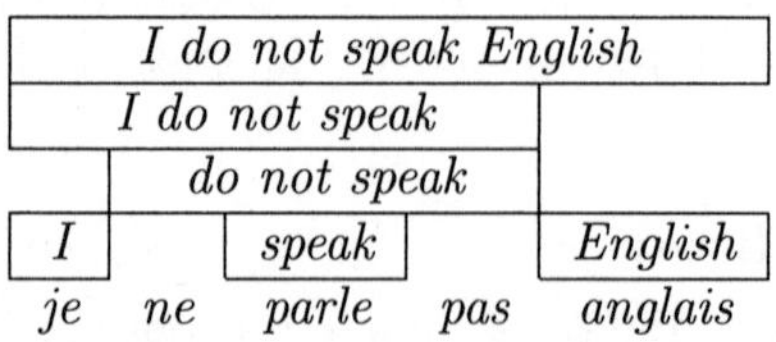

A rough sketch of the chart-decoding algorithm is given in Algorithm 10–3. In practice, a number of refinements are needed to avoid the loop over all possible sequences (starting in line 4) and all rules (starting in line 5), which is computationally too expensive. When entering new chart entries for a span, an efficient search through the underlying chart entries and available rules has to be carried out, for instance, by using Earley parsing.

10.5.3 Syntactic Models

Having made the leap to hierarchical phrase models, it is not much further to a syntax-based model with real constituents labels such as VP and NP. In addition to a word-aligned parallel

Algorithm 10–3 Sketch of the core chart-decoding algorithm

Input: Foreign sentence $\mathbf{f} = f_1, ...f_{l_f}$
Output: English translation $\mathbf{e}$

```
for span length l = 1 to l_f do
  for start=0 .. l_f-l do            // beginning of span
    end = start+l
    for all sequences s of entries and words in span [start,end] do
      for all rules r do
        if rule r applies to chart sequence s then
          create new chart entry c
          add chart entry c to chart
        end if
      end for
    end for
  end for
end for
return English translation e from best chart entry in span [0,l_f]
```

corpus, we now also need syntactic annotation on the source or target side, or both. See Figure 10–12 for an example.

Syntax on the source side acts as a restriction on which rules may apply. Syntax on the target side requires the syntactic parsing of the output sentence into a tree, thus enforcing syntactic well-formedness in addition to the fluency enforced by the n-gram language model.

To give one example, our French verb negation rule may look like this:

VP: *ne* V *pas* → VP: *do not* V

There are some caveats to keep in mind when adding syntactic labels. Phrases in phrase-based models do not have to match constituents in a syntax tree. However, since each chart entry requires a constituent label, we have two choices: (a) require that the target side phrase is a single constituent, or (b) create artificial constituent labels.

Let us give an example. In a phrase model, we may have the rule:

der große → *the big*

When adding syntactic labels on the English target side, choice (a) requires us to extend the rule to the entire noun phrase that includes *the big*:

der große X → NP: *the big* N

Choice (b) requires us to make a new label, for instance:

der große → DT + J: *the big*

Both choices have drawbacks: choice (a) throws out many phrase pairs as potential rules, limiting the knowledge we extract from the parallel corpus. Choice (b) leads to an explosion of nonterminal labels, making decoding harder.

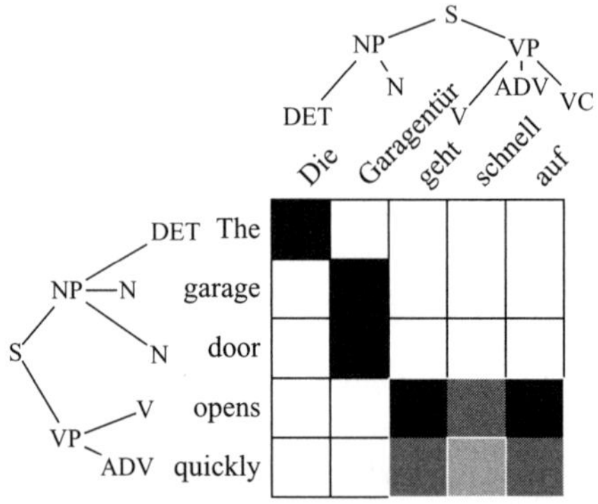

Figure 10–12: Extracting syntactic translation rules. As in the hierarchical phrase pair example from Figure 10–10, the phrase pair *(geht x auf, opens x)* is acquired. The syntactic annotation informs the identity of the nonterminals, giving us the rule VP: *geht* ADV *auf* → VP: *opens* ADV

A third choice that has been used in syntax-based models is the binarization of the syntax tree to make the restriction of limiting phrases to constituents less harsh.

10.6 Linguistic Challenges

So far, we have paid scant attention to the nature of the problem of translation. Most readers, especially if they have learned a second language, will have an intuitive understanding of what makes translation a hard problem: words in the source language have different meanings and thus different translations, the word order between languages differs, and the relationship between words in a sentence are encoded in different ways—be it morphological markup, function words, or order.

All these problems have to be overcome in statistical machine translation systems. Although we pretend that the methods we present here are language-independent, they do in fact work better if the languages between which we translate have mostly the same word order, similar concepts and metaphors, and little morphological complexity on the target side. To give an example, they work very well for French to English but perform worse for Chinese to Turkish.

10.6.1 Lexical Choice

A popular problem in computational linguistics is word sense disambiguation. Words such as *interest* and *bank* have multiple meanings. This shows up in translation as the problem of lexical choice; that is, we have to choose as translation for *bank* into German either *Bank* or *Ufer*, selecting either the money or river sense of the word.

Research in word sense disambiguation has shown that local context (the neighboring words or part-of-speech tags), content words in a larger window, the syntactic role of the word, and syntactic related words are good indicators of word sense.

In fact, by using an n-gram language model, we already capture effectively local context information that is very useful for making the right lexical choice. The prior probability is also helpful: the money sense of *bank* is much more frequent than its river sense. Consequently, statistical machine translation systems handle lexical choice rather well, certainly better than the traditional rule-based systems.

Nevertheless, in recent years, some researchers have targeted word sense disambiguation in statistical machine translation and have shown gains by incorporating the type of additional features we alluded to earlier. It is straightforward to convert the traditional conditional probability distribution—be it at the word or phrase level—into a more sophisticated classifier.

A common choice is to use maximum entropy to incorporate arbitrary features from the source sentence. It is harder to incorporate target side features because they often split states in our beam-search decoding algorithm. If we, say, condition the translation of a word on the first word in our target sentence, we cannot recombine hypotheses that have different first words.

10.6.2 Morphology

The models we have presented so far operate on surface forms of words. For instance, they make no connection between the singular *house* and plural *houses*. Because most of the work in statistical machine translation has focused on English as a target language and English has relatively low morphological complexity, this has not been regarded as a high-priority problem. Yes, we lose some generalization ability by treating *house* and *houses* as two completely different words, but we also keep our model simple and may be able to make better distinctions in the translation of singular and plural forms.

However, when translating into morphologically rich languages such as Turkish, Hungarian, Czech, or German, treating morphology becomes much more important. The first concern is that rich morphology leads to much larger vocabulary sizes and hence sparse data problems in model estimation.

Second, when translating into morphologically rich languages, it is often not clear from the local context which morphological variant to choose. For instance, when translating *the man* into German, we can choose *der Mann*, *des Mannes*, *dem Manne*, or *den Mann*. Which one is correct depends on the relationship of the noun phrase to its syntactic head; for example, is it the subject or object?

Factored translation models [44] propose to represent words not as simple tokens but as vectors of factors such as the lemma, POS tag, gender, count, and so on. Including such additional annotation into our models has two benefits. First, it allows for generalization such as the translation between lemmas instead of surface forms. Second, it enriches the model, which can be exploited for, say, reordering based on POS tags or grammatical coherence checks based on morphological tags.

Adding factored representations to phrase models has been used to enrich the input for better morphological choice in the target, increase grammatical coherence in the output, or improve translation of rare morphological variants. The work has also shown that a risk is involved in breaking up phrase translation into separate mapping steps by assuming independence between them. If we know how to translate morphologically rich phrases because we have seen them very often, there is only harm in decomposing their translation into more fine-grained steps—just as the translation of large phrases (if possible) is better than word-for-word translation.

10.6.3 Word Order

Sentences are made up of one or more clauses, and each clause describes an action that centers on a verb and its arguments and adjuncts. To define which of the entities mentioned in the sentence is the subject and which are the objects and what their roles are, languages such as English use word order.

English is an SVO language, meaning that a clause typically starts with a subject *(English)*, followed by a verb *(is)* and any number of objects *(an SVO language)*. Other languages may have different canonical word order, such as VSO or SOV. This presents a straightforward problem for translation: the words need to be rearranged when mapped into the target language.

The insight that reordering is mostly driven by syntactic differences is one fundamental motivation for the tree-based models discussed in Section 10.5. If we obtain syntactic trees of the input or construct parse trees of the output during translation, then movements that look arbitrary on the surface level (e.g., a word moves nine positions to the left) may be a simple child node reordering in a syntactic tree.

Because the use of tree-based models is generally rather complex, simpler approaches have been proposed to incorporate syntactic trees into statistical machine translation models. One idea is to **pre-reorder** the input before the actual translation process. The goal is to rearrange the input in a way that it still consists of the same input words but now in the expected word order of the output. This may be done via handwritten rules (since we are mostly worried about well-understood long-distance movements) or rules learned automatically from a word-aligned source-annotated parallel corpus, maybe even just using POS tags. We may settle on a unique input sequence or represent potential choices in a reordering lattice. The expectation is that such a rearranged input is easier to translate with traditional phrase-based models, maybe even without allowing any reordering at all afterwards.

Another class of languages, free word order languages, cannot be easily classified as SVO or VSO. Recall that the purpose of a fixed word order is to define the relationship between the different constituents in the sentence, such as the relationships of noun phrases to the verb. Some languages use different means to define this relationship: markers or noun cases. Markers are used, for instance, in Japanese, but also English speakers should be familiar with the concept: prepositions play pretty much the same role (*from the house* vs. *to the house*). Noun cases change the surface form of words; for instance, *der Mann* is a subject, but *dem Manne* is an object.

The mapping between languages that use such different means of defining syntactic relationships has not yet been sufficiently explored in statistical machine translation—partly because of the strong focus on English as the output language where fixed word order is well handled by n-gram language models.

10.7 Tools and Data Resources

Although building a machine translation system is a complex task, it is much facilitated by the tools and data resources that have been made available, often in form of open source software. Look out for any recent developments, but let us quickly review some of the most commonly used resources.

10.7.1 Basic Tools

The training pipeline for statistical machine translation is fairly straightforward to implement, save for two nontrivial steps: sentence alignment and word alignment.

Translated text found out in the wild (think about a book and its translation or a multilingual website) rarely comes in the sentence-aligned format that the methods described in this chapter require. Hence, the first step is to align individual sentences that are translations of each other.

The simplest methods rely on length of sentences as a measure of similarity; more complex methods also utilize translation dictionaries. A widely used tool for sentence alignment is **Hunalign**,[7] which uses both of these knowledge sources to determine the best alignments and also offers filtering functions for potential mismatches.

We discussed the problem of word alignment at length in Section 10.3. The **GIZA++** toolkit[8] is an open source implementation of the popular IBM models presented earlier. It is widely used. More recently, the problem of word alignment has regained attention in the research community. One outcome of this focus is the **Berkeley word aligner**,[9] which integrates the idea of symmetrizing word alignments (recall § 10.3.5) more closely into the alignment method.

The use of language models is essential for machine translation. In almost all cases, machine translation systems integrate existing language model tools and libraries instead of reinventing the wheel. Most popular is the open source **SRILM** toolkit,[10] which has been in use for over a decade. A recent addition is the **IRSTLM** toolkit,[11] which targets compact representation and scalable training tools for very large language models (using billions of words). Worth mentioning is also the **randLM** toolkit,[12] which uses a lossy data structure to even more space-efficiently encode such large language models.

10.7.2 Machine Translation Systems

Entire machine translation systems—including the training process and the decoder—have become available with open source licenses.

The most commonly used toolkit is **Moses**,[13] which implements most of the methods described in this chapter. It draws heavily on existing tools for word alignment and language modeling. More recently, the **Joshua**[14] decoder was developed with a focus on hierarchical and syntax-based models.

We have not discussed rule-based approaches to machine translation in this chapter, but many commercial systems in use today are still based on translation rules written by hand. Typically, such systems allow the integration of more detailed knowledge into translation decision but suffer from the lack of a language model and other probabilistically weighted decision processes. Nevertheless, there is still active work in this area. The open source

7. http://mokk.bme.hu/resources/hunalign/
8. http://www.fjoch.com/GIZA++.html
9. http://nlp.cs.berkeley.edu/Main.html#WordAligner
10. http://www.speech.sri.com/projects/srilm/
11. http://hlt.fbk.eu/en/irstlm/
12. http://sourceforge.net/projects/randlm/
13. http://www.statmt.org/moses/
14. http://sourceforge.net/projects/joshua/

Apertium project[15] aims at the construction of rule-based machine translation system for many language pairs.

10.7.3 Parallel Corpora

Finally, but foremost, you will need to have translated texts as training data for statistical machine translation systems—the more, the better. The more closely tailored to your domain of interest, the better.

Practically all parallel corpora used in machine translation systems are *found* corpora; that is, they have been built for other purposes and co-opted by machine translation research. The main source of such corpora are governments (e.g., Canada for French-English) and international institutions (UN, European Union). Most translations are currently produced in the commercial sector (product documentation, marketing material), but they are usually closely guarded by their content owners. A promising new direction is the exploitation of collaborative efforts on the Internet to create translations—the buzzwords are *wiki translation* and *crowd sourcing*.

Here is a short list of commonly used corpora:

- The **Canadian Hansards**[16] consists of the proceedings of the Canadian parliament, which are translated between French and English.
- The **Europarl corpus**[17] consists of the translated proceedings of the European parliament. It offers about 40 million words in 11 languages each.
- The **Acquis corpus**[18] consists of the legal documents that member countries of the European Union have to submit. The corpus covers 22 languages with up to 40 million words per language.
- The **OPUS project**[19] collects parallel corpora from a wide variety of sources, including open source documentation and movie subtitles.
- The **LDC**[20] is the main source of data for the field of computational linguistics. The organization makes also parallel corpora available, especially for Arabic–English and Chinese–English, which have been the target of recent U.S.-sponsored research programs.

10.8 Future Directions

The field of statistical machine translation is, despite its 20 years of history, very much in motion. The strong focus on evaluation campaigns and hence emphasis of performance over

15. http://www.apertium.org/
16. A part of the corpus is available at http://www.isi.edu/natural-language/download/hansard/; more is available through the LDC.
17. http://www.statmt.org/europarl/
18. http://wt.jrc.it/lt/Acquis/
19. http://urd.let.rug.nl/tiedeman/OPUS/
20. http://www.ldc.upenn.edu/

fanciful ideas leads to rapid adoptions of new methods that have shown to be successful. Current research focuses on a number of issues that we briefly touch upon here.

Statistical machine translation models have a lot of numbers in them, and the estimations of these parameter values is a core problem. While the reliance on probability distributions mirrored in the training data has brought us a long way, there is intense interest in applying more advanced machine learning methods. Current systems rely on a mix of generative models (e.g., the phrase translation probabilities) and discriminate training (parameter tuning; see §10.4.5).

Research on syntactic models is in full swing, and there are many open questions about representation, such as phrase structure grammars versus dependency grammars, specific grammar formalisms, and efficient decoding algorithms.

The reliance on parallel data to train statistical models places a lot of importance on an often very scarce resource. How can we also use comparable or purely monolingual data? How do we deal with small in-domain data and large out-of-domain data? Can we exploit user interactions with machine translation systems as additional training data to improve our systems?

Finally, because machine translation closely interacts with other information processing applications, there is keen interest in integrating statistical machine translation into such applications.

Two applications have been explored in recent work. First, speech translation aims at the integration of speech recognition, machine translation, and speech synthesis. Second, because high-quality translation still requires a human in the loop, recent computer-aided translation tools exploit methods in statistical translations.

10.9 Summary

The application of data-driven methods to machine translation has turned the field into a hotbed of activity.

Machine translation is a seemingly strightforward task: translating text written in one language into text in another language, but with the same meaning. But exactly how to measure if a translation of a sentence is correct is still an open question, as we discussed in Section 10.2 on evaluation.

An important step in learning translation models from a parallel corpus is word alignment (§10.3). A word-aligned parallel corpus allows the estimation of phrase-based (§10.4) and tree-based models (§10.5), currently the most commonly followed approaches.

Machine translation has made great progress; for instance, translating news stories from French to English with today's technology produces very readable and accurate output. But many challenges remain, especially for language pairs with divergent word order and rich morphology (§10.6).

Research in the area is facilitated by a large array of open source tools and resources (§10.7), and many future directions remain to be explored (§10.8).

Bibliography

[1] P. F. Brown, J. Cocke, S. A. Della-Pietra, V. J. Della-Pietra, F. Jelinek, R. L. Mercer, and P. Rossin, "A statistical approach to language translation," in *Proceedings of the International Conference on Computational Linguistics (COLING)*, 1988.

[2] C. Callison-Burch, C. S. Fordyce, P. Koehn, C. Monz, and J. Schroeder, "Further meta-evaluation of machine translation," in *Proceedings of the NAACL 3rd Workshop on Statistical Machine Translation*, pp. 70–106, 2008.

[3] C. Callison-Burch, P. Koehn, C. Monz, and J. Schroeder, "Findings of the 2009 Workshop on Statistical Machine Translation," in *Proceedings of the NAACL 4th Workshop on Statistical Machine Translation*, pp. 1–28, 2009.

[4] M. Przybocki, K. Peterson, and S. Bronsart, "Official results of the NIST 2008 metrics for machine translation challenge (MetricsMATR08)," 2008. http://nist.gov/speech/tests/metricsmatr/2008/results/.

[5] P. Koehn and B. Haddow, "Interactive assistance to human translators using statistical machine translation methods," in *Proceedings of the 12th Machine Translation Summit (MT Summit XII)*, 2009.

[6] L. Truss, *Eats, Shoots & Leaves—The Zero Tolerance Approach to Punctuation.* London: Profile Books, 2003.

[7] D. A. Jones, T. Anderson, S. Atwell, B. Delaney, J. Dirgin, M. Emots, N. Granoein, M. Herzog, T. Hunter, S. Jabri, W. Shen, and J. Sottung, "Toward an interagency language roundtable based assessment of speech-to-speech translation capabilities," in *Proceedings of the 5th Conference of the Association for Machine Translation in the Americas (AMTA)*, 2006.

[8] K. Papineni, S. Roukos, T. Ward, and W.-J. Zhu, "BLEU: A method for automatic evaluation of machine translation," in *Proceedings of the 40th Annual Meeting of the Association of Computational Linguistics (ACL)*, 2002.

[9] G. A. Miller, R. Beckwith, C. Fellbaum, D. Gross, and K. J. Miller, "Introduction to WordNet: An online lexical database," Tech. Rep. CSL 43, Cognitive Science Laboratory Princeton University, 1993.

[10] S. Banerjee and A. Lavie, "METEOR: An automatic metric for MT evaluation with improved correlation with human judgments," in *Proceedings of the ACL Workshop on Intrinsic and Extrinsic Evaluation Measures for Machine Translation and/or Summarization*, pp. 65–72, 2005.

[11] S. Vogel, H. Ney, and C. Tillmann, "HMM-based word alignment in statistical translation," in *Proceedings of the 16th International Conference on Computational Linguistics (COLING)*, 1996.

[12] F. J. Och and H. Ney, "A systematic comparison of various statistical alignment models," *Computational Linguistics*, vol. 29, no. 1, 2003.

[13] E. Matusov, R. Zens, and H. Ney, "Symmetric word alignments for statistical machine translation," in *Proceedings of the Conference on Computational Linguistics (COLING)*, pp. 219–225, 2004.

[14] D. Ren, H. Wu, and H. Wang, "Improving statistical word alignment with various clues," in *Proceedings of the 11th Machine Translation Summit (MT Summit XI)*, 2007.

[15] Y. Ma, S. Ozdowska, Y. Sun, and A. Way, "Improving word alignment using syntactic dependencies," in *Proceedings of the ACL-08: HLT Second Workshop on Syntax and Structure in Statistical Translation (SSST-2)*, pp. 69–77, 2008.

[16] V. L. Fossum, K. Knight, and S. Abney, "Using syntax to improve word alignment precision for syntax-based machine translation," in *Proceedings of the 3rd Workshop on Statistical Machine Translation*, pp. 44–52, 2008.

[17] R. C. Moore, "A discriminative framework for bilingual word alignment," in *Proceedings of Human Language Technology Conference and Conference on Empirical Methods in Natural Language Processing*, pp. 81–88, 2005.

[18] R. C. Moore, W.-T. Yih, and A. Bode, "Improved discriminative bilingual word alignment," in *Proceedings of the 21st International Conference on Computational Linguistics and 44th Annual Meeting of the Association for Computational Linguistics*, pp. 513–520, 2006.

[19] A. Ittycheriah and S. Roukos, "A maximum entropy word aligner for Arabic-English machine translation," in *Proceedings of Human Language Technology Conference and Conference on Empirical Methods in Natural Language Processing*, pp. 89–96, 2005.

[20] N. F. Ayan, B. J. Dorr, and C. Monz, "NeurAlign: Combining word alignments using neural networks," in *Proceedings of Human Language Technology Conference and Conference on Empirical Methods in Natural Language Processing*, pp. 65–72, 2005.

[21] B. Taskar, L.-J. Simon, and D. Klein, "A discriminative matching approach to word alignment," in *Proceedings of Human Language Technology Conference and Conference on Empirical Methods in Natural Language Processing*, pp. 73–80, 2005.

[22] H. Wu and H. Wang, "Boosting statistical word alignment," in *Proceedings of the 10th Machine Translation Summit (MT Summit X)*, 2005.

[23] H. Wu, H. Wang, and Z. Liu, "Boosting statistical word alignment using labeled and unlabeled data," in *Proceedings of the COLING/ACL 2006 Main Conference Poster Sessions*, pp. 913–920, 2006.

[24] C. Cherry and D. Lin, "Soft syntactic constraints for word alignment through discriminative training," in *Proceedings of the COLING/ACL 2006 Main Conference Poster Sessions*, pp. 105–112, 2006.

[25] P. Blunsom and T. Cohn, "Discriminative word alignment with conditional random fields," in *Proceedings of the 21st International Conference on Computational Linguistics and 44th Annual Meeting of the Association for Computational Linguistics*, pp. 65–72, 2006.

[26] J. Niehues and S. Vogel, "Discriminative word alignment via alignment matrix modeling," in *Proceedings of the 3rd Workshop on Statistical Machine Translation*, pp. 18–25, 2008.

[27] S. Venkatapathy and A. Joshi, "Discriminative word alignment by learning the alignment structure and syntactic divergence between a language pair," in *Proceedings of SSST, NAACL-HLT 2007/AMTA Workshop on Syntax and Structure in Statistical Translation*, pp. 49–56, 2007.

[28] A. Fraser and D. Marcu, "Measuring word alignment quality for statistical machine translation," *Computational Linguistics, Squibs & Discussion*, vol. 3, no. 33, pp. 293–303, September 2007.

[29] G. Foster, R. Kuhn, and H. Johnson, "Phrasetable smoothing for statistical machine translation," in *Proceedings of the 2006 Conference on Empirical Methods in Natural Language Processing*, pp. 53–61, 2006.

[30] K. Knight, "Decoding complexity in word-replacement translation models," *Computational Linguistics*, vol. 25, no. 4, pp. 607–615, 1999.

[31] F. J. Och, "Minimum error rate training in statistical machine translation," in *Proceedings of the 41st Annual Meeting of the Association for Computational Linguistics* pp. 160–167, 2003.

[32] C. Callison-Burch, C. Bannard, and J. Schroeder, "Scaling phrase-based statistical machine translation to larger corpora and longer phrases," in *Proceedings of the 43rd Annual Meeting of the Association for Computational Linguistics (ACL'05)*, pp. 255–262, 2005.

[33] R. Zens and H. Ney, "Efficient phrase-table representation for machine translation with applications to online MT and speech translation," in *Human Language Technologies 2007: The Conference of the North American Chapter of the Association for Computational Linguistics; Proceedings of the Main Conference*, pp. 492–499, 2007.

[34] H. Johnson, J. Martin, G. Foster, and R. Kuhn, "Improving translation quality by discarding most of the phrasetable," in *Proceedings of the 2007 Joint Conference on Empirical Methods in Natural Language Processing and Computational Natural Language Learning (EMNLP-CoNLL)*, pp. 967–975, 2007.

[35] H. Wu and H. Wang, "Comparative study of word alignment heuristics and phrase-based SMT," in *Proceedings of the 11th Machine Translation Summit (MT Summit XI)*, 2007.

[36] L. Zettlemoyer and R. C. Moore, "Selective phrase pair extraction for improved statistical machine translation," in *Human Language Technologies 2007: The Conference of the North American Chapter of the Association for Computational Linguistics; Companion Volume, Short Papers*, pp. 209–212, 2007.

[37] C. Quirk and A. Menezes, "Do we need phrases? Challenging the conventional wisdom in statistical machine translation," in *Proceedings of the Human Language Technology*

Conference of the North American Chapter of the Association for Computational Linguistics, Main Conference, pp. 9–16, 2006.

[38] J. B. Mariño, R. E. Banchs, J. M. Crego, A. de Gispert, P. Lambert, J. A. R. Fonollosa, and M. R. Costa-jussà, "N-gram-based machine translation," *Computational Linguistics*, vol. 32, no. 4, 2006.

[39] M. R. Costa-jussà, J. M. Crego, D. Vilar, J. A. R. Fonollosa, J. B. Mariño, and H. Ney, "Analysis and system combination of phrase- and N-gram-based statistical machine translation systems," in *Human Language Technologies 2007: The Conference of the North American Chapter of the Association for Computational Linguistics; Companion Volume, Short Papers*, pp. 137–140, 2007.

[40] M. Eck, S. Vogel, and A. Waibel, "Estimating phrase pair relevance for translation model pruning," in *Proceedings of the 11th Machine Translation Summit (MT Summit XI)*, 2007.

[41] M. Eck, S. Vogel, and A. Waibel, "Translation model pruning via usage statistics for statistical machine translation," in *Human Language Technologies 2007: The Conference of the North American Chapter of the Association for Computational Linguistics; Companion Volume, Short Papers*, pp. 21–24, 2007.

[42] T. Kutsumi, T. Yoshimi, K. Kotani, I. Sata, and H. Isahara, "Selection of entries for a bilingual dictionary from aligned translation equivalents using support vector machines," in *Proceedings of the 10th Machine Translation Summit (MT Summit X)*, 2005.

[43] D. Chiang, "A hierarchical phrase-based model for statistical machine translation," in *Proceedings of the 43rd Annual Meeting of the Association for Computational Linguistics (ACL'05)*, pp. 263–270, 2005.

[44] P. Koehn and H. Hoang, "Factored translation models," in *Proceedings of the 2007 Joint Conference on Empirical Methods in Natural Language Processing and Computational Natural Language Learning (EMNLP-CoNLL)*, pp. 868–876, 2007.

Chapter 11

Multilingual Information Retrieval

Philipp Sorg and Philipp Cimiano

Research on monolingual information retrieval (IR) dates back at least to the 1960s and represents by now an established and mature research field. The subfield of crosslingual information retrieval has observed a surge of interest in recent years. The reasons for this surge are many. First, it is certainly the case that improvements in related technologies, especially in machine translation (MT), have fostered the development of effective multilingual retrieval systems. Second, the number of non-English Internet users has been growing at a fast rate.[1] As a consequence, we find much more non-English content on the Web compared to several years ago. Further, the advent of Web 2.0 technologies has accelerated the need for crosslingual retrieval techniques. The reason is that, although professional websites are usually translated into all relevant languages, it is clearly not the case for the massive amount of user-generated content in Web 2.0 applications such as Flickr, Yahoo! Answers, Facebook, and Twitter. Finally, for multinational companies or globally acting organizations and communities, crosslingual retrieval is an essential need.

In this chapter we present current approaches to crosslingual information retrieval (CLIR) and multilingual information retrieval (MLIR). CLIR involves two languages—the query language and the collection language—and consists in answering documents in the query language on the basis of a language-homogeneous document collection. In contrast, MLIR involves arbitrarily many languages and consists in answering queries in any language supported by the system on the basis of a document collection containing documents in different languages.

Because the main approaches applied to CLIR and MLIR are based on fundamental IR techniques, we also introduce the IR foundations that are needed to understand these approaches. We present alternative design choices for the development of CLIR and MLIR systems along with best practices. The chapter should thus be of interest to both researchers looking for an overview of the main methods used in CLIR and MLIR and developers implementing multilingual information systems. We discuss alternative choices for document models, retrieval functions, and translation approaches depending on the languages that are supported by the retrieval systems. This includes a discussion of language-specific document preprocessing, statistical retrieval models, MT systems, and how the outcome of IR systems can be evaluated.

1. http://www.internetworldstats.com/stats7.htm

11.1 Introduction

Information retrieval deals with the representation, storage, organization of, and access to information items [1]. IR systems with suitable representation and organization of the information items allow users with a specific information need to access the information they are interested in.

Typically, users manifest their information need in the form of a query, usually a bag of keywords, to convey the need to the IR system. The IR system then retrieves items it believes are relevant to the user's information need. In contrast to question answering (QA) systems, which return direct answers to questions, the goal of an IR system is to deliver a list of documents ranked by relevance to the user's query. The target of an IR system is to rank the relevant documents as high as possible and the nonrelevant as low as possible.

In this chapter, we focus on multilingual aspects of information retrieval. In CLIR and MLIR, the information need and the corresponding query of the user may be formulated in a different language than the relevant information is expressed in. While relevance is in principle a language-independent notion, the user must also be able to understand the retrieved items. Multilingual search systems have to ensure that only items in languages supported by the user are returned or that the information items are translated to one of these languages.

11.2 Document Preprocessing

In this section we cover the preprocessing of documents. Preprocessing takes a set of raw documents as input and produces a set of **tokens** as output. Tokens are specific occurrences of terms (types) in a document that represent the smallest unit of meaning. This output defines the **vocabulary** that can be used to index a collection of documents, as described in Section 11.3.

As in most extant IR models and systems, we make the simplifying assumption that the order of tokens in a document is irrelevant. **Phrase indices** or **positional indices** are examples of approaches making use of the order of tokens (see Manning, Raghavan, and Schtze [2] for an introduction).

Depending on language, script, and other factors, the process for identifying terms can differ substantially. For Western European languages, terms used in IR systems are often defined by the words of these languages. However, terms can also be defined as a fixed number of characters in sequence, which is often the case in IR systems applied to Asian languages. Taking Chinese as an example, words are not separated by whitespaces, such that defining terms by character sequences bypasses the problem of having to recognize words.

In the following sections we introduce common techniques used for document preprocessing. In our discussion, we emphasize the differences in preprocessing for different languages and scripts. This includes, in particular, a discussion of the differences with respect to document syntax, encoding, tokenization, and normalization of tokens. The complete preprocessing pipeline is illustrated in Algorithm 11–1. This pipeline shows the dependencies of the different preprocessing steps described in the following.

Algorithm 11–1 The preprocessing pipeline of document d that results in a set of tokens T

```
d ← INPUT
T ← ∅
[c_1, c_2, ...] ← character-stream(d)
B ← tokenize([c_1, c_2, ...])
while B ≠ ∅ do
  t ← POLL(B)
  if is-compound(t) then
    B ← B ∪ compound-split(t)
  end if
  if not is-stop-word(t) then
    t = normalize(t)
    T ← T ∪ {t}
  end if
end while
return T
```

11.2.1 Document Syntax and Encoding

The first step in the preprocessing pipeline is to identify documents in the given data stream [2]. In many cases, this is a straightforward task because the researcher can assume that one file or web site corresponds to exactly one document. However, there are other scenarios with files containing several documents (e.g., XML retrieval) or documents spread over several files (e.g., web pages). The definition of what exactly constitutes a document is thus essentially a design choice of the developer and depends on the search task, that is, the kind of information items that should be retrieved.

The next step is to transform documents into character streams representing the content of documents. The goal of this step is to get a unified representation with respect to encoding, script and direction of script. Two documents with the same content in the same language thus should have identical character streams after this step. The following challenges have to be addressed:

Document Syntax The content of documents is usually encoded in a syntax specific for the given **file type**. Based on the file type specification, the textual content of a document has to be extracted before indexing, avoiding, in particular, that vocabulary elements containing formatting instructions or metadata information are indexed.

Examples for file types that require content extraction are PDF files or web pages. For both cases, many libraries are available that parse PDF or HTML files and extract the textual content.

In many scenarios only parts of the textual content contribute to the semantic content of an individual document. Other parts might be equal across documents (e.g., header or footer parts). In these cases, indexing the complete text also introduces noise. For specific document formats, extractors based on the structure of documents are usually applied to identify the relevant text parts. In the case of web pages for example, the extraction depends on the individual layout of the site. While elements from the header, such as title or keywords, might describe content and should be extracted, the top bar or menus, which are identical on all web pages in the collection, should be ignored.

Encoding and Script Encoding is the representation of letters through a number of bytes in a computer system. Historically, the ASCII character encoding scheme was widely used to encode English documents. Because this scheme is mainly limited to the Latin alphabet, it cannot be used for scripts having different letters. As an encoding scheme supporting most common languages, Unicode [3] established itself as the de facto standard for internationalized applications. The unique number of every character across all languages ensures high portability across platforms and avoids errors introduced by conversion. Unicode also supports right-to-left scripts and can be used to encode, for example, Arabic or Hebrew. Because most operating systems and most current programming languages support Unicode, it is highly recommended to use this character encoding as default.[2]

For IR systems, it is essential that queries and documents are represented in the same script. At some level, retrieval boils down to matching characters, which is unsuccessful when query and document scripts are not compatible. Korean is an example of a language that has different common scripts, namely, Hangul and Hanja. The process of mapping text into another script is called **transliteration**. This must not be confused with translation, as the language is not changed. Transliteration attempts to mimic the sound of the word in the original language by using the spelling of a different language. It is therefore a phonetic transformation that is typically reversible.

For preprocessing of data sets containing documents in heterogeneous scripts, **romanization** is a common technique used to get a unified representation. Romanization is the transliteration of any script to the Latin (Roman) alphabet. For retrieval systems, this is especially useful when searching for common names. Applying romanization, common names used in documents of different languages and scripts are mapped to the same character sequence in most cases. As part of the United Nations Group of Experts on Geographical Names (UNGEGN), the Working Group on Romanization Systems [4] provides romanization resources for various languages. The motivation of this working group is to introduce unique representations of geographic names. However, the resources provided can be used for romanization of any text.

Direction of Script Because scripts are used to record spoken language, a natural order of words and characters is defined by their order in the speech stream [2]. Usually byte representations of text also reflect this natural order. The actual direction of script is handled by the visualization layer in applications, which is part of the user interface. The main problems are typically documents containing text in different languages with different directions of script. An example is Arabic texts with English common names. As we focus on the core functionality and models of MLIR in this chapter, we do not discuss these difficulties any further. We only operate on the data level of documents, which is usually independent of the direction of the script. When designing user interfaces, this is a more important issue.

---

2. Technically, Unicode is a mapping from characters to code points. The set of Unicode encodings includes UTF-8 and UTF-16.

11.2.2 Tokenization

Tokenization is the process of splitting a character stream into tokens. Tokens are instances of terms and correspond to the smallest indexation unit. The set of all terms is typically called the vocabulary. In the following we introduce three common types of vocabularies that require different tokenization approaches. The choice of vocabulary is an important design choice for any IR system. Guidelines for this decision can be found in Section 11.2.4.

To illustrate the different tokenization approaches, we use the following sentence as running example:

```
It is a sunny day in Karlsruhe.
```

Word Segmentation The most common approach to tokenization is splitting text at word borders. Thus, tokens refer to words of a language, and the vocabulary is equivalent to a lexicon (including morphemes).

For languages that use whitespaces to separate words, this is a successful approach used in most IR systems. Whitespaces and punctuations are thereby used as clues for splitting the text into tokens. Examples for such languages are Western European languages. The problem of this approach is that simply splitting text at all whitespaces and punctuations will also split parts of the text that should be represented by a single token. Examples of such error sources are hyphens *(co-education)*, white spaces in proper nouns *(New York)*, dates *(April 28, 2010)*, and phone numbers [2]. In many cases heuristics are used to decide whether or not to split. Classifiers can also be trained on this decision. For our running example, splitting using whitespaces results in the following tokens:

```
[It], [is], [a], [sunny], [day], [in], [Karlsruhe]
```

Tokenization at word borders is a much harder problem for scripts without whitespaces, such as Chinese. Approaches can be classified into two classes: lexical and linguistic. Lexical approaches match terms from a lexicon to the token stream to get a complete coverage. Usually this matching is not deterministic. To get the most accurate matching, heuristics can be applied, such as always preferring to match longer terms. A problem for such approaches is unknown terms that are not in the lexicon and will not be matched but should be detected as such. Linguistic approaches make use of background knowledge consisting of already tokenized text. Using statistical measures based on the frequency of tokens, the goal is to find the most probable segmentation of the current text. Hidden Markov models can be used to compute this in an efficient way [5]. Machine learning techniques like conditional random fields have also been successfully applied to this problem [6]. Because no approach ever achieves a perfect segmentation, wrong tokens will be used for indexing and search and will therefore influence the retrieval performance.

Phrase Indices Phrase indices are based on word segmentation. Tokens are thereby defined not as single words but as tuples of words. Phrase indices are also known as ***n*-gram models**, with n defining the number of words in each token. The character stream that has been already split into words is mapped to tokens by moving a window of n words iteratively over the text. These tokens preserve the context of words. However, this process comes at the cost of a very huge vocabulary. Another problem for search is the sparseness of terms; that is, many terms in queries will not be present in the collection at all. To circumvent this problem, phrase indices can be used on top of a retrieval approach based on single-word segmentation. For our running example, a 3-gram model results in the following tokens:

`[It is a], [is a sunny], [a sunny day], [sunny day in], ...`

Character *n*-Gram Models Character n-gram models define terms as n subsequent characters. Character streams are tokenized by moving a window of n characters over the text. In this case terms do not correspond to words. The vocabulary is defined as the set of sequences having n characters, including whitespaces and punctuation. Term lengths of 4 or 5 have been shown to be reasonable. For our running example, a character 4-gram model results in the following tokens:

`[_It_], [It_i], [t_is], [_is_], [is_a], [s_a_], [_a_s], ...`

This approach can be applied to any character stream and does not depend on word border clues such as whitespaces. It can therefore be used to tokenize text of any script. Because no segmentation is needed, it also avoids errors introduced by word segmentation. In the literature, this approach has been proven superior to word-based segmentation in several scenarios [7]. It has also been applied to the problem of spelling correction [2]. In the context of multilingual retrieval, character n-gram tokenization can be used only if no mapping of terms into different languages is needed. Terms do not correspond to words and thus cannot be mapped or translated across languages. Another drawback using character n-grams is the more difficult visualization of search results. Because only n-grams are matched, it is not possible to highlight matching words for search results.

11.2.3 Normalization

The goal of normalization is to map different tokens describing the same concept to the same terms. An English example is the mapping of plural forms to their singular forms, like *cars* to *car*. Normalization can be defined as building equivalence classes of terms. In a search scenario, normalization can be used to increase the number of relevant documents retrieved and thus also increase the recall of the system. The same normalization methods have to be applied to the collection before indexing and to the query before search. This ensures that all tokens are mapped to equivalent terms, which is crucial for matching queries to documents.

The approach to normalization differs between languages. For languages having complex morphology, a common approach is to map (compound) terms to their lemma(s). Examples are Roman and Germanic languages. There are two main approaches to this problem. First, **lemmatizers** use lexical information to map terms to lemmas. For this approach, rich linguistic resources are required. Second, **stemmers** use a set of simple rules to map terms to stems. For the plural example, the rule of deleting a trailing *s* would map both terms to the same equivalence class. Stemmers do not require rich language resources. The drawback is that terms are not mapped to lemmas but to stems, which do not necessarily correspond to a word. In many cases terms describing different concepts might also be mapped to the same stem. For example, the terms *organize*, *organizing*, and *organization*, would be mapped to *organ*, which makes it impossible to distinguish these terms in the index. In contrast, a lemmatizer would correctly normalize *organize* and *organizing* to the lemma *organize* without changing the term *organization*.

Normalization might also be useful for scripts using diactritics. If the use of diactritics is not consistent, it is useful to delete them in the normalization step. For example, if users do not specify diactritics in queries, normalization should also delete them before indexing. Simple rule-based approaches are normally applied to remove diactritics.

For fusional languages (for example, German, Dutch, Italian) **compound splitting** is another form of normalization. In such languages, compound terms are typically split into the composing lemmas to increase recall. The problem of compound splitting is quite similar to the problem of word segmentation in Asian languages as described earlier. Lexical approaches use a lexicon to match terms in compounds. Linguistic approaches additionally use background knowledge. Many approaches compare the frequency of the compound itself and the frequency of its constituent terms to decide whether or not to split. When applying compound splitting, usually both compounds and split components are added to the token stream. In the search process, this still allows the matching of compounds.

Removal of **stop-words** is a normalization step that deletes frequent terms from the token stream. These terms occur in almost all documents and are therefore not useful to discriminate between relevant and nonrelevant documents. Stop-words are usually articles, prepositions, or conjunctions. For many languages, compiled lists of stop-words exist that can be used to match and filter tokens.

Coming back to our running example, stemming and stop-word removal would result in the following tokens:

```
[sunny], [day], [karlsruh]
```

11.2.4 Best Practices for Preprocessing

After introducing different steps and variants of preprocessing in the previous section, we now present some guidelines for preprocessing distinguishing different types of languages.

Languages Using Latin or Cyrillic Alphabet Because these languages use whitespaces to separate words, word segmentation is the preferable tokenization approach. This approach should be enhanced—depending on the search task—with special treatment for common names, dates, phone numbers, and so on. Stemming or lemmatization usually improves retrieval results for these languages, but this improvement is not always significant [1]. Stemming can be implemented at a modest cost, so it is typically worth doing it. If high precision in finding relevant documents is required, normalization can, however, decrease the retrieval quality. For fusional languages, compound splitting has shown to improve performance up to 25% [8].

Languages Using Arabic, Devanagari or Hebrew Script Word segmentation using whitespaces can be used for these languages and is therefore recommended. Because these languages are not morphologically rich, morphological analysis (stemming or lemmatizing) is not crucial, but diacritics in these languages have to be handled with care. In particular, preprocessing needs to ensure that query and document tokens are transformed into a canonical representation with respect to diacritics.

Languages Using Logographic or Syllabic Scripts Some of these languages (e.g., Korean, Japanese) use more than one writing system, so queries and/or documents might be written in various scripts. In this case, transliteration of queries/documents is needed to ensure compatibility in the search process. In these scripts, words are usually not separated by whitespaces. If rich language resources are available for a language (e.g., Chinese), word segmentation based on heuristic rules or machine learning has been shown to produce good results [6]. However, without these resources, character n-gram tokenization can be applied. This approach is language-independent and avoids sophisticated approaches to word-border detection. It has been shown to be robust and to achieve comparable results to other systems based on word segmentation on European languages [7].

11.3 Monolingual Information Retrieval

Most approaches to MLIR are either directly based on monolingual IR techniques or make use of standard IR models. MLIR can be seen as the problem of aggregating the results of IR systems in different languages. Apart from aggregation, language-specific preprocessing of queries is needed, particularly translation (covered in §11.5). In general, MLIR is based on the same index structures and relies on similar document and retrieval models as known from monolingual information retrieval. In this chapter, we therefore give a short overview of monolingual information retrieval, including document representation, index structures, retrieval models, and document a priori models. We focus on those aspects of information retrieval that are also relevant for CLIR and MLIR. For more details concerning monolingual information retrieval, see Manning et al. [2] and Baeza-Yates and Ribeiro-Neto [1].

11.3.1 Document Representation

In Section 11.2, we described the preprocessing of documents. It results in **token stream** representations of documents. The tokens are instances of terms, which are defined by words, stems or lemmas of words, or character n-grams. The IR models presented in this chapter are independent of the used vocabulary and can be applied to any term model. For the sake of presentation, we make the simplifying assumption that terms correspond to words in spoken language throughout this chapter, as this yields the most intuitive vocabulary for humans.

Most current retrieval approaches use document models based on the **independence assumption** of terms. This means that occurrences of terms in documents are assumed to be independent of the occurrences of other terms in the same document. Although this assumption is certainly overly simplistic, retrieval models based on this assumption achieve reasonable results with current IR technology.

Given the independence assumption, documents can be represented using the **vector space model**. This vector space is spanned by the vocabulary in such a way that each dimension corresponds to a specific term. Documents are represented as vectors by a mapping function f, which maps token streams of documents d to term vectors $\vec{d}$. Different functions f are used in literature, the most prominent being

- *Boolean document model:* The value of a term dimension is set to 1 if the term occurs at least once in the document, otherwise to 0.

- *TF document model:* The value of each dimension depends on the number of occurrences of terms in the document token stream, that is, the **term frequency**. The term frequency can be directly used as value in the term vector. Variants are, for example, the normalization of the term frequency by document length.
- *TF.IDF document model:* These models additionally multiply term frequency values by the **inverse document frequency** of terms. The document frequency of a term is the number of documents in the collection containing this term. The inverse document frequency therefore puts more weight on infrequent terms and less weight on frequent terms that do not discriminate well between documents in the collection. In most cases, the logarithm of the inverse document frequency is used in TF.IDF models.

Given a collection of documents, the document term vectors can be aligned to form the **term-document matrix**. This matrix is spanned by terms as rows and documents as columns. We illustrate the different document representations using the following documents:

```
Doc1: It is a sunny day in Karlsruhe.
Doc2: It rains and rains and rains the whole day.
```

For the different document models discussed, this results in the following term-document matrices:

	Boolean		*TF*		*TF.IDF*	
Term	Doc1	Doc2	Doc1	Doc2	Doc1	Doc2
sunny	1	0	1	0	$1 \log 2/1 = 0.7$	0.0
day	1	1	1	1	$1 \log 2/2 = 0.0$	$1 \log 2/2 = 0.0$
Karlsruhe	1	0	1	0	$1 \log 2/1 = 0.7$	0.0
rains	0	1	0	3	0.0	$3 \log 2/1 = 2.1$

11.3.2 Index Structures

An important aspect of information retrieval is time performance. Users expect retrieval results in almost real time and delays of only 1 second might be perceived as a slow response. The simplistic approach to scan through all documents given a query obviously does not scale to large collections. The high time performance of current retrieval systems is achieved by using an **inverted index**. The idea is to store for each term the information in which documents it occurs. This relation from terms to documents is called **posting list**; a detailed example can be found in Manning et al. [2]. During retrieval, only posting lists of query terms have to be processed. Because queries usually consist of only a few terms, the scores can be computed with low average time complexity.

For the preceding example documents, we get the following posting lists:

```
sunny     -> doc1(1x)
day       -> doc1(1x), doc2(2x)
Karlsruhe -> doc1(1x)
rains     -> doc2(3x)
```

A remaining bottleneck using inverted indices is memory consumption. Loading of posting lists from storage to main memory is the slowest part and should be avoided. Heuristics are therefore needed to decide which posting lists should be kept in memory and which should be replaced. General approaches to reduce memory usage, for example by compression or by usage of suffix trees, are described in Baeza-Yates and Ribeiro-Neto [1]. For very large corpora, distributed indexing can be applied. Posting lists are distributed to several servers. Each server therefore indexes the posting lists of a subset of the vocabulary.

To reduce the time complexity of retrieval, **inexact retrieval models**—also known as **top-k** models—can be applied. These models determine documents that are most likely to be relevant without processing all matching documents. Using these methods, retrieval time can be reduced without getting significant losses in retrieval performance [9].

11.3.3 Retrieval Models

Retrieval models are used to estimate relevance of documents to queries. Different theoretical models have been used to derive these relevance functions. In the following we describe three main families of retrieval models: **boolean models**, **vector space models**, and **probabilistic models**. Depending on the retrieval model, queries are represented in different ways. Boolean queries used for boolean models are modeled as a binary term vector. As defined earlier, the order of query terms is lost in this representation, as only the presence or absence of terms is captured. For vector space and probabilistic models, queries are represented in real-valued vector space, and scores for each query term are accumulated [2].

Boolean Models Boolean models were the first retrieval models used in the beginning of information retrieval. In the case of the Boolean retrieval model, relevance is binary and is computed by matching binary vectors representing term occurrence in the query to binary document vectors representing term occurrence. Because current vector space or probabilistic models outperform boolean models, we focus on these models in this chapter. The interested reader is referred to Manning et al. [2] for details.

Vector Space Models Vector space models are based on vector space representations of documents. As described earlier, this vector space is spanned by the vocabulary, and entries in the term-document matrix are usually defined by term frequencies. There are different models to assess the relevance of documents to a given query:

1. *Accumulative model:* The retrieval function computes scores for each query term. The query term scores are summed up per document to get a final accumulated score for each document. Functions computing scores for a single query term t are based on the following measures:

    - $\mathrm{tf}_d(t)$. Term frequency in the document.
    - $|d|$. Length of the document.
    - $\mathrm{df}(t)$. Document frequency of the query term.
    - $\mathrm{tf}_D(t)$. Number of tokens of the query term in the whole collection.
    - $|D|$. Number of documents in the collection.

For example, the accumulated score of a simple retrieval model based on term frequency and inverse document frequency is computed as follows:

$$\text{score}(q,d) = \sum_{t \in q} \text{tf}_d(t) \log \frac{|D|}{\text{df}(t)}$$

2. *Geometric model:* The vector space representation of the query q can be interpreted as term vector $\vec{q}$. In this case, geometric similarity measures in the term vector space can be used as retrieval models [2]. For example, the **cosine similarity** has been applied successfully in retrieval scenarios:

$$\text{score}(q,d) = \text{cosine}(\vec{q},\vec{d}) = \frac{\langle \vec{q},\vec{d} \rangle}{||\vec{q}||||\vec{d}||}$$

Probabilistic Models In probabilistic retrieval models, the basic idea is to estimate the likelihood that documents are relevant to a given query. Relevance is thereby modeled as a random variable R taking values $\{1, 0\}$. A document d is relevant for a given query q, if and only if $P(R = 1|d,q) > P(R = 0|d,q)$ [2, p. 203]. It has been shown that, given a binary loss function and the most accurate estimation of all probabilities based on all available information, these models achieve optimal performance [10]. However, in practice, it is not possible to get accurate estimations. Probabilistic models have also been used to justify design choices in heuristic functions used in vector space models; the use of the inverted document frequency is an example (see Manning et al. [2] for more details).

The BM25 model [11] is an example of a probabilistic retrieval model that has been proven to be very successful in practice. The scoring function is defined as follows:

$$\begin{aligned}\text{score}(q,d) &= \sum_{t \in q} \text{idf}(t) \frac{\text{tf}_d(t)}{k_1 \left((1-b) + b\frac{|d||D|}{\sum_{d'} |d'|}\right) + \text{tf}_d(t)} \\ \text{idf}(t) &= \log \frac{|D| - \text{df}(t) + 0.5}{\text{df}(t) + 0.5}\end{aligned}$$

Common values for the parameters of this model are $k_1 = 2$ and $b = 0.75$, but they should be adjusted to the search task and data set.

Language Models In recent years, language models have established themselves as powerful alternative retrieval models. Language models are a subclass of probabilistic models. Documents, queries, or whole collections are represented by generative models. These models are represented by probability distributions over terms, such as the probability that a document, query, or collection generate a certain term [12].

Maximum likelihood estimation is often used to define document models. The probability of a term t being generated by document d is then defined as:

$$P(t|d) = \frac{\text{tf}_d(t)}{|d|}$$

In information retrieval, language models are used to estimate the probability $P(d|q)$, which is then interpreted as relevance score. Using **Bayes theorem**, this can be transformed to:

$$P(d|q) = \frac{P(q|d)P(d)}{P(q)}$$

Because $P(q)$ is constant for a query and $P(d)$ can be assumed to be uniform, ranking of documents is based on the value of $P(q|d)$. When modeling queries as sets of independent terms, this probability can be estimated using document language models:

$$P(q|d) = \prod_{t \in q} P(t|d)$$

This score will be zero for all documents not containing all query terms, so **smoothing** is often applied. Using background knowledge, a priori probabilities of terms $P(t)$ are estimated, and a mixture model is used for retrieval:

$$P(q|d) = \prod_{t \in q} (1-\alpha)P(t|d) + \alpha P(t)$$

Often the whole collection is used as background knowledge and the a priori probability is estimated by the language model of the collection:

$$P(t) = \frac{\sum_{d \in D} \mathrm{tf}_d(t)}{\sum_{d \in D} |d|}$$

11.3.4 Query Expansion

Query expansion is an established technique to improve retrieval performance, which is of special interest in the context of CLIR and MLIR. The query is expanded by additional terms that further characterize the information need. The goal is to match more relevant documents that contain relevant content but use other terms to describe it.

Expanded queries can be used in all retrieval models presented previously. Usually, expanded query terms are given less weight than the original query terms. The weight depends on the confidence of each expanded term and the overall weight put into query expansion. Using probabilistic retrieval models, query expansion can be used to improve the estimation of probabilities, such as the estimation of the query language model. We distinguish two different sources for expansion terms:

Background Knowledge Additional knowledge sources are exploited to find expansion terms for a given query. An example is the use of a thesaurus to expand the query with synonyms of the query terms. For CLIR or MLIR, a special case of query expansion is the translation of the query. In this case the query is expanded using the terms of its translation into different languages.

Relevance Feedback Using **relevance feedback** for query expansion is a two-step retrieval process. First, the original query is matched to the document collection. Then, relevance assessments are used to identify the relevant documents in the retrieval results.

Using an expansion model based on term frequency and document frequency in this set of **expansion documents**, promising terms are identified and used in a second retrieval step for query expansion.

The selection of relevant documents in the first step can be either manual or automatic. In the first case the user selects relevant documents manually out of the retrieval results of the first step. In the case of **pseudo-relevance feedback** (PRF), the top k documents of the first retrieval step are assumed to be relevant. This enables to implement automatic query expansion without user interaction. For this reason, PRF is often referred to as **blind relevance feedback**.

11.3.5 Document A Priori Models

In all retrieval models presented earlier, the a priori probability of documents is assumed to be uniform; that is, the probability of retrieving documents independently of a specific query is the same for all documents. However, in many scenarios this assumption does not hold. For example, documents have different perceived quality and popularity. Such factors could definitely influence the a priori probability of a document in the sense that very popular or high-quality documents should intuitively have a higher likelihood of being relevant.

For the different types of retrieval models, there are different approaches to integrate document priors. When using vector space models, these a priori probabilities can be multiplied with the IR score of each document [1]. Another option is the linear combination of scores and a priori probabilities. Weights in this linear combination have to be optimized for the special application scenario. For probabilistic and language models, the estimation of document priors $P(d)$ is required as part of the retrieval model. In the standard case without background knowledge, document priors are assumed to have equal distribution over all documents. However, if document a priori models are available, they can be integrated directly into the retrieval model by replacing the uniform model used before.

The way document priors are modeled clearly depends on the target application. In web search, for example, the web graph consisting of pages and hyperlinks can be exploited to compute authority measures, which can be used as document priors. Pagerank [13] and HITS [14] are established algorithms to compute authority in web graphs. Another example is search in community portals. Ratings of users, usage patterns, or other evidence can be used to compute document priors [15].

11.3.6 Best Practices for Model Selection

The main criteria for selecting retrieval models is retrieval performance. Both costs of indexing and costs of searching are similar across models. All are based on similar inverted indices and use arithmetic operations in the same complexity class to compute document scores.

When comparing the performance on reference data sets, vector space models, probabilistic models, and language models show no significant difference. The top results on the TEL data set published at Cross Language Evaluation Forum (CLEF) 2009 (see §11.6 for more details on evaluation campaigns) were achieved by retrieval systems based on different models. On English documents, for instance, a vector space model implemented by the University of Chemnitz outperformed a language model of the University of Dublin by only

0.4% in mean average precision.[3] On French documents, a probabilistic model implemented by the University of Karlsruhe outperformed the best vector space model by 1.4% [16]. As can be seen for the results on different languages, these differences are specific to certain data sets, such that it is difficult to decide in general which models perform best.

The choice of retrieval model also depends on the available training data—for example, in the form of relevance assessments of sample queries—and the richness of document models. Without training data, the use of established standard models with standard parameters is recommended, such as BM25 (defined in §11.3.3). This ensures a baseline performance on new data sets. When training data is available, parameters of these models can be optimized. When rich models of documents are available, language models offer the flexibility of integrating this new evidence of relevance. The estimation of probabilities can be adapted to a specific task to improve performance. On top of a well-performing search system, query expansion using PRF can be used to further improve retrieval results in most cases. Query expansion in particular has the goal of increasing recall. However, it should be applied with care if the precision of the system is the main evaluation criteria.

11.4 CLIR

CLIR is the task of retrieving documents relevant to a given query in some language (query language) from a collection of documents in some other language (collection language).

> **Definition 11–1. Crosslingual information retrieval** Given a collection D containing documents in language l_D (collection language), CLIR is the task of retrieving a ranked list of relevant documents for a query in language l_q (query language). Hereby, D is a monolingual collection; that is, all documents in D have the same language.

Essentially, we can distinguish between two different paradigms of CLIR. On the one hand, we have translation-based approaches that translate queries and/or documents into the language supported by the retrieval system. Such approaches reduce the task of crosslanguage retrieval to a standard monolingual IR task to which standard retrieval techniques can be applied. On the other hand, there are also approaches that map both documents and queries into an interlingual (concept) space. The relevance functions are then defined on the basis of this interlingual space.

11.4.1 Translation-Based Approaches

Translation-based approaches translate the query and/or the document collection into some language supported by the retrieval system. Translation-based approaches differ in the choice of translation techniques as well as in the choice of whether only the query, the document collection, or both are translated. We describe several alternative choices for the latter. Further, translations can be obtained either by involving manual translators or through the application of MT techniques.

3. Mean average precision (MAP) is a standard evaluation measure used to evaluate the performance of IR systems. Higher values correspond to more relevant documents being retrieved at lower ranks. A precise definition of MAP is presented in §11.6.

Translating Queries The default strategy for CLIR is the translation of the query into the language of the document collection. This effectively reduces the problem of CLIR to monolingual information retrieval. In what follows, we list some of the advantages (PRO) and disadvantages (CON) of such an approach:

PRO

- Only the query has to be translated, which is usually a short text.
- The index can be used to evaluate queries in arbitrary languages provided they can be translated into the language of the collection/index.

CON

- An online query translation is needed. Because the response time of the retrieval system is the sum of the translation time and the retrieval time, an efficient MT system is needed to maintain system performance at reasonable levels.
- The accuracy of the retrieval system is partially dependent on the quality of the MT system used.

Translating Documents A further strategy is to translate the complete document collection into the query language and create an inverted index for the query language. This might be useful in search scenarios having a fixed query language, such as in portals that have only users of one language. In the following, we also summarize the advantages and disadvantages of such an approach:

PRO

- The translation is part of the preprocessing, as indices will be based on the translated documents. Thus, there is (almost) no temporal constraint on the translation step, such that researchers can resort to manual translation if needed for quality reasons.

CON

- The query language has to be known and fixed in advance. Because the index is specific for this language, queries in other languages are not supported.
- The whole collection has to be translated, which might be costly.

Pivot Language As a combination of the first two approaches, both queries and documents can be translated into a **pivot language**. The pivot language is either a natural or artificial language for which translation systems are available from many languages. English is most often used as such a pivot language because of the large amount of available translation systems. Because no direct translation from query language to document language is needed, the pivot language approach is useful if no language resources supporting this translation are available.

Using a pivot language reduces CLIR to the problem of standard monolingual information retrieval because an existing IR system in the pivot language can be applied to any pairs of query and document languages. However, the performance depends on an adequate translation for both the query language and the collection language into the pivot language. Advantages and disadvantages here can be summarized as follows:

PRO

- Translation systems to a pivot language can be used for CLIR between languages for which direct translation is not available.
- Existing IR systems in the pivot language can be used for CLIR for any pair of query and document language.

CON

- Online translation of the query as well as offline translation of documents (as part of document preprocessing) is required.

Query Expansion Query expansion techniques can also be applied in CLIR settings in the following ways:

Pretranslation expansion expands the query before it is translated. The expanded query is then processed by the translation system. This has the advantage that more context is given as input to the translation process. In CLIR settings, this was shown to improve precision of the retrieval results [17].

Posttranslation expansion is equivalent to query expansion used in monolingual information retrieval. In a CLIR setting, it has been shown that posttranslation expansion can even alleviate translation errors because wrong translations can be spotted by using local analysis of the results of the query (e.g., using PRF) [17].

11.4.2 Machine Translation

As described earlier a translation step is necessary for translation-based CLIR. Either the query or documents need to be translated before queries can be evaluated using the (language-specific) inverted index. Manual translation, for example, by professional translators, typically incurs high costs. The manual translation of documents does not scale to large corpora, and it is not possible to have real-time translation of queries, a crucial requirement in retrieval systems that need response times in fractions of a second (e.g., in web search). This clearly motivates the use of machine translation for CLIR.

In this chapter we present the two main approaches to machine translation used in CLIR systems—**dictionary-based translation** and **statistical machine translation**.

Dictionary-Based Translation A straightforward approach to query translation is the use of bilingual dictionaries for term-by-term translation. There are different strategies to cope with alternative translations of terms, ranging from choosing the most common translation to taking into account all possible translations. Interestingly, Oard [18] showed that there are no significant differences between the different strategies in a CLIR setting. When using all alternative translations, query terms are usually weighted by their translation probability.

Ballesteros and Croft [17] argue that posttranslation expansion can be used to minimize translation errors in dictionary-based query translation. They showed that using PRF for query expansion removes extraneous terms introduced by the translation and therefore improves the retrieval performance.

Statistical Machine Translation In contrast to dictionary-based translation, statistical machine translation (SMT) aims at translating complete sentences. Thus, in principle, SMT can be applied to both query and document translation. (See Chapter 10 for a full discussion of approaches to SMT.)

Most current SMT systems are based on the IBM models introduced by Brown et al. [19]. These models are iteratively induced for language pairs on the basis of a training corpus in which sentences are aligned across languages. In two subsequent steps, the term alignment of translated sentences and the translation model of terms are optimized. The final model then is a product of the iterative optimization of these two steps. These models can be further improved by additionally translating phrases. In this case not only alignment and translation of single terms but also of phrases like *New York* are learned and applied. Using additional background knowledge can also improve translation, for example, by including language models derived from large monolingual training corpora.

The drawbacks of applying SMT systems to translate the query on the fly is the potentially longer execution time of the retrieval step and the requirement of a training corpus. The execution time bottleneck seems less problematic given the continuous advances in computer hardware and the fact that providers of online translation systems build on a large and distributed computer infrastructure. Indeed, recent systems can already be applied to real-time query translation. However, training corpora are still missing for many language pairs [20].

11.4.3 Interlingual Document Representations

An alternative to translation-based CLIR are interlingual document representations. The essential idea is that both query and documents are mapped to an interlingual **concept space**. In contrast to term-based representations of documents, concepts represent **units of thought** and are thus assumed to be language-independent. Language-specific mapping functions are needed, however, to map documents into the interlingual concept space. Such a mapping might for instance rely on a quantification of the degree of association for terms in different languages (and by aggregation also for a document) to the given set of interlingual concepts. By mapping queries to the same concept space as documents, information retrieval can be reduced to the comparison of query and document concept vectors. This enables the application of standard similarity measures such as the cosine of the angle enclosed by the two vectors representing the query and the document to compute a ranking. In the following, we present two approaches to interlingual concept spaces that have been applied to CLIR.

Latent Semantic Indexing In the monolingual case, latent semantic indexing (LSI) is used to identify latent topics in a text corpus. These topics, which correspond to concepts as described previously, are extracted by exploiting co-occurrences of terms in documents. This is achieved by singular value decomposition of the term-document matrix [21]. The latent topics then correspond to the eigenvectors having the largest singular values. This also results in a mapping function from term vectors to **topic vectors**. LSI was originally used for dimensionality reduction of text representation and for improved retrieval of synonyms or similar terms. By using parallel training corpora, LSI can also been applied to CLIR [22]. In this case the extracted topics span terms of different languages, and the mapping function maps documents of all languages to the latent topic space.

Explicit Semantic Analysis Recently, explicit semantic analysis (ESA) has been proposed as an alternative concept-based retrieval model [23]. Concepts are explicit and defined with respect to some external knowledge source. Textual descriptions of each concept are used to map documents into the concept space. Examples of such resources including concepts and their descriptions that have been used for ESA are Wikipedia and Wiktionary. ESA can be applied to CLIR if textual descriptions of concepts are available in all languages supported by the retrieval system. When using Wikipedia as a multilingual knowledge resource, crosslanguage links can be used to build multilingual concept definitions. Cimiano et al. [24] have shown that ESA can be extended to crosslanguage retrieval settings.

11.4.4 Best Practices

In most cases, query translation is the most flexible way to implement a CLIR system. While supporting arbitrary query languages, the same index can be used for retrieval in any language that can be translated into the language of the collection/index. However, its success depends on the availability of a real-time translation system from query to document language. Given limited resources, translating queries and documents into a pivot language having the best support in terms of translation resources might be the best approach.

Oard showed that SMT systems outperform dictionary-based approaches for query translation. It is therefore recommended to use existing SMT systems, whether commercial or open source. However, if the retrieval system is domain-specific, dictionary-based query translation based on a bilingual dictionary containing all relevant technical terms is likely to outperform generic SMT systems applied to CLIR on this particular domain [18]. If such resources are available for this specific scenario, dictionary-based query translation paired with postretrieval expansion is the best choice for the design of a CLIR system.

11.5 MLIR

In contrast to CLIR, multilingual information retrieval (MLIR) considers corpora containing documents written in different languages. It can be defined as follows:

> **Definition 11–2. Multilingual information retrieval** Given a collection D containing documents in languages $l_1, \ldots, l_n$, MLIR is the task of retrieving a ranked list of relevant documents for a query q in language l_q. These relevant documents may thereby be distributed over all languages $l_1, \ldots, l_n$.

MLIR finds application in all those settings where a data set consists of documents in different languages and users of the retrieval system have at least passive knowledge of some of the languages the documents are written in. In most cases, people have indeed basic reading and understanding skills in some language other than their mother tongue (the one the collection is queried with). Such settings can be found in particular on the web but also in large corporate multinationals. Further, still if the users do not understand the language of a returned document, MT techniques can be applied to produce a text in the native language of the user.

In general, MLIR systems are based on techniques similar to those used for CLIR systems, and essentially the same translation approaches can be applied. However, the multilingual scenario requires a different index organization and relevance computation strategies than are used in monolingual and crosslingual retrieval. In the following, we briefly describe different strategies ranging from unified indices to multiple language-specific indices. If the language of the documents is not known a priori, language identification is required as part of the preprocessing.

11.5.1 Language Identification

Language identification is the problem of labeling documents with the language in which the content of the document is expressed. In the following, we assume that documents are monolingual; that is, they contain text in one language. The more complex case of mixed documents is briefly touched upon at the end of this section.

The problem of language identification can be reduced to a standard classification problem with discrete classes. The target classes are given by a set of languages, and the task is to classify documents to one of these classes representing each of the relevant languages. Given monolingual training corpora for each language, supervised machine learning approaches can be applied to this task. The most successful reported classification method is based on character n-gram representations of documents. Cavnar and Trenkle [25] present language identification results with 99% precision using a set of 14 languages. They build term vectors for each document by extracting character n-grams for $n = 1 \ldots 5$. An important aspect here is that the classifiers can be trained on monolingual input for each of the languages so that an aligned data set is not necessary. Thus, the approach is applicable in principle to any set of languages. Further, the method requires no preprocessing because character n-grams are based on the character streams without word splitting. It has been demonstrated that the accuracy of this language identification method is dependent on document length because longer documents provide more evidence for the language they are written in. The results of Cavnar and Trenkle show that precision of 99% or more can be expected for documents having more than 300 characters.

Applying the proposed classifier on mixed documents having content in multiple languages results in unpredictable classification. The language-specific distribution of terms or n-grams (that is exploited by the classifier) is lost as the characteristics of the individual languages overlay each other. These documents have to be split into their monolingual components beforehand. As the splitting is done on sections, paragraphs, or sentences, this produces shorter documents that are more difficult to classify, thus degrading results.

11.5.2 Index Construction for MLIR

There are two main approaches to index construction for MLIR, differing in whether a single or multiple indices are used. Single-index approaches build one index for the documents in the different languages. We distinguish three techniques for constructing such an index:

Document translation: By translating all documents into a pivot language, the problem of MLIR can be reduced to CLIR. The single index then contains all the translated documents.

Language token prefixes: Nie [26] proposes the creation of a unified index by adding language prefixes to all tokens. This ensures that terms having the same character representation in different languages can be distinguished. The lexicon of the unified index consists of terms in all languages. Nie argues that this unified index preserves term distribution measures like term frequency and document length.

Concept index: As discussed earlier, language-independent concept indices can also be applied to MLIR. As documents of different languages are mapped to the same interlingual concept space, only a single concept index is needed for the multilingual corpus.

Approaches based on multiple indices build different indices for each language of the corpus. There are two different techniques:

Language-specific indices: Each document in a multilingual collection is added to the index for the corresponding language, whereby the language needs to be identified such that the language-specific preprocessing can be applied. For monolingual documents, the set of documents contained in each index are thus disjointed. For mixed documents having content in different languages, only document parts in the language of the index are added. In this case a document can appear in many of the language-specific indices.

Specific preprocessing: For each language, an index is constructed containing all documents of the corpus. However, preprocessing of these documents is specific to the language associated to each index. For each index, documents are therefore assumed to be in the index language. As a consequence, each document is contained in all indices.

11.5.3 Query Translation

The different approaches to index construction require different query translation strategies. For single indices based on document translation or concept indices, refer to Section 11.4 because the query translation is analogous to query translation used in CLIR.

For all other approaches, queries need to be translated into all document languages. Depending on the index used, these translations are applied in different ways:

Language token prefixes: A query for the unified index with language prefixes for each term is built by concatenation of all query translations into a single query and by adding language prefixes to all query tokens. Standard IR models can then be used to query the unified index.

Multiple indices: When using multiple indices for the different languages, the translation of the query into each language is used to query the index of the corresponding language. This produces different language-specific rankings for each language, and the rankings must be combined into an aggregated score determining an aggregated ranking. We discuss some of the most important aggregation models next.

11.5.4 Aggregation Models

Retrieval based on multiple indices requires score aggregation models because the rankings based on evidence in each language need to be combined to yield a final ranking. Given a set of languages $L = \{l_1, \ldots, l_n\}$, a query q, and language-specific scores for each document—$\text{score}_l(d, q)$—a straightforward approach is to sum up the scores for all the languages:

$$\text{score}(q, d) = \sum_{l \in L} \text{score}_l(q, d)$$

The aggregated score can then be used to sort all documents and produce an overall ranking of the documents.

The main problem of this aggregation strategy is the potential incompatibility of the scores. In fact, by simply adding scores, it is assumed that the absolute score values express the same relevance level in each ranking. However, for most retrieval models, this is not the case. The absolute values of scores depend on collection statistics and term weights, such as the number of documents, number of tokens, average document length, or document frequency. For each index, these values differ, and therefore the absolute scores are not necessarily comparable. To overcome this problem, normalization typically is applied to each ranking before aggregation. A standard approach for MLIR is the Z-score normalization [27]. Each ranking is normalized by using statistical measures on its scores: the minimal score, the mean score, and the standard deviation. Given training data in the form of queries and relevance judgments for documents, machine learning techniques can be used to compute optimal weights by which scores can be combined (see Croft [28]).

A complete aggregation step using Z-score normalization is presented in Algorithm 11–2. Given a set of rankings $R = \{r_1, \ldots, r_n\}$, the algorithm computes the combined ranking r_c. In the first step, each ranking r_i is normalized using the minimum value, the mean value, and the standard deviation of its values. In the second step, combined scores are computed by summing the scores of each document across all rankings. Finally, the combined ranking is built by reordering documents according to descending values of the aggregated scores.

11.5.5 Best Practices

By analogy to CLIR, indexing documents in their original language and using translated queries for retrieval is the most flexible approach to MLIR because it directly supports new query languages and can usually be adopted to new retrieval and aggregation models. An interesting feature is that if the translation system is changed or updated, there is no need to rebuild the indices. An analysis of the results of recent evaluation campaigns for MLIR—the results of the CLEF workshop 2009 [16]—reveals that the most successful systems are based on multiple language-specific indices. SMT systems are thereby used for query translation, and score aggregation is based on Z-score normalization [29].

Using a unified index with language prefixes is a good option for MLIR systems that are built on top of existing IR systems. Because the indexing and retrieval steps remain unaffected, only the preprocessing of documents (adding language prefixes on tokens) and queries (translation and language prefixes) needs to be adjusted.

Algorithm 11–2 Aggregation of multiple rankings $r_1, \ldots, r_n$ based on Z-score normalization. For ranking r, $r[i]$ defines the score at rank position i, $\text{score}_r(d)$ defines the score of document d. MIN, MEAN, and STD-DEVIATION are defined on the set of score values of ranking r

```
R ← {r_1, ..., r_n}
for all r ∈ R do                          // Normalization
  μ ← MEAN(r)
  σ ← STD-DEVIATION(r)
  δ ← (μ − MIN(r)) / σ
  for i = 1..|r| do
    r(i) ← (r(i) − μ) / σ + δ
  end for
end for

r_c ← {}
for all d ∈ D do                          // Aggregation
  s ← 0
  for all r ∈ R do
    s ← s + score_r(d)
  end for
  score_{r_c}(d) ← s
end for
r_c ← DESCENDING-SORT(r_c)
return r_c
```

11.6 Evaluation in Information Retrieval

Ultimately, the goal of any IR system is to satisfy the information needs of its users. Needless to say, user satisfaction is very hard to quantify. Thus, IR systems are typically evaluated building on the notion of **relevance**, where relevance is assessed by a team performing the evaluation of the system rather than by the final. We can adopt a binary notion of relevance, where a document is either relevant to a query or it isn't, or a real-valued notion of relevance, where we consider the degree of relevance of a document to a query. The former case is the most frequent one in IR evaluation. Given a specification of which documents are relevant to a certain query and which ones are not, the goal of any IR system is to maximize the number of relevant documents returned while minimizing the amount of nonrelevant documents returned. If the IR system produces a ranking of documents, then the goal is clearly to place relevant documents on top and nonrelevant ones on the bottom of the ranked list. Several evaluation measures have been proposed to capture these intuitions. In addition, several reference collections with manual relevance judgments have been developed over the years. Because results on such data sets are thus reproducible, they allow different system developers to compete with each other and support the process of finding out which retrieval models, preprocessing, indexing strategies and so on perform best on certain tasks.

In this section we first describe the experimental setup that was introduced as the **Cranfield paradigm**. Then we introduce and motivate different evaluation measures. These measures are based on relevance assessments. We describe manual and automatic approaches to create relevance assessments. Finally, we provide an overview of established datasets that can be used to evaluate CLIR and MLIR systems.

11.6.1 Experimental Setup

The experimental setup used to evaluate IR systems has to ensure that an experiment is reproducible, which is the primary motivation for the development of the Cranfield evaluation paradigm [30]. According to this paradigm, we have to fix a certain corpus as well as a minimum number of **topics** consisting of a textual description of the information need as well as a query to be used as input for the IR system. The systems under evaluation are expected to index the collection and return (ranked) results for each topic (query). To reduce the bias toward outliers, a reasonable number of topics must be used in order to yield statistically stable results. A number of at least 50 topics is typically recommended.

For each topic, a gold standard defines the set of relevant documents in the collection [2]. The notion of relevance is hereby typically binary—a document is relevant or not to a given query. Using this gold standard, the IR system can then be evaluated by examining whether the returned documents are relevant to the topic and whether all relevant documents are retrieved. These notions can be quantified by certain evaluation measures, which are supposed to be maximized (see §11.6.3). Because user satisfaction is typically difficult to quantify and such experiments are difficult to reproduce, an evaluation using a gold standard—with defined topics and given relevance assessments—is an interesting and often adopted strategy.

11.6.2 Relevance Assessments

Experimentation in information retrieval usually requires **relevance assessments** that are used to create the gold standard. Whereas for smaller collections, such as the original Cranfield corpus, the manual examination of all the documents for each topic by assessors is possible, it is unfeasible for larger document collections [2]. Thus, a technique known as **result pooling** is used to avoid the need for assessors to scan the whole document collection for each topic. The idea is that the top-ranked documents are pooled from a number of IR systems to be evaluated. For each topic, the top k documents retrieved by different systems, where k is usually 100 or 1,000, are typically considered. As relevance assessments vary between assessors, each document/topic pair is usually judged by several assessors. The final relevance decision as contained in the gold standard is an aggregated value, for example, based on majority votes. The measurement of the interannotator agreement, for example, through the kappa statistic [2], is an indicator for the validity of an experiment. A low agreement might, for instance, result from the ambiguous definition of information needs.

By involving several systems in the pooling, the researcher tries to reduce the bias of the relevance judgments toward any single system. Moreover, the test collection should be sufficiently complete so that the relevance assessments can be reused to test IR techniques or systems that were not present in the initial pool.

For CLIR or MLIR systems, an alternative evaluation method is provided by the **mate retrieval** setup. This setup avoids the need to provide relevance judgments by using a parallel or aligned data set consisting of documents and their translation into all relevant languages. The topics used for evaluation correspond to a set of documents in the corpus. The **mates** of this topic—the equivalents of the document in different languages—are regarded as the only relevant documents, such that the goal of any system is to retrieve exactly these mates. The gold standard can therefore be constructed automatically. The values of evaluation measures are clearly underestimated using this gold standard, as other documents might be relevant as well.

11.6.3 Evaluation Measures

To quantify the performance of an IR system on a certain data set with respect to a given gold standard consisting of relevance judgments, we require the definition of certain evaluation metrics. The most commonly used evaluation measures in information retrieval are **precision** and **recall**. Precision measures the percentage of the retrieved documents that are actually relevant, and recall measures the percentage of the relevant documents that are actually retrieved.

Computation of these measures can explained on the basis of the contingency table of retrieval results for a single query, as presented in Table 11–1. Precision P and recall R are then defined as:

$$P = \frac{TP}{TP + FP} \qquad R = \frac{TP}{TP + FN}$$

To choose an appropriate evaluation metric, it is crucial to understand how the retrieval system will be used. In some scenarios, users are likely to read all documents, for example, to compile a report, while in other scenarios, such as ad hoc search in the web, users are likely to only examine the top-ranked documents. It should be clear from these very extreme examples of usage that the choice of an evaluation metric is not independent of the way the IR system is supposed to be used.

For retrieval systems in which both precision and coverage (i.e., returning all relevant documents) is important—which is not necessarily the case for web search—a reasonable choice is average precision (AP), which averages the precision at certain positions in the ranking. In particular, these are the positions at which relevant documents are found.

For ranking r of n documents, the set of relevant documents REL, the binary function $rel : D \rightarrow \{0, 1\}$ mapping relevant documents to 1 and nonrelevant to 0 and P_k as precision

Table 11–1: Contingency table of retrieval results for a single query

	relevant	*nonrelevant*
retrieved	TP	FP
nonretrieved	FN	TN

at cutoff level k, AP is computed as follows:

$$AP(r) = \frac{\sum_{i=1}^{n} P_i \times rel(r_i)}{|REL|}$$

Mean average precision (MAP) averages AP over all topics and can be used to evaluate the overall performance of an IR system.

A common feature of measures such as MAP—others are bpref [31] and infAP [32]—is that they are primarily focused on measuring retrieval performance over the entire set of retrieved documents for each query, up to a predetermined maximum (usually 1,000). As already mentioned, such evaluation measures are a reasonable choice for scenarios in which users require as many relevant documents as possible. However, it is likely that users will not read all 1,000 retrieved documents provided by a given IR system. For this reason, other measures have been proposed to assess the correctness of the retrieval system given that users typically examine only a limited set of (top-ranked) documents. For example, precision can be calculated at a given rank (denoted P@r). Precision @ rank 10 (P@10) is commonly used to measure the accuracy of the top-retrieved documents. Where there is an importance to get the top-ranked document correct, mean reciprocal rank of the first relevant document is often used.

In some cases, relevance assessments contain multiple levels of relevance in combination with a measure such as normalized discounting cumulative gain (NDCG) [33], which takes into account the preference to have highly relevant documents ranked above less relevant ones.

11.6.4 Established Data Sets

IR experiments become reproducible and results comparable by reusing shared data sets consisting of a common corpus of documents, topics/queries and relevance assessments. In the field of information retrieval, different evaluation initiatives defining various retrieval tasks and providing appropriate data sets have emerged.

Apart from data sets published by evaluation campaigns, parallel corpora are also of high interest to CLIR and MLIR. They are used as language resources, for example, to train SMT systems or to identify crosslanguage latent concepts as in LSI. Additionally, they are used as test collection, for example, in mate retrieval scenarios.

Evaluation Campaigns

Text REtrieval Conference (TREC) is organized yearly with the goal of providing a forum where IR systems can be systematically evaluated and compared. TREC is organized around different tracks (representing different IR tasks such as ad hoc search, entity search, or search in special domains). For each track, data sets and topics/queries (and relevance judgments) are typically provided that participants can use to develop and tune their systems. Since its inception in 1992, TREC has been applying the pooling technique that allows for a cross-comparison of IR systems using incomplete assessments for test collections. TREC and similar conferences are organized in a competitive spirit in the sense that different groups can compete with their systems on a shared task and data set, thus making results comparable. Such shared evaluations have indeed contributed substantially to scientific progress in terms of understanding which retrieval models, weighting methods, and so on, work better compared to others on a certain task. However, the main goal of TREC is not only to foster competition but also to provide shared data sets to the community as a basis for systematic, comparable, and reproducible results. The main focus of TREC is monolingual retrieval of English documents such that the published data sets consist only of English topics and documents.

Crosslingual Evaluation Forum (CLEF) was established as the European counterpart of TREC with a strong focus on multilingual retrieval. In the ad hoc retrieval track, different data sets have been used between 2000 and 2009, such as a large collection of European newspapers and news agency documents with documents in 14 languages, the TEL data set containing bibliographic entries of the European Library in English, and French, German, and Persian newspaper corpora. For all data sets, topics in different languages are available, which makes these data sets suitable for CLIR and MLIR. The TEL data set also contains mixed documents with fields in different languages.

NII Test Collection for IR Systems (NTCIR) defines a series of evaluation workshops that organize retrieval campaigns for Asian languages, including Japanese, Chinese, and Korean. A data set of scientific abstracts in Japanese and English as well as news articles in Chinese, Korean, Japanese, and English with topics in different languages has been released. In addition, a data set for Japanese-English patent retrieval has been published.

Forum for Information Retrieval Evaluation (FIRE) is dedicated to Indian languages. It has released corpora built from web discussion forums and mailing lists in Bengali, English, Hindi, and Marathi. Topics are provided in Bengali, English, Hindi, Marathi, Tamil, Telugu, and Gujarati.

Parallel Corpora

JRC-Acquis is a document collection extracted from the Acquis Communautaire, the total body of European Union law that is applicable in all EU member states. It consists of parallel texts in the following 22 languages: Bulgarian, Czech, Danish, German, Greek, English, Spanish, Estonian, Finnish, French, Hungarian, Italian, Lithuanian, Latvian, Maltese, Dutch, Polish, Portuguese, Romanian, Slovak, Slovene, and Swedish.
http://langtech.jrc.it/JRC-Acquis.html

Multext Dataset is a document collection derived from the Official Journal of European Community in the following five languages: English, German, Italian, Spanish, and French.
http://aune.lpl.univ-aix.fr/projects/multext/

Canadian Hansards consists of pairs of aligned text chunks (sentences or smaller fragments) from the official records (Hansards) of the 36th Canadian Parliament in English and French.
http://www.isi.edu/natural-language/download/hansard/

Europarl is a parallel corpus containing the proceedings of the European Parliament from 1996 to 2009 in the following languages: Danish, German, Greek, English, Spanish, Finnish, French, Italian, Dutch, Portuguese, and Swedish.
http://www.statmt.org/europarl/

11.6.5 Best Practices

We have clearly argued that the ideal evaluation method and metric for CLIR and MLIR systems are dependent on the way the system will be used.

If the system is designed for research purposes and the goal is to advance the state-of-the-art in information retrieval by analyzing a specific research question, using established data sets and standard evaluation measures is highly advised to ensure that results are comparable to existing systems. In many cases existing gold standards can also be used to compute evaluation measures.

If the retrieval system is part of an application involving real users, the data set is usually defined by the task. To evaluate the system, topics covering the expected information needs of users have to be defined, and relevance assessments are required in order to construct an appropriate gold standard. As described previously, pooling techniques help to reduce the effort to come up with a gold standard of relevance judgments.

In all cases, standard evaluation measures like MAP or mean reciprocal rank are the preferred measures to assess retrieval performance. For specific scenarios, different measures can be used to focus on specific aspects of the desired outcome, for example, if high precision at low ranks is required.

11.7 Tools, Software, and Resources

The development of a complete IR system includes many different aspects, such as the implementation of preprocessing steps, file structures for inverted indices, and efficient retrieval algorithms. Building a system from scratch therefore constitutes an enormous effort. It is essential to build on existing tools to reduce the costs related to implementation.

In a specific project, it might be the case that only the retrieval model or ranking function needs to be adapted, while the other components of the system can be used off-the-shelf. Fortunately, several libraries provide standard IR components or even complete frameworks where certain components can be replaced.

Following are selected tools and software libraries supporting the development of IR systems. We focus on established tools that are widely used and also have community support. The most popular IR framework is Lucene, which also contains wrappers for many other tools we present.

Preprocessing

Content Analysis Toolkit (Tika) is a toolkit to extract text from documents of various file types, such as PDF or DOC, implemented in Java. The detection of file types is also supported. Tika evolved from the Lucene project.
http://lucene.apache.org/tika/

Snowball Stemmer is a stemmer for several European languages. The implementation is very fast and also supports stop-word removal. Lists of stop-words for the supported languages are provided on the project website.
http://snowball.tartarus.org

HTML Parser is a tool for parsing HTML documents. It can be used to extract textual content from websites, ignoring tags and parts not related to the semantic content.
http://htmlparser.sourceforge.net/

BananaSplit is a compound splitter for German based on dictionary resources.
http://www.drni.de/niels/s9y/pages/bananasplit.html

Translation The web portal http://www.statmt.org is an excellent entry point to get information about statistical machine translation systems. It provides software and data sets to train translation models.

As an example of a commercial SMT system, the Google Translate Service[4] provides an API for translation into various languages. However, because translation is part of preprocessing and is usually not deeply integrated into the retrieval framework, any commercial translation system might be plugged into a CLIR or MLIR system.

IR Frameworks

Lucene is a widely used IR framework implemented in Java. It is available as open source software under the Apache License and can therefore be used in both commercial and open source programs. It has reached a mature development status and is used in various applications. The main features of Lucene are scalability and reliability, which come at the price of a decreased flexibility, making it more difficult to exchange components. For instance, in Lucene the index construction is dependent on the retrieval model selected, so the retrieval model cannot be exchanged without rebuilding the index.
http://lucene.apache.org

Terrier and Lemur are tools used for research purposes. Terrier (implemented in Java) and Lemur (implemented in C++) are both flexible IR frameworks that can be easily extended and modified. Because of their different focus, they do not match the stability and performance of Lucene.
http://terrier.org
http://www.lemurproject.org

4. http://translate.google.com/

Evaluation

trec_eval (evolved from TREC) is a tool that can be used to compute various evaluation measures for a given document ranking with respect to a gold standard. The input is expected as plain text files with simple syntax. Creating output in the TREC format enables to use trec_eval for any IR system. The IR frameworks presented earlier also support output in the TREC format.
http://trec.nist.gov/trec_eval/

11.8 Summary

In this chapter we provided an overview of methods that can be used to implement IR systems to access documents in different languages. We distinguished two flavors of this problem: crosslingual and multilingual information retrieval. CLIR retrieves documents in one language given topics in another language, and MLIR can be applied to multilingual document collections with topics in different languages.

We discussed what types of preprocessing (tokenization, stemming, etc.) are required depending on the languages supported. We further discussed foundational approaches to information retrieval that can be reused as building blocks when developing CLIR and MLIR systems. In particular, we showed that most of the standard document models used in information retrieval can be reused in CLIR and MLIR systems. We discussed two main approaches to CLIR and MLIR: translation-based approaches and interlingual representation-based approaches. In this context, we also discussed different machine translation techniques and how they can be applied in CLIR and MLIR settings. Advances in statistical machine translation have made it possible to reduce CLIR and MLIR to a standard monolingual retrieval task by supporting the translation of queries into several languages in real time. We also discussed approaches to identify the language of a document, a crucial step if several language-specific indices are constructed and maintained. We briefly touched upon the problem of aggregating different scores obtained from different language-specific indices as a way to yield an overall score and ranking. This is a nontrivial problem in multilingual retrieval.

Because evaluation is crucial for the field of information retrieval, we examined how IR systems are typically evaluated. In particular, we presented methodologies to obtain relevance judgments, either manually or automatically, and introduced standard IR evaluation measures. Finally, we provided an overview of standard data sets, evaluation campaigns, as well as software libraries and general resources.

Acknowledgments

This work was funded by the German Research Foundation (DFG) under the Multipla project (grant 38457858) and by the European Commission under the Monnet Project (grant FP7-ICT-4-248458).

Bibliography

[1] R. Baeza-Yates and B. Ribeiro-Neto, *Modern Information Retrieval.* Boston: Addison-Wesley, 1999.

[2] C. D. Manning, P. Raghavan, and H. Schtze, *Introduction to Information Retrieval.* New York: Cambridge University Press, 2008.

[3] The Unicode Consortium, *The Unicode Standard, Version 5.2.0.* Mountain View, CA: The Unicode Consortium, 2009.

[4] Working Group on Romanization Systems, "United Nations Group of Experts on Geographical Names (UNGEGN)," updated 2011. http://www.eki.ee/wgrs/.

[5] H. Zhang, Q. Liu, X. Cheng, H. Zhang, and H. Yu, "Chinese lexical analysis using hierarchical hidden markov model," in *Proceedings of the 2nd SIGHAN Workshop on Chinese Language Processing*, vol. 17, pp. 63–70, 2003.

[6] F. Peng, F. Feng, and A. McCallum, "Chinese segmentation and new word detection using conditional random fields," in *Proceedings of the 20th International Conference on Computational Linguistics*, p. 562, 2004.

[7] P. McNamee and J. Mayfield, "Character N-Gram tokenization for European language text retrieval," *Information Retrieval*, vol. 7, no. 1, pp. 73–97, 2004.

[8] C. Monz and M. de Rijke, "Shallow morphological analysis in monolingual information retrieval for dutch, german, and italian," in *Evaluation of Cross-Language Information Retrieval Systems* (C. A. Peters, ed.), pp. 1519–1541, Berlin: Springer, 2002.

[9] V. N. Anh, O. de Kretser, and A. Moffat, "Vector-space ranking with effective early termination," in *Proceedings of the 24th International Conference on Research and Development in Information Retrieval (SIGIR)*, pp. 35–42, 2001.

[10] C. J. van Rijsbergen, *Information Retrieval* (2nd ed.). London: Butterworths, 1979.

[11] S. E. Robertson and S. Walker, "Some simple effective approximations to the 2-Poisson model for probabilistic weighted retrieval," in *Proceedings of the 17th International Conference on Research and Development in Information Retrieval (SIGIR)*, pp. 232–241, 1994.

[12] J. M. Ponte and W. B. Croft, "A language modeling approach to information retrieval," in *Proceedings of the 21st International Conference on Research and Development in Information Retrieval (SIGIR)*, pp. 275–281, 1998.

[13] S. Brin and L. Page, "The anatomy of a large-scale hypertextual web search engine," *Computer Networks and ISDN Systems*, vol. 30, no. 1-7, pp. 107–117, 1998.

[14] J. M. Kleinberg, "Authoritative sources in a hyperlinked environment," *Journal of the ACM*, vol. 46, no. 5, pp. 604–632, 1999.

[15] E. Agichtein, C. Castillo, D. Donato, A. Gionis, and G. Mishne, "Finding high-quality content in social media," in *Proceedings of the International Conference on Web Search and Web Data Mining (WSDM)*, pp. 183–194, 2008.

[16] N. Ferro and C. Peters, "CLEF 2009 ad hoc track overview: TEL & Persian tasks," in *Working Notes of the Annual CLEF Meeting*, 2009.

[17] L. Ballesteros and W. B. Croft, "Phrasal translation and query expansion techniques for cross-language information retrieval," in *Proceedings of the 20th International Conference on Research and Development in Information Retrieval (SIGIR)*, pp. 84–91, ACM, 1997.

[18] D. Oard, "A comparative study of query and document translation for cross-language information retrieval," in *Machine Translation and the Information Soup* (D. Farwell, L. Gerber, and E. Hovy, eds.), pp. 472–483, Berlin: Springer, 1998.

[19] P. F. Brown, V. J. D. Pietra, S. A. D. Pietra, and R. L. Mercer, "The mathematics of statistical machine translation: Parameter estimation," *Computational Linguistics*, vol. 19, no. 2, pp. 263–311, 1993.

[20] P. Resnik and N. A. Smith, "The web as a parallel corpus," *Computational Linguistics*, vol. 29, no. 3, pp. 349–380, 2003.

[21] S. C. Deerwester, S. T. Dumais, T. K. Landauer, G. W. Furnas, and R. A. Harshman, "Indexing by latent semantic analysis," *Journal of the American Society of Information Science*, vol. 41, no. 6, pp. 391–407, 1990.

[22] S. T. Dumais, T. A. Letsche, M. L. Littman, and T. K. Landauer, "Automatic cross-language retrieval using latent semantic indexing," in *Procedings of the AAAI Spring Symposium on Cross-Language Text and Speech Retrieval*, pp. 15–21, 1997.

[23] E. Gabrilovich and S. Markovitch, "Computing semantic relatedness using Wikipedia-based explicit semantic analysis," in *Proceedings of the 20th International Joint Conference on Artificial Intelligence (IJCAI)*, pp. 1606–1611, 2007.

[24] P. Cimiano, A. Schultz, S. Sizov, P. Sorg, and S. Staab, "Explicit versus latent concept models for cross-language information retrieval," in *Proceedings of the 21st International Joint Conference on Artificial Intelligence (IJCAI)*, pp. 1513–1518, 2009.

[25] W. Cavnar and J. M. Trenkle, "N-gram-based text categorization," *Proceedings of the 3rd Annual Symposium on Document Analysis and Information Retrieval (SDAIR)*, pp. 161–175, 1994.

[26] J. Nie, "Towards a unified approach to CLIR and multilingual IR," in *Proceedings of the Cross-Language Retrieval Workshop at SIGIR*, pp. 8–14, 2002.

[27] J. Savoy, "Data fusion for effective European monolingual information retrieval," in *Multilingual Information Access for Text, Speech and Images*, pp. 233–244, 2005.

[28] W. B. Croft, "Combining approaches to information retrieval," in *Advances in Information Retrieval*, pp. 1–36, 2000.

[29] J. Krsten, "Chemnitz at CLEF 2009 Ad-Hoc TEL task: Combining different retrieval models and addressing the multilinguality," in *Working Notes of the Annual CLEF Meeting*, 2009.

[30] C. Cleverdon, "The Cranfield tests on index language devices," *Aslib Proceedings*, vol. 19, no. 6, pp. 173–194, 1967.

[31] C. Buckley and E. M. Voorhees, "Retrieval evaluation with incomplete information," in *Proceedings of the 27th International Conference on Research and Development in Information Retrieval (SIGIR)*, pp. 25–32, 2004.

[32] E. Yilmaz and J. A. Aslam, "Estimating average precision with incomplete and imperfect judgments," in *Proceedings of the 15th ACM International Conference on Information and Knowledge Management*, p. 111, 2006.

[33] K. Jrvelin and J. Keklinen, "IR evaluation methods for retrieving highly relevant documents," in *Proceedings of the 23rd Annual International ACM SIGIR Conference on Research and Development in Information Retrieval*, pp. 41–48, 2000.

Chapter 12

Multilingual Automatic Summarization

Frank Schilder and Liang Zhou

12.1 Introduction

Automatic summarization has been a very active field within computational linguistics, and researchers have looked at this problem from various angles. In the past, the focus has been on texts written in a single source language. However, in recent years multilingual summarization has been generating a lot of interest where texts written in multiple languages are used by summarization systems.

We can distinguish between single- and multidocument summarization. A summary can be driven by a specific query or provide a general summary of the document (or document collection). The summary itself can have different purposes. An **informative** summary, for example, is a compressed version of the original covering the most important facts reported in the input text(s) (e.g., summary of a journal article). A summary can be **indicative** of topics covered in the input text without providing further details (e.g., keywords for scientific papers). Another type of summary can be found in the form of reviews. Such an **evaluative** summary gives an opinion on the input text most often by comparing it to similar documents. An **elaborative** summary can provide more details of parts of a large document or the document linked to by the current document to help navigation through large documents or linked collections such as Wikipedia [1].

Most basically, we can distinguish between a summary as being an extract or an abstract, with rather different implications. An extract is a summary constructed mostly by choosing the most relevant pieces of text, perhaps with some minor edits. An abstract is a gloss that describes the contents of a document without necessarily featuring any of that content. Most current summarization systems produce extracts, but some attempts have been made to produce abstracts [2] or propose solutions for sentence compressions that would keep only the important part of a (longer) sentence [3].

Recent variations include generation summaries for bibliographic information, update summarization (i.e., only report the latest changes of a developing story), or guided summarization in which the goal is to extract semantic information from the source documents depending on the text type (e.g., accidents/natural disasters).

Multilingual summarization inherits all features (and challenges) from monolingual automatic summarization and adds an additional dimension to the overall task. Loosely defined, multilingual summarization involves more than one language in the process of automatically summarizing a text.

To be more specific, summarization can be carried out on one source language (e.g., Arabic), and the resulting summary is presented in one target language (e.g., English). We call this specific multilingual summarization task **translingual** summarization.

Even more complex is a task called **crosslingual** summarization. Here the summarization task is spread out over multiple source languages, and the resulting summary is presented in one (or more) target languages.

Crosslingual summarization is the more challenging task because it requires the integration of multiple source documents coming from different languages. All multilingual summarization tasks, whether they involve two or multiple languages as source or target languages, face a host of problems.

The first problem is crossdocument coreference resolution. Named entities are often transcribed differently in different languages. *Al-Qaida*, *al-Qa'ida*, *el-Qaida*, or *al Qaeda* are different transliterations for *Al-Qaeda* in English and *El Kaida* in German, for example. A summarization system needs to normalize these variants and map them to a unique entity.

Similarly, anaphora resolution in a multilingual setting needs to be addressed. Languages encode number and gender agreement differently. English lacks grammatical gender, but other Indo-European languages, for example, use grammatical gender to indicate reference to antecedents with the respective pronoun (e.g., French: *la lune* (FEM)-*elle*; German: *der Mond* (MASC)-*er*).

Other problems a multilingual summarization system may encounter could be due to different discourse structures commonly used in different languages. Discourse relations may be expressed differently in different languages. Hence, it may be difficult to generate a coherent summary in the target language.

Even more complex problems are created if language-dependent concepts need to be summarized. The summarization of legal concepts in different languages, for instance, may be difficult, if not impossible, to carry out.

Many of these problems already exist in monolingual summarization (e.g., anaphora resolution), but they get more severe because languages encode anaphora, discourse structure, or concepts differently. The quality of a summary therefore hinges on the quality of the machine translation systems, which are still far from perfect. A general strategy of minimizing errors induced by machine translation is to find ways to minimize the impact of the problems described previously. Summarization systems can, for example, include knowledge-poor approaches to anaphora resolution [4] that rely on easy-to-extract features and graph-based approaches that cluster similar sentences according to word-based similarity metrics [5].

History SUMMARIST, one of the first summarization systems, which also generated summaries in languages other than English, was developed by Ed Hovy and Chin-Yew [6] in 1998. The system was able to produce extracts from newspaper articles written in English, Spanish, French, German, and Indonesian.[1]

1. Some older versions of the system also generated summaries in Arabic and Japanese.

In 2001, SummBank—the first crosslingual summarization framework for research in this field—was developed. This resource was the product of a Johns Hopkins Research Workshop [7] and comprises 360 multidocument, human-written summaries for 40 news clusters in English and Chinese.[2]

In 2002, the EU-sponsored project MLIS-MUSI (Multilingual Summarization for the Internet) offered multilingual summarization for English and Italian scientific articles [8].

A couple of years later, the NewsBlaster summarization system was developed by Columbia University enabling users to browse news written in multiple languages from multiple sites on the Internet [9].[3]

In 2005, the Multilingual Summarization Evaluation (MSE) project at the Linguistics Data Consortium (LDC) advanced the research yet further.[4] The 25 news topics used for this evaluation were derived from the output of Columbia's NewsBlaster topic clustering system. The summarization task captured English and Arabic news messages. However, annotators generated their 100-word summaries from the English news documents, but only from the English translations of the Arabic articles and not directly from the Arabic source documents.

Another milestone in multilingual research was reached when the GATE-based summarizer SUMMA by Horacio Saggion was released in 2006 [10, 11]. Given the open architecture of the GATE system [12], it was straightforward to integrate language-specific tools (e.g., tokenizers, sentence splitters) into the SUMMA system supporting also summaries in Latvian, Swedish, and Finnish.[5]

Recent papers that address specific problems of multilingual summarization or offer approaches to trans- or crosslingual summarization systems include work by Mani, Yeh, and Condon, who describe a system that finds names across different languages and show that it can match names from English to Chinese with an F-measure of up to 97.0 [14]. Another summarization problem that requires processing multiple languages is described by Mille and Wanner [15], who propose a system that processes patents in different languages.

Systems that allow users to summarize text in a language other than English have been proposed in recent years. Leuski et al. [16] describe a system that translates English headlines into Hindi. Orăsan and Chiorean [17] utilize maximal marginal relevance (MMR) [18] for summarizing Romanian news messages.

12.2 Approaches to Summarization

12.2.1 The Classics

Automatic summarization is the extraction and modification of material from a source document to create a more succinct description of the original content to satisfy the user's information need. If text is extracted verbatim (with minimal modifications), the summary

2. http://www.summarization.com/summbank/

3. The website http://newsblaster.cs.columbia.edu summarizes news (and images) from (English) news websites.

4. http://projects.ldc.upenn.edu/MSE/

5. These language resources were developed in the context of the Clarity project [13].

is called an **extract**; if the text is abstracted to capture the gist of the content on a more abstract level, the summary is called an **abstract**. Most current automatic summarization systems produce extracts, not abstracts.

A wide body of research has focused on how user needs can be addressed. This research led to the introduction of different variations of the summarization task, such a multi-document summarization and query-based summarization. Multidocument summarization provides summaries of multiple documents concerned with the same topic, and query-based summarization guides the summarization process by a user query instead of providing a general-purpose summary. Query-based summarization can be carried out for a single document or multiple documents.

In general, every summarization system can be divided into three stages:

Analysis The source text is analyzed, and some internal representation is generated. This representation can be a collection of feature vectors (e.g., counts of most frequent words in a sentence) or a logical representation of the described content. For a translingual system, this part is particularly crucial because the representation needs to be in some way compatible across different languages.

Transformation The internal representation is manipulated in such a way that the content of the source document is condensed (e.g., ranking sentences according to a scoring function). Again, such transformations may be language-dependent on the way the internal representation is chosen.

Realization The summary is generated by producing a shorter piece of text than the source document. A shallow approach could just output the n highest-scoring sentences according to a scoring function, but most likely other operations are necessary to produce a coherent summary (e.g., coreference resolution). A multilingual summarization system has to employ a machine translation component at this point, if it has not done so earlier in the progress, to ensure that the summary is readable in the target language. Alternatively, language generation can produce the summary directly from an abstract semantic representation.

Research on automatic summarization can be traced back into the late 1950s with Luhn's work on summarization [21]. Luhn investigated the influence of frequent terms in a sentence and came up with a scoring function that computes a score for each sentence in the document.

Other early systems on summarization relied on surface-based features for extracting important sentences. In general, sentences at the beginning (or the end) of the document were found to be often important [22]. Hence, the position of a sentence in a document is often a good feature to determine the importance of a sentence because an author would like to put such sentences at a salient position in the document.

Many of the early approaches as well as recent ones used these surface features that are easy to extract [21, 22, 23].

- indicative phrases such as *in summary*
- distribution of terms

- overlap with words from headings, titles
- position of sentence in the text, paragraph, and so on

These general features can also easily be adopted for multilingual summarization. Term distribution and position are mostly language-independent features where position is more genre-dependent than language-dependent. For example, news messages tend to have important sentences at the beginning, whereas legal text tends to show summarization information at the end.

The problem that is often observed with these surface-based approaches is that the generated summaries are not always coherent. As a result, discourse theories that predict the coherence of a text were incorporated in the summarizer. Because discourse is often seen as a graph structure, graph-based theories are discussed in the following subsection.

12.2.2 Graph-Based Approaches

This section discusses approaches that model text in the form of graphs and how this representation can help to improve automatic summarization of text. On the one hand, discourse theories such as rhetorical structure theory (RST) [24] model the coherence of a text via a tree structure, and on the other hand, graph-based ranking approaches such as PageRank [25] have been shown to be helpful for scoring sentences according to their importance.

Whereas the former approaches require deep linguistic knowledge of the respective language, there are graph-based approaches that translate the text into a graph representation with similarity scores as weights for the links between nodes representing the sentences. The second part of this section focuses on such approaches that use PageRank as a scoring mechanism for extracting the summary.

Coherence and Cohesion

Extractive summaries automatically generated from the source document(s) often suffer from poor linguistic quality. Because sentences are extracted out of context, important connections in the form of anaphoric expressions (e.g., pronouns) or discourse structure (e.g., discourse markers such as *therefore*) can be broken and make the summary incoherent and hard to read.

Several approaches to improving the linguistic quality have been introduced. We discuss two main concepts that are important in this context. First, **cohesion** is the link that connects sentences in a meaningful way [26]. It is typically done via anaphoric (or cataphoric) references between sentences. Other linguistic phenomena that support cohesion include substitution, ellipsis, or lexical collocation.

John went to the bank. He wanted to swim in the river.

The two sentences are well connected because we can resolve the anaphoric reference *he* to John and can infer the meaning of *bank* (i.e., *sloping land, especially the slope beside a body of water*) correctly because of the lexical collocation with the words *swim* and *river*.

Related to the concept of cohesion that is often restricted to the sentence-sentence connection is **coherence**. Coherence is often used in the context of a discourse theory modeling how sentences are connected within the entire text. Summaries need to be coherent to be understood and helpful for a user. Hence, the question of how sentences in an extract should be ordered and possibly modified to make the summary more readable becomes important.

To maximize the coherence of a summary, several approaches have been proposed [27, 28, 29]. They are mostly grounded in discourse theories such as RST [24]. The main assumption of RST is based on the observation that text segments are connected via rhetorical relations. A rhetorical relation between text segments can either be explicitly marked via a discourse marker (e.g., *because*) or inferred from the context. Rhetorical relations can express causality between events, elaborate a situation, or move the narration forward.

Work by Marcu and Echihabi [30] built on RST and proposed a rhetorical parser that can also be used for summarization. One of the core ideas of RST is the generation of a discourse tree. The nodes of the tree can combine text spans. Two types of nodes are possible:

- Nucleus & Satellite (hypotactic): The Nucleus contains the more important information supported by the information extracted by the Satellite. The ELABORATION relation, for example, possesses a Nucleus and a Satellite, as in:

  Lactose is milk sugar: the enzyme lactase breaks it down.

- Nucleus & Nucleus (paratactic): The multinuclear relation CONTRAST, on the other hand, establishes a contrast between two equally important facts, as in:

  For want of lactose, most adults cannot digest milk. In populations that drink milk, the adults have more lactase, perhaps through natural selection.

Figure 12–1 contains an RST discourse tree for the following example text about Mars exploration, as analyzed by Marcu [31]:

> [With its distant orbit [1]] [— 50 percent farther from the sun than Earth — [2]] [and slim atmospheric blanket, [3]] [Mars experiences frigid weather conditions. [4]] [Surface temperatures typically average about 60 degrees Celsius (76 degrees Fahrenheit) at the equator [5]] [and can dip to 123 degrees C near the poles. [6]] [Only the midday sun at tropical latitudes is warm enough to thaw ice on occasion, [7]] [but any liquid water formed in this way would evaporate almost instantly [8]] [because of the low atmospheric pressure. [9]] [Although the atmosphere holds a small amount of water, [10]] [and water-ice clouds sometimes develop, [11]] [most Martian weather involves blowing dust or carbon dioxide. [12]] [Each winter, for example, a blizzard of frozen carbon dioxide rages over one pole, [13]] [and a few meters of this dry-ice snow accumulate [14]] [as previously frozen carbon dioxide evaporates from the opposite polar cap. [15]] [Yet even on the summer pole, [16]] [where the sun remains in the sky all day long, [17]] [temperatures never warm enough to melt frozen water.[18]]

The textual units into which this example text is broken are based on clauses and indicated by square brackets. Clause 12 (i.e., *most Martian weather involves blowing dust or carbon dioxide*), for example, states an example for the statement in clause 4 (i.e., *Mars experiences frigid weather conditions*). Here, clause 4 is the Nucleus and clause 12 is the Satellite. The

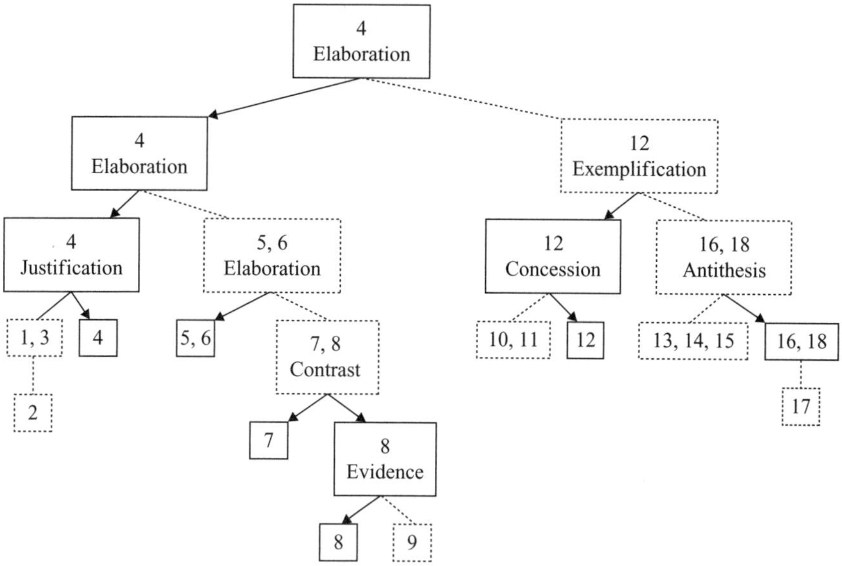

Figure 12–1: The RST structure of the Mars example text (Reproduced from Marcu [31])

Nucleus & Satellite node is defined in such a way that the Satellite could be deleted from the discourse tree, and the entire discourse would still be coherent. This feature can also be used for summarization purposes, and a discourse tree can be pruned to generate a more concise representation of the entire text [31, 28, 29]. The full text on Mars exploration could therefore be summarized as follows:

> Mars experiences frigid weather conditions. Surface temperatures typically average about 60 degrees Celsius (76 degrees Fahrenheit) at the equator and can dip to 123 degrees C near the poles. Only the midday sun at tropical latitudes is warm enough to thaw ice on occasion, but any liquid water formed in this way would evaporate almost instantly.
>
> Most Martian weather involves blowing dust or carbon dioxide. Yet even on the summer pole, temperatures never warm enough to melt frozen water.

Even though these approaches based on discourse theories such as RST provide a coherent summary, they are not easily transferrable to other languages [31] [32].[6]

Discourse parsers for English [31], Japanese [28], and German [29] have been used in the context of summarization systems, but discourse parsers are not widely developed for many other languages.

Even the translation of discourse markers may be difficult because they may cover different semantics. The English marker *since*, for example, can have a causal or purely temporal

6. Learning discourse parsers from discourse markers, as suggested by Marcu and Echihabi [30] has proven to be difficult, as shown by Sporleder and Lascarides [33].

meaning. To translate this marker correctly into German, the researcher has to choose between *weil* (causal) or *seit* (temporal).

Nevertheless, researchers must consider how coherence can be maintained in a different source language. This area is likely to be a new area to be explored.

Text as Graph

TextRank is an approach to summarization that also utilizes a graph representation [19]. TextRank is related to PageRank, but instead of generating a graph consisting of linked documents, the graph is derived from the text. The sentences in the text are represented as the vertices, whereas the edges between the vertices are weighted by a similarity metric. Similar to PageRank, vertices that are highly connected are "recommended" by other sentences and receive a high rank.

Formally, a graph representation is used for the text where a directed graph $G = (V, E)$ with a set of vertices V and a set of edges $E \subseteq V \times V$ represents links between sentences. The PageRank score is computed on the basis of the number of inlinks $in(V_i)$ pointing to a vertex and the number of outlinks $out(V_i)$ pointing away from a vertex. The PageRank score is then computed via the following formula, where d is the dampening factor indicating the probability of jumping to a new page:[7]

$$S(V_i) = (1 - d) + d * \sum_{j \in in(V_i)} \frac{1}{|out(V_j)|} S(V_j) \tag{12.1}$$

For TextRank, the directed graph becomes an undirected graph and consequently $in(V_i) = out(V_i)$. Instead, the links have weights w_{jk} based on similarity scores between the sentences. The similarity metric defined by Mihalcea and Tarau [19] counts the number of words two sentences share and normalizes by the length of the sentences.

$$Similarity(S_i, S_j) = \frac{|\{w_k | w_k \in S_i \wedge w_k \in S_j\}|}{log(|S_i|) + log(|S_j|)} \tag{12.2}$$

The weighted PageRank score is defined as follows:

$$WS(V_i) = (1 - d) + d * \sum_{V_j \in in(V_i)} \frac{1}{\sum_{V_k \in out(V_j)} w_{jk}} WS(V_j) \tag{12.3}$$

A sample newspaper article is shown in Table 12–1. Given the equation in 12.2, similarity scores between all sentences can be computed. The resulting graph that connects all sentences via links contains the scores as the respective weights for each link, as illustrated in Figure 12–2.

The PageRank scores for each sentence are derived from the graph, giving high scores to sentences that have links with high weights pointing to them.

TextRank was evaluated with the Document Understanding Conference (DUC) 2002 data, and it was shown that the system was comparable to the top systems within this competition. Given that this approach is unsupervised and does not require any further

7. The parameter d is normally set to 0.85.

Table 12–1: A sample newspaper article used as input for TextRank. The output graph is shown in Figure 12–2

4: BC–Hurricane Gilbert, 0348

3: BC–Hurricane Gilbert, 0–11 339

5: Hurricane Gilbert heads toward Dominican Coast

6: By Ruddy Gonzalez

7: Associated Press Writer

8: Santo Domingo, Dominican Republic (AP)

9: Hurricane Gilbert Swept toward the Dominican Republic Sunday, and the Civil Defense alerted its heavily populated south coast to prepare for high winds, heavy rains, and high seas.

10: The storm was approaching from the southeast with sustained winds of 75 mph gusting to 92 mph.

11: "There is no need for alarm," Civil Defense Director Eugenio Cabral said in a television alert shortly after midnight Saturday.

12: Cabral said residents of the province of Barahona should closely follow Gilbert's movement.

13: An estimated 100,000 people live in the province, including 70,000 in the city of Barahona, about 125 miles west of Santo Domingo.

14: Tropical storm Gilbert formed in the eastern Carribean and strenghtened into a hurricane Saturday night.

15: The National Hurricane Center in Miami reported its position at 2 a.m. Sunday at latitude 16.1 north, longitude 67.5 west, about 140 miles south of Ponce, Puerto Rico, and 200 miles southeast of Santo Domingo.

16: The National Weather Service in San Juan, Puerto Rico, said Gilbert was moving westward at 15 mph with a "broad area of cloudiness and heavy weather" rotating around the center of the storm.

17: The weather service issued a flash flood watch for Puerto Rico and the Virgin Islands until at least 6 p.m. Sunday.

18: Strong winds associated with Gilbert brought coastal flooding, strong southeast winds, and waves up to 12 feet to Puerto Rico's south coast.

19: There were no reports on casualties.

20: San Juan, on the north coast, had heavy rains and gusts Saturday, but they subsided during the night.

21: On Saturday, Hurricane Florence was downgraded to a tropical storm, and its remnants pushed inland from the U.S. Gulf Coast.

22: Residents returned home, happy to find little damage from 90 mph winds and sheets of rain.

23: Florence, the sixth named storm of the 1988 Atlantic storm season, was the second hurricane.

24: The first, Debby, reached minimal hurricane strength briefly before hitting the Mexican coast last month.

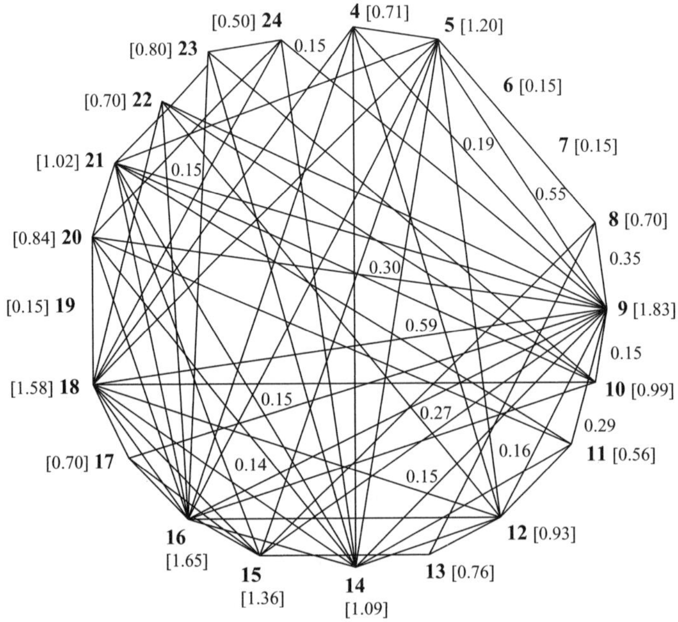

Figure 12–2: A sample graph generated from a text (Reproduced from Mihalcea and Tarau [19])

language-dependent tools except for a similarity metric, this approach would work also with other languages.

A similar approach, called LexPageRank, was developed by Erkan and Radev [5]. LexPageRank also utilizes PageRank, but the similarity scores are computed via cosine similarity, and thresholds for the weights are introduced. They offer LexPageRank as part of the MEAD summarization system, described in more detail in Section 12.2.4.

12.2.3 Learning How to Summarize

Starting with Kupiec, Pedersen, and Chen [23], the idea of learning a classifier that determines which sentences to be included in the summary was introduced. Many different approaches developed over the last decades fall into this category, and they all share the following components listed in Table 12–1 [34, 35]:

1. *An aligned corpus between summaries and their respective document(s).* Some method (e.g., word overlap) has to be employed to match summary sentences and sentences from the text to be summarized.

2. *Feature extractors that generate feature vectors for each sentence.* A feature may be the length of a sentence, the position in the text/paragraph, the overlap of words in the sentence with the title/headings, or the word frequency of the words in the sentence.

3. *A machine learning algorithm that classifies a sentence.* This can be a binary classifier, a multiclass classifier, or a regression model in which a sentence would receive an overall score.

In recent years, several methods for learning the rank of a sentence have evolved. They can be classified via these three categories that differ in terms of what is learned:

Score Each sentence from the training set is assigned a score. This score may be computed by the word overlap of document sentences with the sentences from model summaries. Given the sentence-score combinations, a regression model can be learned. Support vector regression (SVR) can be employed for learning a score for each sentence [36, 37].

Partial order Pairs of sentences are ranked in order to receive a partial order of sentences. A learning to rank method expects pairs of sentences that learns a partial order. Svore, Vanderwende, and Burges [38], for example, use RankNet [39] employing pairwise cross-entropy as a loss function similar to Amini et al. [40], who use an exponential loss function for XML summarization.

Ranks Another way of learning summary sentences is to learn how sentences are ranked in a list. Instead of pairwise ranking, sentences are ranked as a full-order list or at least in several "buckets." Approaches that chose this direction include ListNet [41] and web-based summarization by Wang et al. [42].

To give an example for one of the three machine learning approaches, we describe the partial order–based approach by Amini et al. [40] in more detail. The proposed learning framework uses a scoring function $h : R^n \rightarrow R$ reflecting the best linear combination of sentence features with respect to the learning criterion. The goal of the classification task is to minimize the error of a ranking loss function L_R. The ranking loss L_R is the average number of relevant sentences scored below irrelevant ones in every document $d \in D$.

$$L_R(h, D) = \frac{1}{\mid D \mid} \sum_{d \in D} \frac{1}{\mid S_d^{pos} \mid\mid S_d^{neg} \mid} \sum_{s \in S_d^{pos}} \sum_{s' \in S_d^{neg}} [[h(s) \geq h(s')]] \qquad (12.4)$$

where $[[h(s) \geq h(s')]]$ is a predicate that equals 1, $h(s) \geq h(s')$ and 0 otherwise. $L_R(h, D)$ iterates through all combinations of positive and negative sentences and increases the value for the loss function if the score for a positive sentence is lower than the score for a negative sentence. Given this loss function, the goal of the ranking algorithm is to learn a scoring function h where higher scores are assigned to relevant sentences rather than to irrelevant sentences in the same document.

The loss function should be expressed as an exponential loss function, because [[]] cannot be differentiated. Moreover, the difference between the sentence scores can be computed via the difference in the feature representations of the sentences s, s' as in $\sum_{i=1}^{n} \beta_i (s_i - s'_i)$:

$$L_{exp}(D, B) = \frac{1}{\mid D \mid} \sum_{d \in D} \frac{1}{\mid S_d^{pos} \mid\mid S_d^{neg} \mid} \sum_{(s,s') \in S_d^{pos} \times S_d^{neg}} e^{\sum_{i=1}^{n} \beta_i (s'_i - s_i)} \qquad (12.5)$$

Using the exponential loss function has an advantage regarding the computational complexity of the learning algorithm. Equation 12.5 can be simply rewritten, leading to a linear time complexity for computing the exponential loss function:

$$L_{exp}(D, B) = \frac{1}{\mid D \mid} \sum_{d \in D} \frac{1}{\mid S_d^{pos} \mid\mid S_d^{neg} \mid} \sum_{s' \in S_d^{neg}} e^{\sum_{i=1}^{n} \beta_i s'_i} \sum_{s \in S_d^{pos}} e^{\sum_{i=1}^{n} \beta_i s_i} \qquad (12.6)$$

Algorithm 12–1 Pseudocode for ranking-based trainable extractive summarizer: LinearRank

---

Input: $\bigcup_{d \in D} S_d^{pos} \times S_d^{neg}$, where D is a collection of documents and S^{pos} the set of positive (summary) sentence and S^{neg} the set of negative (non-summary) sentences.

Output: Each sentence vector s is normalized such that $\sum_{s_i} = 1$; feature weights $F = (\beta_1 ... \beta_n)$ are set to arbitrary values; t=0;

repeat
    for $i = 1$ **to** n **do**
        $\beta_i^{(t+1)} = \beta_i^{(t)} + \Sigma^t$
    end for
    t = t+1
until Convergence of $L_{exp}(D, F)$
return B^F
Create a summary for each new document d by taking the first n sentences in d with regard to the linear combination of sentence features with B^F.

Amini et al. chose a linear ranking function $h(s, B)$ given a list of features represented as a feature weight vector $B = (\beta_1, \ldots, \beta_n)$ called LinearRank (Algorithm 12–1). The iterative scaling of the feature vector optimizes the loss function described in Equation 12.6 via an update rule $B^{(t+1)} = B^{(t)} + \Sigma^t$. More precisely, the update function can be described as follows (see Amini et al. [40] for more details):

$$\beta_i^{(t+1)} = \beta_i^{(t)} + \frac{1}{2} log \frac{\sum_{d \in D} \frac{1}{|S_d^{neg}||S_d^{pos}|} \sum_{s' \in S_d^{neg}} e^{h(s', B^{(t)})} \sum_{s \in S_d^{pos}} e^{-h(s, B^{(t)})} (1 - s_i' + s_i)}{\sum_{d \in D} \frac{1}{|S_d^{neg}||S_d^{pos}|} \sum_{s' \in S_d^{neg}} e^{h(s', B^{(t)})} \sum_{s \in S_d^{pos}} e^{-h(s, B^{(t)})} (1 + s_i' - s_i)} \tag{12.7}$$

After generating training data using one of these three approaches, features need to be generated for each sentence. The feature engineering is important because it decides how well the classification task can be learned.

Assuming a setting of a query-based multidocument summarization such as in the DUC or Text Analysis Conferences (TAC) summarization competition, we can utilize frequency information from the overall topic, the query, and the document, as well as the other documents in the clusters. The DUC/TAC task includes at least a set of 25 to 50 documents grouped according to a topic (e.g., steps toward introduction of the Euro) and a query (e.g., describe steps taken and worldwide reaction prior to introduction of the Euro on January 1, 1999). Given this information, the following features have been used by past systems (e.g., Schilder and Kondadadi [37]):

Topic title frequency: ratio of number of words t_i in the sentence s that also appear in the topic title $\mathcal{T}$ to the total number of words $t_{1..|s|}$ in the sentence s: $\frac{\sum_{i=1}^{|s|} f_{\mathcal{T}}(t_i)}{|s|}$, where

$$f_{\mathcal{T}} = \begin{cases} 1 & : \quad t_i \in \mathcal{T} \\ 0 & : \quad otherwise \end{cases}$$

Topic description frequency: ratio of number of words t_i in the sentence s that also appear in the topic description $\mathcal{D}$ to the total number of words $t_{1..|s|}$ in the sentence s: $\frac{\sum_{i=1}^{|s|} f_{\mathcal{D}}(t_i)}{|s|}$, where $f_{\mathcal{D}} = \begin{cases} 1 & : \quad t_i \in \mathcal{D} \\ 0 & : \quad otherwise \end{cases}$

Content word frequency: the average content word probability $p_c(t_i)$ of all content words $t_{1..|s|}$ in a sentence s. The content word probability is defined as $p_c(t_i) = \frac{n}{N}$, where n is the number of times the word occurred in the cluster and N is the total number of words in the cluster: $\frac{\sum_{i=1}^{|s|} p_c(t_i)}{|s|}$

Document frequency: the average document probability $p_d(t_i)$ of all content words $t_{1..|s|}$ in a sentence s. The document probability is defined as $p_d(t_i) = \frac{d}{D}$, where d is the number of documents the word t_i occurred in for a given cluster and D is the total number of documents in the cluster: $\frac{\sum_{i=1}^{|s|} p_d(t_i)}{|s|}$

Other features that turned out to be useful include headline frequency (the average headline probability of all content words in a sentence s), sentence length, sentence position, TF-IDF score for the words, n-gram frequency, and named entity frequency in a sentence.

These machine learning approaches work well if an aligned corpus exists for all languages in a multilingual setting or could be easily generated. However, this may not always be the case. To work around the data problem, approaches have been proposed to bridge the gap between documents written in different languages. Ji and Zha [20] propose an algorithm that aligns the (sub-)topics of a pair of multilingual documents and summarizes their correlation by sentence extraction. They carry out this alignment via a weighted bipartite graph representing sentences of the two documents. Then, sentences are translated via a machine translation program into the other language, and a weight matrix is generated that consists of the similarity scores between the translated sentences and the sentences in the original language. Note that the machine-translated sentences do not need to be perfect translations, because the goal is to capture the similarity between the sentences.

From the weight graph, a subgraph of highly correlated sentences can be derived. These sentences present the main topic the two documents share. In addition, a biclustering algorithm is employed to derive further subtopics represented by clustered sentences from each document.

12.2.4 Multilingual Summarization

Challenges

We reviewed the most important approaches to summarization with pointers to how some of the techniques would fare with multilingual summarization and that most of the current summarization approaches often rely on language-dependent resources or tools (e.g., rhetorical parsers, cue phrase lexicons). Some approaches exist that allow for language-independent summarization by generating summaries from a representation that is abstracted from the source language.

The following list is a summary of features that need to be considered for a multilingual summarization system. In particular, these are challenges we must face when working with multiple languages.

Tokenization Because languages encode word boundaries differently, tokenization is a first obstacle to overcome when building a summarization for different languages. Languages such as English identify token boundaries via whitespace and punctuation, but other languages such as Chinese require a more complex segmenter to extract tokens from a stream of text that does not contain any whitespaces. A token is a word in languages such as English but may be something else in different languages. Other languages (e.g., Arabic) that possess a rich morphology may require an even more fine-grained tokenization up to the morph level.

Anaphoric expressions The identification of anaphora (i.e., pronouns, discourse markers, and definite noun phrases) can help to make a summary more cohesive. Some techniques exist for monolingual summarization, but multilingual summarization also faces the challenges that names are written differently and that discourse markers have different semantics in different languages.
A knowledge-poor approach to anaphora resolution proposed by Mitkov [4] uses, in addition to number and gender agreement, a number of simple indicators (e.g., definiteness, givenness, verb classes) that are aggregated to generate a score for potential antecedent candidates.

Discourse structure The identification of document structure can help to improve the coherence of a summary. Different languages, however, may express the structure of a text differently.

Machine translation The state-of-the-art machine translation technology has not yet reached a level sufficient to guarantee high-quality translation. When designing a multilingual summarization system, developers must answer the question of when machine translation should be employed in the system. If text is generated at the start, components developed for the source language can be reused (e.g., tokenizer). If translation is done after identifying the summary-worthy sentences, language-dependent systems have to be used to preprocess the text accordingly.

Systems

There are three major summarization systems available that have some multilingual capabilities: MEAD, Summa, and NewsBlaster.

The **MEAD**[8] platform for multilingual summarization and evaluation offers several different summarization algorithms based on position, centroid, longest common subsequence, and keywords. MEAD is a publicly available platform for multilingual summarization and evaluation written in Perl. This framework can be used to easily adapt surface-based approaches discussed earlier or to train a classifier for detecting summary-worthy sentences. Moreover, it allows users to train their own summarization approach by offering support for

8. http://www.summarization.com/mead/

machine learning algorithms such as decision trees, support vector machines, and maximum entropy.

The centerpiece of the MEAD framework is the centroid-based summarization approach. A centroid is a set of words that are significant for a cluster of documents. Relevant documents and summary sentences within these cluster of documents are extracted on the basis of the centroids they contain.

The algorithm that generates the clusters is called CIDR [43]. CIDR generates clusters of documents that share the same words among them. Starting with one document, the algorithm compares the similarity to other clusters. Documents are represented via word vectors. The values for the words are derived from the document frequency and the inverse document frequency (TF-IDF).

Each cluster has a centroid that can be described as a pseudodocument containing only the most important words with the highest TF-IDF scores. The word vector representing the cluster is composed of the weighted averages of the corresponding TF-IDF values from the documents that are already clustered.

The algorithm starts with the first document and puts it in a cluster containing only this document. New documents are compared to the word vector representing the cluster and are assigned to the respective cluster if the cosine similarity between the cluster vector and the document vector falls below a predefined threshold.

The cosine similarity is the cosine of the angle between two (word) vectors:

$$\text{sim}(A, B) = \text{cosine}\ \theta = \frac{A \cdot B}{|A||B|} \tag{12.8}$$

If the document cannot be assigned to any cluster, a new cluster is formed containing so far only this single document.

Another graph-based algorithm also comes with MEAD: LexPageRank [5] is based on computing the PageRank score of the sentences in the lexical connectivity matrix with a defined threshold. LexPageRank is similar to TextRank in using PageRank for scoring the sentences. It differs from PageRank in the way the weights for the graph are generated. LexPageRank uses the cosine similarity to generate the weights between sentences, and it allows for using thresholds on the cosine similarity: a link between sentences is generated only if the cosine similarity is above a certain threshold (e.g., 0.1).

An alternative summarization system is **SUMMA**—a summarization tool that can run as a GATE plug-in or as a standalone application. The tool is extendable and allows users to add their own scoring functions in addition to the provided position- or centroid-based scoring functions. Various similarity metrics such as cosine and n-gram similarity are also included in this tool.

Finally, the **NewsBlaster** summarization system from Columbia University (see Figure 12–3) possesses a multilingual extension [9][9] and enables users to browse news written in multiple languages from multiple sites on the Internet. The approach utilizes a well-tested approach to document clustering [44] on machine-translated English text.

9. The website http://newsblaster.cs.columbia.edu summarizes news (and images) from (English) news websites.

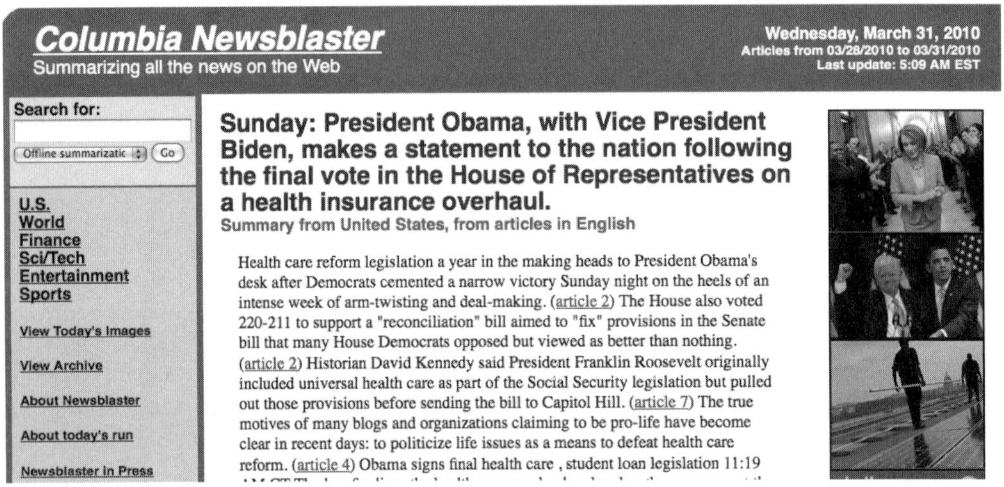

Figure 12–3: A sample page generated by NewsBlaster (Courtesy Columbia University)

The summarization is carried out by the Columbia summarizer [45] that clusters machine-translated text from non-English documents. The English version is online, but no multilingual version seems to be available.

12.3 Evaluation

Determining the quality of system-generated summaries is one major challenge in summarization research. There are two ways to measure summary quality. Indirectly, **extrinsic** evaluations measure the usefulness of summaries by measuring how much they can help in performing another information-processing task. However, **intrinsic** evaluations are being actively pursued because they directly measure and reflect summary quality and can be used in various stages in a summarization development cycle. Summary comparison (i.e., content coverage calculation) is used as the preferred intrinsic evaluation method. Comparisons are performed by assessing how much information from a reference summary is included in a peer summary. **Reference** summaries are usually written by humans to serve as the gold-standard summaries in a comparison. A **peer** summary can refer to any summary whose quality is being measured and thus can be a system-generated summary if we are measuring the quality of a summarization system or can be a human-written summary if we are analyzing the reference summaries for their qualities.

Two directions in designing evaluation methodologies for summarization are manual evaluation and automated evaluation. Naturally, there is a great amount of confidence in manual evaluations because humans can infer, paraphrase, and use world knowledge to relate text units with similar meanings but different wording. Human efforts are preferred if the evaluation task is easily conducted and managed and does not need to be performed repeatedly. However, when resources are limited, automated evaluation methods become more desirable. Creating such an automatic evaluation methodology that can be readily applied to a wide range of summarization tasks proves to be quite complicated. This section discusses both manual and automatic evaluation methodologies in detail.

12.3.1 Manual Evaluation Methodologies

One fascinating aspect of automatic summarization is the high degree of freedom when summarizing or compressing information presented in either single or multiple input texts. The process of choosing and eliminating informational pieces largely depends on task definition, topic in question, and domain and prior knowledge. When asked to perform the summarization task, even human summarizers would disagree on what goes into the summaries from original texts. This curious fact was discovered and analyzed through performing manual evaluation exercises.

Three most noticeable efforts in manual evaluation are the Summary Evaluation Environment (SEE) of Lin and Hovy ([46] and [47]), Factoid of Van Halteren and Teufel [48], and Pyramid of Nenkova and Passonneau [49].

Summary Evaluation Environment

SEE provides a user-friendly environment in which human assessors evaluate the quality of a system-produced peer summary by comparing it to an ideal reference summary. Summaries are represented by a list of summary units (sentences, clauses, etc.). Assessors can assign full or partial content coverage scores to peer summary units in comparison to the corresponding reference summary units. Grammaticality can also be graded unit-wise. One unique feature of this work is that it allows systematic identification of summary units and facilitates partial matches.

The Factoid Method

The goal of the Factoid work is to compare the information content of different summaries written on the same text and determine the minimum number of summaries needed to achieve stable consensus among human-written summaries. Van Halteren and Teufel studied 50 summaries that were created on the basis of one single text. For each sentence, its meaning is represented by a list of atomic semantic units called **factoids**. Here semantic atomicity means the amount of information associated with a factoid can vary from a single word to an entire sentence. Factoids from all summaries are collected and analyzed. Those expressing the same meaning or carrying the same amount of information across multiple summaries are identified manually as semantically similar. As the number of manually created summaries increases and reaches a certain level, the set of factoids stabilizes and remains largely unaffected even when new summaries and their corresponding factoids are added to the set. Ideally, the gold-standard human-written summaries should be a stable set before we start using them in measuring the quality of the system-generated summaries through content comparison. The Factoid method shows 15 summaries are needed to achieve stable consensus among reference summaries. In practice, the number of human-written summaries is much lower than the required quantity because of the resource-intensive nature of information-processing tasks.

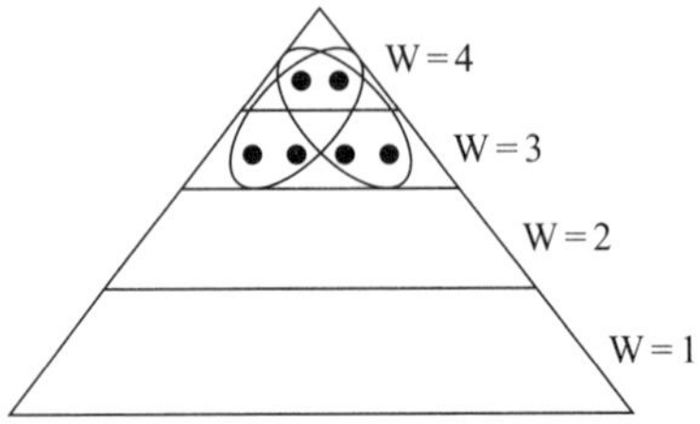

Figure 12–4: A pyramid of four levels (Reproduced from Nenkova and Passonneau [49])

The Pyramid Method

The Pyramid method is an extension of the Factoid method carried out on a larger scale. Nenkova and Passonneau show that only six summaries are required to form stable consensus from reference summaries. This lowered requirement on the number of reference summaries is empirically proven by the authors and achieves the primary goal of reliably differentiating the scoring of summaries. Summarization content units (SCUs) were originally defined as units that are not bigger than a clause but later were redefined as larger than a word but smaller than a sentence because clauses can still carry multiple semantic units.

The process of finding similar SCUs starts by finding similar sentences and proceeds to identifying finer-grained inspection of more tightly related subparts. After all the SCUs are identified and compared, they can be partitioned into a pyramid structure, as illustrated in Figure 12–4. A specific level in the pyramid indicates the number of summaries in which this level's SCUs occurred. SCUs that appeared in all summaries appear at the top of the pyramid because there are only a small number of them. SCUs from lower levels of the pyramid can be used to show the differences in human summary writers' understanding, interests, and knowledge of the summary topics. And the large number of these SCUs from the bottom levels demonstrates the difficulty in summarization. Using the example from Nenkova and Passonneau [49], the variety of summaries can be shown by the following summaries where underlined text indicates the SCUs that are shared (these four sentences come from four different summaries):

A. In 1998 <u>two Libyans indicted in 1991</u> for the Lockerbie bombing were still in Libya.

B. <u>Two Libyans were indicted in 1991</u> for blowing up a Pan Am jumbo jet over Lockerbie, Scotland, in 1988.

C. <u>Two Libyans, accused</u> by the United States and Britain of bombing a New York-bound Pan Am jet over Lockerbie, Scotland, in 1988, killing 270 people, for 10 years were harbored by Libya who claimed the suspects could not get a fair trial in America or Britain.

D. <u>Two Libyan suspects were indicted in 1991</u>.

we obtain two SCUs:
SCU1(weight=4): two Libyans were officially accused by the Lockerbie bombing

A. [two Libyans] [indicted]

B. [Two Libyans were indicted]

C. [Two Libyans,] [accused]

D. [Two Libyan suspects were indicted]

SCU2(weight=3): the indictment of the two Lockerbie suspects were in 1991

A. [in 1991]

B. [in 1991]

D. [in 1991]

The scoring of peer summaries is precision based. A peer summary would receive a score that is a ratio of the sum of the weights of its SCUs to the sum of the weights of an optimal summary with the same number of SCUs. Suppose we created a pyramid of SCUs from a set of reference summaries and found 10 SCUs in the peer summary, and only one SCU from the peer summary is found to have matched the SCUs from the pyramid. The SCU that is found in the pyramid had a weight of 1 (only one occurrence in all of the reference summaries). Then the pyramid score for the peer summary is $1/10 = 0.1$.

Although the Pyramid method shares the same high cost as other manual evaluation exercises, it has gained community acceptance as the preferred manual evaluation methodology. It has been carried out by conference and task participants in the DUC and DUC's follow-up program, TAC.

Another positive side effect from running the Pyramid experiment on a large scale and on a repeated basis is the large set of human-written summaries and their corresponding semantic units. In designing and tuning summarization systems, the semantic units can be used as gold-standard data that can facilitate research beyond sentence-level extraction.

Responsiveness

In addition to providing content coverage evaluations through manual efforts, at TAC a score of 1 to 5 (1 to 10 since TAC 2009) on responsiveness is also given for a summary in question. This score does not reflect a comparison with the reference summary but solely reflects the quality of the evaluated summary on both content coverage and linguistic quality (two qualities that were measured separately at previous DUCs).

12.3.2 Automated Evaluation Methods

Evaluation systems that take reference and peer summaries as input and perform text comparison to produce evaluation results are called automated evaluations. To test and validate the effectiveness of an automatic evaluation metric, researchers must show that the automatic evaluation results correlate with human assessments highly, positively, and consistently [50].

ROUGE

ROUGE (Recall-Oriented Understudy for Gisting Evaluation) [50, 51] is one of the first automatic summarization evaluation metrics proposed. It is an automatic evaluation package that measures a number of n-gram co-occurrence statistics between peer and reference summary pairs. ROUGE was inspired by BLEU [52], which was adopted by the machine translation community for automatic machine translation evaluation. While BLEU is precision related, ROUGE is a recall-oriented metric.

Instead of producing one figure that quantifies the summary quality, ROUGE produces a set of scores that can be used to interpret system-generated results:

- *ROUGE-N*: computes the n-gram recall score between a peer summary over all of its corresponding reference summaries. The following formula shows how to compute the ratio of matched n-grams from the peer summary and the total number of n-grams from the reference summaries:

$$ROUGE - N = \frac{\sum_{S\in\{\text{Reference Summaries}\}} \sum_{\text{gram}_n \in S} \text{Count}_{match}(\text{gram}_n)}{\sum_{S\in\{\text{Reference Summaries}\}} \sum_{\text{gram}_n \in S} \text{Count}(\text{gram}_n)} \tag{12.9}$$

- *ROUGE-L*: matches the longest common sequence (LCS) between two textual units, which finds the longest in-sequence matches instead of consecutive matches. It is not necessary to predefine a length limit as with n-gram matches. This metric also reflects the possible differences in sentence structure among the units being compared. To estimate the similarity between two summaries X of length m and Y of length n, a LCS-based F-measure is computed as follows:

$$R_{\text{lcs}} = \frac{\text{LCS}(X,Y)}{m} \tag{12.10}$$

$$P_{\text{lcs}} = \frac{\text{LCS}(X,Y)}{n} \tag{12.11}$$

$$F_{\text{lcs}} = \frac{(1+\beta^2)R_{\text{lcs}}P_{\text{lcs}}}{R_{\text{lcs}} + \beta^2 P_{\text{lcs}}} \tag{12.12}$$

  $\text{LCS}(X,Y)$ is the longest common subsequence between X and Y, and $\beta = P_{\text{lcs}}/R_{\text{lcs}}$ when $\partial F_{\text{lcs}}/\partial R_{\text{lcs}} = \partial F_{\text{lcs}}/\partial P_{\text{lcs}}$.

- *ROUGE-W*: computes the weighted LCS. While *ROUGE-L* finds the LCS, it does not penalize matches that have gaps in them. It simply indicates words appeared in the same sequence if there is a match. *ROUGE-W* differentiates matched word sequences that are consecutive and those that are nonconsecutive by charging a gap penalty. This gap penalty is reflected in a weighting function that gives higher reward to consecutive matches than to nonconsecutive matches.

- *ROUGE-S*: calculates the skip-bigram co-occurrence statistics. A skip-bigram is any two ordered words that occurr in a sentence, with arbitrary gaps between them. With a gap of 0, it is equivalent to *ROUGE-N* where *n=2* on bigram matchings. Skip-bigram-cased F-measure is computed as follows:

$$R_{\text{skip2}} = \frac{\text{SKIP2}(X,Y)}{C(m,2)} \tag{12.13}$$

$$P_{\text{skip2}} = \frac{\text{SKIP2}(X, Y)}{C(n, 2)} \tag{12.14}$$

$$F_{\text{skip2}} = \frac{(1+\beta^2) R_{\text{skip2}} P_{\text{skip2}}}{R_{\text{skip2}} + \beta^2 P_{\text{skip2}}} \tag{12.15}$$

- *ROUGE-SU*: supplements *ROUGE-S* with a fallback-counting strategy, unigram matching, to address the case where two sentences do not have any skip-bigram matches. Without this supplement, *ROUGE-S* punishes sentences that have different word-order occurrences but could have the same content.

Evaluation results produced by ROUGE are highly correlated with human-based evaluation such as responsiveness. Correlations are expressed by Spearman ranking and Pearson correlation coefficients. Spearman correlation coefficient is used to show the correlation between the ranking orders:

when there are n rank pairs (x_i, y_i)

$$p = 1 - \frac{6 \sum (x_i - y_i)^2}{n(n^2 - 1)} \tag{12.16}$$

Pearson correlation coefficient is computed on raw scores (X_i, Y_i) instead of ranks, as follows:

$$r = \frac{\sum_{i=1}^{n} (X_i - \bar{X})(Y_i - \bar{Y})}{\sqrt{\sum_{i=1}^{n} (X_i - \bar{X})^2} \sqrt{\sum_{i=1}^{n} (Y_i - \bar{Y})^2}} \tag{12.17}$$

One added advantage with ROUGE as an automatic evaluation package is that it does not have dependencies on other language-processing tools, such as various types of parsers, though it provides options to have stemming and part-of-speech tagging activated if so desired.

Basic Elements (BE)

BE [53] was proposed as an approach to automatic evaluation based on the concept of minimal semantic units. A basic element is a semantic unit extracted from a sentence such as subject-object relation, modifier-object relation. Several different syntactic and dependency parsers can be utilized to produce BEs: Charniak's parser [54], Collins's parser [55], Minipar [56], and Microsoft Logical Forms [57]. The BE breaker model takes in a parse tree and applies a set of heuristics to extract from the tree a set of smaller constituents, or BEs. Collins's and Charniak's parse trees are syntactic and do not include the semantic relations between head and modifier words. Minipar, however, is a dependency parser that automatically produces <*head*; *modifier*; *relation*> triples. The default version of the BE package creates BEs from Minipar's dependency trees. Systems are graded by measuring the overlap between system-generated summary BEs and the human-written summary BEs.

To show that BE is effective in evaluating summarization systems, it was tested on DUC 2003 results, comparing system-produced peer summaries against gold-standard reference summaries. Correlation figures are calculated by comparing rankings and average coverage scores of systems (peers and baselines) of those documented by DUC and produced by BE. Spearman rank-order correlation coefficient and Pearson correlation coefficient are computed for the validation tests. While multiple options are available when running the BE package, the authors show that running BE-F, where Minipar is used to extract BEs, without differentiating relations between the head and modifier, and taking the lemma of all words, has the highest correlations on both Spearman and Pearson when evaluating multidocument results.

When developing and tuning a summarization system, it is common to run both ROUGE and BE to analyze system-produced results thoroughly. However, because of BE's dependency on parsers, researchers may not be able to run the BE package in a multilingual scenario if the underlining parser is not available in that particular language.

Related Work

Both ROUGE and BE are used frequently because of their simplicity and high correlations with human judgments. However, the textual unit comparisons between peer and reference summaries are still limited to the matching of lexical identities. Efforts have been made to move toward measuring semantic closeness using paraphrases and synonyms. The ParaEval [58] method facilitates paraphrase matching in an overall three-level comparison strategy. At the top level, favoring higher coverage in reference, it performs a greedy search to find multiword to multiword paraphrase matches between phrases in the reference summary (usually human-written) and those in the peer summary (system-generated). The nonmatching fragments from the previous level are then searched by a greedy algorithm to find single-word paraphrase/synonym matches. At the third and the lowest level, ROUGE-1 matching is run on the remaining texts. This tiered design for summary comparison guarantees at least a ROUGE-1 level of summary content matching if no paraphrases are found. Compared to the initial release of ROUGE, ParaEval gained slightly on correlations. The paraphrases were extracted using machine translation alignment data based on the assumption that phrases that are frequently translated interchangeably are likely to be paraphrases of each other [59]. This method is most effective for machine translation evaluations [60] because in translation the goal is to produce text in a target language that completely corresponds to the original text without any compression and redundancy complications that result in more word choices.

12.3.3 Recent Development in Evaluating Summarization Systems

In 2004, Filatova and Hatzivassiloglou [61] defined **atomic events** as major constituents of actions described in a text linked by verbs or action nouns. They believe that major constituents of events are marked as named entities in text, and an atomic event is a triplet of two named entities connected by a verb or an action-denoting noun all extracted from the same sentence. Atomic events are used in creating event-based summaries and are not modeled into any evaluation method.

Tratz and Hovy [62] provide an improvement to the original BE method, which facilitates surface transformation of the basic elemental text units, called BE with Transformations for Evaluation (BEwTE). This work is based on the idea that naïve lexical identity matching does not take into account the equivalency between text units that have exact or similar words but are structured differently syntactically or semantically. To perform the transformation automatically, a set of transformation heuristics are written, and the sequence in which they are to be run is defined. This rule-building process is manually performed. The scoring on BEs in the peer summaries is produced on the basis of a greedy matching algorithm and is normalized by total weights of corresponding reference BEs. Correlation tests performed on past DUCs and TACs results show higher correlations compared to the original BE method and ROUGE. In addition to the dependency of language-processing tools, BEwTE requires significant human efforts and linguistics knowledge to create the transformation rules and the order of executing them when operating in a multilingual environment.

Louis and Nenkova [63] show that automatic summarization evaluations can be run without manually written reference summaries. This work hypothesizes that gold-standard summaries have low divergence with texts on word probability distributions where low divergence indicates high similarity. Kullback Leibler (KL) and Jensen Shannon (JS) divergence between reference and peer summaries are used as summary scores. Topic signatures [64], a useful summary creation feature, are shown to be also indicative in terms of summary evaluation where a high concentration of signatures show higher summary content quality.

Another innovative work, AutoSummENG (Automatic Summary Evaluation based on n-gram Graphs [65]), creates summary graphs where nodes are n-grams and edges are relations between the n-grams. Summary comparison is a comparison between the reference and peer summary graphs. Relations are modeled by taking the fixed-length windows of context information surrounding the n-grams. Relation edges are weighted to indicate the distance between the n-gram nodes and the number of occurrences in text. This work shows higher correlations than other automatic methods. An added advantage of this work is its language neutrality, not needing language-dependent tools.

12.3.4 Automatic Metrics for Multilingual Summarization

Summarization is a complex natural language processing task, and its evaluation presents challenges that facilitate active research development. Even though most of the automatic evaluation methods are lexical-identity matching based, it is important to keep in mind that statistically they do provide a reliable measure of system-generated summaries' quality. While good systems and bad systems are easily distinguishable by these methods, they have difficulties in identifying nuances presented by comparable systems. Given the imperfections from these various evaluation methods, it is essential for summarization system designers to understand the task being undertaken and conduct their own detailed error analyses. When moving toward multilingual summarization, there are even fewer evaluation packages that can be used. Table 12–2 summarizes the language neutrality of all the automated methods discussed in this section.

Table 12–2: Evaluation metrics used for summarization and their requirements on language-dependent processing tools

Method Name	Language-Processing Tool Dependent	Notes
ROUGE	No	
BE	Yes	Syntactic and/or dependency tree parsers
ParaEval	No	Machine translation alignment data
BEwTE	Yes	Basic element dependencies and linguistic knowledge
Divergence ([63])	No	
AutoSummENG	No	

12.4 How to Build a Summarizer

This section provides a blueprint for building a summarization system. We do not assume any particular programming language or development framework, because a summarizer can be built in any programming language. This section contains pointers to different tools and frameworks that can be used for building a multilingual summarization system either from scratch or on an already existing framework.

A general schema of a multilingual summarization system is shown in Figure 12–5. The general schema reflects the three stages commonly used for summarization described in Section 12.2.1. First, the documents must be analyzed. Depending on what type of multilingual summarization system we intend to build, our input documents are of one language (i.e., translingual) or multiple languages (i.e., crosslingual). Multiple multilingual corpora are listed in Section 12.5. The choice of languages influences which subsequent tools we need (§12.4.2).

After collecting the input data, tokenization tools need to be applied. Tokenization will probably go beyond simple whitespace tokenization, particularly for languages that do not separate words with whitespace or punctuation (e.g., Chinese). It may also be necessary to tokenize into finer categories than words if the language in question possesses a rich morphology (e.g., Arabic) or allows for generating many compound expressions such as compound nouns in German. This analysis step also includes other separation and chunking techniques, such as sentence splitting, chunking, and parsing. During the tokenization process, some bookkeeping regarding the frequency of all tokens, n-grams, chunks, and so on, needs to be carried out.

The next step involves further analysis of the tokenized text and leads to linking tokens via coreference resolution (i.e., *Microsoft-the company*) or simply the preceding or succeeding context (e.g., *Today–Microsoft–announced*).

The final component in the analysis step is concerned with translating the input content. This may happen after or before the tokenization and linking. It may also be postponed until after the transformation step.

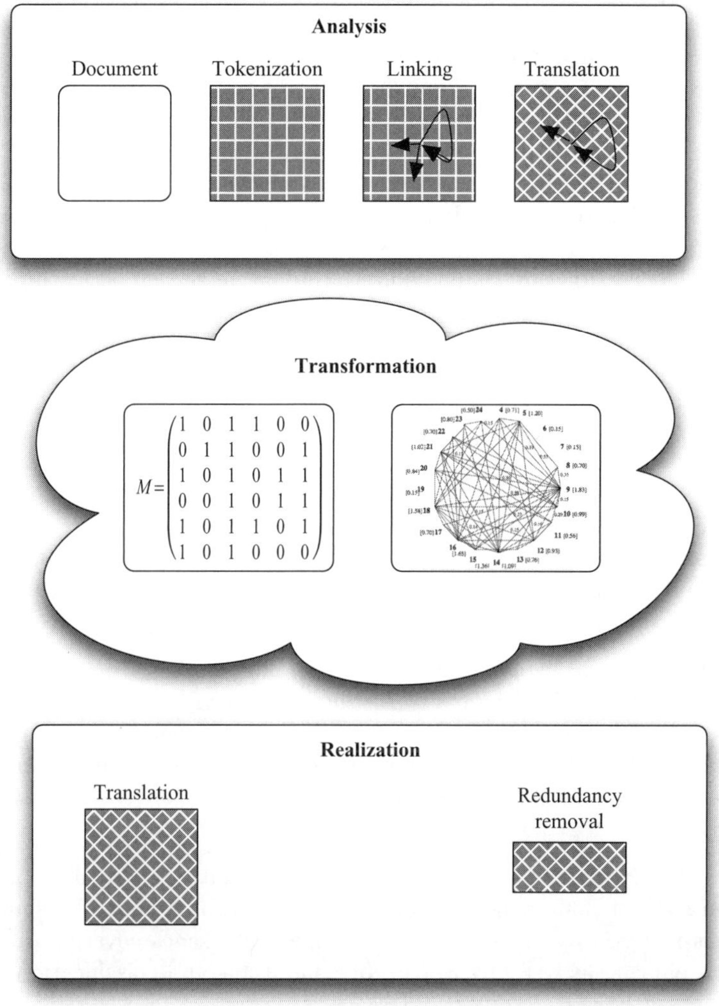

Figure 12–5: A blueprint for a multilingual summarization system

The second step in a summarization system is concerned with the transformation of the analyzed text. The choices made in the analysis text determine what kind of representation goes into the transformation modules. Section 12.2 offered different approaches to summarization to choose from. The output of this step consists of a reranked list of sentences/chunks where top-ranked text units are most summary-worthy.

Eventually, the summary is generated in the final realization step. Redundancies in the output text can be removed by applying different redundancy removal techniques described in the literature (e.g., QR, cosine similarity). If no machine translation has been applied to the input text, it now needs to be carried out to produce text in the target language.

12.4.1 Ingredients

To develop a multilingual automatic summarization program, data in various forms is a prerequisite. Ideally, we could draw from the different summarization corpora provided by NIST[10] and the LDC.[11]

In most cases, however, we will not have any data available, and creating gold-standard data may be too expensive. In such cases, we can either train and test on available data and transfer the system to this new domain or try to adapt the system to the new domain. Clearly, new domain adaptation is an interesting research direction on its own, and we refer to recent efforts, as described by Daumé and Marcu [66] or presented at the Association for Computational Linguistics 2010 workshop on domain adaptation.[12]

A good starting point for training your summarizer is the collection of data provided by the National Institute of Standards and Technology for DUC and TAC:

The system can be implemented in different frameworks. We list some here as possible suggestions but do not want to imply in any way that this is an exclusive list:

- **UIMA**[13] stands for Unstructured Information Management Architecture. It was developed by IBM and is now an Apache project. It has a component architecture and software framework implementation for the analysis of unstructured content like text, video, and audio data. This framework is Java-based but also available in C++.
- **GATE**,[14] a General Architecture for Text Engineering, was developed and first released in 1996 by the University of Sheffield. GATE is a general framework for natural language processing that contains many different language processing tools mainly written in Java that are useful for developing a summarization system. Moreover, the SUMMA toolkit developed by Horacio Saggion can be used as a GATE plug-in.
- **NLTK**,[15] the Natural Language ToolKit, offers natural language processing tools written in Python. The toolkit was developed for teaching natural language processing techniques in Python and offers a wide range of packages covering different taggers, stemmers, parsers, as well as corpus processing tools and classification and clustering algorithms.
- **R**[16] is a free software environment for statistical computing and graphics and not a natural language processing tool, but it offers easy access to many of the techniques discussed in Section 12.2. There are many machine learning packages[17] as well as tools for graph processing,[18] including implementations for running PageRank.

10. http://www.nist.gov/tac/data/index.html
11. http://www.ldc.upenn.edu/
12. http://sites.google.com/site/danlp2010/home
13. http://uima.apache.org/
14. http://gate.ac.uk
15. http://www.nltk.org/
16. http://www.r-project.org/
17. http://cran.r-project.org/web/views/MachineLearning.html
18. http://igraph.sourceforge.net/

In addition to the general frameworks that provide some initial support for writing your own summarization system, you may also start with one of the open source summarization systems introduced earlier: MEAD and SUMMA.

12.4.2 Devices

A number of tools are required for building a summarization system. In particular, at least a machine translation program is needed if more than one language is used that is different from the target language.

The following is an "ingredients" list that offers lots of suggestions on how to substitute one ingredient with another one.

Tokenizer/sentence splitter Different tools mentioned earlier (e.g., NLTK, GATE) contain tokenizers and sentence splitters. Here are some other natural language processing tools that offer similar functionalities:

lingPipe offers several different Java libraries for the linguistic analysis of human language, including sentence segmentation, Chinese word segmentation, and tokenization for English.

openNLP combines different open source projects related to natural language processing and offers a sentence splitter and tokenizer.

Machine translation program Several machine translation toolkits are available that allow researchers to train their own statistical machine learning model:

Giza++ http://fjoch.com/GIZA++.html

Thot http://sourceforge.net/projects/thot/

Moses http://www.statmt.org/moses/

Joshua http://www.cs.jhu.edu/c̃cb/joshua/index.html

Another way of integrating machine learning is via the Google translation API: http://code.google.com/p/google-api-translate-java/

Feature extractors To run machine learning experiments or to generate a graph representation, researchers must extract features from the documents for each sentence (or word). There are tools available that facilitate this process and offer out-of-the-box feature extractors that researchers are likely to use (e.g., n-gram-based features). A tool that works with the UIMA framework was developed by the University of Boulder, Colorado, and is called ClearTK[19] [67].

12.4.3 Instructions

The two previous sections contain enough pointers to get all the necessary ingredients and devices for creating your own summarization system. At the end of this chapter, we discuss how to utilize the blueprint of a summarization system (see Figure 12–5).

19. http://code.google.com/p/cleartk/

First, you must decide where to use the machine translation part. There are two possibilities. You can either translate first or translate later. The latter method has two advantages: a summary system that adopts this approach would probably be faster because only the best summary sentences need to be translated, a fact you should consider when large documents need to be summarized. Moreover, translation errors may degrade the summarization process if that is done on the target language only. This will surely be true if summarization techniques require high-level linguistic features such as a parse tree, but it may not be such a problem if clustering or graph-based approaches based on bag-of-words or n-gram features are chosen. Depending on this decision, the other components need also to be available and need to produce output of a certain quality (e.g., tokenizer, chunker).

Second, the overall approach needs to be determined. We summarized different approaches in Section 12.2 and pointed in particular to clustering and graph-based approaches that should work well with crosslingual or translingual summarization. The decision for this part of the system should be guided by the available language resources and the quality of the machine translation component. The output will be a ranked list of sentences with the best sentences being the best summary sentences.

An additional (optional) component would address the generation part of the system. For multidocument summarization, this component would have to make sure that no redundant sentences are selected, and for a multilingual summarization system, it must ensure that the correct translation for an entity or concept has been selected. Some systems offer a solution for this problem of redundancy removal (e.g., Carbonell and Goldstein [18]) or the selection of names in other languages (e.g., Mani, Yeh, and Condon [14]).

Finally and most importantly, you must to determine which evaluation methods should be used. The method should depend on how the system is used and may be intrinsic or extrinsic. It is recommended to set up experiments with the different parameters of your system and record the achieved results. These records will help you to decide on which parameters lead to the best system configuration.

12.5 Competitions and Data Sets

12.5.1 Competitions

DUC The Document Understanding Conference was carried out by the National Institute of Standards and Technology from 2001 to 2007 and focused on making progress in summarization research and providing a forum for researchers to participate in large-scale experiments. The tasks investigated include single summarization as well as multidocument summarization, mostly in English with the exception of DUC 2003, which involved summarization from Arabic to English translations.

TAC The Text Analysis Conference is the successor meeting for DUC since 2008. Tasks include query-based multidocument summarization, opinion-based summarization, as well as update summarization. In 2011, TAC included a multilingual pilot task. In 2012, the TAC entity linking task will be truly multilingual, covering English, Chinese and Spanish.

MSE The Multilingual Summarization Evaluation (MSE) 2005 and 2006 focused on multi-document summarization of the English and Arabic portions of the TDT-4 corpus, which contains 41,728 Arabic documents and 23,602 English documents. As for the DUC 2003 summarization task, summarizations were generated from the Arabic translations from the original English news articles. First, clusters were created by running a clustering algorithm developed by the University of Columbia over the the TDT4 corpus. Next, the Information Sciences Institute's machine translation system was used to translate the Arabic data. Interestingly enough, the best system in 2005 used only English sentences as input.

12.5.2 Data Sets

- SummBank (Cantonese, English) consists of 18,147 aligned bilingual (Cantonese and English) article pairs from the Information Services Department of the Hong-Kong Special Administrative Region of the People's Republic of China:
http://clair.si.umich.edu/clair/CSTBank/
http://www.ldc.upenn.edu/Catalog/CatalogEntry.jsp?catalogId=LDC2003T16
- Document Understanding Conference (English, Arabic [DUC 2003])[20]
- Text Analysis Conference (English)[21]
- Multilingual Summarization Evaluation (Arabic, English)
- Crossdocument Structure Theory Bank (CSTBank) (English): data annotated according to crossdocument structure theory (CST), a functional theory for multidocument discourse structure related to rhetorical structure theory
(http://clair.si.umich.edu/clair/CSTBank/)
- The New York Times Annotated Corpus (English) contains over 1.8 million articles written and published by the *New York Times* between January 1, 1987, and June 19, 2007, with article metadata provided by the New York Times Newsroom. The corpus provides over 650,000 article summaries written by library scientists. Although it is a monolingual corpus, it offers a normalized index for people, organizations, locations, and topic descriptors, which could be helpful for mapping entities across documents.
http://www.ldc.upenn.edu/Catalog/CatalogEntry.jsp?catalogId=LDC2008T19
- The Language Understanding Annotation Corpus (Arabic, English) contains over 9,000 words of English text (6,949 words) and Arabic text (2,183 words) annotated for committed belief, event and entity coreference, dialog acts, and temporal relations.
http://www.ldc.upenn.edu/Catalog/CatalogEntry.jsp?catalogId=LDC2009T10
- Topic Detection and Tracking (TDT) corpora covered multiple years of data creation (English, Arabic, Mandarin Chinese). TDT2 Multilanguage Text corpus contains news data collected daily from nine news sources in two languages (American English and

20. http://www-nlpir.nist.gov/projects/duc/data.html
21. http://www.nist.gov/tac/data/index.html

Mandarin Chinese) over a period of six months (January through June 1998).
http://www.ldc.upenn.edu/Catalog/CatalogEntry.jsp?catalogId=LDC2001T57
TDT 3 contains data from the same nine sources found in TDT2 plus two additional English television sources. For this corpus, the daily collection took place over a period of three months (October through December 1998).
http://www.ldc.upenn.edu/Catalog/CatalogEntry.jsp?catalogId=LDC2001T58
Finally, TDT4 contains the complete set of English, Arabic, and Chinese news text (broadcast news transcripts, and newswire data) used in the 2002 and 2003 Topic Detection and Tracking technology evaluations.
http://www.ldc.upenn.edu/Catalog/CatalogEntry.jsp?catalogId=LDC2005T16

12.6 Summary

In this chapter we presented the main approaches to summarization and showed how they need to be extended in order to work in a multilingual environment. Multilingual summarization presents an additional complexity to automatic summarization systems designed for one source/target language.

After providing a brief history to multilingual summarization, we gave an overview to the major approaches to summarization. Most monolingual summarization systems are divided into three stages: analysis, transformation, and realization. The same is true for multilingual systems.

1. For the analysis stage, summarization systems may represent the text in the form of a graph. This may be a linguistically motivated discourse tree or a matrix representation based on sentence-to-sentence similarity.

2. The transformation process can be carried out via graph-based algorithms such as PageRank or by machine learning–based classifiers that learn to classify sentences according to their relevancy.

3. Multilingual approaches have to face many language-dependent challenges such as tokenization, anaphoric expressions, and discourse structure for the realization of the summary.

Many natural language processing research areas can be encompassed into the summarization process, such as language modeling and understanding, coreference resolution, anaphora resolution, and surface realization. Each of these tasks elicits rich problems and solution representations, adding complexity and variability to summarization problem solutions.

This complexity in turn complicates the evaluation process in terms of task definition and solution comparison. As part of the continuing research effort, many manual and automated evaluation methodologies have been created to suit various task needs, such as query-based and single- and multidocument summarizations. We discussed all major approaches to evaluation. The approaches range from manual annotation to automatically generated metrics that are sometimes language-independent but also require language-specific resources such as parsers.

We then discussed the different concrete ingredients that can be used for building a summarization system. Many natural language processing tools already are available, although perhaps not for all languages. Machine translation systems may be able to bridge some of the gaps, but often new resources need to be developed in order to build a summarization system in not-well-researched languages.

Finally, we compiled a list of data sets that can be used to develop and train your own summarization system in languages other than English.

Bibliography

[1] S. Wan and C. Paris, "In-browser summarisation: Generating elaborative summaries biased towards the reading context," in *HLT '08: Proceedings of the 46th Annual Meeting of the Association for Computational Linguistics on Human Language Technologies*, pp. 129–132, 2008.

[2] U. Hahn and I. Mani, "The challenges of automatic summarization," *Computer*, vol. 33, no. 11, pp. 29–36, 2000.

[3] K. Knight and D. Marcu, "Summarization beyond sentence extraction: A probabilistic approach to sentence compression," *Artificial Intelligence*, vol. 139, no. 1, pp. 91–107, 2002.

[4] R. Mitkov, "Robust pronoun resolution with limited knowledge," in *Proceedings of the 18th International Conference on Computational Linguistics (COLING'98)/ACL'98 Conference*, pp. 869–875, 1998.

[5] G. Erkan and D. R. Radev, "LexPageRank: Prestige in Multi-Document Text Summarization," in *Proceeding of the Conference on Empirical Methods on Natural Language Processing (EMNLP)*, 2004.

[6] E. Hovy and C.-Y. Lin, "Automated text summarization and the SUMMARIST system," in *Advances in Automated Text Summarization* (I. Mani and M. Maybury, eds.), Cambridge, MA: MIT Press, 1998.

[7] D. R. Radev, S. Teufel, H. Saggion, W. Lam, J. Blitzer, H. Qi, A. Çelebi, D. Liu, and E. Drabek, "Evaluation challenges in large-scale multi-document summarization: the mead project," in *Proceedings of the Association for Computational Linguistics 2003*, 2003.

[8] A. Lenci, R. Bartolini, N. Calzolari, A. Agua, S. Busemann, E. Cartier, K. Chevreau, and J. Coch, "Multilingual summarization by integrating linguistic resources in the MLIS-MUSI project," in *Proceedings of the 3rd International Conference on Language Resources and Evaluation (LREC'02)*, 2002.

[9] D. K. Evans, J. L. Klavans, and K. R. McKeown, "Columbia NewsBlaster: Multilingual news summarization on the web," in *Proceedings of the Human Language Technology Conference of the North American Chapter of the Association for Computational Linguistics (HLT/NAACL): Demonstration Papers at HLT-NAACL 2004*, pp. 1–4, 2004.

[10] H. Saggion, "Multilingual multidocument summarization tools and evaluation," in *Proceedings of the 5th International Conference on Language Resources and Evaluation*, 2006.

[11] H. Saggion, "SUMMA: A robust and adaptable summarization tool," *Traitement Automatique des Langues*, vol. 49, no. 2, 2008.

[12] H. Cunningham, D. Maynard, K. Bontcheva, and V. Tablan, "GATE: An architecture for development of robust HLT applications," in *Proceedings of the 40th Annual Meeting on Association for Computational Linguistics*, pp. 168–175, 2002.

[13] G. Demetriou, I. Skadina, H. Keskustalo, J. Karlgren, D. Deksne, D. Petrelli, P. Hansen, G. Gaizauskas, and M. Sanderson, "Cross-lingual document retrieval categorisation and navigation based on distributed services," in *Proceedings of the First Baltic Conference. Human Language Technologies: the Baltic Perspective*, 2004.

[14] I. Mani, A. Yeh, and S. Condon, "Learning to match names across languages," in *Proceedings of the Workshop on Multi-source Multilingual Information Extraction and Summarization*, pp. 2–9, 2008.

[15] S. Mille and L. Wanner, "Multilingual summarization in practice: The case of patent claims," in *Proceedings of the 12th Annual Conference of the European Association for Machine Translation (EAMT)*, pp. 120–129, 2008.

[16] A. Leuski, C.-Y. Lin, L. Zhou, U. Germann, F. J. Och, and E. Hovy, "Cross-lingual C*ST*RD: English access to Hindi information," *ACM Transactions on Asian Language Information Processing (TALIP)*, vol. 2, no. 3, pp. 245–269, 2003.

[17] C. Orăsan and O. A. Chiorean, "Evaluation of a cross-lingual romanian-english multi-document summariser," in *Proceedings of the Sixth International Language Resources and Evaluation*, European Language Resources Association (ELRA), 2008.

[18] J. Carbonell and J. Goldstein, "The use of mmr, diversity-based reranking for reordering documents and producing summaries," in *Proceedings of the 21st Annual International ACM SIGIR Conference on Research and Development in Information Retrieval*, pp. 335–336, 1998.

[19] R. Mihalcea and P. Tarau, "Textrank: Bringing order into texts," in *Conference on Empirical Methods in Natural Language Processing*, 2004.

[20] X. Ji and H. Zha, "Correlating summarization of a pair of multilingual documents," *Research Issues in Data Engineering, International Workshop on*, vol. 0, p. 39, 2003.

[21] H. P. Luhn, "The automatic creation of literature abstracts," *IBM Journal of Research Development*, vol. 2, no. 2, pp. 159–165, 1958.

[22] H. P. Edmundson, "New methods in automatic extracting," *Journal of the ACM*, vol. 16, no. 2, pp. 264–285, 1969.

[23] J. Kupiec, J. Pedersen, and F. Chen, "A trainable document summarizer," in *Proceedings of the 18th Annual International ACM SIGIR Conference on Research and Development in Information Retrieval*, pp. 68–73, 1995.

[24] W. C. Mann and S. A. Thompson, "Rhetorical structure theory: Toward a functional theory of text organization," *Text*, vol. 8, no. 3, pp. 243–281, 1988.

[25] S. Brin and L. Page, "The anatomy of a large-scale hypertextual web search engine," in *Computer Networks and ISDN Systems*, pp. 107–117, Elsevier Science Publishers B. V., 1998.

[26] M. A. K. Halliday and R. Hasan, *Cohesion in English.* London: Longman, 1976.

[27] D. Marcu, *The Theory and Practice of Discourse Parsing and Summarization.* Cambridge, MA: MIT Press, 2000.

[28] K. Ono, K. Sumita, and S. Miike, "Abstract generation based on rhetorical structure extraction," in *Proceedings of the 15th Conference on Computational Linguistics*, pp. 344–348, 1994.

[29] F. Schilder, "Robust discourse parsing via discourse markers, topicality and position," *Natural Language Engineering*, vol. 8, no. 2/3, pp. 235–255, 2002.

[30] D. Marcu and A. Echihabi, "An unsupervised approach to recognizing discourse relations," in *Proceedings of the 40th Annual Meeting on Association for Computational Linguistics*, pp. 368–375, 2002.

[31] D. Marcu, "Discourse trees are good indicators of importance in text," in *Advances in Automatic Text Summarization* (I. Mani and M. Maybury, eds.), Cambridge, MA: MIT Press, 1999.

[32] H. Lüngen, C. Puskas, M. Bärenfänger, M. Hilbert, and H. Lobin, "Discourse segmentation of german written text," in *Proceedings of the 5th International Conference on Natural Language Processing (FinTAL 2006)*, 2006.

[33] C. Sporleder and A. Lascarides, "Using automatically labelled examples to classify rhetorical relations: An assessment," *Natural Language Engineering*, vol. 14, no. 3, pp. 369–416, 2008.

[34] C. Aone, M. E. Okurowski, and J. Gorlinsky, "Trainable, scalable summarization using robust nlp and machine learning," in *Proceedings of the 17th International Conference on Computational Linguistics*, pp. 62–66, 1998.

[35] C.-Y. Lin, "Training a selection function for extraction," in *Proceedings of the 8th International Conference on Information and Knowledge Management*, pp. 55–62, 1999.

[36] Y. Ouyang, S. Li, and W. Li, "Developing learning strategies for topic-based summarization," in *Proceedings of the 16th ACM Conference on Information and Knowledge Management*, pp. 79–86, ACM, 2007.

[37] F. Schilder and R. Kondadadi, "Fastsum: Fast and accurate query-based multi-document summarization," in *Proceedings of the Association for Computational Linguistics: HLT, Short Papers*, pp. 205–208, 2008.

[38] K. M. Svore, L. Vanderwende, and C. J. C. Burges, "Using signals of human interest to enhance single-document summarization," in *Proceedings of the 23rd National Conference on Artificial Intelligence*, pp. 1577–1580, 2008.

[39] C. J. C. Burges, T. Shaked, E. Renshaw, A. Lazier, M. Deeds, N. Hamilton, and G. N. Hullender, "Learning to rank using gradient descent," in *Proceedings of the 22nd International Conference on Machine Learning*, pp. 89–96, 2005.

[40] M.-R. Amini, A. Tombros, N. Usunier, and M. Lalmas, "Learning based summarization of xml documents," *Journal of Information Retrieval*, vol. 10, no. 3, pp. 233–255, 2007.

[41] Z. Cao, T. Qin, T.-Y. Liu, M.-F. Tsai, and H. Li, "Learning to rank: from pairwise approach to listwise approach," in *Proceedings of the 24th International Conference on Machine Learning*, (New York, NY, USA), pp. 129–136, ACM, 2007.

[42] C. Wang, F. Jing, L. Zhang, and H.-J. Zhang, "Learning query-biased web page summarization," in *Proceedings of the 16th ACM Conference on Information and Knowledge Management*, pp. 555–562, 2007.

[43] D. Radev, V. Hatzivassiloglou, and K. R. Mckeown, "A description of the CIDR system as used for tdt-2," in *DARPA Broadcast News Workshop*, 1999.

[44] V. Hatzivassiloglou, L. Gravano, and A. Maganti, "An investigation of linguistic features and clustering algorithms for topical document clustering," in *Proceedings of the 23rd ACM SIGIR Conference on Research and Development in Information Retrieval*, pp. 224–231, 2000.

[45] K. R. McKeown, R. Barzilay, D. Evans, V. Hatzivassiloglou, J. L. Klavans, A. Nenkova, C. Sable, B. Schiffman, and S. Sigelman, "Tracking and summarizing news on a daily basis with Columbia's NewsBlaster," in *Proceedings of the 2nd International Conference on Human Language Technology Research*, pp. 280–285, 2002.

[46] C. Lin and E. Hovy, "Manual and automatic evaluation of summaries," in *Proceedings of the Document Understanding Conference (DUC-02)*, 2002.

[47] C. Lin, "Summary evaluation environment," 2001 http://www.isi.edu/ cyl/SEE.

[48] H. V. Halteren and S. Teufel, "Examining the consensus between human summaries: Initial experiments with Factoid analysis," in *Proceedings of the Human Language Technology Conference of the North American Chapter of the Association for Computational Linguistics (HLT/NAACL) Workshop*, 2003.

[49] A. Nenkova and R. Passonneau, "Evaluating content selection in summarization: The Pyramid method," in *Proceedings of the Human Language Technology Conference of the North American Chapter of the Association for Computational Linguistics (HLT/-NAACL)*, 2004.

[50] C. Lin and E. Hovy, "Automatic evaluation of summaries using n-gram co-occurrence statistics," in *Proceedings of the Human Language Technology Conference of the North American Chapter of the Association for Computational Linguistics (HLT/NAACL)*, 2003.

[51] C. Lin, "ROUGE: A package for automatic evaluation of summaries," in *The Workshop on Text Summarization Branches Out*, 2004.

[52] K. Papineni, S. Roukos, T. Ward, and W. Zhu, "IBM research report BLEU: A method for automatic evaluation of machine translation," in *IBM Research Division Technical Report, RC22176*, 2001.

[53] E. Hovy, C.-Y. Lin, L. Zhou, and J. Fukumoto, "Automated summarization evaluation with basic elements," in *Proceedings of the 5th International Conference on Language Resources and Evaluation (LREC)*, 2006.

[54] E. Charniak, "A maximum-entropy-inspired parser," in *Proceedings of the Conference of the North American Chapter of the Association for Computational Linguistics*, 2000.

[55] M. Collins, "Three generative lexicalized models for statistical parsing," in *Proceedings of the Conference of the Association for Computational Linguistics*, 1997.

[56] D. Lin, "A dependency-based method for evaluating broad-coverage parsers," in *IJCAI-95*, 1995.

[57] G. Heidorn, "Intelligent writing assistance," in *A Handbook of Natural Language Processing: Techniques and Applications for the Processing of Language as Text* (R. Dale, H. Moisl, and H. Somers, eds.). New York: Marcel Dekker, 2000.

[58] L. Zhou, C. Lin, D. Munteanu, and E. Hovy, "Paraeval: Using paraphrases to evaluate summaries automatically," in *Proceedings of the Human Language Technology Conference of the North American Chapter of the Association for Computational Linguistics (HLT/NAACL)*, 2006.

[59] C. Callison-Burch, P. Koehn, and M. Osborne, "Improved statistical machine translation using paraphrases," in *Proceedings of the Human Language Technology Conference of the North American Chapter of the Association for Computational Linguistics (HLT/NAACL)*, 2006.

[60] L. Zhou, C. Lin, and E. Hovy, "Re-evaluating machine translation results with paraphrase support," in *Proceedings of the Conference on Empirical Methods on Natural Language Processing (EMNLP)*, 2006.

[61] E. Filatova and V. Hatzivassiloglou, "Event-based extractive summarization," in *ACL Workshop on Summarization*, 2004.

[62] S. Tratz and E. Hovy, "Summarization evaluation using transformed basic elements," in *Text Analytics Conference (TAC-08)*, 2008.

[63] A. Louis and A. Nenkova, "Summary evaluation without human models," in *Text Analytics Conference (TAC-08)*, 2008.

[64] C. Y. Lin and E. Hovy, "The automated acquisition of topic signatures for text summarization," in *Proceedings of the Conference of the Association for Computational Linguistics (HLT/NAACL)*, 2000.

[65] G. Giannakopoulos, V. Karkaletsis, G. Vouros, and P. Stamatopoulos, "Summarization system evaluation revisited: N-gram graphs," in *ACM Transactions on Speech and Language Processing*, vol. 5, no. 3, 2008.

[66] H. Daumé III and D. Marcu, "Bayesian query-focused summarization," in *Proceedings of the Conference of the Association for Computational Linguistics*, 2006.

[67] P. V. Ogren, P. G. Wetzler, and S. Bethard, "ClearTK: A UIMA toolkit for statistical natural language processing," in *UIMA for NLP workshop at Language Resources and Evaluation Conference (LREC)*, 2008.

Chapter 13

Question Answering

Nico Schlaefer and Jennifer Chu-Carroll

13.1 Introduction and History

Question answering (QA) systems retrieve answers to user questions from information sources. In contrast to the keyword search paradigm adopted by most traditional information retrieval (IR) systems, QA systems can be asked questions in natural language, which is more intuitive and also more expressive than mere keywords. In addition, while IR systems return passages or documents in response to the user queries, QA systems attempt to provide answers that are accurate and to the point. Often, the web is utilized as a large, redundant, and up-to-date information source. However, local text corpora are frequently used for advanced search techniques that require the sources to be preprocessed, for restricted domains (e.g., medical, legal, or intranet data), and in evaluations that require results to be comparable and reproducible.

Question types that have been best studied to date are **factoid questions**, which ask for concise answers such as named entities (e.g., *What is the capital of Turkey?*), and **list questions** seeking lists of such factoid answers (e.g., *Which countries are in NATO?*). Attempts have been made to tackle questions with complex answers, such as **definitional questions** requesting information on a given topic, including biographies for people (e.g., *Who is Albert Einstein?*), **relationship questions** (e.g., *What is the relationship between the Taliban and Al-Qaeda?*), and **opinion questions** (e.g., *What do people like about IKEA?*). In this chapter we focus on techniques and algorithms that are deployed in factoid QA systems and can be adapted to answer list questions. Factoid questions are well suited for illustrating the principles underlying modern QA systems, and the algorithmic solutions and evaluation methodologies deployed in factoid QA are more mature than those used for questions with complex answers. Refer to Section 13.11 for recommended reading on other question types.

What makes question answering a challenging task is the flexibility, richness, and ambiguity of natural language, causing frequent mismatches between the information expressed in the question and in answer-bearing passages. While simple keyword matches can successfully identify the correct answer for many questions, general knowledge and the ability to perform logical inference, such as technologies developed under the RTE (recognizing textual entailment) task [1], are often inevitable. Additional challenges arise from temporal expressions and statements whose validity is time sensitive. Some of these difficulties are encountered when answering the question *Which car manufacturer has been owned by VW since 1998?* given a 1998 newspaper article containing the passage *Volkswagen today announced the acquisition of Bentley.* To be capable of identifying the correct answer, a QA system would need to know that *Volkswagen* and *VW* refer to the same entity and that *Bentley* is a *car manufacturer.* It would also need to infer that *acquisition* implies *ownership* and that the temporal expression *today* is consistent with the year *1998.*

Furthermore, the answer to a question may not be found in a single source document, in which case it becomes necessary to combine evidence from multiple sources. Consider the question *In which country is Sony headquartered?* Even if it is not explicitly stated in the sources that Sony's headquarters are located in Japan, two independent documents may mention that the headquarters are in Tokyo and that Tokyo is a city in Japan. In other cases it may be necessary to divide a question into multiple subquestions and compose a final answer from the answers to those questions. For instance, the question *Which countries have won both the soccer World Cup and the European championship?* can be answered by intersecting the lists of winners of the two tournaments.

QA research dates back to the 1960s, when several expert systems for **restricted domains** were developed [2]. The BASEBALL system [3] was designed to answer questions about the US baseball league, while LUNAR [4] could answer questions about rock samples retrieved from the moon in the Apollo missions. Both systems relied on **structured knowledge** sources that were manually constructed by experts of the respective domains, and they could not easily be extended to more general domains. Some early natural language dialog systems also included basic QA capabilities. For instance, the SHRDLU system described by Winograd [5] could carry on a dialog in natural language about a toy world containing a small number of objects, and the user could ask it to manipulate objects or inquire about the state of the world. Another early application of QA technologies was reading comprehension systems such as QUALM [6], which could process a text and answer questions about its content. These systems no longer relied on handcrafted knowledge bases but were still constrained to rather narrow domains. The 1990s brought a transition toward **open-domain** QA, leading to systems that can answer questions about almost any topic based on large collections of **unstructured text**. One of the first examples of this new generation of QA systems was MURAX [7], which answered factoid-style questions about general knowledge using an online encyclopedia.

A major driver of English QA research has been the annual evaluation conducted by the Text REtrieval Conference (TREC) starting in 1999 [8]. Participating systems had to answer factoid questions and later list, definitional, and relationship questions based on newswire corpora and other unstructured document collections. In 2008, the QA track was moved to the Text Analysis Conference (TAC) [9] and the focus shifted to opinion questions. The Cross-Language Evaluation Forum (CLEF) established a similar evaluation platform for other European languages [10], and the NTCIR (NII Test Collection for IR Systems) workshop performs annual evaluations of QA systems for Asian languages [11]. Whereas TREC and TAC focused on monolingual QA tasks in which the questions and information sources are both in English, CLEF and NTCIR also introduced crosslingual tasks where the languages in which the questions are posed differ from the languages of the sources.

Today a number of QA systems provide web interfaces and can be tested online, including the START system[1] developed at MIT, Ask.com, and Wolfram Alpha.[2] Microsoft and Google have also integrated basic QA capabilities for restricted types of questions into their web search engines. Recently, two former TREC systems, Carnegie-Mellon University's OpenEphyra[3] and MIT's Aranea,[4] have been released into open source and are available for download.

13.2 Architectures

Although a variety of QA architectures have been adopted in recent years, the vast majority of QA systems are based on a core pipeline comprising components for question analysis, query generation, search, candidate answer generation, and answer scoring. The **question analysis** component derives syntactic and semantic information from the question, using techniques such as answer type classification, syntactic and semantic parsing, and named entity recognition. In the **query generation** stage, this information is transformed into a set of search queries, often with some degree of query expansion, which are passed to the **search** component to retrieve relevant content from a collection of **knowledge sources**. The search results are processed by the **candidate generation** component, which extracts or generates candidate answers of the desired granularity (e.g., factoid answers or definitional phrases). The **answer scoring** component estimates confidence scores for the candidate answers and often merges similar candidates. At this stage, the knowledge sources can be reused to retrieve supporting evidence for individual candidates. The final output is a list of answers ranked by confidence estimates.

Figure 13–1 illustrates this canonical architecture and shows how a question is processed by a sample implementation. The input is the question *Which computer scientist invented the smiley?* given in text format. In this simple example, the QA component determines that the question is seeking an answer of the type *computer scientist*, and it extracts the additional keywords *invented* and *smiley*. The query generation component constructs a search engine query from the answer type and extracted keywords. Given this query, the search component retrieves passages such as the one shown in Figure 13–1 from a textual corpus (say, the web). In the candidate generation stage, named entities are extracted as candidate answers. Finally, an answer scoring component estimates a confidence score for each candidate, using features such as the retrieval rank, the number of occurrences of a candidate in the search results, and whether it matches the predicted answer type. The highest scoring candidate, *Scott E. Fahlman*, is returned as the most probable answer.

Most QA systems in principle follow this canonical architecture, although some have introduced variations either to incorporate additional components or to alter the flow between system components. For example, Harabagiu et al. [12] introduced feedback loops into their system architecture so that multiple strategies can be attempted in turn, with

1. http://start.csail.mit.edu/
2. http://www.wolframalpha.com/
3. http://sourceforge.net/projects/openephyra/
4. http://www.umiacs.umd.edu/~jimmylin/downloads/Aranea-r1.00.tar.gz

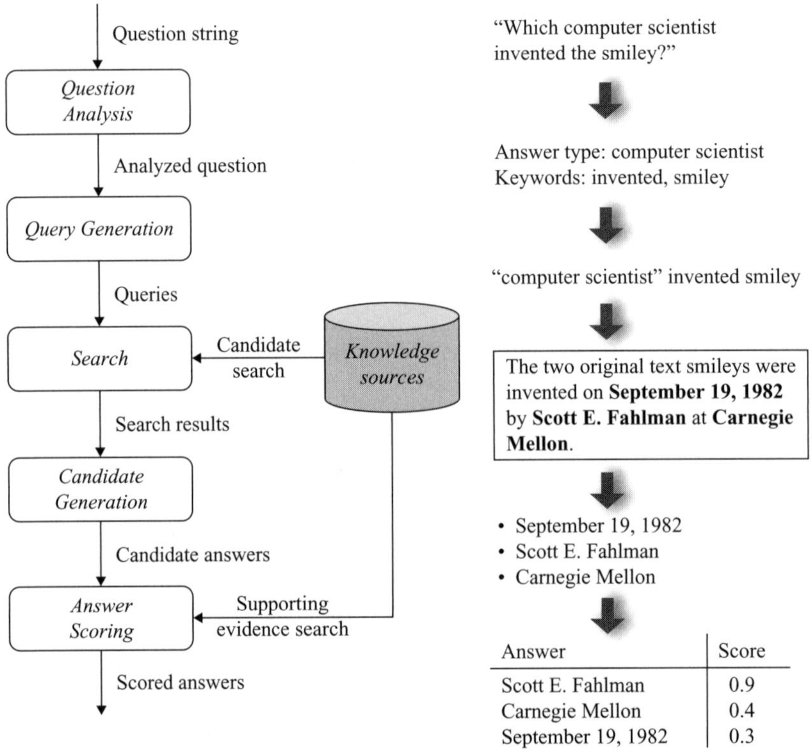

Figure 13–1: Canonical question answering architecture (left) and sample question processed in the pipeline (right)

higher recall strategies being applied when earlier, more precise strategies failed. The START QA system [13] diverged from the canonical QA architecture by enabling complex questions to be decomposed and answered in a nested fashion. For instance, the question *Where was the 20th U.S. president born?* can be answered by first retrieving the president's name *(James A. Garfield)* and then using this information to find his birthplace *(Orange Township)*. Finally, modern QA systems often adopt a multistrategy approach to question answering in which several independent algorithms are applied in parallel and their results are combined (e.g., Chu-Carroll et al. [14] and Nyberg et al. [15]). This parallel QA approach can be computationally expensive, but it also proved to be very effective because multiple components can reinforce or complement one another, and final decisions can be postponed until the outcomes of all execution paths are known.

QA systems commonly rely on existing information retrieval engines to search a local document collection or the web for relevant documents or passages. Thus the question analysis and query generation components can be viewed as preprocessing stages that transform natural language questions into abstract queries that are supported by the underlying search engines. The candidate generation and answer scoring components can then be regarded as postprocessing stages that generate precise, to-the-point answers from the search results.

Here we focus on this search-based approach to question answering. Note, however, that there are systems that manage without a conventional text search. For instance, Clifton and Teahan [16] automatically extract knowledge relations from textual sources and store them in a knowledge base, and the more recent Wolfram Alpha system uses as its answer source human-curated knowledge bases. At runtime, the QA system matches questions with entries in the knowledge bases rather than performing a search over unstructured text.

The QA architecture outlined here is mostly language-independent. Systems for Asian languages and European languages other than English use similar architectures, and there are instances of systems that have been adapted to other languages with only minimal modifications to their pipeline layouts. An example is the JAVELIN system [17], which was originally developed for English and was later adapted to Chinese and Japanese. However, the underlying natural language processing (NLP) tools such as segmenters, parsers, and named entity recognizers can be significantly different across languages, and tasks that are trivial in one language can be challenging in another. For instance, tokenization can be performed with high accuracy in English but is much harder in Chinese and Japanese because of the lack of spacing between words. Furthermore, though a wealth of NLP tools is publicly available for English, some of these core technologies are unavailable or less accurate in other languages. QA system developers have to accommodate for these differences by instantiating each of the pipeline components with algorithms that are feasible in the respective languages.

In crosslingual QA (§13.7), it further becomes necessary to incorporate translation steps in the QA architecture. Most commonly, questions or query terms are translated to the languages of the sources in the QA component. Alternatively, the entire sources can be translated to the languages of the questions in an offline preprocessing step, in which case the pipeline does not need to be modified but is essentially the same as for monolingual QA.

In the following, we discuss offline processing steps for building relevant source material (§13.3) and then describe each stage in a QA pipeline in more detail (§§13.4–13.6). Although most of the algorithms and techniques presented in these sections are applicable to various languages, we point out differences between languages that affect the feasibility or effectiveness of some approaches.

13.3 Source Acquisition and Preprocessing

The World Wide Web is by far the largest, broadest, and most up-to-date source of digitized text and has therefore been used extensively for question answering. However, there are also definite advantages in using smaller, locally available sources. Although the algorithmic details of web search engines are unknown, local sources can be indexed with IR systems that give developers full control over their retrieval algorithms and search results. In addition, the web, if searched with existing search engines, has to be used as is, whereas locally available sources can be preprocessed, consolidated, and augmented with useful information. Web content and the features and algorithms used by web search engines also change over time, and hence evaluation results based on the web are often not comparable or reproducible. Consequently, comparative evaluation efforts such as the QA tracks of TREC, TAC, CLEF, and NTCIR have all used static collections as their reference corpora, although systems have been allowed to optionally utilize additional resources such as the web. Practical applications of QA technologies may also require fast response times and high availability, which can make a live web search and subsequent retrieval of relevant websites infeasible. Local indexing and retrieval become unavoidable if the knowledge domain includes confidential data or specialized knowledge that is not available on the web.

An initial set of sources can be selected on the basis of an analysis of the knowledge domain. For instance, newswire corpora can be a useful resource for questions about political events, the economy, or sports, encyclopedias have good coverage for questions about common knowledge and well-known entities, and blog sources may be appropriate for answering opinion questions. The availability of information sources greatly depends on the language, and some of the sources frequently used for English QA are less comprehensive than or do not exist in other languages. For example, online resources that are commonly utilized for QA, such as Wikipedia, are still predominantly in English. Relevant sources may be incrementally added to a QA system if they are found to improve the search performance on a development set, but note that this practice can result in overfitting if sources are selected on the basis of a small sample of questions.

Before a collection of text documents can be indexed, it usually undergoes a series of preprocessing steps. First, most QA systems normalize the text by converting the characters to a uniform encoding and replacing symbols and foreign characters. This is a necessary step to improve search results, to facilitate the merging of similar answers, and to support automatic evaluations based on answer keys. In addition, low-quality sources such as web crawls may require further processing, including the removal of noise (e.g., advertisement, text in unsupported languages) and spelling correction. Next, documents are often segmented into sentences to support the retrieval of individual sentences and passages that align with sentence boundaries. Depending on the language of the sources, sentences are further tokenized into words or smaller units of text, such as morphemes, character n-grams, or individual characters. In English and other European languages, words are usually used as the basic unit of text for indexing and retrieval. Often, words are stemmed to increase search recall and reduce the index size, but this may also cause mismatches between words that carry different meanings.

In Japanese QA, text is most commonly segmented into morphemes. Tokenization is harder because of the lack of spacing between words but can be performed relatively effectively using statistical approaches such as sequential modeling [18]. Usually multiple character types (katakana, hiragana, and kanji) are used in a single sentence, and changes between character types provide useful clues about boundaries. Some Japanese QA systems also index individual characters or character bigrams, which may improve search recall but can also lead to more noise in the search results. Currently, there is no consensus on which approach is most effective. Chinese also lacks spacing between words, and usually only one character type is used in a document, which makes it hard to recognize and separate unknown words that cannot be found in a dictionary. Therefore, most Chinese QA systems index and retrieve text at the character level, although recent advances in Chinese word segmentation [19] made word-based indexing feasible.

A few systems also perform coreference resolution (also known as **anaphora resolution**) on the source text. Common types of coreferences are pronouns and nominals referring to named entities mentioned earlier in the text. For instance, the pronoun *he* may be a reference to a specific person, and the nominal *the city* may refer to a specific city mentioned previously. Coreference resolution can improve passage search by ensuring that related terms appear in close proximity, but a sufficiently precise algorithm is required. Hickl et al. [20] adopt a conservative approach that uses heuristics to resolve pronominal and nominal coreferences. In addition, the performance on questions containing time constraints can be improved by normalizing temporal expressions in questions and the sources. For example, Moldovan, Clark, and Bowden [21] report that their system replaces expressions such as *annually* and *each year* with canonical forms, which enables it to retrieve a candidate passage containing the string *Fulbright awards approximately 4,500 new grants annually* when answering the question *How many grants does the Fulbright Program award each year?* (TREC 16, Question 249.5).

Some information sources also provide metadata that can be mined by a QA system and utilized at various stages in the pipeline. For example, the anchor texts of internal links in Wikipedia and automatic redirects to articles can be used to expand query terms with related concepts and improve search recall [22, 23]. This information can also be utilized to merge and reinforce similar candidates during answer scoring [24].

Often sources are augmented with various types of syntactic and semantic annotations, such as parts of speech, named entity types, and relations between entities. If incorporated in the index, such annotations can improve search performance because they provide additional layers of information that can be used to formulate more constrained queries. Parts of speech and named entity information can be leveraged by the retrieval component to ensure that a query only matches instances of question terms that are of the correct syntactic or semantic type. For example, if the question is about the *city* Washington, then mentions of the *president* Washington are unlikely to be relevant and should not be retrieved. In addition, the search can be restricted to passages that contain an instance of the expected answer type. This approach can reduce noise in the search results, but relevant passages may be missed if the named entity recognizer has imperfect recall.

Syntactic and semantic relations can also be leveraged to formulate more precise queries. For instance, when answering the question *Which companies did Sun Microsystems acquire?*, a query can impose the syntactic constraint that *Sun Microsystems* is the subject of *acquire* and not the direct object to avoid retrieving passages that discuss the acquisition of Sun by Oracle. On a semantic level, the search can be constrained by requiring Sun to be the agent of an acquisition and not the patient. Prager et al. [25] and Moldovan et al. [26] incorporate named entity type information in the search index to increase the relevancy of their search results. Tiedemann [27] uses multiple layers of annotations for passage retrieval in Dutch. Sentences are processed with a syntactic dependency parser and augmented with word classes, syntactic relations, named entity labels, and compound terms. Queries that make use of these additional layers of information outperformed keyword queries on a set of CLEF questions. Bilotti et al. [28] preprocess a newswire corpus with a sentence segmenter, semantic parser, and named entity recognizer. The annotations are leveraged to formulate structured queries that place constraints on the semantic roles of query terms and their named entity types. In experiments with TREC data, the structured queries retrieved more relevant sentences at higher ranks compared to keyword queries. Examples of structured queries are given in Section 13.5.1 when we discuss the search component.

Apart from the potential impact on search performance, the preannotation of source corpora can reduce the computational costs at runtime considerably. In Section 13.5.2, we discuss structural matching approaches for candidate answer extraction that depend on syntactic or semantic parses of both the question and sentences in the corpus. These techniques benefit greatly from preprocessed sources and may otherwise only be feasible on massively parallel hardware or if the response time is of no importance. For instance, Cui et al. [29] preannotated their sources with named entity types and syntactic dependency parses to accelerate their candidate extraction algorithm at runtime. On the other hand, the annotation of large document collections is computationally expensive, and the integration of new sources can be time consuming and cumbersome. Furthermore, the annotations have to be updated and the search indices rebuilt each time changes are made to the annotation scheme or algorithms.

The processed documents can be indexed with IR systems such as Indri[5] and Lucene,[6] which are both publicly available as open source software. These systems were developed primarily for English but are also applicable to other languages because they support arbitrary sequences of space-delimited tokens, be they words, morphemes, or individual characters. Structured information such as relations between entities extracted during preprocessing is often stored in knowledge bases to support fast and precise answer lookups (see §13.5.3).

13.4 Question Analysis

In the question analysis phase, a variety of core technologies are applied to the question to extract information for use by downstream components. It is common to identify in the question string key terms and phrases that can be used by the search component to retrieve relevant documents or text passages from the sources. Function words that carry little or no semantic information (e.g., articles, pronouns, conjunctions, and auxiliary verbs) are usually discarded. Compound terms such as *pass away*, *computer science*, and *leave of absence* can be recognized via lookups in dictionaries and ontologies such as WordNet [30] or FrameNet [31, 32]. Most systems also apply a repository of named entity recognizers to identify instances of common types, such as person names, locations, and numbers.

In addition, questions are often analyzed and transformed into structural representations using syntactic and shallow semantic parsers. Structural information extracted from the question can be used in the search phase to formulate more precise queries and during candidate extraction to ensure that candidate answers have the correct relationships with regard to entities mentioned in the question. We describe the nature of these syntactic and semantic representations in more detail when discussing structural matching for candidate extraction in Section 13.5.2.

A key function that is performed by the question analysis phase of almost every factoid QA system is answer type classification, which predicts the expected type of the answer on the basis of a predefined set of types. For instance, the question *Who invented the light bulb?* seeks an answer that is a *person*, whereas the question *How many people live in Bangkok?* asks for a *number*. Answer type information can be utilized by the search component to constrain the search to text passages that contain instances of the predicted type, by the

5. http://www.lemurproject.org/indri/
6. http://lucene.apache.org/

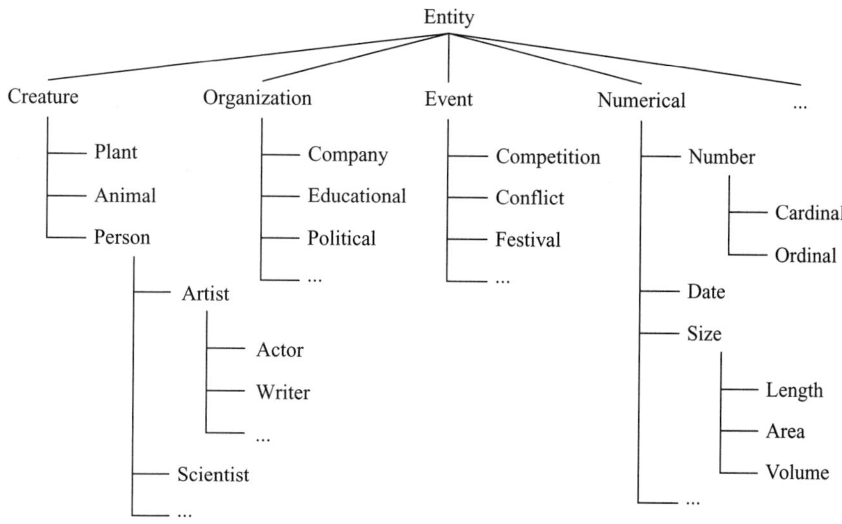

Figure 13–2: Sample answer type ontology

candidate extraction component to identify instances of that type as candidate answers, or during answer scoring to boost candidates that match the type.

Because some questions are more specific about the expected answer type than others (e.g., *In which city is the Colosseum?* as opposed to *Where is the Colosseum?*), the types are usually arranged in an ontology, allowing for classifications at different granularities. A sample type ontology is given in Figure 13–2. Ontologies are typically constructed manually by QA system developers and reflect their perception of the breadth and depth of the domain in which their system is expected to operate. For the open-domain TREC QA task, participants adopted ontologies of a few dozen or at the very most a few hundred types, which has been sufficient to cover most questions in those evaluations [33, 34].

The answer type classifier can be as simple as a set of regular expressions, where each expression is associated with a type in the ontology and matches questions seeking answers of that type. The patterns can be derived from questions in a development set by discarding irrelevant tokens and generalizing the remaining expression to match lexical and grammatical variations. Examples are given in Table 13–1. This approach is easy to implement and can be quite accurate if unseen questions do not deviate from the expected templates. For better generalization performance, however, it is common to devise more generic classification rules based on lexical and syntactic properties of the question or to fit a statistical model to a data set of manually labeled question/answer type pairs to predict the answer type on the basis of these features.

In both approaches, a strong indicator of the answer type is the question focus word (e.g., *country* in the question *Which country is the largest in population?* or *who* in *Who invented the light bulb?*). The focus can be identified fairly easily on the basis of the syntactic parse of the question and can then be mapped to one of the answer types in the static ontology by applying manual mapping rules, through learned correspondences in the training data,

Table 13–1: Sample patterns for answer type classification

Answer Type	Regular Expression
Company	(what|which) (company|corporation)
Date	(when|on which date)
Length	how (long|tall|deep)
Location	(where|which (place|spot|site))
Number	(how many|what (is|was) the number)
Writer	(what|which) (author|writer|novelist)

or by leveraging synonym and hypernym information provided by external resources such as WordNet [35, 36]. For instance, to ensure broad coverage of the answer type classifier, the question foci *company*, *corporation*, and *enterprise* could all be mapped to the answer type *company* in the sample ontology. Other useful features for predicting the answer type are the main verb and the grammatical relation of the focus to that verb. For instance, if the main verb is *eat* and the focus is the direct object, then the question likely asks for a type of *food*.

While QA strategies that are based on static type ontologies are fast, relatively easy to implement, and have been very effective in past QA evaluations, they also have severe limitations. Because a hard decision is usually made during answer type classification, the QA system often cannot recover when an error is made in determining the answer type. Furthermore, the coverage of a static type system is always limited and may be insufficiently specific. For example, while it is simple to recognize the focus *redhead* for *What redhead made Bobbie Gentry's 1970 song "Fancy" a hit again in the 90s?*, it is unlikely that a corresponding ontology entry and named entity recognizer exist. Instead, the system may have to resort to a more general type such as *person* or *singer*. Finally, even when an answer type is correctly identified, the impact on QA performance depends on the ability of downstream components to effectively utilize that information. Entity recognizers adopted by systems to preannotate sources, to generate candidates of the expected types, or to score candidates according to type match tend to be imperfect in terms of both precision and recall: they extract candidates of wrong types or miss instances of the predicted type. For instance, a named entity recognizer for the type *actor* may incorrectly label an instance of a person whose namesake is an actor, and it may fail to recognize actors if they are not famous.

In an interactive QA scenario, questions are not independent, but successive questions can be related and can refer to one another. This would most likely be the case in a dialog with a real user, and recent TREC evaluations attempted to model this behavior by grouping questions into series about common topics and including coreferences to preceding questions, answers, and the topic of a series. For instance, the question *In what city was the 1999 All-Star Game held?* was followed by *What is the name of the ballpark where the game was played?*, referring to part of the first question, and *What is the seating capacity of the ballpark?*, referring to the answer of the previous question (TREC 15, Target 161). To effectively address such dependencies, a QA system must resolve coreferences before extracting key terms and structural information from the question. Coreference (or anaphora) resolution in question series is a hard problem because little context is given, and most systems in

TREC resorted to heuristics to address common types of coreferences encountered in that task (e.g., Hickl et al. [20]).

Because the purpose of this component is to provide analysis results on the question for the consumption in downstream pipeline stages, the types of analyses performed here should depend on the accuracy of the analysis results as well as whether and how the downstream components may leverage them. To develop a baseline factoid QA system, it is common to employ a syntactic parser to help identify the focus of the question, hence the type of the answer sought, and a named entity recognizer to identify candidate answers of the predicted type. Most state-of-the-art QA systems, however, perform additional analyses such as coreference resolution, relation recognition, and semantic parsing. These components are readily available and reasonably accurate for English and a few other (mostly European) languages, but the same cannot be said for less commonly studied languages. Whether or not these technologies should be adopted, and to which degree other system components should depend on their results if they are used, can be determined empirically.

13.5 Search and Candidate Extraction

Modern QA systems usually search unstructured sources for relevant documents or passages and extract candidate answers using named entity recognizers for the expected answer type by aligning the structure of the question and retrieved text or by applying surface patterns that match relevant substrings. Additionally, answers to frequently occurring types of questions can be extracted from structured or semistructured resources that are readily available or have been generated in an offline preprocessing step, as discussed in Section 13.3. These two principal approaches to candidate extraction are described in this section. We discuss candidate **extraction** techniques as a special case of candidate **generation** because most research to date has focused on extracting substrings from textual sources rather than synthesizing new answers from information found in the sources.

13.5.1 Search over Unstructured Sources

Given the question analysis results, most QA systems generate one or more queries and retrieve relevant texts from an index of unstructured documents. These retrieved texts typically serve as the bases used by subsequent system components to identify candidate answers and evaluate them. The queries vary in complexity and can range from simple keyword queries to more complex queries with weights and proximity operators to structured queries that make use of syntactic and semantic annotations of the sources (see §13.3). Sample queries generated from the question *When did Apple buy Coral Software?* (answer: *1989*) for a Google web search and a local search using Indri are shown in Table 13–2.

Keyword queries are the most general and often result in the highest recall, whereas structured queries can encode more constraints and thus reduce the chance of false positives. However, the effectiveness of structured queries is contingent not only on the automatic generation of a correct query from the question but also on the precision and recall of annotations on the reference corpora. For example, the last structured query in Table 13–2 is of limited utility if the relation recognizer that operates on the corpus can only identify

Table 13–2: Queries for the question *When did Apple buy Coral Software?*

Query	Search	Description
Apple buy Coral Software	Google	Simple keyword query.
Apple buy "Coral Software"	Google	Requires an occurrence of the phrase *Coral Software.*
Apple buy OR purchase OR acquire "Coral Software"	Google	Disjunction of related terms.
Apple #weight(1 buy 0.5 purchase 0.3 acquire) #1(Coral Software)	Indri	Less weight on related terms. *#1(...)* in Indri is equivalent to quotations in Google.
#combine[org](Apple) #weight(1 buy 0.5 purchase 0.3 acquire) #combine[org](#1(Coral Software))	Indri	*Apple* and *Coral Software* must be annotated as organizations (*org*) in the sources.
#combine[sentence](#any:date Apple buy Coral Software)	Indri	Retrieves sentences only if they contain a preannotated date.
#combine[sentence](#max(#combine[target](buy #max(#combine[./arg0](Apple)) #max(#combine[./arg1](Coral)))))	Indri	Retrieves sentences containing a *buy* event with agent *Apple* and patient *Coral.*

the *buy* relationship from sentences such as *X bought Y*. On the other hand, if a high coverage relation recognizer was used that can identify the same relation from *X paid \$20M in stock options for Y*, then the structured query could potentially retrieve related texts missed by the less sophisticated queries. As a result, the effectiveness of semantically rich search queries highly depends on the accuracy of the components adopted to recognize those semantic attributes in the question and in the corpus.

Although there have been successful attempts at using structured queries in QA in Dutch and in English [27, 28], the performance gains have been modest. Chu-Carroll and Prager [37] showed that state-of-the-art named entity and relation recognition on English text had positive impact on search performance. However, since search performance is highly sensitive to the accuracy of these analysis components, careful empirical evaluations should be carried out when deciding whether or not to adopt this approach for other languages. Furthermore, structured queries require extensive preprocessing of the sources and are also more expensive at runtime. Therefore, keyword queries, sometimes combined with proximity operators and weights, are still most widely used.

Most QA systems retrieve documents or passages consisting of one or more sentences. A document search usually yields a much higher recall than a passage search with the same hit list length [38] because answers often do not occur in close proximity of question keywords. A common problem is anaphora referring to keywords in previous sentences or the title of the document. Anaphora are particularly frequent in Japanese and Chinese, which have a tendency toward short sentences and omit subjects and objects if they can be inferred from the context (known as zero-anaphora). On the other hand, passages can be processed more efficiently, which is a major concern if an expensive analysis of the search results is performed, such as semantic parsing. Shorter passages that are centered around question keywords also yield fewer irrelevant candidate answers, which impacts answer scoring efficiency and effectiveness.

Some systems implement a two-stage approach in which they retrieve documents and subsequently split them into passages and rank those passages. Different algorithms have been proposed for estimating the relevance of passages on the basis of their similarity to the question, often resembling well-known retrieval models used in IR. For instance, passages have been ranked by the sum of the inverse document frequency (IDF) scores of query terms they contain, the cosine similarity between query and passage term vectors, and Okapi BM25 weights. Tellex et al. [39] performed a quantitative comparison of various passage ranking algorithms.

Some QA systems also use automatic query expansion techniques to retrieve additional relevant results. Often, query terms are augmented with morphological variants [12], related concepts such as synonyms or hypernyms found in WordNet and other ontological resources [40, 41], or related terms extracted from semistructured sources such as Wikipedia anchor texts [22] and Wikipedia redirects [23]. However, due to the polysemous nature of most words, although the contexts in most questions provide sufficient information to disambiguate each term, correctly identifying the word sense and mapping it to the correct interpretation in an ontology to extract related terms is not a trivial task. For instance, the term *star* in *What movie star played the Joker in* The Dark Knight? could be expanded with *celebrity* and *actor*, and the same term in *What star on Orion's belt is most visible to the naked eye?* could be augmented with *celestial body*.

The need to perform query expansion can depend on the degree of redundancy of the reference corpora. When searching the web, which has a high degree of redundancy, one may choose to rely on the natural variation in language present in the corpus in lieu of performing query expansion. On the other hand, in applications where there is little redundancy in the sources, such as QA on an intranet, query expansion may be necessary to achieve reasonable recall. In general, query expansion can improve the average performance of a QA system and has been widely used in evaluations. However, some systems expand a query only if it yields low recall to reduce the risk of corrupting queries by adding irrelevant terms [12, 41].

An alternative to automatic query expansion is pseudo-relevance feedback (PRF), where an initial query is issued to retrieve related text passages from the sources and is then augmented with terms extracted from the search results. Some systems perform a web search and extract terms from the summary snippets produced by the search engine [42, 23]. However, there is no general agreement on whether PRF is helpful for the QA task, and a few groups reported that it actually hurt system performance [43].

13.5.2 Candidate Extraction from Unstructured Sources

Depending on the type of queries, the search results can be documents, passages, or even individual named entities. Different techniques have been proposed for extracting factoid answers from high-level search results. Often, systems use an ensemble of algorithms that address different types of questions and compensate for each other's weaknesses.

Type-Based Candidate Extraction

Perhaps the most common and one of the most effective candidate generation strategies to date utilizes the answer type information extracted during the question analysis phase (see §13.4). The answer type is determined on the basis of a predefined, static type ontology, and named entity recognizers that can identify instances of the predicted answer type are used to extract candidate answers of that type from the sources (e.g., Moldovan et al. [26], Prager et al. [25]). If the instances of a type can be listed exhaustively, such as *U.S. presidents* and *weekday names*, an in-memory dictionary is the most efficient way of recognizing candidates. This approach typically has high recall, but it may suffer from low precision due to the lack of disambiguation in list lookups. Regular expressions are suitable for numeric types, such as numbers or dates. More ambiguous types such as person names, organizations, and locations (e.g., *Washington* is the name of a person, a city, and a state) require more complex heuristics or statistical models that take the context of an occurrence into account.

Candidate Extraction Using Structural Matching

Although candidate extraction based on answer type information has been shown to be effective for the vast majority of factoid questions, the approach does presuppose that an answer type is expressed in the question and that users can reasonably expect an entity recognizer to identify instances of that type. Consider the sample questions *What is Indianapolis known for?* and *What word was coined by Karel Capek for a mechanical man in his play* R.U.R?, whose foci are *what* and *word*, respectively. The first question has no answer type, and the second question has an answer type so general that it is practically useless.

Furthermore, answer type classification is a recall-oriented approach that extracts candidate answers solely based on type information without verifying whether they satisfy the semantic relations in the question. Consequently, an incorrect answer may be selected if it frequently co-occurs with question terms. For instance, a keyword query formed from the question *Who killed Lee Harvey Oswald?* (TREC 8, Question 110) retrieves phrases such as *Lee Harvey Oswald killed John F. Kennedy*, and thus the person name *John F. Kennedy* would likely be extracted as a candidate answer. In addition, candidate sentences often contain multiple instances of the expected answer type, and a purely type-based extraction strategy is incapable of distinguishing between them. Light et al. [44] analyzed a sample of TREC questions and estimated a performance bound of 70% accuracy for type-based candidate extraction if the system does not employ additional techniques to distinguish between multiple entities of the expected type in the same sentence. This upper bound can be reached only under the assumptions of perfect question classification, search, and named entity recognition. The candidate extraction strategies discussed in this section can remedy these deficiencies of type-based extraction and complement it in other cases.

Structural matching approaches parse the question and sentences from the sources and attempt to align their syntactic or semantic structures. These techniques can increase precision by ensuring that candidate answers have the correct relationships with respect to entities in the question. QA developers can often resort to publicly available parsers for extracting the required syntactic or semantic information, though the availability and performance of such tools varies among languages. One possible choice for structural matching is syntactic dependency relations extracted by a dependency parser [41, 45, 29]. Figure 13–3 shows

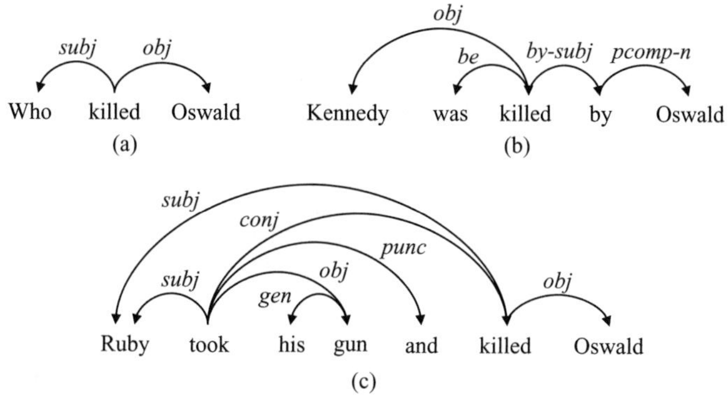

Figure 13–3: Dependency parse trees for a question (a), and two candidate sentences (b, c)

dependency parse trees for the question *Who killed Oswald?* and the candidate sentences *Kennedy was killed by Oswald* and *Ruby took his gun and killed Oswald.* The parse trees were produced by Minipar [46], one among several publicly available dependency parsers for English. Note that a type-based approach would extract person names from both sentences as candidate answers, and *Kennedy* would be selected as the most probable answer if candidates were scored on the basis of their proximity to question keywords. Leveraging structural information, we can extract dependency paths from the parses that link nodes through a sequence of dependency relations. In the example, we can derive (among others) the path *Who* SUBJ OBJ *Oswald* from question (a) and the paths *Kennedy* OBJ *by*-SUBJ PCOMP-N *Oswald* and *Ruby* SUBJ OBJ *Oswald* from sentences (b) and (c) respectively. The dependency path in the question matches the one extract from sentence (c) but not (b), and thus *Ruby* can be identified as a candidate answer instead of *Kennedy*.

A general weakness of this approach are mismatches caused by syntactic variations in questions and candidate sentences. Attardi et al. [41] address this issue by applying simple heuristics to infer additional dependency paths from existing ones and increase the chances of finding a match. For instance, dependency paths can be simplified by removing stop-words and directly linking nodes that were connected through them. In sentence (b), the stopword *by* can be dropped and the path *killed by*-SUBJ PCOMP-N *Oswald* simplified into *killed* SUBJ *Oswald.* Cui et al. [29] use statistical methods to learn similarities between dependency relations from training data and perform approximate matching of dependency paths.

Alternatively, structural matching can be based on shallow semantic information, such as predicate-argument structures [42, 36] and semantic frames [47]. Here we illustrate the use of predicate-argument structures, which capture events and entities that participate in those events. The events are verbs and the participants are subjects, objects, and oblique arguments of the verbs. Each participant is assigned a label that specifies its semantic role in the event, such as *agent* (often labeled as ARG-0), *patient* (often ARG-1), *location* (ARGM-LOC), or *time* (ARGM-TMP). The PropBank corpus [48] has been annotated manually with predicate-argument structures and can be used to train a semantic role labeling (SRL) system that performs the task automatically. A commonly used SRL system is the publicly available parser ASSERT (for Automatic Statistical SEmantic Role Tagger) [49]. The parser is applied to both the question and candidate sentences, and the semantic structures are

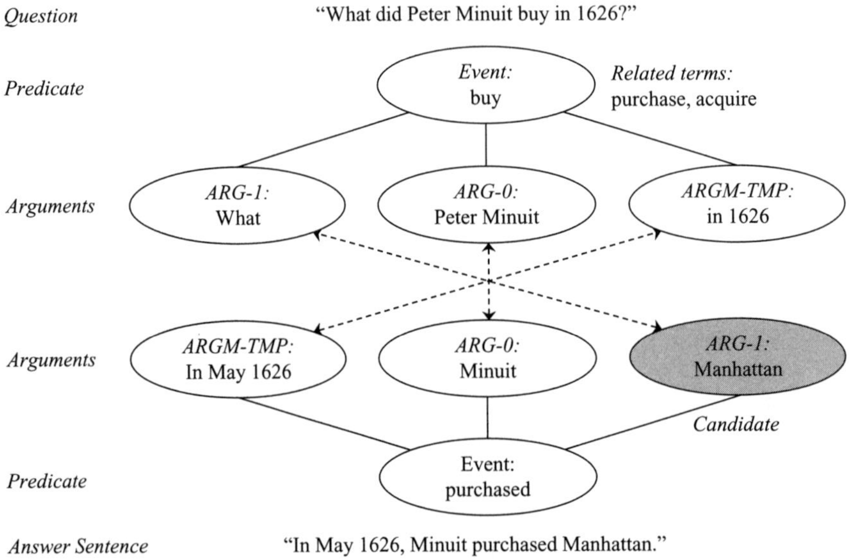

Figure 13–4: Semantic role labeling and matching example

matched. Question terms can be augmented with related concepts to facilitate their alignment with terms in the search results, using the techniques we introduced in Section 13.5.1. Arguments in the parses of candidate sentences that contain the information that is missing in the question can be extracted as candidate answers.

The example in Figure 13–4 illustrates how structural matching based on predicate-argument structures can be applied to answer the question *What did Peter Minuit buy in 1626?* Note that this question does not have an explicit answer type, and therefore type-based candidate extraction is not effective here. The example also shows that this approach preserves relations between entities specified in the question (i.e., *Peter Minuit* must be the agent and *Manhattan* the patient of a *buy* event) and is therefore also applicable to the *Kennedy–Oswald* example.

Compared to type-based extraction strategies, structural matching can be computationally intensive and has a lower recall because it imposes additional constraints and heavily relies on the correctness of the components that extract the meta-information [37]. Semantic parsing, in particular, tends to be slow and error-prone. Often, structural approaches are complemented with answer type analysis to improve their efficiency and increase precision. For instance, Attardi et al. [41] filter out candidate sentences that do not contain an entity of the expected type before they undergo an expensive analysis, and Schlaefer et al. [36] require arguments extracted from semantic parses as candidate answers to match the answer type if one has been predicted.

Surface Patterns for Candidate Extraction

Candidate answers can also be extracted with surface patterns that are solely based on the lexical representation of the search results and do not require a syntactic or semantic analysis. The patterns can take the form of regular expression templates that are instantiated with question terms and match text passages that contain the answer. For instance, the template

< ORG > *was (founded|established) in(the year)?* <ANSWER>.

may be used to extract candidate answers for a question about the *founding date* of a given organization. Questions are categorized by a classification component, and appropriate surface patterns are selected on the basis of the assigned category. The categories are not necessarily identical to answer types but can be of a coarser or finer granularity. For instance, different surface patterns are required for extracting the *date of birth* and the *date of death* from the passage *Johann Sebastian Bach (31 March 1685–28 July 1750) was a German composer*, but a type-based answer extractor could use a single *date* recognizer to extract both dates as candidate answers. The surface patterns can be handcrafted or automatically learned using question–answer pairs as training data [50, 51]. More general patterns that match a wider range of similar formulations can be constructed automatically from specific patterns. For example, common words can be replaced with canonical forms, parts of speech, or even wildcards, and named entity types can be substituted for concrete instances of the types [52].

Similarly to structural matching, surface patterns do not depend on answer type information and are suitable for questions without an explicit useful type, such as *What is Enrico Fermi most known for?* (TREC 14, Question 87.5). Surface patterns can also ensure that semantic relations in questions are preserved. On the other hand, the approach is only applicable to questions that fall into a finite set of predefined categories. For instance, it is feasible to devise categories and surface patterns for common attributes of entities that may be the subject of questions, such as the *nationality* or *profession* of a person, or the *leader* or *size* of an organization. However, the question *What is the legal blood alcohol limit for the state of California?* (TREC 8, Question 41) would require a category *legal blood alcohol limit*, which is too specific to warrant its own set of patterns. In addition, depending on the generality of the patterns, this approach often suffers from either low recall or low precision. Specific patterns can miss instances of correct answers if they occur in previously unseen surface forms, whereas overly general patterns extract incorrect candidates and introduce noise.

Of the candidate extraction approaches discussed here, the most commonly adopted approach is type-based candidate generation, which relies on good named entity recognition against an ontology relevant to the application domain for the language the corpus is in. The structural approach to candidate extraction relies on more sophisticated NLP technologies that are unlikely to exist for languages in which good named entity recognition is not available. The surface pattern approach, on the other hand, can be retrained given sufficient question–answer pairs in the target language for select question categories. The approach is typically employed to augment type-based candidate extraction in English QA and may be leveraged to play an even more important role for QA in languages where the type-based approach is less effective.

13.5.3 Candidate Extraction from Structured Sources

In addition to searches over unstructured corpora, QA systems can perform answer lookups in structured and semistructured sources. Structured data is often represented in relational databases or Resource Description Framework (RDF) stores that have been populated with entities and their properties. For instance, one database table may contain famous actors along with their birth dates, nationalities, movies they have featured in, and awards they have received. The structured sources are typically populated offline, either by importing publicly available resources such as DBpedia[7] and Freebase,[8] by applying automatic relation extraction techniques to unstructured resources [53, 16], or by manually curating data relevant to the application domain.

Examples of semistructured sources are websites that combine structured elements with unstructured text. For instance, a gazetteer may provide common statistics about countries, such as their sizes, populations, and official languages, along with narratives about their political systems and economies. While the common statistics can be represented in a structured format that is identical for all countries, the narratives take the form of unstructured plain text. Similarly, Wikipedia pages often combine unstructured text with tables that summarize important facts in a format that aims to be consistent across pages about entities belonging to the same category, such as presidents or companies. Semistructured resources can either be mined offline and transformed into structured data or accessed at runtime through wrappers that extract only the required and most up-to-date information.

Compared to candidate extraction approaches for unstructured sources, answer lookups in structured and semistructured sources typically have higher precision but much lower recall because the effectiveness is constrained by the system's ability to automatically identify the supported relations in the questions and correctly map the relations sought to the relations represented in the sources. Furthermore, the manual effort involved in constructing and maintaining these sources can be considerable. In practice, it is common to integrate structured and unstructured sources to combine the relative merits of the two approaches [54].

13.6 Answer Scoring

This section gives an overview of common or interesting approaches for answer scoring and validation (§13.6.1). We further discuss how multiple sources of evidence can be integrated and similar candidate answers merged or reinforced (§13.6.2), and we outline how the techniques and algorithms described in this chapter can be extended to answer questions seeking lists of factoid answers (§13.6.3).

13.6.1 Overview of Approaches

If the knowledge sources are semantically redundant, containing numerous instances of the correct answer, a simple frequency-based answer scoring approach can be effective for identifying the answer among other entities of the expected type. For example, Clarke, Cormack, and Lynam [55] extract all instances of the predicted answer type (e.g., *length*) from the search results and rank them using a weighting scheme that is similar to term frequency-inverse document frequency (TF-IDF) scoring in information retrieval. The algorithm boosts

7. http://dbpedia.org/
8. http://www.freebase.com/

candidates that frequently occur in the search results but penalizes answers that are overall frequent in the knowledge sources. The underlying assumption is that the correct answer is also most common in the retrieved text, which is often the case when retrieving short passages centered around question keywords from large, redundant sources such as the web. The approach is easy to implement and can be a good starting point when developing a factoid QA system for any language. However, it often fails if the sources contain few relevant passages or if an incorrect answer frequently co-occurs with question terms, such as in the *Kennedy–Oswald* example discussed in Section 13.5.2.

Type-based candidate extraction can be combined with measures of the word-level similarity between questions and candidate passages to produce more accurate confidence scores. For instance, the number of question keywords (optionally weighted with IDF scores) that occur in a passage and the proximity of those keywords in the passage can be predictive of its relevance [56, 57]. The answer extraction algorithms based on structural matching and surface patterns discussed in Section 13.5.2 can also produce confidence scores for candidate answers. When performing approximate matching of syntactic dependency paths, the similarities between the paths in the question and candidate sentences can be used as confidence estimates [29]. Similarly, structural matching based on shallow semantic information can yield confidence scores that reflect the closeness of a match [42]. When using surface patterns for candidate extraction, the precision of each pattern can be estimated offline on test data and assigned as a confidence estimate to candidates extracted with the pattern [50].

To demonstrate the impact of deeper reasoning methods on question answering, Moldovan and Rus [58] and Moldovan et al. [59] adopted an approach whereby questions and potential answer-bearing passages are transformed into logical representations based on their syntactic parses, and a logic prover, COGEX, is leveraged to unify the two logical representations in the answer scoring phase of their QA system. If unification succeeds, the entity in the passage that unifies with the *wh*-slot in the question is deemed the answer to the question. The utility of this approach over shallower methods is most obvious when vocabulary and structure of the answer-bearing passage do not directly mirror those of the question. For example, consider the question *Which company created the Internet browser Mosaic?* and the passage *A program called Mosaic, developed by the National Center for Supercomputing Applications, has been gaining popularity lately.*[9] In order to unify the logical representations of these two texts, COGEX must be able to unify *create* with *develop* and *Internet browser Mosaic* with *Mosaic* and to recognize that *National Center for Supercomputing Applications* is an organization and unify an instance of *organization* with *company*. COGEX performs this unification with the aid of a large body of world knowledge axioms automatically derived from eXtended WordNet (XWN) glosses [60], which allows it to consider *create* and *develop* equivalent, and a set of manually encoded NLP axioms, from which an axiom that equates the head noun of a complex nominal with the nominal itself, links *Internet browser Mosaic* and *Mosaic*.

More recently, textual entailment techniques have been developed under the PASCAL RTE challenge [1], which required systems to determine whether one sentence *entails* another rather than being equivalent. For instance, the sentence *Judge Drew served as Justice until Kennon returned to claim his seat in 1945* entails the hypothesis *Kennon served as Justice*,

9. Adapted from Moldovan et al. [59].

but not vice versa (RTE-3, Pair 12). Harabagiu and Hickl [61] incorporated textual entailment into their QA system for answer scoring and demonstrated significant performance improvements.

Magnini et al. [62] introduced a web reinforcement algorithm that exploits the redundancy of the web to estimate confidence scores for candidate answers. For each candidate, it constructs a query consisting of question keywords and the candidate, submits it to a web search engine, and retrieves summary snippets. The candidate is then assigned a score that reflects its proximity to the question keywords in the snippets. The rationale behind this approach is that a candidate that is closely related to question keywords is likely to occur in close proximity of the keywords on the web. Some systems also use external semantic resources to verify answers. WordNet and structured information from Wikipedia can be leveraged to verify that a candidate is of the correct type [59, 63]. For example, both the hypernym relation in WordNet and Wikipedia article categories confirm that *Richard Feynman* is a *physicist* and therefore a plausible answer to the question *Which physicist developed the theory of quantum electrodynamics?* Gazetteers provide information that can be leveraged to validate answers to geographical questions [24]. For instance, the *CIA World Factbook*[10] confirms that *Brazil* is a *country in South America* and thus could be the answer to the question *Which country in South America has the largest area?*

An interesting approach for answer validation that uses question inversion is proposed by Prager, Duboue, and Chu-Carroll [64]. As an example, given the question *What was the capital of Germany in 1985?* and the candidate answer *Bonn*, their approach formulates the inverted question *Of what country was Bonn the capital in 1985?* and reruns the QA pipeline. If *Germany* is among the candidate answers for the inverted question, then the QA system increases its confidence in the candidate *Bonn* for the original question. The question inversion approach improved performance on TREC questions but it is computationally expensive.

13.6.2 Combining Evidence

Statistical techniques are often used to combine multiple sources of evidence for answer scoring [56, 57, 24]. Each form of evidence is represented as a numeric or categorical feature, and a statistical model estimates the probability of a candidate being correct given these features. The probability estimates can be used to rank the answers and to decide whether or not the top answer should be presented to the user. In addition to the previously described approaches, it is common to integrate features that are less predictive on their own but are nevertheless indicative of answer correctness, such as the rank and score assigned by the IR engine to the search result from which a candidate was extracted, and whether a candidate matches the expected answer type. Statistical models are also useful for integrating candidates from multiple answer generation algorithms with otherwise incomparable confidence scores. Common choices of statistical techniques include logistic regression [65] and maximum entropy models [66].

The final list of candidate answers produced by a QA system often contains similar and even equivalent entities because the search results can be redundant, and the same concept may be expressed in different ways depending on the source and context. Equivalent answers

10. https://www.cia.gov/library/publications/the-world-factbook/

can be lexical and semantic variations, such as abbreviations (e.g., *VW* versus *Volkswagen*), different spellings (*Al-Qaeda* versus *Al-Qaida*), synonyms (*China* versus *Middle Kingdom*), and measurements with different units ($100°C$ versus $212°F$). In addition, candidates can be similar to varying degrees. For instance, one candidate can be more specific than another (*Rome, Italy* versus *Italy*; *George W. Bush* versus *Bush*), or candidates can differ numerically (*12,049 m* versus *12,053 m*). Related candidate answers provide additional evidence for the correctness of a given candidate and should therefore be taken into account during answer scoring.

Prager, Luger, and Chu-Carroll [67] proposed a rule-based approach for identifying related candidate answers based on answer type information. For instance, different sets of rules were devised for various types of places, organizations, and numeric entities, covering most of the earlier examples. Heuristics are used to boost the score of a candidate answer based on the scores of related candidates, taking the degree of their similarity into account. This approach is prudent if a relatively small set of frequent answer types can be identified a priori, and it has been effective for questions from TREC evaluations. Whereas Prager et al. increase the scores of related candidates in a separate postprocessing step, Ko, Si, and Nyberg [24] proposed an integrated approach for reinforcing similar candidates as part of the answer scoring process. A unified probabilistic framework integrates features that estimate the correctness of candidate answers and features that measure similarities between candidates. String distance metrics such as the Levenshtein distance and the cosine similarity are used to measure the lexical similarity of candidates, whereas a database of synonyms compiled from resources such as WordNet and Wikipedia as well as handwritten rules are used to recognize semantically similar answers.

A challenge that has yet to be addressed is answer merging across different languages. This scenario is likely to occur in crosslingual QA (§13.7), where answers extracted from sources in multiple languages may be aggregated and their supporting evidence combined. Crosslingual answer merging is under consideration for future NII Test Collection for IR Systems (NTCIR) evaluations.

When answering a factoid question, QA systems typically return the highest scoring answer or no answer if the top score falls below a predetermined threshold. Returning no answer is a valid option if the question is ill-posed (e.g., *Who is the prime minister of the United States?*) or if the answer is not covered by the sources. Even if the answer could be found by a perfect QA system, it is still preferable to inform the user that the system failed instead of returning an incorrect and possibly misleading answer.

13.6.3 Extension to List Questions

The techniques discussed in this chapter are illustrated by examples of factoid questions, but are equally applicable to questions seeking lists of factoid answers (e.g., *What books did George Orwell write?*). When answering list questions, it is common to return the top n answers, where n can be given in the question (e.g., *Who were the last ten presidents of the United States?*), or n can be determined dynamically by the estimated confidence scores. For instance, a system may select the top answers up to a given confidence threshold or until a significant drop in answer confidence is observed. Effective merging of similar candidates is particularly important for list questions to avoid returning multiple instances of the same answer (e.g., *Bill Clinton* and *William Jefferson Clinton*).

13.7 Crosslingual Question Answering

In crosslingual QA, the languages in which questions are posed differ from the languages of the knowledge sources. When extending a monolingual system to crosslingual tasks, the developer can either translate the source documents to the languages of the questions, or translate the questions or extracted keywords to the languages of the documents. The debate on which approach is more effective originated in the IR community and has been fueled by the difficulty of obtaining conclusive evidence. Because a different machine translation (MT) system is needed for each translation direction, the performance difference in a comparison of the two approaches could be attributed either to the choice of approach or to the MT systems. McCarley [68] attempted to resolve this issue by performing a comparison of query translation and document translation on crosslingual IR datasets from TREC evaluations. The two translation approaches were compared on both English–French and French–English data sets using MT models trained on the same data. No approach consistently outperformed the other, but a hybrid system that performed both query translation and document translation was more effective than either approach on its own. Surprisingly, it even outperformed human-generated query translations, which suggests that a hybrid approach is the ideal choice if the computational costs are manageable.

In QA, both translation directions have been implemented successfully. A common argument for the source translation approach is its robustness to MT errors. If important question keywords are translated incorrectly, it is unlikely that the correct answer can be found and selected. The sources, on the other hand, often contain multiple relevant passages, and it can be sufficient if one passage is translated correctly. In addition, the translation of sources can be performed during an offline preprocessing step, with no additional costs at runtime and without requiring modifications to the QA pipeline. On the other hand, the offline translation can be computationally expensive if the sources are large or questions in multiple languages are to be supported. As a consequence, researchers may have to resort to more efficient but less accurate MT algorithms. Furthermore, source translation is viable only if the sources can be stored and indexed locally and thus is not applicable to web search. In addition, similarly to other source preprocessing steps discussed in Section 13.3, the translations of the sources need to be updated after making improvements to the MT system.

Bowden et al. [69] performed source translation in the CLEF 2007 English–French and English–Portuguese QA tasks, which included factoid, list, and definition questions. The sources were translated to English offline, and a monolingual QA system extracted answers from the translations. The final answers were mapped back to corresponding text snippets in the original French or Portuguese sources. Thus the QA system could be used without adaptation to the new languages, though some semantic and syntactic constraints in the answer processing component had to be relaxed to compensate for inaccurate translations.

While translating the entire sources is feasible for some QA tasks, it is more common to translate the question, or keywords and phrases extracted from the question, during question analysis and perform subsequent pipeline steps on the original sources. When translating the whole question, it is possible to disambiguate word senses based on context. In addition, the syntactic structure of the question is mapped to the language of the sources and can be used to select syntactically similar sentences in the source corpora for candidate extraction. On the other hand, if the question is complex, it can be difficult to find an accurate and grammatical translation, in which case the translation of individual keywords may be more effective. It may also be preferable to analyze the question in its original language and translate keywords only if more reliable NLP tools are available for that language. Multiple translation systems can be combined in a voting scheme to improve translation accuracy [17]. Useful resources are online tools such as Google Translate[11] and Babel Fish[12] for question translation and Wikipedia links to articles in other languages and Wiktionary[13] for keyword translation.

An additional challenge arises from the translation of proper names in crosslingual QA between European and Asian languages, regardless of the translation approach. For instance, an English person name may have an entirely different Japanese translation, but it can also be transcribed in the katakana writing system or may even be written in Roman characters within a Japanese text. Furthermore, if the name is transcribed in katakana, there is often not a single established spelling, but different authors may use different characters. Such ambiguities can be addressed by considering multiple translations when retrieving and matching relevant text or by replacing proper names in the sources that refer to the same entities with canonical forms during the preprocessing phase (§13.3). The latter approach avoids computational overhead at runtime but requires resources for recognizing expressions that refer to the same entity and mapping them to a unique representation.

13.8 A Case Study

In this section we present a case study that further illustrates concepts and techniques introduced earlier in the chapter. The question *The 2008 Summer Olympics took place in which city?* (answer: *Beijing*) serves as a running example. We show how this question is processed in each stage of the typical QA pipeline introduced in Figure 13–1: question analysis, query generation, search, candidate generation, and answer scoring. We apply some of the most common and effective QA algorithms, but note that this is by no means a complete overview of what has been implemented or what is feasible in QA.

The question analysis component of a typical QA system is outlined in Algorithm 13–1. Given the question string, our sample system extracts the named entities (NEs) *2008* and *Summer Olympics*. This can be accomplished using regular expressions that match instances of the type *year* and a list of common *events* or *sports competitions*. Additional key terms that will later be used as query terms are looked up in dictionaries. For example, the ontology WordNet[14] recognizes *take place* as a compound verb. A list of function words is used to rule out words that are not useful as query terms, leaving the key terms *2008*, *Summer Olympics*, *took place*, and *city*.

11. http://translate.google.com/
12. http://babelfish.yahoo.com/
13. http://www.wiktionary.org/
14. http://wordnet.princeton.edu/

Algorithm 13–1 Question analysis component in a typical QA pipeline

AnalyzeQuestion(String *question*)

  $aq.question \leftarrow question$

  // extract key terms for query generation
  $aq.nes \leftarrow$ extractNamedEntities($question$)
  $aq.keyTerms \leftarrow$ extractKeyTerms($question$, $aq.nes$)

  // extract syntactic dependency relations
  $aq.depParse \leftarrow$ parseSyntacticDependencies($question$)

  // predict answer type for type-based candidate extraction
  $aq.focus \leftarrow$ extractQuestionFocus($aq.depParse$)
  $aq.answerType \leftarrow$ predictAnswerType($aq.depParse$, $aq.focus$)

  return aq

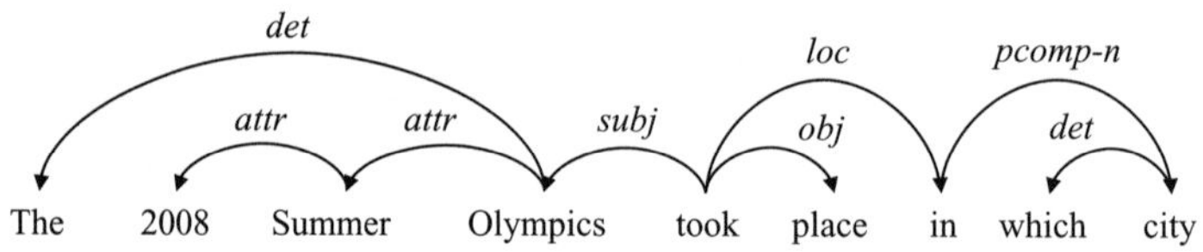

Figure 13–5: Dependency parse tree for the sample question

Figure 13–5 shows a dependency parse tree for the sample question. Dependency parses can be generated with publicly available tools such as Minipar[15] or the Stanford Parser.[16] The key term *city* has the question word *which* as its determiner and thus can easily be identified as the question focus. Our sample system does not have a named entity recognizer for city names, making *city* unsuitable as an answer type. However, in WordNet *city* has the hypernym *location*, and location names can be extracted with various open source toolkits such as OpenNLP.[17] Thus we map the question focus *city* to the more general answer type *location*.

The query generation component, shown in Algorithm 13–2, constructs queries from the key terms extracted in the previous step. We assume that the Indri information retrieval system[18] will be used in the search phase, and thus the queries must conform to the Indri query language. Our QA system also expands question key terms with related terms found in external structured resources. For the sample question, structured information extracted from Wikipedia sidebars can be leveraged to recognize *Olympic Games* as a hypernym of *Summer Olympics* (referring to the winter games or the summer games). Furthermore,

15. http://webdocs.cs.ualberta.ca/~lindek/minipar.htm
16. http://nlp.stanford.edu/software/lex-parser.shtml
17. http://opennlp.sourceforge.net/
18. http://www.lemurproject.org/indri/

Algorithm 13–2 Query generation component in a typical QA pipeline

GenerateQueries(AnalyzedQuestion *aq*)

   queries ← ∅

   // look up related terms in Wikipedia, WordNet etc.
   relatedTerms = getRelatedTerms(*aq.keyTerms*)

   // generate queries from key terms and related terms
   queries ← *queries* ∪ keyTermQuery(*aq.keyTerms*)
   queries ← *queries* ∪ expandedQuery(*aq.keyTerms*, *relatedTerms*)

   return *queries*

WordNet provides the synonym *happen* for the key term *take place*. Given the key terms and related terms, the following queries can be constructed:

1. `#combine[p](2008 #1(Summer Olympics) #1(took place) city)`

2. ```
   #combine[p](2008
           #weight(1 #1(Summer Olympics) 0.3 #1(Olympic Games))
           #weight(1 #1(took place) 0.5 happened)
           city)
   ```

The Indri query operator `#combine[p](...)` is used to retrieve passages that have been preannotated in the sources. Passages can be annotated automatically on the basis of punctuation and existing markup. Terms enclosed in `#1(...)` must occur in the sources as consecutive tokens, similarly to quotations in a web search. The second query includes related terms but gives lower weight to the synonym (0.5) and the hypernym (0.3). The weights were chosen for illustrative purposes but should ideally be tuned to optimize search performance on a set of development questions.

The search component, illustrated in Algorithm 13–3, uses the queries to retrieve text from a collection of Indri indices built from local sources, such as a newswire corpus and a copy of Wikipedia. Each query is issued against each source separately, and the search results are merged. Typical QA systems retrieve on the order of 10 to 100 passages, but for simplicity, we assume that only the following three passages were found for the sample question:

1. The 2008 Summer Olympics took place in Beijing, China, from August 8 to August 24, 2008.

2. The Summer Olympics were held in Peking in 2008, in Athens in 2004, and in Sydney in 2000.

3. When I visited Beijing during my trip to China in 2008, the airport was crowded because of visitors who came to watch the Olympics.

In the candidate generation phase (Algorithm 13–4), two complementary answer extraction strategies are applied to the retrieved passages. A recall-oriented candidate generator
   ```

Algorithm 13–3 Search component in a typical QA pipeline

```
Search(String[] queries, String[] indexPaths)
    passages ← ∅

    foreach query (queries)
        foreach indexPath (indexPaths)
            passages ← passages ∪ retrievePassages(query, indexPath)

    return passages
```

Algorithm 13–4 Candidate generation component in a typical QA pipeline

```
GenerateCandidates(String[] passages, AnalyzedQuestion aq)
    answers ← ∅

    foreach passage (passages)
        // answer type matching
        answers ← answers ∪ extractAnswerType(passage)
        // syntactic dependency path matching
        answers ← answers ∪ extractDepPath(aq.depParse, passage)

    return answers
```

extracts instances of the type *location* from all passages, returning the candidates "Beijing, China," "Peking," "Athens," "Sydney," "Beijing," and "China." A second, more precise candidate extractor performs syntactic dependency parsing on the passages, matches the dependency path `Olympics subj loc pcomp-n city` in the question parse (Figure 13–5) with the similar path `Olympics subj loc pcomp-n Beijing` in the first passage, and extracts "Beijing, China" as its only candidate.

The answer scoring component (Algorithm 13–5) computes features for candidate answers that are predictive of their correctness and estimates confidence scores from the feature values. State-of-the-art systems often combine tens or even hundreds of features, but here we focus on three features that leverage different forms of evidence:

1. The frequency of a candidate answer in the retrieved passages.
2. The text similarity between the question and the passage a candidate was extracted from. We simply estimate the similarity as the fraction of question keywords (i.e., *2008*, *Summer*, *Olympics*, *took*, *place*, and *city*) that occur in the passage.
3. A binary feature indicating whether a candidate answer is entailed by one of the passages. Here we assume that an algorithm for recognizing textual entailment (RTE) is available that predicts that the candidates *Beijing, China, Peking, Beijing and China*, and only those candidates, are entailed as correct answers.

The third passage again illustrates the difficulties involved in RTE. To a human it is quite obvious from reading the passage that *Beijing* is a correct answer. However, a system would

Algorithm 13–5 Answer scoring component in a typical QA pipeline

```
ScoreAnswers(String[] answers, String[] passages, AnalyzedQuestion aq)
    scoredAnswers ← ∅

    foreach answer (answers)
        // feature 1: frequency of answer in retrieved passages
        freq ← countAnswerFrequency(answer, passages)
        // feature 2: text similarity between passage and question
        textSim ← calculateTextSimilarity(answer, passages, aq.question)
        // feature 3: whether one of the passages entails the answer
        entailed ← recognizeEntailment(answer, passages, aq.question)

        // estimate confidence score from feature values
        score ← estimateScore(freq, textSim, entailed)
        scoredAnswers ← scoredAnswers ∪ (answer, score)

    // reinforce similar answers by boosting confidence scores
    scoredAnswers ← reinforceSimilarAnswers(scoredAnswers)

    return scoredAnswers
```

Table 13–3: Features and confidence scores of candidate answers for the question *The 2008 Summer Olympics took place in which city?*

Candidate	Frequency	Text Similarity	Entailed	Score
Beijing, China	1	0.83	1	0.94
Peking	1	0.5	1	0.83
Athens	1	0.5	0	0.50
Sydney	1	0.5	0	0.50
Beijing	2	0.33	1	1.11
China	2	0.33	1	1.11

need to reason that *Olympics* must refer to the Summer Olympics and not the Winter Olympics because at most one of these competitions is held in any given year. Furthermore, it would have to conclude that because visitors came to watch the games, the competition was likely held in Beijing. Fortunately, such sophisticated processing is often not necessary in practice because of semantic redundancy in the sources. In this example, the correct answer can be extracted more easily from the first or second passage.

The evidence represented by the preceding features is combined into a confidence score for each candidate. The feature values and overall confidence scores are given in Table 13–3. Here we simply give equal weight to each feature and use the average feature value as the score. In practice, however, it is more effective to fit a model to a data set of candidate answers that were judged manually, using logistic regression or other statistical techniques. The model can be estimated with a machine learning toolkit such as Weka[19] or MinorThird.[20]

In the example, "Beijing" and "China" are tied for the first rank. However, an answer reinforcement algorithm recognizes that "Beijing, China" is more specific than these candidates by performing string matching, and in WordNet "Peking" is listed as a synonym for "Beijing." The QA system increases its confidence in these similar candidates and returns "Beijing, China" as the top answer because it is most specific. If the score of the top candidate was below a predefined threshold (say, 0.8), the QA system would instead indicate that it could not find the answer.

13.9 Evaluation

Question answering research over the past decade was driven by organized evaluation efforts that created a significant amount of community resources for further development: the Text REtrieval Conference (TREC) and later the Text Analysis Conference (TAC) for English QA, the Cross-Language Evaluation Forum (CLEF) for English and other European languages, and the NTCIR (NII Test Collection for IR Systems) workshop for Asian languages. In the following, we describe each of these evaluation tasks and discuss evaluation methodologies and common performance metrics.

13.9.1 Evaluation Tasks

The TREC conducted annual evaluations of English QA systems in the years 1999 through 2007 (TREC 8–16) [8]. This evaluation forum has been one of the major drivers of research in English QA, and the question sets and answer keys produced in the evaluations have become standard test collections. Initially, TREC focused on factoid questions, but in later years list, definition, and relationship questions were added. While earlier test sets consisted of independent and self-contained questions, in more recent evaluations, questions were grouped into series with a common topic and contained references to the topic, preceding questions and answers. In 2008, the QA track was moved to the newly established TAC [9] and focused on list questions asking about opinions, subjects of opinions, and opinion holders. Table 13–4 illustrates common types of TREC and TAC questions.

In the TREC evaluations, systems were required to retrieve answers from text collections that initially consisted of newspaper articles and were later augmented with a large crawl of blog websites. In TAC, this blog crawl became the only source of candidate answers for opinion questions. The blog corpus posed new challenges because its size did not permit comprehensive preprocessing and the poor text quality created the need for more robust NLP tools. In both TREC and TAC, systems had to support each answer with a document from the source that contains the answer and justifies it. Thus even though the systems were allowed to leverage additional sources such as the web for candidate generation and answer scoring, the justification of the final answers had to come from the sources used in the evaluations.

19. http://www.cs.waikato.ac.nz/ml/weka/
20. http://minorthird.sourceforge.net/

Table 13–4: Examples of common question types in TREC and TAC

Question Type	Sample Questions
Factoid	Who was the first American in space? *(TREC 8, Question 21)* Where is the Valley of the Kings? *(TREC 9, Question 249)*
List	Name 20 countries that produce coffee. *(TREC 10 list task, Question 1)*
Definition	Who is Aaron Copland? *(TREC 12 main task, Question 1901)* What is a golden parachute? *(TREC 12 main task, Question 1905)*
Relationship	Are Israel's military ties to China increasing? *(TREC 14 relationship task, Question 17)*
Opinion	Who likes Mythbusters? *(TAC, Question 1018.1)* Why do people like Trader Joe's? *(TAC, Question 1047.2)*

The NTCIR workshop is concerned with monolingual and crosslingual QA in Asian languages [11]. The QA systems are given factoid questions and, more recently, complex questions about events, biographies, definitions, and relationships, and must identify answers in newswire corpora. Currently, the sources are in Japanese or Chinese (simplified and traditional), and the questions are posed either in the same language (monolingual QA) or in English (crosslingual QA). Back-translation of answers to English is not required in the crosslingual tasks. Whereas TREC focused on end-to-end evaluations of QA systems, NTCIR also provides the opportunity to exchange question analysis and document retrieval results among teams. In this way, participants can evaluate different combinations of algorithms and draw conclusions about the effectiveness of individual components.

CLEF evaluates QA systems for various European languages, including Bulgarian, Dutch, English, French, German, Italian, Norwegian, Portuguese, Romanian, and Spanish [10]. Similarly to NTCIR, the evaluation includes monolingual and crosslingual subtasks, but CLEF features many more question and corpus language pairs. Past evaluations have included factoid and definitional questions, and answers were extracted from sources of varying textual quality, such as news articles, Wikipedia documents, and spontaneous speech transcriptions.

13.9.2 Judging Answer Correctness

Although many questions have multiple acceptable answers, judgment of the correctness of factoid answers is for the most part straightforward, as most acceptable answers are semantically equivalent, such as *Volkswagen* and *VW*. There are several areas where judgment is potentially more complicated, including questions with numeric answers for which a range of correct answers may exist and questions whose answers may change over time. An example of the former is *What was the length of the Wright brothers' first flight?* (TREC 11, Question 1414) where both *120 feet* and *120 ft 4 in* are considered correct, while examples of the latter include asking for the age of a person or the current CEO of a company. In past TREC, TAC, NTCIR, and CLEF evaluations, the answers submitted by participants were judged manually by human assessors. Correct answers identified by the assessors can subsequently be compiled into answer keys to be used for automatic evaluations.[21]

The problem of assessing answer correctness is harder for complex answers, such as answers to definition questions. For instance, it is often difficult to decide whether a fact is important enough to justify its inclusion in the answer or whether it is even essential for the answer to be complete. In TREC, human assessors evaluated the answers on the basis of lists of vital and acceptable information nuggets that had to be part of the answer or could be included without penalty. For instance, a perfect answer to the definition question about *Amazon River* (TREC 15, Question 187.7) had to mention that the *Amazon is the longest river in the world*, and it was acceptable to include the information that *Amazon.com is named after the Amazon River*. Evaluation tools such as Nuggeteer [70] and Pourpre [71] have been developed for automatic evaluations of complex answers.

13.9.3 Performance Metrics

The key in evaluating the performance of a QA system lies primarily in whether or not it provides correct answers to questions. However, over the years, many evaluation methods have been proposed and adopted that attempt to represent in a single performance metric information such as the system's ability to rank answers, its confidence in the correctness of its answers, and so forth.

The simplest and most intuitive performance metric for factoid QA is **accuracy**. Let n be the number of questions in a test set and c the number of questions answered correctly by the top-ranked candidate returned by the system. Then accuracy is defined as

$$Accuracy = \frac{c}{n}.$$

Whereas accuracy is based on only the answers with the highest confidence, the mean reciprocal rank (MRR) metric also gives partial credit to correct answers at lower ranks. For each question q_i in a test set $(i = 1, ..., n)$, let r_i be the rank of the first correct answer in the hit list generated for that question if one has been found. The MRR is computed as follows:

$$MRR = \frac{1}{n}\sum_{i=1}^{n}\begin{cases}\frac{1}{r_i} & \text{if a correct answer was found,}\\ 0 & \text{otherwise.}\end{cases}$$

The MRR is commonly based on only the top answers up to a fixed rank. For instance, MRR@5 takes only the five highest ranked answers for each question into account. This

21. Note that these answer keys are often incomplete and are dependent on the reference corpus, so they usually need to be updated continuously to more accurately reflect system performance in subsequent experiments.

metric is useful in capturing the system's recall while rewarding systems that are able to rank the correct answer higher up in the answer list. The MRR is usually not used to evaluate rankings of more than 5 or 10 candidates because it is most sensitive to the top candidates and is hardly affected by correct answers that occur at low ranks.

A metric that takes into account the confidence a system assigns to an answer is the confidence weighted score (CWS). The questions are sorted by the confidence score of the top answer in descending order. Then the CWS is defined as

$$CWS = \frac{1}{n}\sum_{i=1}^{n} \frac{\#\text{ correct answers up to question } i}{i}.$$

This metric rewards correct answers as well as reliable confidence estimates that are comparable across questions.

The performance on list questions is often measured in terms of F-scores. Let t_i be the total number of correct answers to the i-th list question in a test set, r_i the number of answers returned by a QA system for that question, and c_i the number of those answers that are correct. Further, let the recall and precision on the i-th question be defined as follows:

$$Recall_i = \frac{c_i}{t_i} \quad \text{and} \quad Precision_i = \frac{c_i}{r_i}.$$

Then the F-score is a weighted harmonic mean of precision and recall:

$$F_i(\beta) = \frac{(\beta^2 + 1) \times Precision_i \times Recall_i}{\beta^2 \times Precision_i + Recall_i}.$$

The weight parameter β determines the relative importance of precision and recall. The larger β, the more weight is given to recall, that is, the more important it becomes to find all the correct answers and the less important to avoid incorrect answers. If $\beta = 1$, precision and recall are equally important. The overall performance of a QA system on a set of list questions can now be defined as the arithmetic mean of the F-scores:

$$F(\beta) = \frac{1}{n}\sum_{i=1}^{n} F_i(\beta).$$

F-scores are also used for evaluating definition questions and other types of questions with complex answers. In TREC and TAC, the assessors compiled lists of information nuggets they considered to be vital or acceptable parts of an answer. Recall and precision were defined on the basis of the coverage of those nuggets in the answer produced by a system and the overall length of the answer [8, 9].

The top-performing QA system in the TREC 2007 evaluation had an accuracy of 71% on factoid questions and an $F(1)$ score of 0.48 on list questions. In the CLEF 2008 multilingual QA track [10], the best system in the monolingual tasks reached an accuracy of 64%, and the average over all participants was 24%. The top system in the crosslingual tasks, however, achieved only 19% accuracy, and the average was 13%. In the NTCIR 2007 crosslingual QA task [72], the best reported performance on factoid questions was 34% accuracy in the

Japanese monolingual task and 52% in Chinese monolingual QA. The accuracies of the top crosslingual systems were considerably lower: 18% in the English–Japanese task and 25% in the English–Chinese task. These results illustrate that the query or source translation in crosslingual QA poses a significant additional challenge. The TAC evaluation and more recent NTCIR evaluations focused on questions with complex answers, and evaluation results are not reported here because they are less intuitive but mainly useful for system comparisons.

13.10 Current and Future Challenges

We have seen that QA systems often use simple statistical models and heuristics to extract and rank candidate answers. These techniques tend to work well if the sources are semantically redundant and contain many instances of an answer, which is often the case for large sources or questions about popular topics. However, if there is a lack of redundancy, more sophisticated query expansion techniques may be needed to retrieve answer-bearing documents and passages, and deeper NLP and reasoning techniques may become necessary to identify answers and their justification. In the most extreme case for semantic matching and textual entailment, there is only one answer-bearing passage in the entire source corpus and the QA system must determine whether it entails the answer. Often, the semantic relationship between question and text passage is not obvious but can be revealed only through the use of ontologies and correlation measures for term matching, structural matching based on accurate syntactic and semantic parses, and logical reasoning requiring world knowledge. The *Volkswagen–Bentley* example in the introduction (§13.1) and the examples in the discussion of RTE approaches for answer scoring (§13.6) illustrate the difficulties involved in textual entailment.

The techniques described in this chapter extract answers from the knowledge sources rather than synthesizing answers from information found in the text. Although this approach is adequate for most factoid questions, it fails if the answer does not appear explicitly in the sources but must be derived from other statements. For instance, it may be necessary to resolve temporal expressions that are relative to the publication date of an article (e.g., *Yesterday, the government announced ...*) or to perform calculations such as unit conversions and aggregations of numeric quantities (e.g., *What is the combined net worth of the 10 richest people in dollars?*). Pure candidate extraction techniques are also insufficient for questions with complex answers, where it becomes important to formulate natural, coherent, and nonredundant paragraphs, and answers may need to be compiled from facts found in multiple documents.

It is often not enough for a QA system to generate and rank candidate answers, but reliable confidence estimates for the top answers may be required. If the best available answer is unlikely to be correct, it can be preferable to inform the user that the question cannot be answered. Incorrect answers hurt the user's trust in the reliability of a QA system and therefore adversely affect its utility to the user. Confidence estimation is also important for list questions, where the number of correct answers is often not known a priori but the system must decide how many instances to return. In current systems, confidence estimates are often not consistent across questions but depend on various factors such as the answer type, the redundancy of the sources, or the length of the question.

Crosslingual QA systems such as the ones evaluated in NTCIR and CLEF are an important first step toward full-fledged multilingual systems. Current systems are capable of translating questions to the languages of the information sources and generating answers in those languages. However, answers are not translated back to the language in which the question was asked. Users who are not proficient in the languages of the sources will require systems that accept questions and return answers in their own language but search knowledge sources in various languages.

Evaluation forums such as TREC, CLEF, and NTCIR have undoubtedly advanced the state of the art in QA, but they also led to specialized solutions that are tuned to the respective tasks and often cannot easily be adapted to new domains and real-world applications. To facilitate practical applications of QA technologies, future research must focus on general-purpose QA algorithms and techniques that can be adapted rapidly to new tasks and that achieve high performance across different domains [73].

While most research to date has focused on factoid and list QA, questions with complex answers such as definitional, relationship, and opinion questions have received more attention recently. However, QA systems are still far less effective at providing complex answers, and both improvements to QA algorithms and consistent automatic evaluation methodologies are necessary to advance complex QA to a level of performance that enables practical applications. Particularly hard to answer are *how* and *why* questions seeking explanations or justifications and *yes–no* questions requiring a system to determine whether the combined knowledge in the available information sources entails a hypothesis. Effective algorithms that address these types of questions have yet to be developed.

13.11 Summary and Further Reading

Question answering systems can be regarded as a step beyond the currently prevalent information retrieval systems. They provide intuitive and efficient access to information by supporting natural language questions and returning accurate answers. This view of question answering as an enhancement of information retrieval is reflected in common QA architectures. Most state-of-the-art systems in principle follow a pipeline layout consisting of components for (i) transforming questions into search engine queries, (ii) retrieving related text using existing IR systems, and (iii) extracting and scoring candidate answers. However, there are exceptions and variations of this fundamental design. We have seen that some QA systems perform extensive source preprocessing to support structured queries or to populate a knowledge base with structured information for answer lookups. It is also common to perform additional search iterations if the recall of previous searches was unsatisfactory, and some systems even rerun the entire pipeline or part of it to validate high-confidence candidates.

We discussed various algorithms that have been applied in the question analysis, search and candidate generation, and scoring stages of QA pipelines, ranging from simple heuristics and patterns to statistical models to semantic analysis and inference. A simple yet effective approach for answering most factoid questions leverages answer type information. Questions are classified with regard to their expected types, and named entity recognizers extract candidates of these types from retrieved text passages. This approach is a reasonable starting point for implementing a QA system, but it is limited to a predetermined set of types and heavily relies on redundancy to select a final answer among candidates that all match the expected type.

We introduced answer extraction and scoring algorithms that overcome these limitations by performing a deeper analysis of questions and passages and rejecting or discounting candidates that do not satisfy syntactic, semantic, or logical constraints. These algorithms usually improve QA performance but require a considerable implementation effort and are more fragile than a purely type-based approach. Often QA systems use an ensemble of different algorithms for query generation, answer extraction, and scoring, each with individual strengths and weaknesses. Answer extraction from unstructured text can be complemented with lookups in structured sources to answer common types of questions with high accuracy and efficiency. A statistical model can be used to integrate multiple sources of evidence and exploit similarities between candidates for answer scoring.

Similar architectures and algorithms have been applied to different languages, though language-specific challenges need to be addressed in the implementations. In addition, deep NLP techniques, such as semantic answer extraction and textual entailment, are not viable in some languages because the required NLP tools are not available or are insufficiently accurate. Crosslingual QA systems support questions and sources in different languages by either translating the source documents or by translating the questions or extracted keywords. Both approaches are used in practice because neither approach has consistently outperformed the other.

The discipline of question answering is still in an early stage compared to information retrieval, but it is evolving rapidly. Research over the past decade has been driven by standard evaluation efforts such as TREC, CLEF, and NTCIR, which provided the community with data sets and performance metrics for measuring progress and a forum for sharing research ideas. However, these initiatives also directed the research focus toward specific QA tasks and often led to highly specialized solutions that do not generalize to new knowledge domains, sources, and question types. One of the major open challenges is the development of general algorithms that are applicable to a wide range of QA tasks and that can be adapted easily to new tasks. To effectively address questions with complex answers, we also need to move from answer extraction approaches toward more flexible answer generation algorithms. Deeper NLP techniques are required to find answers in sources that lack semantic redundancy. Finally, to fully utilize multilingual resources such as the web, we need QA systems that support user interactions and information sources in various different languages.

For further reading, we recommend an introduction to question answering [74], which covers basic principles and a survey of interesting systems. There are also two recent books on QA discussing significant developments and innovative approaches [75, 76]. For recent publications on English QA, test collections, and past evaluation results, we refer the reader to the NIST websites for TREC[22] and TAC.[23] The evaluation forums NTCIR[24] and CLEF[25] are excellent resources for monolingual and crosslingual QA in Asian and European languages.

22. http://trec.nist.gov/
23. http://www.nist.gov/tac/
24. http://research.nii.ac.jp/ntcir/
25. http://www.clef-campaign.org/

Although our discussion focused on algorithms and resources for answering factoid and list questions, in recent years considerable efforts have been made to tackle other types of questions with more complex answers, such as definition questions, opinion questions, and relationship questions. Blair-Goldensohn, McKeown, and Schlaikjer [77] describe a hybrid approach to answering definitional questions that combines knowledge-based and statistical methods. Weischedel, Xu, and Licuanan [78] answer biographical questions of the form *Who is X?* by automatically extracting linguistic constructs such as appositives and propositions from sentences mentioning a person. More recently, various strategies for definitional QA have been proposed in the proceedings of TREC 2004–2007. Kaisser, Scheible, and Webber [79] present a simple yet effective web reinforcement approach that scores candidate sentences according to how frequently their keywords occur in web search results. Qiu et al. [80] extract sentences from the sources and rank them with a statistical model that combines syntactic features, retrieval scores, and language models. Definitional QA in languages other than English has been addressed in CLEF [10] and NTCIR [11].

The NRRC Workshop on Multi-Perspective Question Answering (MPQA) [81] explored how to identify and organize opinions in a text corpus. Stoyanov, Cardie, and Wiebe [82] introduced a data set comprising opinion questions and annotated documents and proposed the use of statistical and rule-based filters for dropping factual information when answering opinion questions. QA systems addressing questions about opinions, opinion holders, and subjects of opinions were evaluated in TAC 2008 [9]. The best performing system [83] used a sentiment lexicon to recognize terms indicating positive and negative opinions in candidate passages.

The TREC 2005 QA track [84] included a task in which systems had to address questions about various types of relationships between entities, such as financial dependencies, communication pathways, and organizational ties. Relationship questions were also the subject of the complex interactive QA (ciQA) task in the TREC 2006 and 2007 evaluations [8]. This task was interactive in the sense that systems could present initial results to a human assessor and request relevance feedback before generating the final answers. Recent NTCIR evaluations also included relationship questions [11].

Acknowledgments

The authors would like to thank Eric Nyberg and John Prager for sharing their knowledge and experience in various areas of QA research and Teruko Mitamura and Hideki Shima for insightful comments on crosslingual QA.

Bibliography

[1] D. Giampiccolo, H. Dang, B. Magnini, and I. Dagan, "The fourth PASCAL recognizing textual entailment challenge," in *Proceedings of the 1st Text Analysis Conference*, 2008.

[2] R. Simmons, "Natural language question-answering systems: 1969," *Communications of the ACM*, vol. 13, no. 1, pp. 15–30, 1970.

[3] B. Green, A. Wolf, C. Chomsky, and K. Laughery, "Baseball: An automatic question-answerer," in *Proceedings of the Western Joint IRE-AIEE-ACM Computer Conference*, 1961.

[4] W. Woods, "Progress in natural language understanding: An application to lunar geology," in *Proceedings of the AFIPS National Computer Conference*, 1973.

[5] T. Winograd, *Understanding Natural Language*. New York: Academic Press, 1972.

[6] W. Lehnert, "A conceptual theory of question answering," in *Proceedings of the 5th International Joint Conference on Artificial Intelligence*, pp. 158–164, 1977.

[7] J. Kupiec, "MURAX: A robust linguistic approach for question answering using an on-line encyclopedia," in *Proceedings of the 16th Annual International ACM SIGIR Conference on Research and Development in Information Retrieval*, pp. 181–190, 1993.

[8] H. Dang, D. Kelly, and J. Lin, "Overview of the TREC 2007 question answering track," in *Proceedings of the 16th Text REtrieval Conference*, 2007.

[9] H. Dang, "Overview of the TAC 2008 opinion question answering and summarization tasks," in *Proceedings of the 1st Text Analysis Conference*, 2008.

[10] P. Forner, A. Peñas, E. Agirre, I. Alegria, C. Forăscu, N. Moreau, P. Osenova, P. Prokopidis, P. Rocha, B. Sacaleanu, R. Sutcliffe, and E. T. K. Sang, "Overview of the CLEF 2008 multilingual question answering track," in *Lecture Notes in Computer Science, Vol. 5706*, Springer, 2009.

[11] T. Mitamura, E. Nyberg, H. Shima, T. Kato, T. Mori, C.-Y. Lin, R. Song, C.-J. Lin, T. Sakai, D. Ji, and N. Kando, "Overview of the NTCIR-7 ACLIA tasks: Advanced cross-lingual information access," in *Proceedings of the NTCIR-7 Workshop Meeting*, 2008.

[12] S. Harabagiu, D. Moldovan, M. Paşca, R. Mihalcea, M. Surdeanu, R. Bunescu, R. Gîrju, V. Rus, and P. Morărescu, "The role of lexico-semantic feedback in open-domain textual question-answering," in *Proceedings of the 39th Association for Computational Linguistics Conference*, 2001.

[13] B. Katz, G. Borchardt, and S. Felshin, "Syntactic and semantic decomposition strategies for question answering from multiple resources," in *Proceedings of the AAAI 2005 Workshop on Inference for Textual Question Answering*, pp. 35–41, 2005.

[14] J. Chu-Carroll, J. Prager, C. Welty, K. Czuba, and D. Ferrucci, "A multi-strategy and multi-source approach to question answering," in *Proceedings of the 11th Text REtrieval Conference*, 2002.

[15] E. Nyberg, T. Mitamura, J. Callan, J. Carbonell, R. Frederking, K. Collins-Thompson, L. Hiyakumoto, Y. Huang, C. Huttenhower, S. Judy, J. Ko, A. Kupść, L. Lita, V. Pedro, D. Svoboda, and B. V. Durme, "The JAVELIN question-answering system at TREC 2003: A multi-strategy approach with dynamic planning," in *Proceedings of the 12th Text REtrieval Conference*, 2003.

[16] T. Clifton and W. Teahan, "Bangor at TREC 2004: Question answering track," in *Proceedings of the 13th Text REtrieval Conference*, 2004.

[17] N. Lao, H. Shima, T. Mitamura, and E. Nyberg, "Query expansion and machine translation for robust cross-lingual information retrieval," in *Proceedings of the NTCIR-7 Workshop Meeting*, 2008.

[18] T. Kudo, K. Yamamoto, and Y. Matsumoto, "Applying conditional random fields to Japanese morphological analysis," in *Proceedings of the Conference on Empirical Methods on Natural Language Processing (EMNLP)*, 2004.

[19] J. Gao, M. Li, A. Wu, and C.-N. Huang, "Chinese word segmentation and named entity recognition: A pragmatic approach," *Computational Linguistics*, vol. 31, no. 4, 2005.

[20] A. Hickl, J. Williams, J. Bensley, K. Roberts, Y. Shi, and B. Rink, "Question answering with LCC's CHAUCER at TREC 2006," in *Proceedings of the 15th Text REtrieval Conference*, 2006.

[21] D. Moldovan, C. Clark, and M. Bowden, "Lymba's PowerAnswer 4 in TREC 2007," in *Proceedings of the 16th Text REtrieval Conference*, 2007.

[22] I. MacKinnon and O. Vechtomova, "Improving complex interactive question answering with Wikipedia anchor text," in *Advances in Information Retrieval*, Lecture Notes in Computer Science, pp. 438–445, Springer, 2008.

[23] B. Katz, G. Marton, S. Felshin, D. Loreto, B. Lu, F. Mora, O. Uzuner, M. McGraw-Herdeg, N. Cheung, Y. Luo, A. Radul, Y. Shen, and G. Zaccak, "Question answering experiments and resources," in *Proceedings of the 15th Text REtrieval Conference*, 2006.

[24] J. Ko, L. Si, and E. Nyberg, "Combining evidence with a probabilistic framework for answer ranking and answer merging in question answering," *Information Processing & Management*, vol. 46, no. 5, pp. 541–554, 2010.

[25] J. Prager, E. Brown, A. Coden, and D. Radev, "Question-answering by predictive annotation," in *Proceedings of the 23rd Annual International ACM SIGIR Conference on Research and Development in Information Retrieval*, 2000.

[26] D. Moldovan, S. Harabagiu, M. Paşca, R. Mihalcea, R. Goodrum, R. Gîrju, and V. Rus, "LASSO: A tool for surfing the answer net," in *Proceedings of the 8th Text REtrieval Conference*, 1999.

[27] J. Tiedemann, "Integrating linguistic knowledge in passage retrieval for question answering," in *Proceedings of the Human Language Technology Conference on Empirical Methods in Natural Language Processing (HLT/EMNLP)*, 2005.

[28] M. Bilotti, P. Ogilvie, J. Callan, and E. Nyberg, "Structured retrieval for question answering," in *Proceedings of the 30th Annual International ACM SIGIR Conference on Research and Development in Information Retrieval*, 2007.

[29] H. Cui, K. Li, R. Sun, T.-S. Chua, and M.-Y. Kan, "National University of Singapore at the TREC-13 question answering main task," in *Proceedings of the 13th Text REtrieval Conference*, 2004.

[30] C. Fellbaum, *WordNet: An Electronic Lexical Database.* Cambridge, MA: MIT Press, 1998.

[31] C. Fillmore, C. Johnson, and M. Petruck, "Background to FrameNet," *International Journal of Lexicography*, vol. 16, no. 3, pp. 235–250, 2003.

[32] J. Ruppenhofer, M. Ellsworth, M. Petruck, and C. Johnson, "FrameNet II: Extended theory and practice," *ICSI Technical Report*, 2005.

[33] X. Li and D. Roth, "Learning question classifiers," in *Proceedings of the International Conference on Computational Linguistics (COLING)*, 2002.

[34] A. Hickl, K. Roberts, B. Rink, J. Bensley, T. Jungen, Y. Shi, and J. Williams, "Question answering with LCC's CHAUCER-2 at TREC 2007," in *Proceedings of the 16th Text REtrieval Conference*, 2007.

[35] J. Prager, J. Chu-Carroll, and K. Czuba, "Statistical answer-type identification in open-domain question-answering," in *Proceedings of the Human Language Technology Conference*, 2002.

[36] N. Schlaefer, J. Ko, J. Betteridge, G. Sautter, M. Pathak, and E. Nyberg, "Semantic extensions of the Ephyra QA system in TREC 2007," in *Proceedings of the 16th Text REtrieval Conference*, 2007.

[37] J. Chu-Carroll and J. Prager, "An experimental study of the impact of information extraction accuracy on semantic search performance," in *Proceedings of the 16th ACM Conference on Information and Knowledge Management*, 2007.

[38] C. Clarke and E. Terra, "Passage retrieval vs. document retrieval for factoid question answering," in *Proceedings of the 26th Annual International ACM SIGIR Conference on Research and Development in Information Retrieval*, 2003.

[39] S. Tellex, B. Katz, J. Lin, A. Fernandes, and G. Marton, "Quantitative evaluation of passage retrieval algorithms for question answering," in *Proceedings of the 26th Annual International ACM SIGIR Conference on Research and Development in Information Retrieval*, 2003.

[40] E. Hovy, L. Gerber, U. Hermjakob, M. Junk, and C.-Y. Lin, "Question answering in Webclopedia," in *Proceedings of the 9th Text REtrieval Conference*, 2000.

[41] G. Attardi, A. Cisternino, F. Formica, M. Simi, and A. Tommasi, "PiQASso: Pisa question answering system," in *Proceedings of the 10th Text REtrieval Conference*, 2001.

[42] R. Sun, J. Jiang, Y. Tan, H. Cui, T.-S. Chua, and M.-Y. Kan, "Using syntactic and semantic relation analysis in question answering," in *Proceedings of the 14th Text REtrieval Conference*, 2005.

[43] L. Pizzato, D. Mollá, and C. Paris, "Pseudo relevance feedback using named entities for question answering," in *Proceedings of the Australasian Language Technology Workshop (ALTW)*, 2006.

[44] M. Light, G. Mann, E. Riloff, and E. Breck, "Analyses for elucidating current question answering technology," *Journal of Natural Language Engineering*, vol. 7, no. 4, pp. 325–342, 2001.

[45] B. Katz and J. Lin, "Selectively using relations to improve precision in question answering," in *Proceedings of the EACL-2003 Workshop on Natural Language Processing for Question Answering*, 2003.

[46] D. Lin, "Dependency-based evaluation of MINIPAR," in *Proceedings of the Workshop on the Evaluation of Parsing Systems*, 1998.

[47] S. Narayanan and S. Harabagiu, "Question answering based on semantic structures," in *Proceedings of the 20th International Conference on Computational Linguistics (COLING)*, 2004.

[48] P. Kingsbury and M. Palmer, "PropBank: The next level of TreeBank," in *Proceedings of Treebanks and Lexical Theories*, 2003.

[49] S. Pradhan, W. Ward, K. Hacioglu, J. Martin, and D. Jurafsky, "Shallow semantic parsing using support vector machines," in *Proceedings of the Human Language Technology Conference of the North American Chapter of the Association for Computational Linguistics (HLT/NAACL)*, 2004.

[50] D. Ravichandran and E. Hovy, "Learning surface text patterns for a question answering system," in *Proceedings of the 40th Association for Computational Linguistics Conference*, 2002.

[51] D. Zhang and W. Lee, "Web based pattern mining and matching approach to question answering," in *Proceedings of the 11th Text REtrieval Conference*, 2002.

[52] N. Schlaefer, P. Gieselmann, and G. Sautter, "The Ephyra QA system at TREC 2006," in *Proceedings of the 15th Text REtrieval Conference*, 2006.

[53] M. Fleischman, E. Hovy, and A. Echihabi, "Offline strategies for online question answering: Answering questions before they are asked," in *Proceedings of the 41st Association for Computational Linguistics Conference*, 2003.

[54] J. Lin and B. Katz, "Question answering from the World Wide Web using knowledge annotation and knowledge mining techniques," in *Proceedings of the 12th International Conference on Information and Knowledge Management (CIKM)*, 2003.

[55] C. Clarke, G. Cormack, and T. Lynam, "Exploiting redundancy in question answering," in *Proceedings of the 24th Annual International ACM SIGIR Conference on Research and Development in Information Retrieval*, 2001.

[56] A. Ittycheriah, M. Franz, W.-J. Zhu, A. Ratnaparkhi, and R. Mammone, "IBM's statistical question answering system," in *Proceedings of the 9th Text REtrieval Conference*, 2000.

[57] J. Xu, A. Licuanan, J. May, S. Miller, and R. Weischedel, "TREC2002 QA at BBN: Answer selection and confidence estimation," in *Proceedings of the 11th Text REtrieval Conference*, 2002.

[58] D. Moldovan and V. Rus, "Logic form transformation of WordNet and its applicability to question answering," in *Proceedings of the Association for Computational Linguistics*, 2001.

[59] D. Moldovan, C. Clark, S. Harabagiu, and S. Maiorano, "COGEX: A logic prover for question answering," in *Proceedings of the Human Language Technology Conference of the North American Chapter of the Association for Computational Linguistics (HLT/-NAACL)*, pp. 87–93, 2003.

[60] S. Harabagiu, G. Miller, and D. Moldovan, "WordNet 2 - a morphologically and semantically enhanced resource," in *Proceedings of SIGLEX-99*, 1999.

[61] S. Harabagiu and A. Hickl, "Methods for using textual entailment in open-domain question answering," in *Proceedings of the COLING/ACL 2006 Main Conference Poster Sessions*, 2006.

[62] B. Magnini, M. Negri, R. Prevete, and H. Tanev, "Comparing statistical and content-based techniques for answer validation on the Web," in *Proceedings of the 8th Convegno AI*IA*, 2002.

[63] D. Buscaldi and P. Rosso, "Mining knowledge from Wikipedia for the question answering task," in *Proceedings of the International Conference on Language Resources and Evaluation*, 2006.

[64] J. Prager, P. Duboue, and J. Chu-Carroll, "Improving QA accuracy by question inversion," in *Proceedings of the COLING/ACL 2006 Main Conference Poster Sessions*, 2006.

[65] A. Agresti, *Categorical Data Analysis.* New York: Wiley, 2002.

[66] A. Berger, S. Della Pietra, and V. Della Pietra, "A maximum entropy approach to natural language processing," *Computational Linguistics*, vol. 22, no. 1, 1996.

[67] J. Prager, S. Luger, and J. Chu-Carroll, "Type nanotheories: A framework for term comparison," in *Proceedings of the 16th ACM Conference on Information and Knowledge Management*, 2007.

[68] J. McCarley, "Should we translate the documents or the queries in cross-language information retrieval?," in *Proceedings of the 37th Association for Computational Linguistics Conference*, 1999.

[69] M. Bowden, M. Olteanu, P. Suriyentrakorn, T. d'Silva, and D. Moldovan, "Multilingual question answering through intermediate translation: LCC's PowerAnswer at QA@CLEF 2007," in *Lecture Notes in Computer Science, Vol. 5152*, Springer, 2008.

[70] G. Marton and A. Radul, "Nuggeteer: Automatic nugget-based evaluation using descriptions and judgements," in *Proceedings of the Human Language Technology Conference of the North American Chapter of the Association for Computational Linguistics (HLT/NAACL)*, 2006.

[71] J. Lin and D. Demner-Fushman, "Methods for automatically evaluating answers to complex questions," *Information Retrieval,* vol. 9, no. 5, pp. 565–587, 2006.

[72] Y. Sasaki, C.-J. Lin, K.-H. Chen, and H.-H. Chen, "Overview of the NTCIR-6 cross-lingual question answering (CLQA) task," in *Proceedings of the NTCIR-6 Workshop Meeting*, 2007.

[73] D. Ferrucci, E. Nyberg, J. Allan, K. Barker, E. Brown, J. Chu-Carroll, A. Ciccolo, P. Duboue, J. Fan, D. Gondek, E. Hovy, B. Katz, A. Lally, M. McCord, P. Morarescu, B. Murdock, B. Porter, J. Prager, T. Strzalkowski, C. Welty, and W. Zadrozny, "Towards the open advancement of question answering systems," Tech. Rep., IBM Technical Report RC24789, 2009.

[74] J. Prager, "Open-domain question answering," *Foundations and Trends in Information Retrieval*, vol. 1, no. 2, pp. 91–231, 2006.

[75] M. Maybury, ed., *New Directions in Question Answering*. Menlo Park, CA: AAAI Press, 2004.

[76] T. Strzalkowski and S. Harabagiu, eds., *Advances in Open Domain Question Answering*. Dordrecht: Springer, 2006.

[77] S. Blair-Goldensohn, K. McKeown, and A. Schlaikjer, "Answering definitional questions: A hybrid approach," *New Directions in Question Answering* (T. Strzalkowski and S. Harabagiu, eds.), Dordrecht: Springer, 2006.

[78] R. Weischedel, J. Xu, and A. Licuanan, "A hybrid approach to answering biographical questions," *New Directions In Question Answering* (T. Strzalkowski and S. Harabagiu, eds.), Dordrecht: Springer, 2006.

[79] M. Kaisser, S. Scheible, and B. Webber, "Experiments at the University of Edinburgh for the TREC 2006 QA track," in *Proceedings of the 15th Text REtrieval Conference*, 2006.

[80] X. Qiu, B. Li, C. Shen, L. Wu, X. Huang, and Y. Zhou, "FDUQA on TREC 2007 QA track," in *Proceedings of the 16th Text REtrieval Conference*, 2007.

[81] J. Wiebe, E. Breck, C. Buckley, C. Cardie, P. Davis, B. Fraser, D. Litman, D. Pierce, E. Riloff, and T. Wilson, "NRRC summer workshop on multiple-perspective question answering final report," Technical Report, Northeast Regional Research Center, Bedford, MA, 2002.

[82] V. Stoyanov, C. Cardie, and J. Wiebe, "Multi-perspective question answering using the OpQA corpus," in *Proceedings of the Human Language Technology Conference on Empirical Methods in Natural Language Processing (HLT/EMNLP)*, 2005.

[83] F. Li, Z. Zheng, Y. Tang, F. Bu, R. Ge, X. Zhu, X. Zhang, and M. Huang, "THU QUANTA at TAC 2008 QA and RTE track," in *Proceedings of the 1st Text Analysis Conference*, 2008.

[84] E. Voorhees and H. Dang, "Overview of the TREC 2005 question answering track," in *Proceedings of the 14th Text REtrieval Conference*, 2005.

Chapter 14

Distillation

Vittorio Castelli and Radu Florian

14.1 Introduction

Distillation is an emerging nontraditional branch of natural language processing (NLP), which lies between the now classical fields of information retrieval (IR) and question answering (QA).

Unlike IR, the aim of distillation is to provide answers supported by one or more passages in the searched collection rather than to retrieve documents or passages that are relevant to a user's query. Distillation answers could be excerpts from the passages or could be synthesized. Distillation queries can be very complex and can require complex answers. For example, consider

Describe the reactions of <COUNTRY> to <EVENT>,

where <EVENT> could be specified via one or more natural language sentences. The answers to such questions could be quite elaborate. Thus, the goal of distillation is not merely to return factoids but to identify complex answers to complex queries.

Distillation is not a synonym of full-fledged discourse understanding, as we shall see shortly. A major impetus toward recent developments in the distillation area came from the DARPA Global Autonomous Language Exploitation (GALE) program, which mandates as the goal of distillation to deliver "pertinent, consolidated information in easy-to-understand forms ... in response to direct or implicit requests." The data to be analyzed should be in the form of "huge volumes of speech and text in multiple languages." In this chapter, we closely follow the GALE interpretation of the distillation task, and we discuss its multimodal and multilingual aspects. In GALE, the distillation task can rely on a moderate amount of world knowledge (e.g., knowing that *the White House* commonly denotes *the U.S. Executive branch of the government* rather than a specific building is consistent with the task definition; however, the political affiliation of the current governor of South Carolina is not world knowledge that can be used for distillation). Additionally, only a minor amount of inference is allowed. Thus, a distillation system is not required to pass a Turing test.

In GALE, user queries are specified by means of **templates**. Templates consists of a **question** having one or more **arguments** and, optionally, **equivalent terms** for one or more of the arguments; **related terms** that rephrase all of part of the query; and

restrictions: on the dates of interest, on the dates of the documents, on the source language, on the modality of the source (audio or text), and on characteristics of the source (structured or unstructured).

The approaches to distillation discussed in this chapter are to a large extent language-independent because they rely on basic NLP techniques such as mention detection, parsing, and semantic role labeling, and build on statistical methods. This combination relinquishes most language-specific details to the annotation of corpora and to the development of low-level features for statistical methods while at the same time leaving essentially untouched the high-level methods and the architectures described herein.

We begin the chapter with a motivating example that illustrates the scope of distillation and the main challenges it poses to NLP, and we discuss the two concepts of **relevance** of answers to queries and of **redundancy** of different answers. We then describe in detail the distillation system developed by the Rosetta Consortium for the GALE program and conclude the chapter with an overview of several approaches to various aspects of distillation and to multilingual distillation.

14.2 An Example

Consider the following query:

> WHAT CONNECTIONS ARE THERE BETWEEN [the Israeli pull-out of Gaza] (between 2005-09-01 and 2005-09-30) AND [the Gaza security situation]?

The template is WHAT CONNECTIONS ARE THERE BETWEEN [event] AND [topic]. There are two arguments: the first is the <EVENT> *the Israeli pull-out of Gaza* and the second is the <TOPIC> *the Gaza security situation.* The arguments are restricted to periods of time: the Israeli pull-out of Gaza that is relevant to the query is the one that took place between between 2005-09-01 and 2005-09-30. At the same time, no temporal restriction is put on the security situation in Gaza.

Examples of relevant answers are:

1. Since then, Palestinians have continued to fire rockets from Gaza, and Israel has carried out periodic air strikes.
2. Israeli settlers and troops withdrew from Gaza last September, though the security situation for Gazans has deteriorated since then, with the Palestinian Authority unable or unwilling to confront the gunmen.

In the first answer, *then* is resolved to the end of the Israeli pull-out, and in the second, *September* is resolved to September 2005.

The first answer is relevant because it establishes a temporal relation between the event and two facts that pertain to the topic: (i) the Palestinians have continued to fire rockets from Gaza, and (ii) Israel has carried out periodic air strikes. The second answer similarly establishes a temporal relation between the event and two facts: (i) the security situation has deteriorated, and (ii) the Palestinian Authority is unable or unwilling to confront the gunmen.

The following are examples of **irrelevant** answers:

1. Israeli Prime Minister Ariel Sharon previously pointed out that Egypt's role in the disengagement plan will be solely a security role.
2. Israel on Friday threatened to restrict travel and trade across Gaza's borders if the Palestinians did not respond to Israeli security concerns within 48 hours at the recently reopened Rafah border crossing on Gaza's southern frontier with Egypt.

The first answer describes an aspect of the Israeli pull-out from Gaza but does not provide information on the security situation in Gaza and consequently on the relation between the two events. Similarly, the second answer deals with the security situation in Gaza but not with its relation to the Israeli pull-out.

Consider now the following answer:

> Since the Israeli pullout, Palestinians have continued to fire rockets from Gaza.

This is clearly relevant; however, it does not add information to relevant answer 1. Thus, it becomes redundant if relevant answer 1 is already known.

14.3 Relevance and Redundancy

We base our discussion of relevance and redundancy on the definition of response mandated by the GALE program. A response comprises a main snippet, supporting snippets, and citations.

- A (main) **snippet** can consist of (i) a span of text verbatim extracted from a document, (ii) a translation, (iii) a summarization, or (iv) a paraphrase of this span. For simplicity, in the discussion we identify a snippet with a span of text consisting of a single sentence.
- A **supporting snippet** is a snippet that provides additional support to at least some relevant information contained in the main snippet and does not contain relevant information absent from the main snippet.
- A **citation** is a literal excerpt from which a snippet or a supporting snippet is generated.

In summary, to answer a query, a distillation system must identify sentences that contain text relevant to the query, partition these sentence into sets that are pairwise nonredundant, and appropriately report the content of a representative sentence that characterizes the information contained in the set. The system can additionally report the content of other sentences that further validate the content of the representative sentence. The relevant content of the representative sentence can be reported as an excerpt, summarized, or paraphrased: the result is the main snippet. The set associated with a main snippet has the following characteristic: each sentence in a set contains at least some information of relevance to the query, and all such information is also contained in the representative sentence of that set, which is the set's main snippet. Also, given any pair of answer sets, each of the corresponding representative sentences contains at least some information of relevance to the query that is not contained in the other representative sentence. Thus, each supporting snippet is redundant given the main snippet of its set, and main snippets are pairwise nonredundant. In the GALE program, requirements were made only on pairwise redundancy of main snippets, eliminating the need to identify a set of main snippets such that each is nonredundant with respect to the remaining ones. We adopt this simplifying assumption in the present chapter.

Supporting snippets provide additional evidence for some or all the relevant information described in the main snippet. Because snippets are computed from parts of sentences, the same sentence can be used to produce (different) supporting snippets for different main snippets—albeit not multiple main snippets.

With our general understanding of relevance and redundancy, let us now explore one of the possible precise definitions of these concepts. We begin with a query:

> PROVIDE INFORMATION ON [Former Lebanese Prime Minister Rafik Hariri]

and a relevant sentence:

> A U.N. investigation into the truck bombing that killed Hariri and 20 others on Feb. 14 concluded in a preliminary report that the attack was the work of high-ranking Syrian and Lebanese intelligence officers.

The answer conveys at least four atomic pieces of information: Hariri is dead: he was killed; his death was a result of a truck bombing; he died on February 14 (and this date ought to be resolved by the system to 02/14/2005) and there is some evidence that high-ranking Syrians and Lebanese intelligence officers were involved in the attack. In GALE, atomic pieces of information are called **nuggets**. The following relevant sentence,

> But Khaddam did not specifically accuse Assad of making or participating in the decision to assassinate Hariri.

has at least one nugget in common with the previous one: Hariri was assassinated. If the former sentence is used in its entirety as a main snippet, the latter could serve as a supporting snippet. Next consider another answer to the same question:

> Months before his assassination, the late Hariri, a self-made billionaire and once ally of the Syrian regime, had voiced strong opinions that Syria should stop interfering in Lebanese affairs.

This sentence contains at least four nuggets: (i) Hariri is dead: he was assassinated; (ii) he was a self-made billionaire; (iii) he was at a certain point in time an ally of the Syrian regime; (iv) months before his death he was a vocal opponent to Syria's politics in Lebanon. The sentence could be used as another main snippet because it does not share all its nuggets with the first main snippet we constructed. Thus, it is acceptable that two main snippets share a nugget of information (Hariri is dead: he was assassinated) as long as each contains at least a nugget not contained in the other.

An open question remains: how to partition a sentence into nuggets. The GALE distillation annotation guidelines suggest focusing on verbs and other predicates in the sentence [1] to conceptually subdivide a sentence into simple clauses. A clause that is relevant to the query contains a nugget of information. Nuggets can be grouped in categories that capture the information they convey. In GALE, the following categories of nuggets are considered: person, geopolitical entity (GPE), organization, title, numerical phrase, propositional nugget, temporal phrase, locative phrase, modifier nugget, and statement.

Most nuggets are self-explanatory, with the exception of propositional and modifier nuggets, which we describe in some detail. A prepositional nugget is constructed around the main relevant predicates of the snippet and consists of the predicate and its main arguments. Modifier nugget is an umbrella category for causative, manner, and other modifiers of verbs that are not covered by the temporal and locative categories. Examples are recipient or addressee of a parcel, goals, cause, purposes, and instrumental phrases. They usually result when a clause describes a cause, a response, an explanation, or some influence on another relevant clause. For example, in the sentence

> Making good on his main campaign pledge, Bolivia's President Evo Morales ordered troops to occupy the country's oil and natural gas fields on Monday and issued a decree giving the government majority control over the energy industry,

which is a relevant answer to the question

> LIST FACTS ABOUT EVENT: Bolivian President Evo Morales' takeover of gas fields,

the nugget *Making good on his main campaign pledge* describes a cause or an explanation of why *Bolivia's President Evo Morales ordered troops to occupy the country's oil and natural gas fields.*

We can now define redundancy in terms of nuggets. First, we say that two nuggets n_1 and n_2 are equivalent if they convey the same information; for example, *Pierre Cartier bought the Hope Diamond* and *Cartier purchased the Hope Diamond* (where *Cartier* is resolved to *Pierre Cartier*) are equivalent.

If $\mathcal{S}_1$ and $\mathcal{S}_2$ are two snippets, and $\mathcal{N}_1$ and $\mathcal{N}_2$ are their respective sets of nuggets, we say that $\mathcal{S}_2$ is redundant given $\mathcal{S}_1$ if $\mathcal{N}_2 \setminus \mathcal{N}_1 = \emptyset$.

Thus, if $\mathcal{S}_1$ and $\mathcal{S}_2$ are two main snippets corresponding to the same query, the following hold: $\mathcal{N}_1 \neq \emptyset$, $\mathcal{N}_2 \neq \emptyset$, $\mathcal{N}_2 \setminus \mathcal{N}_1 \neq \emptyset$, and $\mathcal{N}_1 \setminus \mathcal{N}_2 \neq \emptyset$, that is, both main snippets contain at least one nugget, and there is at least one nugget in each main snippet not contained in the other. If $\mathcal{S}_1$ is a main snippet and $\widetilde{\mathcal{S}_1}$ is one of its supporting snippets with nugget set $\widetilde{\mathcal{N}_1}$, then $\widetilde{\mathcal{N}_1} \neq \emptyset$ and $\widetilde{\mathcal{N}_1} \subseteq \mathcal{N}_1$, that is, the nuggets contained in the supporting snippet form a subset of those in the main snippet.

14.4 The Rosetta Consortium Distillation System

In this section, we describe an actual distillation system. This system was built as part of the GALE program by one of the participating consortia, the Rosetta team led by IBM. The system is designed to answer distillation queries run against a large corpus composed of text documents and audio recordings in multiple languages: English, Arabic, and Mandarin.

Text sources are assumed to belong to two main categories: structured (i.e., newswire) and unstructured (i.e., web blogs). Similarly, audio sources are assumed to be structured (i.e., news recorded in a studio) and unstructured (i.e., news coverages from reporters in the field).

The distillation system operates in three distinct stages: document preparation, indexing, and query answering.

14.4.1 Document and Corpus Preparation

During document preparation, audio recordings are transcribed, and text and transcripts in foreign languages are translated into English. Text documents in English and in foreign languages are then analyzed by the IBM information extraction system [2]. During information extraction, documents are tokenized, HTML tags are removed, cases are appropriately restored (in particular, if the document is an automatic transcript), sentences are parsed, and mentions are identified and coreferenced. Using the extracted information, relations are detected between mention pairs and semantic role labels are associated with nodes of the parse tree.

Tokenization, part-of-speech (POS) tagging, parsing, mention detection, and semantic role labeling rely on maximum entropy (MaxEnt) models [3]; sequential decoding is performed via the Viterbi algorithm [4]. The mention detection engine identifies both mentions of named entities and anchors of 17 specific event types. Named, nominal, and pronominal mentions of 36 different entity types are identified, and their span and head extent are marked. The anchors of events are verbs, nominalized verbs, or nouns.

Mentions are coreferenced by a resolution algorithm based on the Bell tree [5]. Mentions are analyzed from left to right. The process of linking mentions to entities is modeled by a tree. The first mention is associated to the first entity, and correspondingly, the root of the tree is created. When the second mention is encountered, it can be linked either to the first entity or to a brand-new entity. This is represented in the tree by creating an edge and a node for each of the two possible actions. The procedure is repeated for each new mention, and the leaves of the resulting tree describe all possible ways of grouping the mentions detected in the document; the number of leaves is known as the Bell number [6]. To expand a node when a new entity is encountered, the coreference algorithm uses a binary MaxEnt classifier that assigns a probability to the event that the mention is linked to an entity; a branch is created for each of the entities in existence (in focus) at that node, plus a branch denoting a new mention. Each branch is decorated with the probability of linking the new mention to the associated entity, calculated by the MaxEnt classifier; the probability of creating a new mention is computed by ensuring that the sum of all probabilities is 1. A canonical mention is associated to each entity, typically the longest named mention in the document.

Relation detection is a preprocessing stage that builds on the other described stages. The relation engine identifies 36 types of relation mentions between pairs of entity mentions or between an entity mention and an event anchor, explicitly supported by the text within individual sentences. These relation mentions are similar in spirit to those in the automatic content extraction (ACE) evaluation [7], of which they can be considered a proper superset. Relation mentions have several attributes, including a relation type (which encompasses type and subtype of ACE relations), the order of the mentions in the relation (to distinguish the role of the mentions in nonsymmetric relations), the tense (present, past, future, or undetermined, where the relation is atemporal), and the specificity (which determines whether the relation is between specific or generic entities). Relations are extracted using a cascaded MaxEnt model that extends the one described by Kambhatla [8]. The first stage of the cascade establishes the existence of a relation mention, and the next stage extracts the attributes described earlier.

As in the case of entity mentions, relation mentions are automatically linked to document-level relations; more specifically, relations having the same type (and order if the relation is symmetric) between mentions of the same entity pair are linked to the same document-level relation. No statistical model is used for this purpose; rather, the task is performed by deterministically following the coreference chain.

ACE-style relations are not sufficient to capture all links that the text establishes between entities. During preprocessing, additional links between entities are extracted that do not satisfy the requirements of being explicitly supported by the text and being described within a sentence. These extended relations are identified by a module that was originally developed for the slot-filling task of the Knowledge Base Population track of the 2009 Text Analysis Conference (TAC-KBP) [9]. Participants in the slot-filling tasks were required to analyze a large text corpus and extract specific attributes of persons, organizations, and geopolitical entities specified at evaluation time. The desired attributes are akin to Wikipedia infobox slots [10], and their values are not constrained to be supported in the text explicitly in a single sentence. Family relations provide us with a simple example: *Bob and his mother Mary went to the mall. His brother John remained at home.* This passage establishes that Mary is John's mother (assuming that *brother* means "full brother") but does do it explicitly or using a single sentence; therefore, ACE-style relations do not capture this fact. The approach to this problem adopted for the TAC-KBP task is centered on a rule-based system built on top of the relation-detection and coreference modules.

This slot system relies on three broad classes of rules: coref rules, relation rules, and irelation rules (for inferred relations). Coref rules follow the coreference chain. Consider the rule:

> IF (X IS-A Person Entity) AND (Y IS-AN Occupation) AND
> (Y ISCOREFERENTWITH X) THEN (X PER:TITLE=Y).

In the excerpt

> Barack Obama concluded his visit to China on Wednesday. The President expressed hope for further Sino-US cooperation.

the rule finds two person mentions: a name (*Barack Obama*) and a nominal describing occupation (*President*); the coreference system links both mentions to the same entity in the document, and therefore rule establishes that the value of the PER:TITLE TAC-KPB slot for Barack Obama is President.

Relation rules perform inference on the basis of one or more relations and on coreference chains. For instance, a relation rule would establish that Mary is John's mother in our motivating example.

Irelation rules extend relation rules by performing inference on slots extracted by other relation and irelation rules as well as on ACE-style relations and on coreference chains. An example IF irelation is the following:

> IF (X IS-A Person) AND (X ISPARTOFMANY G) AND (G HASTITLE T) THEN (X HASTITLE T),

which, applied to the sentence *Fifteen Senators supported the bill, including John McCain* would extract the information that John McCain has title Senator. These rules are applied to individual documents, and the extracted slots, values are treated as if they were ACE-style relations during question answering.

The final step in preparing the corpus for indexing and for answering queries consists of performing crossdocument coreference (XDC), that is, of assigning a unique identifier to each distinct entity in the corpus. Thus, the entity *Barack Obama, 44th U.S. President* must have the same ID in every document in which it appears, while the entities *George Bush, NASCAR driver* and *George W. Bush, 43rd U.S. President* must have distinct IDs. Crossdocument coreference relies on the system built for the 2009 TAC-KPB entity-linking task in which participants are given a database (called a knowledge base) containing one describing document per entity. Queries are in the form of an entity name and a document that provides disambiguation context. Answers are the knowledge-base ID of the entity, if the entity is in the knowledge base, or null otherwise.

The entity-linking system can be extended to become an XDC algorithm. The first extension consists of augmenting the knowledge base; in the Rosetta distillation system, the dbpedia[1] database is merged with the TAC-KBP knowledge base. The second extension consists of selecting text to vicariously provide disambiguation context; the selected text consists of the collection of sentences containing mentions of the document-level entity. With these two changes, XDC can be recast as the problem of assigning to each document-level entity its unique knowledge-based ID.

This leads to the third extension: assigning IDs to entities that are not in the knowledge base. A two-stage process is used to find an entity in the extended knowledge base. The first stage consists of a fast name match based on character trigrams. This simple approach is robust to spelling variations and to typographical errors in that the correct entity is in the top 50 hits in the vast majority of the cases. It is also efficient because it is easily implemented on top of a standard search engine, such as the open source Lucene. The top 50 hits are further analyzed by the second stage, which combines a more sophisticated name similarity score, the SoftTFIDF from the SecondString package [11], and a context-matching score. The context-matching score is based on cosine similarity and measures the overlap between the non-stop-words in the context of the document-level entity with those of the candidate in the knowledge base. The latter are extracted from the Wikipedia infoboxes of the candidate. The process succeeds if both fast match and refined match yield scores that exceed thresholds computed via a hold-out data set. If the process fails, the entity is deemed not to be in the knowledge base, no knowledge base ID is associated with it, and a fallback strategy is then invoked. This strategy consists of assigning an XDC ID only to

1. The dbpedia is available at http://dbpedia.org.

document-level entities for which either the fast or the refined match succeed and of assigning a unique ID to the remaining ones. The XDC ID is the identifier of the closest knowledge-based entity, the one with the highest score for the match that succeeds, prepended by a distinguishing prefix. The rationale of the approach is that two document-level entities that represent the same real-life entity will likely have the same "most similar" knowledge-base entity.

14.4.2 Indexing

Documents are indexed using an open source search engine, Lucene. The index allows both bag-of-word searches on document text and queries on named entities. To support the latter, all mentions of entities except nominal and pronominal mentions are indexed both in their entirety, for exact matches, and in tokenized form, for n-gram matches.

14.4.3 Query Answering

The query answering distillation system takes as input a GALE-style query, described in the introduction, and returns a list of main snippets with associated supporting snippets and citations, sorted in decreasing order of relevance to the query. The architecture of the system consists of five stages: query preprocessing, document retrieval, snippet filtering, snippet processing, and planning.

Query Preprocessing

The query preprocessing stage performs information extraction on the query components: the arguments, the related terms, and the equivalent terms. These are tokenized and parsed, and semantic role labels are computed. Mentions are detected and associated with entities. The XDC system assigns crossdocument IDs to detected entities as appropriate. For arguments of type PERSON, ORGANIZATION, LOCATION, GPE, and COUNTRY, the query preprocessing stage identifies the main entity, detects ancillary mentions, and identifies their relation to the main entity. For arguments of type EVENT, TOPIC, or CRIME, the preprocessing stage additionally computes the dependency tree of the argument, of the related terms, and of the equivalent terms.

As an example, the query

> DESCRIBE INVOLVEMENT OF [Russia] IN [attempts to freeze Iran's nuclear program]

has two arguments, the first of type COUNTRY, the second of type EVENT; there are no equivalent terms or related terms. The XDC system assigns an appropriate crossdocument ID to *Russia*. Information extraction is performed on the EVENT definition: the text is tokenized and parsed, mentions are detected (*Iran*), and the XDC system assigns to *Iran* an XDC ID.

Document Retrieval

The information extracted from the distillation query components is used to search a Lucene index. The Lucene query is composed using the nonterminals and all the entities extracted from all distillation query components. Additionally, all XDC IDs assigned to named entities by the preprocessing stage are used as arguments to the search engine query. The result of the search engine query is a collection of documents, each of which has an associated score. The search engine is provided with the maximum number of documents to return. Because all documents are passed to the subsequent stages, the maximum number of documents is selected by trading off the expected response time and the recall yielded by the entire system. Selecting this parameter can be accomplished in a variety of standard ways, such as using a hold-out set to fix its value. Alternatively, methods that adaptively select the number of documents according to the document scores can also be successfully used. In the Rosetta distillation system, the former solution was adopted, and the number of retrieved documents was fixed to 500.

In the preceding example, the query will require that retrieved documents contain mentions of both Russia and Iran, and will favor documents that contain a larger subset of the non-stop-words *attempts, freeze, nuclear,* and *program.*

Snippet Filtering

The queries submitted to search engine return a set of documents a large fraction of which is typically relevant to the distillation query. The next step is to identify the relevant portions of the documents and produce nonredundant snippets. Some categories of documents, in particular long newsgroup logs and transcribed newscasts, are often for the most part irrelevant to the query; at the same time, their size makes it impractical to analyze them in detail in their entirety. The solution adopted in the Rosetta distillation system was to build a high-recall filtering stage that seeks to pass through relevant sentences with high probability, while at the same time discarding a large fraction of the irrelevant sentences. This stage is based either on heuristics or on a simple statistical model that relies on a small number of features. For example, for the template query DESCRIBE RELATION BETWEEN <PERSON1> AND <PERSON2>, a simple heuristic rule that fires if mentions of both persons appear in the sentence or in nearby sentences achieves the desired high-recall goal while discarding a large fraction of the irrelevant sentences. For other templates, more complex statistical methods are used. These are akin to those used in the snippet processing stage, albeit simpler; we discuss these in more detail in the following section. Whenever appropriate, the system records the score associated with sentences that pass the snippet filtering stage; these scores are used by the fallback strategy of the snippet processing stage.

For the running example, the snippet filter would retrieve all the snippets containing Russia or mentions of representatives of Russia. Because this stage is designed to have high recall, it will pass many irrelevant sentences among the relevant ones; examples of outputs are:

> Russian frustration at Iran's refusal to send uranium to Russia and France for processing into fuel hints at the possibility that Moscow may be open to a new UN Security Council resolution.
>
> Russian President Dmitry Medvedev stated that there is agreement over sanctions for Iran but that this is still not the desired path.
>
> Moscow and Tehran announced that Russia will build a nuclear reactor in Bushehr.

Snippet Processing

The two goals of the snippet processing stage are to assign a relevance score to sentences that pass the snippet filtering stage and to identify information used by the planning stage to construct main snippets, supporting snippets, and citations. Depending on the template, a sentence is relevant for a query if it describes properties of an argument (e.g., for the template PROVIDE INFORMATION ON <ORGANIZATION>), actions or events involving an argument (e.g., for the template PRODUCE A BIOGRAPHY OF <PERSON>), or potentially complex interactions between arguments (e.g., for DESCRIBE THE INVOLVEMENT OF <COUNTRY> IN <EVENT>). This is a complex task: it can be challenging to determine whether a sentence pertains to an argument if the argument is sufficiently complex (e.g., for EVENTS and TOPICS). Although it is possible to manually construct a template-dependent rule-based system that would assign a relevance score to sentences, this approach is neither cheap nor scalable.

The snippet processing stage of the Rosetta distillation system instead relies on template-dependent hierarchical statistical scoring models trained using manually annotated data. Scalability is achieved by training hierarchical models and reusing the annotated data to train different models. Argument models for entity arguments are at the foundations of the model hierarchy. Their goal is to detect whether a sentence contains or describes the main entity of a person, organization, location, country, or a geopolitical entity query argument. The learning algorithm used to learn the argument models is the voted-perceptron [12], which slightly outperformed MaxEnt with small training sets. The training data consists of triples: (QUERY, SENTENCE, LABEL), where the QUERY is a simple question of the form DOES THE SENTENCE CONTAIN <ARGUMENT>, *sentence* is a sentence with a pointer to the document from which it is extracted, and *label* is a binary label manually assigned to the sentence by an annotator who is trained to follow argument-specific guidelines. The annotation guidelines capture the many ways in which arguments of different type can be mentioned in a sentence.

The triples (QUERY, SENTENCE, LABEL) are converted into vectors of features, produced by feature extractors. We can categorize the feature extractors according to their input space: QUERY-ARGUMENT, SENTENCE, QUERY-ARGUMENT × SENTENCE, QUERY-ARGUMENT × DOCUMENT, QUERY-ARGUMENT × SENTENCE × DOCUMENT.

For example, the feature extractor that fires if the specification of a PERSON argument contains a title has input space equal to QUERY-ARGUMENT, and the feature extractor that detects whether a sentence is a fragment has an input space equal to SENTENCE. A more complex extractor that compares the XDC ID of the main argument mention with those of mentions in the sentence of interest is an example of QUERY-ARGUMENT × SENTENCE input space.

Numerous feature extractors, such as those that perform XDC ID matching and approximate text matching between mentions in the argument and in the sentence are extensively used across the argument models. Others are crafted for specific argument types: because countries, for example, are often represented by their officials (Dmitry Medvedev is a valid proxy for Russia) or mentioned using a metonymy (*the White House* refers to the United States, *London* is often a metonymy for United Kingdom), the country model has a feature function that fires when it detects a representative of a country or a metonymy for the country in the sentence.

The models that detect complex arguments, EVENT and TOPIC, are hierarchical: some of their features are constructed from the output of the other argument models we just described. Events and topics are specified via one or more sentences or noun phrases that often involve mentions of persons, organizations, countries, GPEs, or locations: for example, *The collapse of Lehman Brothers* contains a mention of an organization, whereas *AIG sells Alico unit to MetLife* contains mentions of three organizations linked by complex relations. Mentions in the argument are identified during query preprocessing and are used by feature extractors that fire if the appropriate argument model finds a match in the sentence. For example, the sentence *On 9/15 the firm filed for Chapter 11 bankruptcy protection*, where the firm is *Lehman Brothers* is relevant to the first query; the event model contains a feature extractor that selects *Lehman Brothers* from the query argument, matches it to the nominal mention *firm* using the ORGANIZATION model, and fires as a result.

To capture the interdependencies among the mentions in a complex query argument, and how they relate to non-stop-words, the models rely on more advanced features, such as features that match ACE-style relations detected in the argument with those detected in the sentence, or features that match the dependency structure between the non-stop-words and the mentions in the query arguments and those present in the sentence, as described in [13].

The Rosetta distillation system scores sentences using statistical models specifically trained for each template. These models rely on a two-tiered approach to feature extraction. At the first level, we find argument models, which produce appropriate features when they detect the presence of the argument in the sentence, as well as a variety of other features that capture lexical, syntactic, and semantic aspects of the sentence. These feature extractors leave a "trace"; that is, they identify specific portions of the sentence that cause them to fire. The second tier consists of extractors that fire when they identify structural, syntactic, or semantic properties of the traces of other extractors. Second-tier extractors can themselves leave traces and can therefore be hierarchically combined.

Determining the relevance of a sentence to a query is particularly challenging when the query arguments are of complex types: events and topics, for instance. Unlike queries regarding entities, where the absence of entity mentions in the sentence is often an indicator that the sentence is irrelevant, information on events and topics is typically conveyed in sentences that do not contain the description of the argument. For instance, newswire articles about a specific topic commonly start by mentioning the topic and then provide information without explicitly referring back to the topic. To address this challenge, the Rosetta distillation template models extract features from a context consisting of a window of sentences surrounding the one being scored. Selected feature extractors are applied to the sentences in the window, and statistics on which fire and where are analyzed to produce what we call **context features**.

Sentences analyzed by the template models are scored, and the trace of the firing features are recorded. The sentences having a score that denotes relevance are passed to the planning stage, while the remaining ones are discarded. If the number of relevant sentences falls below a user-specified threshold, a fallback strategy is invoked, consisting of adding to the result set the sentences with the highest scores produced by the filtering stage.

Referring to our running example, the snippet processing is designed to select as relevant the following two sentences:

> Russian frustration at Iran's refusal to send uranium to Russia and France for processing into fuel hints at the possibility that Moscow may be open to a new UN Security Council resolution.
>
> Russian President Dmitry Medvedev stated that there is agreement over sanctions for Iran but that this is still not the desired path.

and to reject

> Moscow and Tehran announced that Russia will build a nuclear reactor in Bushehr.

Planning

The snippet processor produces a set of relevant sentences that are potentially redundant. The planning stage analyzes these sentences and identifies nonredundant snippets, supporting citations, and supporting snippets. The planner relies heavily on the scores and the feature traces produced by the snippet processor. Sentences are analyzed in order of decreasing score. The highest scoring sentence automatically becomes the citation of a main snippet. A main snippet is constructed from the citation by selecting the span of the sentence that contains all its feature traces, identifying in the parse tree the constituent farthest from the root that covers this span, and selecting the part of the sentence corresponding to this constituent. Each remaining sentence is compared to the current main snippets. Each sentence containing at least one feature trace that is not in any of the main snippets becomes a new main snippet. Each sentence containing a subset of the feature traces of a main snippet becomes a citation of a supporting snippet. The supporting snippet is constructed in the same fashion as the main snippet. An enhancement of the described strategy consists of setting a threshold smaller than 1; all sentences with scores larger than the threshold times the score of the best sentence are considered as candidates for main snippet and supporting snippet, while the remaining ones are only allowed to become citations of supporting snippets. The system is forced to select as main snippets only sentences that the snippet processor considers relevant with sufficiently high certainty.

Referring to our running example, the planner is designed to mark

> Moscow might be open to a new UN Security Council Resolution

and

> Russian President Dmitry Medvedev stated that there is agreement over sanctions for Iran but that this is still not the desired path

as the portions of the sentences containing the relevant information. The features that fire to retrieve the snippets have different traces, and therefore the planner selects the two sentences as separate main snippets.

14.5 Other Distillation Approaches

After describing in detail a specific distillation system, we briefly review some of the approaches to distillation described in the literature. In particular, we discuss system architectures and approaches to relevance detection and redundancy reduction. We conclude the section with a brief review of approaches to multimodal approaches that use both speech and transcription data and multilingual approaches that rely on both the data in the source language and their translations. We are not aware of alternative document retrieval approaches that are unique to distillation, so document retrieval is not covered in this section.

14.5.1 System Architectures

Distillation systems typically conform to the general framework of retrieving documents first, using information retrieval techniques, and analyzing the individual document sentences afterwards [14, 15, 16]. An alternative approach can be found in Lin [17], where the author discusses the role of information extraction in answering complex questions. This paper addresses two main questions: whether IR techniques alone can be used to identify sentences that are relevant to questions more complex than factoid-style questions and whether IR techniques can be used to reduce or eliminate redundancy among the retrieved sentences. The author concludes that IR alone cannot satisfactorily retrieve sentences that are relevant to complex questions; conversely, the results hint at the ability of IR techniques to address the redundancy problem.

14.5.2 Relevance

A precursor to distillation can be found in Lin [17], where the author addresses the problem of answering relationship questions. Relationship questions were formally introduced in 2005 as part of the TREC Question Answering track [18]. A relationship question asks how X and Y interact or how X influences Y, where X and Y are entities, events, or topics. For example, a user could ask how the Treaty of Versailles influenced the creation of the League of Nations. Lin investigates how far traditional information retrieval techniques, in particular, sentence retrieval, can go toward answering relationship questions. The author constructs simple features: a passage-matching score computed from the inverse document frequency (IDF) values of the unique terms appearing in the query and the candidate sentence; term IDF and recall; and length of the sentence. The features are combined by a linear regression model with a relevance measure as response. This simple model outperforms a baseline system that relies only on IR score, especially when the answer length is restricted to 1,000 characters or less.

Levit et al. [15] describe the statistical approach to relevance detection used in the IXIR distillation system. The high-level structure of IXIR is similar to that of the Rosetta system, a noticeable difference being the combination of the snippet filtering and snippet processing stages. As in the Rosetta system, relevance to a query is established by a template-specific statistical system that relies on a broad spectrum of features. The gist of the approach is as follows. For each sentence, the IXIR system construct a graphical representation that combines these features, called a **chart**. A chart is a graph over the words of a sentence whose edges are annotated with the features that fire over the nodes connected by the edges.

The simplest lexical features have the form A immediately followed by B, where A and B are words in the sentence. Syntactic relations, dependency relations, semantic role labeling relations, and so on can similarly be represented by edges in the chart. When presented with a named entity argument, IXIR attempts to detect whether said entity is instantiated in the sentence using a variety of well-known strategies, such as approximate matches, detections of spelling variations, synonym dictionaries, gazetteers, modifier word detectors, and WordNet [19]. If the matching is successful, the system adds a layer to the chart of the sentence describing where and how the matches occur. Once the chart is constructed, it is used to compute features for statistical classifiers that detect whether the argument is present in a sentence. These features are extensions of the traditional lexical n-grams. A lexical n-gram can be generated by following $n-1$ edges in a simple chart containing only lexical features of the form A immediately followed by B. The features in IXIR are n-grams obtained by following a connected path with $n-1$ edges, irrespective of which features generated them. Complex arguments, such as event, are treated somewhat differently; IXIR computes a chart for the argument description and extracts features from both the argument chart and the sentence chart.

Kamangar [20] and Kamangar et al. [21] advocate an unsupervised learning approach to sentence selection. First, the authors identify a small set of likely relevant sentences and likely irrelevant sentences and propose three approaches based on the stemmed non-stop-words of the query argument. The first is selection by total term frequency (TF) and consists of computing the frequencies of the non-stop-words within the candidate sentences, computing the mean frequency, retaining only the words with frequency higher than the mean, and marking as positive the sentences that contain all the retained words and as negative those that contain none. The second is selection by TF-IDF (term frequency–inverse document frequency) and consists of retaining the query argument words with sufficiently large TD-IDF, marking as positive the sentences that contain all these words and as negative the sentences that contain none. The TF-IDF threshold is learned by means of a separate training set. The final method consists of considering all query-argument non-stop-words as equally important, marking as positive the sentences that contain at least a certain fraction of the terms and as negative those that contain none. The initial sets of sentences are then used by an iterative self-training algorithm: a classifier is learned from the automatically generated positive and negative examples and then applied to classify the candidate sentences not in the training set. This classifier must produce a score or a posterior probability estimate. This output is then used to select additional positive examples (those whose score exceeds a threshold learned from the separate training set) and negative examples (those whose score is below another threshold, also learned from the training set). The iterative procedure terminates when no new positive or negative sentence is identified or when a maximum number of iterations is reached.

14.5.3 Redundancy

Redundancy reduction is not unique to distillation and has a noticeable precursor in the TREC novelty track [22]. Lin [17] defines a utility function for a new candidate c to be included in the incrementally constructed answer set A:

$$\text{Utility}(c) = \text{Relevance}(c) - \lambda \max_{s \in A} sim(s, c);$$

where Relevance is computed as described earlier, *sim* is a similarity function such as cosine similarity, and λ is a parameter to be tuned. Lin compares three measures of relevance; the first is based on the regression score using the maximum operator, and the remaining two are his baseline relevance score with *max* and *average* as the aggregation functions. The author tunes λ using the POURPRE score [23] as the evaluation metric. An empirical finding is that the *max* operator outperforms *average* for the purpose of detecting redundancy.

14.5.4 Multimodal Distillation

In the GALE program, evaluations were conducted against large multimodal, multilingual corpora containing hundreds of thousands of documents. A portion of the corpus consisted of voice recordings. The baseline approach to answering questions against voice recordings consists of automatically transcribing them, translating into English the transcriptions of Mandarin and Arabic, and running the standard distillation system against the resulting text documents. Errors in transcription and translation can result in substantial degradation of system performance compared to searching "clean" text, that is, newswires. Yaman et al. [24] analyze the effects of transcription errors on distillation and report a substantial performance degradation of 35%. They propose a solution to this challenge based on using what they call **anchored speech recognition** in the snippet processing stage. They assume the existence of a snippet filtering stage that identifies candidate snippets and discards clearly irrelevant ones. Snippets containing an answer to the query can be divided into two groups: those in which the answer and the question are worded in a similar fashion and those in which the answer and the question are worded differently. The paper describes how to analyze the former and claims that the method can be extended to deal with the latter. Given a collection of queries, the authors bias existing language models toward recognizing word phrases from the questions. For each question, they construct a word network that matches the word sequence of the question while allowing other words around it, but not interspersed with the question words. They then combine the biased lattice from the biased language model with the word network for the specific question and force the decoder to accept only paths that contain the word network from the query. The resulting paths are further rescored, and appropriate corrective actions are taken if no result is returned; these actions consist of relaxing the recognition constraints. Even after relaxing the constraints, the described approach by far works better when the answer contains the exact phrasing of the question without intervening words. The authors' experiments show how the method can help the distillation system recover from 30% of the error induced by errors in transcription and that the relative word-error rate of correct answers is reduced by 37%.

14.5.5 Crosslingual Distillation

Crosslanguage information retrieval is a recent area of investigation [25]. Producing an answer in English by searching a corpus of documents written in different languages poses challenges not encountered in traditional information retrieval. The two simplest solutions to the problem are (i) searching the corpus in the foreign language and translating the retrieval results and (ii) automatically translating the corpus first and performing information retrieval on the translations. The former approach suffers from the limited availability of linguistic resources that can be used to train or build the basic components of an IR or distillation system. The latter approach is impaired by the current state of the art of machine translation: automatically translated documents contain translation errors, nongrammatical sentences, poorly transliterated proper names, and other mistakes that can negatively impact information extraction. These considerations suggest that a hybrid approach could be beneficial. McCarley [26] supports this conclusion. The author compared three strategies for multilingual information retrieval: translating the query, translating the corpus, and a hybrid approach that assigns to documents the arithmetic means of the first two. The hybrid approach consistently outperforms the other two on a variety of data sets, surprisingly even when the queries are translated into the language of the corpus by humans.

Crosslingual information retrieval designed for distillation is the main focus of Parton et al. [27]. The authors approach, called **translingual information retrieval**, departs from McCarley's in how the search index is constructed and the query executed. Whereas McCarley uses separate indexes for the original documents and their translations, Parton et al. propose joint indexing of each document and its translation using a single index. Distillation queries expressed in English are translated; IR queries are constructed from originals and translations and are executed against the translingual index. Finally, the authors propose an approach to correcting potential translation errors by relying on the original and translated query.

Singla and Hakkani-Tür [14] address the problem of crosslanguage snippet processing a Mandarin corpus and an Arabic corpus. The authors build a statistical snippet processing model for English, as described by Hakkani-Tür and Tür [28], and an analogous one for the source language. They propose two approaches to combining them: posterior probability interpolation and cascading. In posterior probability interpolation, a candidate sentence is scored by the source language model, and its translation is scored by the English model; the scores are then combined via convex interpolation. Cascading two models consist of using the probability estimate of a model as an input feature for the other. As an alternative to model combination, the authors propose extracting features from both source and translated sentences and using them as input to a single combined snippet processing model. In the paper, convex model interpolation appears to be superior to the other methods for both English and Arabic queries and to source-language snippet processing.

The promising field of crosslingual distillation is still in its infancy: most of the current results are logical extensions of single-language techniques or constitute preliminary investigations; for example, the results by Singla and Hakkani-Tür [14] rely uniquely on simple lexical (n-gram) features. However, the increasing availability of linguistic resources that can be used to build or improve basic information extraction components clearly indicates that substantial strides are likely in the near future.

14.6 Evaluation and Metrics

The evaluation of distillation systems is more complex than that of QA and IR systems. The classical metrics of precision, recall, and F-measure are the standard for assessing the performance of IR systems. A substantial literature exists on how to evaluate IR systems (see Vorhees [29]).

Three main factors add challenges to the evaluation of distillation results: the complexity of the queries, the format of the answers, and the need to combine multiple aspects of the system output into a single evaluation metric. Even if they are based on templates, distillation queries look for answers to semantically complex questions, such as those that involve events. Deciding whether a passage is relevant to a query can depend on how the query is interpreted, and therefore decisions can often be highly subjective. This consideration holds a fortiori for redundancy detection: given two passages that answer the same query, detecting redundancy implies identifying pieces of information (nuggets) that appear in only one of the passages and deciding whether these nuggets are relevant to the query. As previously mentioned, answers to distillation queries are complex: they consist of a main snippet (a textual passage extracted from a document or its paraphrase), additional supporting snippets that contain all or some of the information of the main snippet, and one or more citations (actual excerpts from documents belonging the corpus being searched) for each snippet. The question arises of how to account for errors in different components of the answer. For example, returning an irrelevant main snippet might be considered a bigger error than returning an irrelevant citation for a relevant snippet supported by other relevant citations. Moreover, many corner cases arise: for example, consider two systems that produce the same main snippet and the same citations but different supporting snippets: Is there an easy way to evaluate which answer is better? The last challenge to building an evaluation metric arises from the desire to capture the relevance of the answers, the redundancy across different main snippets, and the completeness of the returned results.

14.6.1 Evaluation Metrics in the GALE Program

The GALE program has addressed these problems over the years, and we next describe the metric proposed for the Year-4 Go/No Go evaluation [30]. The goal of the GALE metric is to compare the performance of distillation systems to that of human analysts using state-of-the art search engines. More specifically, analysts were allotted between 30 and 60 minutes of time per query and were required to produce answers in the same format as the systems (main snippet, supporting snippets, citations). Responses from analysts and systems were manually analyzed, as follows.

Relevance Analysis

First, each main snippet was labeled as relevant, partially relevant, or irrelevant by at least two human judges. The actual portion of a relevant and partially relevant snippet that contains the answer was marked, and the marked portion was automatically nuggetized, while the rest were treated as context. The results of automatic nuggetization were reviewed and corrected as appropriate by the judges. Irrelevant snippets were also nuggetized to produce wrong nuggets, which affect the computation of precision-related quantities. Each judge assigned a relevance score to each of the nuggets: 1 for completely relevant nuggets, 0.8 for partially relevant nuggets, and 0 for irrelevant nuggets. Scores from different judges were averaged to produce the final relevance score of the nugget.

Redundancy Detection

The judges then analyzed snippets for redundancy. For each pair of main snippets, the judges compared the corresponding nuggets and identified nugget pairs with semantically equivalent information. Two main snippets, A and B, were considered nonredundant if at least one nugget in A had no semantic equivalent in B and at least one nugget in B had no semantic equivalent in A. If each nugget in A had a semantic equivalent in B and vice versa, then A and B were equivalent. Finally, if every nugget in A had a semantic equivalent in B, but the opposite did not hold, then A was redundant with respect to B.

Citation Checking

The judges determined if each citation fully supports the (relevant and nonredundant) main snippet(s) it is associated with. A penalty was assigned to citations that did not fully support the associated snippets. The judges scored slightly differently the citations associated with supporting snippets: such citations were deemed as correct if their associated supporting snippet had at least one nugget in common with the main snippet and if the citation fully supported the supporting snippet.

Primary Task Metrics

The judgments were used to produce two primary task metrics, the information-content metric and the document-support metric, which were then combined into a single performance number. We provide an overview of these metrics and refer the interested reader to the cited official evaluation document [30].

The information-content metric measures performance at the nugget level. A nugget i has a relevance score $R(i)$ and a redundancy score $D(i)$. The relevance score is computed as described previously while the redundancy score is either 0 or 1. Let N_j be the number of nuggets produced by a distiller in response to a query; then the precision is defined as

$$P_j = \frac{\sum_{i=1}^{N_j} R(i)D(i)}{N_j},$$

and the recall is

$$R_j = \frac{\sum_{i=1}^{N_j} R(i)D(i)}{M_j},$$

provided that M_j, the total number of relevant nuggets in the corpus, were known. Because it is unfeasible to manually analyze a corpus with hundred of thousands or millions of documents for each query, the recall measure was computed as

$$R_j = \frac{\sum_{i=1}^{N_j} R(i)D(i)}{\widehat{M_j}},$$

where $\widehat{M_j}$ is the maximum likelihood estimate of M_j. The corresponding F-measure is denoted by F^I.

The document-support metric measures the number of valid citations associated with nonredundant snippets. A citation is said to be valid if it does not share segments with other citations. A valid citation is said to be right if it fully supports the associated snippet and the associated snippet is either a main snippet or a supporting snippet with at least one nugget in common with its main snippet. If R_j is the number of right citations returned by a distiller, V_j is the number of valid citations returned by the same distiller, and W_j is the total number of valid citations for the query in the corpus, then the document-support precision and recall are

$$P_j^D = \frac{R_j}{V_j}$$

and

$$R_j^D = \frac{R_j}{\widetilde{W}_j},$$

where $\widetilde{W}_j$ is an estimate of W_j (in practice, the total number of right citations returned by all the distiller and the analysts). The corresponding F-value is denoted by F^D.

The official metric is obtained by first scaling the information recall by the square root of the document F-value:

$$R^{I^*} = \sqrt{F^D} R^I,$$

and then computing the harmonic mean of the scaled information recall and of the original information precision:

$$F^{I^*} = \frac{2P^I R^{I^*}}{P^I + R^{i^*}}.$$

Additional Metrics

The GALE year-4 evaluation also relied on additional metrics that capture specific aspects of the performance of distillation systems. Additionally, the official evaluation document describes a variety of other methods for measuring information recall. Discussing these methods is beyond the scope of this chapter, and the interested reader is referred to the Formal Evaluation Plan document [30].

Remarks

The metrics proposed in the GALE program over the years suffer from the substantial amount of manual labor entailed. Human judges must analyze each answer returned by a distillation system and compare different answers to detect redundancy. Thus, evaluating a full distillation system is a time-consuming and expensive proposition. This is a potential limitation to the development of distillation systems. An open question is how to construct less demanding metrics to measure the quality of distillation results. In particular, it might be possible to construct meaningful bounds on the performance of a full distillation system using metrics for the individual components of the distillation pipeline.

14.7 Summary

Distillation is a relatively new field of natural language processing that fills the gap between information retrieval and question answering. The DARPA GALE program was very influential in promoting the field and provided the framework for developing and evaluating multilingual and crosslingual distillation.

The current approaches to distillation combine techniques from information extraction and QA with novel statistical methods that allow systems to process complex queries, such as those involving specific events. In the existing systems, queries are specified using templates with one or more arguments. The results are extracted or paraphrased passages retrieved from a corpus and grouped into nonredundant groups.

The two main challenges that distillation faces are the lack of publicly available corpora for measuring the progress of the field and the difficulty and cost of evaluating the outputs of distillation systems due to the lack of automatic metrics.

Bibliography

[1] "Phase 4 GALE distillation annotation guidelines," Tech. Rep., BAE Systems, July 2009.

[2] R. Florian, H. Hassan, A. Ittycheriah, H. Jing, N. Kambhatla, X. Luo, N. Nicolov, and S. Roukos, "A statistical model for multilingual entity detection and tracking," in *Proceedings of the Human Language Technology Conference of the North American Chapter of the Association for Computational Linguistics (HLT/NAACL)*, pp. 1–8, 2004.

[3] A. Berger, S. Della Pietra, and V. Della Pietra, "A maximum entropy approach to natural language processing," *Computational Linguistics*, vol. 22, no. 1, pp. 39–71, 1996.

[4] A. J. Viterbi, "Error bounds for convolutional codes and an asymptotically optimum decoding algorithm," *IEEE Transactions on Information Theory*, vol. IT-13, pp. 260–267, 1967.

[5] X. Luo, A. Ittycheriah, H. Jing, N. Kambhatla, and S. Roukos, "A mention-synchronous coreference resolution algorithm based on the bell tree," in *Proceedings of the 42nd Annual Meeting on Association for Computational Linguistics*, p. 135, 2004.

[6] E. T. Bell, "Exponential numbers," *American Mathematics Monthly*, vol. 41, pp. 411–419, 1934.

[7] NIST, "ACE (automatic content extraction) English annotation guidelines for relations," 2008. http://projects.ldc.upenn.edu/ace/docs/English-Relations-Guidelines_v6.2.pdf.

[8] N. Kambhatla, "Combining lexical, syntactic, and semantic features with maximum entropy models for extracting relations," in *Proceedings of the ACL 2004 on Interactive poster and demonstration sessions*, p. 22, 2004.

[9] "TAC 2009 knowledge base population track," 2009. http://apl.jhu.edu/paulmac/kbp.html.

[10] "Help:infobox." http://en.wikipedia.org/wiki/Help:Infobox.

[11] W. W. Cohen, P. Ravikumar, and S. Fienberg, "A comparison of string metrics for matching names and records," in *KDD Workshop on Data Cleaning and Object Consolidation*, 2003.

[12] Y. Freund and R. E. Schapire, "Large margin classification using the perceptron algorithm," in *Machine Learning*, vol. 37, no. 3, pp. 277–296, 1999.

[13] D. M. Bikel and V. Castelli, "Event matching using the transitive closure of dependency relations," in *Proceedings of the 46th Annual Meeting of the Association for Computational Linguistics on Human Language Technologies*, pp. 145–148, 2008.

[14] A. K. Singla and D. Hakkani-Tür, "Cross-lingual sentence extraction for information distillation," in *Proceedings of the 9th International Conference of the International Speech Communication Association (Interspeech 2008)*, 2008.

[15] M. Levit, D. Hakkani-Tür, G. Tür, and D. Gillick, "IXIR: A statistical information distillation system," *Computer Speech & Language*, vol. 23, no. 4, pp. 527–542, 2009.

[16] M. Levit, B. E., and M. Freedman, "Selecting on-topic sentences from natural language corpora," in *Proceedings of the 8th Conference of the International Speech Communication Association (Interspeech 2007)*, 2007.

[17] J. Lin, "The role of information retrieval in answering complex questions," in *Proceedings of the COLING/ACL on Main Conference Poster Sessions*, pp. 523–530, 2006.

[18] E. V. Hoa, E. M. Voorhees, and H. T. Dang, "Overview of the TREC 2005 question answering track," in *Proceedings of the Text Retrievel Conference (TREC)*, 2005.

[19] G. A. Miller, "WordNet: A lexical database," *Communications of the ACM*, vol. 38, no. 11, 1995.

[20] K. Kamangar, "Unsupervised learning for information distillation," Tech. Rep., Idiap Research Institute, 2007.

[21] K. Kamangar, D. Hakkani-Tür, G. Tür, and M. Levit, "An iterative unsupervised learning method for information distillation," in *Proceedings of the IEEE International Conference on Acoustic Speech and Signal Processing*, pp. 4949–4952, 2008.

[22] I. Soboroff and D. Harman, "Overview of the TREC 2003 novelty track," in *Proceedings of the 12th Text Retrieval Conference (TREC 2003)*, 2003.

[23] J. Lin and D. Demner-Fushman, "Automatically evaluating answers to definition questions," in *Proceedings of the Conference on Human Language Technology and Empirical Methods in Natural Language Processing*, pp. 931–938, 2005.

[24] S. Yaman, G. Tür, D. Vergyri, D. Hakkani-Tür, M. Harper, and W. Wang, "Anchored speech recognition for question answering," in *Proceedings of the North American Chapter of the Association for Computational Linguistics Human Language Technologies Conference*, pp. 265–268, 2009.

[25] F. Gey and D. Oard, "The TREC-2001 cross-language information retrieval track: Searching Arabic using English, French or Arabic queries," in *Proceedings of the 10th Text REtrieval Conference*, pp. 16–25, 2001.

[26] J. S. McCarley, "Should we translate the documents or the queries in cross-language information retrieval?," in *Proceedings of the 37th Annual Meeting of the Association for Computational Linguistics on Computational Linguistics*, pp. 208–214, 1999.

[27] K. Parton, K. R. McKeown, J. Allan, and E. Henestroza, "Simultaneous multilingual search for translingual information retrieval," in *Proceeding of the 17th ACM Conference on Information and Knowledge Management*, pp. 719–728, 2008.

[28] D. Hakkani-Tür and G. Tür, "Statistical sentence extraction for information distillation," in *Proceedings of the IEEE International Conference on Acoustic Speech and Signal Processing*, vol. 4, pp. IV–1–IV–4, 2007.

[29] E. M. Voorhees, "The evaluation of question answering systems: Lessons learned from the trec qa track," in *Proceedings of Question Answering: Strategy and Resources Workshop at LREC-2002*, 2002.

[30] "Phase 4 formal evaluation plan for GALE distillation," Tech. Rep. TR-2458, BAE Systems, Oct. 2009.

Chapter 15

Spoken Dialog Systems

Roberto Pieraccini and David Suendermann

15.1 Introduction

In this chapter we discuss the issues related to the development of commercial spoken dialog systems. A spoken dialog system is a complex machine that manages goal-oriented user interactions. The functional architecture of spoken interaction is generally broken down into three main components: the speech recognition and understanding module, the speech generation module, and the dialog manager. A large amount of literature about research dialog systems and their various development paradigms is available; here we discuss the problems and approaches related to the design, development, deployment, and maintenance of commercial spoken dialog applications. In particular we show how commercial organizations that deploy large-volume dialog systems can use the wealth of data collected to continuously tune the system and improve its performance. One of the issues discussed in this chapter is related to the cost of porting the application to a different language. Although prompt localization is straightforward and typically carried out by professional human translators, the localization of speech recognition and understanding poses a problem of resources and costs. However, because in modern spoken dialog systems grammars are often, but not always, realized by statistical language models and classifiers usually learned from large corpora of annotated utterances, we can recast the problem of grammar localization into that of corpus translation. We show how commercially available machine translation can be used to translate a large corpus of several million utterances and allow for the creation of context-specific grammars that, with very limited human supervision, can achieve a performance comparable to that of manually tuned systems.

15.2 Spoken Dialog Systems

Spoken dialog systems are probably among the most widely adopted applications of speech recognition. A spoken dialog system is an application whereby a machine communicates with humans using speech in a series of sequential interaction turns. In its simplest form, a spoken dialog system can be described by the functional diagram of Figure 15–1.

The **dialog manager**, based on a set of rules called **dialog strategy**, directs a **speech generation** module on what information or request will be spoken after it has received the

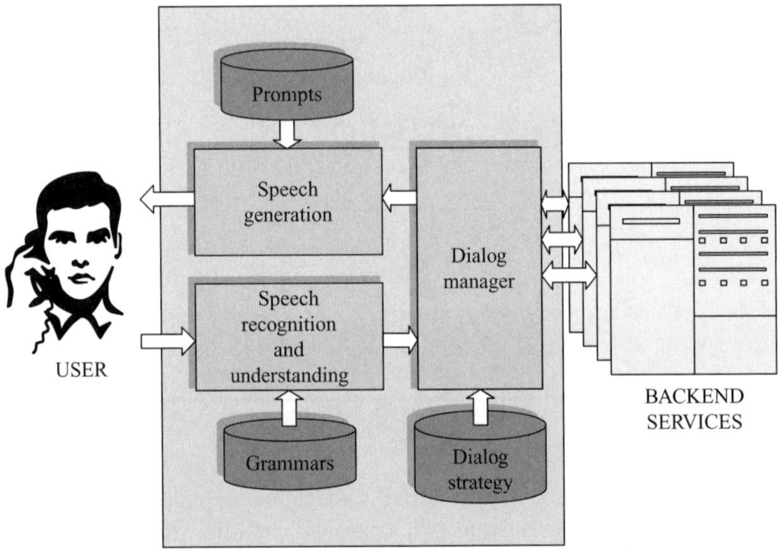

Figure 15–1: A high-level functional diagram of a spoken dialog system

interpretation of the user's speech from a **speech recognition and understanding** module. The dialog manager also interacts with external **backend services**, such as databases, customer relationship management (CRM) systems, or the web, to extract additional information necessary to complete the interaction. We should mention that the approaches described here are in principle language independent. However, some languages may require the application of additional processing, mainly at the level of the speech recognition and understanding module, to deal with different conceptual definitions of token.

15.2.1 Speech Recognition and Understanding

A speech recognition engine is a system that decodes input speech into its constituent words. The understanding module is then responsible for assigning a semantic tag to each string of words returned by the speech recognizer. For instance, imagine the user responds to the prompt: *Have you recently rebooted your PC?* with the expression "You bet." A properly designed understanding module will return the semantic tag YES. Advanced spoken dialog systems developed in research [1] often use large vocabulary recognition at each stage of the interaction on the assumption that a user can and will say anything at any point in the dialog, and thus the system should be able to react accordingly. However, it is also well known that the distribution of what a user will speak is heavily influenced by the specific dialog state; context-specific adaptation of language models has been proven to be beneficial [2] to the performance of spoken dialog systems. But although building a general speech recognizer able to decode words from a very large general vocabulary with tens and often hundreds of thousands of words is possible today, the same is not true for the understanding component. Language understanding, no matter how it is implemented, is always very specific to the domain and often even to the context in which an expression has to be interpreted. For these reasons (the dependency of the language model on the specific dialog context, and the even more specific dependency of the understanding module), and because of the complexity inherent to building effective statistical language models and the lack of specialized resources, the spoken dialog industry, early on, settled on the use of context-specific regular finite state grammars—or **rule-based grammars**. Rule-based grammars are generally written according to the SRGS[1] (Speech Recognition Grammar Specification) standard, even though different recognition engines support other proprietary grammar definition languages. SRGS allows for writing arbitrary context-free grammar rules with embedded ECMAScript[2] code. The rules define the syntax of the expressions accepted and recognized by the recognition engine. ECMAScript defines the interpretation of the return string in terms of semantic slot tags. For example, this is a snippet of an SRGS grammar rule used in a sample department store routing application:

```
  <rule id="selection" scope="public">
 <item repeat='0-1'><ruleref uri='prefixes.xml'/></item>
 <one-of>
   <item><ruleref uri='#rule_Footwear'/>
     <tag>out.answer='Footwear';</tag>
   </item>
   <item><ruleref uri='#rule_Jewelry'/>
     <tag>out.answer='Jewelry';</tag>
   </item>
   <item><ruleref uri='#rule_MensWear'/>
     <tag>out.answer='MensWear';</tag>
   </item>
   <item><ruleref uri='#rule_Mowers'/>
     <tag>out.answer='Mowers';</tag>
   </item>
 </one-of>
</rule>
```

The `<one-of>` element defines a set of alternatives specified by each of the `<item>` elements. `<ruleref>` is a reference to another rule identified by the associated URL. The `<tag>` element includes snippets of ECMAScript. For instance, if the spoken input utterance is parsed by the `#rule_Footwear` rule, the ECMAScript statement `out.answer='Footwear'` is executed. The ECMAScript object `out` is available in the calling application namespace as the return semantics of the speech recognizer. The reference to `prefixes.xml` includes an optional prefix grammar.

The rule reference `#rule_Footwear` can be expanded by the following SRGS snippet:

```
<rule id="rule_Footwear" scope="public">
  <one-of>
    <item>footwear</item>
```

1. http://www.w3.org/TR/speech-grammar/

2. ECMAScript (http://www.ecmascript.org/) is a scripting language standardized by ECMA International. JavaScript is an ECMAScript dialect.

```
    <item>foot wear</item>
    <item>shoes</item>
    <item>boots</item>
  </one-of>
</rule>
```

This rule states that any of the expressions defined by the `<item>` elements can be spoken and, if recognized, the value `'Footwear'` will be assigned to the output slot (`out.answer`). As it is clear from the example, rule-based grammars can be very complex and can include references to other rules and scripts. Their maintenance is equivalent to the maintenance of complex code. Very little can be automated, and every change or improvement needs to be handled manually by grammar experts (known as **speech scientists** by the industry).

From the functional point of view, a grammar can be thought of as two components, as described by Figure 15–2. The language model defines the space of all possible strings of words that the speech recognizer can handle, and the semantic classifier maps any particular string of words into one of a finite set of semantic tags. As we saw earlier in this chapter, the language model can be specified by the rules of a rule-based grammar, and the semantic classifier can be implemented by ECMAScript code. If we move to the realm of statistical grammars, the language model is defined as a set of n-grams, and semantic classification is generally done by a learned statistical classifier operating on the string of words returned by the speech recognition component. Although a rule-based grammar is generally built by hand, statistical grammars are built from a possibly large set of sample utterances that have been **transcribed** into the corresponding strings of words and **annotated** with their corresponding semantic tag. Table 15–1 shows an example of a set of transcribed and annotated utterances from people calling the main technical support number of a large U.S. cable company. The transcribed utterances are the responses to the prompt *Please tell me the reason for your call.*

Once a large number of transcriptions and the corresponding semantic annotations are available, a statistical language model can be built and used to constrain the speech recognizer and a statistical semantic classifier. The statistical language model is in the form of n-grams, typically with $n = 3$, or **trigrams**. A trigram is the set of probabilities for any word in an utterance to be preceded by any possible pair of words. So, if t is the index of a word in an utterance, the set of probabilities that constitute a trigram has the form:

$$p(w_t|w_{t-1}w_{t-2}) \tag{15.1}$$

There are several ways to estimate trigrams, the main problem being for the triplets of words that do not appear in the training set. To that purpose, different backoff techniques have been proposed in the literature; see, for instance, the language modeling Chapter 5.

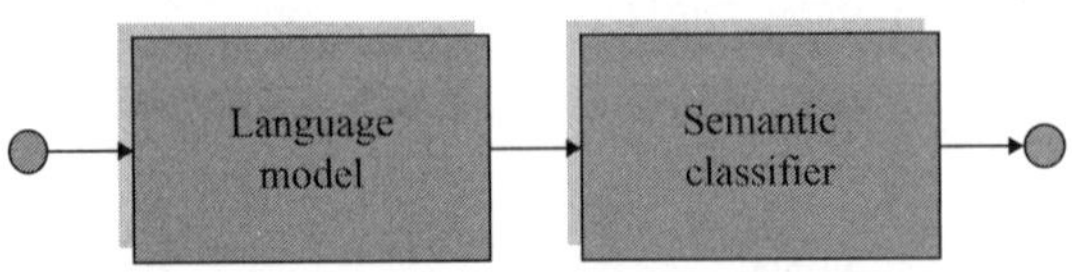

Figure 15–2: Equivalent functional diagram of a spoken dialog grammar

Table 15–1: Example set of transcribed and annotated utterances

TRANSCRIPTION	ANNOTATION
want to cancel the account	SERVICE_CANCEL
cancel service	SERVICE_CANCEL
cancellation of the service	SERVICE_CANCEL
I want to discontinue the service	SERVICE_CANCEL
I can't send a particular message to a certain group of people	CANT_SEND_RECEIVE_EMAIL
I can't get messages on my email and Outlook Express	CANT_SEND_RECEIVE_EMAIL
I can't receive all my email	CANT_SEND_RECEIVE_EMAIL
I'm trying to send an email and it says it's not going through	CANT_SEND_RECEIVE_EMAIL
my emails are not being received at the address I send them to	CANT_SEND_RECEIVE_EMAIL
can't send	CANT_SEND_RECEIVE_EMAIL
can't send large files	CANT_SEND_RECEIVE_EMAIL
bounce message notification	CANT_SEND_RECEIVE_EMAIL
message won't be sent won't send	CANT_SEND_RECEIVE_EMAIL
it concerns mac mail I can't open it	SETUP_EMAIL
when I set up the internet you didn't give the email account	SETUP_EMAIL
I can't set up my email account	SETUP_EMAIL
setting up email account	SETUP_EMAIL
cannot configure the email	SETUP_EMAIL
they registered my modem from my Internet and I need to get my email address	SETUP_EMAIL
all I need is to find out how to set up my sent email box to save my sent email	SETUP_EMAIL
I'd like to set up an additional email account	SETUP_EMAIL

As far as the statistical semantic classifier is concerned, we can use several techniques. A discussion on the performance of different classifiers applied to large corpora of collected utterances can be found in Evanini, Suendermann, and Pieraccini [3].

15.2.2 Speech Generation

The speech generation module in commercial spoken dialog systems is quite limited or nonexistent. Research has experimented with natural language generation (NLG) modules followed by text-to-speech (TTS). However, the quality of a combined NLG and TTS solution is not high enough to support a commercial, widely used spoken dialog system. Even the use of TTS on predefined text is generally limited to situations where the variability of the message makes prerecording of high-quality prompts impractical or impossible. In reality, most of the commercial applications use experienced voiceover actors and voice talents to record all the predefined prompts necessary for an application. For complex applications, such as technical support customer care [4], it is not unusual to record a number of prompts ranging between 5,000 and 10,000. When needed, a simple form of concatenative speech synthesis is used to play variable prompts such as arbitrary numbers.

15.2.3 Dialog Manager

In a typical commercial implementation of a spoken dialog system, the dialog strategy is expressed as a **call-flow** [5]. A call-flow corresponds to the specification of a finite state machine, often structured in a hierarchical fashion, with nodes representing dialog activities and arcs corresponding to conditions. A typical activity can be that of instructing the speech generation module to play a specific recorded prompt and, at the same time, activating the speech recognition module with a specific grammar. Other activities can be querying external backend services, setting and evaluating internal variables, performing any type of arbitrary computation, or invoking another call-flow as a subdialog.

Historically, spoken dialog managers were first implemented programmatically by software developers using traditional procedural languages (C, C++, or Java), each new application hardcoded as a specific finite state machine (or call-flow). With the advent of the VoiceXML standard—initially drafted by the VoiceXML forum[3] during the late 1990s, and then adopted as a recommendation[4] by the World Wide Web Consortium (W3C)—spoken dialog applications started to be implemented as web applications. In analogy with a visual web browser, such as Internet Explorer or Firefox, a voice browser interprets a markup language (e.g., VoiceXML) to control its resources (e.g., speech recognition, TTS) at each turn of the interaction. Again, as with a visual web browser, voice browsers use the HTTP protocol to interact with the application server and receive VoiceXML documents in response to HTTP requests. VoiceXML documents instruct the browser about playing specific prompts and recognizing input speech using a specific speech recognizer and grammar. Prompt-playing resources, TTS, and speech recognition engines are controlled by the browser using specific protocols (such as Media Resource Control Protocol, or MRCP)[5]

The VoiceXML markup language also includes directives to instruct the browser to fetch another document in a conditional manner, thus realizing a static call-flow as a collection of linked documents. However, as the complexity of the application grows, as it happened for traditional visual web applications, developers moved from the static model—a collection of static documents—toward the dynamic, on-demand generation of markup. In this case the application server hosts a program that implements the call-flow finite-state machine and dynamically generates VoiceXML at each turn of interaction to instruct the browser to play prompts and recognize input speech. Moreover, developers can build a generic-purpose call-flow engine—the dialog manager—and specify the topology of the call-flow along with its attributes using a specific, often proprietary call-flow markup language. See Pieraccini and Huerta [6] for a detailed description of the evolution of dialog management.

3. http://www.voicexml.org/
4. http://www.w3.org/TR/2007/REC-voicexml21-20070619/
5. http://tools.ietf.org/html/rfc4463

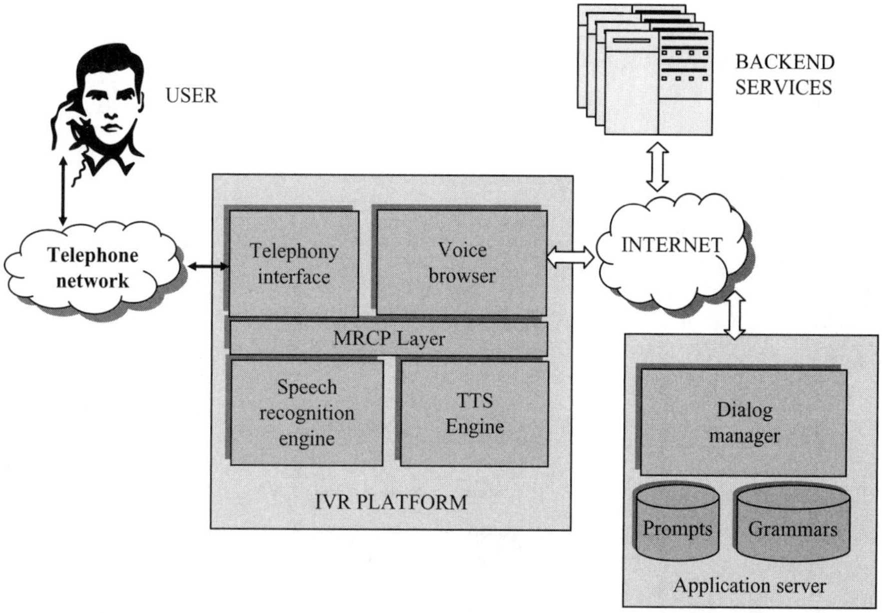

Figure 15–3: Architecture of a modern commercial spoken dialog system

Figure 15–3 shows the architecture of a modern commercial spoken dialog system. The interactive voice response (IVR) platform comprises a VoiceXML browser, which interprets VoiceXML documents, and a telephone interface, which connects to the public telephone network (or equivalently, a Voice over IP gateway). The VoiceXML browser controls standard speech recognition and TTS engines through a MRCP protocol layer.

The interaction is managed by the application server (implemented through a regular Web server), which serves VoiceXML documents upon HTTP requests issued by the IVR platform. Prompts and grammars are generally associated to URLs and may be hosted by the same web server that hosts the application server or elsewhere in the network. The dialog manager may occasionally access backend services, often using SOAP (Simple Object Access Protocol) directives. The IVR platform and the application do not have to be part of the same local network but may be geographically distributed, as it is often the case.

15.2.4 Voice User Interface

The voice user interface (VUI) specification for a given application is what describes the system's prompts, what is the range of expressions accepted by the speech recognizer at each step of the interaction, and the general logic of the application. A call-flow is a finite-state machine description of an application VUI. VUIs are often designed and developed using drag-and-drop WYSIWYG tools that allow visualizing all the details of the interaction as a hierarchical finite-state machine. Call-flow authoring tools compile the graphical representation in a call-flow markup language—typically a proprietary language—which is then used by a call-flow application engine to render the interaction by generating VoiceXML

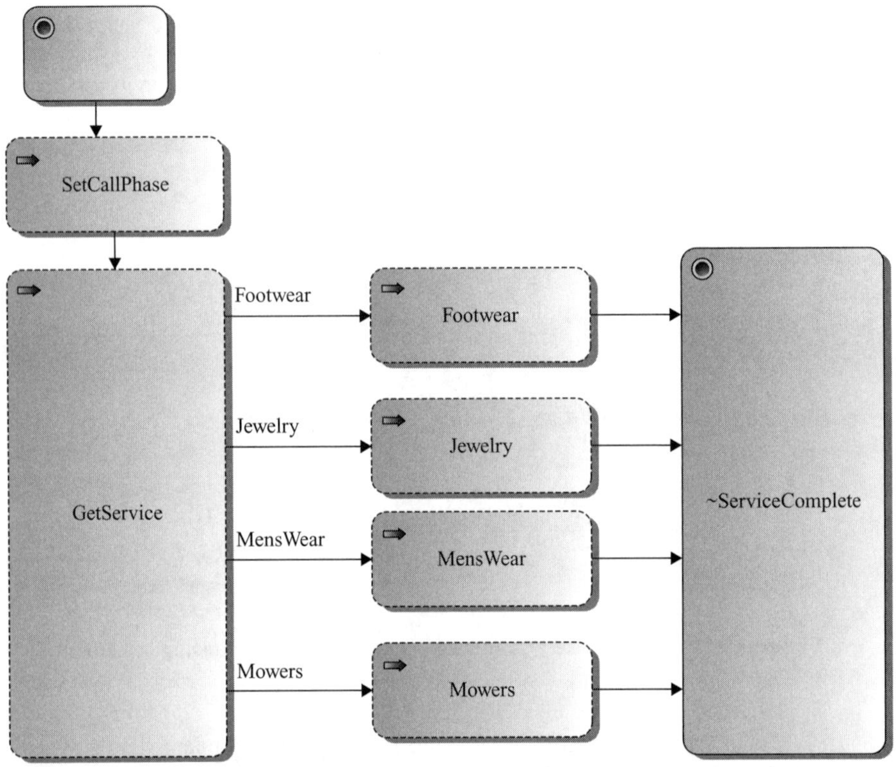

Figure 15–4: Example call-flow specification built with a WYSIWYG authoring tool

dynamically. Figure 15–4 is an example of the graphical specification[6] of a call-flow module (process).

Boxes represent activities, which are the equivalent of the statements of a traditional procedural language. Arcs represent conditional transitions to other activities; that is, they are the equivalent of if-then-else clauses of a traditional procedural language. The first activity in the upper left corner of Figure 15–4 is the entry point of the process, and the activity to the right of the chart, indicated by ∼`ServiceComplete`, indicates the return to the calling process (the `Main` process in this case). All the other activities in Figure 15–4 are process references: they correspond to the invocation of subroutines defined by other graphical specifications (or pages) similar to the one of Figure 15–4. Process references are the equivalent of function calls in a traditional language. For instance, the `GetService` process is specified by the graphical page of Figure 15–5.

6. Here and in the rest of the chapter, we use SpeechCycle's RPA Compose as an example of a tool for the development of advanced spoken dialog systems (see http://www.speechcycle.com). Other research tools are publicly available, such as Olympus (http://accent.speech.cs.cmu.edu/), an open source dialog framework provided by Carnegie Mellon University, and Galaxy (http://groups.csail.mit.edu/sls/technologies/galaxy.shtml), provided by MIT.

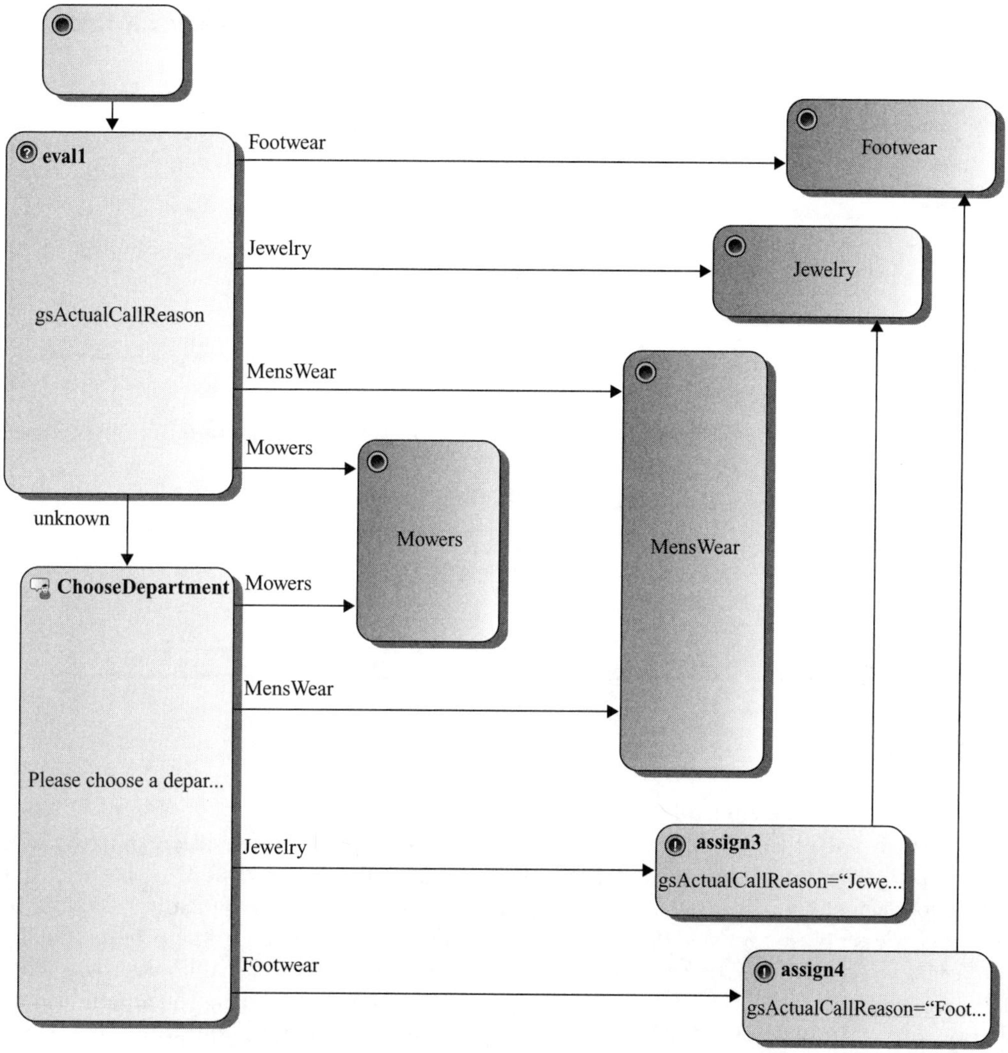

Figure 15–5: Expansion of the `GetService` process referenced in Figure 15–4

The activity called `eval1` (upper left of Figure 15–5) corresponds to the evaluation of the variable `getActualCallReason`. If the variable evaluates as one of the four possible values (`Footwear, Jewelry, MensWear, Mowers`), the current process returns to the calling one with the appropriate return value. If the variable is unassigned (value is unknown), the process proceeds to the activity named `ChooseDepartment`, which is a question activity (as indicated by the top left icon in the box), also known as DM, or dialog module [7]. In its simplest form, a DM plays a prompt and activates the speech recognition engine with a given grammar or a set of grammars. However, a DM needs to deal with several discourse issues, such as timeouts, repromptings, and confirmations. So, the proper configuration of a DM requires the designer to set several functional parameters.

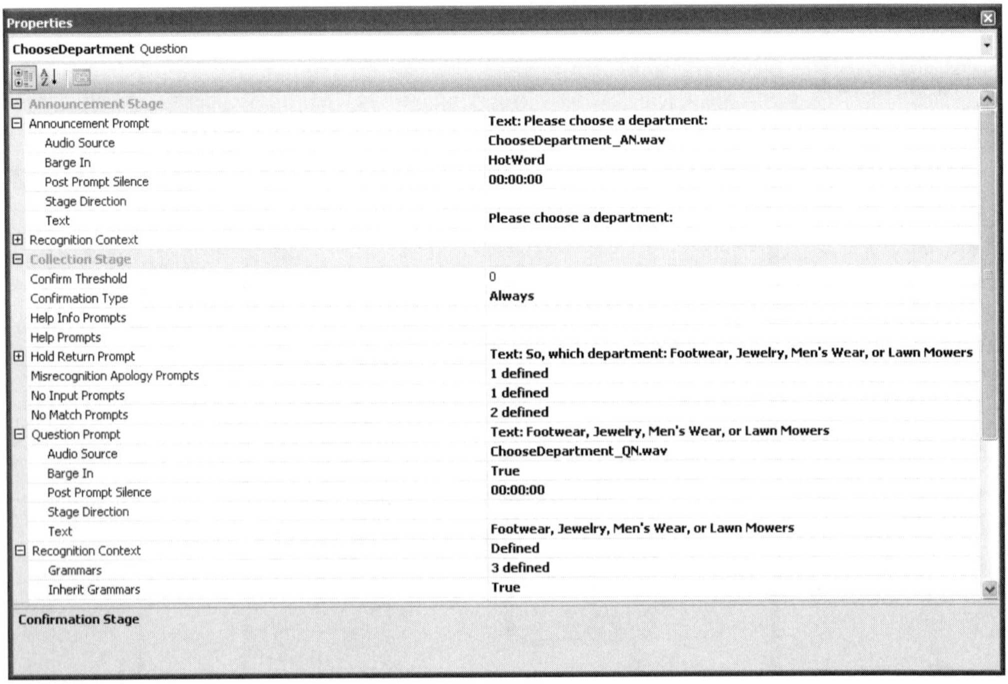

Figure 15–6: Properties of a dialog module

Describing the meaning of all the properties of a DM, as shown in Figure 15–6, is beyond the scope of this chapter, but it is enough to take into consideration that the most important properties are the various prompts and grammars used by the DM. For example, the announcement is the first part of a prompt where barge-in is typically disabled, for instance, *Please choose a department.* Question is the content portion of the prompt, such as *Footwear, Jewelry, Men's Wear,* or *Lawn Mowers.* Typically only general hot words, such as *help* or *operator*, and thus the corresponding grammars, are active during the announcement portion of a DM. All other content grammars are active during the question. The active grammars are indicated by the Recognition Context property. More than one grammar can be used in parallel. For instance, for the DM described here, three grammars are active during the question, as shown by Figure 15–7.

The three active parallel grammars of Figure 15–7 are a voice grammar, including expressions that describe each of the possible departments (see grammar examples in the previous section), a DTMF grammar that describes which keys of the telephone keypad correspond to which choice, and an operator grammar that captures several ways to speak an operator request.

To conclude this section, we remark that building a complex application requires design of a call-flow that fully captures the evolution of the interaction on the basis of activities that include prompts and grammars, along with many other parameters. Building a spoken dialog application requires a coding effort aided by the availability of authoring tools, such as the one described earlier, which allows developing a call-flow while visualizing

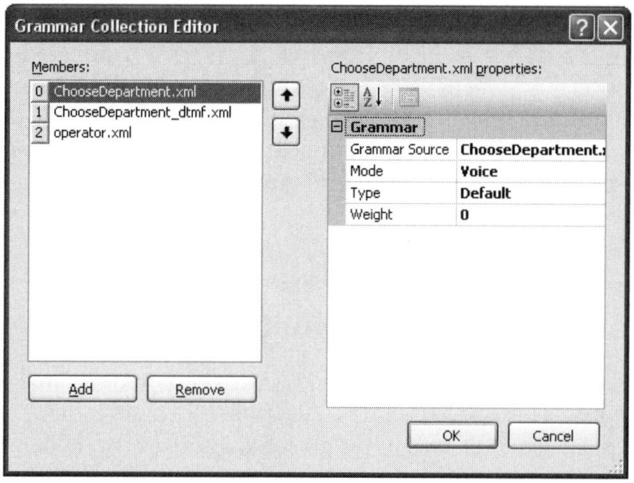

Figure 15–7: Grammars active during the question of the dialog module described by Figure 15–6

it as a hierarchical finite-state machine. Current commercial dialog systems for complex applications such as technical support may include hundreds of pages, like the ones shown in Figures 15–4 and 15–5, and thousands of activities.

15.3 Forms of Dialog

Most deployed commercial dialog systems today follow the **directed dialog** paradigm, meaning that the system generally directs the course of interaction by asking questions and interpreting the user answers. At each step of the interaction, the dialog system asks a specific question by providing a menu of choices, suggesting possible responses, or referring to a list of items known to the user, like a city name or a date.

By contrast, research systems have been targeting the goal of open dialog which, allows for a certain degree of **mixed initiative**. This type of interaction leaves full freedom to the users to express what they want, typically using natural language input, with limited constraints or guidance by the system. Although several research systems have implemented different degrees of mixed initiative in a restricted domain (e.g., ATIS, CMU [8, 9]), commercial spoken dialog systems have always remained as close as possible to the directed dialog paradigm. There are several reasons for that, including the lack of practical and robust representations for mixed-initiative interaction and the difficulty of providing a complete prediction of the behavior of a mixed-initiative system with respect to all possible input situations (known as the **VUI completeness principle** [6]). Moreover, in the presence of open prompts, users often do not know what to say [10, 11]. This causes users to produce underspecified requests, which require a follow-up of the system in a directed dialog fashion, or requests that go beyond the limitations of the system, leading to interaction failure.

For these reasons, in today's commercially deployed systems, mixed-initiative dialog and open prompts are limited or totally absent. Often, only the initial question—typically the identification of the call reason—is based on an open prompt, and the rest of the dialog is conducted in a directed dialog fashion. However, even with a directed dialog interaction, where the prompt strictly instructs users or provides hints on what to say, a certain amount of unconstrained input and input not matching what is requested by the prompt is observed. For instance, when prompting in a billing application *Do you want to pay by credit card or at a payment center?* callers may answer *debit card*, *check*, or *online*, not matching any of the predefined choices.

15.4 Natural Language Call Routing

Although, by and large, users tend to respond with the keywords and phrases suggested by well-crafted prompts, there are several applications in which a directed dialog approach is not practical. Applications of this type are characterized by a domain model that is complex and unknown to the majority of users. Call routing applications, for instance, fall in this category. There can be a huge variety of call reasons to be covered in such applications (sometimes as many as several hundreds [12]), which cannot be handled by single or stacked directed dialogs. Identifying the call reason would require multiple questions even though callers could effectively and clearly express what they need by means of a single utterance.

A possible solution would be providing a menu that includes all possible semantically distinct reasons that users can call about. However, the list of all possible reasons may be too large, and building a grammar that captures all the possible expressions that can be used to describe all of them may be impractical. On the other hand, an elaborated disambiguation using stacked, or hierarchical, directed dialog menus to identify the call reason would require multiple questions to be answered, resulting in an overly long interaction and consequent poor caller experience with the risk of losing the caller. In this type of situation, one of the solutions is to let callers express themselves freely and back the system with a statistical classifier able to assign user utterances to one of the predefined categories, as described earlier. This technique, known as How May I Help You [13], statistical call routing [14, 15], or statistical natural language understanding [16], is just a simplified form of language understanding that combines the robustness of a structured approach (a limited number of categories, or routes) with the flexibility of natural language (an open prompt leading to a large number of possible user expressions). In fact, the dialog can still be structured in a directed dialog manner because the output of the interaction is one of a predefined number of categories. Statistical grammars based on n-grams learned from large amounts of data can generally be applied to this problem, where the semantic interpretation of the message is obtained by a statistical classifier [3], as described earlier.

15.5 Three Generations of Dialog Applications

Since the beginning of the telephony spoken dialog industry in the mid 1990s, we have witnessed the evolution of at least three generations of systems. What differentiates each generation is not only the increase in complexity but also the different architectures used.

Table 15–2: Generations of dialog systems (VXML, Voice Extensible Markup Language; SLU, statistical language understanding)

	Generation		
	First	Second	Third
Time Period	1994–2001	2000–2005	2004–today
Type of Application	Informational	Transactional	Problem Solving
Examples	Package tracking, flight status	Banking, stock trading, train reservation	Customer care, technical support, help desk
Architecture	Proprietory	Static VXML	Dynamic VXML
Complexity (Number of DMs)	10	100	1000
Interaction Turns	Few	10	100
Dialog Modality	Directed	Directed + natural language (SLU)	Directed + natural language (SLU) + limited mixed initiative

Table 15–2 provides a summary of the features that distinguish each generation. The first-generation systems were mostly informational in that they would request some information from the user and provide information in return. Examples of those systems, mostly developed during the mid and late 1990s, are package tracking, simple financial applications, and flight status information. At the time, there were no standards for developing dialog systems, and thus the dialog applications of the first generation were implemented on proprietary platforms, typically evolutions of existing touch-tone IVR architectures.

The number of DMs in a call-flow is generally an indication of the application complexity. First-generation applications showed a range of complexity of a few to tens of DMs, typically spanning a few turns of interaction. Early applications supported strict directed dialog interaction that would also result in a limited grammar or vocabulary at each turn.

The applications of the second generation were typically transactional, in the sense that they could perform actual transactions on behalf of the user, like moving funds between bank accounts, trading stocks, or buying tickets. Most of those applications were developed using the new standards, typically as collections of VoiceXML documents. The complexity moved to the range of dozens of DMs, spanning a number of turns of interactions of an order of magnitude of ten or more. At the same time, some of the applications started using statistical grammars for mapping loosely constrained user utterances to a finite number of predefined semantic categories (SLU, or statistical language understanding). The natural language modality—as opposed to directed dialog—was initially used mostly for call routing.

Whereas the model behind the first and second generations of dialog applications can be described by the form-filling paradigm, and the interaction follows a predetermined simple script, the third-generation systems have risen to a qualitatively different level of complexity. Problem-solving applications, like customer care, help desk, and technical support, are characterized by a level of complexity ranging in the thousands of DMs for a number of turns of dynamic interaction in the dozens that can exceptionally reach 100 or more turns. As the sophistication of the applications evolved, so did the system architecture by moving the logic from the client (VoiceXML browser, or voice browser) to the server [6]. As described previously more and more systems are today based on generic dialog application servers that interpret a dialog specification and serve the voice browser with dynamically generated VoiceXML documents. Finally, the interaction modality of the third-generation systems is moving from the strictly directed dialog application toward using more natural language turns and some degree of mixed initiative.

15.6 Continuous Improvement Cycle

Usually, third-generation dialog systems have integration functionality that communicates with backend databases or remote devices, support multiple input and output modalities, and can sometimes sustain more than 20 minutes of interaction with a user. In order to keep a caller engaged in such environments, the use of advanced VUI techniques such as incorporation of natural language understanding, limited mixed-initiative, and dynamic response generation is critical. As discussed earlier, natural language understanding was first introduced to automate spoken dialog systems as call classifiers, or call routers, in the second generation. The caller was asked a general question at the top of the call, such as *Briefly tell me what you're calling about today.* The caller's utterance was then recognized and the call routed to the appropriate agent on the basis of the result of the semantic classifier. The human agent then interacted with the caller, providing services including, for instance, technical problem solving, billing support, or order processing. Third-generation dialog systems, by contrast, are designed to emulate the human agent's role to a far greater degree.

As dialog systems improved, callers' expectations increased. Several characteristics of modern dialog system design encourage callers to behave as if they were interacting with a human agent. Such characteristics include open-ended questions at the beginning of a conversation and global commands such as "help" and "repeat" at every point in the dialog. This design encourages callers to say things that are not explicitly prompted by the dialog system. Furthermore, explicit directed dialog prompts in which callers are asked to choose an item from a list often unintentionally elicit out-of-grammar utterances that may be incomplete, too vague, or too specific. That causes handcrafted rule-based grammars to break for a not negligible portion of the user inputs. Even listening to hundreds of calls will hardly provide a broad understanding of what expressions will be spoken at every point in a dialog system that receives millions of calls every month. It is barely possible to satisfy this expectation with the still-common approach of using handcrafted, rule-based grammars. Suendermann et al. [17] proposed a method to continuously improve dialog context performance by using caller utterances to tune SLU classifiers and use them at every dialog recognition context, even when directed dialog prompts would request a simple response, such as yes or no. To automate the process as much as possible, collection, transcription, annotation, language model and classifier training, baseline testing, and grammar publishing are carried out programmatically in a continuous cycle that requires very limited expert supervision. The goal is to ensure continual improvement of system behavior and to obtain the highest possible recognition performance reflecting the actual caller behavior in a statistical manner. This process was validated on over 2 million utterances from more than half a million full calls to a complex call-routing and troubleshooting dialog system leading to substantial increase in the performance of the system.

15.7 Transcription and Annotation of Utterances

Tuning large-scale spoken dialog systems of the third generation typically requires several hundreds of thousands, if not millions of utterances to be transcribed and semantically annotated. Although transcription and annotation of such amounts of data is partially automatable, it can still keep several people busy for months. While transcription is a relatively straightforward exercise, semantic annotation (i.e., the mapping of a lexical content to one of a number of semantic symbols) requires knowledge about the application. Not only must annotators understand what a caller utterance means in the context of the system prompt, but there are several aspects to semantic annotation making it a nontrivial undertaking, such as:

- Utterances may have no representation in the given set of semantic categories, suggesting that they are out-of-scope for the grammar.
- When the ratio of out-of-scope utterances grows and well-distinguishable patterns manifest themselves, annotators are to suggest the introduction of new semantic categories that have to be taken into account by the logic of the system.
- Utterances may be ambiguous, vague, too specific, or carry content belonging to multiple semantic categories, making it hard for the annotator to make a decision.
- Annotations have to follow a number of quality assurance criteria to produce powerful and exact results, including criteria for completeness, consistency, congruence, correlation, confusion, coverage, and corpus size, also referred to as C^7 [18].

These issues emphasize that thorough speech recognition tuning in spoken dialog systems requires careful planning and coordination.

15.8 Localization of Spoken Dialog Systems

Large-scale third-generation spoken dialog systems are mostly used by enterprises trying to optimize their customer care telephone portals. Many of these companies operate internationally, producing a need to localize their phone services, including spoken dialog systems. Moreover, some countries have a large multilingual population of users, such as English and Spanish users in the United States and English and French users in Canada.

As we discussed earlier the user interaction in spoken dialog systems is primarily determined by three sources of content: the call-flow, the prompts, and the grammars. In addition, we have to consider the localization of the speech recognition, and if needed, the TTS engines. However, given that commercial recognition and TTS engines are being used and that the major manufacturer of standard commercial engines provide **language packs** (i.e., sets of acoustic and pronunciation model extensions for all the major languages), localizing the speech recognition and TTS engines is as straightforward as acquiring the necessary language extension for the speech engines used in production. Therefore, in the rest of this section we analyze the issues pertaining to call-flow, prompts, and grammars in relation to the localization of a spoken dialog system.

15.8.1 Call-Flow Localization

The call-flow determines the logic of the interaction, including, at a high level, which questions will be asked and which information will be presented to the user at each point of the interaction. However, the particular linguistic form in which questions and statements are presented to the user, that is, the actual prompts, and the grammars that specify what the callers can say and how that is translated into semantic tags, should not be part of the call-flow. Rather, they should be represented by specific placeholders (dynamic variables, table lookups) to realize a clear separation between logic and linguistic content. The call-flow is specified by a large graph where the nodes correspond to system actions and the arcs are associated to conditions, such as the semantic tags returned by the semantic classifier after a successful user interaction. Also, the symbolic semantic tags can be language-independent. An example of this separation between logic and linguistic content is the call-flow layout and the DM properties described earlier.

We generally assume that the logic part of the call-flow does not change across languages. Although this assumption may hold for languages and cultures that are somehow close, such as U.S. English and Spanish, it may break when considering languages and cultures that may be considerably different, such as English and Japanese. Here, porting an application from one language to the other may entail changing the order in which questions are asked and may require modifications of the call-flow because of cultural reasons. However, for the rest of this chapter, we assume that the logic part of the call-flow does not have to be localized.

15.8.2 Prompt Localization

The prompts represent what the system speaks at each step of the interaction. Typically, several prompts are associated to the collection of a single piece of information from the user because information collection through speech recognition may require the engagement in different dialog activities as a result of the issues typical of spoken language interaction, such as speech recognition rejection, timeouts, and low confidence. All these activities are part of the logic of a dialog module. The following is a list of all the typical prompts that need to be designed for the collection of a single piece of information, let's say a telephone number:

- Main collection prompt: This prompt is issued the first time the information is requested. For instance: *Say or enter your ten-digit telephone number.*

- Retry prompt: In case the speech recognizer rejects the first input, a retry prompt encourages the user to speak the same information again. For instance: *I didn't get that. Please say or enter your ten-digit telephone number again.*
- Confirmation prompt: If the recognizer comes back with a medium confidence, the recognition hypothesis is confirmed. For instance: *That was three one zero nine two six seven one two three, right?*
- Repair prompt: In case the user denies the confirmed hypothesis, the system prompts again. For instance: *I am sorry, please say or enter your ten-digit telephone number again.*
- Timeout prompt: This prompt is played if the user does not speak within the amount of time allocated for the input, and the speech recognizer times out. For instance: *I didn't hear anything. Please say or enter your ten-digit telephone number.*
- Help prompt: This prompt is played if the user asks for help. For instance: *Sure, here's some more information. I'm looking for the phone number you are calling from. Please say or enter your telephone number one digit at a time, starting with the area code.*
- Come back prompt: This prompt is played if the system comes back to the same question, after a diversion, such as after a help prompt. For instance: *So, just say or enter your ten-digit telephone number.*
- Operator prompt: This prompt is played if the user explicitly requests an operator or pushes 0. For instance: *I understand you would like to speak to an agent, but I need to get your phone number first in order to route you to the right agent. Please enter or say....*

This list is just a nonexhaustive example, and the set of possible prompts for each dialog module can be larger than that. For instance, there might be different retry and timeout prompts that can be spoken after the first attempt, up to a maximum number after which the system declares failure to collect the information, and you would need prompts for that, too. Or the prompts can be personalized depending on what the system knows about the user, such as different prompts for different levels of user expertise with the dialog system, different prompts for different user age brackets, and so on. Hence, for each piece of information collected, you need not just one prompt but many, often several dozens, to handle all the possible discourse situations. So, even for a simple system, it is not uncommon to end up with hundreds, and for complex systems, thousands or tens of thousands of prompts that need to be designed, managed, and translated into a different language when a system has to be localized.

Because the performance of a spoken dialog system is very sensitive to the quality of the prompts, from both the linguistic and audio points of view, it is important to obtain a high-quality translation of them that takes into account the precise context when they are played. Obviously, the only way to accomplish a high-quality translation is by engaging the service of a professional translator who, with the help of a VUI designer, would have to translate the prompts one by one. Despite that a spoken dialog system may comprise several thousands of prompts, the cost of this operation is not excessive, and it is generally performed without any automated process.

One of the main technology issues in prompt translation is the maintenance of the relationships between the call-flow and the sets of prompts in the different languages. The call-flow maintenance environment needs to include localization and prompt management tools that allow maintaining different versions of prompts for different languages in the face of modifications to the application. The tool needs to flag prompts that have been modified, added, or deleted in one of the languages and require similar operations for the corresponding prompts of the other language. Without such a tool, the maintenance of multilingual spoken dialog systems can become overly unwieldy and expensive.

15.8.3 Localization of Grammars

Localization of grammars is the most problematic part of the porting of a spoken dialog system to a different language. On the one hand, rule-based grammars are hard to translate because one we cannot present them to professional translators or interpreters in their original form, such as the one in the examples of rule-based grammars shown earlier, and expect them to produce an accurate translation. This is because phrases and sentences often are broken into grammatical constituents that are arranged in different levels of hierarchical composition. Making sense of them may be as hard as making sense of software written by someone else. So, the effort of translating a rule-based grammar may be comparable to that of rewriting it from scratch. But a professional translator cannot write grammars, so we need to employ a mother-tongue speech scientist or team up a speech scientist with a professional translator expert in the target language.

On the other hand, statistical grammars, used to a large extent in third-generation applications, cannot be directly translated because they are composed of n-grams and statistical classifiers. If professional translators cannot write rule-based grammars, it is more the case for n-grams and statistical classifiers! Instead it is much easier to retrain n-grams and classifiers from scratch using a corpus of transcriptions and annotations in the target language. But finding a new corpus in the target language may be difficult or impractical, and translating the entire corpus of several hundreds of thousands, if not millions, of utterances from the source to the target language will be financially demanding and hard to complete within a reasonable timeframe using human translators. However, machine translation can be used for that.

In the following, we report on recent work carried out to localize statistical grammars in an automatic way using a commercial machine translation engine, especially useful when not enough data resources are available in the target language.

15.8.4 The Source Data

As a case study of using machine translation for grammar localization, we used source data collected in the scope of a large-scale English dialog system for broadband Internet troubleshooting, as described in further detail by Acomb et al. [4]. Over a time span of more than three years, several millions of calls were processed by this system. For a sizable subset of these calls, utterances were captured, transcribed, and semantically annotated based on a complete list of semantic categories. Table 15–3 provides an overview of the amount of data available for the source language; it lists the number of calls with transcribed utterances, the number of transcribed (also distinct) and annotated utterances, and an

Table 15–3: Summary of the English source data

Calls	1,159,940
Transcribed utterances	4,293,898
Distinct utterances	278,917
Annotated utterances	3,846,050 (89.6%)
DMs	2,332
Grammars	253

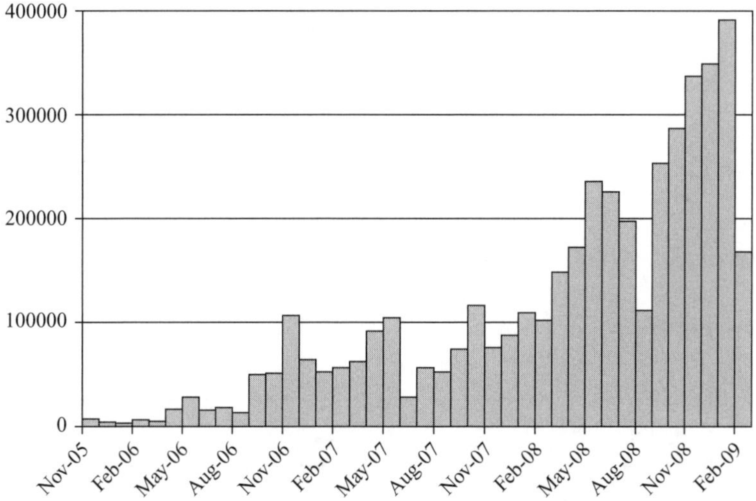

Figure 15–8: Utterance collection monthly volume

indication of the complexity of the system in terms of number of DMs and number of grammars.

The original English dialog system had undergone the continuous improvement cycle—as described earlier—before it was considered for localization. Because the aforementioned human involvement for the generation of transcriptions and annotations decreases as more and more data is collected, the productivity increases, and more and more utterances can be processed in a given timeframe [19]. Figure 15–8 shows the distribution of utterances over the collection time period indicating that the capture volume was continuously increasing since the start of the project.

15.8.5 Training

All 4,293,898 transcribed utterances of Table 15–3 were translated from English into Spanish using commercial statistical machine translation software. In fact, this was done by only translating the 278,917 unique expressions and associating the translations with the source utterances' contexts. Figure 15–9 shows the Zipf-like distribution of the unique expressions in the corpus. The translation was performed in a completely unsupervised fashion. No

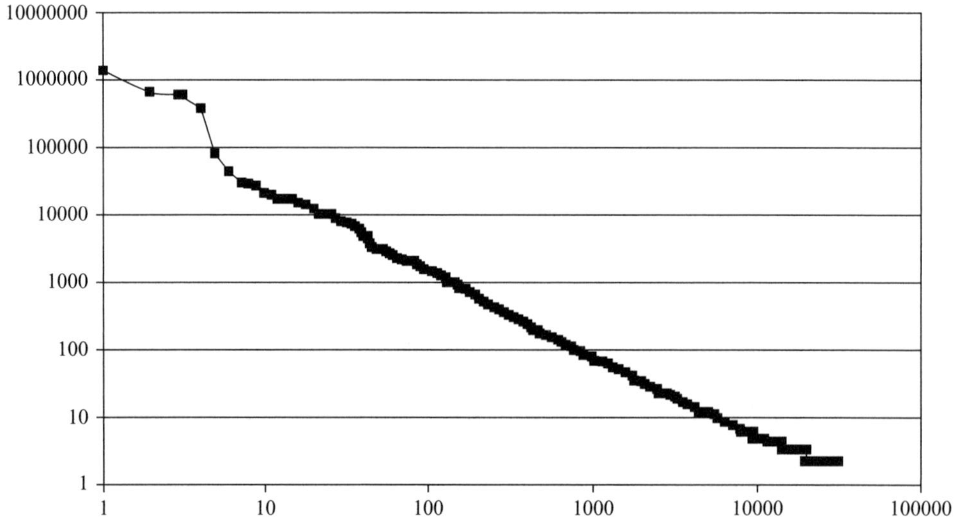

Figure 15–9: Frequency distribution of the unique expressions in the English corpus

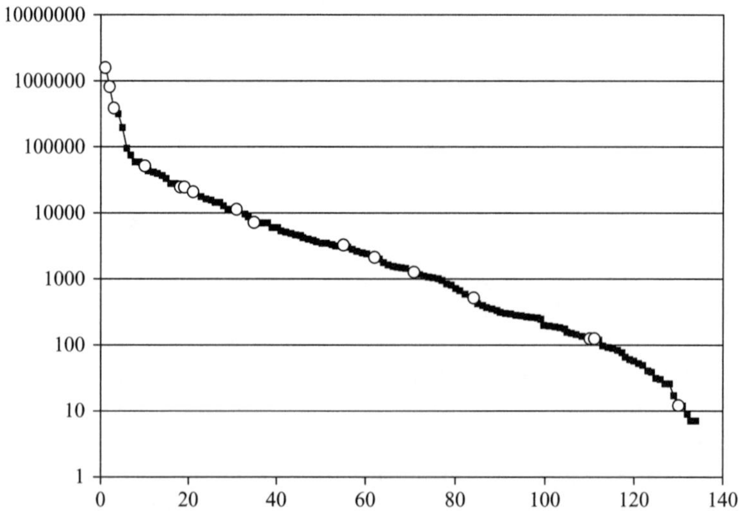

Figure 15–10: Distribution of utterances per grammar in the English corpus

corrections of the output or any tuning of the machine translator was performed. For all distinct grammars, the respective translated Spanish utterances and their original semantic annotations were used to train a statistical language model and a statistical classifier using standard settings for the involved parameters, since no development data was available.

Figure 15–10 shows the distribution of the number of utterances of the English corpus for each of the grammars in descending order showing that there are grammars exceeding

Table 15–4: Characteristics of the Spanish test data

Calls	951
Transcribed utterances	11,470
Annotated utterances	11,470 (100%)
DMs	144
Grammars	17

1 million utterances (a typical yes/no context) as well as numerous grammars facing data sparseness (22 grammars feature less than 100 training utterances).

15.8.6 Test

Because at the time of the grammar generation, the Spanish target system had not yet been deployed, we could perform tests only on a subset of the automatically translated grammars. To that goal, we collected, transcribed, and annotated a limited number of utterances from an existing Spanish version of a similar broadband Internet troubleshooting dialog system. The characteristics of this data are shown in Table 15–4.

The grammars found in the test data are shown as white bullets in Figure 15–10, showing that they are distributed among different magnitudes of amounts of available training data. A batch experiment was carried out performing speech recognition and classification on the complete set of collected utterances using the automatically translated grammars in their respective contexts. For each of the 11,470 utterances, the classification results were now compared to the semantic annotation of the same utterance. The accuracy measure used in the evaluation of the experimental results is the number of acoustic events for which the semantic classification result matched the annotation, divided by the total number of acoustic events. These events include in-scope and out-of-scope utterances as well as noise, background speech, and so on. Overall accuracy for the entire test set was at 85.0%, which is deemed very high compared to the performance of dialog systems based on handcrafted grammars. In fact, it is our experience that rule-based grammar systems often perform at less than 80% average accuracy. To have a more reliable standard of comparison, we looked at the performance of the English source dialog system optimized using several years of continuous tuning and found that the most recent system version performed at 90.7% (measured on 930 full calls, 11,274 completely annotated utterances).

The reason for the performance loss with respect to that achieved by the same system in the source language can be explained by the following:

- Weakness of the target acoustic model. In our experiment, we used an outdated Spanish speech recognizer whose acoustic models obviously did not achieve the same performance as its English counterpart. For example, in yes/no (sí/no) contexts, we saw a significantly higher portion of false accepts and rejects than in equivalent English contexts clearly independent of any linguistic factors.
- Weakness of the translation model. Statistical translation not only produces a lot of commonly known artifacts, but there are cases where even a human translator

would fail: a grammar is normally designed on the basis of utterances a caller says in response to a system prompt restricting the caller's language. For instance, a Spanish prompt may say *Cuando esté desconectado, diga continúe* translated from the English prompt *When it's unplugged, say continue.* Hence, most of the English responses will be *continue*, which a machine as well as a human being most likely would translate into Spanish as *continuar* instead of the prompt-dependent correct *continúe.* So, to achieve a higher accuracy of the translation hypotheses, they could be rescored taking the respective system prompt and other application-dependent information into consideration.

- No development data was available for this experiment because this would have required a (minimal) portion of collected target language utterances, their transcriptions, and annotations. Such data will be available once the first version of the target system goes into production and can be used to tune language models and classifiers.

In any case, we have shown that even with an initial lower performance a dialog system can be deployed in a different language with the minimum amount of human labor. Moreover, once the system is deployed and a reasonable amount of data has been collected, the continuous tuning procedure introduced in a previous section would improve the speech recognition performance to an acceptable level.

15.9 Summary

In this chapter, we described the architecture, technology, and methodology currently used to build commercial dialog systems. The architecture of a commercial dialog system is composed of mainly three modules: speech recognition and understanding, speech generation, and dialog manager. The goal of the speech recognition and understanding module is to assign one or more semantic tags to each speech input. Although the industry still uses rule-based grammars, which encode both the syntax and semantics of possible utterances, there are several advantages in moving to a fully statistical approach. In particular is the possibility of tuning all the grammars in an automated way, provided one has access to the transcriptions and semantic annotations of a substantial sample of the user utterances. Speech generation in commercial dialog systems is mostly implemented on the basis of a set of high-quality prompt recordings. Finally, the dialog manager uses a finite-state machine approach by explicitly encoding the whole interaction into what is generally known as call-flow. Very effective GUI tools are available to VUI designers that allow designing and developing very complex interactions often consisting of thousands of modules. We then describe different types of dialog that have been developed and deployed commercially. The industry of dialog systems evolved from very simple informational applications to transactional to problem-solving systems. We then approached the problem of localization of dialog systems to different languages. We showed that localizing speech recognition using machine translation can be straightforward and reasonably inexpensive when large amounts of transcribed and annotated data of the source language are available and statistical grammars are used throughout the whole application as opposed to traditional rule-based grammars. Testing an example implementation of the proposed methodology indicated that this approach can outperform manual bootstrapping even though it does not achieve the same accuracy as the original dialog system in the source language. Of course, once the system is deployed in the new target language, continuous tuning will bring the performance up to par with that of the source language.

Bibliography

[1] D. Bohus, A. Raux, T. Harris, M. Eskenazi, and A. Rudnicky, "Olympus: An open source framework for conversational spoken language interface research," in *Proceedings of the Human Language Technology Conference of the North American Chapter of the Association for Computational Linguistics (HLT/NAACL)*, 2007.

[2] A. Gruenstein, C. Wang, and S. Seneff, "Context-sensitive statistical language modeling," in *Proceedings of the Annual Conference of the International Speech Communication Association*, 2005.

[3] K. Evanini, D. Suendermann, and R. Pieraccini, "Call classification for automated troubleshooting on large corpora," in *Proceedings of the IEEE Automatic Speech Recognition and Understanding (ASRU) Workshop*, 2007.

[4] K. Acomb, J. Bloom, K. Dayanidhi, P. Hunter, P. Krogh, E. Levin, and R. Pieraccini, "Technical support dialog systems: Issues, problems, and solutions," in *Proceedings of the Human Language Technology Conference of the North American Chapter of the Association for Computational Linguistics (HLT/NAACL)*, 2007.

[5] W. Minker and S. Bennacef, *Speech and Human-Machine Dialog*. New York: Springer, 2004.

[6] R. Pieraccini and J. Huerta, "Where do we go from here? Research and commercial spoken dialog systems," in *Proceedings of the SIGdial Workshop on Discourse and Dialogue*, 2005.

[7] E. Barnard, A. Halberstadt, C. Kotelly, and M. Phillips, "A consistent approach to designing spoken-dialog systems," in *Proceedings of the IEEE Automatic Speech Recognition and Understanding (ASRU) Workshop*, 1999.

[8] C. Hemphill, J. Godfrey, and G. Doddington, "The ATIS spoken language systems pilot corpus," in *Proceedings of the Workshop on Speech and Natural Language*, 1990.

[9] A. Rudnicky and W. Xu, "An agenda-based dialog management architecture for spoken language systems," in *Proceedings of the IEEE Automatic Speech Recognition and Understanding (ASRU) Workshop*, 1999.

[10] S. Oviatt, "Predicting spoken disfluencies during human-computer interaction," *Computer Speech and Language*, vol. 9, no. 1, 1995.

[11] J. Williams and S. Witt, "A comparison of dialog strategies for call routing," *Speech Technology*, vol. 7, no. 1, 2004.

[12] D. Suendermann, P. Hunter, and R. Pieraccini, "Call classification with hundreds of classes and hundred thousands of training utterances . . . and no target domain data," in *Proceedings of the 4th IEEE Tutorial and Research Workshop on Perception and Interactive Technologies for Speech-Based Systems: Perception in Multimodal Dialogue Systems*, 2008.

[13] A. Gorin, G. Riccardi, and J. Wright, "How may I help you?," *Speech Communication*, vol. 23, no. 1/2, 1997.

[14] J. Chu-Carroll and B. Carpenter, "Vector-based natural language call routing," *Computational Linguistics*, vol. 25, no. 3, 1999.

[15] I. Zitouni, "Constrained minimization and discriminative training for natural language call routing," *IEEE Transactions on Audio, Speech and Language Processing*, vol. 16, no. 1, 2008.

[16] V. Goel, H. Kuo, S. Deligne, and C. Wu, "Language model estimation for optimizing end-to-end performance of a natural language call routing system," in *Proceedings of the International Conference on Acoustics, Speech, and Signal Processing*, 2005.

[17] D. Suendermann, J. Liscombe, K. Evanini, K. Dayanidhi, and R. Pieraccini, "From rule-based to statistical grammars: Continuous improvement of large-scale spoken dialog systems," in *Proceedings of the International Conference on Acoustics, Speech, and Signal Processing*, 2009.

[18] D. Suendermann, J. Liscombe, K. Evanini, K. Dayanidhi, and R. Pieraccini, "C^5," in *Proceedings of IEEE Workshop on Spoken Language Technologies*, 2008.

[19] D. Suendermann, J. Liscombe, and R. Pieraccini, "How to Drink from a fire hose: One person can annoscribe 693 thousand utterances in one month," in *Proceedings of the SIGdial Workshop on Discourse and Dialogue*, 2010.

Chapter 16

Combining Natural Language Processing Engines

John F. Pitrelli and Burn L. Lewis

16.1 Introduction

Many early speech and natural language processing (NLP) applications were based on single processing engines, such as a speech-to-text (STT, a.k.a. speech recognition) engine for dictation or a translation engine for text translation. However, many engines are now attaining accuracy sufficient to enable combining them to serve more complex tasks than were possible before, despite the compounding of errors inherent in such a combination. Example applications in the text domain include semantic search, enterprise reporting and other business intelligence, question answering, medical-abstract mining, and crosslingual search. Examples of audio processing include audio/video search and cataloging, speech-to-speech translation, and foreign broadcast news analysis.

Applications like these share many common engines, such as speaker identification, speech-to-text, text tokenization, grammatical parsing, named entity detection, coreference analysis, part-of-speech labeling, and translation. The benefits of sharing, plus the sheer complexity of these applications, motivate implementing such applications as a sequence of simpler steps performed by separate engine components. Doing so also yields the benefit of enabling components to be developed and tested in isolation, avoiding the difficulty of debugging a large application.

Prototyping applications like these often entails taking the output of one engine, reformatting it to the requirements of the next engine, inputting it to that engine, and so on. But application builders can realize many benefits by creating an **aggregate** processor that automatically moves the data from one engine to the next, reformatting it as needed. These benefits include:

- single-point invocation of a set of engines,
- efficient transfer of data between engines—no manual transfer and conversion,
- fault-tolerance, failover—automatic switching to a backup if an engine fails, and
- system-combination techniques to improve accuracy [7, 12].

However, aggregation poses several challenges:

- Heterogeneous computing environments: Different engines are often developed by different groups, using different operating systems, programming languages, byte order, and so on.
- Remote operation: Engines are often developed and maintained at different sites, making remote processing advantageous to avoid the need for porting engines from one site to another, propagate software updates, and so on. Even engines sharing a site may need to be run on separate machines due to processing requirements.
- Data formats: Different engines often require conflicting data formats. For example, speech-to-speech translation can be decomposed into speech-to-text, text translation, and text-to-speech synthesis. However, the natural input to speech-to-text is an audio signal, and its natural output associates texts, often one word at a time, with time ranges of that signal, whereas a text-translation engine has nothing to do with audio and simply expects text strings as inputs, typically in chunks larger than one word. Aggregation thus requires appropriate data conversion/reorganization to and from each engine's format.
- Exception handling: When an engine encounters a problem, it often reports it in a manner that is not recognized correctly by independently developed engines later in the aggregate, perhaps causing the error to be ignored or even causing the aggregate to fail. Exception-handling facilities and conventions are needed, handling, for example, errors that can be tolerated, those that cause an acceptable loss of data, and those that necessitate termination of the application.

In this chapter, we examine software frameworks created to address such challenges and discuss several example aggregate systems assembled to perform complex tasks.

16.2 Desired Attributes of Architectures for Aggregating Speech and NLP Engines

Several basic attributes are required of a software framework to facilitate realizing fully the advantages of aggregating engines. In the following sections we categorize them into four areas: modular components, computational efficiency, data management, and robustness.

16.2.1 Flexible, Distributed Componentization

Fundamental to addressing complex applications is the need to support a modular design. Engine functions such as speech-to-text, translation, and information extraction predate complex applications requiring combinations of these functions, and it is impractical and often undesirable to integrate the engines that perform each function. Therefore, our first requirement is for a simple componentization design. The framework should be designed so that it is easy to adapt to run in this framework any existing engine written in any common programming language and running under any common operating system. Such adaptation might take the form of a simple wrapper to make the engine conform to a simple application programming interface. Once engines are adapted, configuring an aggregate should also be easy, specifying a process flow through the engines and any needed data reorganization in between.

In general, components may be developed independently, and so the framework must be able to handle heterogeneous operating systems and programming languages. Engines should not need to be converted to a common operating system and programming language; rather, the framework should enable each engine to be run in its native computing environment.

In addition, the framework should allow the application to define the data interfaces between components. A customizable extendable data model would allow components to be replaced or upgraded and allow new components with new data formats to be easily added.

Engines should not need to be ported to a common location. Permitting engines to operate from their home sites eases maintenance and facilitates upgrade as the technologies advance. Hence the framework should support remote operation, enabling each engine to be deployed as a server accessible via Internet, with an aggregate application to function as a remote client of such distributed engines.

Further, many of these engine components are useful to many applications, and so an aggregation framework should provide for engines to serve multiple application clients, for example, by queueing requests from them. Load balancing should be enabled by a facility by which multiple instances of long-running and/or heavily demanded engines can be provisioned to serve such queues.

16.2.2 Computational Efficiency

Various engines require different amounts of context in order to perform their function. For example, a translation engine may operate best when processing a sentence or paragraph of context, whereas a news-topic-clustering engine would typically assign a label to an entire news story. For this reason, the framework must be able to handle segments of content whose sizes—how many minutes of audio, characters of text, and so on—must be controllable by the application.

Efficient processing of these segments requires some fundamental capabilities. The first is pipelining, the ability to process multiple content segments simultaneously, each at a different stage in the aggregate. An N-engine sequential aggregate will suffer up to an N-fold throughput suboptimality if the first engine only begins work on the second segment when the aggregate finishes the first rather than going to work on it as soon as the second engine receives the first segment.

Often, however, an aggregate includes a set of engines whose processing is mutually independent. An example is the use of multiple speech-to-text and/or translation engines preceding a system-combination component, such as Rover [7] or multiengine machine translation [12]. Exploiting this opportunity to minimize latency requires that an aggregation framework provide for parallel invocation of independent engines on the same data segment and recombination of the results produced in parallel.

A further issue is that often one or two particular engine functions, such as speech-to-text, become clear bottlenecks in a processing aggregate due to long processing time. It is often advantageous for the framework to support deploying multiple instances of an engine servicing its processing queue so that multiple data segments can be processed at a time, transparently to the client application, thereby improving throughput.

Finally, the framework should provide the capability to run components as services shared by multiple client applications. In conjunction with the preceding capabilities, this attribute provides the flexibility needed for dynamic load balancing for a set of distributed engines of varying computational footprint to serve a set of distributed client applications efficiently.

16.2.3 Data-Manipulation Capabilities

As stated earlier, different data types are fundamental to different engine functions. Speech-to-text and text-to-speech engines associate a text string with a span of audio signal, whereas a translation engine associates text strings in two different languages, so a speech-to-speech-translation application configured from these three engines must coordinate two languages' audio and text while driving a translation engine that does not deal with audio and two speech-processing engines that deal with only one language at a time. Therefore, the framework must provide the capability to coordinate multiple data types in different modalities representing a single piece of content. It must be able to maintain alignments among various video, audio, and text representations of the data in the segment and organize the data in such a way that each engine can focus on the representations appropriate to it while ignoring the others. This capability must be easily extendable as new engines are added.

In some cases, engines will have conflicting segmentation requirements, or one engine's output will play a role in determining the correct segmentation for data input to a subsequent engine. For example, speech-to-text may have created the text that is used by a story-boundary-detection engine to determine the proper boundaries for segments to be passed on to a topic-clustering engine. All text, audio, and other representations of the content would have to be combined and resegmented while maintaining the correct alignment linkages between them. So another requirement for the framework is that it be able to handle dynamic re-segmentation of content.

16.2.4 Robust Processing

Inevitably, exceptions will occur in various engines, and on occasion, an engine or a network connection between an application client and an engine service will fail. An aggregation framework must facilitate flexible error handling and flow control in order to manage such exceptions. Exceptions from engine processing should be caught so that unintended output from one engine does not become problematic input to another, potentially multiplying the failures. Configuration of an aggregate must include the ability to stipulate criteria and consequences for engine/connection failure. These conditions may include timeouts, number of failures before giving up on retries, and action to take upon giving up on an engine, such as proceeding without it, invoking a backup component, or terminating processing altogether.

In addition, along with remote services comes the need for remote monitoring and management. A life-cycle management system should provide a notification mechanism that would warn of problems with any of the remote services and enable the monitoring, starting, and stopping of the services from an administration console.

16.3 Architectures for Aggregation

Some existing architectures support many of these attributes. A few popular and promising ones are described in the following sections.

Note that there are a number of sets of libraries of text-based NLP tools that support only simple sequential processing, in essence relying on the application author to implement the aggregation, such as OpenNLP, NLTK, Ellogon, OpenCalais, Weka, Kea, OpenCalais, LingPipe, or FreeLing. Hence these are not useful by themselves for complex aggregation, but some of the following frameworks have developed wrappers for these that facilitate their integration into more complex applications.

16.3.1 UIMA

The Unstructured Information Management Architecture (UIMA) is an architecture and software framework for creating, discovering, composing, and deploying a broad range of multimodal analysis capabilities and integrating them with search technologies. The architecture has been accepted as an Open Standard by the Organization for the Advancement of Structured Information Standards (OASIS) [15].

UIMA allows multiple analytic engines to be combined in an aggregate and provides a customizable type system that enables different engines to share their results in a common data structure. Each engine implements the UIMA Annotator interface and is passed the analysis data in a common analysis structure (CAS), which contains all of the data produced by earlier annotators. A UIMA analysis engine (AE) may be a single annotator or an aggregate of analysis engines, where the flow among the AEs is managed by a customizable flow controller. Each CAS contains one or more representations of the data being analyzed (e.g., a text document, image, or segment of audio or video) as well as the metadata (annotations) added by the engines. The CAS also contains a representation of the type system and an index repository for efficient access to the type instances that are indexed by position in the document.

Apache UIMA is an open source implementation available on the Apache Software Foundation website [4] that provides the following features:

- a common analysis structure to organize and maintain a segment of data (e.g., text, audio) and all the analysis results on it,
- an extensible type-system mechanism used to formalize the format for all input and output data,
- an extensible component-based framework that simplifies the integration and deployment of UIMA-compliant analytics,

- support for analytics written in Java, C++, Perl, Python, and Tcl,
- support for Linux, Windows, and MacOS X,
- tools for developing and testing components individually,
- ability to run components as shared services on the Internet,
- ability to create custom analysis flow with complex error-handling options,
- ability to process multiple data segments simultaneously through different stages in the aggregate for increased throughput,
- ability to process the same segment through multiple engines in parallel to reduce latency, and
- ability to resegment data.

Flexible, Distributed Componentization

The Apache UIMA framework is implemented in Java, but AEs can be written in Java, C++, or scripting languages such as Perl, Python, and Tcl. AEs can be combined into aggregates with a simple linear flow or a user-defined flow. Communication with remote services is provided by Apache ActiveMQ [3], an open source implementation of the Java Message Service (JMS).

The fundamental data element in UIMA is an annotation of a region of the data being analyzed. For a text document, the region is usually a span of characters, but for other modalities could be a sequence of audio samples or video frames. UIMA annotations are based on the TIPSTER [20] architecture and contain the begin and end offsets of the region in the immutable representation of the data being analyzed. Each component specifies the types of data in the CAS that it processes, and the framework forms a complete type system for the application by merging all these requirements. Components only need access the subset of data in the CAS matching their defined types and are unaffected by changes to the other data in the CAS. For remote services, the data in each CAS is transmitted in a platform-independent format (either XML or binary), and only the changes to the CAS need be returned.

Computational Efficiency

In an aggregate of AEs, each one can run independently (remotely or locally) on different segments of the data, allowing each CAS to ripple through the aggregate with minimal delay. As a further speed-up, some AEs can be run in parallel, processing the same CAS, with their results being merged when the slowest one completes. Because the slowest AE can become a bottleneck, multiple instances can be deployed to increase the throughput. For remote services, the instances can be distributed across multiple processors, all servicing the same JMS queue, providing load balancing as well as robustness to individual failures.

Data-Manipulation Capabilities

A CAS may contain more than one "view" of the analysis data or document. For example, a speech-to-speech application might start with a view containing a segment of audio, later adding a view containing a text transcript produced by a speech-to-text engine, and then a view holding a translation produced by a translation engine. Each view contains its representation of the data along with annotations and indexes, providing a consistent and natural interface for an engine, independent of the original form of the data. A web crawler may start with an HTML view, then create a view containing the detagged text, then a view of the translation of that text. This would enable a translation engine service to process CASes from both audio and web applications, analyzing just the view containing the transcript or the detagged text. Certain types in the type system can provide cross-references between views, so alignments can be preserved.

AEs usually take a single CAS as input and add their results to it, but they can also create new CASes derived from their input CAS. In this way an AE could partition its analysis data into smaller segments or duplicate it for processing by different parts of the aggregate or resegment the original sequence of CASes into a sequence based on features detected in the data. An application may initially segment a long audio stream into shorter fixed-length segments and later resegment it into variable-length segments based on boundaries detected in the transcribed text.

Robust Processing

Apache UIMA provides a number of error-handling options configurable for each AE. Errors may be caused by infrastructure problems, such as a remote service or the connection to it failing, or by application problems, such as invalid data. In both cases the flow controller can decide whether to retry the process, to let the CAS continue in the flow without the processing by that AE, or to terminate the application. Retrying is appropriate if the connection failure is brief or if the service has deployed multiple AEs. If a remote service generates an unacceptable number of errors, the flow controller can be configured to divert the flow around that AE or perhaps to an alternative AE.

Usage statistics for remote services can be monitored to help identify bottlenecks or underutilized resources. Apache UIMA does not yet have an integrated life-cycle management system, but some applications have used external resources such as IBM WebSphere Application Server Community Edition or JCraft (SSH under Java) to achieve much of this functionality.

16.3.2 GATE: General Architecture for Text Engineering

The General Architecture for Text Engineering (GATE) [10] was developed at the University of Sheffield as a tool to aid experimentation in NLP. It includes a development environment with a graphical interface as well as a set of reusable components comprising both language and processing resources. It supports a simple pipeline of annotators implemented as JavaBeans with the document and its annotations augmented by feature maps of Java objects. Currently, GATE is restricted to processing a predefined corpus of text documents, no remote execution, and sequential execution of the components with some data-dependent skipping. Because UIMA and GATE share a similar concept of ordered, overlapping, typed annotations, wrappers have been developed that allow a GATE application to run as a UIMA analysis engine and vice versa, via an XML mapping file that describes how particular annotations can be converted. In this way, GATE applications can benefit from the flexible deployment features from UIMA, and UIMA applications from the many plug-ins provided with GATE.

Flexible, Distributed Componentization

Components interfaces are Java-only, so components in other languages such as C++ and Tcl must be wrapped. Data types are easily customizable because annotations are Java objects holding the begin and end offsets to the region of interest, along with additional references to other annotations or Java objects.

Computational Efficiency

Remote excecution, pipelining, parallel processing, and scaleout are not supported.

Data-Manipulation Capabilities

Processing is restricted to text documents only.

Robust Processing

Because all execution is local, there is little opportunity to recover from errors.

16.3.3 InfoSphere Streams

InfoSphere Streams [11] is a commercial offering from IBM designed for the rapid analysis of information streaming from multiple real-time sources, increasing the speed and accuracy of decision making in diverse fields such as health care, astronomy, manufacturing, and financial trading. Applications are developed as stream-processing graphs in which each processing element consumes and produces multiple streams of events, with automatic assignment of the elements of the graph across the available computing resources. Processing elements declare the name and type of each stream they handle, and the framework compiles the flow graph by matching the input requirements of consumers with the appropriate stream producers.

Flexible, Distributed Componentization

Processing elements may be written in Java or C++, but the only platform supported is Linux. There is no restriction on the data streamed between components; each type of stream is named and associated with the input and output streams of the processing elements. The absence of any data encapsulation model complicates the sharing and reuse of components.

Computational Efficiency

Pipelining support is inherent because each component is data-driven. Parallel processing is achieved when components consume the same stream, with the separate output streams feeding a "join" component that combines them back into a single stream. Streams can be filtered into multiple slower streams, distributing the workload among multiple instances of a relatively slow component, and later merged into a single stream.

Data-Manipulation Capabilities

Because there is no inherent data model, the application is responsible for all data management.

Robust Processing

The framework monitors the state of each component and upon failure can restart it or move it to another machine, reconnecting all the streams. Unless it has been declared as a "high-availability" component, some data may be lost. Visualization tools help to optimize the placement of components across the cluster of processing resources, but these must be dedicated resources in the same operating environment.

The focus of the architecture design has been on high-bandwidth, low-latency processing of real-time data such as stock market trades, news feeds, weather data, and RFID events, in applications where the loss of some packets from a stream under overload conditions may be acceptable. It should also be able to handle the larger context-critical data packets associated with NLP streams of audio and documents and may be suitable for some applications with strong real-time requirements.

16.4 Case Studies

In the following three case studies, we describe applications with differing requirements (e.g., remote versus local processing, real-time response versus batch, dedicated versus shared engine services). Because the focus is to describe issues relating to various aggregation scenarios rather than to compare software frameworks for aggregation, and because all three applications require features that are best supported by Apache UIMA, all three case studies discuss UIMA aggregates.

16.4.1 The GALE Interoperability Demo System

One example of a large, distributed aggregate of speech- and text-processing engines is the Interoperability Demo (IOD) [16] system developed within the Global Autonomous Language Exploitation (GALE) research program sponsored by the U.S. Defense Advanced Research Project Agency (DARPA). GALE encompasses research advancing a host of speech- and text-processing technologies, and the objective of IOD is to demonstrate the interoperation of many such engines operating at many GALE sites. UIMA is chosen as the framework for IOD's aggregation because it is well-suited to handle both speech and text and to deal with preexisting engines operating in a variety of computing environments. The description of IOD in this section exemplifies and explains how an aggregate system is created from a set of engines using UIMA.

IOD consists of two applications that draw from 15 engines operating in universities and companies in the United States and Europe. One application, IOD-video, employs all

15 engines to make Arabic broadcast news browsable as English-text stories and audible using English speech synthesis. The other, IOD-web, uses a subset of the same engines to make Arabic web text news similarly browsable and audible as English. To accomplish this, IOD runs a wide variety of engine functions: dialect identification, gender/speaker detection, speech-to-text (STT), named-entity detection, machine translation (MT) to English, multiengine machine translation (MEMT) that performs a system-combination function, story-boundary detection, topic-clustering of stories, multidocument summarization to produce topic summaries, headline generation for stories and topics, and text-to-speech synthesis. These engines operate in their native operating systems—Linux or Microsoft Windows—in their native programming languages—C++, Java, Tcl, Perl, and combinations thereof—at their home sites. Currently these sites include IBM [1, 8, 9, 18] and Columbia University [19] in New York, Carnegie Mellon University [12, 14] in Pennsylvania, Raytheon BBN Technologies [5] in Massachusetts, RWTH Aachen University [6] in Germany, Systran Company in France, and University of Massachusetts at Amherst [2]. These applications are diagrammed in Figure 16–1.

IOD has been processing approximately 4 hours of news shows daily from two Arabic news networks, Al-Arabiya and Al-Jazeera, for over 3 years. IOD's input consists of these shows segmented into 2-minute segments, the duration chosen to provide sufficient context for audio processing while avoiding excessive latency. During processing, the aggregate resegments the content according to the story boundaries it detects. At the end, it outputs, to a browser interface, a menu of topic headlines, and optionally English audio synthesized from the translation. Clicking on the topic headlines enables drilling down to topic summaries, story headlines, entity mentions, and story translations aligned to video keyframes, all produced by the aggregate.

IOD-web processes content originating as text and therefore skips the audio-processing engines. This aggregate begins with a component to strip HTML tags and related material away from the content to be processed. The IOD-web application also skips story-boundary detection, as the majority of web pages processed are already stories.

Functional Description

IOD's engines are depicted by bold boxes in Figure 16–1. IOD-video begins by determining time spans of various Arabic dialect and speaker gender. It also determines speaker-identity time spans in the case of known speakers such as recurring anchors and world leaders. Then segments are passed simultaneously to a bank of STT engines, yielding parallel Arabic transcripts of the speech. When all STT engines have completed processing, Arabic entity detection is invoked on the resulting texts, after which segments are sent simultaneously to a bank of MT engines. Multiple STT and MT engines are included for two reasons. One is to enable MEMT, a system-combination engine, to mine a better translation from those provided by each STT-MT combination. The other reason is to provide fault-tolerance in case of failure of one or two engines of either type or the network connection to them. Story-boundary detection exploits both the Arabic transcripts and the timing information, such as pauses detected by STT. Topic clustering assigns a topic identifier to each story such that stories classified as being about the same topic share the same identifier. Multidocument summarization annotates each story segment with a cumulative summary of all stories labeled with the same topic identifier. The headline-generation engine adds a headline derived

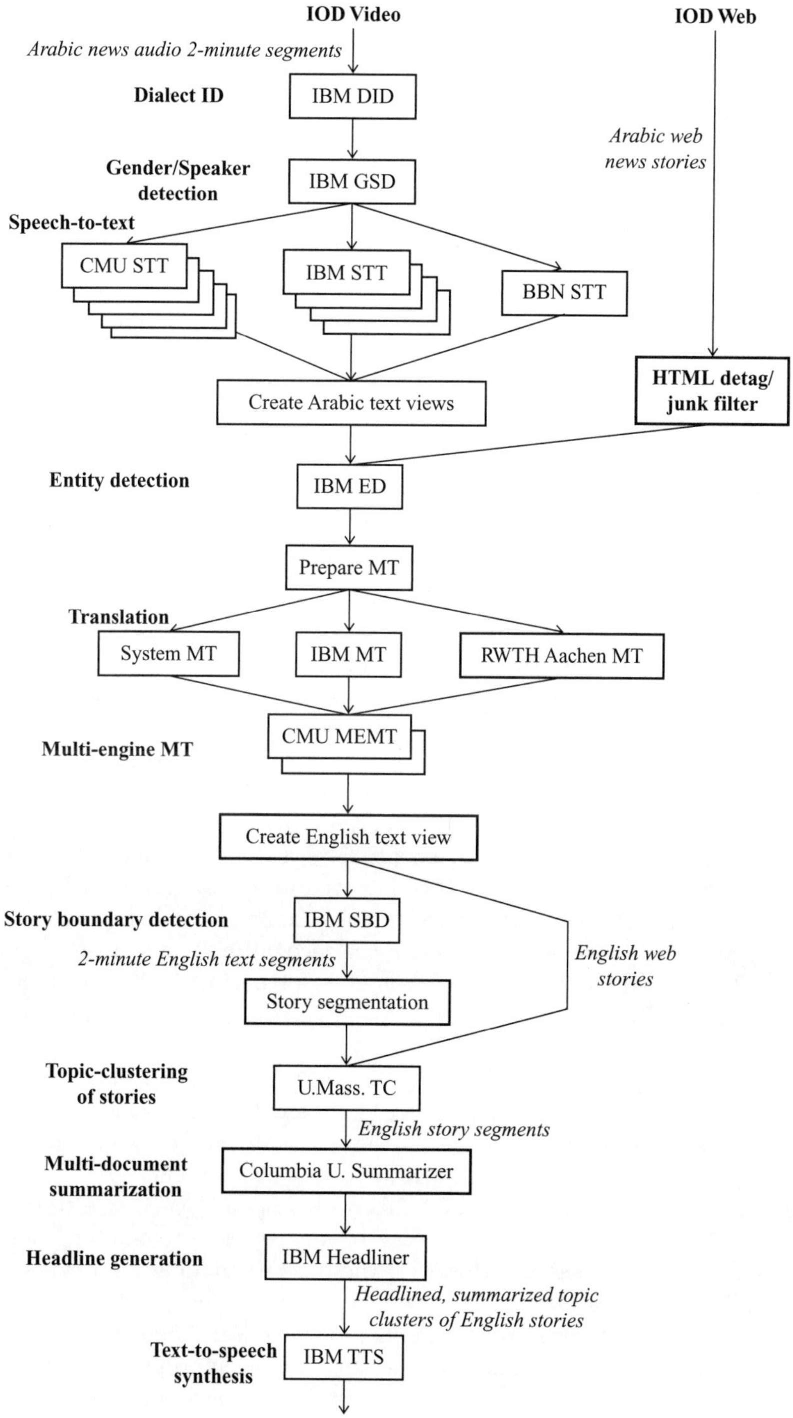

Figure 16–1: System diagram of IOD applications' engine aggregates. Solid thin arrows indicate data flow for the IOD-video application; dotted, IOD-web; and thick, both applications

from the story's translation and another derived from the summary, and the text-to-speech synthesis engine creates an audio stream from the translation.

Implementation

Views IOD uses three kinds of views to provide each engine just the input data it requires:

- an **audio view** representing a segment's content as a sequence of waveform samples,
- one **Arabic-text view** corresponding to each STT engine, representing the segment's content as a sequence of Arabic characters based on the transcript's output by an STT engine, and
- an **English-text view** representing the content as a sequence of English characters, typically based on the translation output by the MEMT engine.

This arrangement enables audio-processing engines to look at only the audio view, while text-processing engines can look at only text views. Monolingual engines look only at the relevant views without being confused by content in the other language.

Type System The GALE Type System (GTS) [17] was created for UIMA aggregates of NLP engines such as IOD. GTS defines data types suitable for audio and text views to hold the inputs and outputs of a wide variety of speech- and text-processing engines. The type system, as a common data format, serves as a foundation for interoperability among engines.

GTS specifies data types that represent the inherent attributes of each engine type's inputs and outputs. For example, an STT engine naturally operates on an audio view of content, that is, an array of speech samples representing a time sequence, and its natural output is transcripts of spoken words. GTS provides a data type named `AudioToken`[1] to represent this output; this type provides a string attribute `spelling` to hold the word, and float attributes `begin`, `end`, and `confidence` to hold the begin- and end-time of the word in the audio view and a measure of confidence in the recognition result if the engine provides one. Another GTS type used by some STT engines for output is `SU` ("sentence unit"); it likewise has `begin` and `end` attributes, and its presence signifies that the engine believes these time points bracket a sentence.

Similarly, natural inputs to a text-processing engine, such as an MT engine, are represented by the GTS types named `WordToken` and `Sentence`, each of which has integer `begin` and `end` attributes representing indices into the character array comprising a text view, which for text-processing engines is the natural view of the content.

It should be noted `AudioToken`s and `SU`s likely correspond one-to-one respectively with `WordToken` and `Sentence` objects in the case of an aggregate containing speech-to-text followed by text processing engines. However, these corresponding data types are not the same. Specifically, speech data types are oriented toward a time-based view like the audio view, as appropriate for a speech-processing engine, while `WordToken` and `Sentence` reflect positions in a character string with no reference to time, as appropriate for text-processing

---

1. `Typewriter font` is used to indicate GTS types and attributes.

engines knowing nothing of audio and time. So when aggregating such engines, a data-reorganization component, as described in Section 16.4.1, is invoked following speech-to-text but before text processing in order to create the appropriate text views and text-oriented object types within those views by harvesting the data the speech-to-text engines had placed in the audio view. In addition, GTS provides cross-reference types such as `AudioXref`, which map across these views to keep various representations of the same content aligned with each other. Such types enable, for example, synchronizing translation outputs with audio time, facilitating automatic subtitling of audio.

GTS specifies many more data types, geared for many other types of engines, such as entity detection, story-boundary detection, and speaker recognition.

Note that specification of a type system does not comprise a complete data "contract" among engines in forming an aggregate. In addition to a shared type system like GTS, the design of an aggregate requires specification of how the type system will be used. This includes issues such as which engines are responsible for creating which types and which types and which attributes are required versus optional. In IOD, for example, STT engines are required to produce `AudioTokens`, but `confidence` attributes are optional, and `SU` types are optional as well.

Adapting Engines to UIMA Because the engines employed by IOD preexisted the aggregate, they required adaptation to the UIMA framework and the GTS data model. UIMA has a simple API with only one required method, to process a data segment. Other methods may also be implemented if the engine requires special initialization or termination operations. GTS provides data types natural to each engine function. Therefore, adaptation essentially consists of providing a thin wrapper around an engine to conform to the API and data format. Specifically, when a preexisting engine is "wrapped" for UIMA, the wrapper's processing function typically converts the GTS types representing input to the engine from the GTS format to the format specified by the engine, runs the engine, and then converts its output into the appropriate GTS output types for that engine function. These conversions tend to be straightforward, as the GTS types are designed to reflect the inputs and outputs inherent to each engine function. Code for an AE that wraps a simulated STT engine is shown in Section 16.7 at the end of this chapter.

Data Reorganization As indicated earlier, assembling an application including STT and text-processing engines requires the use of a data-reorganization component following STT responsible for

1. creating text views by concatenating the strings from `AudioTokens`,
2. creating a set of `Sentence` annotations that convert the `SU`s from spans of time in the audio view to spans of characters on the text views,
3. creating `AudioXrefs` that explicitly align words in the text view back to the `AudioTokens` that generated them so that time alignments can be maintained, and
4. creating `WordToken` annotations on the text views for use later by text-processing engines.

In this way, the aggregate bridges across the incompatibilities between STT and text processing and the discrepancy between the inherent output of STT and the input of text-processing engines. This component is depicted in Figure 16–1 as Create Arabic Text Views. Note that aggregates containing multiple STT engines will produce multiple parallel transcripts, each resulting in another Arabic-text view of the content.

Data-reorganization components are conceptually very different from "engines" like STT, MT, and so on, in that the latter often represent experimental NLP technologies that are the subject of ongoing research, whereas data-reorganization components perform more "mechanical" data-manipulation tasks. However, as far as the UIMA framework is concerned, both types of components look the same, all being implemented as AEs. Code for an AE that implements the last step of this data-reorganization component is shown in Section 16.7 at the end of this chapter.

Similarly, other data-reorganization components, depicted by non-bold boxes in Figure 16–1, are needed for analogous purposes of interfacing among the engines in IOD. A component similar to the one described earlier creates the English text view from the English translation strings that MT and MEMT annotated onto Arabic text spans and maps annotations, such as named entities, between English and Arabic. This is necessary because translation engines inherently deal with multiple languages and thus produce GTS objects called `TranslationResults`, which annotate a span of characters in one language's text view with a string of characters in another language. Most other text-processing engines work within a single language at a time, however, so engines processing the output of MT need a view in the target language, hence the Create English Text View data-reorganization component to create an English-text view serving subsequent engines that process English while knowing nothing of Arabic.

Before MT, another data-reorganization component, Prepare MT, creates another GTS data type, `Translatables`, to designate chunks to be translated one at a time. Currently, these simply mirror the `Sentences` but could be defined by some other algorithm to segment the text string, for example, into longer units for MT engines that benefit from more context or into shorter units for specialized translation engines such as for names. Yet another component, Story Segmentation, resegments the content into story segments an the basis of story boundaries detected by the engine preceding it. Story Segmentation creates new CASes with data elements corresponding to those in the original 2-minute segments but reindexed according to the new boundaries. This reorganization serves the following engines whose natural input is stories, such as topic clustering, summarization, and headline generation.

Finally, two components, not shown, book-end the whole process, reading collections of input data and creating CASes from them at the beginning of the aggregate and extracting data from the CASes into formats desired by the application at the end of the aggregate. In UIMA these are called **collection readers** and **CAS consumers** respectively.

Context-Dependent Processing IOD's processing of a segment requires context outside of that segment, in two different ways. One involves the immediately surrounding segments. Story-boundary detection's model provides outputs for the middle 2 minutes of a 6-minute window. Given IOD's 2-minute segments, this engine must therefore buffer one segment, emitting its output on segment N of a show only after receiving segment $N + 1$ so that the output can be based on the 6-minute window consisting of segments $N - 1$, N, and $N + 1$.

The other dependence applies to topic clustering and summarization, which must maintain a history of past content associated with each topic cluster so that they can respectively determine the proper cluster to which to assign the current segment and generate a cumulative summary of that topic's content. The histories that these two engines maintain must also be segregated according to client application instances, so that different users' histories do not get conflated.

Computational Efficiency As mentioned, IOD invokes multiple engines serving the same function in parallel on a segment, as these engines produce the same output types from the same input types and thus have no interdependences. IOD also pipelines multiple segments through the aggregate at a time, so the second segment enters the first engine as soon as the first segment leaves the first engine rather than waiting for the first segment to exit the entire aggregate.

In addition to parallel invocation of engines and pipelining of segments, IOD makes use of other features of UIMA's capability for configurable flow control. Aggregates are configured with processing timeouts for each engine service and consequent actions to take in case of a timeout. One example is that when an STT or entity-detection engine is lost due to failure of the engine or the network connection to it, the aggregate continues processing without that engine because the presence of other STT engines. Another example, in contrast, is that when the summarization engine is lost, IOD substitutes as a backup a simple component that concatenates all the story translations for a topic, which does not substitute for a summary but does serve as a credible input for the subsequent engine to generate a headline for the topic. Yet another flow criterion applies to when MEMT is lost; in this case, processing proceeds with one of the translations resulting from an STT-MT combination being used as the preferred translation. However, when story-boundary detection fails, with no backup for this function essential to subsequent processing, the application terminates.

As it happens, one engine function, STT, requires far more computation than the others. To mitigate the effect on throughput, multiple instances of two STT engines are deployed to service those engines' queues of client jobs, as depicted by stacked boxes in Figure 16–1. For IOD-web, MEMT is the bottleneck, and accordingly two instances of the MEMT engine are similarly deployed.

IOD exploits UIMA's ability for an engine service to be shared by multiple applications. IOD-video and IOD-web simultaneously queue requests for many of the IOD engine services. This capability and the multiple-instance-deployment capability are the keys to dynamic load balancing for the scaled deployment of an array of applications employing an array of engine services.

Flexible Application Building

In addition to IOD-video and IOD-web, a GUI-based application-configuration tool known as UIMA Component Container (UCC) has been deployed at Carnegie Mellon University. UCC enables users to upload data and configure aggregates of IOD engines to process it. UCC automatically completes the aggregate by adding the necessary data-reorganization components.

16.4.2 Translingual Automated Language Exploitation System (TALES)

TALES is an IBM aggregate that bears some resemblance to IOD in that it performs speech recognition, information, and translation and is implemented using UIMA. However, TALES represents a different aggregation scenario in that it operates on a co-located cluster of machines, it processes multiple languages, and it is closer to a production system, including real-time requirements on part of its operation.

TALES incorporates both a video- and a web-processing aggregate, as depicted in Figure 16–2. TALES's aggregates include entity detection, translation to English, and provision for several types of data search, browsing, and monitoring. In addition, TALES's video-processing aggregate contains STT, gender and speaker recognition, language/dialect identification, and English text-to-speech synthesis. Several instances of TALES are deployed, with varying numbers of machines processing varying numbers of video channels in varying sets of languages, such as Arabic, Chinese, Spanish, and English.

TALES's top priority is to keep up with its incoming video streams, achieved primarily by tuning the STT models to take under 2 minutes for each 2-minute video segment and by dedicating an aggregate and its processing hardware to each channel of video. The exception is MT, owing to the large size of its language models: several instances of MT are shared among the aggregates, with requests from the web-processing aggregates taking second priority due to the real-time requirement for processing video.

TALES is designed to run with no external network connections, just feeds from video and a web crawler. TALES aggregates terminate in several components enabling varied uses of the output:

- browsing of current shows by segment, enabling the user to play video with English captions, dialect/speaker annotation, entity highlighting, and optionally English speech synthesis dubbed over the original audio;
- English-keyword search of processed content, including capability to narrow the search according to date, language of origin, video versus web; and
- alerts, whereby the user issues a standing keyword query, and upon processing of new content matching that query, an alert is sent to that user by means he or she specifies, such as e-mail.

16.4.3 Real-Time Translation Services (RTTS)

IBM's RTTS enables two-way, free-form speech translation that assists human communication for people who do not share a common language. For each utterance from one of the parties in the conversation, it employs three engines, STT, MT, and TTS, to deliver the translated speech to the other party. Thus, while the priorities of IOD and TALES are, respectively, distributed processing and throughput to keep up with an incoming video stream, RTTS's priority is to handle multiple simultaneous with low latency. RTTS accomplishes this by deploying clusters of each type of engine as UIMA services. Each call is handled by a UIMA client, which sends requests to the JMS queues that provide the desired services. Because the application is directly implementing the pipelining of the services, it can easily

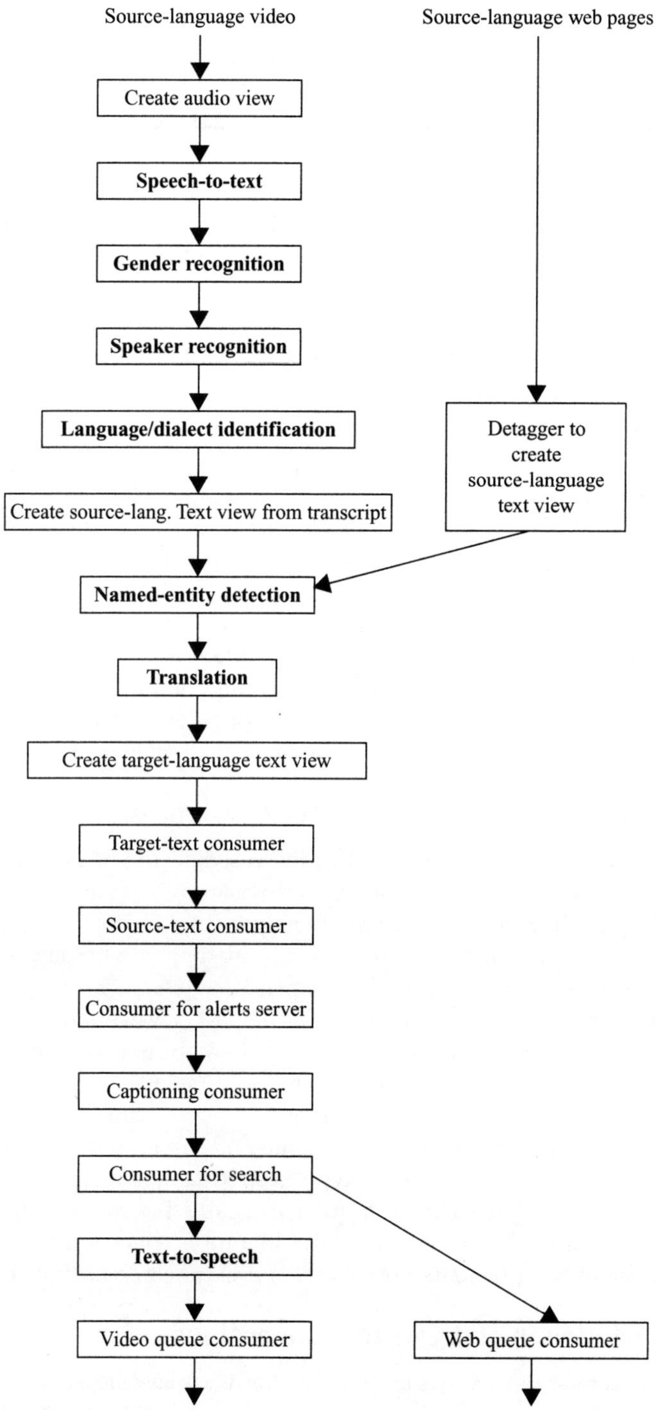

Figure 16–2: System diagram of TALES aggregates

monitor the progress of the translation and handle any delays caused by an overloaded service. This could also be done by using a UIMA custom flow controller.

16.5 Lessons Learned

A number of challenges intrinsic to engine aggregation of this sort have been exposed by the experience of configuring NLP applications with UIMA. It is instructive to address the issues discussed next.

16.5.1 Segmentation Involves a Trade-off between Latency and Accuracy

When processing audio or video, we have gradually converged toward the practice of processing 2-minute segments. Each segment cut limits how much context is available for engines to exploit for the sake of accuracy. However, when one engine must complete a segment before a succeeding engine begins work on it, long segments cause high latency.

Operation would be improved by equipping the framework with a generalized "streaming" operating mode. Rather than explicit segmentation, the data would be passed from component to component in arbitrary small increments, with the components themselves taking responsibility for working with enough context and accordingly lagging their output behind their input. Such a change would add significant complexity to the framework, particularly to manage the gathering of data following parallel invocation of multiple engines and to reconcile this capability with multiple-instance deployment of single-engine services.

16.5.2 Joint Optimization versus Interoperability

Joint optimization of engine functions can yield increased accuracy. For example, coordinating the language models of an STT engine and a translation engine can reduce occurrences of untranslatable words. Tighter integration of engines can benefit accuracy more generally by reducing the degree to which "hard" decisions must be made by one engine to limit the space of hypotheses to be considered by the following engine.

The interoperability of a large aggregate of engines, however, requires a shared data model, a contract of sorts stipulating fairly standard characteristics of data input and output for each engine function. Such a common-denominator model will tend toward relatively thin data streams between engines. For example, it is easier to reconcile the format of a text string as a standardized output of a speech-to-text engine and input to a translation engine than it is to reconcile the format of a lattice of hypothesized transcripts. Some benefits of joint optimization typically must be foregone in order to enable interoperation. While one site's STT and MT engines may be coordinated, interoperation enables use of multiple engines for each function, facilitating benefits derived from system-combination strategies.

16.5.3 Data Models Need Usage Conventions

Aggregation essentially requires a two-level model for data passing. For the aggregate to run at all, a set of mutually agreed-upon data types, such as a UIMA-type system like GTS, is necessary. As discussed earlier, the type system is effectively the data component of the API for engines coordinating in the aggregate so that they can communicate using a common data format.

However, it is further necessary to specify usage conventions for the format's data types. A common understanding of which data types must be or may optionally be created by each component, and how to represent various exceptional cases using the data format must be agreed upon. Engines developed independently often encode exceptional cases using a local convention in their standard output stream, such as a textual code for an unknown word, which may itself be misinterpreted as a distinct word by a succeeding engine in an aggregate if proper care is not taken.

16.5.4 Challenges of Performance Evaluation

Quantitative evaluation of accuracy of such aggregates is complicated by several factors. One is simply the combinatorics of aggregation. From a collection of 10 engine functions, the potential number of aggregates that can be drawn from them ranges from 45 to 1,013, depending on interdependences among the engines.[2] Thus, evaluation of accuracy of topic clustering of translated stories transcribed by STT engines will be distinct from that of topic clustering of translated stories that originated as text, and so on. Many evaluation criteria are needed.

A related challenge is the complexity of obtaining ground-truth data for comparison with results from large aggregates. In general, each distinct aggregate requires its own reference corpus for evaluation, an expensive undertaking.

Finally, some engine functions, even in isolation, lack well-defined evaluation metrics. For example, evaluation of summarization and topic-clustering algorithms is necessarily somewhat subjective.

Efforts have begun to define a formal methodology for evaluation of various aspects of accuracy for engine aggregates, with the goal of formulating evaluations designed to quantify the contribution of various engines to the overall error rate of the aggregate [13].

16.5.5 Ripple-Forward Training of Engines

Ideally, each statistical engine is trained on data representative of what it will receive at operating time. In the case of an aggregate, the typical engine's input is the output of engines that precede it in the aggregate. For this reason, when engines are upgraded, whether due to new algorithms, new training data, or changed model formats, any resulting accuracy improvement risks being lost in the aggregate because of the resultant mismatch introduced between its output data and the now-obsolete training conditions of the following engines. Thus, the accuracy of an aggregate depends on ripple-forward training of engines. Ideally, the first engine is updated and run to generate new input data for succeeding engines,

---

2. If every engine $N = 1, ..., 10$ has the constraint that it must either be preceded by engine $N - 1$ or begin the aggregate, and must either be followed by engine $N + 1$ or end the aggregate, then the number of possible aggregates is the number of choices of start and end engines $= 10(10 - 1)/2 = 45$ possible aggregates. At the other extreme, however, if the engines lack mutual dependences and so every engine can be included or not in an aggregate, then $2^{10} - 10 - 1 = 1{,}013$ aggregates are possible, that is, all combinations of each engine being included or not, minus the 10 of these cases that include only one engine (hence not an aggregate) and the one case that has zero engines.

which are then retrained using that data, and the aggregate through those engines is run to generate new training data for the engines following those, and so on.

16.6 Summary

Speech- and text-processing algorithms have advanced to the point that large aggregates of such disparate engine functions as speech-to-text, translation, named entity detection, text-to-speech, and other specialized information-extraction processors can provide useful output, despite errors compounding across engines. Aggregating these engines opens the door to a wealth of crosslingual NLP applications. Enabling flexible aggregation of existing engines requires a software framework like UIMA that provides for heterogeneous computing environments, remote operation across that Internet, and management of multiple application-clients' requests that are queued to be run by multiple instances of engine services. It also requires shared conventions for data representation and components to reorganize the data so that one engine can contend with the data output by engines preceding it in the aggregate. Such a platform enables complex, distributed tasks to be performed by single-point invocation of distributed engines operating in their home environments to facilitate their maintenance and upgrade by their authors. High accuracy requires coordination of upgrades so that each engine remains tuned to the type of data it is processing; however, formal evaluation of aggregates' accuracy remains in its infancy because of the challenges of establishing suitable evaluation metrics and test corpora. Nevertheless, an increasing number of applications are operational, ranging from multiple-research-lab prototypes to real-time deployed systems.

16.7 Sample UIMA Code

Several annotators are packaged as part of Apache UIMA at http:/uima.apache.org in the UIMA Sandbox; others may be found in the UIMA Component Repository hosted by CMU at http://uima.lti.cs.cmu.edu/UCR.

The following is a simple analysis engine implementing part of the data reorganization described in Section 16.4.1.

```
import java.util.Iterator;
import java.util.regex.Matcher; import
java.util.regex.Pattern;

import org.apache.uima.analysis_component.JCasAnnotator_ImplBase;
import org.apache.uima.analysis_engine.AnalysisEngineProcessException;
import org.apache.uima.cas.CASException;
import org.apache.uima.jcas.JCas;
import org.gale.WordToken;

/**
 * Tokenizes all Transcription views creating
 * whitespace-delimited WordToken annotations
```

```
 */

public class TokenizeMT extends JCasAnnotator_ImplBase {

  public void process(JCas aJcas) throws
      AnalysisEngineProcessException {

    Pattern p = Pattern.compile("\\S+");
    try {
      Iterator<JCas> viewIter = aJcas.getViewIterator("SourceText");
      while (viewIter.hasNext()) {
        JCas view = viewIter.next();
        Matcher m = p.matcher(view.getDocumentText());
        while (m.find()) {
          (new WordToken(view, m.start(), m.end())).addToIndexes();
        }
      }
    } catch (CASException e) {
      throw new AnalysisEngineProcessException(e);
    }
  }
}
```

All UIMA annotators must have an XML component descriptor describing the implementation, name, data types, and any required parameters. A simple one for this annotator is:

```
 <?xml version="1.0" encoding="UTF-8"?>
 <analysisEngineDescription
   xmlns="http://uima.apache.org/resourceSpecifier">
  <frameworkImplementation>org.apache.uima.java
  </frameworkImplementation>
  <primitive>true</primitive>
  <annotatorImplementationName>org.gale.pipe.TokenizeMT
  </annotatorImplementationName>
  <analysisEngineMetaData>
    <typeSystemDescription>
      <imports>
        <import name="GaleTokenTypes"/>
      </imports>
    </typeSystemDescription>
  </analysisEngineMetaData>
</analysisEngineDescription>
```

The following code illustrates how an existing STT engine might be wrapped to create an analysis engine that processes audio defined by a URL and annotates the Audio view with AudioTokens for each decoded word. See Section 16.4.1.

```
package org.gale.gus;

import java.io.BufferedInputStream;
import java.util.ArrayList;
```

```
import org.apache.uima.UimaContext;
import org.apache.uima.analysis_component.JCasAnnotator_ImplBase;
import org.apache.uima.analysis_engine.AnalysisEngineProcessException;
import org.apache.uima.cas.CASException;
import org.apache.uima.jcas.JCas;
import org.apache.uima.resource.ResourceInitializationException;
import org.apache.uima.util.Level;
import org.apache.uima.util.Logger;

import org.gale.AudioToken;
import org.gale.SU;

/**
 * Demo STT annotator
 */

public class DemoSTT extends JCasAnnotator_ImplBase {

  private Logger logger;
  private String compId;

  public void initialize(UimaContext aContext) throws
     ResourceInitializationException {

    super.initialize(aContext);
    logger = aContext.getLogger();
    compId = (String) aContext.getConfigParameterValue("ComponentId");
  }

  public void process(JCas jcas) throws AnalysisEngineProcessException {

    try {
      jcas = jcas.getView("Audio");
    } catch (CASException e) {
      throw new AnalysisEngineProcessException(e);
    }
    logger.log(Level.INFO, compId + ": Processing audio URL '"
                          + jcas.getSofaDataURI() + "'");

    String audioMimeType = jcas.getSofaMimeType();
    BufferedInputStream audioStream = new
      BufferedInputStream(jcas.getSofaDataStream());

    // Run a pretend STT that puts its results in two arrays
    ArrayList<String> words = new ArrayList<String>(100);
    ArrayList<Float> endTimes = new ArrayList<Float>(100);
    runSTT(audioStream, audioMimeType, words, endTimes);

    // Get the STT results and add AudioTokens to CAS
    float time = 0;
    for (int i = 0; i < words.size(); ++i) {
```

```
      AudioToken atok = new AudioToken(jcas);
      atok.setSpelling(words.get(i));
      atok.setBegin(time);
      time = endTimes.get(i);
      atok.setEnd(time);
      atok.setComponentId(compId);
      atok.addToIndexes();
    }

    // Add one SU spanning all of the audio
    SU su = new SU(jcas);
    su.setBegin(0);
    su.setEnd(time);
    su.setComponentId(compId);
    su.addToIndexes();
  }


  // Demo code pretending to perform STT

  private void runSTT(BufferedInputStream in, String mimeType,
          ArrayList<String> words, ArrayList<Float> endTimes) {
    logger.log(Level.INFO,
              "runSTT: pretending to process audio ... creating 2 fake words");
    words.add("hello");
    endTimes.add(0.65f);
    words.add("world");
    endTimes.add(1.35f);
  }

}
```

Its descriptor file includes a parameter used to identify the creator of the entries in the CAS.

```
<?xml version="1.0" encoding="UTF-8"?>
<analysisEngineDescription
   xmlns="http://uima.apache.org/resourceSpecifier">
  <frameworkImplementation>org.apache.uima.java
  </frameworkImplementation>
  <primitive>true</primitive>
  <annotatorImplementationName>org.gale.gus.DemoSTT
  </annotatorImplementationName>
  <analysisEngineMetaData>
    <configurationParameters>
      <configurationParameter>
        <name>ComponentId</name>
        <description>Name of STT engine</description>
        <type>String</type>
        <mandatory>true</mandatory>
      </configurationParameter>
```

```
    </configurationParameters>
    <configurationParameterSettings>
      <nameValuePair>
        <name>ComponentId</name>
        <value>
          <string>STTx</string>
        </value>
      </nameValuePair>
    </configurationParameterSettings>
    <typeSystemDescription>
      <imports>
        <import name="GaleSpeechTypes"/>
      </imports>
    </typeSystemDescription>
  </analysisEngineMetaData>
</analysisEngineDescription>
```

The following XML describes the GTS types that are used in these code samples. The Apache UIMA SDK includes an Eclipse plug-in that greatly facilitates the creation and development of analysis engine and type system descriptors.

```
<typeDescription>
  <name>org.gale.WordToken</name>
  <description>A basic unanalyzed word
  </description>
  <supertypeName>org.gale.NonWhiteSpaceToken</supertypeName>
</typeDescription>

<typeDescription>
  <name>org.gale.NonWhiteSpaceToken</name>
  <description>A span of characters that meet the Unicode
    definition of non-whitespace.
  </description>
  <supertypeName>org.gale.Token</supertypeName>
</typeDescription>

<typeDescription>
  <name>org.gale.Token</name>
  <description>Tokenizer output - these should be
    non-overlapping.  Frequently the set of Tokens
    will cover the entire document, but this is not
    required.  The type hierarchy derived from Token
    is used purely for constructing specific iterators,
    not for data inheritance.
  </description>
  <supertypeName>uima.tcas.Annotation</supertypeName>
</typeDescription>

<typeDescription>
  <name>org.gale.AudioToken</name>
```

```
  <description>Word-like units</description>
  <supertypeName>org.gale.AudioSpan</supertypeName>
  <features>
    <featureDescription>
      <name>spelling</name>
      <description>Spelling of the word; typically does not
        include capitalization, optional diacritics, or
        punctuation</description>
      <rangeTypeName>uima.cas.String</rangeTypeName>
    </featureDescription>
    <featureDescription>
      <name>confidence</name>
      <description>Value representing the "score" of this AudioToken, such
  as the probability that the span actually contains the annotated
        word spoken within.
      </description>
      <rangeTypeName>uima.cas.Float</rangeTypeName>
    </featureDescription>
  </features>
</typeDescription>

<typeDescription>
  <name>org.gale.SU</name>
  <description>Sentence-like units.  An SU spans one or more AudioTokens.</description>
  <supertypeName>org.gale.AudioSpan</supertypeName>
</typeDescription>

<typeDescription>
  <name>org.gale.AudioSpan</name>
  <description>The basic unit of a time duration (similar to an Annotation). This is
   a base class that should not be instantiated.</description>
  <supertypeName>uima.cas.TOP</supertypeName>
  <features>
    <featureDescription>
      <name>begin</name>
      <description>Begin time in seconds from the beginning of the segment</description>
      <rangeTypeName>uima.cas.Float</rangeTypeName>
    </featureDescription>
    <featureDescription>
      <name>end</name>
      <description>End time in seconds from the beginning of the segment</description>
      <rangeTypeName>uima.cas.Float</rangeTypeName>
    </featureDescription>
    <featureDescription>
      <name>componentId</name>
      <description>ID of the STT component that created this annotation</description>
      <rangeTypeName>uima.cas.String</rangeTypeName>
    </featureDescription>
  </features>
</typeDescription>
```

Bibliography

[1] Y. Al-Onaizan and K. Papineni, "Distortion models for statistical machine," in *Proceedings of the Association for Computational Linguistics*, pp. 529–536, 2006.

[2] J. Allan, S. Harding, D. Fisher, A. Bolivar, S. Guzman-Lara, and P. Amstutz, "Taking topic detection from evaluation to practice," in *Proceedings of the Hawaii International Conference on System Sciences*, 2005.

[3] Apache ActiveMQ, http://activemq.apache.org

[4] Apache UIMA, http://uima.apache.org

[5] http://bbn.com/products_and_services/bbn_broadcast_monitoring_system/; BMS includes BBN's AMC STT engine.

[6] O. Bender, E. Matusov, S. Hahn, S. Hasan, S. Khadivi, and H. Ney, "The RWTH Arabic-to-English spoken language translation system," in *Proceedings of the IEEE Automatic Speech Recognition and Understanding (ASRU) Workshop*, pp. 396–401, 2007.

[7] J. G. Fiscus, "A post-processing system to yield reduced word error rates: Recognizer output voting error reduction (ROVER)," in *Proceedings of the IEEE Automatic Speech Recognition and Understanding (ASRU) Workshop*, pp. 347–354, 1997.

[8] R. Florian, H. Hassan, A. Ittycheriah, H. Jing, N. Kambhatla, X. Luo, N. Nicolov, and S. Roukos, "A statistical model for multilingual entity detection and tracking," in *Proceedings of the Human Language Technology Conference of the North American Chapter of the Association for Computational Linguistics (HLT/NAACL)*, 2004.

[9] M. Franz and J.-M. Xu, "Story segmentation of broadcast news in Arabic, Chinese and English using multi-window features," in *Proceedings of the International ACM Special Interest Group on Information Retrieval (SIGIR) Conference*, 2007.

[10] GATE, http://gate.ac.uk/

[11] InfoSphere Streams, http://www.ibm.com/software/data/infosphere/streams/

[12] S. Jayaraman and A. Lavie, "Multi-engine machine translation guided by explicit word matching," in *Proceedings of the 10th Annual Conference of the European Association for Machine Translation*, pp. 143–152, 2005.

[13] U. Murthy, J. F. Pitrelli, G. Ramaswamy, M. Franz, and B. L. Lewis, "A methodology and tool suite for evaluation of accuracy of interoperating statistical natural language processing engines," in *Proceedings of the Annual Conference of the International Speech Communication Association*, 2008.

[14] M. Noamany, T. Schaaf, and T. Schultz, "Advances in the CMU/InterACT Arabic GALE transcription system," in *Proceedings of the Human Language Technology Conference of the North American Chapter of the Association for Computational Linguistics (HLT/NAACL)*, 2007.

[15] UIMA as OASIS Standard, http://www.oasisopen.org/committees/uima

[16] J. F. Pitrelli, B. L. Lewis, E. A. Epstein, M. Franz, D. Kiecza, J. L. Quinn, G. Ramaswamy, A. Srivastava, and P. Virga, "Aggregating distributed STT, MT, and information extraction engines: The GALE Interoperability-Demo System," in *Proceedings of the Annual Conference of the International Speech Communication Association,* 2008.

[17] J. F. Pitrelli, B. L. Lewis, E. A. Epstein, J. L. Quinn, and G. Ramaswamy, "A data format enabling interoperation of speech recognition, translation and information extraction techniques: The GALE type system," in *Proceedings of the Annual Conference of the International Speech Communication Association,* 2008.

[18] G. Saon, D. Povey, and G. Zweig, "Anatomy of an extremely fast LVCSR decoder," in *Proceeding of the 9th European Conference on Speech Communication and Technology,* 2005.

[19] B. Schiffman, A. Nenkova, and K. McKeown, "Experiments in Multidocument Summarization," in *Proceedings of the Human Language Technologies Conference,* 2002.

[20] TIPSTER Text Program, http://www.itl.nist.gov/iaui/894.02/related_projects/-tipster/overv.htm, including R. Grishman, *TIPSTER Architecture Design Document Version 2.3,* Technical report, DARPA, 1997; see http://www.itl.nist.gov/-iaui/894.02/related_projects/tipster/

Index

Viral Data in SOA
An Enterprise Pandemic
Neal A. Fishman
Search Engine Marketing, Inc.
Driving Search Traffic to Your Company's Web Site
Second Edition
Mike Moran and Bill Hunt
The New Language of Business
SOA & Web 2.0
Sandy Carter
The Greening of IT
How Companies Can Make a Difference for the Environment
John Lamb
Understanding DB2
Learning Visually with Examples